What's Online...

Print More Coupons Online!

SAVE THOUSANDS MORE!

HOW?

Simply activate your online benefits at
www.entertainment.com/activate
using your Membership Card number.

Flip page for Membership Card 👉

More online benefits:

- Sign up for our complimentary e-newsletter and get coupons not found in your membership book emailed to you!

- Print Repeat Savings® coupons— additional monthly coupons from your favorite places.

- Print local coupons not found in your book... new discounts are added throughout the year!

- Get $1,000s in travel savings, including discounts at over 35,000 hotels.

- View a map of all the offer locations near you!

- Access hundreds of offers from top online retailers.

- Purchase discounted movie tickets (great gift idea!).

YOU MUST REGISTER ONLINE TO FULLY ACTIVATE YOUR MEMBERSHIP

Purchase an additional
Entertainment® Membership Card

ONLY $15

Get Double... *Dining Out offers, online prints and more!*

Order at **www.entertainment.com/getcards**
while supplies last.

Activate at
www.entertainment.com/activate
using your Membership Card number.

Use Your Card For:

- **Dining Out:** Present your Membership Card at restaurants found in the blue Dining Out section with this symbol  on the offer page.

- **Travel & Hotels:** Use your card for Travel & Hotels discounts. See the section for details.

- **Online:** Print additional coupons!

Rules of Use can be found in the back of the book.

SAFEWAY

save $20 at your local Safeway store

SAFEWAY COUPON

Valid 11/01/2009 - 1/31/2010

Use your Safeway
Club Card to enjoy

$5.00 OFF

**any grocery purchase of
$50 or more during any
single shopping trip.***

*Maximum discount of $5.00 per shopper, per
quarter. Valid at all Washington stores. Also
valid at all Idaho and Oregon stores. Offer valid
Quarterly. Restrictions apply. See reverse side of
coupon for more information.

See reverse side for details

SAFEWAY COUPON

Valid 2/01/2010 - 4/30/2010

Use your Safeway
Club Card to enjoy

$5.00 OFF

**any grocery purchase of
$50 or more during any
single shopping trip.***

*Maximum discount of $5.00 per shopper, per
quarter. Valid at all Washington stores. Also
valid at all Idaho and Oregon stores. Offer valid
Quarterly. Restrictions apply. See reverse side of
coupon for more information.

See reverse side for details

SAFEWAY COUPON

Valid 5/01/2010 - 7/31/2010

Use your Safeway
Club Card to enjoy

$5.00 OFF

**any grocery purchase of
$50 or more during any
single shopping trip.***

*Maximum discount of $5.00 per shopper, per
quarter. Valid at all Washington stores. Also
valid at all Idaho and Oregon stores. Offer valid
Quarterly. Restrictions apply. See reverse side of
coupon for more information.

See reverse side for details

SAFEWAY COUPON

Valid 8/01/2010 - 10/31/2010

Use your Safeway
Club Card to enjoy

$5.00 OFF

**any grocery purchase of
$50 or more during any
single shopping trip.***

*Maximum discount of $5.00 per shopper, per
quarter. Valid at all Washington stores. Also
valid at all Idaho and Oregon stores. Offer valid
Quarterly. Restrictions apply. See reverse side of
coupon for more information.

See reverse side for details

SAFEWAY

Grilled Chicken Salad

Visit **www.daphnes.biz** for locations and to order online.

FEATURED OFFERS

Portland Locations

Beaverton
(503) 644-4048

Portland
(503) 222-5758

Tanasbourne
(503) 533-4130

Subject to Rules of Use. Coupons VOID if purchased, sold or bartered for cash.

Subject to Rules of Use. Coupons VOID if purchased, sold or bartered for cash.

Subject to Rules of Use. Coupons VOID if purchased, sold or bartered for cash.

Subject to Rules of Use. Coupons VOID if purchased, sold or bartered for cash.

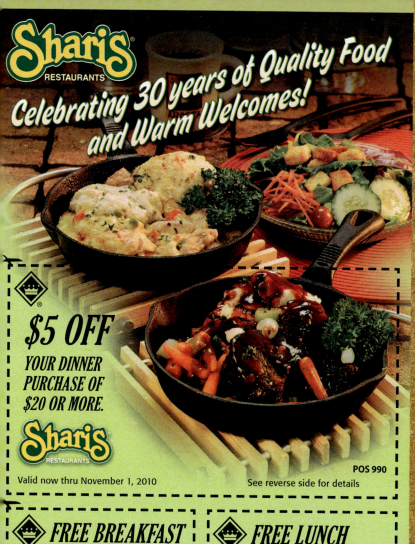

Shari's RESTAURANTS®

Celebrating 30 years of Quality Food and Warm Welcomes!

$5 OFF
YOUR DINNER PURCHASE OF $20 OR MORE.

Shari's RESTAURANTS®

POS 990

Valid now thru November 1, 2010

See reverse side for details

FREE BREAKFAST

Purchase any breakfast entrée and two beverages and receive a breakfast entrée of equal or lesser value **FREE!**

(Up to a $9 Value)

Shari's RESTAURANTS®

Valid now thru November 1, 2010
See reverse side for details

POS 949

FREE LUNCH

Purchase any lunch entrée and two beverages and receive a lunch entrée of equal or lesser value **FREE!**

(Up to a $9 Value)

Shari's RESTAURANTS®

Valid now thru November 1, 2010
See reverse side for details

POS 950
A2

SHARI'S TO-GO!

Don't forget the pie!

Take home a delicious whole Shari's pie or enjoy a slice with your meal.

Perfect with a cup of Arösta, Down to Earth Great Coffee!

www.Sharis.com

All the best in one giant sizzling platter!!!

Chevys
FRESH MEX®
chevys.com

Mixed Grill

All the best in one giant sizzling platter!!!

Chevys
FRESH MEX®
chevys.com

Mixed Grill

GIVE ME MORE FRiDAY'S®

TWO GREAT DEALS FOR TWO GREAT MEALS!

BRUSCHETTA CHICKEN PASTA

GET $5 OFF A PURCHASE OF $15 OR MORE

Valid now thru November 1, 2010
See reverse side for details

BUY ONE LUNCH GET ONE FREE
MONDAY-FRIDAY 11-3

Valid now thru November 1, 2010
See reverse side for details

A4

TUSCAN SPINACH DIP

GiVE ME MORE STRiPES™

Go to GiveMeMoreStripes.com to sign up.

JUMP THE **LINE**

FREE APPETIZER

8 BUCKS FOR EVERY $100

GET THE CARD.
GET FREE STUFF.

Sign up for our GiVE ME MORE STRiPES™ guest recognition program and get perks like free appetizers, desserts and more. Go to givememorestripes.com or head to your nearest Friday's® location and tell them you want GiVE ME MORE STRiPES!™

Smothered Steak Fajitas

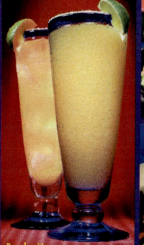
Borderita

Guacamole Live!

Border Brownie Sundae

ON THE BORDER. OFF THE MAP.

Hillsboro

Vancouver

ON THE BORDER MEXICAN GRILL & CANTINA

"BEST BBQ"

WINNER OF OVER 300 BBQ AWARDS!

WORLD'S GREATEST RIBS!

DINE-IN TO GO CATERING

Famous Dave's®

Legendary Pit Bar-B-Que®

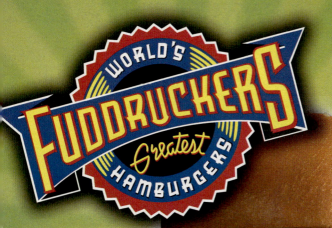

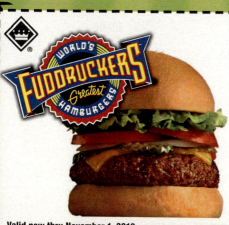

$5.00
value

Enjoy $5 off any purchase of $25 or more.

(Excluding tax, tip and alcohol.)

Valid anytime.

Valid now thru November 1, 2010

See reverse side for details

A7

Fuddruckers Is Forkin' It Out For You!

Earning money for your school, sports team or club has never been so easy or so delicious. You pick the day and we will write you a check for up to 20% of whatever your organization spends for the entire day.

Call to book your event today! 1.877.844.1990

CALIFORNIA
Concord
1975 Diamond Blvd., E-260
(925) 825-1443

Dublin
4910 Dublin Blvd.
(925) 551-8052

Emeryville
5614 Bay St., #232
(510) 655-5902

Walnut Creek
1940 N. Main St.
(925) 943-1450

IDAHO
Boise
1666 S. Entertainment Blvd.
(208) 246-8640

Meridian
3421 N. Eagle Rd.
(208) 887-2194

OREGON
Lake Oswego
17815 S. W. 65th
(503) 620-5119

Union City location
coming soon!

CALIFORNIA
Concord
1975 Diamond Blvd., E-260
(925) 825-1443

Dublin
4910 Dublin Blvd.
(925) 551-8052

Emeryville
5614 Bay St., #232
(510) 655-5902

Walnut Creek
1940 N. Main St.
(925) 943-1450

IDAHO
Boise
1666 S. Entertainment Blvd.
(208) 246-8640

Meridian
3421 N. Eagle Rd.
(208) 887-2194

OREGON
Lake Oswego
17815 S. W. 65th
(503) 620-5119

Union City location
coming soon!

Subject to Rules of Use. Coupons VOID if purchased, sold or bartered for cash.

We do entertainment **BIG!**

REGAL
ENTERTAINMENT
G R O U P

REGAL CINEMAS · UNITED ARTISTS Theatres · EDWARDS THEATRES

Go to the Attractions section for more offers from this merchant.

REDEEM AT THEATRE - MOVIE TICKETS

 **PURCHASE $7.00 TICKETS AT BOX OFFICE**

Purchase up to two (2) *VIP Super Saver Admission Tickets for only $7.00 each.

Upgrade to an "UNRESTRICTED" Premiere Super Saver Admission Ticket for only $1.50 extra per ticket.

Limit 2 Admission Tickets Per Coupon.

Subject to Rules of Use. Coupons VOID if purchased, sold or bartered for cash.

Valid now thru November 1, 2010
See reverse side for details

REDEEM AT THEATRE - MOVIE TICKETS

 PURCHASE $7.00 TICKETS AT BOX OFFICE

Purchase up to two (2) *VIP Super Saver Admission Tickets for only $7.00 each.

Upgrade to an "UNRESTRICTED" Premiere Super Saver Admission Ticket for only $1.50 extra per ticket.

Limit 2 Admission Tickets Per Coupon.

Subject to Rules of Use. Coupons VOID if purchased, sold or bartered for cash.

Valid now thru November 1, 2010
See reverse side for details

FREE POPCORN

 FREE POPCORN

Free Small Popcorn with the purchase of a Large Soft Drink. Present this coupon at the concession stand for redemption.

Subject to Rules of Use. Coupons VOID if purchased, sold or bartered for cash.

Valid now thru November 1, 2010
See reverse side for details

FREE ADMISSION

 FREE MOVIE ADMISSION ON YOUR BIRTHDAY

One (1) FREE Movie Admission on your birthday! Present this coupon at the box office for redemption.

Valid only on the date of your birthday.

Valid Driver's License or Birth Certificate required.

Subject to Rules of Use. Coupons VOID if purchased, sold or bartered for cash.

Valid now thru November 1, 2010
See reverse side for details   A8

FEATURED OFFERS

i'm lovin' it®

FEATURED OFFERS

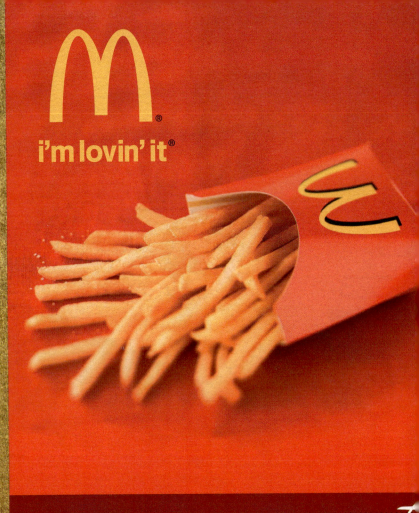

Valid at participating locations in Aloha, Astoria, Beaverton, Canby, Clackamas, Forest Grove, Gladstone, Goldendale, Gresham, Hillsboro, Hood River, Lake Oswego, McMinnville, Milwaukie, Molalla, Newberg, North Plains, Oregon City, Portland, Sandy, Scappoose, Seaside, Sherwood, Silverton, St. Helens, The Dalles, Tigard, Tualatin, West Linn, Wilsonville, Woodburn, Battle Ground, Bingen, Camas, Kelso, Longview, Long Beach, Vancouver and Woodland.

YOU know what GOOD is.

FEATURED OFFERS

USE THIS COUPON
FOR YOUR NEXT CATERING EVENT!

Church's CHICKEN SINCE 1952

$10 OFF
CATERING ORDER OF
$100 OR MORE

Valid now thru November 1, 2010

At Participating locations only and at regular menu price only. Not valid with other offers, promotions or discounts. Void where prohibited. © 2009 Cajun Operating Company, under license by Cajun Funding Corp. Subject to Rules of Use. Coupons VOI D if purchased, sold or bartered for cash.

Coupon Code: 244

YOU know what GOOD is.

Church's CHICKEN SINCE 1952

SPICY, SAUCY, SAVORY AND SWEET
A DOMINO'S® MEAL MAKES THE DAY COMPLETE!

MAKE THE MOST OF YOUR MEAL TODAY WITH THESE DELICIOUS DEALS FROM DOMINO'S®!

FEATURED OFFERS

THERE'S NO BETTER DEAL ON VARIETY
ENJOY A FULL MEAL FROM DOMINO'S® TONIGHT!

ORDER ONLINE ▶ DOMINOS.COM

www.samuraisams.net

FREE EGG ROLL

FREE Egg Roll.

Valid anytime.
No purchase necessary.
Not valid with any other offer.

Valid now thru November 1, 2010
See reverse side for details

FREE TERIYAKI CHICKEN BOWL

Buy one regular Teriyaki Chicken Bowl and receive a FREE Teriyaki Chicken Bowl with the purchase of 2 regular drinks.

Valid anytime.
Not valid with any other offer.

Valid now thru November 1, 2010
See reverse side for details

FREE KID'S BOWL

Buy one regular Teriyaki Chicken Bowl and receive a FREE Kids Bowl at no additional charge.

Valid anytime.
Not valid with any other offer.

Valid now thru November 1, 2010
See reverse side for details

FREE CHICKEN YAKISOBA BOWL

Buy one Chicken Yakisoba Bowl and a receive FREE Chicken Yakisoba Bowl with the purchase of 2 regular drinks.

Valid anytime.
Not valid with any other offer.

Valid now thru November 1, 2010
See reverse side for details

A12

FEATURED OFFERS

Valid at participating locations only.

www.samuraisams.net

Valid at participating
locations only.

Valid at participating
locations only.

Valid at participating
locations only.

Valid at participating
locations only.

FRESH
FLAVORFUL
FLAME-GRILLED
MEXICAN
CHICKEN
FREE!!!

Fresh, natural, citrus-marinated and masterfully grilled right before your eyes by expert cooks.

El Pollo Loco
Flame-Grilled Mexican Chicken

A13

Let Us Cater Your Next Event

Citrus-marinated, Flame-grilled Mexican Chicken!

From kids' parties and school team lunches to office events and family gatherings—we know you've got hungry mouths to feed. Our tasty, juicy, flame-grilled chicken fits the bill and it's good for you! Take advantage and save big on a healthy, satisfying meal for everyone!

CALL US WITH YOUR CATERING ORDER

888-EPL-ToGo
(888-375-8646)

©2009 El Pollo Loco, Inc.

Pick your passion.

Every piece a celebration.

**Valid at all participating
Oregon
Cold Stone Creamery locations.**

Price excludes tax. Served in a cup. Waffle products and
extra mix-ins available for additional charge. Limit one per
customer per visit. Valid only at participating locations.
No cash value. Not valid with other offers or fundraisers
or if copied, sold, auctioned, exchanged for payment or
prohibited by law. 16.0147 ©2009 Cold Stone Creamery,
Inc. All rights reserved. PLU#98 Expires 11/01/10.

**Subject to Rules of Use. Coupons VOID if purchased,
sold or bartered for cash.**

**Valid at all participating
Oregon
Cold Stone Creamery locations.**

Served in a cup. No substitutions. Waffle products and
extra mix-ins available for additional charge. Valid for
children 12 and under only. Limit one per customer per
visit. Valid only at participating locations. No cash value.
Not valid with other offers or fundraisers or if copied, sold,
auctioned, exchanged for payment or prohibited by law.
16.0147 ©2009 Cold Stone Creamery, Inc. All rights
reserved. PLU#99 Expires 11/01/10.

**Subject to Rules of Use. Coupons VOID if purchased,
sold or bartered for cash.**

**Valid at all participating
Oregon
Cold Stone Creamery locations.**

Limit one per customer per visit. Valid only at participating
locations. No cash value. Not valid with other offers or
fundraisers or if copied, sold, auctioned, exchanged for
payment or prohibited by law. 16.0147 ©2009 Cold Stone
Creamery, Inc. All rights reserved.
PLU#93 Expires 11/01/10.

**Subject to Rules of Use. Coupons VOID if purchased,
sold or bartered for cash.**

**Valid at all participating
Oregon
Cold Stone Creamery locations.**

Limit one per customer per visit. Excludes pies and petite
cakes. Valid only at locations listed. No cash value. Not
valid with other offers or fundraisers or if copied, sold,
auctioned, exchanged for payment or prohibited by law.
16.0147 ©2009 Cold Stone Creamery, Inc. All rights
reserved. PLU#97 Expires 11/01/10.

**Subject to Rules of Use. Coupons VOID if purchased,
sold or bartered for cash.**

Pretzel Withdrawal Ain't Pretty.

FEATURED OFFERS

SO MANY PRETZELS, SO LITTLE TIME.

 AuntieAnne's

PRETZEL PERFECT

Free pretzel must be of equal or lesser value. One coupon per person; one-time use only. Not valid with any other offer. Tax extra where applicable. Valid at participating Auntie Anne's locations. Not a cash substitute. Duplicated or altered coupons will not be accepted. **Offer valid through November 1, 2010.** ©2009 Auntie Anne's, Inc. All rights reserved.

Subject to Rules of Use. Coupons VOID if purchased, sold or bartered for cash.

Please present coupon when ordering. One coupon per person; one-time use only. Not valid with any other offer. Tax extra where applicable. Valid at participating Auntie Anne's locations. Not a cash substitute. Duplicated or altered coupons will not be accepted. **Offer valid through November 1, 2010.** ©2009 Auntie Anne's, Inc. All rights reserved.

Subject to Rules of Use. Coupons VOID if purchased, sold or bartered for cash.

DINING OUT INDEX

To search by area, see the **Neighborhood Index** located at the back of your book.

= **Print more coupons online at www.entertainment.com,** up to once a month, with these Repeat Savings® merchants. See the Rules of Use for more details.

DINING OUT INDEX

GET YOUR BOOK*
FIRST EACH YEAR

With FREE Shipping!

Join the Entertainment®
Annual Renewal Program Today!

What is it?

- Get Entertainment® hot off the presses each fall!

- You get 15 full months to use your coupons!

- Receive exclusive online offers on your customized Web site!

- Buy additional editions at 10% off our best available rate. Great for gift-giving!

- You can credit a fundraiser with up to 50% of the purchase price every year.

Convenience, extra time to save, free shipping, and credit for your favorite fundraiser—you just can't lose!

Just sign up during online activation at
www.entertainment.com/activate

*The Entertainment® Book is part of your Entertainment® Membership.

CHANG'S
MONGOLIAN GRILL

Experience 1000 ways of Creative Eating!

EXPERIENCE AUTHENTIC MONGOLIAN COOKING IN THE TRADITION OF GENGHIS KHAN
- Choose from a variety of meats, fresh vegetables and exotic seasonings.
- NO MSG in our cooking! • Reservations accepted for 10 or more.

SEE REVERSE SIDE FOR SIX CONVENIENT LOCATIONS

DINING OUT

CHANG'S
MONGOLIAN GRILL

Six convenient locations in Oregon

PORTLAND
San Rafael Shopping Center
1610 NE 122nd Ave
(503) 253-3535

MILWAUKIE
18925 SE McLoughlin Blvd
(503) 655-2323

JANTZEN BEACH
12055 N Center Ave
(503) 240-0205

BEAVERTON
1935 NW 167th Pl
(503) 645-7718

GRESHAM
2502 E Powell Blvd
(503) 665-8998

SALEM
Evergreen Plaza
3928 Center St NE
(503) 373-9779

CHANG'S
MONGOLIAN GRILL

SEE REVERSE SIDE FOR DISCOUNT

PORTLAND
San Rafael Shopping Center • 1610 NE 122nd Ave • (503) 253-3535
MILWAUKIE
18925 SE McLoughlin Blvd • (503) 655-2323
JANTZEN BEACH
12055 N Center Ave • (503) 240-0205
BEAVERTON
1935 NW 167th Pl • (503) 645-7718
GRESHAM
2502 E Powell Blvd • (503) 665-8998
SALEM
Evergreen Plaza • 3928 Center St NE • (503) 373-9779

Subject to Rules of Use. Coupons VOID if purchased,
sold or bartered for cash.

CHANG'S
MONGOLIAN GRILL

SEE REVERSE SIDE FOR DISCOUNT

PORTLAND
San Rafael Shopping Center • 1610 NE 122nd Ave • (503) 253-3535
MILWAUKIE
18925 SE McLoughlin Blvd • (503) 655-2323
JANTZEN BEACH
12055 N Center Ave • (503) 240-0205
BEAVERTON
1935 NW 167th Pl • (503) 645-7718
GRESHAM
2502 E Powell Blvd • (503) 665-8998
SALEM
Evergreen Plaza • 3928 Center St NE • (503) 373-9779

Subject to Rules of Use. Coupons VOID if purchased,
sold or bartered for cash.

Fresh Food & Smooth Ales

DINING OUT

4765 NE FREMONT | PORTLAND, OR | 503-460-9025 | ALAMEDABREWHOUSE.COM

"Black Bear Stout" Turkey Pot Pie **$12.95**

Gingered Tahini-Soy Tiger Prawn & Scallop Skewers **$12.95**

Beer Battered Halibut + Chips **$13.95**

Bacon-Wrapped Filet Mignon **$18.95**

Greek Seafood Linguini **$12.95**

Grilled Tequila-Lime Ahi Tuna **$13.95**

Menu Sampler - Prices and menu subject to change.

Subject to Rules of Use. Coupons VOID if purchased, sold or bartered for cash.
Tipping should be 15% to 20% of the total bill before discount.

LOCATED IN THE BEAUMONT DISTRICT • NON-SMOKING + CHILD FRIENDLY

Featuring our award-winning hand-crafted ales.

< Black Bear XX Stout – Winner of the coveted **Gold Medal** at the **Great American Brew Festival** in 2003 and 2005 and the **Silver** in 2006 and 2008!

4765 NE FREMONT | **PORTLAND, OR** | **503-460-9025** | **ALAMEDABREWHOUSE.COM**

豪城

Ambassador
restaurant & lounge

THE FINEST SZECHUAN, HUNAN & CANTONESE CUISINE &
PORTLAND'S OLDEST & MOST ELABORATE KARAOKE LOUNGE!

Family Karaoke every Sunday!
Two Stages of Karaoke, no long wait!
Featuring a massive song selection, gigantic Big Screen with multiple
monitors throughout the bar and the highest quality sound.

- Amazing Stage Lighting and Effects • Terrific Sound System
- Contemporary Lounge • Dancing Nightly

4744 NE SANDY BLVD. • PORTLAND, OR
503.280.0330

DINING OUT

PLEASE PRESENT YOUR ENTERTAINMENT® CARD TO RECEIVE DISCOUNT

Enjoy $7 off your dinner entree when a second dinner entree of greater or equal value is purchased.

CARD # 113 • VALID ANYTIME, DINE IN ONLY

Subject to Rules of Use. Coupons VOID if purchased, sold or bartered for cash.
Tipping should be 15% to 20% of the total bill before discount.

KARAOKE 7 NIGHTS A WEEK!

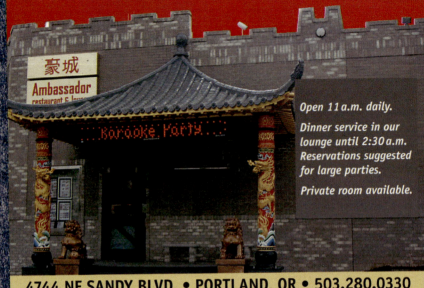

豪城
Ambassador
restaurant & lounge

:::Karaoke Party:::

Open 11 a.m. daily.

Dinner service in our lounge until 2:30 a.m. Reservations suggested for large parties.

Private room available.

4744 NE SANDY BLVD. • PORTLAND, OR • 503.280.0330
WWW.AMBASSADORRESTAURANT.NET • WWW.AMBASSADORKARAOKE.COM

DINING OUT

isabel
www.isabelscantina.com

Come try our delicious, creative, & bold-flavored cuisine combining Latin and Asian influences. Healthy, nutritious, & lower-calorie specialties that sacrifice nothing to extraordinary taste. Many vegetarian and vegan options available. Modern, light, and spacious central-Pearl location. Open for breakfast (meetings..), lunch, and romantic dinners 7 days/week.

LETTUCE WRAPS 7.00
Marinated chicken served with peanut sauce
AHI WONTONS 9.00
Wonton crisps topped with seared ahi, avocado, sweet soy, and wasabi cream
PLANTAINS WITH CARNITAS 6.00
Carnitas, chipotle sour cream, and avocado on crispy plantains
OVER ROASTED DRAPER VALLEY FREE RANGE HALF CHICKEN 17.00
Latin Style: black beans, brown rice, crispy salted plantains and salsa cruda
Asian Style: Coconut rice, edemamae and peanut sauce
Dragon Style: Roasted red and sweet potatoes and chipotle cream sauce
Isabel Style: Steamed broccoli, brown rice and pesto
DOUBLE HAPPINESS LETTUCE WRAPS 14.00
Marinated steak and chicken served with green leaf lettuce, jasmine rice, cucumber kimchee and peanut sauce
ASIA GRILL 12.00
Grilled eggplant, sweet potatoes, mushrooms, and roasted peppers, served with marinated tofu, brown rice and peanut sauce
BUDDHA BOWL 8.00
Lemongrass, miso and coconut broth with shitake mushrooms, noodles, veggies and cilantro
BRAZIL BOWL 12.00
Brown rice or coconut rice, black beans served with mango-papaya salsa and crispy plantains
TEMPTATIONS
Flourless Chocolate Cake 6.00
Coconut Flan 6.00
Bananas Cantina 7.00
Flamed bananas with run served a la mode

Menu Sampler - Prices and menu subject to change.

DINING OUT

Up To $20.00 Value

Classic Cuisine **Amadeus** Manor

www.amadeusrestaurants.com

Enjoy the romance of classical Continental cuisine served within a beautifully restored three story manor set along the Willamette river. The food, decor, music and ambiance of Amadeus Manor will indulge your senses and delight your soul. You will be sure to return time and time again.

Enjoy one complimentary ENTREE when a second ENTREE of equal or greater value is purchased with 2 BEVERAGES.

valid any evening

Excluding holidays

2122 Sparrow St., Milwaukie, OR (503)659-1735

PRINT MORE ONLINE

Card No. 10

CORDON BLEU
Chicken stuffed with Black Forest Ham and Swiss Cheese, breaded and served with an regano demi-glace.

SEAFOOD PASTA
A mixture of seafood sauteed with garlic, white wine, artichoke hearts and tossed over pasta.

BOUILLABAISSE
A French classic. Assorted Seafood nestled together in a delicate seafood broth.

RACK OF LAMB PROVENCAL
Succulent Lamb roasted with a crust of fresh herbs and bread crumbs and served with port wine demi-glace.

SCHNITZEL AMADEUS
Austrian Classic! Hand trimmed Tenderloin of Pork, lightly breaded and sauteed to a crisp golden brown.

STEAK Au POUIVRE MADAGASCAR
A French classic. Choice cut of New York Strip grill. Served with peppercorn cognac demi-glace and mango chutneys.

Menu Sampler - Prices and menu subject to change.

DINING OUT

Up To $12.00 Value

www.kinarathai.com

Enjoy one complimentary LUNCH OR DINNER ENTREE when a second LUNCH OR DINNER ENTREE of equal or greater value is purchased.

valid anytime

1126 S.W. 18th Ave. (between S.W. Madison & S.W. Main St.), **Portland, OR (503)227-5161**

A delightful interpretation of traditional Thai cuisine, served in contemporary, intimate atmosphere. Be sure to ask about our daily specials! Kinara rolls our specialty. Stop by before the game at PGE park or your trip to the MAC Club. Open 11 a.m. - 9 p.m. Mon. - Thurs.; 11 a.m. - p.m. Fri. & 3 p.m. - 9:30 p.m. Saturday. Please visit our website.

PRINT MORE ONLINE

Card No. 3

APPETIZERS

Kinara Rolls   9
A Kinara essential! Slices of roasted duck meat, cucumber, carrots, cilantro, and scallions wrapped in a delicious hoi-sin flour tortilla.

Blue Crab Wontons   8
Our delicious fried wontons stuffed with sweet Blue crab and cream cheese.

NOODLES

Pad Thai
Kinara's own recipe for this popular noodles dish! Rice noodles stir-fried in sweet tamarind sauce with bean sprouts, green onions, egg and crushed peanuts.

Drunken Noodles
Flat rice noodles stir-fried with basil, bell peppers, onions, tomatoes, garlic, and Thai chili.

CURRIES

Pineapple Curry Prawns   11
Prawns, pineapple, broccoli, and bell pepper in a light red curry.

Duck Curry   11
Roasted duck, cherry tomatoes, and bell peppers in a red curry.

FROM THE WOK

Garlic and Pepper Chicken   10
Delicious cuts of all natural chicken stir fried in fresh garlic and black pepper in our fabulous Kinara sauce. Steamed vegetables on the side.

Cashew Nuts Chicken Delight   10
Delicious cuts of all natural chicken with golden roasted cashews, onions, green onions, carrots, roasted chili and sweet chili paste.

Menu Sampler - Prices and menu subject to change.

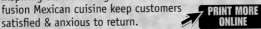
AVES

Pollo a la Costita $13.50

A Soltero family recipe! Tender chunks of chicken breast sautéed in our signature Monterey Jack cream sauce, butter and onions. Served with tortillas, rice and refried beans.

Pollo en Mole $13.50

"Mole" derives from "mulli," a holistic Nahuatl word encompassing sauce, mixture, concoction and/or stew. Of the multiple versions of mole, we serve a dark brown concoction created with unsweetened chocolate, various chile peppers and spices. It is sautéed with sliced chicken breast and chopped onions, and served with white rice and tortillas.

CARNES

Cane En Su Jugo $14.00

Another signature dish from Guadalajara, Mexico that is sure to please your soul. This Mexican stew is cooked with marinated steak in a beef consommé, whole pinto beans, bits of bacon and is accompanied by grilled green onions, tomatillo salsa, cilantro and handmade corn tortillas.

Tacos Tijuana $14.00

Another T.J. classic that's here to please your tastebuds! Five soft corn tortillas, with carne asada, chopped onions, cilantro, sliced avocados and queso fresco. Served with frijoles de la hoya (whole pinto beans).

PESCADOS Y MARISCOS

Camarones Costa Azul $14.50

Big prawns wrapped in bacon and placed over a bed of sliced onions, red peppers and zucchini then covered with Jack cheese and baked. This dish is served with rice and refried black beans, garnished with sour cream, guacamole and pico de gallo.

Camarones con Naranja y Tequila $14.50

Shrimp sautéed in butter, chopped onion, garlic, jalapeno, cilantro, orange peel strips and lightly mixed with a touch of tequila reposado. Served over white rice. ¡¡Magnífico!!

Menu Sampler - Prices and menu subject to change.

DINING OUT

THE RESERVE
VINEYARDS AND GOLF CLUB

www.reservegolf.com

The Vintage Room Restaurant & Bar is a premium dining experience with a fantastic view of 2 of Oregon's best golf courses. We feature delicious Northwest cuisine & fine wines. With the addition of the Bar & Kids menus, The Vintage Room truly offers something for everyone. Visit our website for current hours of operation.

Up To $25.00 Value

Enjoy one complimentary LUNCH OR DINNER ENTREE when a second LUNCH OR DINNER ENTREE of equal or greater value is purchased.

Dine in only

valid anytime

Holidays & special events excluded

4805 SW 229th Ave., Aloha, OR (503)848-2986

PRINT MORE ONLINE

 Card No. 6

Appetizers

Spinach Artichoke Dip
Served with grilled flat bread
8-

Crab Cakes
Pan-seared crab cakes, mustard artichoke aioli, micro cilantro greens
14/21-

Potato Croquettes
Milled potatoes and Crater Lake blue cheese rolled in herbed bread crumbs and pan fried, scallion Dijon sauce
8-

Sea Scallops
Sesame seared scallops, soy ginger glaze, field greens, grilled spring onions
11-

Entrees

Peppered New York Steak
12oz. Oregon County strip with four pepper crust, blue cheese-potato gratin, asparagus, sauce Madeira
28-

Filet Mignon
8oz. Pancini crusted Cascade Natural filet over garlic whipped white rose potatoes, sauce Robert, crispy onions
32-

Wild King Salmon
Grilled Wild Salmon, spring wild rice, baby spring onions, with sweet lime buerre blanc sauce
28-

Halibut Cheeks
Pan seared Alaskan Halibut cheeks, fresh masted red pepper linguini, sauteed spinach, pancetta vinaigrette
26-

Diver Scallops and Prawns
Pan seared sea scallops and grilled gulf prawns atop Parmesan risotto, asparagus, blood orange, smoked pork belly
27-

La Bottega Della Pasta
French Spinach and egg linguini served with fresh green peas, Pomodara tomato sauce, Pecarino Ramano cheese
16-

Menu Items Subject to Change Based on Seasonal Availability

Menu Sampler - Prices and menu subject to change.

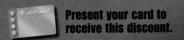
DINING OUT

Sam's

MONARCH HOTEL
& CONFERENCE CENTER

www.monarchhotel.cc

Sam's Restaurant & Lounge provides the perfect atmosphere for good food, good wine & good times. Sample the finest Pacific Northwest seafood, steaks & specialty pastas, & for the hearty appetite, our slow-roasted prime rib is a Monarch classic! Also choose from a wine selection featuring Oregon's finest. Reservations recommended.

Up To $16.00 Value

Enjoy one complimentary DINNER ENTREE when a second DINNER ENTREE of equal or greater value is purchased or enjoy one SUNDAY BRUNCH when a second SUNDAY BRUNCH of equal or greater value is purchased.

Valid any evening except holidays

For holidays-see Rules of Use

12566 S.E. 93rd Ave., Clackamas, OR (503)652-7505

Card No. 93

APPETIZERS, SOUPS AND SALADS

TERIYAKI CHICKEN SALAD — 12.95
CRISP ROMAINE TOPPED WITH TERIYAKI-GLAZED CHICKEN BREAST, SAUTÉED ORIENTAL VEGETABLES, FRESH PINEAPPLE AND MANGO, TOSSED WITH TOASTED SESAME DRESSING. GARNISHED WITH SESAME SEEDS.

NORTHWEST PEAR SALAD
SPRING GREENS AND CRISP ROMAINE TOSSED WITH LEMON-GARLIC VINAIGRETTE, FINISHED WITH DICED PEAR, BLEU CHEESE AND CHOPPED HAZELNUTS. — 10.95
TOPPED WITH GRILLED CHICKEN BREAST — 12.95
TOPPED WITH SLICED FLAT IRON STEAK — 14.95

SEAFOOD

FILET OF SALMON — 19.95
GRILLED, BLACKENED CAJUN STYLE, ALMOND ENCRUSTED OR SAUTÉED.

HALIBUT AMANDINE — 23.95
FILET OF HALIBUT SAUTÉED WITH WHITE WINE AND FINISHED WITH ALMONDS AND BUTTER.

HOUSE SPECIALTIES

PORK FRANGELICO — 16.95
SAUTÉED MEDALLIONS OF PORK, FINISHED WITH FRANGELICO AND CHOPPED HAZELNUTS. SERVED WITH ROASTED GARLIC MASHED POTATOES AND SEASONAL VEGETABLES.

BARBECUED BABY BACK RIBS — 21.95
SLOW ROASTED AND FINISHED WITH A TANGY BARBEQUE SAUCE. SERVED WITH CHOICE OF FRENCH FRIES, ROASTED GARLIC MASHED POTATOES OR BAKED POTATO.

CHICKEN MONARCH — 16.95
LIGHTLY BREADED AND BAKED BREAST OF CHICKEN FILLED WITH SPINACH, MOZZARELLA AND PARMESAN. TOPPED WITH MORNAY SAUCE. SERVED WITH HERBED PASTA AND SEASONAL VEGETABLES.

STEAKS

SAM'S PRIME RIB
SLOW ROASTED WITH OUR SECRET BLEND OF SPECIAL SEASONINGS, SERVED WITH CREAMED HORSERADISH.
10oz 23.95
12oz 26.95

Menu Sampler - Prices and menu subject to change.

Present your card to receive this discount.

DINING OUT

the STOCKPOT BROILER

Steaks, Seafood & Spirits

"Comfort food" in an elegant setting, using choice hand-cut steaks, fresh salads, and many local ingredients prepared individually to order. Try our chef's unique recipes using Northwest and international ingredients to create a delicious fusion.

$22.00 Value

Enjoy one complimentary dinner entree when a second dinner entree of equal or greater value is purchased.

Dining room only

For holidays-see Rules of Use

8200 SW Scholls Ferry Road at the Red Tail Golf Course, **Beaverton, OR (503)643-5451**

  Card No. 32

Grilled Wild King Salmon $25
Warm Potato Salad with Arugula & Pepper Bacon~
Smoked Salmon Beurre Blanc

Tuscan Beef Tenderloin $26
Fresh Herb Marinade ~ Garlic
Mashed Potatoes ~ Veal Glacé

Idaho Potato Crusted Mahi Mahi $22
Savory Herb Potato Gnocchi & Wilted
Spinach ~ Tomato-Vodka Sauce

Draper Valley Chicken $19
Pan Seared Breast with Chicken & Wild Mushroom
Cannelloni ~ Spicy Romaine & Tomato-Thyme Sauce

Braised Niman Ranch Lamb Shank $22
Creamy Parmesan Polenta, Summer Vegetable Ragout
with an Orange Spice Broth

Menu Sampler - Prices and menu subject to change.

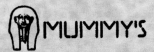

DINING OUT

Up To $14.00 Value

MUMMY'S

"For the ultimate in Middle East ambiance, a place where you get everything but the sand in your shoes. Mummy's is your destination." --The Oregonian. Enjoy Egyptian cuisine among hieroglyphs, pyramids, a sculptured mummy & glass etchings of Egyptian artifacts. Sample roast leg of lamb, chicken coriander of bouftiek (delectable marinated veal dish).

Enjoy one complimentary DINNER ENTREE when a second DINNER ENTREE of equal or greater value is purchased.

valid any evening

622 S.W. Columbia, Portland, OR (503)224-7465

 Card No. 87

-Entrees-

All entrees served with green salad, your choice of dressing, fresh vegetables, rice, bread and butter.

chicken kabob $13.95

Boneless breast of chicken, marinated in fresh lemon juice and herbs, skewered with onion, then broiled.

shish kabob $13.95

Tender pieces of lamb marinated with herbs and spices, skewered with onion, then broiled.

kabob combination $13.95

Includes chicken kabob and shish kabob.

chicken with hot sauce $14.25

Chicken breast baked in an aromatic almond and hot sauce.

daoud basha $13.95

Specially spiced meatballs in an exotic sauce of onion, green pepper and tomato.

bouftaek $16.25

Veal marinated with salt, pepper and lemon, dipped in whipped eggs and bread crumbs, then sauteed in butter.

lamb $16.25

Specialty of the house. Lamb marinated in a savory sauce of herbs and spices, then baked.

Menu Sampler - Prices and menu subject to change.

4th Street Specialties

On the Bayou Jambalaya
Cajun seasoned chicken, Andouille sausage, ham, fire roasted tomatoes, peppers & onions served with dirty rice . 12.95
With Shrimp 15.95

I'd Do Anything For Meatloaf
Made from scratch, oven roasted & topped with Powell Porter sweet caramelized onions. Served with fresh veggies, garlic mashed potatoes & gravy. 10.95

Yankee Shepherd's Pie
We have Americanized this traditional English pub fare. We bake to perfection seasoned ground beef in homemade gravy then mix with green peas and corn. Topped with garlic mashed potatoes and Tillamook cheddar cheese. 11.95

Mac Attack
Creole seasoned Tillamook cheddar cheese & ziti pasta topped with bread crumbs, then baked & served with spicy Andouille sausage. 12.95
Without the spicy sausage 9.95

Amber Ale Fish & Chips
Hand-cut Alaskan halibut, dipped in Amber Ale batter, deep fried & served with our house tartar sauce, fries & coleslaw.
5 Piece 15.95

Duke of New York
USDA Choice ten ounce New York steak charbroiled to perfection. Served with baked potato and fresh veggies. 21.95
Three Steak Toppings to choose from:
Melted Bleu Cheese / Sautéed Mushrooms & Onions / Pinot Noir Butter

Burgers

Brew Your Own Tillamook Cheese Burger
Your choice of cheese included.
Tillamook cheddar, pepper jack, Swiss
8.95
You add the toppings; pepper bacon or ham 1.50 each. fried egg, jalapenos, grilled onions, grilled peppers, sautéed mushrooms, onion rings....95 each.

Sandwiches

Reinheitsgebot Reuben
Choice of turkey or corned beef with Swiss cheese, sauerkraut & 1000 island dressing on grilled rye bread. 7.95

Northwest Dip
Thinly sliced tender roast beef, sautéed mushrooms & bleu cheese crumbles, served on a hoagie roll with a side of au jus. 8.95

The Porky
Tender smoked pulled pork in our homemade sweet & tangy BBQ sauce. Served with coleslaw. 8.50

Menu Sampler - Prices and menu subject to change.

CHUTNEYS

Enjoy $10.00 off with a minimum purchase of forty dollars (excluding tax, tip & alcoholic beverages).

valid anytime

3000 SE 164th Ste. 100, Vancouver, WA (360) 254-7254

Located in the heart of Vancouver's Fishers landing area, Chutney's offers authentic and delicious Indian cuisine. Enjoy our warm and cozy atmosphere, friendly staff and excellent service. Most of all, come visit us for our outstanding food.

  Card No. 16

CHICKEN   *Served with Basmati Rice*

2. BUTTER CHICKEN   10.99
Boneless chicken pieces cooked in creamy tomato gravy

3. CHICKEN CHETTINAD   10.50
Chicken prepared in South Indian style

LAMB   *Served with Basmati Rice*

2. MUTTON HYDERABADI   12.99
Lamb meat prepared in traditional Hydera-badi style

4. LAMB BHUNA   14.99
Lamb fried in traditional Indian spices

SEAFOOD   *Served with Basmati Rice*

1. FISH CURRY   12.50
Seasonal fish in a curry sauce

4. SHRIMP MASALA   12.99
Shrimp in Indian spices

Menu Sampler - Prices and menu subject to change.

DINING OUT

MarKum Inn

Up To $12.00 Value

Enjoy one complimentary ENTREE when a second ENTREE of equal or greater value is purchased.

valid anytime

36903 S. Hwy. 213, Marquam, OR (503)829-9853

Howdy! We're a little informal here, so come in and enjoy a heapin' helpin' of our hospitality. Just a short drive from Salem or Portland, the MarKum Inn serves home cooked soups, sandwiches and unbelievable dinners. Sample a jumbo MarKum burger, New York steak, New England cod or lasagna, all under one roof. Ask about our full service BBQ and catering.

 Card No. 143

- PRIME RIB -
SUNDAY ONLY

RARE - cold red center
MEDIUM RARE - warm red center
MEDIUM - pink center
MEDIUM WELL - hot, slightly pink center
WELL - hot grey center

Mama Cut, 10-oz	14.25
Papa Cut, 14-oz	16.25
New York Steak, 7-oz	12.75
New York Steak, 10-oz	14.75
Top Sirloin Steak, 7-oz	12.25
Petite Filet, 6-oz	12.75
Rib Eye Steak, 10-oz	14.25
Ground Sirloin Steak	9.25
Salisbury Steak	9.50
New England Cod	10.50
Grilled Salmon Fillet	11.75
Grilled Halibut Steak	12.25
Deep Fried Shrimp	12.95
Deep Fried or Sauteed Scallops	12.95
New York Steak & Shrimp	16.25
New York Steak & Scallops (sauteed or deep fried)	16.25
Low Calorie Plate	8.50
Perfect Potato	8.25
Baked potato stuffed with chicken, bacon, cheese, vegetables & ranch dressing	
Chicken Parmesan & Spaghetti	10.95
Lasagna	10.25
Chicken Monte	12.95
Grilled Chicken Breast with Bay Shrimp & jack Cheese	
Liver & Onions	8.50
Chicken Fried Steak w/ mashed potatoes & gravy	8.95

Menu Sampler - Prices and menu subject to change.

DINING OUT

Up To $12.00 Value

Walter Mitty's

RESTAURANT AND BAR

Enjoy one complimentary DINNER ENTREE when a second DINNER ENTREE of equal or greater value is purchased.

valid any evening

11830 Kerr Parkway, Lake Oswego, OR (503) 246-7153

Come to Walter Mitty's where all our tables are quaint & cozy. Enjoy your meal in the dining room or on our beautiful spacious patio. Try one of our specialties including steaks, fresh pasta, wilted spinach salad & Halibut fish & chips.

PRINT MORE ONLINE

Card No. 54

HALIBUT FISH AND CHIPS 12.95
Alaskan halibut batter-dipped, deep-fried and served with tossed salad or clam chowder, French fries or baked potato.

BLACK TIGER PRAWNS 14.95
Our prawns are sautéed in a light herb wine sauce but can be prepared tempura style, on request.

Our prawns are sautéed in a light herb wine sauce but can be prepared tempura style, on request.

NEW YORK STEAK 18.95
Ten ounces of well trimmed and correctly aged beef.

FILET MIGNON 18.95
An excellent half pound of U.S.D.A. beef tenderloin .

STEAK AND PASTA 15.95
Mitty's steak and pasta combination is on the menu by popular demand. Our six ounce top sirloin steak is served with fresh pasta Al burro. Sautéed with butter, lots of garlic and parmesan cheese.

APRICOT DIJON BREAST OF CHICKEN 13.95
Charbroiled breast of fresh Oregon chicken basted with our special apricot dijon glaze.

CHICKEN PICCATA 14.95
Fresh chicken breast prepared in a delicate lemon, mushrooms and caper sauce and served with fresh vegetables and sourdough bread.

* CHICKEN & ARTICHOKE FETTUCINI 12.95
Prepared with fresh, boneless, skinless, charbroiled breast of chicken and artichoke hearts sauteed in our creamy white sauce.

* SHRIMP AND MUSHROOM FETTUCINI 12.95
Pacific bay shrimp and fresh white mushrooms with our white sauce.

* SMOKED PACIFIC SALMON FETTUCINI 14.95
Smoked Pacific salmon, sun dried tomatoes and noodles in a lemon-basil cream sauce

FRESH PASTA

Walter is famous for his fresh fettucini pasta. Our dinners are prepared al dente and with just the right sprinkling of herbs and spices and freshly grated cheese (Garlic toast, soup or tossed salad is included.) Noted* items may be Cajuned for an additional fifty cents.

Menu Sampler - Prices and menu subject to change.

DINING OUT

INDIA PALACE

Authentic Indian Cuisine

Up To $12.00 Value

Enjoy one complimentary LUNCH OR DINNER ENTREE when a second LUNCH OR DINNER ENTREE of equal or greater value is purchased.

valid anytime

Special Feasts Excluded

2401 N.E. Cornell Rd., Suite Q Cornell Square behind Burgerville, **Hillsboro, OR** (503)844-6161

Specializing in North and South Indian cuisine. Tandori bread, Roti, Naan, stuffed Paratha. Spiciness from mild to very spicy. Wide selection of vegetarian, chicken and lamb entrees. Open 7 days a week.

   Card No. 8

Tandoori

Tandoori Chicken — $ 9.95
Chicken marinated in yogurt & mild spices cooked in its own juices over red-hot charcoal, and roasted in the "tandoori"

Mixed Grill — $13.95
A scrumptious combination of Tandoori Chicken, Chicken Tikka, Sheesh Kabob, Lamb Boti Kabob, and Shrimp

Lamb Boti Kabob — $10.95
Marinated lamb meat in morsel-sized pieces, skewered over red-hot charcoal with mint chutney and onion

Palace Specialties

Butter Chicken (Chicken Makhani) — $10.95
Boneless Tandoori chicken cooked in a creamy sauce

Lamb Fraizee — $10.95
Specialty of India Palace, cooked in special gravy with onions, tomatoes & bell pepper and tossed in Indian iron skillet

Karahai Shrimp & Potatoes — $12.95
Fresh jumbo shrimp marinated with Indian spices cooked with ginger, fresh tomatoes, onions and bell pepper, tossed in Indian iron skillet

Vegetable Jal Fraizee — $ 8.95
Fresh blend of vegetables cooked in mixed Indian spices

Palak Paneer — $ 8.95
Fresh spinach cooked curry style with homemade cheese, cream & seasoned with aromatic herbs

Chili Vegetable — $ 8.95
Vegetables mixed and cooked in a hot sauce made predominately from chilies

Menu Sampler - Prices and menu subject to change.

Present your card to receive this discount.

DINING OUT

Up To $15.00 Value

Enjoy one complimentary ENTREE when a second ENTREE of equal or greater value is purchased.

valid anytime

225 W 4th St, La Center, WA (360)263-1255

The New Phoenix Casino Restaurant serves lunch and dinner from 11 a.m. until midnight. After midnight, menu items can be ordered in the showroom. Of course, Black Jack tables and video pull tabs offer exciting entertainment too!

PRINT MORE ONLINE

Card No. 68

House Specials

Served with Steamed Rice

Dragon & Phoenix   12.50
Breast of chicken, prawns, broccoli, water chestnuts, snow peas, fresh mushrooms, zucchini, carrots, onions – stir fried in our spicy hot garlic sauce, served on a sizzling hot plate.

Happy Family   12.50
Prawns, BBQ pork, breast of chicken, broccoli, snow peas, water chestnuts, zucchini, mushrooms, carrots, onions – stir fried in our garlic brown sauce, served on a sizzling hot plate.

Moo Goo Guy Pinn   9.50
Breast of chicken, broccoli, water chestnuts, snow peas, fresh mushrooms, shitake mushrooms, zucchini, carrots, onions – stir fried in a rich oyster sauce.

Curry Tomato Chicken Noodles   9.50
Breast of chicken, fresh tomatoes, broccoli, water chestnuts, snow peas, fresh mushrooms, zucchini, carrots, onions – stir fried in a curry sauce, over noodles, or rice.

General Tso' Chicken   9.50
Lightly battered breast of chicken and broccoli combined with our delicious spicy hot szechwan sauce.

Lemon Chicken   9.50
Lightly battered breast of chicken with our tangy lemon sauce.

Menu Sampler - Prices and menu subject to change.

DINING OUT

The Last • Frontier Casino

Up To $17 00 Value

Enjoy one complimentary ENTREE when a second ENTREE of equal or greater value is purchased.

valid anytime

105 W 4th Ave, La Center, WA (360)263-1255

The Last Frontier Casino Restaurant features breakfast, lunch and dinner, with an emphasis on unique and regional menu specialties. Fresh seafood, pasta, steaks and salads are created using the highest grades of local and seasonal food products. Look for value and quality in our portions and pricing.

 PRINT MORE ONLINE

 Card No. 162

BISTRO STEAK AND SEAFOOD CAKES
Beef Medallion in a Green Peppercorn Sauce, Three Seafood Cakes topped with Lemon Beurre Blanc Sauce and Garnished with a Red Pepper Pesto $16.99

SMOKED PORK CHOP
Two 5oz Chops Cooked in a Sweet Mango Butter Sauce $13.99

COUNTRY MEATLOAF WITH WILD MUSHROOM GRAVY
Old Fashion Meatloaf Kicked Up a Notch $10.99

BABY BACKS
Slow Cooked, Fall off the Bone Tender Baby Backs Basted with our Signature Jalapeño Jelly

Half Rack $16.99   Full Rack $22.99

FISHERMAN'S FETTUCCINI
White Fish, Tiger Prawns, Bay Scallops and Crab in a Roasted Red Pepper Pesto Wine Sauce $15.99

MANGO BARBEQUED SALMON
Fresh Grilled Salmon Basted with Our "House Recipe" Mango Flavored Barbeque Sauce $14.99

PESTO PRAWNS AND GRILLED CHICKEN
8oz Chicken Breast Topped with Five Prawns Marinated in Roasted Red Pepper Pesto and Sautéed with Shallots and Tomatoes $15.99

T-BONE STEAK 16oz
Best of Both Worlds a Tender Piece of Filet and a Flavorful Piece of Strip Loin $26.99

Menu Sampler - Prices and menu subject to change.

Up To $**14**$ ^{00} Value

The Restaurant at the Holiday Inn
—Wilsonville—

Enjoy one LUNCH or DINNER ENTREE at 50% OFF when a second LUNCH or DINNER ENTREE of equal or greater value is purchased.

valid anytime

For holidays-see Rules of Use

25425 S.W. 95th Ave., Wilsonville, OR (503)682-2211

The Garlic Onion Ristorante offers you a delicious selection of menu items for breakfast, lunch and dinner. Located within the Holiday Inn in Wilsonville, our upscale casual dining atmosphere brings you your favorite meals while staying close to home.

Card No. 1

Specialties

Add Soup or Salad to any entrée

Dry Aged Prime Rib

Rubbed with cracked pepper and garlic, slow roasted, and sliced to order. Served with Au Jus, Horseradish Mousse, White Cheddar Mashed Potatoes, and Fresh Seasonal Vegetables.

eight ounce cut

Northwest Cioppino

Our "Fisherman's Stew" with Clams, Prawns, Scallops, Bay Shrimp, and White Fish in a zesty Tomato and Pinot Noir Sauce with Mushrooms, Peppers, Onions, and Parmesan Cheese.

Halibut Fish and Chips

Dusted with Rice Flour (Gluten Free) and quick fried for the perfect fish and chips. Served with Coleslaw, Fries, Lemon, and Tartar Sauce.

Aged New York Steak

with a Juniper Demi Glaze and Crumbled Oregon Blue Cheese. Served with White Cheddar Mashed Potatoes and Sautéed Greens

eight ounce

Pork Tenderloin Arago

Medallions of Pork Tenderloin, seared and served on Juniper Demi with Red Onion Confite. Served with Corn Pudding and Fresh Seasonal Vegetables.

Menu Sampler - Prices and menu subject to change.

DINING OUT

Up To $10.00 Value

FUJI'S GRILL & SUSHI
HIBACHI STYLE COOKING AT YOUR TABLE

Enjoy your own personal chef, while he amuses & amazes you with the art of preparing ancient hibachi-style Japanese food. Featuring steak & chicken, scallops, shrimp & more. Each meal includes a side of delicious yaki soba & all are served in a rural Japanese atmosphere. Come & try our sushi bar now available. Offer is valid on all holidays.

Enjoy $10 off any COMBINATION DINNER when a second COMBINATION DINNER of equal or greater value is purchased.

valid any evening

**16155 N.E. Cornell Rd. #100, Beaverton, OR
(503)466-1111**

**16062 S.W. Tualatin-Sherwood Rd., Sherwood, OR
(503)625-7849**

 Card No. 81

Fuji's Combination Dinners

Choice of any 2 Items $20. 95

Chicken, Tenderloin Steak

New York Steak, Scallops,

Shrimps, Calamari, Tofu

Additional side item $4. 95

All Dinners include salad with house dressing, steamed rice, onions, zucchini, mushrooms and yakisoba noodles.

Menu Sampler - Prices and menu subject to change.

Present your card to receive this discount.

DINING OUT

$5.00 Value

THAI CABIN
Restaurant

Enjoy $5 off a minimum purchase of twenty dollars or more (excluding tax, tip and alcoholic beverages).

Dine in only

valid any evening

16165 SW Regatta Ln. Ste. 300, Beaverton, OR
(503)617-4602

Thai Cabin offers traditional Thai cuisine customized to your taste. Our modern style restaurant gives you a feeling of home. The comfortable atmosphere along with smooth music will invite you to sit back and relax after a long day of work. Our food will keep you coming back. Private dining section available for parties or meetings.

Card No. 2

APPETIZERS Crab Puff(6)...6.50
Crab meat mixed with cream cheese wrapped in wonton skin, deep fried served w/ sweet & sour sauce.

Cabin Roof(5)...6.50
Deep fried wonton skin stuffed w/chicken and shrimp served w/ sweet & sour sauce.

CURRY   Peanut Sauce Red Curry 9.00
Red curry in coconut milk w/peanut sauce ,broccoli,eggplants, bell peppers and basil.

FRIED RICE   green curry fried rice...............................10.00
Fried rice with eggs, bamboo slice, eggplant and basil in spicy green curry sauce.

SPECIALTIES Spicy Telapia Fish...............................11.00
Deep fried Telapia topped with onions, basil and bell peppers stir fried in spicy sauce.

Pad Thai Volcano...............................12.00
Thin rice noodle stir fried with **chicken & shrimp** , eggs, bean spouts, green onions, ground peanuts in Pad Thai sauce wrapped with scramble eggs.

Crispy **salmon** Green Bean 12.00
Crispy **salmon** stir fried with green beans, bell peppers in our special sauce.

Garlic Prawns...............................16.50
Stir fried prawns with garlic and black pepper, served over steamed broccoli and spinach served with steamed rice.

Menu Sampler - Prices and menu subject to change.

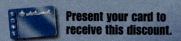

Present your card to receive this discount.

DINING OUT

$5⁰⁰ Value

MI PUEBLO

Enjoy *$5 off with the minimum purchase of twenty dollars or more (excluding tax, tip and alcoholic beverages.).*

valid anytime

10543 S.E. Fuller Rd., Milwaukie, OR (503)653-5094

More authentic options than most Mexican restaurants around. Original flavors, spices and traditional family recipes. From favorite enchiladas to savory seafood specialties, our menu will satisfy one and all. Family owned and operated, Mi Pueblo is open for lunch and dinner 7 days a week.

  Card No. 11

ESPECIALIDADES- HOUSE SPECIALS

TACOS AL CARBON   **$11.50**
Three charbroiled steak tacos topped with pico de gallo and cotija cheese.

ARROZ CON POLLO   **$9.75**
Sliced chicken breast sautéed with mushrooms and onions. Served on a bed of rice and topped with tomato and melted cheese.

ENCHILADAS

ENCHILADAS DE ESPINACA   **$10.50**
Two enchiladas filled with baby shrimp, spinach, mushrooms and pico de gallo. Topped with our special white sauce and melted cheese.

MARISCOS-SEAFOOD

CAMARONES MONTERREY   **$12.75**
Sauteed bacon wrapped prawns on a bed of rice. Topped with monterrey jack cheese. Garnished with guacamole.

BURRITOS GRANDES

PUEBLO BURRITO   **$9.50**
10" flour tortilla filled with ground beef, chicken, al pastor, carnitas or asada, guacamole, rice and beans. Topped with burrito sauce, melted cheese, lettuce, tomato, and sour cream.

VEGGIE BURRITO   **$7.25**
Broccoli, cauliflower, carrots, mushrooms, bell pepper and onion Sautéed and seasoned with the best flavors.

Menu Sampler - Prices and menu subject to change.

Present your card to receive this discount.

DINING OUT

Up To $**15**.^{00} Value

Sweet Basil Thai
www.sweetbasilor.com

Enjoy one complimentary DINNER
ENTREE when a second DINNER
ENTREE of equal or greater value is
purchased.

valid anytime

Come enjoy from-scratch, homemade
Thai cooking in an authentic Thai
ambiance. We prepare the best sauces
in Oregon; try our special curry!
Our full bar and restaurant are open
for lunch M-F 11:30-2:30 and dinner
every day from 5-9; 5-10 F & SA.

1639 NW Glisan St. (Between 16th & 17th), **Portland, OR**
(503)473-8758

3135 NE Broadway (Between 31st & 32nd), **Portland, OR**
(503)281-8337

NEW   Card No. 20

Appetizers:

Gai Satay: 7.5- Skewers of BBQ chicken, marinated in a light curry served with peanut sauce, toasts and cucumber salad.

Sample Plate: 9.5- Combination of Popia Tod, Fresh Wrapped, Fried Wonton, and Fried Tofu, served w/ plum sauce & peanut sauce.

Salads:

Larb:* 8.75- Ground chicken or tofu mixed with shallot and green onions, lemongrass, cilantro, and mint tossed with spicy lime sauce and served with fresh lettuce.

House Specials:

King Salmon Curry:*16.5- Grilled Salmon to perfection, with a touch of smooth, Homemade Curry Sauce on a bed of vegetables.

Phad Phet Talay:* 18- Stir-fried combination of seafood /w homemade curry paste & fresh Thai pepper, onions, bell peppers & sweet basil

Crispy Honey Duck: 17- crispy-fried sliced duck on the bed of broccoli & spinach topped w/ honey, ginger & Sweet Basil special sauce.

Oriental Eggplant:* 9.5- Stir-fried Thai eggplant, fried tofu, assorted mushrooms, bell peppers, onions, black bean sauce & basil leaves.

Chef's Choices: (No. 60-61, 63-66, 68-69 Served with Jasmine Rice)

Thai Grilled Seafood Curry:* 16.75- Grilled Tiger prawns, scallops, crab leg, green curry sauce, green beans, bamboo shoots, bell pepper and fresh spinach topped w/ our delicious

Thai Pasta: 16- Thai style egg noodles with crab legs, black tiger prawns, bean sprouts, cilantro, green onion and lettuce in a zesty garlic sauce

Roasted Duck Curry:*17- Roasted duck with pineapple chunks, basil leaves, bell peppers, and tomatoes with a smooth red curry sauce.

Panang Seafood:* 21- Sautéed Black tiger prawns, green mussel, calamari, salmon, scallops, crab claws, basil leaves with a delicious Panang curry sauce

Moo Yang with Peanut Sauce: 14- Marinated pork loin grilled to perfection, topped with peanut sauce.

House Salmon Noodle: 16.5- Sautéed Pacific Salmon with famous Pad Thai sauce and garlic, on a bed of Broccoli, spinach and egg noodle, topped with green onion and cilantro

Menu Sampler - Prices and menu subject to change.

DINING OUT

Cha Taqueria & Bar

chaportland.com

Serving only sustainable seafood and all-natural meat using the healthiest of ingredients. Our restaurant is an authentic, elegant, and upscale southern-Mexican-style taqueria. We happily accommodate special diets. Enjoy our unique tequila-tasting bar at lunch or dinner every day.

Up To $15.00 Value

Enjoy one complimentary LUNCH OR DINNER ENTREE when a second LUNCH OR DINNER ENTREE of equal or greater value is purchased.

valid anytime

305 N.W. 21st Ave. (at Everett St.), **Portland, OR** (503)295-4077

Card No. 34

Enchiladas
Served with Mexican rice
Del Mar Crab & Prawns in our creamy garlic-white wine sauce 14

Mole Poblano
Our Famous Mole Poblano over grilled chicken breast served with Mexican rice and Anita's handmade tortillas 13

Salmon en Chipotle
Grilled wild salmon in a light garlic chipotle pepper sauce over seasonal vegetables & Mexican rice 15

Chile Verde
Tender pork, green beans and potatoes slow cooked in a traditional verde sauce served with Anita's handmade tortillas, pinto beans & Spanish rice 14

Lomo de Puerco
Grilled pork medallions marinated in a tequila achiote sauce brushed with a habanero butter and served with sauteed seasonal veggies & roasted potatoes 14

Menu Sampler - Prices and menu subject to change.

DINING OUT

$10.00 Value

fuji's clackamas

www.myfujis.com

Enjoy $10.00 off with a minimum purchase of forty dollars (excluding tax, tip & alcoholic beverages).

valid anytime

12270 SE Sunnyside Rd, Clackamas, OR (503)698-3941

Enjoy the unique Fuji's dining experience as you watch our personal chefs entertain you while preparing your choice of steak, seafood or poultry right at your table. Selections include succulent Filet Mignon and Rib-Eye cuts of beef, chicken and fresh seafood featuring Sea Scallops, Black Tiger Prawns, grilled Calamari and Rock Lobster served with drawn butter.

  Card No. 15

Hibachi-Style Dinner
*** *all dinners include grilled vegetables (zucchini, mushrooms, and onions), tossed side salad, steamed white rice and your choice of fresh yakisoba noodles or fried rice*

Chicken Dark
Chicken Breast
Grilled Calamari
Flat-Iron Steak
Grilled Beef Short-Ribs
Black Tiger Prawns
Premium Rib-Eye Steak
Premium Beef Tenderloin
Large Sea Scallops

Samurai Combinations
*** *enjoy one of our fantastic combinations featuring your choice of any two items above*

New Family-Style Meals
*** *all family-style meals include grilled vegetables, tossed side salad, steamed white rice, and your choice of fresh yakisoba noodles or fried rice*

*** Choose from any three featured selections

Menu Sampler - Prices and menu subject to change.

DINING OUT

Present your card to receive this discount.

The London Grill

The Benson
HOTEL · PORTLAND

For over 50 years The London Grill has offered the finest in dining traditions; elegant decor, award winning cuisine & attentive service. Located in the historic Benson Hotel, the staff strives to make every occasion special & your dining experience a memorable one.

Up To $27.00 Value

Enjoy one complimentary LUNCH OR DINNER ENTREE when a second LUNCH OR DINNER ENTREE of equal or greater value is purchased.

valid anytime

309 S.W. Broadway (located in the Benson Hotel), **Portland, OR (503)228-2000**

 Card No. 5

Lunch

Stone Ground Buccatini Pasta
Sautéed with wild mushrooms, oven dried tomatoes, spinach garlic and parmesan cheese $14

Oven Roasted Halibut Filet
Mussels and shrimp in a white wine and parsley sauce, rice pilaf $20

Grilled Chicken Breast Wrapped in Prosciutto
Olive, basil and cherry tomato relish, and Couscous $14

Warm Brie and Ham Sandwich
French baguette, cornichons, and sweet onions $14

Dungeness Crab Salad
Tomatoes, asparagus, sweet onion and Louis dressing $16

Dinner

Scallop and Crab Crusted Halibut
Beet couscous and saffron beurre blanc $34

Roasted Umpqua Valley Lamb Rib Eye
Eggplant orange marmalade, yogurt sauce with a hint of curry $48

Flash Cured Atlantic Salmon
Yukon Gold mash, piquillo and white truffle oil $29

Grilled Jumbo Prawns
Black sweet rice, Madras curry vinaigrette and yucca chips $32

Menu Sampler - Prices and menu subject to change.

DINING OUT

Up To $23.00 Value

VINOTOPIA.

www.cinetopiatheater.com

Enjoy one complimentary ENTREE when a second ENTREE of equal or greater value is purchased.

Dining room only

valid anytime

11700 SE 7th Street, Vancouver, WA (360)213-2811

Enjoy our upscale American Grill restaurant located within the Cinetopia complex. Serving a fine selection of seafood, meat and pasta dishes complemented by over 100 wines available by the glass. Come enjoy an evening in our elegant dining area, or catch a quick meal before or after a movie.

   Card No. 18

Dungeness Crab - Mango, Avocado, Asparagus and Hearts of Palm with Toasted Pine Nut Vinaigrette $16.95
suggested wine: 2007 Kim Crawford Sauvignon Blanc Marlborough, NZ
oz.: $1.50 glass: $7.50

Alaska Halibut – Coconut Braised Halibut with Pineapple, Cilantro, Relish and Passion Fruit Sauce Accompanied by Wasabi Mashed Potatoes with Local Asparagus $28.95
suggested wine: 2006 A to Z Pinot Noir, Oregon
oz.: $1.80 glass: $9.00

Grilled Chicken Penne - Sun-Dried Tomatoes, Broccoli, Goat Cheese and Pine Nuts with Balsamic Chicken-Roasted Garlic Reduction $14.95
suggested wine: 2005 Sportoletti Merlot/Sangiovese Umbria, Italy
oz.: $1.50 glass: $7.50

Risotto Milanese - with Tenderloin of Beef, Saffron, Peas and Parmesan $20.95
suggested wine: 2006 Razer's Edge Shiraz, McLaren Valley, Australia
oz.: $1.80 glass: $9.00

Pinot Short Rib - with Mashed Potatoes and Roasted Vegetables $15.95
suggested wine: 2006 Elk Cove Pinot Noir, Willamette Valley, OR
oz.: $2.30 glass: $11.50

Rosemary Chicken Pot Pie - Puff Pastry Crust with Peas, Carrots, Potatoes, and Chicken $11.95
suggested wine: 2005 Robert Mondavi Chardonnay, Napa Valley, CA
oz.: $1.60 glass: $8.00

Menu Sampler - Prices and menu subject to change.

DINING OUT

Café Allegro

Up To $14.00 Value

Come join us at our quaint little cafe in downtown Tigard. Sample some of our delicious pasta dishes or specialties all made with fresh ingredients. If pizza is more to your taste, we have a wonderful selection, all hearth baked. Also available, banquet facilities & catering, perfect for business luncheons, friendly gatherings or intimate get togethers.

Enjoy one complimentary DINNER ENTREE when a second DINNER ENTREE of equal or greater value is purchased.

valid any evening

Friday & Saturday seating after 8 p.m.

12386 SW Main St., Tigard, OR (503)684-0130

Card No. 33

Low Carb Specials

Sautéed Chicken Breast, Greens and Roasted Veggies 9.95
*Italian seasonings, broccoli, mushroom, bell pepper, red onions,
zucchini, tomato and carrot sautéed in olive oil and garlic
and served over a bed of fresh spinach*

Pasta Sautés

Veggie Sauté 11.95
*Artichoke hearts, sundried tomato, mushroom, zucchini,
red and green onion sautéed in olive oil and garlic served
over lingine and marinara sauce*

Spicy Chicken Alfredo 11.95
*Tender pieces of chicken breast sautéed in a spicy cream sauce
and served over egg linguine*

Entrées

Sea Scallops 14.95
*Fresh sea scallops seared with a spicy herb crust, finished with a
reduced balsamic vinaigrette*

Chicken Picatta 13.95
Breast of chicken sautéed with lemon, garlic, red onion and capers

Grilled Salmon 15.95
Fresh salmon grilled and served with a lemon-herb vinaigrette

Menu Sampler - Prices and menu subject to change.

DINING OUT

Up To $11.00 Value

Enjoy one complimentary DINNER or A LA CARTE ENTREE when a second DINNER or A LA CARTE ENTREE of equal or greater value is purchased.

valid anytime

312 E Evergreen Blvd, Vancouver, WA (360)750-7475

Fresh Mexican Food With a Flair

Treat your tastebuds to traditional Mexican cuisine and your disposition to a festive, cheery atmosphere. Enjoy a variety of authentic and specially created house recipes. Dinner is served until 1:00 am.

  Card No. 19

Especialidades

Carnitas De Pollo 9.95
White meat (fried and sliced) with green peppers, onions and spices.

Suizas 9.95
Two corn tortillas filled with chicken, topped with tomatillo sauce and sour cream.

Arros con Pollo 9.95
Boneless breast of chicken sautéed in a special sauce and served over a bed of rice and melted cheese.

Carne Asada 9.95
Slices of skirt steak cooked over charcoal, served with tortillas, guacamole and pico de gallo.

Chile Verde 9.95
Lean diced pork simmered with green chile peppers and spices.

Chile Colorado 9.95
Cubes of lean tender beef cooked in red chile sauce blended with Mexican spices.

Pollo en Mole 9.95
Chicken covered with our own sweet and spicy Mexican sauce.

Steak Presidente 9.95
Tip sirloin steak cooked over charcoal and served with a cheese enchilada.

Enchiladas Rancheras 9.95
Two corn tortillas rolled and stuffed with cheese, topped with ranchera, guacamole and sour cream.

Flautas 9.95
Two crisp flour tortillas stuffed with chicken and served with guacamole and sour cream.

Steak Picado 9.95
Marinated chunks of steak simmered with tomatoes, bell peppers and onions.

Carnitas *(Mexican Roast Pork)* 9.95
Large chunks of fresh pork, slowly simmered in its own juices, along with onion, garlic and seasonings. With sour cream and pico de gallo.

Taquitos Rancheros 9.95
Deep fried crisp corn tortillas stuffed with beef and served with guacamole and sour cream.

Menu Sampler - Prices and menu subject to change.

DINING OUT

www.marcoscafe.com

Up To $17.00 Value

Enjoy one complimentary LUNCH OR DINNER ENTREE when a second LUNCH OR DINNER ENTREE of equal or greater value is purchased.

valid anytime

7910 SW 35th Ave. (On the corner of 35th & Multnomah Blvd. in Multnomah Village), **Portland, OR**
(503) 245-0199

Marco's Cafe is located in SW Portland's historic Multnomah Village. Since 1983 we have served delicious breakfasts, lunches & dinners. Our dinner menu changes daily & always includes 2 vegetarian entrees. We use only all-natural & hormone-free meats & chicken. Our fish is approved by the Monterey Bay Aquarium "Seafood Watch".

  Card No. 36

Andouille and Asparagus Omelette
natural pork andouille sausage, asparagus, red peppers, onion and pepperjack cheese $11.25

Veggie Burrito
chipotle flour tortilla filled with brown rice, black bean chili, corn, tomato, avocado and pepper jack cheese, topped with Spanish sauce and sour cream $10.25

Gouda Mouda
roasted turkey, gouda, chipotle grilled onion, lettuce, tomato and roasted garlic red pepper aioli on grilled hazelnut bread $10.50

Lemon Broiled Halibut
Fresh Alaskan halibut fillet lightly coated with lemon breadcrumbs, broiled and topped with maple apple butter OR spicy remoulade; served with lemon steamed rice. $16.50

Southwestern Salad
grilled sweet corn, salsa, avocado, black bean chili, crisp chipotle tortillas, jack and cheddar cheese over crisp romaine lettuce, topped with lime, smoked chili, avocado and cilantro vinaigrette dressing $10.00 Half Salad $7.00

Menu Sampler - Prices and menu subject to change.

DINING OUT

GASTRO PUB

Established 1947

Caint, Ceol agus Ól

www.theleakyroof.com

The Leaky Roof, Portland's first Gastro Pub, is where high-end casual meets neighborhood comfortable. Serving Portland since 1947. Parking close by.

Up To **$21⁰⁰ Value**

Enjoy one complimentary LUNCH OR DINNER ENTREE when a second LUNCH OR DINNER ENTREE of equal or greater value is purchased.

valid anytime

1538 SW Jefferson St. (At the corner of 16th & Jefferson, across from KGO TV), **Portland, OR (503)222-3745**

PRINT MORE ONLINE

NEW

Card No. 37

Prosciutto Wrapped Sea Scallops
Prosciutto, vodka sauce & salsa verdé
14.50

Guinness Battered Onion Rings
Served with house made rémoulade
8.5

Apple & Pear Salad
Apples, pears, bleu cheese, candied walnuts tossed in balsamic vinaigrette and served over mixed greens
9.5

The Leaky Roof Special
Tillamook Cheddar, apple wood smoked bacon, ham, egg, and mayonnaise
11.95

Hand Formed Vegetarian Black Bean Burger
Black beans & barley infused with cilantro, lime & jalapeño, topped with Tillamook Cheddar, chipotle aioli & avocado
9

Osso Bucco
Braised pork shank, mashed potatoes, red wine demi-glace, seasonal vegetables
22

Stuffed Meatloaf
Certified Angus Beef, ham, spinach, mushrooms, Parmesan cheese, mashed potatoes, mushroom gravy, seasonal vegetables
16

Guinness Battered Fish & Chips
Two piece - 12.5   Three piece - 15

Menu Sampler - Prices and menu subject to change.

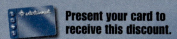

Present your card to receive this discount.

DINING OUT

Sungari
Classic Szechwan

www.sungarirestaurant.com

Recognized as one of Portland's top Szechwan restaurants, Sungari takes pride in preparing the unique and exotic flavorings and food of Szechwan cuisine. Award-winning food, sophisticated atmosphere and courteous service make Sungari a definite must try.

Up To **$20.00** Value

Enjoy one complimentary DINNER ENTREE when a second DINNER ENTREE of equal or greater value is purchased.

Dine in only

valid any evening

735 SW 1st Ave, Portland, OR (503)224-0800

  Card No. 22

House Specialties

芝 麻 牛
Spicy Sesame Beef   13.95
Marinated slices of beef glazed with a spicy sweet sauce, topped with toasted sesame seeds and served on a bed of crispy rice noodles.

黑 椒 豬 柳
Peppered Pork Tenderloin   16.95
Sautéed mushrooms and bell peppers in a spicy black pepper sauce, served over seared pork tenderloin medallions.

糖 醋 里 肌
Tung-Chou Pork   13.95
Szechwan Sweet & Street Pork
Sautéed diced pork in lemon-honey sauce with rice vinegar.

左 宗 棠 雞
General Tso's chicken   13.95
Chunks of boneless chicken sauteed in a savory sauce with dry chili peppers.

本 樓 鴨 片
Sungari Duck Slices   13.95
Boneless duck slices sauteed with snow peas and black mushrooms in our Kung Pao sauce.

核 桃 蝦
Crispy Prawns with Honeyed Walnuts   17.95
Jumbo prawns with a light lemon glaze, topped with toasted honey walnuts.

Menu Sampler - Prices and menu subject to change.

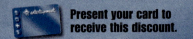
DINING OUT

Up To $17⁰⁰ Value

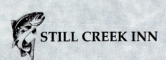

STILL CREEK INN

Savor the creations of Chef Brigette Romeo at the Still Creek Inn. Enjoy a Northwest style menu highlighting local produce, fresh meats & seafood. Featuring all natural burgers from Shadow Mountain Ranch & USDA Choice Grade Steaks. The Still Creek Inn is sure to become a regular stop on your trip to Mt. Hood. Stop by & find out what the locals already know.

Enjoy one complimentary ENTREE when a second ENTREE of equal or greater value is purchased.

Specials excluded

valid anytime

73365 E. Hwy 26, Rhododendron, OR (503)622-4618

  Card No. 25

Still Creek Seafood & Chicken & Pasta

Still Creek Oysters
Willapa Bay oysters pan-fried or deep fried crispy with spicy cocktail sauce
$16.95

Portobello Chicken
Chicken filled with brie cheese & thyme Served with portobello linguine
$16.95

Alpine Pan Fried Chicken
Takes 20 minutes to prepare, and it is well worth the wait
$15.95

Alder Smoked Salmon Fettuccini
Alder smoked salmon tossed with fettuccini mushrooms, spinach & garlic cream sauce
$15.95

Camp Fire Steaks

Flat Iron Steak
8oz Flat Iron with a mesquite rub, grilled then glazed with pine nut herb butter
$17.95

Rosemary Crusted Prime Rib
(Served only on Friday & Saturday evenings Slow Roasted with garlic, rosemary & pepper served with creamy horseradish & au jus

Queen Cut	10 oz -	$19.95
King Cut	15 oz -	$22.95
Still Creek Cut	20 oz-	$26.95

Peppered Baseball Top Sirloin
10 oz. Baseball cut sirloin rubbed with pepper spice, grilled and topped with crispy sweet onions
$18.95

Menu Sampler - Prices and menu subject to change.

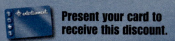

Present your card to receive this discount.

DINING OUT

Bush Garden
TUALATIN

Up To $16.00 Value

Enjoy one complimentary DINNER ENTREE when a second DINNER ENTREE of equal or greater value is purchased.

Sushi & Specials excluded

valid any evening

Not valid with any other discounts or promotions

8290 S.W. Nyberg Rd., Tualatin, OR (503)691-9744

The Bush Garden Tualatin, located on the lake in the heart of downtown Tualatin, offers the finest in Japanese cuisine. Choose from an outstanding selection of sashimi, sushi, seafood, tempura, salmon or beef teriyaki & more. Outside dining by the lake is available, weather permitting.

PRINT MORE ONLINE

 Card No. 56

DINNERS
W/ MISO SOUP, EDAMEME AND RICE

ディナー
御飯、味噌汁、枝豆付

EBI TEMPURA
Prawns and Vegetables in our ultra-light Tempura batter & quickly deep-fried

えび天麩羅   *13.00*

CHICKEN TERIYAKI
Tender Chicken with our TERIYAKI sauce

チキンテリヤキ   *12.00*

TONKATSU
Lean Pork Cutlet lightly breaded and deep-fried

とんかつ   *13.50*

SUSHI DINNER
Tuna Roll & A varied assortment of Finest Sushi : chef's choice

寿司ディナー   *19.50*

COMBO DINNER
W/ MISO SOUP, EDAMAME AND RICE

コンボディナー
御飯、味噌汁、枝豆付

SALMON COMBO
Combination of SALMON TERIYAKI & TEMPURA

サーモンコンボ   *17.00*

YAKINIKU COMBO
Combination of Spicy BBQ Beef w/ sliced onion & TEMPURA

焼肉コンボ   *16.00*

Menu Sampler - Prices and menu subject to change.

Offer validity is governed by the Rules of Use and excludes defined holidays. Offers are not valid with other discount offers, unless specified. Coupons void if purchased, sold or bartered. Discounts exclude tax, tip and/or alcohol, where applicable. Tipping should be 15% to 20% of the total bill before discount.

DINING OUT

Up To **$20.00** Value

PiZZA MiA
RISTORANTE E SPORTS BAR

Offering gourmet pizzas & great
Italian dishes. Complemented by
a fine selection of beer & wine,
featuring Banfi wines, the number 1
winery of Italy. Casual fine dine
environment with 10 beers on tap and
a full bar, TVs & big screen. Close to
Delta Park.

*Enjoy one complimentary LUNCH OR
DINNER ENTREE when a second
LUNCH OR DINNER ENTREE of equal
or greater value is purchased or for
those who prefer - buy any one pizza,
get one free.*

valid anytime

915 N. Anchor Way (Marine Dr. E. exit), **Portland, OR**
(503) 285-8889

 Card No. 47

ANTIPASTI

MOZZARELLA WITH RADICCHIO AND TOMATOES
GRILLED RADICCHIO, SLICED
TOMATOES AND MOZZARELLA
SERVED WITH PESTO
DRESSING, OLIVE OIL, CRACKED
PEPPER, AND SEA SALT

ARANCINI
TENDER SAFFRON RISOTTO STUFFED
WITH BLACK FOREST HAM
AND 3 CHEESES, DEEP FRIED AND
SERVED WITH PESTO MAYONNAISE

TUSCAN PRAWNS
MARINATED CHARBROILED
TIGER PRAWNS, WRAPPED IN
BASIL AND PROSCIUTTO
PAIRED WITH A RICH PESTO
DIPPING SAUCE.

HOUSE SPECIALTY PIZZAS

BBQ CHICKEN
ROSEMARY DOUGH, TOPPED
WITH BBQ SAUCE, PEPPERS,
ROASTED CHICKEN AND
OUR HOUSE 3 CHEESE BLEND

DI MARE
FRESH SHRIMP, CALAMARI,
AND CRAB ON PIZZA
DOUGH, TOPPED WITH AN
ALFREDO CHEESE
SAUCE GARNISHED WITH
ARTICHOKES AND FRESH
DILL

ANATRA AGLI AROMI
ROASTED DUCK, RED SAUCE,
AND OUR HOUSE 3 CHEESE
BLEND, FINISHED WITH
ORANGE ZEST

SECONDI

GRILLED TUNA STEAK
MARINATED YELLOW FIN TUNA
STEAK CHARBROILED TO
PERFECTION. TOPPED WITH A
HERB AIOLI SAUCE AND SERVED
WITH SAFFRON RISOTTO AND
MIXED VEGETABLES.
$14.95

SCALOPPINE AL LIMONE
TENDER VEAL CUTS
MARINATED IN ITALIAN
SEASONING AND SAUTÉED TO
PERFECTION AND FINISHED
WITH A LEMON VERMOUTH
SAUCE. SERVED WITH
PARMESAN POTATOES AND
MIXED VEGETABLES.
$19.95

BISTECCA ALL PIZZAIOLA
THICK RIB-EYE STEAK GRILLED TO
YOUR LIKING, SMOTHERED IN A
WHITE WINE, OREGANO
FLAVORED TOMATO SAUCE.
SERVED WITH PARMESAN
POTATOES AND MIXED
VEGETABLES.
$19.95

Menu Sampler - Prices and menu subject to change.

DINING OUT

PORCELLI'S

Up To $18.00 Value

Enjoy one complimentary ENTREE when a second ENTREE of equal or greater value is purchased.

valid anytime

6500 S.W. Virginia Ave., Portland, OR (503)245-2260

John's Landends neighborhood Italian restaurant. Featuring the best in authentic Italian cuisine complemented with a intimate dining experience. Fresh flavors, daily specials, a seasonal menu will please your palate. Come and visit. Open for breakfast, lunch & dinner.

 PRINT MORE ONLINE   **NEW**   Card No. 12

CAPELLINI AGLIO E OLIO CON GAMBERI — $14.00
Tiger shrimp sautéed with garlic, mushrooms, zucchini, extra virgin olive oil in angel hair pasta

PENNE CON SALMONE E ASPARAGI — $14.00
Chunks of salmon as asparagus sautéed with white wine, garlic and extra virgin olive oil tossed with penne pasta

FETTUCCINE ALFREDO — $ 9.00
Classic alfredo sauce with heavy cream and parmesan

w/ mushrooms — $11.00

w/ chicken or shrimp — $12.00

VITELLO MILANESINE — $15.00
Thinly sliced veal, lightly breaded, oven roasted, topped with marinara and fresh tomatoes

POLLO PARMAGGIANO — $13.00
Breast of chicken, lightly breaded, oven roasted, topped with marinara

CARPACCIO DI SALMONE AFFUMICATO — $9.00
Thinly sliced smoked salmon on a bed of mixed greens with capers, lemon juice and extra virgin olive oil

PROSCIUTTO E MELONE — $8.50
Thinly sliced Prosciutto and melon on a bed of mixed greens

INSALATA PORCELLI — $9.50
Oven roasted chicken breast on a bed of mixed greens tossed in a balsamic vinaigrette, topped with caramelized Pecans and gorgonzola cheese

Menu Sampler - Prices and menu subject to change.

DINING OUT

Up To $15.00 Value

Shilo INNS.

Enjoy one complimentary DINNER ENTREE when a second DINNER ENTREE of equal or greater value is purchased.

valid any evening

11707 N.E. Airport Way, Portland, OR (503)252-4300

An exceptional array of entrees are prepared with a touch of creativity. We take great pride in offering fresh Northwest regional fare. Start off with an order of Coconut Prawns or delicious crab & artichoke dip. Enjoy such specialties as Seared Salmon, Portobello Ravioli or Filet Mignon. Open daily. Reservations are suggested.

Card No. 39

Appetizers

Ohana Blackened Ahi $11
With a spicy soy mustard

Szechuan Pork Ribs $9
In a zesty sesame glaze

Avocado and Ahi Shilotini $10
With tomato & onion In a sesame-garlic wasabi aoili

Dinner Entrées

Roasted Portobello Mushroom $14
Char-broiled and served with garlic mashed potatoes

Mai Ke Kai Broiled Ahi $22
Seared to perfection in blackened spices and served with jasmine rice

Shilo Asian Noodle Primavera $13
With fresh vegetables in a lemon kalbi glaze

Mai K'Aina Rustic Grilled Ribeye $20
Served with Roquefort sauce and garlic mashed potatoes

Menu Sampler - Prices and menu subject to change.

DINING OUT

Up To $15.00 Value

Kesone
Thai Lao bistro
Cuisine of Home Cooking

Offering the fine essence of Thai & Lao home cooking. Every dish is prepared with the kind of perfection that can only be found with many years of practice. Family owned & operated on N.E. Sandy across from Pepsi Cola Company.

Enjoy one complimentary LUNCH OR DINNER ENTREE when a second LUNCH OR DINNER ENTREE of equal or greater value is purchased.

Dine in only

valid anytime

2600 N.E. Sandy Blvd., Portland, OR (503)228-5775

Card No. 7

CHEF'S SPECIALTIES

NAMM KAO VIENTIANE – Crispy rice with coconuts shaving with choice of Chicken, Pork or Tofu, Tossed with mints, lime juice, house seasoning with roasted peanuts, cilantro, green onions, served with lettuce leaves and herbs.   9.00

KING OF TIGERS – Grilled beef tenderloin marinated in lemon grass seasoning served with spicy ginger lime sauce.   9.00

KANG PHED PED YANG – Boasted duck in red curry, pineapple, peas, carrots and sweet basil.   12.00

Each dish is prepared with your choice of;
Vegetarian, chicken, beef, or pork...........$8.50
Prawns or Squid.................................$9.50
Scallops or Combination Seafood..............$13.50
Noodles, Salad and Fried rice entrees do not include Jasmine rice.

SWEET PRINCESS – Sweet green curry sauce with eggplants, zucchin bell peppers, kaffir lime leaves and sweet basil.

PAD KRA PRAUW – Garlic sauce sautéed fresh chili, mushroom, bell pepper, onion and sweet basil.

PAD THAI – Pan-fried rice noodles, house sauce, egg and scallion with roasted ground peanuts served with bean sprouts and a sliced of lime.

PAD KEE MAO – Pan fried wide rice noodles, egg, bell pepper, broccoli and sweet basil with fresh garlic chili sauce.

Menu Sampler - Prices and menu subject to change.

DINING OUT

Up To $15.00 Value

BIGRED'S
A WESTERN CAFE

Big Red's is a Western Cafe where the cowboy legend lives on. Enjoy sumptuous BBQ, delectable grilled chicken and mouthwatering Tex-Mex. Sit back and enjoy in our Western themed, comfortable dining room, or stroll on in to our cowboy cantina. Fun and family-friendly, Big Red's will be your favorite night out.

Enjoy one complimentary DINNER ENTREE when a second DINNER ENTREE of equal or greater value is purchased.

valid any evening

5515 SW Canyon Ct. (On Sylvan), **Portland, OR** **(503)297-5568**

 PRINT MORE ONLINE

 NEW

 Card No. 21

SOUPS AND SALADS

CLASSIC TACO SALAD
With seasoned ground beef, cheddar and pepperjack cheese, tomatoes, olives and green onions over crisp greens. Served with guacamole, sour cream and salsa.
9.50

CHICKEN FIESTA SALAD
Deep fried chicken tenders with cheddar and pepperjack cheese, tomatoes, olives and green onions over crisp greens. Served with guacamole, sour cream and Southwest Ranch.
9.50

SOUTHWESTERN COBB
Tomatoes, black olives, bacon, pepperjack, guacamole and grilled chicken breast over crisp greens. Your choice of dressing.
9.50

SANDWICHES

RED'S BURGER
7.00
Add cheddar, Swiss or pepperjack .75
Add pepper bacon .95

BUFFALO BURGER
Two 1/4 pound buffalo patties with cheddar and pepperjack cheese.
9.50

BRONCO BURGER
Tillamook cheddar, pepper bacon and guacamole.
8.75

BBQ BRISKET
Slow smoked beef brisket slathered in BBQ sauce on a toasted roll.
9.50

CHICKEN FRIED STEAK SANDWICH
Tender battered Angus beef fried to a golden brown. Served on a toasted roll with country gravy
8.95

HALIBUT SANDWICH
Beer battered halibut with cheddar cheese and tartar sauce on a sesame bun.
9.50

BIG RED'S BBQ

BABY BACK RIBS
A long time house favorite. We smoke them slow for maximum tenderness.
Half Rack 14.95   Full Rack 19.95

SANTA FE BBQ CHICKEN
Grilled chicken breast smothered with Red's BBQ sauce, pepper bacon, cheddar and jack cheese. Topped with diced tomatoes and green onions. 13.50

Menu Sampler - Prices and menu subject to change.

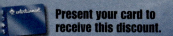

MAXURI
INDIAN RESTAURANT
Traditional Home Style Cooking

Sample our savory selection of traditional home style cooking with made from scratch recipes, tandoori, Biriyani, curry & vegetarian dishes. Buffet lunch. Open 7 days a week. Catering available.

Enjoy one complimentary DINNER ENTREE when a second DINNER ENTREE of equal or greater value is purchased.

valid anytime

16175 S.W. Walker Rd. (near Fred Meyer)**, Beaverton, OR**
(503)533-9050

 PRINT MORE ONLINE

 Card No. 52

Dinner
Non-Vegetarian Entrees

	A La Carte	Thali Dinner
Chicken Curry	11.95	15.95
Boneless chicken cooked in spiced masala sauce		
Lamb Tikka Masala	12.95	16.95
Boneless Lamb tikka cooked in spiced creamy sauce		
Shrimp Curry	13.95	17.95
Shrimp cooked in spicy curry sauce		

South Indian Specialties

Dosas are crepes made with different lentil flours stuffed with vegetable curry, served with sambar and hot & mild sauces

Plain Dosa	5.50
Thin crepe made of rice and lentil flour over griddle served with sambar and chutney	
Mysore Masala Dosa	6.95
Crepe layered with spicy chutney and potato masala	
Chicken Dosa	9.95
Thin crepe filled with spicy chicken curry	

Dinners (Vegetarian Entrees)

	A La Carte	Thali Dinner
Aloo Gobi	10.95	14.95
Potatoes & cauliflower cooked with special spices		
Malai Kofta Curry	10.95	14.95
Paneer stuffed vegetable patties simmered in a creamy sauce		

Menu Sampler - Prices and menu subject to change.

DINING OUT

Up To $14.00 Value

The Rutherglen Mansion

Elegant Old World dining & an exceptional view 600 ft. above the Columbia River Valley. Views of Longview, Mt. St. Helen & the Columbia River. Dinner served Tues.-Sat. from 5 p.m. Earlybirds: 4:30 p.m.-5:30 p.m. same menu, smaller portions, at 30% less! I5 N. to Kelso, W. on Ocean Beach Hwy 4, left on 38th Ave. & just ahead on the right. Welcome! Reservations please.

Enjoy one complimentary DINNER ENTREE when a second DINNER ENTREE of equal or greater value is purchased.

valid any evening

420 Rutherglen Rd., Longview, WA (360)425-5816

 Card No. 135

CHEF BORNEMAN'S PASTA SPECIALTIES

ROMA TOMATO & BASIL LINGUINE
Roma Tomato, Garlic, Fresh Basil, Olives, Feta and Parmesan Cheese

SCALLOP & BAY SHRIMP PENNE
Sweet Red Peppers, Mushrooms, Creamy Lobster Sherry Sauce

STEAKS & CHOPS

STEAK & PRAWNS
12 oz. Rib Eye, Jumbo Prawns, Sauteed Scampi Style

PORTERHOUSE PORK STEAK 12 OZ.
Served with Raspberry, Pineapple, and Almond Chutney

GOURMET POULTRY

MEDITERRANEAN CHICKEN
Sun Dried Tomatoes, Capers, Artichoke Hearts, Sweet Vermouth

CITRON CHICKEN
Breast of Chicken, Three Citrus Sauce, Slivered Almonds, Fresh Cilantro

Menu Sampler - Prices and menu subject to change.

DINING OUT

Up To $14.00 Value

THAI ELEPHANT

Enjoy one complimentary LUNCH OR DINNER ENTREE when a second LUNCH OR DINNER ENTREE of equal or greater value is purchased.

valid anytime

2225 N.W. Allie Ave. #915, Hillsboro, OR (503)645-5959

Thai Elephant embodies the many distinctive flavors of Thailand. Our recipes are strictly prepared in traditional Thai-style cooking using exotic spices & ingredients, then served in the traditional, family style. Thai Elephant is conveniently located in the Street of Tanasborne. Open daily.

 Card No. 41

Entrees
$10.95-13.95

Kra Prow (Garlic Basil)
Him Man Pan (Cashew)
Pud Khing (Ginger)
Pud Ma Khur (Eggplant)
Kra Tiam (Garlic Black Pepper)
Pud Pric (Chili Bamboo)
Pud Kaw Pod On (Baby Corn)
Pud Kanah (Meat and Broccoli)

Curry
$10.50-15.95

Red Curry
Green Curry
Panang Curry
Massaman Curry
Yellow Curry
Red Curry Duck

Chef's Specials
$11.50-13.95

Emerald Chicken
Kang Kua Kung
Pla Rad Prik (Flaming)
Spicy Chicken (Sizzling)

Menu Sampler - Prices and menu subject to change.

DINING OUT

CHEN'S DYNASTY
RESTAURANT & LOUNGE
Hunan & Szechuan Cuisine

Szechuan & Mandarin cuisine. Family-style combinations. Specializing in seafood dishes. Crispy beef, barbecued pork & many other favorites. Come join us for a peaceful family dinner. Open 11 a.m. - 10 p.m. every day.

Enjoy one complimentary LUNCH OR DINNER ENTREE when a second LUNCH OR DINNER ENTREE of equal or greater value is purchased.

valid anytime

Take-out excluded. Combination meals excluded. Not valid with other discounts, cards or coupons

4840 NW Bethany Blvd. (on the corner of Laidlaw & Bethany, next to Walgreen's), **Portland, OR**
(503)439-8898

PRINT MORE ONLINE

Card No. 4

---

* 鴛鴦茄子　LOVER'S EGGPLANT $6.75
Skinned eggplant, fresh jalapeno, garlic slices, pickled vegetable, and bamboo shoots sauteed in kung pao sauce.

* 魚香茄子　EGGPLANT with TANGY SAUCE $6.95
Skinless eggplant strips sauteed with spicy garlic sauce.

素什錦　BUDDHA'S DELIGHT $7.25
Splendid presentation of sugar peas, carrot, baby corn, straw mushrooms, broccoli, napa, bamboo shoots, regular mushrooms, water chestnuts, sauteed in brown sauce.

海鮮大會　NEPTUNE'S DELIGHT $12.50
Shrimp, scallops, squid, winter bamboo shoots, straw mushrooms, and sugar peas sauteed in white sauce.

長江明蝦　LONG RIVER PRAWNS $10.50
Prawns, bamboo shoots, straw mushrooms, baby corn, and red bell pepper sauteed in spicy tomato sauce.

* 四川芝麻雞柳　SZECHUAN SESAME CHICKEN $9.95
Chicken strips sauteed in excessive house special Szechuan sauce, sprinkled with sesame seeds.

* 長沙雞柳　CHIANG SIA CHICKEN $10.25
Chicken strips, red bell pepper, and black mushrooms sauteed in kung pao sauce circled by steamed broccoli. A dish originated by "Uncle Chen".

* 雀巢芝麻牛肉　SESAME BEEF in the NEST $11.25
Sliced beef sauteed in kung pao sauce and sprinkled with sesame, delicately placed in a bird nest made of shredded fresh potato.

* 陳皮牛肉　BEEF with ORANGE FLAVOR $10.95
Sliced beef, orange peel, and ginger sauteed in specially made brown sauce.

Menu Sampler - Prices and menu subject to change.

Up To $13.00 Value

Enjoy one complimentary LUNCH OR DINNER ENTREE when a second LUNCH OR DINNER ENTREE of equal or greater value is purchased.

valid anytime

June 15 - Sept. 15 excluded

34450 Brooten Rd., Pacific City, OR (503)965-6722

Riverhouse is right on the scenic Nestucca River. Our ambiance is very warm & casual. We feature selective seafood & steak dinners, gourmet sandwiches, homemade soups & desserts. For your dining pleasure we have an extensive list of N.W. beers, wines & cocktails. Pacific City is located 19 miles north of Lincoln City. We are open daily & look forward to serving you!

 Card No. 167

BURGERS

THE HOUSE BURGER
Charbroiled ¼ lb. beef pattie with cheese, bacon, avocado, lettuce, tomato, pickles and onion.

SALADS

DUNGENESS CRAB OR PACIFIC SHRIMP
Chilled greens with tomato, egg slices, olives, and lemon.

SPINACH SALAD
Fresh spinach leaves with bacon, mushrooms, avocado tomato, egg slices, and artichoke hearts.

SPECIALTY DINNERS

Available after 5:00 p.m.

COQUILLE ST. JACQUES
Scallops and mushrooms sauteed in a lightly spiced cream sauce with parmesan.

OYSTERS KIRKPATRICK
Oysters oven broiled with bacon and swiss cheese in a spiced tomato puree.

FILET MIGNON
Our finest tenderloin steak wrapped in bacon and charbroiled to perfection.

Menu Sampler - Prices and menu subject to change.

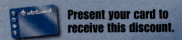

DINING OUT

 Present your card to receive this discount.

The Essence of China
RESTAURANT

武
江

At Essence of China, friendly service is efficient & the menu is seasoned with diversity. Serving authentic Cantonese & Mandarin cuisine. Our amazing menu offers new & familiar entrees, dishes are piled high with the freshest ingredients & special spices are used to ensure the best tasting Chinese food.

Up To $12.00 Value

Enjoy one complimentary DINNER ENTREE when a second DINNER ENTREE of equal or greater value is purchased.

Dine in only

valid any evening

510 S.W. 3rd Ave., Portland, OR (503)235-1976

1727 Willamette Falls Dr., West Linn, OR (503)656-6578

 PRINT MORE ONLINE

Card No. 95

CHEF'S SUGGESTIONS

General Tso's Chicken *$9.75*

Chicken Trio *$11.95*

Kung Pao Three Kinds *$10.95*

Garlic Scallop and Shrimp *$9.95*

Shrimp with Crispy Rice *$9.95*

Tien Fu Chicken *$8.75*

Triple Delight *$9.75*

House Special Sizzling Rice *$9.95*

Chicken and Shrimp Combination *$8.95*

Sesame Chicken (Beef) *$9.75*

Happy Family *$10.95*

Orange Chicken (Beef) *$9.75*

Sweet and Sour Combination *$8.75*

WAIST WATCHERS (VEGETABLE AND TOFU)

Broccoli with Garlic Sauce *$6.75*

Hot and Spicy Eggplant *$6.75*

Vegetable Delight *$6.75*

Tofu with Vegetables *$6.75*

DINNER SPECIALS

Asparagus with Chicken, Beef or Pork *$7.95*

Asparagus with Shrimp *$8.95*

Squid *$8.95*
Choice of flavor (Kung Pao, Garlic or salt and pepper)

Crispy Tofu *$6.95*

Menu Sampler - Prices and menu subject to change.

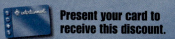

DINING OUT

Nicola's Pizza & Pasta

Capture the tastes, sights & sounds of Italy. Close & open your eyes & you are there, in the middle of a Piazza with all its beauty & history. Celebrate food & festivity surrounded by murals of the landscapes of Rome. Even the bathrooms reveal the riches of the Sistine Chapel or a vineyard from the Tuscan hills. The outdoor Patio.. simply BELLA!

Up To $13.00 Value

Enjoy one complimentary DINNER ENTREE when a second DINNER ENTREE of equal or greater value is purchased.

valid any evening

Friday & Saturday nights seating before 5 or after 8 p.m.

4826 N Lombard St., Portland, OR (503)285-1119

 Card No. 27

Nicola's Pasta with Peppers and Sausage

We sauté fresh red and green peppers with onions, garlic, spices and spicy Italian sausage. Then simmer it all in our delicious marinara sauce and serve it over spaghetti noodles. 11.99

Nicola's Lasagna

Layers of pasta with rich ricotta cheese and meat sauce. A house specialty! 11.99

Cannelloni con Salsa

Rolled pasta stuffed with a flavorful blend of veal, beef and chicken and topped with Nicola's famous meat sauce. Baked with mozzarella cheese on top. 10.99

Menu Sampler - Prices and menu subject to change.

DINING OUT

Up To $12.00 Value

DeNicola's
Italian Restaurant

Mrs. DeNicola & her family invite you to the DeNicola's Restaurant. The DeNicolas prepare each entree with fine ingredients from recipes they brought with them from Italy. They serve the kind of Italian food you've been looking for.

Enjoy one complimentary DINNER ENTREE when a second DINNER ENTREE of equal or greater value is purchased.

Dine in only; Pizza excluded

valid any evening

Saturday night seating before 6:30pm or after 8:30pm

3520 S.E. Powell, Portland, OR (503)234-2600

 Card No. 77

Entrees

	A LA CARTE	DINNER
VEAL PICCATA	15.95	17.95
(Tender veal sauteed in butter and lemon juice, with capers optional).		
VEAL PARMIGIANA STEAK	14.95	16.95
(Baked veal steak covered with meat sauce and melted cheeses).		
CHICKEN CACCIATORA	12.95	14.95
(Hunter's style with fresh mushrooms and light red sauce splashed with wine).		
CHICKEN PICCATA	12.95	14.95
(Boneless chicken sauteed in butter and lemon juice, with capers optional).		
CHICKEN PARMIGIANA	12.95	14.95
(Baked boneless chicken breast covered in a meatless red sauce and our own blend of cheeses).		

"House Specialties"

	A LA CARTE	DINNER
LASAGNA ALLA NAPOLITANA	10.95	12.95
(Layered noodles with meat & cheese blend)		
EGGPLANT PARMIGIANA	10.95	12.95
(Eggplant covered with meatless sauce & melted cheeses)		
FETTUCINE ALFREDO	8.95	10.95
SMOKED SALMON FETTUCINE ALFREDO	12.95	14.95
CHICKEN FETTUCINE ALFREDO	11.95	13.95
FETTUCINE PESTO SUPREME	10.95	12.95
(Fettucine prepared with pesto (basil) and romano cheese in a light cream sauce)		

Menu Sampler - Prices and menu subject to change.

DINING OUT

Up To $12.00 Value

SHANGHAI
海 上
NOBLE HOUSE

Specializing in Shanghai, Szechuan & Mandarin style cuisine, the experienced chefs at Shanghai Noble House strive to bring the taste of Shanghai to their distinctive dishes. Choose from specials such as Maine lobster & chicken trio. Open nightly. Banquet facilities available for up to 120 people.

Enjoy one complimentary DINNER or A LA CARTE ENTREE when a second DINNER or A LA CARTE ENTREE of equal or greater value is purchased or one FAMILY-STYLE DINNER at $7.00 off the regular price.

Peking duck excluded; Dine in only

valid any evening

5331 S.W. Macadam Ave. (Johns Landing Water Tower Bldg.), **Portland, OR** (503)227-3136

 PRINT MORE ONLINE

 Card No. 62

生猛龍蝦 **Live Maine Lobster** ....**Seasonal**
Cooked in butter or soybean or black bean or ginger scallion sauce

生猛螃蟹 **Live Dungeness Crab** ....**Seasonal**
Cooked in butter or soybean or black bean or ginger scallion sauce

鮮蒸貝殼 **Steamed Young Scallops (seasonal)** 9.50
Steamed with half shell in chef's special sauce (looks & tastes like magic)

豉汁大蜆 **Butter Clams** 8.95
Live clams sauteed with black bean sauce

龍鳳雀巢 **Lovers Bird's Nest** 12.95
General Tso's chicken and shrimp cooked in spicy sauce served with crispy birds nest

蜜桃蝦 **Honey Prawns** 10.95
Crispy prawns in light batter covered with chef's special sauce garnished with candied walnuts

一雞三味 **Chicken Trio** 10.95
Tso's chicken, cashew nut chicken and lemon chicken

雞崧生菜包 **Shanghai Moo-Shu Chicken** 9.50
Chef's recommendation
Chicken breast cooked in special way, wrapped with green lettuce, (tasty and healthy, you've never ever had it before)

黑椒牛柳 **Sizzling Marinated Beef** 10.95
Beef tenderloin sauteed with green pepper & onion with strong black pepper flavor

京都肉扒 **Imperial Porkloin** 8.75
Tender porkloin cooked with tomato sauce

脆皮干貝 **Golden Scallops** 9.95
Crispy fried scallops in spicy sauce

Menu Sampler - Prices and menu subject to change.

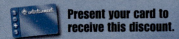
DINING OUT

Caro Amico
Est. 1949

Celebrating 58 years!!

Still here after all these years! We served our first pizza in 1949 and have been privileged to have scores of pizza lovers become friends and customers since then. Now it's our turn to welcome you! We hope you are pleased. Enjoy our ongoing tradition of good food and friendly dining in our cozy little restaurant.

Up To $12.00 Value

Enjoy one complimentary DINNER ENTREE when a second DINNER ENTREE of equal or greater value is purchased.

Or for those who prefer - any one pizza at 50% off the regular price - maximum discount $7

valid anytime

Reservations recommended

3606 SW Barbur Blvd, Portland, OR (503)223-6895

  Card No. 9

Steak Marsala $21.50
Pan-seared flat iron steak topped with sautéed mushrooms, sun-dried tomatoes and garlic in a Marsala sauce. Served with penne pasta and marinara sauce.

Pan Seared Scallops $21.50
Sea scallops seared in butter, sautéed with white pepper, garlic and dill weed. Deglazed with lemon juice & white wine. Served on a bed of linguine Alfredo.

Baked Ravioli with Prawns & Sausage $21.50
Tiger prawns sautéed with sliced Italian link sausage, mushrooms and red and yellow peppers. Tossed in a Marinara sauce with Asiago ravioli, topped with freshly grated Parmesan cheese.

Chicken Picatta $19.00
Tender breast of chicken sautéed with shallots and capers in a lemon-white wine-butter sauce. Served with fresh seasonal veggies and a side of fettuccine Alfredo.

Eggplant Parmigiana $16.00
Layers of roasted eggplant, marinara sauce and mozzarella cheese. Topped with Parmesan cheese and baked until golden brown.

Pasta Putanesca 15.00
Classic Neapolitan dish of spaghetti, anchovies, kalamata olives and crushed red pepper flakes in marinara sauce

Cannelloni 14.00
Pasta stuffed with ground meats and herbs. Baked in an individual casserole, covered with meat sauce, topped with mozzarella

Menu Sampler - Prices and menu subject to change.

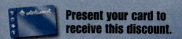

Present your card to receive this discount.

DINING OUT

HOUSE OF LAMTHONG
THAI RESTAURANT

Experience Oregon's very first Thai restaurant! Since 1980, the House of Lamthong has delighted diners with the tastes & flavors of authentic Thai cuisine. Choose from chicken, beef, pork, seafood or tofu or try one of our chef's selections.

Up To $11.00 Value

Enjoy one complimentary LUNCH OR DINNER ENTREE when a second LUNCH OR DINNER ENTREE of equal or greater value is purchased.

Dine in only

valid anytime

**1503 S.E. Tualatin Valley Hwy., Hillsboro, OR
(503)693-9222**

PRINT MORE ONLINE

Card No. 51

House Favorites

Sweet Basil
Your choice of meat. Stir-fried with basil, Thai chilies, bell pepper, carrot, onion.

Fresh Ginger
Your choice of meat, Stir-fried with fresh ginger, carrot, onion, green onion.

Garlic and Black Peppers
Your choice of meat. Stir-fried with oyster sauce, carrot, onion, mushroom.

Broccoli with Oyster Sauce
Your choice of meat. Stir-fried with oyster sauce, carrot, onion, broccoli

Chef's Selections
Served with Jasmine Rice

Fantastic Combination..$13.95
A combination of chicken, beef, pork stir-fried with broccoli, carrot, bokchoi, bell pepper, onion, tofu

Shrimp in Ceramic Pot..$15.95
Steamed shrimp with clear noodles, bokchoi, carrot, onion

Menu Sampler - Prices and menu subject to change.

DINING OUT

Up To $10.00 Value

Jerusalem Cafe
www.thejerusalemcafe.com

Enjoy one complimentary ENTREE when a second entree & two beverages are purchased.

valid anytime

516 S.E. Chkalov Dr., Vancouver, WA (360)891-1490

Welcome to the best authentic Mediterranean cuisine in Vancouver. If you haven't dined at the Jerusalem, you haven't dined out! Our goal is to offer our customers traditional dishes with only the freshest & healthiest ingredients complemented with a warm & inviting dining atmosphere. Family owned & operated. Valid at this location only.

Card No. 28

~Lunch and Dinner Entrees~
All meals include selected appetizers, pocket pita bread, and your choice of rice, tabouli, and Mediterranean salad (excluding #9 and #12).

1. **Shish Kabob**
   - Your choice of specially seasoned meat.
   Chicken....$9.99   Pork....$10.99   Beef....$11.99   Lamb.....$11.99
2. **Kofta Kabob**..$10.99
   - Mix of ground lamb and beef with onion, parsley, and our special seasoning.
3. **Jerusalem Special**..$9.99
   - Chicken and pork grilled with chopped onions and bell peppers with our special seasoning.
4. **Chicken on Fire**...$10.99
   - Boneless skinless chicken charbroiled with our special seasoning.
5. **Shish Tawouk**...$11.99
   - Pieces of chicken served on grilled pita bread smothered with sautéed onions and mushroom sauce.
6. **Garlic Chicken**..$11.99
   -boneless skinless chicken grilled with lemon garlic sauce.
7. **Saniha**...$11.99
   - Mix of ground lamb and beef with onions, parsley, and our special seasonings cooked with tahini or tomato.
9. **Hummus Bel-laham**
   - Hummus topped with your choice of specially seasoned meat.
   Chicken....$8.99   Pork....$9.99   Beef....$9.99   Lamb.......$9.99

~Sandwiches~
Served in pocket pita bread stuffed with hummus, tahini, tabouli, Turkish salad, with red and green pickled cabbage.

Hummus Sandwich...$3.99
Babagahnooj Sandwich...$3.99
Falafel Sandwich...$4.99
Shish Kabob Sandwich   Chicken....$4.99   Pork....$5.99   Beef....$5.99   Lamb....$5.99

Menu Sampler - Prices and menu subject to change.

DINING OUT

TEQUILA Grill

Up To $9.00 Value

Enjoy one complimentary LUNCH OR DINNER ENTREE when a second LUNCH OR DINNER ENTREE of equal or greater value is purchased.

valid anytime

325 N. Hwy. 99, McMinnville, OR (503)474-1776

A warm welcome of Mexican hospitality awaits you. Come & enjoy traditional Mexican dishes prepared just to your liking along with a collection of your favorite appetizers & great margaritas. We invite you & your family to come & enjoy the freshest & best Mexican foods. Open daily.

   Card No. 164

CARNES AL ESTIL TEQUILA
STEAKS MADE EL TEQUILA STYLE

Carne Asada 9.95
Top sirloin charcoal broiled in a special way, topped with fried onions & bell peppers, chunky sauce & guacamole

Chile Colorado 8.95
Chunks of beef cooked in a tasty red chile sauce

Carnitas De Res 8.95
Slices of beef cooked with green peppers & onions w/guacamole

Tacos Al Carbon 8.95
Corn tortillas dipped in a special red sauce w/charbroiled Steak or chicken w/guacamole, chunky sauce & lettuce. Topped w/permesan cheese

Steak Mexicano 9.25
Tender loin sliced & fried w/onions, bell peppers & carrots covered with our secret sauce

Steak Macho 9.25
Tender loin sliced & fried w/onions & mushrooms

PORK MEAT

Pork Carnitas 9.95
Roasted pork w/chunky sauce with guacamole

Pork Chile Verde 8.95
Chunks of Pork cooked in a tasty green chile sauce

Pork Adobado 9.95
Marinated, served with guacamole and chunky sauce

Pork Machaca or Beef Machaca 9.95
Cooked with eggs, tomatoes and onions

Menu Sampler - Prices and menu subject to change.

Present your card to receive this discount.

DINING OUT

Up To $12.00 Value

湘帅
CHINA MOON
Chinese Restaurant

Enjoy one complimentary LUNCH OR DINNER ENTREE when a second LUNCH OR DINNER ENTREE of equal or greater value is purchased or for those who prefer 50% off the regular price of any ONE BUFFET.

Dine in only

valid anytime

10743 SW Beaverton Hillsdale Hwy, Beaverton, OR
(503)350-1888

1001 S.E. TV Hwy. (Shute Park Plaza), **Hillsboro, OR**
(503)615-8898

Card No. 90

Welcome to the ultimate in Chinese dining including an exquisite buffet with the most authentic chef's special dishes from our menu. We cater to every preference from meat lover, seafood fanatic to vegetarian & those with dietary restrictions. There is always something for everyone-in abundance! Allow us to fulfill your catering needs. We hope you'll visit us soon!

CHEF'S SPECIALITIES

芝 麻 鶏 **CRISPY SESAME CHICKEN** 9.25
Chicken marinated in egg white, deep fried , then sautéed in house special sauce with a touch of sweet coating and sesame seeds. Surrounded with broccoli.

左 宗 鶏 **GENERAL TSO'S CHICKEN** 9.25
Chunky chicken dipped in special batter, pan fried to perfection, sautéed with chef's special sauce. Surrounded with broccoli.

沙 茶 鶏 **SHA-CHA CHICKEN** 8.95
White meat chicken with black mushroom and corn in a special hot sauce.

陳 皮 鶏 **ORANGE CHICKEN** 8.95
Fried marinated chicken, pan seared to perfection with orange peels and sautéed in a chef's special sauce.

芝 麻 牛 **SESAME BEEF**...9.95
Chunks of beef marinated in egg white, deep fried then sautéed in House special sauce with a touch of sweet coating and sesame seeds, served on dried noodles.

全 家 福 **HAPPY FAMILY**...11.95
Jumbo shrimp, sliced chicken, beef, scallop sautéed with broccoli, red pepper, snow peas, mushrooms and baby corn in brown sauce.

BEEF

四 季 豆牛 **Beef with String Beans**...7.75

POULTRY

宮 保 鶏丁 **Kung Pao Chicken** 7.50
Diced chicken sautéed in spicy hot sauce with peanuts and diced vegetables.

Menu Sampler - Prices and menu subject to change.

DINING OUT

I Love Sushi

JAPANESE KOREAN RESTAURANT
www.ilovesushi.net

Food for mind & body. Fresh hand rolled sushi, Japanese & Korean entrees. Special fish each weekend. Satisfaction guaranteed. Open daily for lunch & dinner.

Up To $**15**.00 Value

Enjoy one complimentary LUNCH OR DINNER ENTREE when a second LUNCH OR DINNER ENTREE of equal or greater value is purchased or for those who prefer: 25% off any sushi order (up to max value) - maximum discount $10.00.

valid anytime

3486 S.W. Cedar Hills Blvd., Beaverton, OR
(503)644-5252

Card No. 17

SUSHI BAR DINNER SPECIALS

KOREAN CHIRASHI — $12.95
ASSORTED CHOPPED RAW FISH AND SPICY SALAD OVER RICE.

MAKI (ROLL) **SUSHI COMBO** — $13.95
CALIFORNIA SURPRISE, SWEET AVOCADO ROLLS AND SPICY TUNA ROLLS.

UNAGI DONBURI — $14.95
FRESH WATER EEL OVER RICE COVERED WITH SWEET UNAGI SAUCE.

DINNERS

BULKOGI — $9.95
THINLY SLICED BONELESS BEEF MARINATED AND STIR-FRIED WITH ONIONS.

SPICY PORK BULKOGI — $9.95
THINLY SLICED BONELESS PORK WITH SWEET YELLOW ONIONS AND A SECRET KOREAN PEPPER SAUCE.

TERIYAKI CHICKEN — $8.95
BONELESS CHICKEN WITH HOMEMADE TERIYAKI SAUCE.

YASAI TEMPURA DINNER — $8.95
ASSORTED FRESH SEASONAL VEGETABLES, BATTER DIPPED AND DEEP FRIED IN THE TRADITIONAL JAPANESE STYLE.

Menu Sampler - Prices and menu subject to change.

DINING OUT

Springwater Grill

Up To $13.00 Value

Enjoy one complimentary DINNER ENTREE when a second DINNER ENTREE of equal or greater value is purchased.

valid any evening

Not valid with any other discounts or promotions; Friday & Saturday night seating before 5:30 p.m. or after 8:30 p.m.

6716 S.E. Milwaukie Ave., Portland, OR (503)232-2442

Located in the heart of Sellwood, Springwater Grill offers a warm atmosphere with a modern flair. Indulge yourself in exquisite pastas, fresh seafood, tender beef or lamb. Happy hour from 4:30 p.m. - 6:00 p.m. & 9:00 p.m. to close. Have your favorite cocktail with fresh squeezed juice & the best liquor. Open daily.

 Card No. 98

Entrees

Rotini Pasta With Crawfish
With corn and a pumpkin seed cilantro pesto sauce. 15.75

Pan Seared Juniper and Rosemary Salmon
With coconut rice, vegetables and an apple honey glaze. 16.75

Oven Roasted Breast of Oregon Chicken
With fresh herbs, roast vegetables, garlic mashed potatoes and natural jus. 13.75

Ribeye Steak
With garlic mashed potatoes, vegetables and topped with a rosemary blue cheese butter. 19.50

Razor Clams
With coconut rice and vegetables. 17.00

Lamb Shanks in a Mole Sauce
Served with mashed potatoes and grilled asparagus. 18.50

Menu Sampler - Prices and menu subject to change.

DINING OUT

www.sternwheelerrose.com

The Sternwheeler Rose is a unique, relaxing & entertaining way to enjoy Portland's enchanting skyline & river life. Enjoy our slow roasted prime rib or raspberry chicken while sipping on your favorite beverage. Reservations & payment in advance required.

Up To $15.00 Value

Enjoy one ADULT DINNER CRUISE at $15 off the regular price when a second ADULT DINNER CRUISE is purchased.

valid any evening

On availability basis

Board at OMSI (next to Submarine - free parking),
Portland, OR (503)286-7673

 Card No. 44

River Cruise Dining Rules of Use

1. You must make advance reservations at (503) 286-7673 and identify yourself as an Entertainment member or the discount will not apply. Have your fine dining card number ready when you call. Remember a maximum of 3 cards will be accepted in a party of 6 or more.
2. Total amount due will reflect the discount and must be paid in advance by check, cash or credit card.
3. When you arrive for boarding you must present your Entertainment card(s) for your discount to apply. If you do not present your card at time of boarding you will be responsible for paying the Entertainment discount by cash or credit card before boarding.
4. If you did not identify yourself as a Entertainment member at time of reservations, we cannot issue credits or make adjustments at the time of boarding.

Important Notice: Reservations are non-refundable, they are transferrable by name only.

DINNER ENTREES
Boneless Raspberry Chicken Breast
Carved Prime Rib

ALL DINNERS SERVED WITH:
Gourmet Greens
Herbed and Wild Rice Pilaf
Seasonal Vegetables, sauteed
Gourmet Rolls with butter
Seasonal Fruit Platter
Varied Desserts

BUFFET STYLE SERVICE

Menu Sampler - Prices and menu subject to change.

DINING OUT

Up To $12.00 Value

Republic Cafe 共和樓

Restaurant and Ming Lounge

The Republic Cafe is conveniently located in Portland's Chinatown. Choose an intimate atmosphere within private booths, or enjoy open dining with unique & ornate decorum. An extensive menu offers Mandarin selections as well as spicy Szechuan dishes. A full service cocktail lounge provides any accompaniment to your dining experience.

Enjoy one complimentary DINNER ENTREE when a second DINNER ENTREE of equal or greater value is purchased.

valid any evening

222 N.W. 4th Ave., Portland, OR (503)226-4388

PRINT MORE ONLINE

Card No. 74

CHEF'S SUGGESTIONS
Served with rice.

ABC Salad 10.95
A Republic Café original.
Jumbo shrimp, ham, & chicken stir fried with garden fresh vegetables. Garnished with Tomato Slices and Crushed Almonds.

Mushroom Duck 9.95
Our special mushroom sauce on crispy pressed duck.

Beef with Black Mushrooms 9.95
Choice tenderloin beef with fresh vegetables and pea pods with delicious imported black mushrooms.

Moo Goo Gai Pan 8.95
Chicken filets sautéed with garden fresh mushrooms, pea pods, and onion.

SEAFOOD
Served with rice.

Shrimp in a Lobster Sauce 12.75

Sauteéd Scallops with Fresh Mushroom & Pea Pods 12.50

DESSERTS

Deep Fried Bananas 4.50

Three Flavor Ice Cream (Chocolate, Vanilla, Strawberry) 2.50

Menu Sampler - Prices and menu subject to change.

DINING OUT

THE QUAY RESTAURANT

Enjoy classic American cuisine featuring char-grilled steaks, fresh seafood and pasta entrees - all while overlooking the beautiful Columbia River and the lights of Portland. Located within the Red Lion Hotel, The Quay Restaurant offers fine dining atmosphere.

Up To $20.00 Value

Enjoy one complimentary LUNCH OR DINNER ENTREE when a second LUNCH OR DINNER ENTREE of equal or greater value is purchased.

valid anytime

Not valid on Christmas Ship nights, Holiday and Sunset specials; For holidays-see Rules of Use; Not valid with any other discounts or promotions

100 Columbia St., Vancouver, WA (360)750-4941

  Card No. 23

Entrée Salads

Combo Louie $16.75
House Greens with Louie Dressing Topped with Crab and Shrimp Meat
With Dungeness Crab Only $18.75

Pacific Seafood Salad $18.25
Salmon, Halibut, Shredded Lobster and Shrimp on House Greens with Avocado, Egg, Asparagus, Tomato, and Cucumber. Served in a Parmesan Basket with Cusabi Dressing

Specialties

Lobster and Shrimp Stuffed Scallops $23.75
Jumbo Sea Scallops Stuffed with Lobster and Bay Shrimp Topped With Rouge River Blue Cheese
Chef's Suggested Wine: Robert Mondavi "Coastal" Chardonnay

Atlantic King Salmon $19.50
Alder Planked, Bronzed, Char-grilled, or Poached
Chef Suggested Wine: St. Chapelle Johannisberg Riesling

BEEF & CHICKEN
Served with Choice of Chowder or Green Salad and Fresh Baked Bread

10 oz. Top Sirloin $22.75
Char-Grilled Top Sirloin with Sautéed Mushrooms
Add Dungeness Crab or Scampi Prawns $27.00
Chef's Suggested Wine: Robert Mondavi Cabernet

12 oz. New York Steak $26.75
With Chipotle Butter and Rouge River Bleu Cheese
Chef's Suggested Wine: Gallo of Sonoma Cabernet

Bistro Filets Wrapped in Bacon $21.75
Tender Steaks Wrapped with Smoked Bacon and Topped with Bleu Cheese. Served Atop Grilled Portobello Mushrooms
Chefs Suggested Wine: Wyndham Bin 555 Shiraz

Pesto Parmesan Chicken $16.95
Parmesan Crusted Breast of Chicken,
Served over Fettuccine with Pesto Cream Sauce
Chef's Suggested Wine: Columbia Crest "Two Vines" Chardonnay

Macadamia & Pineapple Chicken $15.50
Seasoned and Char-Grilled Topped with Macadamia Nut and Pineapple Chutney
Chef's Suggested Wine: Woodbridge Chardonnay

Roast Prime Rib of Beef
1/2 Pound Cut $23.50   3/4 Pound Cut $27.50
Served with Natural Juices and Creamed Horseradish
Also Available Blackened Upon Request
Chef's Suggested Wine: Columbia Crest "Two Vines" Cabernet

Menu Sampler - Prices and menu subject to change.

DINING OUT

Mandarin Cove
HUNAN & SZECHUAN CUISINE

好 運

Up To $10⁰⁰ Value

Awarded "Best Chinese Restaurant 1993 & 1994" -- People's Choice Downtowner, we feature authentic Hunan & Szechuan cuisine. Mandarin Cove chooses each dish with an eye to color, texture & taste. The ingredients & methods of preparation will assure you the ultimate dining pleasure. Free parking after 5 p.m. in Columbia Square parking. "Between 1st & 2nd on Jefferson".

Enjoy one complimentary DINNER ENTREE when a second DINNER ENTREE of equal or greater value is purchased or for those who prefer, enjoy one special/family dinner when a second special/family dinner is purchased - maximum discount $8.00.

One entree per person or plate charge may apply

valid any evening

111 S.W. Columbia, Portland, OR (503)222-0006

 Card No. 35

POULTRY

Kung Pao Chicken 9.95
Diced chicken, peanuts & hot peppers sauteed with our special sauce.

Moo Goo Gai Pan 9.95
Sliced chicken breast, mushrooms & pea pods in wine sauce.

SEAFOOD

Kung Pao Shrimp 11.95
Shrimp, peanuts & hot pepper blended with our special sauce.

Shrimp in Black Bean Sauce 11.95
Shrimp sauteed with black bean, green pepper, onion & carrots.

PORK

Sweet & Sour Pork 9.95

Szechuan Pork 9.95

VEGETABLES

Assorted Vegetables 8.95

Dry Sauteed String Beans .9.50
Available with or without meat.

Menu Sampler - Prices and menu subject to change.

CASUAL & FAMILY DINING INDEX

To search by area, see the **Neighborhood Index** located at the back of your book.

= **Print more coupons online at www.entertainment.com,** up to once a month, with these Repeat Savings® merchants. See the Rules of Use for more details.

CASUAL & FAMILY DINING INDEX

Casual & Family Dining Index

Looking for a certain merchant?

Go to **www.entertainment.com** to search for hundreds of online printable coupons not found in your book.

OR

Visit **www.entertainment.com/choice** to tell us about a place you'd like to see a coupon for.

To search by area, see the **Neighborhood Index** located at the back of your book.

= **Print more coupons online at www.entertainment.com,** up to once a month, with these Repeat Savings® merchants. See the Rules of Use for more details.

CASUAL & FAMILY DINING INDEX

Qdoba

Enjoy one complimentary MENU ITEM when a second MENU ITEM of equal or greater value is purchased.

Offer Conditions on reverse side.

Valid now thru November 1, 2010

Up To $**7**$⁰⁰ Value

www.qdoba.com

See Reverse Side for Locations

C1

Qdoba

Enjoy one complimentary SIGNATURE BURRITO when a second SIGNATURE BURRITO of equal or greater value is purchased.

Offer Conditions on reverse side.

Valid now thru November 1, 2010

FREE SIGNATURE BURRITO

www.qdoba.com

See Reverse Side for Locations

C2

Qdoba

Enjoy $5.00 off a purchase of twenty-dollars.

Offer Conditions on reverse side.

Valid now thru November 1, 2010

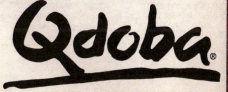

$**5**$⁰⁰ Value

www.qdoba.com

See Reverse Side for Locations

C3

Qdoba

- Fresh ingredients; innovative flavors
- Handcrafted preparations
- Signature salads & sauces
- Many entrée options for vegetarians
- Each entrée is as unique as the person ordering it!
- Open daily for breakfast, lunch and dinner
- Family-friendly
- Catering for any size group

Qdoba®

4655 SW Griffith Dr.
(in the City Hall Plaza)
Beaverton, OR
(503)643-5820

2288 NW Allie Ave.
(In the Streets of Tanasbourne Mall)
Hillsboro, OR
(503)645-2244

505 SW Taylor St.
(Taylor St. at Fifth Ave.)
Portland, OR
(503)241-1144

7132 SW Hazel Fern Rd.
(The Pointe at Bridgeport)
Tigard, OR
(503)670-7800

Offer Conditions: Valid anytime.

00781226

Qdoba

- Fresh ingredients; innovative flavors
- Handcrafted preparations
- Signature salads & sauces
- Many entrée options for vegetarians
- Each entrée is as unique as the person ordering it!
- Open daily for breakfast, lunch and dinner
- Family-friendly
- Catering for any size group

Qdoba®

4655 SW Griffith Dr.
(in the City Hall Plaza)
Beaverton, OR
(503)643-5820

2288 NW Allie Ave.
(In the Streets of Tanasbourne Mall)
Hillsboro, OR
(503)645-2244

505 SW Taylor St.
(Taylor St. at Fifth Ave.)
Portland, OR
(503)241-1144

7132 SW Hazel Fern Rd.
(The Pointe at Bridgeport)
Tigard, OR
(503)670-7800

Offer Conditions: Valid anytime.

00781232

Offer validity is governed by the Rules of Use and excludes defined holidays. Offers are not valid with other discount offers, unless specified. Coupons void if purchased, sold or bartered. Discounts exclude tax, tip and/or alcohol, where applicable.

Qdoba

- Fresh ingredients; innovative flavors
- Handcrafted preparations
- Signature salads & sauces
- Many entrée options for vegetarians
- Each entrée is as unique as the person ordering it!
- Open daily for breakfast, lunch and dinner
- Family-friendly
- Catering for any size group

Qdoba®

4655 SW Griffith Dr.
(in the City Hall Plaza)
Beaverton, OR
(503)643-5820

2288 NW Allie Ave.
(In the Streets of Tanasbourne Mall)
Hillsboro, OR
(503)645-2244

505 SW Taylor St.
(Taylor St. at Fifth Ave.)
Portland, OR
(503)241-1144

7132 SW Hazel Fern Rd.
(The Pointe at Bridgeport)
Tigard, OR
(503)670-7800

Offer Conditions: Valid anytime.

00781718

Offer validity is governed by the Rules of Use and excludes defined holidays. Offers are not valid with other discount offers, unless specified. Coupons void if purchased, sold or bartered. Discounts exclude tax, tip and/or alcohol, where applicable.

Stardust Diner

Enjoy $5 off of a minimum purchase of $20 or more (excluding tax, tip and alcoholic beverages.).

Offer Conditions on reverse side.

Valid now thru November 1, 2010

1110 S.E. 164th Ave., Vancouver, WA
(360)828-1648

C4

Bill's Chicken & Steak House

Enjoy one complimentary DINNER ENTREE when a second DINNER ENTREE of equal or greater value is purchased.

Offer Conditions on reverse side.

Valid now thru November 1, 2010

Up$ To **15**⁰⁰ Value

2200 St. Johns Blvd., Vancouver, WA
(360)695-1591

C5

Darcelle XV

Enjoy one complimentary DINNER ENTREE when a second DINNER ENTREE of equal or greater value is purchased.

Offer Conditions on reverse side.

Up$ To **15**⁰⁰ Value

DARCELLE XV

Valid now thru November 1, 2010

208 N.W. 3rd St., Portland, OR
(503)222-5338

C6

Stardust Diner

- Vancouver's classic 1950's diner
- Delicious home style meals
- Breakfast served all day
- Fun, retro atmosphere with super friendly staff
- Biggest, best chicken fried steak in town!

1110 S.E. 164th Ave.
Vancouver, WA
(360)828-1648

Offer Conditions: Valid anytime.

00765978

Bill's Chicken & Steak House

- A Vancouver tradition since 1965
- Bill's features delicious chicken, steaks & seafood in a warm family dine atmosphere
- Banquet facilities & catering available
- Open daily
- Separate full service lounge

2200 St. Johns Blvd.
Vancouver, WA
(360)695-1591

Offer Conditions: Valid any evening. Dine in only.

Offers not valid holidays and subject to Rules of Use
Tipping should be 15% to 20% of the total bill before discount

00654695

Darcelle XV

- Join Darcelle & other female impersonators for a lively, fun-filled evening
- Dinner seating from 5:00 p.m. - 7:00 p.m.
- Showtimes: Wed. & Thur. 8:30 p.m. Fri. & Sat. 8:30 p.m. & 10:30 p.m.
- Show cover $15 per person

DARCELLE XV

208 N.W. 3rd St.
Portland, OR
(503)222-5338

Offer Conditions: Valid any evening.

Offers not valid holidays and subject to Rules of Use
Tipping should be 15% to 20% of the total bill before discount

00005943

Amadeus Manor

Enjoy $10 off ONE SUNDAY BRUNCH, upon the payment for a SECOND SUNDAY BRUNCH of the same of equal or greater value and 2 BEVERAGES.

Offer Conditions on reverse side.

Classic Cuisine **Amadeus** Manor

Valid now thru November 1, 2010

www.amadeusrestaurants.com

2122 Sparrow St., Milwaukie, OR
(503) 659-1735

C7

Thai Fresh

Enjoy one complimentary ENTREE when a second ENTREE of equal or greater value is purchased.

Offer Conditions on reverse side.

Valid now thru November 1, 2010

www.thaifreshpdx.com

8409 SE Division St, Portland, OR
(503) 774-2186

C8

La Fogata

Enjoy one complimentary LUNCH OR DINNER ENTREE when a second LUNCH OR DINNER ENTREE of equal or greater value is purchased.

Offer Conditions on reverse side.

Up To $10.00 Value

La Fogata

Valid now thru November 1, 2010

3905 S.W. 117th, Ste. H, Beaverton, OR
(503) 526-8808

C9

Amadeus Manor
- Enjoy the romance of classical Continental cuisine served within a beautifully restored three story manor set along the Willamette river.
- The food, decor, music and ambiance of Amadeus Manor will indulge your senses and delight your soul.
- You will be sure to return time and time again.

Classic Cuisine **Amadeus** Manor

2122 Sparrow St.
Milwaukie, OR
(503)659-1735

Offer Conditions: Valid anytime.

00740583

Thai Fresh
- Delicious selection of Thai cuisine
- Fresh and prepared to your taste, with tofu, veggies, shrimp, squid, beef, chicken, pork or a seafood combo
- Inviting dining atmosphere
- See our website at www.thaifreshpdx.com for details and directions

8409 SE Division St
Portland, OR
(503)774-2186

Offer Conditions: Valid anytime.

00759199

La Fogata
- For a taste of Old Mexico in a contemporary atmosphere, come try La Fogata
- Featuring seafood plates & many combination meals
- We offer a large selection of bottled beer, wine, cocktails & margaritas
- Dinner is served from 5 p.m. daily

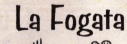

3905 S.W. 117th, Ste. H
(corner of 117th & Canyon Rd.)
Beaverton, OR
(503)526-8808

Offer Conditions: Valid anytime. Dine in only.

Offers not valid holidays and subject to Rules of Use
Tipping should be 15% to 20% of the total bill before discount

00207519

Walter Mitty's Restaurant & Bar

Enjoy one complimentary LUNCH ENTREE when a second LUNCH ENTREE of equal or greater value is purchased.

Offer Conditions on reverse side.

Valid now thru November 1, 2010

Up$ **7**^{00}
To Value

11830 Kerr Parkway, Lake Oswego, OR
(503) 246-7153

C10

Big Al's

Enjoy $5 off a minimum purchase of $20 or more (excluding tax, tip and alcoholic beverages.).

Offer Conditions on reverse side.

Tracking Code: Code #4002

Valid now thru November 1, 2010

$ **5**^{00}
Value

BIG AL's

www.ilovebigals.com

16615 S.E. 18th St., Vancouver, WA
(360) 944-6118

C11

---

entertainment.com

The Quay Restaurant

Enjoy one complimentary SUNDAY BRUNCH when one complimentary SUNDAY BRUNCH of equal or greater value is purchased.

Offer Conditions on reverse side.

Valid now thru November 1, 2010

FREE SUNDAY BRUNCH

THE QUAY RESTAURANT

100 Columbia St., Vancouver, WA
(360) 750-4941

C12

Walter Mitty's Restaurant & Bar

- Come to Walter Mitty's where all our tables are quaint & cozy
- Enjoy your meal in the dining room or on our beautiful spacious patio
- Try one of our specialties including steaks, fresh pasta, wilted spinach salad & Halibut fish & chips

Walter Mitty's
RESTAURANT AND BAR

11830 Kerr Parkway
Lake Oswego, OR
(503)246-7153

Offer Conditions: Valid anytime.

Offers not valid holidays and subject to Rules of Use
Tipping should be 15% to 20% of the total bill before discount

00715605

Big Al's

- Visit the next generation of entertainment
- 60,000 sq. ft. of awe-inspiring fun
- 30 traditional bowling lanes
- 12 lounge-style bowling lanes
- Up-scale sports bar and grill with 8'x36' Jumbo-tron
- Full menu with a variety of amazing appetizers, impressive entrees and delectable desserts
- See www.ilovebigals.com for more information

16615 S.E. 18th St.
Vancouver, WA
(360)944-6118

Offer Conditions: Valid anytime. Valid in restaurant only; Code: 4002.

00765986

The Quay Restaurant

- Enjoy classic American cuisine featuring char-grilled steaks, fresh seafood and pasta entrees - all while overlooking the beautiful Columbia River and the lights of Portland. Located within the Red Lion Hotel, The Quay Restaurant offers fine dining atmosphere

THE
QUAY
RESTAURANT

100 Columbia St.
Vancouver, WA
(360)750-4941

Offer Conditions: Valid any Sunday Brunch except for Holidays - see Rules of Use.

00768602

The Oak Tree Restaurant

- The Oak Tree Restaurant's reputation is as solid as the legendary wood it's named after
- A fixture in Woodland for decades, The Oak Tree invites you for breakfast, lunch or dinner
- Delicious, quality food served with our family and friends in mind

1020 Atlantic Ave.
Woodland, WA
(360)887-8661

Offer Conditions: Valid anytime.

00765994

Peachtree Restaurant & Pie House

- Two locations in Vancouver
- Start your morning with eggs benedict, ranch skillet or chicken fried steak
- Or how about a California crispy salad or grilled halibut for lunch?
- Seniors menu, handicap access
- Open daily for breakfast, lunch and dinner - and don't forget dessert!

4400 E. Fourth Plain
Vancouver, OR
(360)694-8880

6600 N.E. Hwy. 99
Hazel Dell, WA
(360)693-6736

Offer Conditions: Valid anytime.

00765900

Sayler's Old Country Kitchen

- A landmark of more than 50 years in Portland!
- Home of the famous 72 ounce steak dinner
- Steaks, prime-rib, seafood & more
- Dinner served from 4:00 p.m. Mon. - Thurs.
- Dinner served from 3:00 p.m. Sat. & from 12:00 noon on Sun.

Sayler's
OLD COUNTRY KITCHEN

10519 S.E. Stark St.
Portland, OR
(503)252-4171

Offer Conditions: Valid any evening. Friday & Saturday seating after 8:30 p.m.; Banquets excluded.

Offers not valid holidays and subject to Rules of Use
Tipping should be 15% to 20% of the total bill before discount

00712938

The Grove Restaurant and Bar

Enjoy $5.00 off a minimum purchase of twenty dollars or more (excluding tax, tip and alcoholic beverages.).

Offer Conditions on reverse side.

Valid now thru November 1, 2010

15300 S.E. McLoughlin Blvd., Milwaukie, OR
(503)653-1930

C16

Los Jalapenos Mexican Restaurant

Enjoy $5 OFF a minimum purchase of $20 or more (excluding tax, tip & alcoholic beverages).

Offer Conditions on reverse side.

Valid now thru November 1, 2010

11711 N.E. 99th St., Vancouver, WA
(360)883-6588

C17

Pyzano's Lounge & Grill

Enjoy one complimentary MENU ITEM when a second MENU ITEM of equal or greater value is purchased.

Offer Conditions on reverse side.

Valid now thru November 1, 2010

www.pyzanosgrill.com

20255 S.W. TV Hwy., Aloha, OR
(503)591-1507

C18

The Grove Restaurant and Bar

- Delicious pizza, pasta and more
- Great menu including burgers, sandwiches and salads
- Daily specials
- Friendly and relaxing - with 17 flat screen TVs, 2 fireplaces and 3 pool tables
- Full bar

15300 S.E. McLoughlin Blvd.
Milwaukie, OR
(503)653-1930

Offer Conditions: Valid anytime. Dine in only.

00767734

Offer validity is governed by the Rules of Use and excludes defined holidays. Offers are not valid with other discount offers, unless specified. Coupons void if purchased, sold or bartered. Discounts exclude tax, tip and/or alcohol, where applicable.

Los Jalapenos Mexican Restaurant

- Enjoy a wonderful, authentic Mexican meal at Los Jalapenos, a family operation from the Jalisco region of Mexico
- You can dine 7 days a week from 11:00 a.m. - 10:00 p.m., weekends until 11:00 p.m.
- Frosty, traditional margaritas complete the experience
- Try our new location in Washougal, or the original Orchards site

11711 N.E. 99th St.
Vancouver, WA
(360)883-6588

Offer Conditions: Valid anytime.
Tipping should be 15% to 20% of TOTAL bill before discount

00312130

Offer validity is governed by the Rules of Use and excludes defined holidays. Offers are not valid with other discount offers, unless specified. Coupons void if purchased, sold or bartered. Discounts exclude tax, tip and/or alcohol, where applicable.

Pyzano's Lounge & Grill

- Famous New York style recipe pizza
- Full service bar
- All Oregon lottery games
- Subs, burgers, broasted chickens
- Breakfast, lunch & dinner
- 21 & over please

20255 S.W. TV Hwy.
Aloha, OR
(503)591-1507

Offer Conditions: Valid anytime. Dine in only. Excludes daily specials.
Tipping should be 15% to 20% of TOTAL bill before discount

00713793

Offer validity is governed by the Rules of Use and excludes defined holidays. Offers are not valid with other discount offers, unless specified. Coupons void if purchased, sold or bartered. Discounts exclude tax, tip and/or alcohol, where applicable.

Enjoy $5 off the minimum purchase of $20 or more (excluding tax, tip & alcoholic beverages).

Offer Conditions on reverse side.

Valid now thru November 1, 2010

See Reverse Side for Locations

C19

Wichita Pubs

Enjoy one LUNCH or DINNER ENTREE when a second LUNCH or DINNER ENTREE & 2 BEVERAGES are purchased.

Offer Conditions on reverse side.

Up To $8.00 Value

WICHITA Pubs

Valid now thru November 1, 2010

See Reverse Side for Locations

C20

Rib City

Enjoy one complimentary ENTREE when a second ENTREE of equal or greater value is purchased.

Offer Conditions on reverse side.

Up To $20.00 Value

Valid now thru November 1, 2010

See Reverse Side for Locations

C21

- Come join us for fresh, authentic Mexican food Jalisco style!
- Lunch specials 11 a.m. - 3 p.m.
- Different dinner platter specials every day
- Fajitas, Pollo la crema, comarones la plancha specialties of the House
- Open 11 a.m. - 10 p.m. every day

San Blas Mexican Restaurant
1585 W. Main St., Ste. K
Molalla, OR
(503)829-9478

Ixtapa Mexican Restaurant
321 Westfield St.
Silverton, OR
(503)874-9111

Ixtapa Mexican Restaurant
29030 S.W. Town Center Loop East
Wilsonville, OR
(503)582-1226

Offer Conditions: Valid anytime.

Tipping should be 15% to 20% of TOTAL bill before discount

00737802

Wichita Pubs
- Lotto games, video games & pool tables
- Large screen TV to watch your favorite sporting events
- Friendly neighborhood pub
- Serving breakfast, lunch & dinner

11481 S.E. Hwy. 212
*(*family friendly)*
Clackamas, OR
(503)657-8344

6106 S.E. King Rd.
*(*21 and over)*
Milwaukie, OR
(503)654-4201

19140 Molalla Ave. S.
*(*family friendly)*
Oregon City, OR
(503)557-0277

Offer Conditions: Valid anytime.

Tipping should be 15% to 20% of TOTAL bill before discount

00320389

Rib City
- Real BBQ and Great Ribs
- If you have to pick up a knife to eat our baby Back Ribs, we will pick up your meal!
- Smokehouse meats including BBQ chicken, St. Louis style ribs, smoked turkey and of course our signature baby backs!
- And don't forget the sides - baked beans, cole slaw and more
- See www.ribcity.com for more information

3655 S.W. Hall Blvd.
Beaverton, OR
(503)643-RIBS

14415 S.E. Mill Plain Blvd.
Vancouver, WA
(360)882-8005

Offer Conditions: Valid anytime.

00766330

Village Inn

Enjoy one complimentary DINNER ENTREE when a second DINNER ENTREE of equal or greater value is purchased.

Offer Conditions on reverse side.

Valid now thru November 1, 2010

FREE DINNER ENTREE

See Reverse Side for Locations

C22

Village Inn

Enjoy one complimentary SLICE OF PIE when a second SLICE OF PIE of equal or greater value is purchased.

Offer Conditions on reverse side.

Valid now thru November 1, 2010

FREE SLICE OF PIE

See Reverse Side for Locations

C23

Village Inn

Enjoy one complimentary ENTREE when a second ENTREE of equal or greater value is purchased.

Offer Conditions on reverse side.

Valid now thru November 1, 2010

FREE ENTREE

See Reverse Side for Locations

C24

Village Inn

- For nearly 50 years, Village Inn has provided Good Food...Good Feelings
- Enjoy great-tasting food and extra-friendly service in a clean and comfortable family environment
- Offering 18 varieties of award winning pie
- Mouth-watering breakfasts served all day!

10650 SW Beaverton Hillsdale Hwy Beaverton, OR (503)644-8848

1621 NE 10th Ave (by Lloyd Center) Portland, OR (503)284-4141

17070 SW 72nd (By Bridgeport Village) Tualatin, OR (503)620-2515

Offer Conditions: Valid any evening. Dine in only. Not valid with any other discounts or promotions.

00114537

Village Inn

- For nearly 50 years, Village Inn has provided Good Food...Good Feelings
- Enjoy great-tasting food and extra-friendly service in a clean and comfortable family environment
- Offering 18 varieties of award winning pie
- Mouth-watering breakfasts served all day!

10650 SW Beaverton Hillsdale Hwy Beaverton, OR (503)644-8848

1621 NE 10th Ave (by Lloyd Center) Portland, OR (503)284-4141

17070 SW 72nd (By Bridgeport Village) Tualatin, OR (503)620-2515

Offer Conditions: Valid anytime. Dine in only. Not valid with any other discounts or promotions.

00114536

Village Inn

- For nearly 50 years, Village Inn has provided Good Food...Good Feelings
- Enjoy great-tasting food and extra-friendly service in a clean and comfortable family environment
- Offering 18 varieties of award winning pie
- Mouth-watering breakfasts served all day!

10650 SW Beaverton Hillsdale Hwy Beaverton, OR (503)644-8848

1621 NE 10th Ave (by Lloyd Center) Portland, OR (503)284-4141

17070 SW 72nd (By Bridgeport Village) Tualatin, OR (503)620-2515

Offer Conditions: Valid Mon-Fri all day; Sat-Sun after 2 p.m. Dine in only. Not valid with any other discounts or promotions.

00115570

Cha Cha Cha

Enjoy one complimentary
LUNCH OR DINNER ENTREE
when a second LUNCH OR
DINNER ENTREE of equal or
greater value is purchased.

Offer Conditions on reverse side.

See Reverse Side for Locations

Valid now thru November 1, 2010

C25

La Isla Bonita

Enjoy one complimentary
LUNCH OR DINNER ENTREE
when a second LUNCH OR
DINNER ENTREE of equal or
greater value is purchased.

Offer Conditions on reverse side.

LA ISLA BONITA

Family Mexican Restaurant

See Reverse Side for Locations

Valid now thru November 1, 2010

C26

Players

Enjoy one complimentary
LUNCH OR DINNER ENTREE
when a second LUNCH OR
DINNER ENTREE of equal or
greater value is purchased.

Offer Conditions on reverse side.

www.eatdrinkbowlplay.com

17880 SW McEwan, Lake Oswego, OR
(503)726-4263

Valid now thru November 1, 2010

C27

Cha Cha Cha

- Serving only natural meats & wild sustainable fish
- Casual Mexican taquerias offering delicious creations
- We have four locations to serve you; all have outdoor seating available!
- Try our delicious margaritas to accompany our exceptional food
- Beer & wine also available at all locations
- Take-out too
- Every location is open daily

1208 N.W. Glisan St.
(at 12th Ave. in the Pearl)
Portland, OR
(503) 221-2111

2635 N.E. Broadway
(at 26th Ave. in the Irvington neighborhood)
Portland, OR
(503) 288-1045

3433 S.E. Hawthorne
(at 35th Ave.)
Portland, OR
(503) 236-1100

4727 N.E. Fremont
(at 47th Ave. in the Beaumont neighborhood)
Portland, OR
(503) 595-9131

Offer Conditions: Valid anytime.

00779020

La Isla Bonita

- Enjoy the fresh flavors Mexico has to offer
- Friendly staff & amazing margaritas
- Try regional favorites or your traditional favorite-whatever your choice-we are sure to be your favorite Mexican restaurant

LA ISLA BONITA
Family Mexican Restaurant

302 NE 122nd Ave.
Portland, OR
(503) 252-3460

7670 SW Nyberg Rd.
Tualatin, OR
(503) 692-0803

Offer Conditions: Valid anytime.

00767094

Players

- Players is more than just great fun, we serve up amazing food daily
- You'll find your favorite dishes packed with flavor
- Mouth watering appetizers
- Gourmet burgers
- Hand tossed pizzas
- Fresh seafood specials
- Decadent desserts
- We can satisfy any craving!
- In a hurry? No problem, our delicious food is available to go!
- Visit us online at www.eatdrinkbowlplay.com

17880 SW McEwan
(1/4 mile E. off I-5 at the Lower Boones Ferry/Durham exit)
Lake Oswego, OR
(503) 726-4263

Offer Conditions: Valid anytime.

00779090

The Sage Restaurant

Enjoy one complimentary
MENU ITEM when a second
MENU ITEM of equal or greater
value is purchased.
Offer Conditions on reverse side.

Up $8.00 To Value

The Sage
RESTAURANT

Valid now thru November 1, 2010

406 Third St., McMinnville, OR
(503)472-4445

C28

Hula Boy Charbroil

Enjoy $5.00 off a minimum
purchase of twenty dollars or
more (tax, tip & alcoholic
beverages excluded).
Offer Conditions on reverse side.

Up $5.00 To Value

HULA BOY CHARBROIL

www.hulaboycharbroil.com

See Reverse Side for Locations

Valid now thru November 1, 2010

C29

Goose Hollow Inn

Enjoy one complimentary
LUNCH OR DINNER ENTREE
when a second LUNCH OR
DINNER ENTREE of equal or
greater value is purchased.
Offer Conditions on reverse side.

$14.00 Value

Bud Clark's
Goose hollow Inn
Since 1967
www.goosehollowinn.com

Valid now thru November 1, 2010

1927 SW Jefferson Street, Portland, OR
(503)228-7010

C30

The Sage Restaurant

- Award-winning sandwich & soup shop in historic downtown McMinnville
- Everything made from scratch, including daily bread
- Best sandwiches west of Mississippi
- Famous creamy broccoli soup
- A destination since 1976 and under the same ownership since 1977!
- Open Monday-Sunday for lunch
- Take-out & special order available too

The Sage
RESTAURANT

406 Third St.
(On the Main St. of historic McMinnville)
McMinnville, OR
(503)472-4445

Offer Conditions: Valid anytime.

00775555

Hula Boy Charbroil

- The best Hawaiian style restuarant around!
- Bento & sandwiches
- Teriyaki, stir fry, kalua pork, coconut shrimp - all your Island favorites
- Let us cater your next party or meeting
- Visit our website for more information
- Mahalo!

HULA BOY
CHARBROIL

1109 Washington St.
Vancouver, OR
(360)859-3954

11820 N.E. 4th Plain Rd., Ste. G
Vancouver, WA
(360)896-3355

Offer Conditions: Valid anytime. Dine in only.

00775151

Goose Hollow Inn

- Former Mayor Bud Clark's classic Portland pub!
- Home of "The Best Reuben on the Planet"
- Homemade soups and salad dressings
- 13 taps, great beer and wine selection.
- Huge heated deck.
- Ride MAX to our door!
- Close to PGE Park, the Rose Gardens and the Japanese Garden in Washington Park
- Visit our Oregon Coast location in Seaside where we have live music weekly

Bud Clark's
Goose Hollow Inn
Since 1967

1927 SW Jefferson Street
(at the corner of SW 19th Avenue)
Portland, OR
(503)228-7010

Offer Conditions: Valid anytime.

00775924

La Terrazza

Enjoy one complimentary
LUNCH OR DINNER ENTREE
when a second LUNCH OR
DINNER ENTREE of equal or
greater value is purchased.
Offer Conditions on reverse side.

Valid now thru November 1, 2010

Up To $**14**.00 Value

LaTerrazza
www.laterrazzaonline.com

933 S.W. 3rd Ave., Portland, OR
(503)223-8200

C31

Pattie's Home Plate Cafe

Enjoy one complimentary
MENU ITEM when a second
MENU ITEM of equal or greater
value is purchased.
Offer Conditions on reverse side.

Valid now thru November 1, 2010

Up To $**9**.00 Value

Pattie's Home Plate Cafe

8501 N. Lombard St., Portland, OR
(503)289-7285

C32

Taste of Mexico

Enjoy one complimentary
LUNCH OR DINNER ENTREE
when a second LUNCH OR
DINNER ENTREE of equal or
greater value is purchased.
Offer Conditions on reverse side.

Valid now thru November 1, 2010

Up To $**16**.00 Value

TASTE *of* MEXICO

716 N.W. 21st, Portland, OR
(503)295-4944

C33

More Offers Online!

CASUAL & FAMILY DINING

entertainment.com

La Terrazza
- Open Mon.-Sat. for lunch & dinner
- Privately-owned

LaTerrazza

933 S.W. 3rd Ave.
(3rd Ave. at Salmon St.)
Portland, OR
(503)223-8200

Offer Conditions: Valid anytime.

00773254

Pattie's Home Plate Cafe
- Original 1950s era Rexall Drugs diner!
- Original horseshoe counter, serving handmade shakes, old-fashioned sodas & malts
- Bring the kids!
- Classic diner cooking prepared right in front of you
- Reasonable prices-practically from way-back-when!
- Serving breakfast all day, every day
- Open 7 days/week for breakfast, lunch & early dinner
- Gift & costume shop too!
- Come enjoy!

Pattie's
Home Plate Cafe

8501 N. Lombard St.
(Right over the St. John's bridge to Lombard)
Portland, OR
(503)289-7285

Offer Conditions: Valid anytime.

00775550

Taste of Mexico
- Mexico's colorful, stimulating & festive culture is mirrored at the Taste of Mexico
- Experience the home made tastes & flavor of a variety of regions
- Savor our specialties, including mole poblano de pollo, salmon con cremada tequila or chille relleno de queso & picadillo

716 N.W. 21st
Portland, OR
(503)295-4944

Offer Conditions: Valid anytime.
Offers not valid holidays and subject to Rules of Use
Tipping should be 15% to 20% of the total bill before discount

00721814

Via Delizia

Enjoy one complimentary LUNCH OR DINNER ENTREE when a second LUNCH OR DINNER ENTREE of equal or greater value is purchased.

Offer Conditions on reverse side.

Valid now thru November 1, 2010

Up To $7.00 Value

Dessert ♦ Espresso ♦ Gelato ♦ Panini

VIA DELIZIA™

*'Street of Delights'™
...In the Pearl*

www.viadelizia.com

1105 NW Marshall St., Portland, OR
(503)225-9300

C34

---

entertainment.com

Juan Colorado

Enjoy one complimentary LUNCH OR DINNER ENTREE when a second LUNCH OR DINNER ENTREE of equal or greater value is purchased.

Offer Conditions on reverse side.

Valid now thru November 1, 2010

Up To $9.00 Value

JUAN COLORADO
MEXICAN RESTAURANT

See Reverse Side for Locations

C35

---

entertainment.com

China Bay Restaurant & Lounge

Enjoy one complimentary DINNER OR A LA CARTE ENTREE when a second DINNER OR A LA CARTE ENTREE of equal or greater value is purchased or for those who prefer - any one FAMILY STYLE DINNER at $8.00 off the regular price.

Offer Conditions on reverse side.

Valid now thru November 1, 2010

Up To $12.00 Value

福 CHINA BAY Restaurant LOUNGE 興

13281 SW Canyon Rd., Beaverton, OR
(503)350-1688

C36

More Offers Online!

CASUAL & FAMILY DINING

entertainment.com

Via Delizia

- Fresh grilled panini sandwiches
- Coffee & espresso
- Salads, soups, pasta
- Artfully plated desserts
- Handcrafted gelato
- Visit our website
- Open 7 days: 7:30 a.m. - 9 p.m. Mon. & Tues.
- 7:30 a.m. - 10 p.m. Wed. & Thurs.
- 7:30 a.m. - 11 p.m. Fri. & Sat.
- 8 a.m. - 9 p.m. Sun.
- Breakfast Menu: Italian Omelettes, Euro Breakfast, Breakfast Paninis
- Beer & Wine

Dessert ◆ Espresso ◆ Gelato ◆ Panini

VIA DELIZIA™

'Street of Delights'™
...In the Pearl

1105 NW Marshall St.
(corner of NW Marshall & NW 11th St.)
Portland, OR
(503)225-9300

00742021

Offer Conditions: Valid anytime. Dinner only. Dine in only.

Offer validity is governed by the Rules of Use and excludes defined holidays. Offers are not valid with other discount offers, unless specified. Coupons void if purchased, sold or bartered. Discounts exclude tax, tip and/or alcohol, where applicable.

Juan Colorado

- Enjoy the best Mexican food west of the Rockies!
- Each entree is custom prepared to your order
- Shrimp enchiladas, specialty burritos, steak & chicken fajitas & more
- We make the best margaritas!

14795 S.W. Murray Scholls, Ste. 111
Beaverton, OR
(503)524-8005

16755 S.W. Baseline Rd., Ste. 110
Beaverton, OR
(503)531-8359

1716 NW Fairview Dr
Gresham, OR
(503)665-4402

8750 SW Citizens Dr.
Wilsonville, OR
(503)682-2171

Offer Conditions: Valid anytime. Dine in only.

00114431

Offer validity is governed by the Rules of Use and excludes defined holidays. Offers are not valid with other discount offers, unless specified. Coupons void if purchased, sold or bartered. Discounts exclude tax, tip and/or alcohol, where applicable.

China Bay Restaurant & Lounge

- Enjoy China Bay for fine food & excellent service
- Visit our new location on Canyon Road in Beaverton where we are serving Mandarin, Szechuan & Hunan cuisine
- You'll enjoy our new atmosphere with colorfully painted mural walls, lots of greenery & warm lighting
- Serving lunch, dinner, appetizers & cocktails
- Parking & banquet rooms available
- Open daily

13281 SW Canyon Rd.
Beaverton, OR
(503)350-1688

00385597

Offer Conditions: Valid any evening. Dine in only. Friday & Saturday seating before 6pm or after 8pm
For holidays-see Rules of Use.

Offers not valid holidays and subject to Rules of Use
Tipping should be 15% to 20% of the total bill before discount

Offer validity is governed by the Rules of Use and excludes defined holidays. Offers are not valid with other discount offers, unless specified. Coupons void if purchased, sold or bartered. Discounts exclude tax, tip and/or alcohol, where applicable.

Skipper's Seafood & Chowder

Enjoy one complimentary TWO PIECE FISH when a second TWO PIECE FISH of equal or greater value is purchased.

Offer Conditions on reverse side.

Tracking Code: #15

Valid now thru November 1, 2010

FREE TWO PIECE FISH

www.skippers.net

See Reverse Side for Locations

C37

Skipper's Seafood & Chowder

Enjoy ONE CUP of our AWARD WINNING CHOWDER when a second CUP of our AWARD WINNING CHOWDER of equal or greater value is purchased.

Offer Conditions on reverse side.

Tracking Code: #7

Valid now thru November 1, 2010

ONE CUP OF OUR AWARD WINNING CHOWDER

www.skippers.net

See Reverse Side for Locations

C38

Steakburger

Enjoy one complimentary BREAKFAST ENTREE when a second BREAKFAST ENTREE of equal or greater value is purchased.

Offer Conditions on reverse side.

Valid now thru November 1, 2010

FREE BREAKFAST ENTREE

7120 N.E. Hwy. 99, Vancouver, WA
(360) 694-3421

C39

Skipper's Seafood & Chowder

- Signature fish & seafood
- Healthy grilled menu & much more!
- Original fish & chips
- Fish bites & chips
- Grilled fish
- All-you-can-eat
- Specialty seafood baskets
- Award winning clam chowder
- Family value meals
- Delicious salads
- Find more coupons at www.skippers.net

IDAHO
Lewiston
719 21st St.
(208)746-0242

Nampa
1124 Caldwell Blvd.
(208)475-3286

Pocatello
303 E. Alameda
(208)668-0011

MONTANA
Kalispell
1260 Hwy 2 West
(406)752-5400

OREGON
Albany
2987 Santiam Hwy SE
(541)928-9264

Bend
61165 S Hwy. 97
(541)382-7851

Grants Pass
1950 NE 7th
(541)476-8898

Klamath Falls
1737 Avalon
(541)884-2757

Portland
10859 SE 82nd Ave.
(503)653-6672

Roseburg
2090 Stewart Pkwy
(541)672-0909

Salem
1735 Lancaster Dr. NE
(503)399-0727

Springfield
1865 Olympic
(541)726-7022

The Dalles
1465 W 6th St.
(541)296-1327

UTAH
Murray
880 East 5600 S.
(801)263-3643

West Valley City
3455 S. 5600 W.
(801)963-5808

WASHINGTON
Auburn
1202 Auburn Way N.
(253)887-1619

Burien
901 SW 148th St.
(206)248-1219

Everett
12811 - 4th Ave. W
(425)353-7144

Kennewick
3307 W Kennewick Ave.
(509)735-3030

Lacey
3812 Pacific Ave. SE
(360)456-4133

Mt. Vernon
323 E. College Way
(360)424-4500

Puyallup
3932 S. Meridian
(253)841-0123

Renton
17808 108th Ave. SE
(425)226-6326

Silverdale
10725 Silverdale Way NW
(360)692-6601

Sunnyside
2150 Yakima Valley Hwy
(509)839-0555

Tacoma
13721 Pacific Ave.
(253)537-3444

Vancouver
6304 Hwy. 99
(360)693-7639

Wenatchee
1512 N. Wenatchee Av
(509)662-5612

Offer Conditions: Valid anytime. No cash value. Not valid with any other discounts or promotions; One coupon/card per customer per visit; Valid a locations listed only; Tracking code: #15.

00736339

Offer validity is governed by the Rules of Use and excludes defined holidays. Offers are not valid with other discount offers, unless specifie
Coupons void if purchased, sold or bartered. Discounts exclude tax, tip and/or alcohol, where applicable.

Skipper's Seafood & Chowder

- Fish facts - researchers suggest:
- Eating grilled fish several times a week is good for you
- Reduces the chance of strokes
- Important factor in preventing heart disease
- Omega-3 fatty acids in salmon may reduce many ailments
- Find more coupons at www.skippers.net

IDAHO
Lewiston
719 21st St.
(208)746-0242

Nampa
1124 Caldwell Blvd.
(208)475-3286

Pocatello
303 E. Alameda
(208)668-0011

MONTANA
Kalispell
1260 Hwy 2 West
(406)752-5400

OREGON
Albany
2987 Santiam Hwy SE
(541)928-9264

Bend
61165 S Hwy. 97
(541)382-7851

Grants Pass
1950 NE 7th
(541)476-8898

Klamath Falls
1737 Avalon
(541)884-2757

Portland
10859 SE 82nd Ave.
(503)653-6672

Roseburg
2090 Stewart Pkwy
(541)672-0909

Salem
1735 Lancaster Dr. NE
(503)399-0727

Springfield
1865 Olympic
(541)726-7022

The Dalles
1465 W 6th St.
(541)296-1327

UTAH
Murray
880 East 5600 S.
(801)263-3643

West Valley City
3455 S. 5600 W.
(801)963-5808

WASHINGTON
Auburn
1202 Auburn Way N.
(253)887-1619

Burien
901 SW 148th St.
(206)248-1219

Everett
12811 - 4th Ave. W
(425)353-7144

Kennewick
3307 W Kennewick Ave.
(509)735-3030

Lacey
3812 Pacific Ave. SE
(360)456-4133

Mt. Vernon
323 E. College Way
(360)424-4500

Puyallup
3932 S. Meridian
(253)841-0123

Renton
17808 108th Ave. SE
(425)226-6326

Silverdale
10725 Silverdale Way NW
(360)692-6601

Sunnyside
2150 Yakima Valley Hwy
(509)839-0555

Tacoma
13721 Pacific Ave.
(253)537-3444

Vancouver
6304 Hwy. 99
(360)693-7639

Wenatchee
1512 N. Wenatchee Av
(509)662-5612

Offer Conditions: Valid anytime. No cash value. Not valid with any other discounts or promotions; One coupon/card per customer per visit; Valid a locations listed only; Tracking code: #7.

00736340

Offer validity is governed by the Rules of Use and excludes defined holidays. Offers are not valid with other discount offers, unless specifie
Coupons void if purchased, sold or bartered. Discounts exclude tax, tip and/or alcohol, where applicable.

Steakburger

- Great food and fun for the whole family.
- Family owned and operated since 1962

steakburger

7120 N.E. Hwy. 99
Vancouver, WA
(360)694-3421

Offer Conditions: Valid anytime. Present coupon/card before ordering; Excludes additional toppings; Not valid with any other discounts or promotions; One coupon/card per customer per visit.

00767067

Offer validity is governed by the Rules of Use and excludes defined holidays. Offers are not valid with other discount offers, unless specifi
Coupons void if purchased, sold or bartered. Discounts exclude tax, tip and/or alcohol, where applicable.

3rd St. Pizza Company

- Voted "Best of Mac" for pizza & theater
- Start with our delicious hand tossed three cheese pie & create your own personal combination, or choose one of our house specialties
- Also serving delicious calzones, chicken wings & salads
- Dine in, pickup & delivery
- Call (503)434-9515 for Moonlight Theater shows & times
- Open Mon.-Sat., 11 a.m.-10 p.m., Sun., 12 noon-9 p.m.

433 N.E. 3rd St.
McMinnville, OR
(503)434-5800

Offer Conditions: Valid anytime. Dine in only.

Offers not valid holidays and subject to Rules of Use
Tipping should be 15% to 20% of the total bill before discount

---

Coyote's Bar & Grill

- Coyote's offers you the best in food & fun
- Come for our signature Bison ribeye or ultimate kobe beef burger
- Or grab an Oregon hazelnut or grilled chicken caesar salad & sit back, relax & enjoy!

BAR AND GRILL
5301 W. Baseline Rd.
Hillsboro, OR
(503)640-7225

Offer Conditions: Valid anytime.

Jin's Steak & Lounge

- A flavorful menu of meat, chicken & seafood dishes
- Serving USDA steak & prime rib everyday
- A great variety of sides & selections
- Comfortable dining area, great for families
- Open for lunch & dinner
- Full service lounge with music Friday & Saturday
- Lottery
- Banquet facilities available

Jin's
STEAK & LOUNGE

1656 S. Beavercreek Rd.
Oregon City, OR
(503)723-9855

Offer Conditions: Valid anytime. Dine in only.

Izgara

Enjoy one complimentary
LUNCH OR DINNER ENTREE
when a second LUNCH OR
DINNER ENTREE of equal or
greater value is purchased.
Offer Conditions on reverse side.

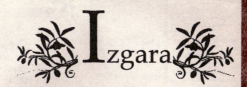

Valid now thru November 1, 2010

2036 Main Street, Forest Grove, OR
(503)352-9306

C43

Farmhouse Restaurant & Lounge

Enjoy one complimentary
LUNCH OR DINNER ENTREE
when a second LUNCH OR
DINNER ENTREE of equal or
greater value is purchased.
Offer Conditions on reverse side.

Valid now thru November 1, 2010

3500 NE Cornell Road, Hillsboro, OR
(503)648-0759

C44

Crazy Grille at The Island Casinos

Enjoy one complimentary
ENTREE when a second
ENTREE of equal or greater
value is purchased.
Offer Conditions on reverse side.

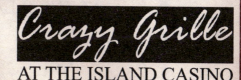

Valid now thru November 1, 2010

See Reverse Side for Locations

C45

Izgara

- We use local & organic ingredients whenever possible
- Healthy, Mediterrean-style cuisine
- We make everything fresh everyday
- All our meats are served grilled
- Several vegetarian options: falafel, hummus & much more
- Pizza too-on lafah flat bread
- Located in an historic building in downtown Forest Grove
- Fri. night belly dancing, Sat. night live music
- Exceptional desserts

00780563

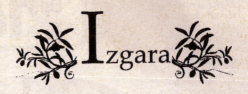

2036 Main Street
(Between 20th & 21st Ave.)
Forest Grove, OR
(503)352-9306

Offer Conditions: Valid anytime.

Farmhouse Restaurant & Lounge

- Classic, specially-prepared dishes for breakfast, lunch, and dinner daily
- Many vegetarian and/or light preparations available
- Large menu with great variety!
- Open-flame grilling for those who choose
- Our food is served with pride--come visit and taste in our relaxed and comfortable atmosphere!
- Wide selection of beers and lovely wines, as well as a full bar

00772847

RESTAURANT & LOUNGE

3500 NE Cornell Road
Hillsboro, OR
(503)648-0759

Offer Conditions: Valid anytime.

Crazy Grille at The Island Casinos

- Breakfast lunch & dinner
- Located in the Island Casino

00757466

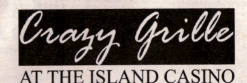

8524 W. Gage Blvd.
Kennewick, WA
(509)374-3289

1125 Commerce Ave
Longview, WA
(360)501-4328

Offer Conditions: Valid anytime.

Smoky Hearth Pizza Company

Enjoy one complimentary ENTREE when a second ENTREE of equal or greater value is purchased or for those who prefer - buy any one pizza, get one free.

Offer Conditions on reverse side.

Valid now thru November 1, 2010

Up$ To 18 00 Value

SMOKY HEARTH PIZZA COMPANY

16607 Champion Way, Ste. 100, Sandy, OR
(503)668-4466

C46

Eastmoreland Golf Course Bar & Grill

Enjoy one complimentary ENTREE when a second ENTREE of equal or greater value is purchased.

Offer Conditions on reverse side.

PRINT MORE ONLINE   NEW

Valid now thru November 1, 2010

Up$ To 15 00 Value

EASTMORELAND Golf Course BAR & GRILL

2425 SE Bybee Blvd, Portland, OR
(503)775-5910

C47

Pacific Grill

Enjoy one complimentary LUNCH OR DINNER ENTREE when a second LUNCH OR DINNER ENTREE of equal or greater value is purchased.

Offer Conditions on reverse side.

Valid now thru November 1, 2010

$15 00 Value

7101 NE 82nd Ave., Portland, OR

C48

Smoky Hearth Pizza Company

- Wood-fired gourmet pizza cooked on a smoky hearth
- Pizza, soups, salads, wraps & desserts
- 19 Specialty pizzas
- Free wireless internet
- Comfortable, cozy dining area
- Catering available

SMOKY HEARTH
PIZZA COMPANY

16607 Champion Way, Ste. 100
(next to Sandy Cinema)
Sandy, OR
(503)668-4466

Offer Conditions: Valid anytime. Dine in only.

Offers not valid holidays and subject to Rules of Use
Tipping should be 15% to 20% of the total bill before discount

00685726

Eastmoreland Golf Course Bar & Grill

- Open at dawn 365 days a year
- Prime rib burger, salads & the best fish & chips you've ever had!
- Banquet facilities perfect for weddings, private parties, business meetings & more
- Patio dining along Eastmoreland Golf Course

EASTMORELAND
Golf Course
BAR & GRILL

2425 SE Bybee Blvd
Portland, OR
(503)775-5910

Offer Conditions: Valid anytime.

00760739

Pacific Grill

- Healthy large menu of all-American food to be enjoyed in our informal atmosphere
- Open-flame grilling
- Sumptuous wraps, as well as burgers, sandwiches, pastas, and appetizers
- Fresh soups and salads daily
- Kids' menu available at a very low price
- Substitutions accomodated, of course
- Full bar, and a wide range of non-alcohol beverages
- Free parking

7101 NE 82nd Ave.
(near Portland Airport--enter at either Alderwood or Frontage Road and 82nd)
Portland, OR

Offer Conditions: Valid anytime.

00772846

Yuki Japanese Restaurant

Enjoy one complimentary LUNCH OR DINNER ENTREE when a second LUNCH OR DINNER ENTREE of equal or greater value is purchased.

Offer Conditions on reverse side.

Up To $15.00 Value

YUKI
Japanese Restaurant

PRINT MORE ONLINE   NEW

Valid now thru November 1, 2010

1337 N.E. Broadway, Portland, OR
(503)281-6804

C49

Bangkok Corner

Enjoy one complimentary LUNCH OR DINNER ENTREE when a second LUNCH OR DINNER ENTREE of equal or greater value is purchased.

Offer Conditions on reverse side.

Up To $14.00 Value

Bangkok Corner.

Authentic Thai Cuisine

PRINT MORE ONLINE

Valid now thru November 1, 2010

7113 S.W. Macadam Ave., Portland, OR
(503)452-2656

C50

Cafe Reese

Enjoy one complimentary LUNCH OR DINNER ENTREE when a second LUNCH OR DINNER ENTREE of equal or greater value is purchased.

Offer Conditions on reverse side.

Up To $12.00 Value

CAFE REESE

NEW

www.cafereese.com

1037 NW 23rd Avenue, Portland, OR
(503)219-0633

C51

More Offers Online!

CASUAL & FAMILY DINING

entertainment.com

Yuki Japanese Restaurant

- Relax within our cozy Japanese dining area
- Enjoy traditional Japanese cuisine featuring an expansive selection of sushi, fresh fish & entrees
- Serving lunch & dinner daily

Japanese Restaurant

1337 N.E. Broadway
Portland, OR
(503)281-6804

Offer Conditions: Valid anytime. Sushi excluded.

00753810

Bangkok Corner

- Authentic Thai Cuisine
- No MSG, many vegetarian choices
- All curries are made on site
- Lao dishes a house specialty
- Brown rice available
- Located next to Zupan's at Taylor's Ferry Rd.
- Hours: Mon. - Fri. 11 a.m. - 9:30 p.m., Sat. 12 p.m. - 9:30 p.m., Sun. 12 p.m. - 9 p.m.
- Dine in & take out

Bangkok Corner.
Authentic Thai Cuisine

7113 S.W. Macadam Ave.
(corner of S.W. Nevada & S.W. Macadam)
Portland, OR
(503)452-2656

Offer Conditions: Valid anytime.

Tipping should be 15% to 20% of TOTAL bill before discount

00741378

Cafe Reese

- Warm ambiance featuring evening candlelight table service
- Delicious food from special appetizers and skewers to salads, pastas, panini, & wraps
- Carefully chosen selection of excellent wines
- Open daily - all day
- Adjacent to streetcar
- Eat outdoors in nice weather

CAFE REESE

1037 NW 23rd Avenue
(at Marshall)
Portland, OR
(503)219-0633

Offer Conditions: Valid anytime.

00771286

Muchas Gracias

Enjoy one complimentary
ENTREE when a second
ENTREE of equal or greater
value is purchased.

Offer Conditions on reverse side.

See Reverse Side for Locations

Valid now thru November 1, 2010

C52

Muchas Gracias

Enjoy one complimentary
ENTREE when a second
ENTREE of equal or greater
value is purchased.

Offer Conditions on reverse side.

MUCHAS GRACIAS

See Reverse Side for Locations

Valid now thru November 1, 2010

C53

Muchas Gracias

Enjoy one complimentary
ENTREE when a second
ENTREE of equal or greater
value is purchased.

Offer Conditions on reverse side.

MUCHAS GRACIAS

See Reverse Side for Locations

Valid now thru November 1, 2010

C54

Muchas Gracias
- Authentic Mexican favorites
- Breakfast burritos
- Tacos, burritos, specials and children's menu

MUCHAS GRACIAS

MEXICAN FOOD

660 N.W. Eastman Parkway
Gresham, OR
(503)489-0815

1898 NW 188th Ave
Hillsboro, OR
(503)466-2819

10100 SW Park Way
(Cedar Hills Shopping Center)
Portland, OR
(503)297-1356

Offer Conditions: Valid anytime. Combinations Excluded.

00114209

Muchas Gracias
- Authentic Mexican favorites
- Breakfast burritos
- Tacos, burritos, specials & children's menu

MUCHAS GRACIAS

550 Redwood Hwy.
Grants Pass, OR
(541)955-9284
112 Robbins St.
Molalla, OR
(503)759-3559

707 NE Weidler St
(By Lloyd Center)
Portland, OR
(503)281-0570
155 N. Columbia River Hwy.
St. Helens, OR
(503)366-1075

1006 Washington Way
Longview, WA
(360)575-1595

Offer Conditions: Valid anytime. Combinations excluded.

00113525

Muchas Gracias
- Valid at participating locations

MUCHAS GRACIAS

1999 NE 7th St.
Grants Pass, OR
(541)472-9423

220 NE 12th St.
McMinnville, OR
(503)434-6367

1412 Capital NE
Salem, OR
(503)371-7678

Offer Conditions: Valid anytime.
Tipping should be 15% to 20% of TOTAL bill before discount

00470889

entertainment.com

Me Too! Cafe

Enjoy one complimentary
ENTREE when a second
ENTREE of equal or greater
value is purchased.
Offer Conditions on reverse side.

Up To $12.00 Value

Me Too!
Café for Grown-ups – Play-time for Kids!

NEW

www.metoobeaverton.com

Valid now thru November 1, 2010

16755 Baseline Rd. #102, Beaverton, OR
(503)439-6586

C55

entertainment.com

**El Tapatio Mexican Restaurant
Salmon Creek**

Enjoy one complimentary
LUNCH OR DINNER ENTREE
when a second LUNCH OR
DINNER ENTREE of equal or
greater value is purchased.
Offer Conditions on reverse side.

Up To $12.00 Value

EL TAPATIO

SALMON CREEK

PRINT MORE
ONLINE

Valid now thru November 1, 2010

910 N.E. Tenney Rd., Ste. 105, Vancouver, WA
(360)571-3207

C56

entertainment.com

Hot Seat Sports Bar

Enjoy one complimentary
ENTREE when a second
ENTREE of equal or greater
value is purchased.
Offer Conditions on reverse side.

Up To $12.00 Value

HOT SEAT
BAR & GRILLE

TUALATIN, OREGON

www.hotseatbarandgrill.com

Valid now thru November 1, 2010

18791 S.W. Martinazzi, Tualatin, OR
(503)885-8787

C57

More Offers Online!

CASUAL & FAMILY DINING

entertainment.com

Me Too! Cafe

- Cafe for grown-ups...playtime for kids
- A friendly, comfortable environment where you can relax, while your kids play in a fun, educational, attended childcare area
- Wholesome, fresh foods including paninis and salads for lunch and baked salmon and chicken enchilada verde for dinner
- Me Too is a place that your child will be just as excited to visit as you are

Café for Grown-ups – Play-time for Kids!

16755 Baseline Rd. #102
(Down the street from Beaverton Costco)
Beaverton, OR
(503)439-6586

Offer Conditions: Valid anytime. Dine in only.

00747177

El Tapatio Mexican Restaurant Salmon Creek

- El Tapatio is a name for the locals that are born in Guadalajara, in the state of Jalisco
- We are proud to offer you a sampling of our heritage through our delicious food, friendly services & festive atmosphere
- Come & enjoy!

EL TAPATIO

SALMON CREEK

910 N.E. Tenney Rd., Ste. 105
Vancouver, WA
(360)571-3207

Offer Conditions: Valid anytime.
Offers not valid holidays and subject to Rules of Use
Tipping should be 15% to 20% of the total bill before discount

00660446

Hot Seat Sports Bar

- Offering you generous portions of South-Western & American fare, all at affordable prices
- Enjoy the friendly, fun atmosphere with a full bar, summer patio dining & all your favorite sporting events on 10 TV's
- Test your knowledge with a game of NTN trivia or come after work for the $2 & $3 bar menu
- Served from 3:00 p.m. - 6:00 p.m.
- 21 & over only please

18791 S.W. Martinazzi
Tualatin, OR
(503)885-8787

Offer Conditions: Valid anytime. Karaoke Friday & Saturday from 9 p.m. to 2 a.m.

Offers not valid holidays and subject to Rules of Use
Tipping should be 15% to 20% of the total bill before discount

00314243

El Valle Mexican Grill

Enjoy one complimentary LUNCH OR DINNER ENTREE when a second LUNCH OR DINNER ENTREE of equal or greater value is purchased.

Offer Conditions on reverse side.

Valid now thru November 1, 2010

Up To $12.00 Value

MEXICAN Grill

6700 NE 162nd Ave. Suite 713, Vancouver, WA
(360)891-6868   C58

Wok Inn Restaurant

Enjoy one complimentary BUFFET when a second BUFFET of equal or greater value is purchased.

Offer Conditions on reverse side.

Valid now thru November 1, 2010

Up To $12.00 Value

Wok Inn
Restaurant
www.wokinnbuffet.com

29970 S.W. Town Center Loop, N., Wilsonville, OR
(503)682-0998   C59

Big Lou's Texas BBQ

Enjoy one complimentary LUNCH OR DINNER ENTREE when a second LUNCH OR DINNER ENTREE of equal or greater value is purchased.

Offer Conditions on reverse side.

Up To $11.00 Value

BIG LOU'S TEXAS BBQ MESQUITE SMOKED

www.bigloustexasbbq.com

1924 NE 3rd Ave., Camas, WA
(360)834-4114   C60

Valid now thru November 1, 2010

El Valle Mexican Grill

- Taste the difference-Taste authentic Mexican cuisine
- Seafood, steak & chicken specialties
- Burritos, enchiladas & combinations
- Lunch specials
- Full service bar
- Open at 11am daily

El Valle
MEXICAN
Grill

6700 NE 162nd Ave. Suite 713
(Heritage Shopping Center)
Vancouver, WA
(360)891-6868

Offer Conditions: Valid anytime.

00745176

Wok Inn Restaurant

- The place where you can be your own chef!
- Choose from a wide variety of fresh vegetables & meats, then have our chef prepare it your way in our open wok kitchen
- Enjoy in our comfortable dining room
- It's sure to please any appetite!

Wok Inn
Restaurant

29970 S.W. Town Center Loop, N.
Wilsonville, OR
(503)682-0998

Offer Conditions: Valid anytime.

Offers not valid holidays and subject to Rules of Use
Tipping should be 15% to 20% of the total bill before discount

00722246

Big Lou's Texas BBQ

- Traditional Texas BBQ
- Smoked brisket, ribs, chicken, sausage, pulled pork
- Eat in or drive through- either way, you'll be back!

1924 NE 3rd Ave.
Camas, WA
(360)834-4114

Offer Conditions: Valid anytime. Not valid with any other discounts or promotions.

Offers not valid holidays and subject to Rules of Use
Tipping should be 15% to 20% of the total bill before discount

00695150

Thai Cottage

Enjoy one complimentary
LUNCH OR DINNER ENTREE
when a second LUNCH OR
DINNER ENTREE of equal or
greater value is purchased.
Offer Conditions on reverse side.

Up To $11⁰⁰ Value

www.thaicottagepdx.com

Valid now thru November 1, 2010

8620 N. Lombard St., Portland, OR
(503)283-4321

C61

Best Salsa Mexican Grill

Enjoy one complimentary
LUNCH OR DINNER ENTREE
when a second LUNCH OR
DINNER ENTREE of equal or
greater value is purchased.
Offer Conditions on reverse side.

Up To $11⁰⁰ Value

Valid now thru November 1, 2010

6159 SW Murray Blvd, Beaverton, OR
(503)574-3503

C62

El Torero Mexican Restaurant

Enjoy one complimentary
LUNCH OR DINNER ENTREE
when a second LUNCH OR
DINNER ENTREE of equal or
greater value is purchased.
Offer Conditions on reverse side.

Up To $10⁰⁰ Value

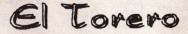

Valid now thru November 1, 2010

2009 Main St., Forest Grove, OR
(503)359-8471

C63

Thai Cottage

- Come enjoy healthy, creative Thai food in a cozy, warm, cottage-like ambiance (even brown rice is available!)
- Many exciting vegetable dishes
- Exotic curry specialties
- In the heart of St. John's, right near the park
- Lunch specials, if desired
- Easy street parking
- Open daily for lunch & dinner
- Dine in or takeout - catering available too

Thai Cottage

8620 N. Lombard St.
(@ Philadelphia)
Portland, OR
(503)283-4321

Offer Conditions: Valid anytime. Dine in only.

00775347

Best Salsa Mexican Grill

- Fresh is best!
- All your favorites, delicious & made to order
- Friendly casual dining great for families
- Try one of our house specials like our Carne Asada or Chile Verde

6159 SW Murray Blvd
Beaverton, OR
(503)574-3503

Offer Conditions: Valid anytime.

00766828

El Torero Mexican Restaurant

- A family Mexican restaurant serving you since 1987
- Specialties include Chile Reliano, Chimichangas, Enchiladas, Fajitas & much more
- Let us help you celebrate your next special occasion in our private dining & event room

El Torero

A Family Mexican Restaurant

2009 Main St.
Forest Grove, OR
(503)359-8471

Offer Conditions: Valid anytime.

00766838

Plaza Jalisco

Enjoy one complimentary
LUNCH OR DINNER ENTREE
when a second LUNCH OR
DINNER ENTREE of equal or
greater value is purchased.
Offer Conditions on reverse side.

Valid now thru November 1, 2010

400 W Main St, Kelso, WA
(360)425-7476

C64

The Village Hut

Enjoy one complimentary
MENU ITEM when a second
MENU ITEM of equal or greater
value is purchased.
Offer Conditions on reverse side.

Valid now thru November 1, 2010

Up $10.00 To Value

The Village Hut

7647 SW Capitol Hwy, Portland, OR
(503)768-3975

C65

Curry Leaf X'press

Enjoy one complimentary
LUNCH OR DINNER ENTREE
when a second LUNCH OR
DINNER ENTREE of equal or
greater value is purchased.
Offer Conditions on reverse side.

Valid now thru November 1, 2010

Up $10.00 To Value

Curry Leaf X'press
GOURMET INDIAN FLAVORS

www.curryleafpdx.com

14845 SW Murray Scholls Dr. #102, Beaverton, OR
(503)590-4442

C66

Plaza Jalisco
- Bienvenidos Amigos!
- Welcome to Kelso's Best Mexican
- Friendly staff, comfortable dining & delicious traditional Mexican cuisine
- Serving all your favorites - Seafood, Pollo (Chicken) Burritos, Enchiladas

Plaza Jalisco

400 W Main St
Kelso, WA
(360)425-7476

Offer Conditions: Valid anytime.

00766835

The Village Hut
- Small kitchen-big taste
- Proudly serving healthy, delicious food in Multnomah Village since 2005
- We shop daily to bring you the freshest ingredients, serving free range, wild & natural dishes
- Our menu has something for everyone; special requests are welcome!
- Dine in, enjoy our three patios, carry out or call in
- Catering available
- Open Mon.-Sat. 11 a.m until 8 p.m

The Village Hut

7647 SW Capitol Hwy
(At SW 31st)
Portland, OR
(503)768-3975

Offer Conditions: Valid anytime.

00781652

Curry Leaf X'press
- North & South Indian cuisine
- Specials: MalabarVeg Kurma, Kofta NazaKat, Chili Paneer, Karaikudi Chicken, Lamb Pepper Fry, Goan Fish Curry, kids menu, desserts
- Beer & wine
- Vegan & gluten free options
- Catering, eat in, take out, delivery
- Lunch buffet 11:30 - 3 p.m.; dinner 4 - 9 p.m. weekdays; 4-9:30 p.m. Fri. & Sat.
- Closed Mon.
- Visit our website

Curry Leaf
X'press
GOURMET INDIAN FLAVORS

14845 SW Murray Scholls Dr. #102
(in Murray Scholls Ferry Towncenter)
Beaverton, OR
(503)590-4442

Offer Conditions: Valid anytime.

00742033

AJ on the Rails

Enjoy one complimentary
LUNCH OR DINNER ENTREE
when a second LUNCH OR
DINNER ENTREE of equal or
greater value is purchased.
Offer Conditions on reverse side.

Up$ **10^{00}** Value
To

Valid now thru November 1, 2010

1022 SW Morrison St, Portland, OR
(503)445-0832

C67

The Blue Pig Cafe

Enjoy one complimentary
ENTREE when a second
ENTREE of equal or greater
value is purchased.
Offer Conditions on reverse side.

Up$ **9^{00}** Value
To

NEW

Valid now thru November 1, 2010

5026 SE Division St, Portland, OR
(503)231-2775

C68

Po'Shines Cafe De La Soul

Enjoy one complimentary
ENTREE when a second
ENTREE of equal or greater
value is purchased.
Offer Conditions on reverse side.

Up$ **9^{00}** Value
To

PO'SHINES
CAFÉ · DE · LA · SOUL

Valid now thru November 1, 2010

8139 N. Denver Ave., Portland, OR
(503)978-9000

C69

More Offers Online!

CASUAL & FAMILY DINING

entertainment.com

AJ on the Rails

- Bold, flavorful food
- Everything cooked from scratch
- All chefs original recipes
- Weekly specials
- Decadent homemade desserts
- Just off the Morrison Street Trolley Shop
- Occasional live, local music
- TV
- Karaoke

**1022 SW Morrison St
Portland, OR
(503)445-0832**

Offer Conditions: Valid anytime.

00772339

The Blue Pig Cafe

- Quality Breakfast and Lunch
- Prices that won't break your piggy bank!
- Try one of our local breakfast favorites like our Corned Beef Hash or Chicken Fried Steak

THE BLUE PIG CAFE

**5026 SE Division St
Portland, OR
(503)231-2775**

Offer Conditions: Valid anytime. Dine in only.

00744738

Po'Shines Cafe De La Soul

- Contemporary soul food
- A part of the Teach Me to Fish Organization where we provide training and counseling to the youth and young adults of our community
- Try a Po' Pork Philly, Catfish Sandwich or some good home cooked BBQ
- Our mission is simple: feed the community and feed it well
- Mind, Body & Soul
- Open for breakfast, lunch and dinner

PO'SHINES CAFÉ · DE · LA · SOUL

**8139 N. Denver Ave.
Portland, OR
(503)978-9000**

Offer Conditions: Valid anytime.

00745130

Sellwood Public House

Enjoy one complimentary ENTREE when a second ENTREE of equal or greater value is purchased or for those who prefer - any one pizza at 50% off the regular price - maximum discount $9.00.

Offer Conditions on reverse side.

Valid now thru November 1, 2010

Up To $9.00 Value

SELLWOOD
PUBLIC HOUSE

www.sellwoodpublichouse.com

8132 13th Ave, Portland, OR
(503)736-0179

C70

Hockinson Kountry Cafe

Enjoy one complimentary ENTREE when a second ENTREE AND TWO DRINKS are purchased of equal or lesser value.

Offer Conditions on reverse side.

Valid now thru November 1, 2010

Up To $8.00 Value

Hockinson Kountry Café

www.hockinsonkountrycafe.com

17407 NE 159th St, Brush Prairie, WA
(360)254-6726

C71

Urban Decanter Wine Collection and Bar

Enjoy one complimentary A LA CARTE ENTREE when a second A LA CARTE ENTREE of equal or greater value is purchased.

Offer Conditions on reverse side.

Valid now thru November 1, 2010

Up To $8.00 Value

URBAN DECANTER
WINE COLLECTION AND BAR

2030 Main St, Forest Grove, OR
(503)359-7678

C72

Sellwood Public House

- Enjoyable, Fun, Friendly and Comfortable
- Full bar with wide selection of micro brews; family friendly until 8pm nightly
- Great place to meet with friends - take in a round of darts or ping pong
- Nightly cash buy-in poker tournaments
- Live acoustic music four nights a week
- All topped off with Mel's cooking and nightly specials

SELLWOOD

PUBLIC HOUSE

8132 13th Ave
(1/2 block south of Tacoma - Step Upstairs)
Portland, OR
(503)736-0179

Offer Conditions: Valid anytime.

00745502

Hockinson Kountry Cafe

- Friendly service, great food
- We'll become your home away from home
- Daily specials, homemade pies
- Try our biscuits & gravy for breakfast or chicken fried steak for lunch or dinner
- Open Mon. - Wed. 6 a.m. - 3 p.m.
- Thurs. - Fri. 6 a.m. - 8 p.m.
- Sat. 6 a.m. - 3 p.m.
- Sun. 7 a.m. - 3 p.m.

Hockinson Kountry Café

17407 NE 159th St
Brush Prairie, WA
(360)254-6726

Offer Conditions: Valid anytime. Not valid with any other discounts or promotions.

00771450

Urban Decanter Wine Collection and Bar

- Come for the Wine, Stay for the Experience
- Showcasing a fine variety of wines from the Pacific Northwest as well as specialty regions around the world
- Complement your wine selection with any of our delicious small plate menu items, including Anti Pasta, Salads and Paninis

URBAN DECANTER

WINE COLLECTION AND BAR

2030 Main St
Forest Grove, OR
(503)359-7678

Offer Conditions: Valid anytime.

00752300

Julia's Cafe

Enjoy one complimentary ENTREE when a second ENTREE of equal or greater value is purchased.

Offer Conditions on reverse side.

Up To $8.00 Value

julia's cafe

Valid now thru November 1, 2010

2130 N. E. Broadway, Portland, OR
(503)284-1066

C73

---

 entertainment. entertainment.com

The Original Chicken Bar - Beaverton Town Sq.

Enjoy one complimentary LUNCH OR DINNER ENTREE when a second LUNCH OR DINNER ENTREE of equal or greater value is purchased.

Offer Conditions on reverse side.

Up To $7.00 Value

Valid now thru November 1, 2010

11733 S.W. Beaverton Hillsdale Hwy., Beaverton, OR
(503)643-6300

C74

---

entertainment. entertainment.com

Geraldi's The Italian Eating Place

Enjoy one complimentary MENU ITEM when a second MENU ITEM of equal or greater value is purchased.

Offer Conditions on reverse side.

Up To $7.00 Value

Geraldi's
THE ITALIAN EATING PLACE

Valid now thru November 1, 2010

226 NE 3rd St, McMinnville, OR
(503)472-7868

C75

Julia's Cafe
- Great grilled and traditional sandwiches
- Fresh salads, pizza, daily specials
- Imported beer and wine
- Espresso, loose leaf tea
- Desserts
- Lottery games

julia's cafe

2130 N. E. Broadway
Portland, OR
(503)284-1066

Offer Conditions: Valid anytime.

00764425

The Original Chicken Bar - Beaverton Town Sq.
- Outrageously healthy & delicious food!
- Low fat, low sodium entrees & salads
- Great tasting boneless, skinless chicken breast
- Flavorful sauces
- White or brown rice & steamed veggies
- Enjoy your meal!

11733 S.W. Beaverton Hillsdale Hwy.
Beaverton, OR
(503)643-6300

Offer Conditions: Valid anytime. This location only.
Tipping should be 15% to 20% of TOTAL bill before discount

00731678

Geraldi's The Italian Eating Place
- Locally owned
- Specials daily
- Great family atmosphere

Geraldi's
THE ITALIAN EATING PLACE

226 NE 3rd St
McMinnville, OR
(503)472-7868

Offer Conditions: Valid anytime.

00759519

Mary's Kitchen

Enjoy one complimentary
ENTREE when a second
ENTREE of equal or greater
value is purchased.

Offer Conditions on reverse side.

Up To $7.00 Value

Valid now thru November 1, 2010

200 W. Baseline, Cornelius, OR
(503)357-1313

C76

Jett Burger Cafe

Enjoy one complimentary
ENTREE when a second
ENTREE of equal or greater
value is purchased.

Offer Conditions on reverse side.

Up To $7.00 Value

Jett Burger Cafe

Valid now thru November 1, 2010

3531 S.E. 2nd Ave., Camas, WA
(360)335-1430

C77

Deli in the Grove

Enjoy one complimentary
ENTREE when a second
ENTREE of equal or greater
value is purchased.

Offer Conditions on reverse side.

Up To $7.00 Value

Valid now thru November 1, 2010

2014 Main St., Forest Grove, OR
(503)357-3513

C78

Mary's Kitchen

- Wake up at Mary's Kitchen
- A home cooked meal with a friendly smile & service

**200 W. Baseline
Cornelius, OR
(503)357-1313**

Offer Conditions: Valid anytime.
Tipping should be 15% to 20% of TOTAL bill before discount

00729908

Jett Burger Cafe

- One bite and we gotcha!
- In Camas since 1992
- Delicious breakfast, mouth-watering burgers, salads, bento, espresso & more!
- Featuring nightly dinner specials

**3531 S.E. 2nd Ave.
(in the One Step Shpg. Ctr.)
Camas, WA
(360)335-1430**

Offer Conditions: Valid anytime.
Offers not valid holidays and subject to Rules of Use
Tipping should be 15% to 20% of the total bill before discount

00695111

Deli in the Grove

- Serving breakfast & lunch in heart Forest Grove
- Great food, affordable prices
- Clean, family friendly casual dining atmosphere
- Open 7 days 6:30 a.m.-3 p.m.
- Breakfast all day

**Deli
in
the
Grove**

**2014 Main St.
Forest Grove, OR
(503)357-3513**

Offer Conditions: Valid anytime.
Offers not valid holidays and subject to Rules of Use
Tipping should be 15% to 20% of the total bill before discount

00692027

Maggie's Buns

Enjoy one complimentary ENTREE when a second ENTREE of equal or greater value is purchased.

Offer Conditions on reverse side.

Up To $6.00 Value

Valid now thru November 1, 2010

2007 21st Ave., Forest Grove, OR
(503)992-2231

C79

The East Bank Saloon

Enjoy one complimentary DINNER ENTREE when a second DINNER ENTREE of equal or greater value is purchased.

Offer Conditions on reverse side.

$6.00 Value

Valid now thru November 1, 2010

727 S.E. Grand Ave., Portland, OR
(503)231-1659

C80

Norma's Kitchen

Enjoy one complimentary ENTREE when a second ENTREE of equal or greater value is purchased.

Offer Conditions on reverse side.

Up To $10.00 Value

NORMA'S
KITCHEN

Valid now thru November 1, 2010

12010 N Jantzen Dr, Portland, OR
(503)240-3447

C81

Maggie's Buns
- Hot savory entrees served daily
- Try our Greek chicken, eggplant parmesan, pork roast or Thai curry chicken
- Complement your meal with fresh baked breads or dessert
- Fun, eclectic dining area
- Delicious!

**2007 21st Ave.
Forest Grove, OR
(503)992-2231**

00692026

Offer Conditions: Valid anytime.

Offers not valid holidays and subject to Rules of Use
Tipping should be 15% to 20% of the total bill before discount

---

The East Bank Saloon
- A unique ol' place full of great food & fine conversations in an 1800's style setting
- Relax in our fresh air patio (weather permitting)
- Sporting events showing on 9 TV's
- Cocktails, beer & wine
- Dinner served daily 3:00 p.m. - 1:00 a.m.

**727 S.E. Grand Ave.
Portland, OR
(503)231-1659**

00010267

Offer Conditions: Valid any evening. Dine in only.

Offers not valid holidays and subject to Rules of Use
Tipping should be 15% to 20% of the total bill before discount

---

Norma's Kitchen
- Savor the flavors of Creole and Cajun Cuisine
- Louisiana Gumbo, Pulled Pork Sandwiches, BBQ Ribs, Muffalatas and more
- Specials, Spicey Sweet Tea, Beer and Wine, Patio Seating
- Come by on FRYday for our Bayou Good Catfish and Fries

NORMA'S
KITCHEN

**12010 N Jantzen Dr
Portland, OR
(503)240-3447**

00744730

Offer Conditions: Valid anytime.

The Parkside Deli & Fine Foods

Enjoy one complimentary ENTREE when a second ENTREE of equal or greater value is purchased.

Offer Conditions on reverse side.

Up $8⁰⁰ Value To

The Parkside Deli
& Fine Foods

6031 SE Belmont, Portland, OR
(503)236-6005

Valid now thru November 1, 2010

C82

---

 entertainment.com

Primetime Pizza

Enjoy any one complimentary PIZZA when a second PIZZA of equal or greater value is purchased.

Offer Conditions on reverse side.

FREE PIZZA

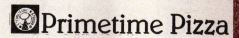 Primetime Pizza

See Reverse Side for Locations

Valid now thru November 1, 2010

C83

Casa Colima

Enjoy one complimentary LUNCH OR DINNER ENTREE when a second LUNCH OR DINNER ENTREE of equal or greater value is purchased.

Offer Conditions on reverse side.

PRINT MORE ONLINE

Up $11⁰⁰ Value To

MEXICAN RESTAURANT
& CANTINA

See Reverse Side for Locations

Valid now thru November 1, 2010

C84

More Offers Online!

CASUAL & FAMILY DINING

entertainment.com

The Parkside Deli & Fine Foods

- House baked breads
- Daily specials
- Mouth watering meals
- Try one of our favorite sandwiches, like our Prosciutto Di Parma with roasted red pepper sauce, onion, tomato, organic greens and provolone on a fresh french baguette
- Catering available

The Parkside Deli

& Fine Foods

6031 SE Belmont
(At the foot of Mt. Tabor)
Portland, OR
(503)236-6005

Offer Conditions: Valid anytime.

00741959

Primetime Pizza

- Every pizza place has its own unique qualities, ours just happens to be TASTE!
- Build your own pizza or choose one from our All-Star Line-Up
- Also serving cheezy garlic bread, garden fresh salads & hot buffalo wings
- Open Sun. - Thurs., 11:00 a.m. - 11:00 p.m., Fri. - Sat., til 12:00 midnight

Primetime Pizza

5025 River Rd. N.
Keizer, OR
(503)390-0098

1350 N. Baker St.
(Baker St. Square)
McMinnville, OR
(503)434-6666

3985 Rich Dr.
Salem, OR
(503)584-0222

5070 Commercial St. S.E.
Salem, OR
(503)588-3232

Offer Conditions: Valid anytime. Delivery excluded. Free 2 liter soda special excluded; Not valid with an other discounts or promotions.

Offers not valid holidays and subject to Rules of Use
Tipping should be 15% to 20% of the total bill before discount

00388069

Casa Colima

- Come join Alonso & Elsa Ochoa in celebrating the best flavors & festivities that Mexico has to offer
- Try traditional favorites with beef, chicken, seafood or veggies
- Compliment your meal with the biggest margaritas in town!
- Party room available for all occasions

CASA COLIMA

MEXICAN RESTAURANT & CANTINA

140 S.W. Oak St.
Hillboro, OR
(503)726-8449

6319 S.W. Capitol Hwy.
Portland, OR
(503)892-9944

Offer Conditions: Valid anytime.
Offers not valid holidays and subject to Rules of Use
Tipping should be 15% to 20% of the total bill before discount

00676403

El Pollo Yucateco

Enjoy one complimentary
LUNCH OR DINNER ENTREE
when a second LUNCH OR
DINNER ENTREE of equal or
greater value is purchased.
Offer Conditions on reverse side.

Up To $**11**.00 Value

EL POLLO YUCATECO

PRINT MORE ONLINE

Valid now thru November 1, 2010

2020 NE Cornell Rd. Ste. D, Hillsboro, OR
(503)648-4822

C85

Fireside Cafe

Enjoy one complimentary
ENTREE when a second
ENTREE of equal or greater
value is purchased.
Offer Conditions on reverse side.

Up To $**10**.00 Value

Fireside Cafe

Valid now thru November 1, 2010

5055 N. Meeker Dr., Kalama, WA
(360)673-3473

C86

La Flor De Michoacan

Enjoy one complimentary
LUNCH OR DINNER ENTREE
when a second LUNCH OR
DINNER ENTREE of equal or
greater value is purchased.
Offer Conditions on reverse side.

Up To $**10**.00 Value

LA FLOR DE MICHOACAN
MEXICAN RESTAURANT AND CANTINA

PRINT MORE ONLINE

Valid now thru November 1, 2010

1075 S.E. Baseline St., Ste. K, Hillsboro, OR
(503)693-7782

C87

More Offers Online!

CASUAL & FAMILY DINING

entertainment.com

El Pollo Yucateco

- Flame broiled chicken & much, much, more!
- Pollo Asada, Codzitos, Empanadas & more
- Specialties from the heart of the Yucatan
- We are here to serve you!

00662033

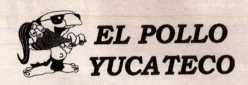

EL POLLO YUCATECO

2020 NE Cornell Rd. Ste. D
Hillsboro, OR
(503)648-4822

Offer Conditions: Valid anytime.

Offers not valid holidays and subject to Rules of Use
Tipping should be 15% to 20% of the total bill before discount

---

Fireside Cafe

- Where home cookin' is the best!
- Open for breakfast, lunch & dinner
- Prime rib Fri. - Sat.
- Homemade desserts
- Friendly staff, great dining atmosphere
- Located in Camp Kalama

00729149

5055 N. Meeker Dr.
Kalama, WA
(360)673-3473

Offer Conditions: Valid anytime.

Tipping should be 15% to 20% of TOTAL bill before discount

La Flor De Michoacan

- Authentic Michican - style food
- Unique traditional cooking
- Specialty plates from popular Mexican states
- Karaoke & dance music every Friday & Saturday nights

00692038

LA FLOR DE MICHOACAN

MEXICAN RESTAURANT AND CANTINA

1075 S.E. Baseline St., Ste. K
Hillsboro, OR
(503)693-7782

Offer Conditions: Valid anytime.

Offers not valid holidays and subject to Rules of Use
Tipping should be 15% to 20% of the total bill before discount

Thai Home

- A delicious experience in downtown Sandy near Mt. Hood
- Come explore our unique Thai cuisine, like Sizzling Spinach and Spicy Soft-shell Crab
- "Alike but different Thai cuisine"
- Family-friendly restaurant with lovely outdoor patio and private parking
- Open daily for lunch and dinner
- Take-out and catering also available

38676 Pioneer Blvd.
(downtown Sandy)
Sandy, OR
(503)668-0779

Offer Conditions: Valid anytime. Dine in only; Specials excluded. Not valid with any other discounts or promotions.

00780165

Copper Monkey

- Northwest with a Caribbean flair
- Eat well in a relaxing, casual dine atmosphere
- Enjoy a unique blend of food & regional styles
- Sauces from all over Western Caribbean
- Pulled pork, steaks, chicken, seafood, pasta
- Next door to Laserport - a perfect combination for families, parties or corporate events.

6540 S.W. Fallbrook Place
(Right beside Laserport)
Beaverton, OR
(503)352-3399

Offer Conditions: Valid anytime.

Offers not valid holidays and subject to Rules of Use
Tipping should be 15% to 20% of the total bill before discount

00626930

Goose Hollow at the Cove

- Sister site of Portland's Goose Hollow Inn, founded by (former Portland Mayor) Bud Clark
- Best Reuben on the Planet
- Outstanding clam chowder
- 14 brews on tap--one of the North Coast's largest selections of microbrews!
- Free Wi-Fi
- Live music
- Outdoor seating
- Family friendly

Goose Hollow
at the cove

220 Avenue U
(at S Columbia Street on Seaside's south end)
Seaside, OR
(503)717-1940

Offer Conditions: Valid anytime.

00775864

Lucky Fortune

- Featuring a large selection of Mandarin & Cantonese cuisine.
- Enjoy favorites such as Kung Pao Chicken, Barbequed Pork, Mandarin Beef and Szechuan Shrimp.
- Relax in a friendly, family oriented atmosphere.
- Compliment your meal with a beverage from our full service bar.
- Open daily.

LUCKY FORTUNE
幸 運 酒 家
RESTAURANT & LOUNGE

400 E. First
Newberg, OR
(503)538-1661

Offer Conditions: Valid anytime. Dine in only. Combination & family style dinners excluded.

Offers not valid holidays and subject to Rules of Use
Tipping should be 15% to 20% of the total bill before discount

00299071

Paradise Restaurant and Lounge

- Enjoy a family friendly atmosphere with a menu that agrees to all appetites
- Everything from soups to seafood
- Located at Park Lanes Entertainment Center where we specialize in family fun
- 32 Lanes of bowling, 9 batting cages, billards, arcade, bumper & monte carlo bowling, party rooms, full service lottery & more

PARADISE
Restaurant and Lounge

6360 SE Alexander St.
(at Park Lanes Family Entertainment Ctr.)
Hillsboro, OR
(503)642-2161

Offer Conditions: Valid anytime.

Offers not valid holidays and subject to Rules of Use
Tipping should be 15% to 20% of the total bill before discount

00361662

J&M House

- Sushi Rolls, Teriyaki, Wokking, hot grilled sandwiches, burgers and more
- All our dishes are prepared in the healthiest manner by using the best ingredients
- Wireless Internet
- Bright comfortable dining area

J&M House

8981 SW Barbur Blvd
Portland, OR
(503)452-7909

Offer Conditions: Valid anytime.

00748237

Fong Huong Seafood Restaurant & Lounge

Enjoy one complimentary MENU ITEM when a second MENU ITEM of equal or greater value is purchased or for those who prefer, 25% off any DIM SUM order.

Offer Conditions on reverse side.

Valid now thru November 1, 2010

Fong Huong
鳳凰海鮮酒家
Seafood Restaurant & Lounge

12525 SW Canyon Rd., Beaverton, OR
(503) 626-6111

C94

Thai Garden Restaurant

Enjoy one complimentary LUNCH OR DINNER ENTREE when a second LUNCH OR DINNER ENTREE of equal or greater value is purchased.

Offer Conditions on reverse side.

Thai Garden Restaurant

Valid now thru November 1, 2010

620 S.E. 122nd Ave., Portland, OR
(503) 262-8002

C95

Asabache

Enjoy one complimentary LUNCH OR DINNER ENTREE when a second LUNCH OR DINNER ENTREE of equal or greater value is purchased.

Offer Conditions on reverse side.

Valid now thru November 1, 2010

See Reverse Side for Locations

C96

Fong Huong Seafood Restaurant & Lounge

- Authentic Cantonese Hong Kong-style Dim Sum
- Voted one of the top 100 Chinese restaurants in the U.S
- Happy hour Mon.-Fri. until 6:30 p.m
- Pool tables, dancing, karaoke & live music in the lounge
- Ideal location; catering for any budget

Fong Huong
鳳凰海鮮酒家
Seafood Restaurant & Lounge

12525 SW Canyon Rd.
(Across from Beaverton Honda)
Beaverton, OR
(503)626-6111

Offer Conditions: Valid anytime.

00781977

Thai Garden Restaurant

- Open Mon. - Thurs. 11:00 a.m. - 9:30 p.m., Fri. 11:00 a.m. - 10:00 p.m., Sat. 12 noon - 10:00 p.m., & Sun. 12 noon - 9:30 p.m.
- Fresh curry, seafood & vegetables
- Vegetarian friendly
- Beer & wine available
- We do catering banquets & parties! Just ask us we would be happy to help!

Thai Garden Restaurant

620 S.E. 122nd Ave.
Portland, OR
(503)262-8002

Offer Conditions: Valid anytime. Dine in only.

Offers not valid holidays and subject to Rules of Use
Tipping should be 15% to 20% of the total bill before discount

00529872

Asabache

- The best & most authentic Mexican food from the old country
- Great family dining with a children's menu available
- Serving lunch, dinner & cocktails
- Two locations to serve you in Tigard & Sheridan

518 S. Bridge St.
Sheridan, OR
(503)843-2333

13815 S.W. Pacific Hwy.
(corner of 138th & SW Pacific Hwy.)
Tigard, OR
(503)598-3907

Offer Conditions: Valid anytime.

Offers not valid holidays and subject to Rules of Use
Tipping should be 15% to 20% of the total bill before discount

00140568

California Chicken

Enjoy one complimentary ENTREE when a second ENTREE of equal or greater value is purchased.

Offer Conditions on reverse side.

Up$ **7**^{00} To Value

California **CHICKEN**

"HEALTHY FLAME-BROILED MEXICAN FOOD"

Valid now thru November 1, 2010

2210 W. Main St., Battleground, WA
(360)687-4500

C97

Taqueria Hermanos Ochoa

Enjoy one complimentary LUNCH OR DINNER ENTREE when a second LUNCH OR DINNER ENTREE of equal or greater value is purchased.

Offer Conditions on reverse side.

Up$ **6**^{00} To Value

Taqueria
Hermanos Ochoa

PRINT MORE ONLINE

Valid now thru November 1, 2010

943 S.E. Oak St., Hillsboro, OR
(503)640-4755

C98

Takahashi Japanese Restaurant

Enjoy one complimentary DINNER ENTREE when a second DINNER ENTREE of equal or greater value is purchased.

Offer Conditions on reverse side.

Up$ **10**^{00} To Value

The Takahashi
Japanese Restaurant

Valid now thru November 1, 2010

10324 S.E. Holgate, Portland, OR
(503)760-8135

C99

California Chicken
- Flame broiled chicken served with a Mexican flare
- Our chicken is 100% fresh, no additives, no hormones, no preservatives
- Salads & salsa made in our kitchen & served fresh daily

California CHICKEN
"HEALTHY FLAME-BROILED MEXICAN FOOD"

2210 W. Main St.
Battleground, WA
(360)687-4500

Offer Conditions: Valid anytime.

Offers not valid holidays and subject to Rules of Use
Tipping should be 15% to 20% of the total bill before discount

00696118

Offer validity is governed by the Rules of Use and excludes defined holidays. Offers are not valid with other discount offers, unless specified. Coupons void if purchased, sold or bartered. Discounts exclude tax, tip and/or alcohol, where applicable.

Taqueria Hermanos Ochoa
- Authentic Mexican food
- Try one of our specialties including pork carnitas & fajitas
- House special - steak enchilada, chile rellanos & two tacos
- Fresh salsa made daily
- Open daily

Taqueria Hermanos Ochoa

943 S.E. Oak St.
Hillsboro, OR
(503)640-4755

Offer Conditions: Valid anytime.

Offers not valid holidays and subject to Rules of Use
Tipping should be 15% to 20% of the total bill before discount

00691019

Offer validity is governed by the Rules of Use and excludes defined holidays. Offers are not valid with other discount offers, unless specified. Coupons void if purchased, sold or bartered. Discounts exclude tax, tip and/or alcohol, where applicable.

Takahashi Japanese Restaurant
- Romantic Japanese rural atmosphere
- Sushi, teriyaki chicken & beef, salmon, sukiyaki & tempura & miso soup
- Ice cream
- Green tea
- Sake & Japanese & American beer
- Hours: Wed. - Sun., 5 p.m. - 9 p.m.
- Closed Monday & Tuesday
- Visa & Mastercard accepted

The Takahashi Japanese Restaurant

10324 S.E. Holgate
Portland, OR
(503)760-8135

Offer Conditions: Valid any evening. Dine in only.

Offers not valid holidays and subject to Rules of Use
Tipping should be 15% to 20% of the total bill before discount

00024895

Offer validity is governed by the Rules of Use and excludes defined holidays. Offers are not valid with other discount offers, unless specified. Coupons void if purchased, sold or bartered. Discounts exclude tax, tip and/or alcohol, where applicable.

Malai Thai Restaurant

Enjoy one complimentary MENU ITEM when a second MENU ITEM of equal or greater value is purchased.

Offer Conditions on reverse side.

Valid now thru November 1, 2010

MALAI THAI

www.malaithairestaurant.com

14297 SW Pacific Hwy., Tigard, OR
(503)684-9749

C100

Pepper's Mexican Grill

Enjoy one complimentary LUNCH OR DINNER ENTREE when a second LUNCH OR DINNER ENTREE of equal or greater value is purchased.

Offer Conditions on reverse side.

Valid now thru November 1, 2010

976 S.E. Baseline St., Hillsboro, OR
(503)681-8226

C101

The Works Family Restaurant & Catering

Enjoy one complimentary ENTREE when a second ENTREE of equal or greater value is purchased.

Offer Conditions on reverse side.

Valid now thru November 1, 2010

The Works
Family Restaurant and Catering

1073 14th Ave, Longview, WA
(360)577-1136

C102

Malai Thai Restaurant

- Intimate, small restaurant serving family recipes from Old Siam
- All our food is homemade
- Take-out, delivery & catering available
- Easy parking
- Open Mon.-Fri. 11 a.m.-3 p.m. & 5 p.m.-9 p.m., Sat. 12 p.m.-3 p.m. & 5 p.m.-9 p.m., Sun. 12 p.m.-3 p.m. & 5 p.m.-8 p.m

MALAI THAI

14297 SW Pacific Hwy.
(In the Canterbury Shopping Center)
Tigard, OR
(503)684-9749

Offer Conditions: Valid anytime.

00781983

Pepper's Mexican Grill

- Authentic Mexican food
- Rated 4.5 out of 5 by Yahoo visitors!
- Privately-owned, single location
- Come try our famous chili rellenos
- Casa of the best margaritas in town
- All our dishes are homemade from scratch
- Moles are one of our specialties
- One of the best values anywhere
- Open daily

976 S.E. Baseline St.
(at corner of N.E. Cornell Rd.)
Hillsboro, OR
(503)681-8226

Offer Conditions: Valid anytime.

00496401

The Works Family Restaurant & Catering

- Family owned & operated
- Home cooked favorites
- Cozy family friendly atmosphere
- Meeting rooms
- Breakfast lunch & dinner
- M- W 8am-3pm
- Th-Sat 8am-6pm
- Catering for all your events

The Works
Family Restaurant and Catering

1073 14th Ave
Longview, WA
(360)577-1136

Offer Conditions: Valid anytime.

00757465

El Ranchito

Enjoy one complimentary
LUNCH OR DINNER ENTREE
when a second LUNCH OR
DINNER ENTREE of equal or
greater value is purchased.
Offer Conditions on reverse side.

Up $9.00 To Value

El Ranchito
a family mexican restaurant

Valid now thru November 1, 2010

329 S.W. 2nd St., Lake Oswego, OR
(503) 636-0331

C103

El Tapatio Mexican Restaurant

Enjoy one complimentary
LUNCH OR DINNER ENTREE
when a second LUNCH OR
DINNER ENTREE of equal or
greater value is purchased.
Offer Conditions on reverse side.

Up $9.00 To Value

Valid now thru November 1, 2010

6202 Hwy. 99, Vancouver, WA
(360) 693-2443

C104

Firehouse Cafe

Enjoy one complimentary
MENU ITEM when a second
MENU ITEM of equal or greater
value is purchased.
Offer Conditions on reverse side.

Up $8.00 To Value

FIREHOUSE
CAFE

PRINT MORE
ONLINE

Valid now thru November 1, 2010

582 Old Pacific Hwy., La Center, WA
(360) 263-0522

C105

El Ranchito

- Enjoy delicious Mexican food
- Each entree is custom prepared to your order by a skilled chef
- Our family recipes have been handed down through generations
- Cocktails served nightly
- Open 7 days for lunch & dinner

a family mexican restaurant

329 S.W. 2nd St.
Lake Oswego, OR
(503)636-0331

Offer Conditions: Valid anytime. Dine in only. Valid at the Lake Oswego location only.

Offers not valid holidays and subject to Rules of Use
Tipping should be 15% to 20% of the total bill before discount

00010330

El Tapatio Mexican Restaurant

- Welcome amigos!
- We serve the finest food & spirits
- Offering traditional selections as well as house favorites
- Reservations accepted

6202 Hwy. 99
(in Hazel Dell)
Vancouver, WA
(360)693-2443

Offer Conditions: Valid anytime.

Offers not valid holidays and subject to Rules of Use
Tipping should be 15% to 20% of the total bill before discount

00010945

Firehouse Cafe

- Cozy neighborhood cafe serving fresh deli sandwiches, soup, salads & espresso
- Comfortable casual dining area
- Friendly staff, ready & happy to assist you

582 Old Pacific Hwy.
La Center, WA
(360)263-0522

Offer Conditions: Valid anytime.

00650036

Sandwich Express

Enjoy one complimentary
MENU ITEM when a second
MENU ITEM of equal or greater
value is purchased.
Offer Conditions on reverse side.

See Reverse Side for Locations

Valid now thru November 1, 2010

C106

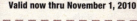

Parkway Station Bar & Grill

Enjoy one complimentary
MENU ITEM when a second
MENU ITEM of equal or greater
value is purchased.
Offer Conditions on reverse side.

Parkway Station Pub

5245 NE Elam Young Pkwy., Hillsboro, OR
(503) 648-6885

Valid now thru November 1, 2010

C107

Gringo's Mexican Restaurant & Lounge

Enjoy one complimentary
DINNER ENTREE when a
second DINNER ENTREE of
equal or greater value is
purchased.
Offer Conditions on reverse side.

Gringo's
MEXICAN RESTAURANT & LOUNGE

419 'E' Street, Washougal, WA
(360) 835-1103

Valid now thru November 1, 2010

C108

More Offers Online!

CASUAL & FAMILY DINING

entertainment.com

Sandwich Express

- 25 Different sandwiches on fresh-baked bread
- Gourmet soups in a bread bowl
- 5 Delicious dinner-size salads
- Bakery delights to satisfy your craving
- Home of the Maxi
- Newberg hrs: Mon.-Fri. 10:00 a.m.-7:30 p.m., Sat. 10:00 a.m.-4:00 p.m., Sun. 11:00 a.m.-3:00 p.m.
- McMinnville hrs: Mon.-Fri. 10:00 a.m.-9:00 p.m., Sat. 10:00 a.m.-7:30 p.m., Sun. 10:00 a.m.-4:00 p.m.

00281726

YAMHILL COUNTY'S PREMIERE

SANDWICH EXPRESS

SANDWICHES

711 N. Hwy. 99 W.
McMinnville, OR
(503)472-3500

901 B Brutscher St.
(next to Fred Meyer)
Newberg, OR
(503)554-8636

Offer Conditions: Valid anytime. Specials excluded.

Offers not valid holidays and subject to Rules of Use
Tipping should be 15% to 20% of the total bill before discount

Offer validity is governed by the Rules of Use and excludes defined holidays. Offers are not valid with other discount offers, unless specified. Coupons void if purchased, sold or bartered. Discounts exclude tax, tip and/or alcohol, where applicable.

Parkway Station Bar & Grill

- Come try us
- New Ownership
- Lunch & dinner
- Full bar, beer on tap
- Lottery
- Across the street from Yahoo!
- Hours: Mon. - Sat. 11 a.m. - 11 p.m.

00740489

Parkway Station Pub

5245 NE Elam Young Pkwy.
Hillsboro, OR
(503)648-6885

Offer Conditions: Valid anytime.

Tipping should be 15% to 20% of TOTAL bill before discount

Offer validity is governed by the Rules of Use and excludes defined holidays. Offers are not valid with other discount offers, unless specified. Coupons void if purchased, sold or bartered. Discounts exclude tax, tip and/or alcohol, where applicable.

Gringo's Mexican Restaurant & Lounge

- Authentic Mexican food in a relaxing, family atmosphere
- American cuisine served, too
- Wide variety of margaritas & Mexican beers
- Banquet rooms available
- Hours: 11:30 a.m. - 9:00 p.m. daily
- Lounge open until 2:00 a.m.

00197513

Gringo's

MEXICAN RESTAURANT & LOUNGE

419 'E' Street
Washougal, WA
(360)835-1103

Offer Conditions: Valid any evening.

Offers not valid holidays and subject to Rules of Use
Tipping should be 15% to 20% of the total bill before discount

Offer validity is governed by the Rules of Use and excludes defined holidays. Offers are not valid with other discount offers, unless specified. Coupons void if purchased, sold or bartered. Discounts exclude tax, tip and/or alcohol, where applicable.

El Charrito

Enjoy one complimentary
DINNER ENTREE when a
second DINNER ENTREE of
equal or greater value is
purchased.
Offer Conditions on reverse side.

Up To $8.00 Value

Valid now thru November 1, 2010

117 E. Main St., Molalla, OR
(503)829-3017

C109

Z Best Pizza

Enjoy any one PIZZA at 50%
off the regular price or for
those who prefer - one
complimentary MENU ITEM at
50% off the regular price -
maximum discount $7.00.
Offer Conditions on reverse side.

Up To $7.00 Value

Z Best PizzaCo.

Valid now thru November 1, 2010

3801 Main St., Vancouver, WA
(360)750-0445

C110

Country Cafe

Enjoy one complimentary
MENU ITEM when a second
MENU ITEM of equal or greater
value is purchased.
Offer Conditions on reverse side.

Up To $7.00 Value

Valid now thru November 1, 2010

6370 Pioneer St, Ridgefield, WA
(360)887-8201

C111

El Charrito

- Sample Sabor de Mexico w/beef, pork, or a combination dinner
- Lite or vegetarian dishes
- American dishes also
- Kid's menu
- Margaritas, beer & wine
- Family owned & operated

EL CHARRITO
FAMILY MEXICAN RESTAURANT

117 E. Main St.
Molalla, OR
(503)829-3017

Offer Conditions: Valid any evening. Specials excluded.

00459445

Z Best Pizza

- Z BEST is truly z best!
- Generous pizzas with the finest toppings & ingredients
- Soups, salads, hot & cold sandwiches, calzone, lasagna & spaghetti
- Hours: Mon. - Fri., 11:00 a.m. - 9:00 p.m., Sat., 12 noon - 9:00 p.m., Sun., 12 noon - 7:00 p.m.

Z Best PizzaCo.

3801 Main St.
Vancouver, WA
(360)750-0445

Offer Conditions: Valid anytime.

Offers not valid holidays and subject to Rules of Use
Tipping should be 15% to 20% of the total bill before discount

00194506

Country Cafe

- Home cooked breakfast & lunch
- Open everyday except holidays
- Sandwiches & soups

6370 Pioneer St
Ridgefield, WA
(360)887-8201

Offer Conditions: Valid anytime.

00759501

Island Teriyaki

Enjoy one complimentary ENTREE when a second ENTREE of equal or greater value is purchased.

Offer Conditions on reverse side.

ISLAND TERIYAKI

Valid now thru November 1, 2010

37333 Hwy. 26, Sandy, OR
(503)668-0133

C112

The Red Fig @ Beaumont Village

Enjoy one complimentary LUNCH OR DINNER ENTREE when a second LUNCH OR DINNER ENTREE of equal or greater value is purchased.

Offer Conditions on reverse side.

THE RED FIG @ BEAUMONT VILLAGE

www.redfig.net

Valid now thru November 1, 2010

4537 NE Fremont, Portland, OR
(503)335-7068

C113

Bentoz Teriyaki

Enjoy one complimentary MENU ITEM when a second MENU ITEM of equal or greater value is purchased.

Offer Conditions on reverse side.

Bentoz Teriyaki

Valid now thru November 1, 2010

9107 SW Barbur Blvd., Portland, OR
(503)245-7152

C114

Island Teriyaki
- Fresh chargrilled marinated teriyaki chicken
- Teriyaki tenderloin beef
- Pan fried yakisoba noodles
- Our teriyaki sauce is a 60-year-old secret family recipe
- No added MSG
- Fresh hand cut veggies with every box-vegetarian dishes available
- Beer, pop, Sobe, & Hawaiian Sun drinks
- Call for hours or directions

37333 Hwy. 26
(located in DMV bldg.)
Sandy, OR
(503)668-0133

Offer Conditions: Valid anytime.

Offers not valid holidays and subject to Rules of Use
Tipping should be 15% to 20% of the total bill before discount

00532981

The Red Fig @ Beaumont Village
- Wide variety of healthy bentos
- Homemade soups, salads & sandwiches
- Outside patio seating
- Call ahead for carry out orders
- Ask us about catering your next event!
- We offer beer & wine
- Don't forget dessert! We carry Tillamook Ice Cream!

4537 NE Fremont
Portland, OR
(503)335-7068

Offer Conditions: Valid anytime. Dine-in or carry out.

Offers not valid holidays and subject to Rules of Use
Tipping should be 15% to 20% of the total bill before discount

00515464

Bentoz Teriyaki
- We use a minimum of pure vegetable oil & only when necessary
- We grill all our meats
- We offer brown rice, mixed grains & steamed vegetables
- We use NO MSG
- Choose from 17 different bento boxes
- Your food is made to order
- We look forward to serving you
- Dine in or take out
- Open Mon.-Sat. for lunch & early dinner
- Call for exact hours

9107 SW Barbur Blvd.
(In Barbur Square across Barbur Blvd. from Capitol Plaza)
Portland, OR
(503)245-7152

Offer Conditions: Valid anytime. Specials excluded.

00781844

Little River Cafe'

Enjoy one complimentary
ENTREE when a second
ENTREE of equal or greater
value is purchased.
Offer Conditions on reverse side.

FREE ENTRÉE

Little River Café

Valid now thru November 1, 2010

0315 S.W. Montgomery St., #310, Portland, OR
(503)227-2327

C115

Sportsmen's Bar & Grill

Enjoy one complimentary
LUNCH OR DINNER ENTREE
when a second LUNCH OR
DINNER ENTREE of equal or
greater value is purchased.
Offer Conditions on reverse side.

PRINT MORE ONLINE

Up To $14.00 Value

Valid now thru November 1, 2010

121 N. Main Ave., Ridgefield, WA
(360)887-3141

C116

The Rutherglen Mansion

Enjoy one complimentary
SUNDAY BRUNCH ENTREE
when a second SUNDAY
BRUNCH ENTREE of equal or
greater value is purchased.
Offer Conditions on reverse side.

Up To $9.00 Value

The Rutherglen Mansion

Valid now thru November 1, 2010

420 Rutherglen Rd., Longview, WA
(360)425-5816

C117

Little River Café'
- Stroll down the esplanade on the waterfront, outdoor seating with a panoramic view
- Full breakfasts, salads, homemade soups, entrees & specialty sandwiches
- Espresso, ice cream & frozen yogurt
- Beer & Wine

Little River Café

0315 S.W. Montgomery St., #310
Portland, OR
(503)227-2327

Offer Conditions: Valid anytime.

Offers not valid holidays and subject to Rules of Use
Tipping should be 15% to 20% of the total bill before discount

00194058

Sportsmen's Bar & Grill
- Ridgefield's premier bar & grill
- Great steaks, burgers, fish & chips & entree salads
- Kid's menu
- Family friendly
- In the old downtown Ridgefield

121 N. Main Ave.
Ridgefield, WA
(360)887-3141

Offer Conditions: Valid anytime.

Offers not valid holidays and subject to Rules of Use
Tipping should be 15% to 20% of the total bill before discount

00724602

The Rutherglen Mansion
- Grand Champagne Sunday Brunch!
- Carved prime rib, ham, boneless pork ribs
- Crepes, crab & angel hair pasta, salmon with dill sauce, fresh fruits, muffins, biscotti, & fresh homemade desserts
- Brunch served 10:00 a.m. - 2:00 p.m.

The Rutherglen Mansion

420 Rutherglen Rd.
Longview, WA
(360)425-5816

Offer Conditions: Valid during Sunday brunch hours.

Offers not valid holidays and subject to Rules of Use
Tipping should be 15% to 20% of the total bill before discount

00308894

Chevys Fresh Mex®

Buy any entrée and receive a second entrée of equal or lesser value for $3.99.

Offer Conditions on reverse side.

Valid now thru November 1, 2010

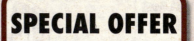

SPECIAL OFFER

Valid only at Participating Locations

C118

Country Bill's

Enjoy one complimentary DINNER ENTREE when a second DINNER ENTREE of equal or greater value is purchased.

Offer Conditions on reverse side.

Valid now thru November 1, 2010

Up To $15.00 Value

Welcome To

Country Bills

Established 1964

4415 S.E. Woodstock, Portland, OR
(503)774-4198

C119

Odessa Cafe

Enjoy one complimentary LUNCH OR DINNER ENTREE when a second LUNCH OR DINNER ENTREE of equal or greater value is purchased.

Offer Conditions on reverse side.

Valid now thru November 1, 2010

Up To $14.00 Value

ODESSA'S CAFÉ

3445 N.E. Broadway, Portland, OR
(503)288-3369

C120

More Offers Online!

CASUAL & FAMILY DINING

entertainment.com

Chevys Fresh Mex®

Valid only at Participating Locations

Country Bill's

- In Southeast Portland since 1964
- Country Bill's is famous for its prime rib & aged choice steaks
- This family owned & operated restaurant provides a casual atmosphere & friendly service
- Dine in the dining room or cocktail lounge
- Mon.-Thur. dinner served from 4 p.m.-10 p.m., Fri.-Sat., 4 p.m.-11 p.m.
- Closed Thanksgiving & Christmas
- Honored all other holidays

Welcome To

Country Bills

Established 1964

4415 S.E. Woodstock
Portland, OR
(503)774-4198

Offer Conditions: Valid any evening. Offer valid all day on Sundays.

Offers not valid holidays and subject to Rules of Use
Tipping should be 15% to 20% of the total bill before discount

---

Odessa Cafe

- Bar-B-Q on Broadway
- Savor the smells of BBQ brisket, ribs & chicken at our front door
- Lunch or dinner with sides including collard greens, baked beans & mac & cheese

ODESSA'S CAFÉ

3445 N.E. Broadway
Portland, OR
(503)288-3369

Offer Conditions: Valid anytime.

El Burro Loco

Enjoy one complimentary
LUNCH OR DINNER ENTREE
when a second LUNCH OR
DINNER ENTREE of equal or
greater value is purchased.

Offer Conditions on reverse side.

Up To $13.00 Value

Valid now thru November 1, 2010

67211 E. Hwy. 26, Welches, OR
(503)622-6780

C121

Dingo's Fresh Mexican Grill

Enjoy one complimentary
ENTREE when a second
ENTREE of equal or greater
value is purchased.

Offer Conditions on reverse side.

Up To $13.00 Value

www.dingosonline.com

4612 S.E. Hawthorne, Portland, OR
(503)233-3996

Valid now thru November 1, 2010

C122

Royal Panda

Enjoy one complimentary DINNER or
A LA CARTE ENTREE when a second
DINNER or A LA CARTE ENTREE of
equal or greater value is purchased or or
for those who prefer- one COMPLETE
COMBINATION OR SPECIAL DINNER
at $8.00 off the regular price.

Offer Conditions on reverse side.

Up To $12.00 Value

WASHINGTON SQUARE TOO

"Delivery & Banquet Service Available"

7200 S.W. Hazel Fern Rd., Tigard, OR
(503)620-8858

Valid now thru November 1, 2010

C123

El Burro Loco

- Enjoy authentic Mexican favorites
- Try our Wild Boar Tacos or Burro Blaster Burritos
- Vegetarian & kids menu also available

67211 E. Hwy. 26
Welches, OR
(503)622-6780

Offer Conditions: Valid anytime.

Offers not valid holidays and subject to Rules of Use
Tipping should be 15% to 20% of the total bill before discount

00725817

Dingo's Fresh Mexican Grill

- Voted 'Best Place to Sample Tequila' by Sunset magazine May, 2006
- Fresh Mexican specialties including fish tacos & lime chicken enchiladas
- Your place for fun, food & friends!
- Now two locations!!
- Open lunch & dinner

4612 S.E. Hawthorne
Portland, OR
(503)233-3996

Offer Conditions: Valid anytime.

Tipping should be 15% to 20% of TOTAL bill before discount

00699595

Royal Panda

- Join us for authentic Northern Chinese, Szechuan, & Hunan cuisine.
- Chicken with fresh vegetables, honey coated shrimp with walnuts, sesame beef or chicken & shrimp in a flower basket.
- Large banquet facilities for corp. or social gatherings.
- Full service bar available including exotic tropical cocktails.
- Open daily for lunch & dinner.
- One check per party please.

WASHINGTON SQUARE TOO

"Delivery & Banquet Service Available"

7200 S.W. Hazel Fern Rd.
Tigard, OR
(503)620-8858

Offer Conditions: Valid any evening. Dine in only. ONE ENTREE PER PERSON REQUIRED.

Offers not valid holidays and subject to Rules of Use
Tipping should be 15% to 20% of the total bill before discount

00312620

Yummy Mongolian Grill

Enjoy 25% off the regular price of any BUFFET for up to 4 people.

Offer Conditions on reverse side.

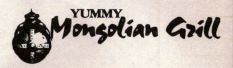

Valid now thru November 1, 2010

316 SE 123rd Ave., Vancouver, WA
(360)256-2468

C124

Happy Fortune Chinese Restaurant & Lounge

Enjoy one complimentary A LA CARTE ENTREE when a second A LA CARTE ENTREE of equal or greater value is purchased.

Offer Conditions on reverse side.

Happy Fortune
Chinese Restaurant & Lounge
寶利華酒家

Valid now thru November 1, 2010

10420 S.W. Barbur Blvd., Portland, OR
(503)244-8356

C125

Chino Sai-Gon

Enjoy one complimentary DINNER ENTREE when a second DINNER ENTREE of equal or greater value is purchased.

Offer Conditions on reverse side.

Valid now thru November 1, 2010

835 N.E. Broadway, Portland, OR
(971)230-1600

C126

Yummy Mongolian Grill

- Full Mongolian Grill, prepared without MSG or preservatives
- Choose your own chicken, beef, pork, shrimp or salmon
- Add your veggies, sauce and we will grill it up for you
- All meals include our Appetizer Bar with orange chicken, charbroiled chicken, honey wings, vegetable tempura, wonton chips, fried rice, steamed rice and 3 soups
- We cook your creation

00745126

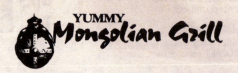

YUMMY Mongolian Grill

316 SE 123rd Ave.
(Mill Plain and 123rd)
Vancouver, WA
(360)256-2468

Offer Conditions: Valid anytime.

Happy Fortune Chinese Restaurant & Lounge

- Family dining & separate full lounge with lottery
- Traditional Chinese dishes prepared fresh with seafood, chicken, beef & pork
- Vegetarian dishes also available
- Hot & spicy or to your taste
- Open daily
- Banquet facilities available for up to 60

00653763

Happy Fortune
Chinese Restaurant & Lounge
寶利華酒家

10420 S.W. Barbur Blvd.
Portland, OR
(503)244-8356

Offer Conditions: Valid anytime. Dine in only.
Offers not valid holidays and subject to Rules of Use
Tipping should be 15% to 20% of the total bill before discount

---

Chino Sai-Gon

- Vietnamese, Thai & Chinese cuisine
- Green beans specialties
- Salad rolls
- Beef, seafood, chicken & vegetarian
- Open daily

00707874

835 N.E. Broadway
(Located on Broadway near Lloyd Ctr.)
Portland, OR
(971)230-1600

Offer Conditions: Valid any evening. Combination dinners excluded.

Bleacher's Bar & Grill

Enjoy one complimentary ENTREE when a second ENTREE of equal or greater value is purchased.

Offer Conditions on reverse side.

Up To $9.00 Value

Bleachers BAR AND GRILL

Valid now thru November 1, 2010

575 N.W. Saltzman, Portland, OR
(503)643-1711

C127

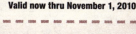

Bento Plus

Enjoy one complimentary LUNCH OR DINNER ENTREE when a second LUNCH OR DINNER ENTREE of equal or greater value is purchased.

Offer Conditions on reverse side.

Up To $9.00 Value

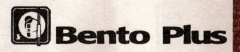

Bento Plus

PRINT MORE ONLINE

Valid now thru November 1, 2010

2354 E. Powell Blvd., Gresham, OR
(503)492-2853

C128

Kelso Theater Pub

Enjoy any one PIZZA at 50% off the regular price or for those who prefer, one MOVIE ADMISSION when a second MOVIE ADMISSION of equal or greater value is purchased.

Offer Conditions on reverse side.

50% OFF

www.ktpub.com

Valid now thru November 1, 2010

214 S. Pacific Ave., Kelso, WA
(360)414-9451

C129

Bleacher's Bar & Grill

- World famous B.U.F.F. burger
- Chichi's chicken enchilada
- Sports bar - big screen TV's, memorabilia
- Sunny outdoor seating
- Enjoy spicy wings or fish & chips with your favorite beer or wine
- Full service bar
- All Oregon Lottery Games
- Open daily

00008972

BAR AND GRILL

575 N.W. Saltzman
(off Cornell Rd. in Cedar Mill)
Portland, OR
(503)643-1711

Offer Conditions: Valid anytime. Dine in only.

Offers not valid holidays and subject to Rules of Use
Tipping should be 15% to 20% of the total bill before discount

Offer validity is governed by the Rules of Use and excludes defined holidays. Offers are not valid with other discount offers, unless specified. Coupons void if purchased, sold or bartered. Discounts exclude tax, tip and/or alcohol, where applicable.

Bento Plus

- A Japanese sushi & teriyaki house
- Try our delicious chicken or beef bento!
- Freshly prepared
- Comfortable dining atmosphere
- Come in & try our new taste
- Open Mon. - Sat. 11:00 a.m. - 9:00 p.m.

00571587

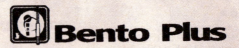

2354 E. Powell Blvd.
(located within Food-4-Less Mall)
Gresham, OR
(503)492-2853

Offer Conditions: Valid anytime.

Offers not valid holidays and subject to Rules of Use
Tipping should be 15% to 20% of the total bill before discount

Offer validity is governed by the Rules of Use and excludes defined holidays. Offers are not valid with other discount offers, unless specified. Coupons void if purchased, sold or bartered. Discounts exclude tax, tip and/or alcohol, where applicable.

Kelso Theater Pub

- 1923 Theater Pub where you can dine while you view late release movies!
- A 25 ft. screen, handcrafted pizza, sandwiches, beer, wine & bottomless popcorn
- See WWF on the big screen!
- Under 21 must be with parent
- Call for show times or check us out at www.ktpub.com

00505857

214 S. Pacific Ave.
Kelso, WA
(360)414-9451

Offer Conditions: Valid anytime. Special events excluded.

Offers not valid holidays and subject to Rules of Use
Tipping should be 15% to 20% of the total bill before discount

Offer validity is governed by the Rules of Use and excludes defined holidays. Offers are not valid with other discount offers, unless specified. Coupons void if purchased, sold or bartered. Discounts exclude tax, tip and/or alcohol, where applicable.

entertainment
entertainment.com

Joe's Cellar Café

Enjoy one complimentary
LUNCH OR DINNER ENTREE
when a second LUNCH OR
DINNER ENTREE of equal or
greater value is purchased.
Offer Conditions on reverse side.

Up To $9.00 Value

Joe's Cellar

Valid now thru November 1, 2010

1332 N.W. 21st Ave., Portland, OR
(503)223-8825

C130

---

entertainment
entertainment.com

McGillacuddy's Sports Bar & Grill

Enjoy one complimentary
LUNCH OR DINNER ENTREE
when a second LUNCH OR
DINNER ENTREE of equal or
greater value is purchased.
Offer Conditions on reverse side.

Up To $8.00 Value

Valid now thru November 1, 2010

11133 N.E. Halsey, Portland, OR
(503)257-2337

C131

---

entertainment
entertainment.com

Da-Kine's RC's Cafe

Enjoy one complimentary
ENTREE when a second
ENTREE of equal or greater
value is purchased.
Offer Conditions on reverse side.

Up To $8.00 Value

Valid now thru November 1, 2010

11700 N.E. 95th St., Ste. 104, Vancouver, WA
(360)253-9160

C132

Joe's Cellar Café
- Breakfast served all day
- Lunch & dinner specials everyday
- Locally-owned & managed
- Open 8-5 everyday

Joe's Cellar

1332 N.W. 21st Ave.
(at the corner of Pettygrove St.)
Portland, OR
(503)223-8825

Offer Conditions: Valid anytime.

00780929

McGillacuddy's Sports Bar & Grill
- Hot & cold sandwiches
- Homemade soups & chili
- Full service bar, local microbrews, domestic & imported beers
- All lottery games & satellite sports
- Pool, darts, fooseball, shovelboard & NTN Trivia
- Open Sun. - Thurs., 11:00 a.m. - 12:00 midnight, Fri. & Sat. 11:00 a.m. - 2:30 a.m.

11133 N.E. Halsey
Portland, OR
(503)257-2337

Offer Conditions: Valid anytime. Dine in only.

Offers not valid holidays and subject to Rules of Use
Tipping should be 15% to 20% of the total bill before discount

00013721

Da-Kine's RC's Cafe
- Mainland food with a Hawaiian flair
- Espresso, breakfast served all day!
- Lunch & other "Ono-licious" stuff
- Burgers, sandwiches, panini's, bento, Kalua pig
- Awesome daily specials

11700 N.E. 95th St., Ste. 104
Vancouver, WA
(360)253-9160

Offer Conditions: Valid anytime.

Offers not valid holidays and subject to Rules of Use
Tipping should be 15% to 20% of the total bill before discount

00695135

Nosh on Seventh

Enjoy one complimentary
ENTREE when a second
ENTREE of equal or greater
value is purchased.
Offer Conditions on reverse side.

Up To $8.00 Value

NOSH
on seventh

Valid now thru November 1, 2010

2030 S.E. 7th Ave., Portland, OR
(503)239-NOSH

C133

The Hangout Sports Bar & Grill

Enjoy one complimentary
LUNCH OR DINNER ENTREE
when a second LUNCH OR
DINNER ENTREE of equal or
greater value is purchased.
Offer Conditions on reverse side.

Up To $8.00 Value

The Hangout
Sports Bar & Grill

Valid now thru November 1, 2010

576 N.E. Burnside, Gresham, OR
(503)667-7936

C134

Lydia's Restaurant & Lounge

Enjoy one complimentary
ENTREE when a second
ENTREE of equal or greater
value is purchased.
Offer Conditions on reverse side.

Up To $8.00 Value

PORTLAND
www.lydiasrestaurantandlounge.com

Valid now thru November 1, 2010

18330 E. Burnside, Gresham, OR
(503)666-2516

C135

More Offers Online!

CASUAL & FAMILY DINING

entertainment.com

Nosh on Seventh
- Nosh: Noun - A snack or a light meal; Verb - To eat, grab a bite, grub
- Nosh on our specialty sandwiches, soups, salads & daily specials
- Contemporary casual dining area or pick up a Nosh box lunch for back at the office

NOSH
on seventh

2030 S.E. 7th Ave.
Portland, OR
(503)239-NOSH

Offer Conditions: Valid anytime.

Offers not valid holidays and subject to Rules of Use
Tipping should be 15% to 20% of the total bill before discount

00722845

The Hangout Sports Bar & Grill
- Fun, friendly atmosphere
- The biggest medalist dart bar in Gresham
- Pool tables, lottery, 2 big screens, 10 TV's
- Great burgers, steaks, snacks & sandwiches
- Must be over 21

The Hangout
Sports Bar & Grill

576 N.E. Burnside
Gresham, OR
(503)667-7936

Offer Conditions: Valid anytime.

Offers not valid holidays and subject to Rules of Use
Tipping should be 15% to 20% of the total bill before discount

00526340

Lydia's Restaurant & Lounge
- Family friendly home-style dining
- Full lounge with lottery, big screen T.V.'s & live music on weekends
- Try Lydia's famous Rueben sandwich - Delicious!!

of

PORTLAND
18330 E. Burnside
Gresham, OR
(503)666-2516

Offer Conditions: Valid anytime. Dine in only.

00707890

Riverwalk Cafe

Enjoy one complimentary ENTREE when a second ENTREE of equal or greater value is purchased.
Offer Conditions on reverse side.

Up To $7.00 Value

Valid now thru November 1, 2010

2100 S.W. River Pkwy., Portland, OR
(503) 241-0307

C136

The Country Inn

Enjoy one complimentary LUNCH OR DINNER ENTREE when a second LUNCH OR DINNER ENTREE of equal or greater value is purchased.
Offer Conditions on reverse side.

Up To $11.00 Value

Valid now thru November 1, 2010

18786 S.W. Boones Ferry Rd., Tualatin, OR
(503) 692-2765

C137

Pho Thien

Enjoy one complimentary LUNCH OR DINNER ENTREE when a second LUNCH OR DINNER ENTREE of equal or greater value is purchased.
Offer Conditions on reverse side.

Up To $6.00 Value

PRINT MORE ONLINE

Valid now thru November 1, 2010

10041 N.E. Glisan, Portland, OR
(503) 256-0217

C138

More Offers Online!

CASUAL & FAMILY DINING

entertainment.com

Riverwalk Cafe

- Located in the Riverplace neighborhood
- The Riverwalk Cafe offers a convenient stop for breakfast & lunch for both residents & business people alike
- Open cafe setting
- Daily specials

2100 S.W. River Pkwy.
Portland, OR
(503)241-0307

Offer Conditions: Valid anytime.
Tipping should be 15% to 20% of TOTAL bill before discount

00727950

Offer validity is governed by the Rules of Use and excludes defined holidays. Offers are not valid with other discount offers, unless specified. Coupons void if purchased, sold or bartered. Discounts exclude tax, tip and/or alcohol, where applicable.

The Country Inn

- Featuring homemade daily specials
- Full service bar, karaoke nightly
- Open for breakfast at 6:30 a.m.
- Hours 6:30 a.m.-2:30 a.m.
- VISA, MasterCard & ATM machine

18786 S.W. Boones Ferry Rd.
Tualatin, OR
(503)692-2765

Offer Conditions: Valid anytime.
Offers not valid holidays and subject to Rules of Use
Tipping should be 15% to 20% of the total bill before discount

00013821

Offer validity is governed by the Rules of Use and excludes defined holidays. Offers are not valid with other discount offers, unless specified. Coupons void if purchased, sold or bartered. Discounts exclude tax, tip and/or alcohol, where applicable.

Pho Thien

- Flavorful Vietnamese specialties
- Try our lemongrass curry, pad Thai or sweet & sour shrimp
- Delicious beef noodle soup -" Pho"
- Dine in or take out
- Espresso available
- Lunch & dinner served 7 days a week

VIETNAMESE CUISINE
FOOD TO GO

10041 N.E. Glisan
Portland, OR
(503)256-0217

Offer Conditions: Valid anytime. Specials excluded.
Offers not valid holidays and subject to Rules of Use
Tipping should be 15% to 20% of the total bill before discount

00672519

Offer validity is governed by the Rules of Use and excludes defined holidays. Offers are not valid with other discount offers, unless specified. Coupons void if purchased, sold or bartered. Discounts exclude tax, tip and/or alcohol, where applicable.

Galaxy Restaurant & Lounge

Enjoy one complimentary
DINNER ENTREE when a
second DINNER ENTREE of
equal or greater value is
purchased.

Offer Conditions on reverse side.

Valid now thru November 1, 2010

Up$ **9**^{00} To Value

THE GALAXY

RESTAURANT & KARAOKE LOUNGE

909 E. Burnside, Portland, OR
(503)234-5003

C139

Longbottom Coffee House & Roasting Factory

Enjoy one complimentary
MENU ITEM when a second
MENU ITEM of equal or greater
value is purchased.

Offer Conditions on reverse side.

Up$ **9**^{00} To Value

www.longbottomcoffee.com

4893 N.W. 235th Ave., Hillsboro, OR
(503)924-4470

Valid now thru November 1, 2010

C140

Maya's Restaurant

Enjoy one complimentary
DINNER ENTREE when a
second DINNER ENTREE of
equal or greater value is
purchased.

Offer Conditions on reverse side.

Up$ **8**^{00} To Value

970 S.E. Oak St., Hillsboro, OR
(503)681-0707

Valid now thru November 1, 2010

C141

Galaxy Restaurant & Lounge

- The Galaxy is a casual, all-American cuisine restaurant
- The fare includes steaks, seafood, pasta, chicken, burgers & sandwiches
- Karaoke is offered nightly & "after hours" on weekends
- The fish tank bar invites engaging entertainment while you dine
- Open 7 days a week

00187085

THE GALAXY
RESTAURANT & KARAOKE LOUNGE

909 E. Burnside
Portland, OR
(503)234-5003

Offer Conditions: Valid any evening. Dine in only.

Offers not valid holidays and subject to Rules of Use
Tipping should be 15% to 20% of the total bill before discount

---

Longbottom Coffee House & Roasting Factory

- Not just coffee... but delicious fresh roasted coffee, specialty sandwiches, homemade soups, BBQ, breakfast, in-house bakery & a great cafe environment
- Free WI-FI available
- Catering - your place or ours
- Open 7days a week

00569173

4893 N.W. 235th Ave.
Hillsboro, OR
(503)924-4470

Offer Conditions: Valid anytime.

Offers not valid holidays and subject to Rules of Use
Tipping should be 15% to 20% of the total bill before discount

---

Maya's Restaurant

- Authentic Mexican food
- Everything made from scratch
- Dine in & carry out
- Family owned & operated
- Open daily, Mon. - Fri. 10:00 a.m. - 9:00 p.m., Sat. & Sun. 8:00 a.m. - 9:00 p.m.
- Breakfast, lunch, dinner

00634644

970 S.E. Oak St.
Hillsboro, OR
(503)681-0707

Offer Conditions: Valid any evening.

Offers not valid holidays and subject to Rules of Use
Tipping should be 15% to 20% of the total bill before discount

entertainment.com

Amigo's Mexican Restaurants

Enjoy one complimentary
LUNCH OR DINNER ENTREE
when a second LUNCH OR
DINNER ENTREE of equal or
greater value is purchased.
Offer Conditions on reverse side.

Up $8 00 To Value

AMIGOS
Mexican Restaurant

Valid now thru November 1, 2010

17683 S.W. Farmington, Aloha, OR
(503)649-3699

C142

---

entertainment.com

Mazatlan Restaurant

Enjoy one complimentary
MENU ITEM when a second
MENU ITEM of equal or greater
value is purchased.
Offer Conditions on reverse side.

Up $7 00 To Value

Mazatlan
R E S T A U R A N T

PRINT MORE ONLINE

Valid now thru November 1, 2010

2714 N. Hwy. 99, McMinnville, OR
(503)472-9711

C143

entertainment.com

Red Fox Bakery & Cafe

Enjoy one complimentary
MENU ITEM when a second
MENU ITEM of equal or greater
value is purchased.
Offer Conditions on reverse side.

Up $6 00 To Value

RED FOX
bakery & cafe

Valid now thru November 1, 2010

328 N.E. Evans St., McMinnville, OR
(503)434-5098

C144

More Offers Online!

CASUAL & FAMILY DINING

entertainment.com

Amigo's Mexican Restaurants

- The best & most authentic Mexican food north of the Rio Grande
- You get the whole enchilada!
- Mexican cuisine at its best
- Cocktails, beer & wine
- Open daily

AMIGOS
Mexican Restaurant

17683 S.W. Farmington
Aloha, OR
(503)649-3699

Offer Conditions: Valid anytime. Dine in only.

Offers not valid holidays and subject to Rules of Use
Tipping should be 15% to 20% of the total bill before discount

00007792

Mazatlan Restaurant

- Family owned restaurant using our family recipes
- Healthy, fresh ingredients
- Homemade corn tortillas on weekends
- Steak, hamburgers, children's & senior menus
- Happy Hour 3 p.m. - 6 p.m. everyday
- Full bar - try our specialty drinks
- Hours: Sun. - Thurs. 11 a.m. - 10 p.m.
- Fri. & Sat. 11 a.m. - Midnight

Mazatlan
RESTAURANT

2714 N. Hwy. 99
McMinnville, OR
(503)472-9711

Offer Conditions: Valid anytime.

Tipping should be 15% to 20% of TOTAL bill before discount

00736058

Red Fox Bakery & Cafe

- European influenced artisan breads & pastries
- Fresh daily
- Serving breakfast & lunch
- We strive to use local seasonal produce whenever possible
- You can taste the difference at Red Fox!
- Gourmet sandwiches, salads, soups & awesome breakfasts

RED FOX
bakery & cafe

328 N.E. Evans St.
McMinnville, OR
(503)434-5098

Offer Conditions: Valid anytime.

Offers not valid holidays and subject to Rules of Use
Tipping should be 15% to 20% of the total bill before discount

00677131

Treasure Island Buffet

Enjoy 25% off the regular price of any BUFFET for up to 4 people.

Offer Conditions on reverse side.

Up To **$10**⁰⁰ Value

Treasure Island Buffet 我家

Chinese Buffet & Mongolian Grill

 PRINT MORE ONLINE NEW

treasurebuffet.com

15930 SW Regatta Ln, Beaverton, OR
(503) 690-0298

Valid now thru November 1, 2010

C145

---

 entertainment. entertainment.com

Yen Ha Vietnamese Restaurant

Enjoy one complimentary LUNCH OR DINNER ENTREE when a second LUNCH OR DINNER ENTREE of equal or greater value is purchased.

Offer Conditions on reverse side.

Up To **$15**⁰⁰ Value

Yen - Ha
Vietnamese Restaurant and Lounge

Valid now thru November 1, 2010

6820 N.E. Sandy Blvd., Portland, OR
(503) 287-3698

C146

---

entertainment. entertainment.com

The Tao of Tea

Enjoy one complimentary MENU ITEM when a second MENU ITEM of equal or greater value is purchased - maximum discount $7.00.

Offer Conditions on reverse side.

Up To **$7**⁰⁰ Value

The Tao of Tea

The leaf,
the art,
the way...

www.taooftea.com

See Reverse Side for Locations

PRINT MORE ONLINE

Valid now thru November 1, 2010

C147

Treasure Island Buffet

- Chinese Buffet PLUS Mongolian Grill
- Choose from our buffet or menu
- Open for lunch and dinner - dine in or take out
- Catering and private parties available
- We promise you will be happy and satisfied with your visit to Treasue Island
- Ask about our FREE Birthday meal

Treasure Island Buffet 我家
Chinese Buffet & Mongolian Grill

**15930 SW Regatta Ln
Beaverton, OR
(503) 690-0298**

Offer Conditions: Valid anytime.

00751362

Yen Ha Vietnamese Restaurant

- Yen Ha Vietnamese Restaurant invites you to experience dishes carefully selected from the best of North, South & Central Vietnamese cuisine
- With gracious hospitality, special requests are always considered with advance notice for special family occasions, such as birthdays, anniversaries & wedding receptions
- Full cocktail service
- Karaoke on weekends

Yen - Ha
Vietnamese Restaurant and Lounge

**6820 N.E. Sandy Blvd.
Portland, OR
(503) 287-3698**

Offer Conditions: Valid anytime.
Offers not valid holidays and subject to Rules of Use
Tipping should be 15% to 20% of the total bill before discount

00495956

The Tao of Tea

- Begin your journey....
- Enjoy teas & sample ethnic foods from around the world
- Tea snacks & desserts
- International ambience
- Experience the "way" of tea
- The leaf, the art, the way...

The Tao of Tea

*The leaf,
the art,
the way...*

**2112 N.W. Hoyt
Portland, OR
(503) 223-3563**

**239 N.W. Everett St.
Portland, OR
(503) 224-8455**

**3430 S.E. Belmont St
Portland, OR
(503) 736-0119**

Offer Conditions: Valid anytime.
Offers not valid holidays and subject to Rules of Use
Tipping should be 15% to 20% of the total bill before discount

00460076

La Fonda Restaurante

Enjoy one complimentary
MENU ITEM when a second
MENU ITEM of equal or greater
value is purchased.
Offer Conditions on reverse side.

Valid now thru November 1, 2010

320 S.W. Alder. St., Portland, OR
(503)227-4128

C148

Abhiruchi

Enjoy one complimentary
DINNER or **A LA CARTE
ENTREE** when a second
DINNER or **A LA CARTE
ENTREE** of equal or greater
value is purchased.
Offer Conditions on reverse side.

Valid now thru November 1, 2010

Up $11.00 To Value

3815 S.W. Murray Blvd., Beaverton, OR
(503)671-0432

C149

Marsan's Restaurant

Enjoy one complimentary
LUNCH OR DINNER ENTREE
when a second **LUNCH OR
DINNER ENTREE** of equal or
greater value is purchased.
Offer Conditions on reverse side.

Up $11.00 To Value

Valid now thru November 1, 2010

7101 N.E. 82nd Ave., Portland, OR
(503)255-6722

C150

La Fonda Restaurante

- Come visit one of, if not the only Mexican restaurant downtown
- Authentic home-style dishes with flavors you've not experienced before
- We cook all our meats on our special grill
- La Fonda offers "heart-healthy" options too
- Family owned & operated
- Please join us for breakfast, lunch or dinner!
- We open daily at 10 am
- Full bar, including beer & wine
- Catering available

00779406

320 S.W. Alder. St.
(between 3d & 4th Avenues downtown)
Portland, OR
(503)227-4128

Offer Conditions: Valid anytime.

Abhiruchi

- The very best Indian cuisine awaits you
- We serve a wide variety of South & North Indian entrees, including vegetarian dishes
- Every entree is prepared fresh from our kitchen
- Our Tandoori dinners are cooked in a clay oven with a blend of herbs & spices
- South Indian Specialties including Masala Dosa, Uttapam and many others
- We look forward to serving you

00135053

ABHIRUCHI
Authentic South & North
Indian Cuisine

3815 S.W. Murray Blvd.
(corner of SW Murray & TV Hwy in K-Mart Shpg Ctr)
Beaverton, OR
(503)671-0432

Offer Conditions: Valid any evening. Dine in only.

Offers not valid holidays and subject to Rules of Use
Tipping should be 15% to 20% of the total bill before discount

---

Marsan's Restaurant

- Marsan's is conveniently located at Howard Johnson's near the airport
- The atmosphere is very attractive & the fare most gratifying
- The menu is extensive offering something to please all tastes, from surf & turf to liver-n-onions
- Plan a visit soon!

00013626

7101 N.E. 82nd Ave.
(Howard Johnson Portland Airport)
Portland, OR
(503)255-6722

Offer Conditions: Valid anytime.

Offers not valid holidays and subject to Rules of Use
Tipping should be 15% to 20% of the total bill before discount

25% OFF

Eddie May Mysteries

Enjoy 25% off the regular price of up to 4 DINNER SHOW ADMISSIONS.

Offer Conditions on reverse side.

www.eddiemaymysteries.com

Valid now thru November 1, 2010

Throughout the Portland Area, Portland, OR
(503)524-4366

C151

---

entertainment.com

Up To $10.00 Value

Spot 79

Enjoy one complimentary MENU ITEM when a second MENU ITEM of equal or greater value is purchased.

Offer Conditions on reverse side.

SPOT 79
BAR AND GRILL

Valid now thru November 1, 2010

7944 S.E. Foster Rd., Portland, OR
(503)775-7339

C152

---

entertainment.com

Up To $10.00 Value

Hidden Bay Cafe

Enjoy one complimentary MENU ITEM when a second MENU ITEM of equal or greater value is purchased.

Offer Conditions on reverse side.

PRINT MORE ONLINE

Valid now thru November 1, 2010

515 N.E. Tomahawk Island Dr., Ste. 105, Portland, OR
(503)240-1871

C153

Eddie May Mysteries
- A typical mystery evening starts with a no-host cocktail period & continues for 2 to 2-1/2 hrs. of fine dining, comedy mystery, mayhem, & "Murder Served Hot!
- Witness a murder over a fabulous dinner with friends & become involved in a live game of "Whodunit?"
- Public shows, private parties & gift certificates

Throughout the Portland Area
Portland, OR
(503)524-4366

Offer Conditions: Valid any performance. Subject to availability; Advance tickets & reservations are required; You must mention coupon upon making reservations; no exceptions; Not valid New Years Eve or with any other offers.

Offers not valid holidays and subject to Rules of Use
Tipping should be 15% to 20% of the total bill before discount

00515199

Spot 79
- Open 365 days a year from 7:00 a.m. - 2:30 a.m.
- Serving select & choice beef
- Also serving a wide variety of seafood
- Full bar & all lotto games
- Please remember you must be 21 & over at Spot 79

SPOT 79
BAR AND GRILL

7944 S.E. Foster Rd.
Portland, OR
(503)775-7339

Offer Conditions: Valid anytime. Specials excluded.

Offers not valid holidays and subject to Rules of Use
Tipping should be 15% to 20% of the total bill before discount

00508085

Hidden Bay Cafe
- Come discover Hayden Island's hidden treasure
- Outdoor BBQ pit & seating overlooking Tomahawk Bay Marina
- Beer & wine available
- Open year round for lunch, 7 days a week in summer, closed Monday in winter
- Fri. night dinners, Sun. morning breakfasts
- Friendly service, fantastic food - burgers, ribs, sandwiches & more!

515 N.E. Tomahawk Island Dr., Ste. 105
Portland, OR
(503)240-1871

Offer Conditions: Valid anytime.

Offers not valid holidays and subject to Rules of Use
Tipping should be 15% to 20% of the total bill before discount

00574237

Eastern Pearl

Enjoy one complimentary A LA CARTE DINNER ENTREE when a second A LA CARTE DINNER ENTREE of equal or greater value is purchased.
Offer Conditions on reverse side.

Up$ **10**^{00} To Value

EASTERN PEARL
NORTHERN AND CANTONESE CHINESE CUISINE

Valid now thru November 1, 2010

8651 S.W. Canyon Dr., Portland, OR
(503)292-8751

C154

Si Senor

Enjoy one complimentary LUNCH OR DINNER ENTREE when a second LUNCH OR DINNER ENTREE of equal or greater value is purchased.
Offer Conditions on reverse side.

Up$ **9**^{00} To Value

FAMILY MEXICAN RESTAURANT

Valid now thru November 1, 2010

4820 S.W. 76th, Portland, OR
(503)203-2999

C155

B.K. Mulligan's

Enjoy one complimentary LUNCH OR DINNER ENTREE when a second LUNCH OR DINNER ENTREE of equal or greater value is purchased.
Offer Conditions on reverse side.

Up$ **8**^{00} To Value

B.K. **Mulligan's**
A Sports Bar

www.bkmulligans.com

266 S.E. Hwy. 101, Lincoln City, OR
(541)996-2468

C156

PRINT MORE ONLINE

Valid now thru November 1, 2010

More Offers Online!

CASUAL & FAMILY DINING

entertainment.com

Eastern Pearl
- Specializing in Northern & Cantonese cuisine
- Buck night 7 nights a week
- Located on the north side of Canyon Dr. at S.W. 86th
- Pool tables
- Open daily

EASTERN PEARL
NORTHERN AND CANTONESE CHINESE CUISINE

8651 S.W. Canyon Dr.
(West Slope)
Portland, OR
(503)292-8751

Offer Conditions: Valid any evening. Dining room only.

Offers not valid holidays and subject to Rules of Use
Tipping should be 15% to 20% of the total bill before discount

00040259

Si Senor
- Savor the romance of Mexico at Si Senor
- Featuring authentic Mexican cuisine
- Choose from favorites such as ranchero burrito, enchiladas rancheras, carne asada & more
- Beer, wine, cocktails & excellent margaritas

FAMILY MEXICAN RESTAURANT

4820 S.W. 76th
(near Raleigh Hills Fred Meyer)
Portland, OR
(503)203-2999

Offer Conditions: Valid anytime. Dine in only; Specials excluded.

Offers not valid holidays and subject to Rules of Use
Tipping should be 15% to 20% of the total bill before discount

00495976

B.K. Mulligan's
- A sports bar
- Multiple sports monitors
- Pool, darts, shuffleboard & golf
- Burgers & appetizers
- 16 Beer taps, full service bar
- Oregon lottery games

266 S.E. Hwy. 101
Lincoln City, OR
(541)996-2468

Offer Conditions: Valid anytime. Specials excluded.

Tipping should be 15% to 20% of TOTAL bill before discount

00618595

Ford's on 5th

Enjoy one complimentary
MENU ITEM when a second
MENU ITEM of equal or greater
value is purchased.
Offer Conditions on reverse side.

Up To $8.00 Value

FORD'S
============on 5th

Famous for great food since 1927

PRINT MORE ONLINE

Valid now thru November 1, 2010

121 N.W. 5th Ave., Portland, OR
(503)226-2828

C157

More Offers Online!

Lynn's Ice Cream, Yogurt & More...

Enjoy one complimentary
MENU ITEM when a second
MENU ITEM of equal or greater
value is purchased.
Offer Conditions on reverse side.

Up To $7.00 Value

Lynn's Ice Cream Yogurt & More...

PRINT MORE ONLINE

Valid now thru November 1, 2010

1232 Commerce, Longview, WA
(360)636-4558

C158

CASUAL & FAMILY DINING

Serranos Mexican Restaurant

Enjoy one complimentary
ENTREE when a second
ENTREE of equal or greater
value is purchased.
Offer Conditions on reverse side.

Up To $7.00 Value

SERRANOS
MEXICAN RESTAURANT
AND MARGARITA HOUSE

NEW

Valid now thru November 1, 2010

33 N.W. 1st, Gresham, OR
(503)666-3151

C159

entertainment.com

Ford's on 5th

- Upscale casual dining famous for certified Angus beef sandwiches & more
- Gourmet hot & cold sandwiches, paninis, salads, & Italian favorites
- Inquire about our featured specials
- Mon.-Thurs., 9 a.m.-7 p.m., Fri., 9 a.m.-4 a.m., Sat., 12 noon-4 a.m., Sun., 10 a.m.-4 p.m.

00621352

FORD'S

============on 5th

Famous for great food since 1927

**121 N.W. 5th Ave.
Portland, OR
(503)226-2828**

Offer Conditions: Valid anytime. Valid at future participating Oregon/Washington locations.
Offers not valid holidays and subject to Rules of Use
Tipping should be 15% to 20% of the total bill before discount

Offer validity is governed by the Rules of Use and excludes defined holidays. Offers are not valid with other discount offers, unless specified.
Coupons void if purchased, sold or bartered. Discounts exclude tax, tip and/or alcohol, where applicable.

Lynn's Ice Cream, Yogurt & More...

- Not just ice cream!
- Try our fresh hot burgers & homemade fries
- Steakburgers with homemade steakburger sauce
- Elephant ears & Umpqua Ice Cream
- Open for breakfast, lunch & dinner Mon. - Sat. 9:00 a.m. - 7:00 p.m.

00566867

Lynn's Ice Cream Yogurt & More...

**1232 Commerce
Longview, WA
(360)636-4558**

Offer Conditions: Valid anytime.

Offers not valid holidays and subject to Rules of Use
Tipping should be 15% to 20% of the total bill before discount

Offer validity is governed by the Rules of Use and excludes defined holidays. Offers are not valid with other discount offers, unless specified.
Coupons void if purchased, sold or bartered. Discounts exclude tax, tip and/or alcohol, where applicable.

Serranos Mexican Restaurant

- Mexican food with an attitude!
- Delicious favorites including burritos, tamales, tacos and quesadillas
- Friendly dining atmosphere with private outdoor courtyard
- Come try the Caldo de Pollo our house specialty

00774973

**33 N.W. 1st
Gresham, OR
(503)666-3151**

Offer Conditions: Valid anytime.

Offer validity is governed by the Rules of Use and excludes defined holidays. Offers are not valid with other discount offers, unless specified
Coupons void if purchased, sold or bartered. Discounts exclude tax, tip and/or alcohol, where applicable.

The Maverick Restaurant & Lounge

Enjoy one complimentary LUNCH OR DINNER ENTREE when a second LUNCH OR DINNER ENTREE of equal or greater value is purchased.

Offer Conditions on reverse side.

$7⁰⁰ Value

The MAVERICK
Restaurant & Lounge

12424 S.E. Division, Portland, OR
(503)761-0170

Valid now thru November 1, 2010

C160

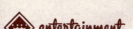

Maguffy's Pub Hillsboro

Enjoy one complimentary LUNCH OR DINNER ENTREE when a second LUNCH OR DINNER ENTREE of equal or greater value is purchased.

Offer Conditions on reverse side.

PRINT MORE ONLINE

Up To $7⁰⁰ Value

Maguffy's Pub

2401 N.E. Cornell, Hillsboro, OR
(503)693-9700

Valid now thru November 1, 2010

C161

Maui Camp 3 Cafe

Enjoy one complimentary ENTREE when a second ENTREE of equal or greater value is purchased.

Offer Conditions on reverse side.

Up To $7⁰⁰ Value

MAUI CAMP 3 CAFE

705 Main St., Oregon City, OR
(503)723-5485

Valid now thru November 1, 2010

C162

More Offers Online!

CASUAL & FAMILY DINING

entertainment.com

The Maverick Restaurant & Lounge

- Everything is homemade!
- Serving breakfast, lunch & dinner
- Try our cajun steaks
- Our stuffed potatos are the best!
- Full service lounge
- Open daily

The MAVERICK

Restaurant & Lounge

12424 S.E. Division
Portland, OR
(503)761-0170

Offer Conditions: Valid anytime.

Offers not valid holidays and subject to Rules of Use

Tipping should be 15% to 20% of the total bill before discount

00013634

Maguffy's Pub Hillsboro

- Serving a tasty selection of appetizers, gourmet burgers, deli-style sandwiches & homemade soups
- Try our specialty, Irish style fish & chips
- Full service bar
- Big screen T.V., 4 pool tables, all lottery games
- ATM available
- Open daily

Maguffy's Pub

2401 N.E. Cornell
(Cornell Square)
Hillsboro, OR
(503)693-9700

Offer Conditions: Valid anytime.

Offers not valid holidays and subject to Rules of Use

Tipping should be 15% to 20% of the total bill before discount

00379938

Maui Camp 3 Cafe

- Open Mon. - Thurs. 11:00 a.m. - 7:30 p.m., Fri. & Sat. 11:00 a.m. - 8:00 p.m.
- Authentic Hawaiian cuisine
- Having an Island party or luau? Ask us about catering your next event!
- We also do family pack meals

MAUI

CAMP 3

CAFE

705 Main St.
Oregon City, OR
(503)723-5485

Offer Conditions: Valid anytime. Dine in only; Buffet excluded.

Offers not valid holidays and subject to Rules of Use

Tipping should be 15% to 20% of the total bill before discount

00544396

Olde Creekside Cafe

Enjoy one complimentary MENU ITEM when a second MENU ITEM of equal or greater value is purchased.

Offer Conditions on reverse side.

Up $**7**00 To Value

Olde Creekside Cafe

Valid now thru November 1, 2010

1323 Commerce Ave., Longview, WA
(360) 423-7225

C163

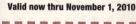

Gator's Pub & Eatery

Enjoy one complimentary ENTREE when a second ENTREE of equal or greater value is purchased.

Offer Conditions on reverse side.

Up $**6**00 To Value

Valid now thru November 1, 2010

11475 S.W. Pacific Hwy., Tigard, OR
(503) 293-0356

C164

Mo Betta Deli

Enjoy one complimentary ENTREE when a second ENTREE of equal or greater value is purchased.

Offer Conditions on reverse side.

Up $**6**00 To Value

MO BETTA DELI

Sandwich, Ice Cream & Espresso Shoppe

Valid now thru November 1, 2010

6110 S.E. King Rd., Milwaukie, OR
(503) 653-5487

C165

Olde Creekside Cafe

- A warm, cozy atmosphere is awaiting you!
- Great food & fantastic service
- Favorites include Hot Thai lettuce wraps, grilled sandwiches & specialty salads
- Check out our daily specials
- Mon. - Fri. 10:00 a.m. - 4:00 p.m., Sat. 11:00 a.m. - 3:00 p.m.
- Closed Sunday

Olde Creekside Cafe

1323 Commerce Ave.
Longview, WA
(360)423-7225

Offer Conditions: Valid anytime.

Offers not valid holidays and subject to Rules of Use
Tipping should be 15% to 20% of the total bill before discount

00566549

Gator's Pub & Eatery

- Gator's Pub & Eatery is where good friends meet for a great time!
- Serving breakfast, lunch & dinner everyday 7:00 a.m. - 2:00 a.m.
- We have pool, darts, pinball, video games & Oregon Lottery
- And of course, the friendliest service staff in town
- 21 years old & over please

11475 S.W. Pacific Hwy.
Tigard, OR
(503)293-0356

Offer Conditions: Valid anytime.

Offers not valid holidays and subject to Rules of Use
Tipping should be 15% to 20% of the total bill before discount

00518736

Mo Betta Deli

- Serving specialty sandwiches
- Gourmet Italia D'Oro Espresso & coffee
- Tillamook ice cream & YoCream soft frozen yogurt
- Open daily

MO BETTA DELI

Sandwich, Ice Cream & Espresso Shoppe

6110 S.E. King Rd.
Milwaukie, OR
(503)653-5487

Offer Conditions: Valid anytime. Dine in only.

Offers not valid holidays and subject to Rules of Use
Tipping should be 15% to 20% of the total bill before discount

00320338

FAST FOOD & CARRYOUT INDEX

FAST FOOD & CARRYOUT INDEX

To search by area, see the **Neighborhood Index** located at the back of your book.

= **Print more coupons online at www.entertainment.com,** up to once a month, with these Repeat Savings® merchants. See the Rules of Use for more details.

Fast Food & Carryout Index

Looking for a certain merchant?

Go to **www.entertainment.com** to search for hundreds
of online printable coupons not found in your book.

OR

Visit **www.entertainment.com/choice** to tell us about
a place you'd like to see a coupon for.

To search by area, see the **Neighborhood Index** located at the back of your book

FAST FOOD & CARRYOUT INDEX

FAST FOOD & CARRYOUT

OREGON

Astoria
740 Astor St.
(503) 325-6400

Beaverton
18021 NW Evergreen Pkwy.
(503) 533-8366

3180 SW Cedar Hills Blvd.
(503) 924-5888

9206 SW Beaverton-
Hillsdale Hwy.
(503) 517-8293

Forest Grove
2042 Main St.
(503) 359-5320

Hillsboro
891 NE 25th Ave.
(503) 601-9007

953 SE Maple St.
(Shute Park Aquatic &
Recreationt Center)
(503) 352-0785

Milwaukie
14624 SE McLoughlin Blvd.
(503) 496-0873

Lake Oswego
14559 Westlake Dr.
(503) 968-7777

31 State St.
(503) 636-1577

Oregon City
19550 Molalla Ave.
(503) 496-1958

Portland
1036 NW Glisan St.
(503) 546-8162

1422 NE Broadway
(503) 517-9981

1811 SW River Dr., #100
(503) 295-0400

320 NW 21st Ave.
(503) 445-7770

405 NW Saltzman Rd.
(503) 924-3645

512 SW Taylor St.
(503) 445-6274

7000 NE Airport Way,
(Portland Airport)
(503) 281-2339

732 SW Yamhill
(503) 227-0888

7535 SW Barnes Rd.
(503) 292-3500

9495 SE 82nd Ave.
(503) 777-2200

9900 SE Washington
(Mall 205)
(503) 261-1100

Sherwood
20661 SW Roy Rogers Rd.
(503) 625-9923

Tigard
12282 SW Scholls Ferry Rd.
(503) 590-7649

West Linn
21700 Salamo Rd.
(503) 657-5799

Wilsonville
8695 SW Jack Burns
Blvd., #J
(503) 582-8210

WASHINGTON
Longview
100 Triangle Center, #140
(360) 578-1500

Redmond
16552 NE 74th St.
(425) 885-2720

Vancouver
910 NE Tenney Rd., #119
(360) 571-4064

- Pizza by the slice, all day long
- Hand-tossed pizza dough fresh every day
- 25 different pizza combinations to choose from, including our infamous Alligator Pizza
- Large selection of exotic drinks, beer & wine
- Salads & breadsticks

www.schmizza.com

Subject to Rules of Use. Coupons VOID if purchased,
sold or bartered for cash.

- Pizza by the slice, all day long
- Hand-tossed pizza dough fresh every day
- 25 different pizza combinations to choose from, including our infamous Alligator Pizza
- Large selection of exotic drinks, beer & wine
- Salads & breadsticks

www.schmizza.com

Subject to Rules of Use. Coupons VOID if purchased,
sold or bartered for cash.

- Pizza by the slice, all day long
- Hand-tossed pizza dough fresh every day
- 25 different pizza combinations to choose from, including our infamous Alligator Pizza
- Large selection of exotic drinks, beer & wine
- Salads & breadsticks

www.schmizza.com

Subject to Rules of Use. Coupons VOID if purchased,
sold or bartered for cash.

- Pizza by the slice, all day long
- Hand-tossed pizza dough fresh every day
- 25 different pizza combinations to choose from, including our infamous Alligator Pizza
- Large selection of exotic drinks, beer & wine
- Salads & breadsticks

www.schmizza.com

Subject to Rules of Use. Coupons VOID if purchased,
sold or bartered for cash.

Domino's Pizza

Enjoy one complimentary Large Pizza with the purchase of any Large Pizza or equal or greater value when purchased online at dominos.com.

Offer Conditions on reverse side.

Tracking Code: EBFP

FREE LARGE PIZZA

Valid at All Participating Locations

Valid now thru November 1, 2010

Domino's Pizza

Enjoy any Bread Side Item for $0.99 with any online purchase at dominos.com.

Offer Conditions on reverse side.

Tracking Code: EB99B

SPECIAL OFFER

Valid at All Participating Locations

Valid now thru November 1, 2010

Domino's Pizza

Enjoy one complimentary Oven Baked Sandwich with the purchase of any Large Pizza at Menu Price when purchased online at dominos.com.

Offer Conditions on reverse side.

Tracking Code: EBFS

FREE OVEN BAKED SANDWICH

Valid at All Participating Locations

D2

Valid now thru November 1, 2010

Domino's Pizza

DOMINOS.COM
Valid at All Participating Locations

Offer Conditions: Limit one offer per household. Valid only for online purchases via dominos.com. Not valid with any other offer. Minimum purchase required for delivery.

00768929

Domino's Pizza

DOMINOS.COM
Valid at All Participating Locations

Offer Conditions: Limit one offer per household. Valid only for online purchases via dominos.com. Not valid with any other offer. Minimum purchase required for delivery.

00768930

Domino's Pizza

DOMINOS.COM
Valid at All Participating Locations

Offer Conditions: Limit one offer per household. Valid only for online purchases via dominos.com. Not valid with any other offer. Minimum purchase required for delivery.

00768932

5 FREE PIECES OF CHICKEN

5 Free pieces of chicken (legs and thighs) with purchase of 15 or more pieces of chicken at regular menu prices.

At participating locations only and at regular menu price only. Not valid with other offers, promotions or discounts. Piece selection at Manager's discretion. Void where prohibited.

©2009 Cajun Operating Company, under license by Cajun Funding Corp

Valid now thru November 1, 2010

See reverse side for details

FREE SIDE

Free regular side with purchase of regular side at regular menu price.

At participating locations only and at regular menu price only. Not valid with other offers, promotions or discounts. Piece selection at Manager's discretion. Void where prohibited.

©2009 Cajun Operating Company, under license by Cajun Funding Corp

Valid now thru November 1, 2010

See reverse side for details

FREE FRIED APPLE PIE

Free Fried Apple Pie with purchase of Fried Apple Pie at regular menu price.

At participating locations only and at regular menu price only. Not valid with other offers, promotions or discounts. Piece selection at Manager's discretion. Void where prohibited.

©2009 Cajun Operating Company, under license by Cajun Funding Corp

Valid now thru November 1, 2010

See reverse side for details

D3

FAST FOOD & CARRYOUT

★ **Valid at all Participating Locations** ★

Subject to Rules of Use. Coupons VOID if purchased, sold or bartered for cash.

★ **Valid at all Participating Locations** ★

Subject to Rules of Use. Coupons VOID if purchased, sold or bartered for cash.

★ **Valid at all Participating Locations** ★

Subject to Rules of Use. Coupons VOID if purchased, sold or bartered for cash.

McDonald's®

Enjoy one complimentary BIG MAC® when a second BIG MAC® of equal or greater value is purchased.

Offer Conditions on reverse side.

Valid now thru November 1, 2010

FREE BIG MAC®

i'm lovin' it®

See Reverse Side for Locations

D4

McDonald's®

i'm lovin' it®

Valid at participating locations in Aloha, Astoria, Beaverton, Canby, Clackamas, Forest Grove, Gladstone, Goldendale, Gresham, Hillsboro, Hood River, Lake Oswego, McMinnville, Milwaukie, Molalla, Newberg, North Plains, Oregon City, Portland, Sandy, Scappoose, Seaside, Sherwood, Silverton, St. Helens, The Dalles, Tigard, Tualatin, West Linn, Wilsonville, Woodburn, Battle Ground, Bingen, Camas, Kelso, Longview, Long Beach, Vancouver, & Woodland

Offer Conditions: Valid anytime. Please present coupon when ordering; Limit one coupon per visit; Limit one offer per coupon; Not valid with any other offer, coupon, or discount; Coupon may not be transferred, copied, or duplicated in any way or transmitted via electronic mail; Price may vary; Prices may vary; Void where prohibited; Cash value 1/20 of 1 cent; Price of required purchase posted on menuboard; ©2009 McDonald's.

00077882

Offer validity is governed by the Rules of Use and excludes defined holidays. Offers are not valid with other discount offers, unless specified. Coupons void if purchased, sold or bartered. Discounts exclude tax, tip and/or alcohol, where applicable.

McDonald's®

i'm lovin' it®

Sandy, Scappoose, Seaside, Sherwood, Silverton, St. Helens, The Dalles, Tigard, Tualatin, West Linn, Wilsonville, Woodburn, Battle Ground, Bingen, Camas, Kelso, Longview, Long Beach, Vancouver, & Woodland

Valid at participating locations in Aloha, Astoria, Beaverton, Canby, Clackamas, Forest Grove, Gladstone, Goldendale, Gresham, Hillsboro, Hood River, Lake Oswego, McMinnville, Milwaukie, Molalla, Newberg, North Plains, Oregon City, Portland,

Offer Conditions: Valid anytime. Please present coupon when ordering; Limit one coupon per visit; Limit one offer per coupon; Not valid with any other offer, coupon, or discount; Coupon may not be transferred, copied, or duplicated in any way or transmitted via electronic mail; Price may vary; Prices may vary; Void where prohibited; Cash value 1/20 of 1 cent; Price of required purchase posted on menuboard; ©2009 McDonald's.

00781621

Offer validity is governed by the Rules of Use and excludes defined holidays. Offers are not valid with other discount offers, unless specified. Coupons void if purchased, sold or bartered. Discounts exclude tax, tip and/or alcohol, where applicable.

McDonald's®

i'm lovin' it®

Sandy, Scappoose, Seaside, Sherwood, Silverton, St. Helens, The Dalles, Tigard, Tualatin, West Linn, Wilsonville, Woodburn, Battle Ground, Bingen, Camas, Kelso, Longview, Long Beach, Vancouver, & Woodland

Valid at participating locations in Aloha, Astoria, Beaverton, Canby, Clackamas, Forest Grove, Gladstone, Goldendale, Gresham, Hillsboro, Hood River, Lake Oswego, McMinnville, Milwaukie, Molalla, Newberg, North Plains, Oregon City, Portland,

Offer Conditions: Valid anytime. Please present coupon when ordering; Limit one coupon per visit; Limit one offer per coupon; Not valid with any other offer, coupon, or discount; Coupon may not be transferred, copied, or duplicated in any way or transmitted via electronic mail; Price may vary; Prices may vary; Void where prohibited; Cash value 1/20 of 1 cent; Price of required purchase posted on menuboard; ©2009 McDonald's.

00781622

Offer validity is governed by the Rules of Use and excludes defined holidays. Offers are not valid with other discount offers, unless specified. Coupons void if purchased, sold or bartered. Discounts exclude tax, tip and/or alcohol, where applicable.

Bullwinkle's/ Family Fun Center

Enjoy any one PIZZA at 50% off the regular price.

Offer Conditions on reverse side.

50%OFF

www.fun-center.com

29111 S.W. Town Center Loop W., Wilsonville, OR
(503)685-5000

Valid now thru November 1, 2010

D7

Tom's Pizza & Sports Bar

Enjoy any one complimentary PIZZA when a second PIZZA of equal or greater value is purchased.

Offer Conditions on reverse side.

FREE PIZZA

See Reverse Side for Locations

Valid now thru November 1, 2010

D8

Bill's Pizza Baron

Enjoy one complimentary MENU ITEM when a second MENU ITEM of equal or greater value is purchased or for those who prefer - any one pizza at 50% off the regular price - maximum discount $8.00.

Offer Conditions on reverse side.

Up$ To 8^{00} Value

PIZZA BARON
SE 122nd

2604 S.E. 122nd, Portland, OR
(503)761-1799

Valid now thru November 1, 2010

D9

More Offers Online!

FAST FOOD & CARRYOUT

entertainment.com

Bullwinkle's/ Family Fun Center

- Tasty pizza, gourmet burgers, heroic sandwiches, desserts and more
- Musical show featuring animated characters
- A delightful experience for the entire family
- See www.fun-center.com for more details

29111 S.W. Town Center Loop W.
Wilsonville, OR
(503)685-5000

Offer Conditions: Valid anytime.

00764755

Tom's Pizza & Sports Bar

- Pizza made from scratch every day - and we mean everything!
- Fresh hand-made dough, secret recipe sauce, the finest meats and 100% real cheese
- Our 18" supreme weighs over 6lbs!
- Over 20 beers on tap along with a full servce bar
- 22 TV's with every sports event played
- Full lottery, including Keno and Video Poker

707 N.E. 181 St.　　　　**2630 N. Lombard St.**
Gresham, OR　　　　　　**Portland, OR**
(503)489-1890　　　　　**(503)283-4217**

Offer Conditions: Valid anytime. Dine in or take out.

00768603

Bill's Pizza Baron

- "Just possibly the greatest anywhere"
- Original sourdough thick crust pizza
- Sandwiches & salad bar
- Banquet & meeting room available
- Hours: Mon. - Thurs. 11:00 a.m. - 12:00 midnight, Fri. & Sat. 11:00 a.m. - 2:00 a.m., Sun. 12:00 noon - 11:00 p.m.

2604 S.E. 122nd
Portland, OR
(503)761-1799

Offer Conditions: Valid anytime. Dine in only.

00008387

Godfather's Pizza

Enjoy one complimentary MEDIUM PEPPERONI PIZZA when a LARGE PIZZA of equal or greater value is purchased at menu price.

Offer Conditions on reverse side.

FREE MEDIUM PEPPERONI PIZZA

See Reverse Side for Locations

Valid now thru November 1, 2010

D10

Godfather's Pizza

Enjoy one complimentary LARGE PEPPERONI PIZZA when a LARGE SPECIALTY PIZZA of equal or greater value is purchased.

Offer Conditions on reverse side.

FREE LARGE PEPPERONI PIZZA

See Reverse Side for Locations

Valid now thru November 1, 2010

D11

Godfather's Pizza

Enjoy one complimentary LUNCH BUFFET when a second LUNCH BUFFET & TWO SOFT DRINKS or equal or greater value is purchased.

Offer Conditions on reverse side.

FREE LUNCH BUFFET

See Reverse Side for Locations

Valid now thru November 1, 2010

D12

Godfather's Pizza

- Lunch buffet, salads & soft drinks
- Groups welcome
- Ask about our group discounts
- Limited delivery area & hours
- VISA, MasterCard accepted
- Beer & wine
- Order online at www.godfathers.com

OREGON
Aloha
17691 S.W. Farmington Mall
(Farmington Ctr.)
(503)649-5600
Canby
1477 S.E. First Ave.
Ste. 101
(503)263-2000

Clackamas
14682 S.E. Sunnyside Rd.
(503)658-2200
Forest Grove
2834-A Pacific Ave.
(Ballad Town Sq.)
(503)359-5405
Hillsboro
7440 S.W. Baseline
(503)848-0100

Portland
11140 S.W. Barnes Rd.
(503)646-1100
4744 N.W. Bethany Blvd.
(503)533-9777
Sherwood
15982 S.W. Tualatin-Sherwood Rd.
(503)625-1600
Tigard
14200 S.W. Barrows Rd.
(503)590-0900

Troutdale
2503 S.W. Cherry Park Rd.
(503)492-3300
WASHINGTON
Vancouver
2100 "A" S.E. 164th
Ste. 107
(360)256-0000
6700 N.E. 162nd Ave.,
Ste. E623
(360)254-5100

Offer Conditions: Valid anytime. Dine-in, carry-out or delivery.

Offers not valid holidays and subject to Rules of Use
Tipping should be 15% to 20% of the total bill before discount

00040615

Offer validity is governed by the Rules of Use and excludes defined holidays. Offers are not valid with other discount offers, unless specified. Coupons void if purchased, sold or bartered. Discounts exclude tax, tip and/or alcohol, where applicable.

Godfather's Pizza

- Lunch buffet, salads & soft drinks
- Groups welcome
- Ask about our group discounts
- Limited delivery area & hours
- VISA, MasterCard accepted
- Beer & wine
- Order online at www.godfathers.com

OREGON
Aloha
17691 S.W. Farmington Mall
(Farmington Ctr.)
(503)649-5600
Canby
1477 S.E. First Ave.
Ste. 101
(503)263-2000

Clackamas
14682 S.E. Sunnyside Rd.
(503)658-2200
Forest Grove
2834-A Pacific Ave.
(Ballad Town Sq.)
(503)359-5405
Hillsboro
7440 S.W. Baseline
(503)848-0100

Portland
11140 S.W. Barnes Rd.
(503)646-1100
4744 N.W. Bethany Blvd.
(503)533-9777
Sherwood
15982 S.W. Tualatin-Sherwood Rd.
(503)625-1600
Tigard
14200 S.W. Barrows Rd.
(503)590-0900

Troutdale
2503 S.W. Cherry Park Rd.
(503)492-3300
WASHINGTON
Vancouver
2100 "A" S.E. 164th
Ste. 107
(360)256-0000
6700 N.E. 162nd Ave.,
Ste. E623
(360)254-5100

Offer Conditions: Valid anytime. Dine-in, carry-out or delivery; Specialty pizza include combo, taco, all-meat combo, veggie, humble pie, hot stuff & bacon cheeseburger.

00743052

Offer validity is governed by the Rules of Use and excludes defined holidays. Offers are not valid with other discount offers, unless specified. Coupons void if purchased, sold or bartered. Discounts exclude tax, tip and/or alcohol, where applicable.

Godfather's Pizza

- Lunch buffet, salads & soft drinks
- Groups welcome
- Ask about our group discounts
- Dine in only
- Limited delivery area & hours
- VISA, MasterCard accepted
- Beer & wine
- Order online at www.godfathers.com

OREGON
Aloha
17691 S.W. Farmington Mall
(Farmington Ctr.)
(503)649-5600
Canby
1477 S.E. First Ave.
Ste. 101
(503)263-2000

Clackamas
14682 S.E. Sunnyside Rd.
(503)658-2200
Forest Grove
2834-A Pacific Ave.
(Ballad Town Sq.)
(503)359-5405
Hillsboro
7440 S.W. Baseline
(503)848-0100

Portland
11140 S.W. Barnes Rd.
(503)646-1100
4744 N.W. Bethany Blvd.
(503)533-9777
Sherwood
15982 S.W. Tualatin-Sherwood Rd.
(503)625-1600
Tigard
14200 S.W. Barrows Rd.
(503)590-0900

Troutdale
2503 S.W. Cherry Park Rd.
(503)492-3300
WASHINGTON
Vancouver
2100 "A" S.E. 164th
Ste. 107
(360)256-0000
6700 N.E. 162nd Ave.,
Ste. E623
(360)254-5100

Offer Conditions: Valid during luncheon hours 11a.m. - 2p.m. Dine in only. Salads excluded.

Offers not valid holidays and subject to Rules of Use
Tipping should be 15% to 20% of the total bill before discount

00040607

Offer validity is governed by the Rules of Use and excludes defined holidays. Offers are not valid with other discount offers, unless specified. Coupons void if purchased, sold or bartered. Discounts exclude tax, tip and/or alcohol, where applicable.

All American Ice Cream and Frozen Yogurt

Enjoy one complimentary LARGE JUICE SMOOTHIE when a second LARGE JUICE SMOOTHIE of equal or greater value is purchased.

Offer Conditions on reverse side.

Valid now thru November 1, 2010

FREE LARGE JUICE SMOOTHIE

See Reverse Side for Locations

D13

All American Ice Cream and Frozen Yogurt

Enjoy one complimentary FRESH HANDMADE WAFFLE CONE when a second FRESH HANDMADE WAFFLE CONE of equal or greater value is purchased.

Offer Conditions on reverse side.

Valid now thru November 1, 2010

FREE FRESH HANDMADE WAFFLE CONE

See Reverse Side for Locations

D14

All American Ice Cream and Frozen Yogurt

Enjoy one complimentary HOT FUDGE SUNDAE when a second HOT FUDGE SUNDAE of equal or greater value is purchased.

Offer Conditions on reverse side.

Valid now thru November 1, 2010

FREE HOT FUDGE SUNDAE

See Reverse Side for Locations

D15

All American Ice Cream and Frozen Yogurt

- 30 Flavors of premium ice cream
- Delicious non-fat frozen yogurt
- Low calorie Glace frozen dessert
- Refreshing hand-made juice smoothies

OREGON
Coquille
29 W. 1st St.
(541)396-5277
Eugene
598 Valley River Ctr.
(Valley River Ctr.)
(541)484-1249
Lincoln City
4095 B Logan Rd.
(541)269-7678

Portland
12000 S.E. 82nd Ave.,
Ste. 1003
(Clackamas Town Ctr.)
(503)654-2852
1600 N. Riverside Dr.
(Rogue Valley Mall)
(541)779-1238
2300 Lloyd Ctr.
(Lloyd Ctr. Mall)
(503)284-5210

Salem
401 Center State St.,
N.E.
(Salem Ctr. Mall)
(503)316-0142
Springfield
3000 Gateway St., #600
(Gateway Mall)
(541)746-4080

WASHINGTON
East Wenatchee
511 Valley Mall Pkwy.
(Wenatchee Valley Mall)
(509)886-2244
Olympia
625 Black Lake Blvd.
(360)753-1424

Offer Conditions: Valid anytime. Valid at participating locations.

00776187

All American Ice Cream and Frozen Yogurt

- 30 Flavors of premium ice cream
- Delicious non-fat frozen yogurt
- Low calorie Glace frozen dessert
- Refreshing hand-made juice smoothies

OREGON
Coquille
29 W. 1st St.
(541)396-5277
Eugene
598 Valley River Ctr.
(Valley River Ctr.)
(541)484-1249
Lincoln City
4095 B Logan Rd.
(541)269-7678

Portland
12000 S.E. 82nd Ave.,
Ste. 1003
(Clackamas Town Ctr.)
(503)654-2852
1600 N. Riverside Dr.
(Rogue Valley Mall)
(541)779-1238
2300 Lloyd Ctr.
(Lloyd Ctr. Mall)
(503)284-5210

Salem
401 Center State St.,
N.E.
(Salem Ctr. Mall)
(503)316-0142
Springfield
3000 Gateway St., #600
(Gateway Mall)
(541)746-4080

WASHINGTON
East Wenatchee
511 Valley Mall Pkwy.
(Wenatchee Valley Mall)
(509)886-2244
Olympia
625 Black Lake Blvd.
(360)753-1424

Offer Conditions: Valid anytime. Valid at participating locations.

00776185

All American Ice Cream and Frozen Yogurt

- 30 Flavors of premium ice cream
- Delicious non-fat frozen yogurt
- Low calorie Glace frozen dessert
- Refreshing hand-made juice smoothies

All American Ice Cream & Frozen Yogurt®

OREGON
Coquille
29 W. 1st St.
(541)396-5277
Eugene
598 Valley River Ctr.
(Valley River Ctr.)
(541)484-1249
Lincoln City
4095 B Logan Rd.
(541)269-7678

Portland
12000 S.E. 82nd Ave.,
Ste. 1003
(Clackamas Town Ctr.)
(503)654-2852
1600 N. Riverside Dr.
(Rogue Valley Mall)
(541)779-1238
2300 Lloyd Ctr.
(Lloyd Ctr. Mall)
(503)284-5210

Salem
401 Center State St.,
N.E.
(Salem Ctr. Mall)
(503)316-0142
Springfield
3000 Gateway St., #600
(Gateway Mall)
(541)746-4080

WASHINGTON
East Wenatchee
511 Valley Mall Pkwy.
(Wenatchee Valley Mall)
(509)886-2244
Olympia
625 Black Lake Blvd.
(360)753-1424

Offer Conditions: Valid anytime. Valid at participating locations.

00776186

Sonic Drive-In

Enjoy one complimentary SONIC BURGER when a second SONIC BURGER is purchased.

Offer Conditions on reverse side.

Valid now thru November 1, 2010

FREE SONIC BURGER

See Reverse Side for Locations

D16

Sonic Drive-In

Enjoy one complimentary EXTRA-LONG CHILI-CHEESE CONEY when a second EXTRA-LONG CHILI-CHEESE CONEY is purchased.

Offer Conditions on reverse side.

Valid now thru November 1, 2010

FREE EXTRA-LONG CHILI-CHEESE CONEY

See Reverse Side for Locations

D17

Sonic Drive-In

Enjoy one complimentary CROISSONIC BREAKFAST SANDWICH when a second CROISSONIC BREAKFAST SANDWICH is purchased.

Offer Conditions on reverse side.

Valid now thru November 1, 2010

FREE CROISSONIC BREAKFAST SANDWICH

See Reverse Side for Locations

D18

Sonic Drive-In
- Now serving breakfast all day!
- Always fast and friendly
- Large selection of shakes, burgers, fries and fresh made onion rings

7380 N.E. Butler Ave
(Cornell and Cornelius Pass Rd)
Hillsboro, OR
(503)648-0150

30129 SW Boones Ferry Rd.
(Exit 283, off I-5 Behind Walgreen's)
Wisonville, OR
(503)855-4642

850 S.E. 192nd Ave.
(192nd at Mill Plain)
Vancouver, WA
(360)891-6646

Offer Conditions: Valid anytime. Valid at these locations only.

00775373

Sonic Drive-In
- Now serving breakfast all day!
- Always fast and friendly
- Large selection of shakes, burgers, fries and fresh made onion rings

7380 N.E. Butler Ave
(Cornell and Cornelius Pass Rd)
Hillsboro, OR
(503)648-0150

30129 SW Boones Ferry Rd.
(Exit 283, off I-5 Behind Walgreen's)
Wisonville, OR
(503)855-4642

850 S.E. 192nd Ave.
(192nd at Mill Plain)
Vancouver, WA
(360)891-6646

Offer Conditions: Valid anytime. Valid at these locations only.

00775372

Sonic Drive-In
- Now serving breakfast all day!
- Always fast and friendly
- Large selection of shakes, burgers, fries and fresh made onion rings

7380 N.E. Butler Ave
(Cornell and Cornelius Pass Rd)
Hillsboro, OR
(503)648-0150

30129 SW Boones Ferry Rd.
(Exit 283, off I-5 Behind Walgreen's)
Wisonville, OR
(503)855-4642

850 S.E. 192nd Ave.
(192nd at Mill Plain)
Vancouver, WA
(360)891-6646

Offer Conditions: Valid anytime. Valid at these locations only.

00768021

Taco Bell®

Enjoy one complimentary
CHALUPA when a second
CHALUPA of equal or greater
value is purchased.
Offer Conditions on reverse side.

CHALUPA

TACO BELL®

See Reverse Side for Locations

Valid now thru November 1, 2010

D19

Taco Bell®

Enjoy one complimentary
BURRITO SUPREME when a
second BURRITO SUPREME
of equal or greater value is
purchased.
Offer Conditions on reverse side.

BURRITO SUPREME

TACO BELL®

See Reverse Side for Locations

Valid now thru November 1, 2010

D20

---

entertainment.com

Taco Bell®

Enjoy one complimentary
CRUNCHY TACO OR BEAN
BURRITO when a second
CRUNCHY TACO OR BEAN
BURRITO of equal or greater
value is purchased.
Offer Conditions on reverse side.

CRUNCHY TACO OR BEAN BURRITO

TACO BELL®

See Reverse Side for Locations

Valid now thru November 1, 2010

D21

Taco Bell®

Gresham
4265 S.E. 182nd
(503)669-7762

Newberg
3420 Portland Rd.
(503)538-7319

Portland
12017 N.E. Glisan
(503)408-1486

12235 N. Jantzen Beach
(503)285-9893

7415 N.E. Martin Luther King
(503)283-2137

Tigard
13305 S.W. Pacific Hwy.
(503)639-2922

Troutdale
560 N.W. Phoenix Dr.
(503)667-6646

Wilsonville
8251 S.W. Wilsonville Rd.
(503)682-2896

Offer Conditions: Valid anytime. One coupon/card per customer per visit; Present coupon/card before ordering; Not valid with any other discount offer; Void if copied or transferred.

00552460

Taco Bell®

Gresham
4265 S.E. 182nd
(503)669-7762

Newberg
3420 Portland Rd.
(503)538-7319

Portland
12017 N.E. Glisan
(503)408-1486

12235 N. Jantzen Beach
(503)285-9893

7415 N.E. Martin Luther King
(503)283-2137

Tigard
13305 S.W. Pacific Hwy.
(503)639-2922

Troutdale
560 N.W. Phoenix Dr.
(503)667-6646

Wilsonville
8251 S.W. Wilsonville Rd.
(503)682-2896

Offer Conditions: Valid anytime. One coupon/card per customer per visit; Present coupon/card before ordering; Not valid with any other discount offer; Void if copied or transferred.

00552463

Taco Bell®

Gresham
4265 S.E. 182nd
(503)669-7762

Newberg
3420 Portland Rd.
(503)538-7319

Portland
12017 N.E. Glisan
(503)408-1486

12235 N. Jantzen Beach
(503)285-9893

7415 N.E. Martin Luther King
(503)283-2137

Tigard
13305 S.W. Pacific Hwy.
(503)639-2922

Troutdale
560 N.W. Phoenix Dr.
(503)667-6646

Wilsonville
8251 S.W. Wilsonville Rd.
(503)682-2896

Offer Conditions: Valid anytime. One coupon/card per customer per visit; Present coupon/card before ordering; Not valid with any other discount offer; Void if copied or transferred.

00552462

A&W Restaurants

Enjoy one complimentary CONEY CHILI DOG when a second CONEY CHILI DOG of equal or greater value is purchased.

Offer Conditions on reverse side.

ONE CONEY CHILI DOG

Valid at All Participating Locations

Valid now thru November 1, 2010

D22

A&W Restaurants

Enjoy one complimentary DELUXE BACON DOUBLE CHEESEBURGER when a second DELUXE BACON DOUBLE CHEESEBURGER of equal or greater value is purchased.

Offer Conditions on reverse side.

ONE DELUXE BACON DOUBLE CHEESEBURGER

Valid at All Participating Locations

Valid now thru November 1, 2010

D23

A&W Restaurants

Enjoy one complimentary A&W ROOT BEER FLOAT when a second A&W ROOT BEER FLOAT of equal or greater value is purchased.

Offer Conditions on reverse side.

ONE A&W ROOT BEER FLOAT

Valid at All Participating Locations

Valid now thru November 1, 2010

D24

Arctic Circle

Enjoy one complimentary SHAKE OR MALT when a second SHAKE OR MALT of equal or greater value is purchased.

Offer Conditions on reverse side.

ONE SHAKE OR MALT

Where the Good Stuff is.

See Reverse Side for Locations

Valid now thru November 1, 2010

D25

Arctic Circle

Enjoy one complimentary TACO SALAD when a second TACO SALAD of equal or greater value is purchased.

Offer Conditions on reverse side.

FREE TACO SALAD

Where the Good Stuff is.

See Reverse Side for Locations

Valid now thru November 1, 2010

D26

Arctic Circle

Enjoy one complimentary BLACK ANGUS RANCHBURGER when a second BLACK ANGUS RANCHBURGER of equal or greater value is purchased.

Offer Conditions on reverse side.

ONE BLACK ANGUS RANCHBURGER

Where the Good Stuff is.

See Reverse Side for Locations

Valid now thru November 1, 2010

D27

Arctic Circle

- Think of us for great tasting food
- 30 Delicious shake flavors
- Milkshakes & malts made the old-fashioned way
- 100% Black Angus beef hamburgers
- Fresh salads
- Fast, friendly service, open daily
- Try our drive thru

Arctic Circle
Where the Good Stuff is.

433 Main St.
Dallas, OR
(503)623-6646

1025 N. Baker
McMinnville, OR
(503)472-3316

16101 S.E. Division St.
Portland, OR
(503)761-1281

318 NW Third
Prineville, OR
(541)447-5075

1415 Capital St., N.E.
Salem, OR
(503)391-6063

00113833

Offer Conditions: Valid anytime. Combo meals excluded.

Offer validity is governed by the Rules of Use and excludes defined holidays. Offers are not valid with other discount offers, unless specified. Coupons void if purchased, sold or bartered. Discounts exclude tax, tip and/or alcohol, where applicable.

Arctic Circle

- Think of us for great tasting food
- 30 Delicious shake flavors
- Milkshakes & malts made the old-fashioned way
- 100% Black Angus beef hamburgers
- Fresh salads
- Fast, friendly service, open daily
- Try our drive thru

Arctic Circle
Where the Good Stuff is.

433 Main St.
Dallas, OR
(503)623-6646

1025 N. Baker
McMinnville, OR
(503)472-3316

16101 S.E. Division St.
Portland, OR
(503)761-1281

318 NW Third
Prineville, OR
(541)447-5075

1415 Capital St., N.E.
Salem, OR
(503)391-6063

00113832

Offer Conditions: Valid anytime. Combo meals excluded.

Offer validity is governed by the Rules of Use and excludes defined holidays. Offers are not valid with other discount offers, unless specified. Coupons void if purchased, sold or bartered. Discounts exclude tax, tip and/or alcohol, where applicable.

Arctic Circle

- Think of us for great tasting food
- 30 Delicious shake flavors
- Milkshakes & malts made the old-fashioned way
- 100% Black Angus beef hamburgers
- Fresh salads
- Fast, friendly service, open daily
- Try our drive thru

Arctic Circle
Where the Good Stuff is.

433 Main St.
Dallas, OR
(503)623-6646

1025 N. Baker
McMinnville, OR
(503)472-3316

16101 S.E. Division St.
Portland, OR
(503)761-1281

318 NW Third
Prineville, OR
(541)447-5075

1415 Capital St., N.E.
Salem, OR
(503)391-6063

00113834

Offer Conditions: Valid anytime. Combo meals excluded.

Offer validity is governed by the Rules of Use and excludes defined holidays. Offers are not valid with other discount offers, unless specified. Coupons void if purchased, sold or bartered. Discounts exclude tax, tip and/or alcohol, where applicable.

Wienerschnitzel

Mix and Match any 5 ORIGINAL CHILI DOGS or CORN DOGS for only $5.

Offer Conditions on reverse side.

5 FOR $5

www.wienerschnitzel.com

8605 N.E. Andresen Rd., Vancouver, WA
(360)892-6223

Valid now thru November 1, 2010

D28

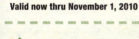

Del Taco

Enjoy one complimentary MENU ITEM when a second MENU ITEM of equal or greater value is purchased.

Offer Conditions on reverse side.

Up To $5.00 Value

See Reverse Side for Locations

Valid now thru November 1, 2010

D29

Emerald City Smoothie

Enjoy one complimentary SMOOTHIE when a second SMOOTHIE of equal or greater value is purchased.

Offer Conditions on reverse side.

FREE SMOOTHIE

nourish your body

See Reverse Side for Locations

Valid now thru November 1, 2010

D30

More Offers Online!

FAST FOOD & CARRYOUT

entertainment.com

Wienerschnitzel
- Dedicated to the art of hot-doggery for over 40 yrs.
- We are the world's largest hot dog chain
- Featuring all beef hot dogs, chili dogs & corn dogs, hamburgers, cheeseburgers & chicken sandwiches
- Tastee Freez ice cream & desserts

8605 N.E. Andresen Rd.
Vancouver, WA
(360)892-6223

Offer Conditions: Valid anytime. Cheese and additional toppings extra.

00697786

Del Taco
- Go Bold or Go Home!
- Mexican & American favorites
- Open for breakfast, lunch & dinner

2164 NE Burnside
Gresham, OR
(503)661-2310

8724 NE Hwy. 99
Vancouver, WA
(360)546-0707

Offer Conditions: Valid anytime. Excludes combinations & fiesta pack.

00760746

Emerald City Smoothie
- Fresh, healthy, nourishing & flavorful smoothies
- Built from scratch with a natural fruit base
- Layered, complete meal smoothies
- Custom-blended to suit your tastes & goals
- Weight Watchers points!
- We sell protein, sports supplements & vitamins
- Comfortable couches with free wi-fi & big-screen TV
- Open daily
- Coming soon to downtown Portland
- Now open in Bend

www.emeraldcitysmoothie.com

11703 S.W. Beaverton-Hillsdale Hwy.
(At Beaverton Town Square next to Moonstruck Chocolate)
Beaverton, OR
(503)372-5676

13504 N.E. 84th. Ste. 101
Vancouver, WA
(360)882-3350

Offer Conditions: Valid anytime.

00115569

Paul Bunyan's Espresso & Deli

Enjoy one complimentary
MENU ITEM when a second
MENU ITEM of equal or greater
value is purchased.

Offer Conditions on reverse side.

Up$ **6**⁰⁰ To Value

PAUL BUNYAN'S
ESPRESSO & DELI

Valid now thru November 1, 2010

8419 N. Denver Ave., Portland, OR
(503)289-0808

D31

Lupe's Escape

Enjoy one complimentary
LUNCH OR DINNER ENTREE
when a second LUNCH OR
DINNER ENTREE of equal or
greater value is purchased.

Offer Conditions on reverse side.

Up$ **8**⁰⁰ To Value

Valid now thru November 1, 2010

19405 S.W. TV Hwy., Aloha, OR
(503)591-5278

D32

For You Only Deli & Gift Shop

Enjoy one complimentary
MENU ITEM when a second
MENU ITEM of equal or greater
value is purchased.

Offer Conditions on reverse side.

Up$ **6**⁰⁰ To Value

"For You Only"

NEW

Valid now thru November 1, 2010

21620 Main St., Aurora, OR
(503)678-2830

D33

Paul Bunyan's Espresso & Deli

- Fresh & delicious cold cut deli sandwiches
- Full selection of coffee drinks
- Fast, friendly service
- Great neighborhood location
- Video poker & lottery games
- Beer & wine
- Right off interstate Max at the Kenton/Denver stop
- Mon. - Fri. 6:00 a.m. - 8:00 p.m., Sat. 8:00 a.m. - 4:00 p.m.

00608608

PAUL BUNYAN'S
ESPRESSO & DELI

8419 N. Denver Ave.
Portland, OR
(503) 289-0808

Offer Conditions: Valid anytime.

Offers not valid holidays and subject to Rules of Use
Tipping should be 15% to 20% of the total bill before discount

Lupe's Escape

- "Best nachos anywhere!"
- Home-style Mexican food in a fun atmosphere
- House especials include torpedo burritos, combination dinners, chimichangas & chile rellenos
- Outdoor dining available
- We feature a variety of cocktails, domestic beers & wines
- Open daily
- Call for hours

00026542

19405 S.W. TV Hwy.
Aloha, OR
(503) 591-5278

Offer Conditions: Valid anytime. Dine in only.

Offers not valid holidays and subject to Rules of Use
Tipping should be 15% to 20% of the total bill before discount

For You Only Deli & Gift Shop

- Soups, sandwiches, homemade pies & pastries
- Old fashioned milk shakes, floats & espresso drinks
- Gifts, antiques & collectables

00579741

"For You Only"

21620 Main St.
Aurora, OR
(503) 678-2830

Offer Conditions: Valid anytime. daily specials excluded.

Offers not valid holidays and subject to Rules of Use
Tipping should be 15% to 20% of the total bill before discount

Papa Murphy's

Enjoy $3.00 off any FAMILY SIZE PIZZA.

Offer Conditions on reverse side.

$3.00 Value

TAKE 'N' BAKE PIZZA

www.papamurphys.com

Valid at All Participating Locations

Valid now thru November 1, 2010   D34

Hungry Howie's Pizza

Enjoy any one complimentary PIZZA when a second PIZZA of equal or greater value is purchased.

Offer Conditions on reverse side.

NEW

FREE PIZZA

Hungry Howie's Pizza

See Reverse Side for Locations

Valid now thru November 1, 2010   D35

Garlic Jim's Famous Gourmet Pizza

Enjoy any one PIZZA at 50% off the regular price.

Offer Conditions on reverse side.

Up To $9.00 Value

Garlic Jim's Famous Gourmet Pizza

www.garlicjims.com

13317 NE 12th Ave., Vancouver, WA
(360)573-8400   D36

Valid now thru November 1, 2010

More Offers Online!

FAST FOOD & CARRYOUT

entertainment.com

Papa Murphy's
- "Simply the Best"
- Take n' Bake Pizza
- The highest quality ingredients
- You'll never go back to the other pizza places

Valid at All Participating Locations

Offer Conditions: Valid anytime.

00698727

Hungry Howie's Pizza
- The original flavored crust pizza
- Choose from: original, butter, butter cheese, garlic herb, ranch, onion, sesame or Cajun
- Subs, Howie wings, salads & breads also available
- Carry out & delivery

727 S.W. 185th Ave.
Aloha, OR
(503)642-9300

19349 Willamette Dr
West Linn, OR
(503)635-5800

Offer Conditions: Valid anytime.

00114313

Garlic Jim's Famous Gourmet Pizza
- Gourmet......Right Away!
- The foundation of a gourmet pizza starts with the dough, the sauce & the cheese
- Garlic Jim's uses only fresh vine-ripened tomatoes for its sauce & 100% whole milk mozzarella for its cheese
- Try our thin crust, complemented with garlic, or our thick crust with parmesan cheese & buttermilk

13317 NE 12th Ave.
(Salmon Creek)
Vancouver, WA
(360)573-8400

Offer Conditions: Valid anytime.

00741909

Round Table Pizza

Enjoy $3.00 off any LARGE PIZZA.

Offer Conditions on reverse side.

Up $3.00 To Value

See Reverse Side for Locations

Valid now thru November 1, 2010

D37

Lone Elder Pizza

Enjoy any one complimentary PIZZA when a second PIZZA of equal or greater value is purchased.

Offer Conditions on reverse side.

Up $18.00 To Value

207 Hwy. 99 Suite 106, Canby, OR
(503)266-1888

Valid now thru November 1, 2010

D38

Nick-N-Willy's Pizza

Enjoy any one complimentary PIZZA when a second PIZZA of equal or greater value is purchased.

Offer Conditions on reverse side.

Up $17.00 To Value

www.nicknwillys.com

7604 N.E. 5th Ave. #110, Vancouver, WA
(360)574-9927

Valid now thru November 1, 2010

D39

Round Table Pizza

Round Table PIZZA

OREGON
Beaverton
14300 S.W. Allen
(503)641-6821
Milwaukie
16550 S.E. McLoughlin
(503)653-6444
Portland
10070 S.W. Barbur Blvd.
(503)245-2211
4141 N.E. 122nd St.
(503)253-3557

6250 S.E. Foster Rd.
(503)777-1461
West Linn
19121 Hwy. 43
(503)635-6654
WASHINGTON
Vancouver
13009 N.E. Hwy. 99., Ste. 205
(360)574-5755
13503 S.E. Mill Plain
(360)253-4921

5016 Thurston Way
(360)892-0450
616 N.E. 81st St.
(JM Plaza)
(360)574-1666

Offer Conditions: Valid anytime. One coupon per order please.

00043451

Lone Elder Pizza
- Build your own or try one of our specialties like our Autodromo Taco Pizza or our Rancho Polo with ranch dressing, chicken, sauteed peppers and onions.
- Canby's neighborhood pizza parlor

LONE ELDER PIZZA

207 Hwy. 99 Suite 106
Canby, OR
(503)266-1888

Offer Conditions: Valid anytime.

00745101

Nick-N-Willy's Pizza
- Always fresh! Always hot!
- Made with the highest quality ingredients in an open-style kitchen & friendly environment
- Eat in, take home hot or take home & bake yourself

NICK-N-WILLY'S PIZZA

7604 N.E. 5th Ave. #110
Vancouver, WA
(360)574-9927

Offer Conditions: Valid anytime.

00741552

Extreme Pizza

Enjoy any one complimentary PIZZA when a second PIZZA of equal or greater value is purchased.

Offer Conditions on reverse side.

Valid now thru November 1, 2010

FREE PIZZA

1888 NW 188th Ave, Hillsboro, OR
(503)645-4200

D40

Lexi'z Pizza Pub

Enjoy any one complimentary PIZZA when a second PIZZA of equal or greater value is purchased.

Offer Conditions on reverse side.

Valid now thru November 1, 2010

Up To $17.00 Value

Lexi'z Pizza Pub

1613 W. Side Hwy., Kelso, WA
(360)575-1960

D41

Sahara Pizza

Enjoy any one complimentary PIZZA when a second PIZZA of equal or greater value is purchased.

Offer Conditions on reverse side.

Valid now thru November 1, 2010

Up To $16.00 Value

www.saharapizza.com

See Reverse Side for Locations

D42

More Offers Online!

FAST FOOD & CARRYOUT

entertainment.com

Extreme Pizza
- Extreme - not Mainstream
- Signature Pizzas, Calzones, Salads and Monster Subs
- Order on-line at www.extremepizza.com

1888 NW 188th Ave
(188th & Cornell at Tanasbourne Central)
Hillsboro, OR
(503)645-4200

Offer Conditions: Valid anytime.

00746760

Lexi'z Pizza Pub
- Family friendly with a fun atmosphere
- Classic & specialty pizzas - try our chili dog or spam pizza!
- Gourmet paninis on house-made bread
- Halibut fish & chip
- Salads & wraps
- Delicious!

1613 W. Side Hwy.
Kelso, WA
(360)575-1960

Offer Conditions: Valid anytime. Dine in only.

00731671

Sahara Pizza
- The hottest place in town
- Gourmet pizzas, delicious pastas & so much more!
- Fast & friendly delivery or come on in & pick it up!

109 N. Market Blvd.
Chehalis, WA
(360)740-0600

2714 NE 114th Ave Suite #B-1
Vancouver, WA
(360)891-1000

Offer Conditions: Valid anytime.

00771473

Westside Pizza

Enjoy any one complimentary PIZZA when a second PIZZA of equal or greater value is purchased.

Offer Conditions on reverse side.

Valid now thru November 1, 2010

316 East Mill Plain Blvd, Vancouver, WA
(360)735-0100

D43

Juliano's Pizzeria

Enjoy $5.00 off the regular price of ANY PIZZA.

Offer Conditions on reverse side.

Valid now thru November 1, 2010

15606 SE Mill Plain Blvd, Vancouver, WA
(360)254-1286

D44

Vernie's Pizza

Enjoy any one complimentary PIZZA when a second PIZZA of equal or greater value is purchased.

Offer Conditions on reverse side.

Vernie's Pizza

Valid now thru November 1, 2010

900 Triangle Ctr., Longview, WA
(360)578-9561

D45

Westside Pizza
- Using only the best ingredients and dough made fresh daily
- Creative pizza combinations of flavorful sauces and toppings
- Fresh salads and sides
- All at an affordable price!

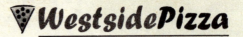

316 East Mill Plain Blvd
Vancouver, WA
(360)735-0100

Offer Conditions: Valid anytime. Carry out only.

00755354

Juliano's Pizzeria
- Open daily for lunch and dinner
- Family friendly dining
- Now serving gluten free pizza
- Savor our generous toppings served over hand-tossed dough
- Juliano's is a great place for your next party or event

15606 SE Mill Plain Blvd
Vancouver, WA
(360)254-1286

Offer Conditions: Valid anytime. Dine in only; Excludes mini pizza.

00753502

Vernie's Pizza
- A family owned, local business supporting our community
- Pizza, sandwiches, salads
- Separate dining area perfect for groups & parties
- Homemade crust, homemade sauce
- Nothing round here is pre-done!

Vernie's Pizza

900 Triangle Ctr.
Longview, WA
(360)578-9561

Offer Conditions: Valid anytime. Dine in only.

00751440

Wingman

Enjoy 10 FREE WINGS with the purchase of 40 WINGS.

Offer Conditions on reverse side.

Valid now thru November 1, 2010

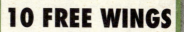

10 FREE WINGS

www.wingmanwings.com

Valid at all Colorado, New Jersey & Washington locations

D46

Wingman

Enjoy 50% off the regular price of any FOOD ORDER.

Offer Conditions on reverse side.

Valid now thru November 1, 2010

$5.00 Value

www.wingmanwings.com

Valid at all Colorado, New Jersey & Washington locations

D47

Wingman

Buy one Sandwich and get a second Sandwich of equal or lesser value at 50% off.

Offer Conditions on reverse side.

Valid now thru November 1, 2010

50% OFF

www.wingmanwings.com

Valid at all Colorado, New Jersey & Washington locations

D48

Wingman
- Burgers, Chicken sandwiches, Philly Cheesesteaks, Boneless Wings, Fish & much more
- Dine in & carry out

Valid at all Colorado, New Jersey & Washington locations

Offer Conditions: Valid anytime. Not valid with any other discounts or promotions; One coupon/card per customer per visit.

00778374

Offer validity is governed by the Rules of Use and excludes defined holidays. Offers are not valid with other discount offers, unless specified. Coupons void if purchased, sold or bartered. Discounts exclude tax, tip and/or alcohol, where applicable.

Wingman
- Burgers, Chicken Sandwiches, Philly Cheesesteaks, Boneless Wings, Fish & much more
- Dine in & carry out

Valid at all Colorado, New Jersey & Washington locations

Offer Conditions: Valid anytime. Not valid with any other discounts or promotions; One coupon/card per customer per visit.

00778373

Offer validity is governed by the Rules of Use and excludes defined holidays. Offers are not valid with other discount offers, unless specified. Coupons void if purchased, sold or bartered. Discounts exclude tax, tip and/or alcohol, where applicable.

Wingman
- Burgers, Chicken sandwiches, Philly Cheesesteaks, Boneless Wings, Fish & much more
- Dine in & carry out

Valid at all Colorado, New Jersey & Washington locations

Offer Conditions: Valid anytime. Not valid with any other discounts or promotions; One coupon/card per customer per visit.

00778375

Offer validity is governed by the Rules of Use and excludes defined holidays. Offers are not valid with other discount offers, unless specified. Coupons void if purchased, sold or bartered. Discounts exclude tax, tip and/or alcohol, where applicable.

Boone's Junction Pizza & Pub

Enjoy any one PIZZA at 50% off the regular price - maximum discount $25.00.

Offer Conditions on reverse side.

50% OFF

Boone's Junction Pizza & Pub

PRINT MORE ONLINE

Valid now thru November 1, 2010

29720 S.W. Boones Ferry Rd., Wilsonville, OR
(503)582-9507

D49

Taco Del Mar

Enjoy one complimentary TACO when a second TACO of equal or greater value is purchased.

Offer Conditions on reverse side.

FREE TACO

Keeping it real.

Valid now thru November 1, 2010

www.tacodelmar.com

Valid at all Oregon & SW Washington locations

D50

Taco Del Mar

Enjoy one complimentary MONDO BURRITO when a second MONDO BURRITO of equal or greater value is purchased.

Offer Conditions on reverse side.

FREE MONDO BURRITO

Keeping it real.

Valid now thru November 1, 2010

www.tacodelmar.com

Valid at all Oregon & SW Washington locations

D51

More Offers Online!

FAST FOOD & CARRYOUT

entertainment.com

Boone's Junction Pizza & Pub

- The Best Pizza in Town!
- Wilsonville's local hangout
- Cozy inside; great deck outside
- Full bar & friendly faces
- Karaoke Fri. & Sat. nights
- Full lottery & darts
- Sorry, no delivery - But it's worth coming in for!!

Boone's Junction Pizza & Pub

29720 S.W. Boones Ferry Rd.
Wilsonville, OR
(503)582-9507

Offer Conditions: Valid anytime. Sorry, no delivery.
Offers not valid holidays and subject to Rules of Use
Tipping should be 15% to 20% of the total bill before discount

00605311

Taco Del Mar

- We bring Baja-craved Mexican flavors to our many OR and SW WA locations
- One of America's Top 10 healthiest fast food restaurants by Health Magazine
- We use real, quality ingredients to balance big taste & nutrition
- Kids' menu, gluten free options & catering service available
- Open everyday for lunch & dinner
- Follow us on facebook & twitter

Valid at all Oregon & SW Washington locations

Offer Conditions: Valid anytime. Not valid with any other discounts or promotions.

00781067

Taco Del Mar

- We bring Baja-craved Mexican flavors to our many OR and SW WA locations
- One of America's Top 10 healthiest fast food restaurants by Health Magazine
- We use real, quality ingredients to balance big taste & nutrition
- Kids' menu, gluten free options & catering service available
- Open everyday for lunch & dinner
- Follow us on facebook & twitter

Valid at all Oregon & SW Washington locations

Offer Conditions: Valid anytime. Not valid with any other discounts or promotions.

00781066

entertainment.com

The Pita Pit

Enjoy one complimentary
MENU ITEM when a second
MENU ITEM of equal or greater
value is purchased.

Offer Conditions on reverse side.

Valid now thru November 1, 2010

Up To $6.00 Value

See Reverse Side for Locations

D52

entertainment.com

Steakburger

Enjoy one complimentary
SANDWICH when a second
SANDWICH of equal or greater
value is purchased.

Offer Conditions on reverse side.

Valid now thru November 1, 2010

Up To $10.00 Value

7120 N.E. Hwy. 99, Vancouver, WA
(360) 694-3421

D53

entertainment.com

Hot Dog on a Stick/Muscle Beach Lemonade

Enjoy one complimentary
MENU ITEM when a second
MENU ITEM of equal or greater
value is purchased.

Offer Conditions on reverse side.

Valid now thru November 1, 2010

FREE MENU ITEM

Valid at All Participating Locations

D54

More Offers Online!

FAST FOOD & CARRYOUT

entertainment.com

The Pita Pit
- Fresh thinking, healthy eating
- Pita Pit's soft healthy pitas are light and tasty and come stuffed with your choice of fresh, tantalizing ingredients.
- Made to order, sizzling hot off the grill!
- One taste and you'll know why we're always smiling

421 SW 10th
Portland, OR
(503)222-6551

16415 S.E. 15th St.
Vancouver, WA
(360)892-7482

7710 N.E. 5th Ave
Vancouver, WA
(360)992-7482

Offer Conditions: Valid anytime.

00114810

Steakburger
- Great food and fun for the whole family.
- Family owned and operated since 1962

7120 N.E. Hwy. 99
Vancouver, WA
(360)694-3421

Offer Conditions: Valid anytime. Present coupon/card before ordering; Excludes additional toppings and excludes combos.; Not valid with any other discounts or promotions; One coupon/card per customer per visit.

00767066

Hot Dog on a Stick/Muscle Beach Lemonade

Valid at All Participating Locations

Offer Conditions: Valid anytime. All Fish and/or Zucchini items excluded; Combo meals & kids meals excluded; Not valid with any other discounts or promotions.

00764113

Black Sheep Bakery and Cafe

Enjoy one complimentary
SANDWICH when a second
SANDWICH of equal or greater
value is purchased.

Offer Conditions on reverse side.

NEW

Valid now thru November 1, 2010

Up to $6.00 Value

See Reverse Side for Locations

D55

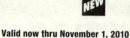

Ay Caramba

Enjoy one complimentary
MENU ITEM when a second
MENU ITEM of equal or greater
value is purchased.
Offer Conditions on reverse side.

Valid now thru November 1, 2010

Up to $6.00 Value

16055 SW Regatta Ln. Ste 500, Beaverton, OR
(503)531-3343

D56

Asian Xpress

Enjoy one complimentary
MENU ITEM when a second
MENU ITEM of equal or greater
value is purchased.
Offer Conditions on reverse side.

Up to $5.00 Value

Asian Xpress

Three Rivers Mall, Kelso, WA
(360)501-6151

D57

Valid now thru November 1, 2010

Black Sheep Bakery and Cafe

- Vegan treats for lovers and haters alike
- Delicious sandwiches, baked goods and drinks galore
- Go ahead, indulge yourself, nourish yourself and impress yourself.

523 NE 19th Ave
Portland, OR
(503)517-5762

833 SE Main St
Portland, OR
(503)473-8534

Offer Conditions: Valid anytime.

00745925

Ay Caramba

- The most "Mexellent"
- Choose from a tasty variety of burritos, tacos, combos, ensaladas & other mexican favorites
- Kid's menu available
- Party platters for all occasions

FRESH MEXICAN GRILL

16055 SW Regatta Ln. Ste 500
(off Walker Rd. in Waterhouse Commons)
Beaverton, OR
(503)531-3343

Offer Conditions: Valid anytime.

00492131

Asian Xpress

- Located in the Three Rivers Mall
- Delicious Chinese food
- Teriyaki chicken, chow mien, fried rice & more
- Take a look & take your choice!

Asian Xpress

Three Rivers Mall
Kelso, WA
(360)501-6151

Offer Conditions: Valid anytime.

00729165

Basco's Burgers

Enjoy one complimentary
MENU ITEM when a second
MENU ITEM of equal or greater
value is purchased.

Offer Conditions on reverse side.

Valid now thru November 1, 2010

1880 SE Baseline, Cornelius, OR
(503)359-0447

D58

Oasis Cafe

Enjoy any FOOD ORDER at
50% off the regular price.

Offer Conditions on reverse side.

Valid now thru November 1, 2010

3701 S.E. Hawthorne Blvd., Portland, OR
(503)231-0901

D59

Super Burrito Express

Enjoy one complimentary
MENU ITEM when a second
MENU ITEM of equal or greater
value is purchased.

Offer Conditions on reverse side.

FREE MENU ITEM

SUPER BURRITO EXPRESS

www.superburritoexpress.com

4210 King Rd., Milwaukie, OR
(503)786-9370

D60

Valid now thru November 1, 2010

Basco's Burgers

- Made with 100% pure beef
- Also fish & chips, chicken, sandwiches & salads
- Come dine in our clean, family friendly dining room

1880 SE Baseline
Cornelius, OR
(503)359-0447

Offer Conditions: Valid anytime.
Tipping should be 15% to 20% of TOTAL bill before discount

00729934

Oasis Cafe

- Try our slices of pizza
- Local microbrews
- Fabulous salads & sandwiches
- Desserts served by "Piece of Cake"
- Open 360 days a year 7 days a week

3701 S.E. Hawthorne Blvd.
Portland, OR
(503)231-0901

Offer Conditions: Valid anytime. Dine in only.

00522379

Super Burrito Express

- Welcome Amigo!
- Join us for the freshest, most delicious Mexican food in Portland
- Choose from a variety of burritos, tacos, & side dishes
- We use only the best steak, chicken & pork
- See you soon!

SUPER BURRITO EXPRESS

4210 King Rd.
Milwaukie, OR
(503)786-9370

Offer Conditions: Valid anytime.

00515745

Burrito Express

Enjoy one complimentary
MENU ITEM when a second
MENU ITEM of equal or greater
value is purchased.

Offer Conditions on reverse side.

FREE MENU ITEM

www.burrito-express.com

52547 Columbia River Hwy., Scappoose, OR
(503)543-4411

Valid now thru November 1, 2010

D61

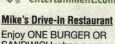

Mike's Drive-In Restaurant

Enjoy ONE BURGER OR
SANDWICH when a second
BURGER OR SANDWICH of
equal or greater value is
purchased.

Offer Conditions on reverse side.

Up To $5.00 Value

MIKE'S DRIVE IN RESTAURANT

See Reverse Side for Locations

Valid now thru November 1, 2010

D62

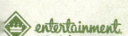

Mike's Drive-In Restaurant

Enjoy ONE BURGER OR
SANDWICH when a second
BURGER OR SANDWICH of
equal or greater value is
purchased.

Offer Conditions on reverse side.

Up To $5.00 Value

MIKE'S DRIVE IN RESTAURANT

See Reverse Side for Locations

Valid now thru November 1, 2010

D63

Burrito Express

- Offering a delicious variety of authentic Mexican burritos, tacos, & side dishes
- Featuring 18 different burritos & 10 different tacos using only the best steak, chicken & pork
- Visit us on the way to the ocean in Scappoose on Hwy. 30

**52547 Columbia River Hwy.
Scappoose, OR
(503)543-4411**

Offer Conditions: Valid anytime.

00515746

Mike's Drive-In Restaurant

- Enjoy good food & friendly service at Mike's
- Featuring halibut fish & chips - one of our favorites
- Wide variety of ice cream, milkshakes & old fashioned banana splits
- Open daily from 10 a.m.

MIKE'S DRIVE IN RESTAURANT

**3045 S.E. Harrison St.
(Hwy. 224 & Harrison St.)
Milwaukie, OR
(503)654-0131**

**905 7th St.
Oregon City, OR
(503)656-5588**

**1707 S.E. Tenino
(Sellwood)
Portland, OR
(503)236-4537**

Offer Conditions: Valid anytime. One coupon per customer per visit.

00036190

Mike's Drive-In Restaurant

- Enjoy good food & friendly service at Mike's
- Featuring halibut fish & chips - one of our favorites
- Wide variety of ice cream, milkshakes & old fashioned banana splits
- Open daily from 10 a.m.

MIKE'S DRIVE IN RESTAURANT

**3045 S.E. Harrison St.
(Hwy. 224 & Harrison St.)
Milwaukie, OR
(503)654-0131**

**905 7th St.
Oregon City, OR
(503)656-5588**

**1707 S.E. Tenino
(Sellwood)
Portland, OR
(503)236-4537**

Offer Conditions: Valid anytime. One coupon per customer per visit.

00036190

Ross Island Grocery & Cafe

Enjoy one complimentary
SANDWICH when a second
SANDWICH of equal or greater
value is purchased.
Offer Conditions on reverse side.

Up To $6.00 Value

Ross Island Grocery & Café

3338 S.W. Corbett, Portland, OR
(503)227-4531

Valid now thru November 1, 2010

D64

Bandito Taco

Enjoy one complimentary
MENU ITEM when a second
MENU ITEM of equal or greater
value is purchased.
Offer Conditions on reverse side.

Up To $5.00 Value

13565 N.W. Cornell Rd., Portland, OR
(503)643-2304

Valid now thru November 1, 2010

D65

Sandwich Depot Deli

Enjoy one complimentary
MENU ITEM when a second
MENU ITEM of equal or greater
value is purchased.
Offer Conditions on reverse side.

Up To $5.00 Value

1652 N.W. Fairview Dr., Gresham, OR
(503)239-4177

Valid now thru November 1, 2010

D66

Ross Island Grocery & Café

Ross Island Grocery & Cafe

- Your new favorite neighborhood cafe
- Start your day with a hot espresso drink
- Drop by for lunch & grab a freshly prepared sandwich
- Pick up your last minute grocery extras on your way home!
- Better yet, kick back & relax with our friendly staff

3338 S.W. Corbett
Portland, OR
(503)227-4531

Offer Conditions: Valid anytime.

00579713

Bandito Taco

- Amigo combination platters are excellent
- Fresh homemade salsa
- 1/2 lb. ultimate burrito
- Something different? Try our Bandito Nachos
- Sunday Crunch - .55 cent tacos
- Approved by Phantom Reviewer

BANDITO TACO

13565 N.W. Cornell Rd.
(Sunset Mall)
Portland, OR
(503)643-2304

Offer Conditions: Valid anytime.

Offers not valid holidays and subject to Rules of Use
Tipping should be 15% to 20% of the total bill before discount

00034126

Sandwich Depot Deli

- Eat in, call ahead to pick-up or we'll deliver (delivery to local area only; delivery charge may apply)
- From simple to simple elegant
- Perfect for large or small meetings, birthdays & weddings
- Any kind of affairs; lunch boxes
- Delicious 3 & 4 foot submarine sandwiches

1652 N.W. Fairview Dr.
Gresham, OR
(503)239-4177

Offer Conditions: Valid anytime.

00614861

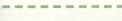

Mexicali Express

- Serving healthy Mexican food
- Try our new breakfast menu available til 11 a.m., Mon.-Sat., 8:30 a.m.-1 p.m. on Sun.
- Featuring Huevos rancheros, Mexicali scramble, Chilaquiles, omelets, pancakes, french toasts & much more
- Other favorites available after 11 a.m.: chicken salad, tacos, veggie burritos, chicken suprema, chicken Kahuna Burrito & combination plates

**12950 S.W. Canyon Rd.
Beaverton, OR
(503) 643-3739**

00036515

Offer Conditions: Valid anytime. Not valid with any other discount offer.

Mexicali Express

- Healthy Mexican food
- Chicken salad & chicken tacos
- Veggie burritos, chicken Suprema & chicken Kahuna burritos
- Combination plates & much more!

**12950 S.W. Canyon Rd.
Beaverton, OR
(503) 643-3739**

00036549

Offer Conditions: Valid anytime. Not valid with any other discount offer.

Mocha Express

- High caffeine espresso blend "Eagle Vision™" available ONLY at Mocha Express, for those wanting that extra kick
- Cool off with an "Eagle Vision Freeze™"
- Great selection of whole bean coffees available by the pound
- All locations open from 6:00 a.m., Mon. - Sat., & from 7:00 a.m. Sun.

**10441 S.E. Holgate
(104th & Holgate)
Portland, OR
(503) 760-8777**

**1951 S.E. 82nd
(4 blocks N. of Division)
Portland, OR
(503) 777-2777**

**3953 S.E. Powell
(39th & Powell)
Portland, OR
(503) 777-2677**

**5111 S.E. Holgate
(51st & Holgate)
Portland, OR
(503) 771-7773**

**7222 S.E. 82nd.
(2 blocks N of Flavel)
Portland, OR
(503) 777-3777**

00238184

Offer Conditions: Valid anytime. Whole bean coffee excluded.

Milo's Espresso

Enjoy one complimentary
MENU ITEM when a second
MENU ITEM of equal or greater
value is purchased.

Offer Conditions on reverse side.

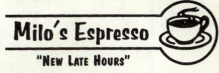
Valid now thru November 1, 2010

16234 SE Division, Portland, OR
(503)761-4048

D70

New York City Sub Shop

Enjoy one complimentary
SANDWICH when a second
SANDWICH of equal or greater
value is purchased.

Offer Conditions on reverse side.

Valid now thru November 1, 2010

D71

Gretchen's Kitchen

Enjoy one complimentary
MENU ITEM when a second
MENU ITEM of equal or greater
value is purchased.

Offer Conditions on reverse side.

Valid now thru November 1, 2010

940 SE Morrison, Portland, OR
(503)234-4086

D72

More Offers Online!

FAST FOOD & CARRYOUT

entertainment.com

Milo's Espresso
- Proudly serving Aroma Coffee
- Winner of the prestigious "Portland Cup" award 2 years in a row
- Freshly baked pastries daily
- Ghiradelli chocolate
- Torani syrups & The Republic of Tea

"NEW LATE HOURS"

16234 SE Division
(next to Plaid Pantry)
Portland, OR
(503)761-4048

Offer Conditions: Valid anytime. Not valid with any other specials or promotions.

00449255

New York City Sub Shop
- Good food fast! Not fast food!
- Subs, Sandwiches, Salads and More!
- Sandwiches made the New York way - no frills and no hassle, just quality meats and cheeses on freshly made bread

1043 N.W. Bond St Bend, OR (541)388-4498	1020B Wasco St. Hood River, OR (541)386-5144	400 E Second St. The Dalles, OR (541)296-4480
1375 SE Wilson St. Bend, OR (541)330-0444	946 SE Veterans Way Redmond, OR (541)548-4400	20 N Jackson St. Jackson, WY (307)733-4414

Offer Conditions: Valid anytime.

00777917

Gretchen's Kitchen
- For over a decade, Gretchen has been supporting Portland's need for a good homemade sandwich
- Sandwiches, salads, soup from scratch
- Catering available
- Specials

940 SE Morrison
Portland, OR
(503)234-4086

Offer Conditions: Valid anytime.

00751445

Up To $6.00 Value

Little Monkey Deli

Enjoy any FOOD/BEVERAGE ORDER at 50% off the regular price.

Offer Conditions on reverse side.

Valid now thru November 1, 2010

1919 Pacific Ave., Forest Grove, OR
(503)357-4500

D73

Up To $7.00 Value

Pogy's Subs

Enjoy one complimentary SUB when a second SUB of equal or greater value is purchased.

Offer Conditions on reverse side.

Valid now thru November 1, 2010

See Reverse Side for Locations

D74

ONE STANDARD SUB

Pogy's Subs

Enjoy one complimentary STANDARD SUB when a second STANDARD SUB of equal or greater value is purchased.

Offer Conditions on reverse side.

Valid now thru November 1, 2010

See Reverse Side for Locations

D75

Little Monkey Deli
- Family-owned & operated
- We make the only bubble tea in Forest Grove!
- Smoothies using local, seasonal fruits
- Bread bowls, sausage dogs, sandwiches, wraps & salads
- Open 7 days a week for your convenience & quick service
- Eat in too, if you'd like

1919 Pacific Ave.
(between Main St. & A St.)
Forest Grove, OR
(503)357-4500

Offer Conditions: Valid anytime.

00780922

Pogy's Subs
- Over 30 varieties of delicious submarine sandwiches
- Cut FRESH for each order
- The "Hot Ones" include meatball, French dip, BBQ beef, & more
- Fresh salads & soups
- Hot toasted hoagies
- French Fries, chips, potato & macaroni salad

6175 S.W. Murray Blvd.
(corner of Allen & Murray Blvd.)
Beaverton, OR
(503)520-9600

125 N. Hwy. 99W
McMinnville, OR
(503)434-9088

17185 S.E. McLoughlin
Milwaukie, OR
(503)652-0120

2855 E. Hayes St.
(behind Yamhill Grill),
(www.pogys.com)
Newberg, OR
(503)538-1000

Offer Conditions: Valid anytime. Delivery excluded. Not valid with any other discount offer or promotions; One coupon per customer per visit; Meal deal excluded.

00046988

Pogy's Subs
- Over 30 varieties of delicious submarine sandwiches
- Cut FRESH for each order
- The "Hot Ones" include meatball, French dip, BBQ beef & many more
- Fresh salads & soups
- Hot toasted hoagies
- French fries, chips, potato & macaroni salad

6175 S.W. Murray Blvd.
(corner of Allen & Murray Blvd.)
Beaverton, OR
(503)520-9600

125 N. Hwy. 99W
McMinnville, OR
(503)434-9088

17185 S.E. McLoughlin
Milwaukie, OR
(503)652-0120

2855 E. Hayes St.
(behind Yamhill Grill),
(www.pogys.com)
Newberg, OR
(503)538-1000

Offer Conditions: Valid anytime. Delivery excluded. Not valid with any other discount offer or promotions; One coupon per customer per visit; Meal deal excluded.

00046993

Sargo's Subs

Enjoy one complimentary Full Standard Sub, Chips and a Medium Drink when a second Full Standard Sub, Chips and a Medium Drink of equal or greater value is purchased.

Offer Conditions on reverse side.

Valid now thru November 1, 2010

FULL STANDARD SUB, CHIPS AND A MEDIUM DRINK

Sargo's Subs

See Reverse Side for Locations

D76

Downtime Deli

Enjoy one complimentary MENU ITEM when a second MENU ITEM of equal or greater value is purchased.

Offer Conditions on reverse side.

Valid now thru November 1, 2010

DOWNTIME

DELI

40 N.E. 2nd, Gresham, OR
(503)667-4969

D77

162nd Street Deli

Enjoy one complimentary SANDWICH when a second SANDWICH of equal or greater value is purchased.

Offer Conditions on reverse side.

Valid now thru November 1, 2010

162nd Street

DELI

2602 S.E. 162nd St., Portland, OR
(503)760-7510

D78

Sargo's Subs

- Over 30 varieties of delicious submarine sandwiches
- Each sandwich is made fresh to order
- Fresh salads, soups and more!
- Specialty and Party Subs available
- Simply the Best!

Sargo's Subs

2699 N.E. Hwy 20
(inside Stop and Go)
Bend, OR
(541)753-7840

29890 SW Town Center Loop W
(Wilsonville Town Center)
Wilsonville, OR
(503)685-6303

22352 NE Park Lane
Wood Village, OR
(503)669-8281

Offer Conditions: Valid anytime. Standard Subs #1-13 only; One coupon/card per customer per visit.

00113978

Downtime Deli

- Full service espresso
- Fresh made deli sandwiches
- Beer & wine
- Full lottery
- Big screen TV, megatouch & games

DOWNTIME

D E L I

40 N.E. 2nd
Gresham, OR
(503)667-4969

Offer Conditions: Valid anytime.

00696146

162nd Street Deli

- We take pride in the high quality meat and ingredients that go into our sandwiches
- Sandwiches, Soups, Hot Dogs and Drinks
- Daily specials
- Private lottery area - all games

162nd Street DELI

2602 S.E. 162nd St.
(1/2 block S. of 162nd)
Portland, OR
(503)760-7510

Offer Conditions: Valid anytime.

00755739

entertainment.com

The Deli Barn

Enjoy one complimentary
MENU ITEM when a second
MENU ITEM of equal or greater
value is purchased.
Offer Conditions on reverse side.

THE DELI BARN

Valid now thru November 1, 2010

2410 S.E. 182nd, Portland, OR
(503) 665-2071

D79

entertainment.com

Phil's 1500 Subs

Enjoy one complimentary 6"
SUB SANDWICH when a
second 6" SUB SANDWICH
of equal or greater value is
purchased.
Offer Conditions on reverse side.

Phil's
1500 subs

Valid now thru November 1, 2010

2834-D Pacific Ave., Forest Grove, OR
(503) 359-1500

D80

entertainment.com

Ozzie's Deli, Gyros

Enjoy one complimentary
SANDWICH when a second
SANDWICH of equal or greater
value is purchased.
Offer Conditions on reverse side.

Up $5.00 To Value

OZZIE'S

Deli, Gyros

Valid now thru November 1, 2010

10010 S.E. Washington, Portland, OR
(503) 255-4222

D81

More Offers Online!

FAST FOOD & CARRYOUT

entertainment.com

The Deli Barn
- Hot & cold sandwiches for lunch & dinner
- Homemade soups
- Daily specials
- Open dining area - great for catching a quick meal on the way home
- Full Oregon lottery
- Beer & wine
- Open Mon. - Fri. 9:00 am. - 9:00 p.m., Sat. 10:00 a.m. - 4:00 p.m.
- Closed Sunday

THE DELI BARN

2410 S.E. 182nd
(182nd & Division)
Portland, OR
(503)665-2071

Offer Conditions: Valid anytime.

00588930

Phil's 1500 Subs
- We feature gourmet subs such as our "warhead" or our homemade meatball sandwich
- Homemade desserts & soups
- Delivery is available, call for restrictions
- A variety of beer & wine to choose from
- Open daily

Phil's
1500 subs

2834-D Pacific Ave.
Forest Grove, OR
(503)359-1500

Offer Conditions: Valid anytime.

00041360

Ozzie's Deli, Gyros
- Excellent submarine sandwiches & gyros
- Pocket bread sandwiches
- Homemade salads
- Frozen yogurt
- Party trays available
- Hours: Mon. - Fri., 7:30 a.m. - 7:00 p.m., Sat., 10:00 a.m. - 6:00 p.m.
- Closed Sunday

OZZIE'S
Deli, Gyros

10010 S.E. Washington
(Inside Mall 205)
Portland, OR
(503)255-4222

Offer Conditions: Valid anytime.

00033223

Seize The Bagel

Enjoy one complimentary
MENU ITEM when a second
MENU ITEM of equal or greater
value is purchased.
Offer Conditions on reverse side.

Seize The Bagel

Valid now thru November 1, 2010

13503 SE Mill Plain Blvd #2, Vancouver, WA
(360)254-1012

D82

Donuts Plus

Enjoy ANY BAKERY ORDER at
50% off the regular price -
maximum discount $5.00.
Offer Conditions on reverse side.

DONUTS *Plus*

Since 1981

Valid now thru November 1, 2010

13500 N.W. Cornell Rd., Portland, OR
(503)644-2168

D83

Donut Nook

Enjoy ANY BAKERY ORDER at
50% off the regular price.
Offer Conditions on reverse side.

Valid now thru November 1, 2010

4403 St. Johns Rd., Vancouver, WA
(360)695-5775

D84

Seize The Bagel

- Freshly made bagels
- Soups, sandwiches, coffee and more
- Try an Eggel sandwich for breakfast
- Variety of bagel flavors and spreads - all delicious and waitng for you!

Seize The Bagel

13503 SE Mill Plain Blvd #2
Vancouver, WA
(360) 254-1012

Offer Conditions: Valid anytime.

00766097

Donuts Plus

- We know P's & Q's about donuts!
- All baked goods made fresh daily
- Coffee & espresso also available
- Open daily from 5:30 a.m.-12:30 p.m.

DONUTS *Plus*

Since 1981

13500 N.W. Cornell Rd.
(Cornell & Murray)
Portland, OR
(503) 644-2168

Offer Conditions: Valid anytime.

00386166

Donut Nook

- All donuts made fresh everyday from scratch
- Donuts, muffins, cookies
- Open 7 days a week
- Hours: Mon. - Thurs., 6:00 a.m. - 4:30 p.m., Fri. - Sun., 6:00 a.m. - 12 noon

DONUT NOOK

4403 St. Johns Rd.
Vancouver, WA
(360) 695-5775

Offer Conditions: Valid anytime.

00388658

entertainment.com

Nestle Toll House Cafe

Enjoy any BAKED GOODS ORDER at 50% off the regular price.

Offer Conditions on reverse side.

Valid now thru November 1, 2010

Up $ To **25**⁰⁰ Value

www.nestlecafe.com

12000 SE 82nd Avenue #2073, Happy Valley, OR
(503) 908-0899

D85

---

entertainment.com

Great Harvest Bread

Enjoy one LOAF OF HONEY WHOLE WHEAT with the purchase of ANY LOAF OF BREAD.

Offer Conditions on reverse side.

Valid now thru November 1, 2010

FREE LOAF OF HONEY WHOLE WHEAT BREAD

See Reverse Side for Locations

D86

---

entertainment.com

Diabetic Bakery

Enjoy any BAKED GOODS ORDER at 50% off the regular price.

Offer Conditions on reverse side.

Valid now thru November 1, 2010

Up $ To **10**⁰⁰ Value

14345 SW. Pacific Hwy., Tigard, OR
(503) 620-3067

D87

Nestle Toll House Cafe

- Let us be your Very Best Dessert Cafe!
- Try our delicious Toll House Cookies, coffees, smoothies, ice cream and more
- Don't forget our famous Cookie Cakes - a festive treat for any occassion!
- See our website for more information - or just come on in!

12000 SE 82nd Avenue #2073
(Clackamas Town Center)
Happy Valley, OR
(503)908-0899

Offer Conditions: Valid anytime.

00780382

Great Harvest Bread

- Our breads are made from hard red spring wheat that we stone-grind into fresh flour in the bakery daily
- Most breads contain no oils or fats, no milk, no eggs & no preservatives
- Come in for a free slice of bread anytime

2105 NW 185th Hillsboro, OR (503)466-1112	540 SW Broadway Portland, OR (503)445-9908	810 S.W. Second Portland, OR (503)224-8583

Offer Conditions: Valid anytime.

00110745

Diabetic Bakery

- Full line dessert bakery that is 100% sugar free
- Tues-Sat 9am-6pm
- Closed Sun-Mon

Diabetic Bakery

14345 SW. Pacific Hwy.
Tigard, OR
(503)620-3067

Offer Conditions: Valid anytime.

00757462

Muno's Bakery

Enjoy up to TWO DOZEN COOKIES at 50% off the regular price.

Offer Conditions on reverse side.

Up To $5.00 Value

Muno's Bakery

Valid now thru November 1, 2010

616 Main St., Oregon City, OR
(503)656-4335

D88

---

 entertainment.com

A Piece of Cake

Enjoy any BAKED GOODS ORDER at 50% off the regular price.

Offer Conditions on reverse side.

Up To $5.00 Value

PIECE OF CAKE
CATERING & DESSERTS

Valid now thru November 1, 2010

8306 S.E. 17th, Portland, OR
(503)234-9445

D89

---

entertainment.com

Scoops Ice Cream Parlor

Enjoy one complimentary MENU ITEM when a second MENU ITEM of equal or greater value is purchased.

Offer Conditions on reverse side.

Up To $7.00 Value

 NEW

Valid now thru November 1, 2010

1339 Commerce Ave., Ste. 103, Longview, WA
(360)423-4986

D90

Muno's Bakery

- Pastries, breads, donuts, pies & cookies
- Established since 1938
- Located downtown Oregon City
- Specializes in cakes for all occassions

Muno's Bakery

616 Main St.
Oregon City, OR
(503)656-4335

Offer Conditions: Valid anytime.

00386129

A Piece of Cake

- Award winning wedding cakes
- Bachelorette & bachelor party cakes
- Fabulous full service catering
- Cakes, cheesecakes, tortes & more
- 9 a.m.-8 p.m. Mon.-Thur., Fri., 9 a.m.-10:30 p.m., & Sat., 10 a.m.-10:30 p.m.

PIECE OF CAKE
CATERING & DESSERTS

8306 S.E. 17th
(Sellwood Area)
Portland, OR
(503)234-9445

Offer Conditions: Valid anytime.

00077177

Scoops Ice Cream Parlor

- Ice cream, sandwiches, chili dogs, espresso & more
- Dining area perfect for families, parties, sports team gatherings
- Ice cream cakes for all occasions

1339 Commerce Ave., Ste. 103
Longview, WA
(360)423-4986

Offer Conditions: Valid anytime.

00751084

MaggieMoo's

Enjoy one complimentary
MENU ITEM when a second
MENU ITEM of equal or greater
value is purchased.

Offer Conditions on reverse side.

 PRINT MORE ONLINE

Valid now thru November 1, 2010

 Up To $6.00 Value

www.maggiemoos.com

9469 SW Washington Square Rd., Tigard, OR
(503)624-1666

D91

Baskin Robbins® Ice Cream

Enjoy one complimentary
SINGLE SCOOP CUP OR
CONE when a second SINGLE
SCOOP CUP OR CONE of
equal or greater value is
purchased.

Offer Conditions on reverse side.

Valid now thru November 1, 2010

FREE SINGLE SCOOP CUP OR CONE

baskin **BR** robbins

See Reverse Side for Locations

D92

Baskin Robbins® Ice Cream

Enjoy any ICE CREAM CAKE
OR PIE at $2.00 off the regular
price.

Offer Conditions on reverse side.

Valid now thru November 1, 2010

$2.00 OFF

baskin **BR** robbins

See Reverse Side for Locations

D93

MaggieMoo's

- It's so fresh, it moos!
- Award-winning ice cream, sorbet, non-fat ice cream
- Variety of special occasion, premium ice cream cakes like Maggiemoo's dream cake!
- Mon. - Sat. 10 a.m. - 9 p.m., Sun. 10 a.m. - 7 p.m.
- Visit our website

9469 SW Washington Square Rd.
(next to JC Penney & Starbucks)
Tigard, OR
(503)624-1666

Offer Conditions: Valid anytime.

00742024

Baskin Robbins® Ice Cream

- New elegant desserts
- Roll cakes, character cakes by Sara Lee®
- Customize your cakes (advance notice required)
- Yogurt or ice cream (where available)

OREGON
Beaverton
11421 Beaverton-Hillsdale Hwy.
(503)626-9727

16015 S.W. Walker Rd.
(503)690-8469

Gresham
1200 E. Burnside
(503)661-1449

475 N.E. 181st
(503)666-3541

Hillsboro
22035 N.W. Imbrie Dr.
(503)640-4442

23053 S.W. Tualatin-Valley Hwy.
(503)649-3299

Lake Oswego
16359 S.W. Bryant
(503)636-8832

17773A SW Lower Boones Ferry
(503)636-1999

Oregon City
1839 Molalla Ave., #F
(503)722-2191

Portland
Jantzen Beach Mall
(503)283-7937

10910 S.W. Barnes Rd.
(503)641-3100

1817 S.E. 82nd Ave.
(82nd & S.E. Mill)
(503)775-0430

4102 S.E. Powell Blvd.
(503)771-0724

5330 N. Lombard
(503)285-9039

6371 S.W. Capitol Hwy.
(503)246-2541

Sandy
36651 Sandy Marketplace Hwy. 26
(503)668-8422

Sherwood
15994 Tualatin Sherwood Rd.
(503)625-2736

Tigard
16200 SW Pacific Hwy
(503)639-3713

Wilsonville
29911 S.W. Boones Ferry Rd.
(503)570-0317

WASHINGTON
Vancouver
7411 N.E. 117th Ave.
(Fred Meyer/Orchards)
(360)254-3210

800 NE Tenney Rd., Ste. 109
(360)566-1119

8700 NE Vancouver Mall Dr. #162
(lower level by Mervyn's)
(360)256-7722

Valid at All Participating Locations

Offer Conditions: Valid anytime.

00111948

Baskin Robbins® Ice Cream

- New elegant desserts
- Roll cakes, character cakes by Sara Lee®
- Customize your cakes (advance notice required)
- Yogurt or ice cream (where available)

OREGON
Beaverton
11421 Beaverton-Hillsdale Hwy.
(503)626-9727

16015 S.W. Walker Rd.
(503)690-8469

Gladstone
19510 S.E. McLoughlin Blvd.
(503)656-0311

Gresham
1200 E. Burnside
(503)661-1449

475 N.E. 181st
(503)666-3541

Hillsboro
22035 N.W. Imbrie Dr.
(503)640-4442

23053 S.W. Tualatin-Valley Hwy.
(503)649-3299

Lake Oswego
16359 S.W. Bryant
(503)636-8832

17773A SW Lower Boones Ferry
(503)636-1999

Oregon City
1839 Molalla Ave., #F
(503)722-2191

Portland
Jantzen Beach Mall
(503)283-7937

10910 S.W. Barnes Rd.
(503)641-3100

1817 S.E. 82nd Ave.
(82nd & S.E. Mill)
(503)775-0430

4102 S.E. Powell Blvd.
(503)771-0724

5330 N. Lombard
(503)285-9039

6371 S.W. Capitol Hwy.
(503)246-2541

Sandy
36651 Sandy Marketplace Hwy. 26
(503)668-8422

Sherwood
15994 Tualatin Sherwood Rd.
(503)625-2736

Tigard
16200 SW Pacific Hwy
(503)639-3713

Wilsonville
29911 S.W. Boones Ferry Rd.
(503)570-0317

WASHINGTON
Vancouver
11600 S.E. Mill Plain Blvd., Ste. A
(360)892-5203

7411 N.E. 117th Ave.
(Fred Meyer/Orchards)
(360)254-3210

800 NE Tenney Rd., Ste. 109
(360)566-1119

8700 NE Vancouver Mall Dr. #162
(lower level by Mervyn's)
(360)256-7722

Valid at All Participating Locations

Offer Conditions: Valid anytime. $12.00 minimum. One coupon per customer per visit; Not valid with any other discount offer.

00113055

TCBY

Enjoy one complimentary
MENU ITEM when a second
MENU ITEM of equal or greater
value is purchased.
Offer Conditions on reverse side.

FREE MENU ITEM

TCBY®

See Reverse Side for Locations

Valid now thru November 1, 2010

D94

TCBY

Enjoy one complimentary
SUNDAE when a second
SUNDAE of equal or greater
value is purchased.
Offer Conditions on reverse side.

FREE SUNDAE

TCBY®

See Reverse Side for Locations

Valid now thru November 1, 2010

D95

TCBY

Enjoy one complimentary
SMALL, REGULAR or LARGE
CUP when a second SMALL,
REGULAR or LARGE CUP of
equal or greater value is
purchased.
Offer Conditions on reverse side.

ONE SMALL, REGULAR OR LARGE CUP

TCBY®

See Reverse Side for Locations

Valid now thru November 1, 2010

D96

TCBY

- The Country's Best Yogurt
- Belgian waffles, crepes & cones
- Tastes like premium ice cream
- Almost one-half the calories
- Lower cholesterol--96% fat free
- Try our new Ultra Slim Fast shakes
- Open daily

TCBY®

10117 S.E. Sunnyside Rd.
(across from Sunnyside Kaiser Hospital)
Clackamas, OR
(503)654-0399

1101 NE Burnside
Gresham, OR
(503)669-8383

933 Lloyd Center Dr
(Lloyd Center)
Portland, OR
(503)287-2432

11681 S.W. Pacific Hwy.
(next to Baja Fresh)
Tigard, OR
(503)684-0551

Offer Conditions: Valid anytime. Quarts, pints, cakes & pies excluded; Toppings extra.

00111960

TCBY

- Hot fudge sundae, black forest sundae
- Waffle bowl sundae, hot caramel sundae
- Hot fudge brownie sundae, fruit sundae
- All our yogurt is 96-97% fat free
- New non-fat & sugar free flavors

TCBY®

10117 S.E. Sunnyside Rd.
(across from Sunnyside Kaiser Hospital)
Clackamas, OR
(503)654-0399

1101 NE Burnside
Gresham, OR
(503)669-8383

933 Lloyd Center Dr
(Lloyd Center)
Portland, OR
(503)287-2432

11681 S.W. Pacific Hwy.
(next to Baja Fresh)
Tigard, OR
(503)684-0551

Offer Conditions: Valid anytime.

00111961

TCBY

- New non-fat & sugar free flavors
- New items: Yog-a-bars & cakes

TCBY®

10117 S.E. Sunnyside Rd.
(across from Sunnyside Kaiser Hospital)
Clackamas, OR
(503)654-0399

3001 West 11 Ave.
Eugene, OR
(541)345-5955

1101 NE Burnside
Gresham, OR
(503)669-8383

933 Lloyd Center Dr
(Lloyd Center)
Portland, OR
(503)287-2432

11681 S.W. Pacific Hwy.
(next to Baja Fresh)
Tigard, OR
(503)684-0551

Offer Conditions: Valid anytime. Toppings extra.

00111959

entertainment.com

Ben & Jerry's Ice Cream & Frozen Yogurt

Enjoy one complimentary ICE CREAM CONE when a second ICE CREAM CONE of equal or greater value is purchased.

Offer Conditions on reverse side.

Valid now thru November 1, 2010

FREE CONE

www.benjerry.com

See Reverse Side for Locations

D97

---

entertainment.com

Ben & Jerry's Ice Cream & Frozen Yogurt

Enjoy one complimentary ICE CREAM CONE when a second ICE CREAM CONE of equal or greater value is purchased.

Offer Conditions on reverse side.

Valid now thru November 1, 2010

2 FOR 1

www.benjerry.com/pearldistrict

See Reverse Side for Locations

D98

---

entertainment.com

ActiveCulture Frozen Yogurt

Enjoy one complimentary MENU ITEM when a second MENU ITEM of equal or greater value is purchased.

Offer Conditions on reverse side.

Valid now thru November 1, 2010

Up To $5.00 Value

ACTIVECULTURE FROZEN YOGURT

www.activeculturepdx.com

820 SE 8th Ave, Portland, OR
(503)608-7742

D99

Ben & Jerry's Ice Cream & Frozen Yogurt

- Cones, cakes, sundaes & more
- We can help you celebrate for any reason, any time & any place!
- From cow to cone, our scoop shops have all the Ben & Jerry's flavors you crave
- Vermont's finest all natural ice cream, frozen yogurt & sorbet

1428 S.E. 36th Ave.
Portland, OR
(503)234-2223

39 N.W. 23rd Place
Portland, OR
(503)295-3033

Offer Conditions: Valid anytime.

00596249

Ben & Jerry's Ice Cream & Frozen Yogurt

- Cones, cakes, sundaes, shakes, baked goods--and now low-cal smoothies!
- Let us help you with your celebrations--we cater!
- We bake our own cookies, brownies, and waffle cones in store!
- We are Vermont's all-natural ice cream, sorbet, and frozen yogurt store.
- From cow to cone, our scoop shops have all the Ben & Jerry's flavors you crave.

301 NW 10th Ave.
(on the corner of Everett Street)
Portland, OR
(503)796-3033

39 NW 23rd Place
(just off Burnside in the Uptown Shopping Center)
Portland, OR
(503)295-3033

Offer Conditions: Valid anytime.

00775431

ActiveCulture Frozen Yogurt

- Proudly serving an All Oregon product
- 50+ flavors served in rotation - 10 served daily
- Fat- free, low in calories and helpful to your digestion and immune system
- Did we mention delicious?!

ACTIVECULTURE FROZEN YOGURT

820 SE 8th Ave
(In the Grand Central Bowl Building)
Portland, OR
(503)608-7742

Offer Conditions: Valid anytime.

00751354

Orange Julius®

Enjoy one complimentary
JULIUS® FRUIT DRINK when a
second JULIUS® FRUIT DRINK
of equal or greater value is
purchased.

Offer Conditions on reverse side.

Valid now thru November 1, 2010

FREE JULIUS® FRUIT DRINK

Orange Julius®

See Reverse Side for Locations

D100

Orange Julius®

Enjoy one complimentary
JULIUS® HOT DOG when a
second JULIUS® HOT DOG
of equal or greater value is
purchased.

Offer Conditions on reverse side.

Valid now thru November 1, 2010

FREE JULIUS® HOT DOG

Orange Julius®

See Reverse Side for Locations

D101

Orange Julius®

Enjoy one complimentary
LIGHT PREMIUM FRUIT
SMOOTHIE when a second
LIGHT PREMIUM FRUIT
SMOOTHIE of equal or greater
value is purchased.

Offer Conditions on reverse side.

Valid now thru November 1, 2010

FREE LIGHT PREMIUM FRUIT SMOOTHIE

Orange Julius®

See Reverse Side for Locations

D102

Orange Julius®

Orange Julius.

OREGON
Albany
1895 14th Ave. S.E.
(Heritage Mall)
(541)791-9524

Eugene
293 Valley River Ctr.
(Valley River Center)
(541)683-8578

Happy Valley
12000 S.E. 82nd
(Clackamas Town Center)
(503)305-6603

Medford
1600 N. Riverside Ave.
(Rogue Valley Mall)
(541)772-8650

North Bend
1611 Virginia
(Pony Village Mall)
(541)756-7775

Portland
2201 Lloyd Ctr.
(Lloyd Center Mall)
(503)287-2627

Roseburg
1444 N.W. Garden Valley Blvd.
(Roseburg Valley Mall)
(503)672-9698

Salem
401 Center St. N.E.
(Salem Center)
(503)364-3503

831 Lancaster Drive N.E.
(Lancaster Mall)
(503)363-8961

Tigard
9585 S.W. Washington Square Rd.
(Washington Square Mall)
(503)620-7282

WASHINGTON
Vancouver
8700 N.E. Vancouver Mall Dr.
(Vancouver Mall)
(360)254-0403

Offer Conditions: Valid anytime.

00193889

Orange Julius®

Orange Julius.

OREGON
Albany
1895 14th Ave. S.E.
(Heritage Mall)
(541)791-9524

Eugene
293 Valley River Ctr.
(Valley River Center)
(541)683-8578

Happy Valley
12000 S.E. 82nd
(Clackamas Town Center)
(503)305-6603

Medford
1600 N. Riverside Ave.
(Rogue Valley Mall)
(541)772-8650

North Bend
1611 Virginia
(Pony Village Mall)
(541)756-7775

Portland
2201 Lloyd Ctr.
(Lloyd Center Mall)
(503)287-2627

Roseburg
1444 N.W. Garden Valley Blvd.
(Roseburg Valley Mall)
(503)672-9698

Salem
401 Center St. N.E.
(Salem Center)
(503)364-3503

831 Lancaster Drive N.E.
(Lancaster Mall)
(503)363-8961

Tigard
9585 S.W. Washington Square Rd.
(Washington Square Mall)
(503)620-7282

WASHINGTON
Vancouver
8700 N.E. Vancouver Mall Dr.
(Vancouver Mall)
(360)254-0403

Offer Conditions: Valid anytime.

00034176

Orange Julius®

Orange Julius.

OREGON
Albany
1895 14th Ave. S.E.
(Heritage Mall)
(541)791-9524

Eugene
293 Valley River Ctr.
(Valley River Center)
(541)683-8578

Happy Valley
12000 S.E. 82nd
(Clackamas Town Center)
(503)305-6603

Medford
1600 N. Riverside Ave.
(Rogue Valley Mall)
(541)772-8650

North Bend
1611 Virginia
(Pony Village Mall)
(541)756-7775

Portland
2201 Lloyd Ctr.
(Lloyd Center Mall)
(503)287-2627

Roseburg
1444 N.W. Garden Valley Blvd.
(Roseburg Valley Mall)
(503)672-9698

Salem
401 Center St. N.E.
(Salem Center)
(503)364-3503

831 Lancaster Drive N.E.
(Lancaster Mall)
(503)363-8961

Tigard
9585 S.W. Washington Square Rd.
(Washington Square Mall)
(503)620-7282

WASHINGTON
Vancouver
8700 N.E. Vancouver Mall Dr.
(Vancouver Mall)
(360)254-0403

Offer Conditions: Valid anytime.

00034181

Firestone Farms Ice Cream Shop

Enjoy one complimentary
MENU ITEM when a second
MENU ITEM of equal or greater
value is purchased.
Offer Conditions on reverse side.

Valid now thru November 1, 2010

ICE CREAM SHOP

18400 N. Hwy. 99 W, Dayton, OR
(503)864-2672

D103

Tropical Smoothie Cafe

Enjoy one complimentary
MENU ITEM when a second
MENU ITEM of equal or greater
value is purchased.
Offer Conditions on reverse side.

Valid now thru November 1, 2010

www.tropicalsmoothie.com

See Reverse Side for Locations

D104

Urban Grind Coffee House & Roasters

Enjoy one complimentary
MENU ITEM when a second
MENU ITEM of equal or greater
value is purchased.
Offer Conditions on reverse side.

Valid now thru November 1, 2010

Coffeehouse & Roasters
www.urbangrindcoffee.com

See Reverse Side for Locations

D105

More Offers Online!

FAST FOOD & CARRYOUT

entertainment.com

Firestone Farms Ice Cream Shop

- Farm fresh fruits & vegetables
- Wine & gifts
- Family owned & operated
- Ice cream shop
- Flower shop
- Open 7 days a week

ICE CREAM SHOP

18400 N. Hwy. 99 W
Dayton, OR
(503)864-2672

Offer Conditions: Valid anytime.

00606767

Tropical Smoothie Cafe

- Smoothies, Sandwiches, Wraps and More!
- Try a supercharged smoothie, low-fat smoothie or maybe a dessert smoothie
- Add a gourmet wrap, sandwich, or breakfast bagel
- Eat better, Feel better

1902 W. Burnside St
Portland, OR
(503)206-6702

16020 SE Mill Plain Blvd #117
Vancouver, WA
(360)891-8418

Offer Conditions: Valid anytime. Excludes Combos.

00765048

Urban Grind Coffee House & Roasters

- Connect with neighbors while enjoying house-roasted coffee and delicious food
- Many vegan and vegetarian options
- We support local and organic suppliers whenever possible
- Event space (and ping pong) available at our NE location
- Open late in the Pearl

Coffeehouse & Roasters

2214 NE Oregon Street
(off Sandy)
Portland, OR
(503)546-0649

911 NW 14th Avenue
(at Kearny St.)
Portland, OR
(503)546-5919

Offer Conditions: Valid anytime.

00771270

Fehrenbacher Hof

Enjoy any FOOD ORDER at 50% off the regular price.
Offer Conditions on reverse side.

$6.00 Value

FEHRENBACHER HOF

Portland, Oregon

NEW

Valid now thru November 1, 2010

1225 SW 19th Avenue, Portland, OR
(503) 223-4493

D106

The Human Bean

Enjoy any BEVERAGE ORDER at 50% off the regular price.
Offer Conditions on reverse side.

$5.00 Value

THE HUMAN BEAN

www.thehumanbean.com

NEW

Valid now thru November 1, 2010

998 SE Oak Street, Hillsboro, OR
(503) 577-3415

D107

Tango Coffee Bar

Enjoy one complimentary MENU ITEM when a second MENU ITEM of equal or greater value is purchased.
Offer Conditions on reverse side.

Up To $7.00 Value

Tango Coffee Bar

NEW

Valid now thru November 1, 2010

1023 S.W. Yamhill St., Portland, OR
(503) 227-0487

D108

Fehrenbacher Hof

- Owned by famous former Portland Mayor, Bud Clark
- Handcrafted espresso and coffees from Ristretto and Longbottom Roasters
- Whole leaf teas and tea lattes
- Cobblestone patio and heated covered porch
- Homemade pastries and soups
- Legendary, satisfying breakfast sandwiches and burritos
- Delicious deli sandwiches made to order
- Free WI-FI; upstairs meeting room too

FEHRENBACHER HOF

Portland, Oregon

1225 SW 19th Avenue
(right next to the Goose Hollow Inn)
Portland, OR
(503)223-4493

Offer Conditions: Valid anytime.

00780964

The Human Bean

- Drive-thru convenience
- Espresso drinks, coffee, tea, smoothies, pastries, sandwiches, and other assorted items.
- New: Cocoa Velvet chocolates!
- We not only purchase and roast exceptional coffees, but we are also committed to being responsible global citizens.
- Check out our Farm-Friendly Direct program on our fun and informative website.

THE HUMAN BEAN

998 SE Oak Street
(at SE 10th)
Hillsboro, OR
(503)577-3415

Offer Conditions: Valid anytime.

00780019

Tango Coffee Bar

- Proudly serving locally-roasted Nossa Familia coffee
- Charming Victorian ambiance with fireplace
- Mid-downtown location
- Free WiFi
- Open daily for breakfast & lunch until 5 p.m.
- Delicious soups, salads, paninis & bagels with fresh toppings
- Across the street from the Central Library

Tango Coffee Bar

1023 S.W. Yamhill St.
Portland, OR
(503)227-0487

Offer Conditions: Valid anytime.

00773252

Tea Chai Te'

- Best bubble tea in Portland
- Over 100 varieties of tea & herbal medicinals
- Chai blends from scratch
- Top-grade specialties, including pastries
- House-brewed Kombucha
- Open every day from 10 a.m.-10 p.m

734 NW 23rd Ave.
(Near NW Johnson, upstairs with an outdoor balcony)
Portland, OR
(503)228-0900

Offer Conditions: Valid anytime.

00781986

Old Town Battle Grounds A Coffee House

- Proudly serving Stumptown coffee
- Best overall coffee in Battle Ground
- Sandwiches, soups & salads daily
- M - F 6 a.m. - 6 p.m.
- Sat 7 a.m. - 5 p.m.
- Sun 7:30 a.m. - 5 p.m.

OLD TOWN
BATTLE GROUNDS
A Coffee House

113 E. Main St.
(on Main St. in Old Town Battle Ground)
Battle Ground, WA
(360)666-2441

Offer Conditions: Valid anytime.

00757806

Sip & Kranz

- Serving famous Stumptown coffee
- Nuvrei Pastries, Kettleman bagels, Portland style cheesecake & cupcakes
- Free WiFi
- Business room for meetings
- Private party hosting
- Outdoor seating on Jameson Park

901 N.W. 10th Ave.
Portland, OR
(503)336-1335

Offer Conditions: Valid anytime.

00773262

Caffe' Umbria

Enjoy any BEVERAGE ORDER at 50% off the regular price.
Offer Conditions on reverse side.

Valid now thru November 1, 2010

303 NW 12th Ave, Portland, OR
(503)241-5300

D112

Guse Coffee Roasters

Enjoy one complimentary MENU ITEM when a second MENU ITEM of equal or greater value is purchased.
Offer Conditions on reverse side.

Valid now thru November 1, 2010

1208 Commerce Ave, Longview, WA
(360)425-8940

D113

Cellar Door Coffee Roasters

Enjoy any BEVERAGE ORDER at 50% off the regular price.
Offer Conditions on reverse side.

www.cellardoorcoffee.com

2001 S.E. 11th, Portland, OR
(505)234-7155

D114

Valid now thru November 1, 2010

Caffe' Umbria

- Authentic Italian Cafe' Bar
- Italian-style espresso & coffee roasted in Seattle
- Panini & other light Italian fare, including pastries & gelato
- Live music every first Thursday of the month
- Televised soccer games & Italian movies
- Open daily

303 NW 12th Ave
(At Davis St.)
Portland, OR
(503)241-5300

Offer Conditions: Valid anytime.

00772343

Offer validity is governed by the Rules of Use and excludes defined holidays. Offers are not valid with other discount offers, unless specified. Coupons void if purchased, sold or bartered. Discounts exclude tax, tip and/or alcohol, where applicable.

Guse Coffee Roasters

- Free WiFi
- Been locally owned 22 years
- All organic
- Roasting daily for 22 years
- Great for meetings

1208 Commerce Ave
Longview, WA
(360)425-8940

Offer Conditions: Valid anytime.

00759514

Offer validity is governed by the Rules of Use and excludes defined holidays. Offers are not valid with other discount offers, unless specified. Coupons void if purchased, sold or bartered. Discounts exclude tax, tip and/or alcohol, where applicable.

Cellar Door Coffee Roasters

- Fresh roasted coffee, roasted in small batches with close attention to detail
- Sample our selection of the finest green coffees from aournd the world
- We are committed to bring you nothing short of excellence

2001 S.E. 11th
Portland, OR
(505)234-7155

Offer Conditions: Valid anytime.

00741553

Offer validity is governed by the Rules of Use and excludes defined holidays. Offers are not valid with other discount offers, unless specified. Coupons void if purchased, sold or bartered. Discounts exclude tax, tip and/or alcohol, where applicable.

Doctor's Choice Coffee Roasters

Enjoy one complimentary
MENU ITEM when a second
MENU ITEM of equal or greater
value is purchased.

Offer Conditions on reverse side.

Up To $5.00 Value

Valid now thru November 1, 2010

1250 Atlantic Ave, Woodland, WA
(360)225-5200

D115

Blue Star Espresso

Enjoy one complimentary
MENU ITEM when a second
MENU ITEM of equal or greater
value is purchased.

Offer Conditions on reverse side.

Up To $5.00 Value

Valid now thru November 1, 2010

See Reverse Side for Locations

D116

Backspace

Enjoy one complimentary
MENU ITEM when a second
MENU ITEM of equal or greater
value is purchased.

Offer Conditions on reverse side.

Up To $7.00 Value

BACKSPACE
NETWORK GAMING :: CAFE :: GALLERY

Valid now thru November 1, 2010

www.backspace.biz

115 N.W. 5th, Portland, OR
(503)248-2900

D117

Doctor's Choice Coffee Roasters

- Freshly Roasted
- None better
- Meeting space available

1250 Atlantic Ave
Woodland, WA
(360)225-5200

Offer Conditions: Valid anytime.

00759509

Blue Star Espresso

- Serving long bottom coffee & tea
- Full service coffee bar
- Delicious pastries & treats
- Fruit smoothies
- Drive Thru

1101 Main Ave.
Tillamook, OR
(503)842-0011

940 N. Main Ave.
Tillamook, OR
(503)842-2583

Offer Conditions: Valid anytime.

00687836

Backspace

- An exciting entertainment mecca in an industrial funk atmosphere
- Network gaming
- Wireless computers & work areas
- Cafe proudly serving Stumptown coffee & Hot Lips pizza
- Open til 2:00 a.m. nightly

115 N.W. 5th
Portland, OR
(503)248-2900

Offer Conditions: Valid anytime.

00650048

Park Place Coffee

Enjoy one complimentary
MENU ITEM when a second
MENU ITEM of equal or greater
value is purchased.
Offer Conditions on reverse side.

Up 5^{00} To Value

www.parkplacecoffee.com

1288 S.E. 182nd, Portland, OR
(503) 808-1244

PRINT MORE ONLINE

Valid now thru November 1, 2010

D118

Java The Hut

Enjoy one complimentary
MENU ITEM when a second
MENU ITEM of equal or greater
value is purchased.
Offer Conditions on reverse side.

Up 5^{00} To Value

PRINT MORE ONLINE

Valid now thru November 1, 2010

2900 Haworth, Newburg, OR
(503) 554-0956

D119

Coffee Romance

Enjoy any BEVERAGE ORDER
at 50% off the regular price.
Offer Conditions on reverse side.

Up 5^{00} To Value

Valid now thru November 1, 2010

7901 SE Powell #K, Portland, OR
(503) 777-8626

D120

More Offers Online!

FAST FOOD & CARRYOUT

entertainment.com

Park Place Coffee

- Coffee, Crepes & Community
- One step inside our door & you are invited to become part of something bigger - a community
- Offering a variety of drinks, snacks & crepes

1288 S.E. 182nd
Portland, OR
(503)808-1244

Offer Conditions: Valid anytime.

00720821

Java The Hut

- More than just coffee
- Full espresso bar
- Flavored coffee drinks, hot or cold
- Italian sodas, smoothies
- Tasty pastries
- Fast friendly service

Java The Hut

2900 Haworth
Newburg, OR
(503)554-0956

Offer Conditions: Valid anytime.

00614849

Coffee Romance

- Serving gourmet Longbottom coffee & tea
- Specialty baked goods
- Special espresso drinks & Italian sodas
- Have a coffee & relax in our comfortable lounge chairs
- Open 7 days a week

7901 SE Powell #K
Portland, OR
(503)777-8626

Offer Conditions: Valid anytime.

00303285

entertainment.com

Koffee Krazy

Enjoy one complimentary
MENU ITEM when a second
MENU ITEM of equal or greater
value is purchased.
Offer Conditions on reverse side.

Up 5^{00} To Value

KOFFEE KRAZY

PRINT MORE
ONLINE

Valid now thru November 1, 2010

9113 S.W. Barbur Blvd., Portland, OR
(503)244-3202

D121

entertainment.com

Francesca's Coffee House

Enjoy one complimentary
MENU ITEM when a second
MENU ITEM of equal or greater
value is purchased.
Offer Conditions on reverse side.

Up 5^{00} To Value

**Francesca's
Coffee House**

PRINT MORE
ONLINE

Valid now thru November 1, 2010

1220 N. Pacific Hwy., Woodburn, OR
(503)981-0665

D122

---

entertainment.com

Incahoots

Enjoy one complimentary
MENU ITEM when a second
MENU ITEM of equal or greater
value is purchased.
Offer Conditions on reverse side.

Up 5^{00} To Value

Plants ❀ Flowers ❀ Gifts
incahoots

Valid now thru November 1, 2010

905 N.E. Baker St., McMinnville, OR
(503)472-4923

D123

More Offers Online!

FAST FOOD & CARRYOUT

entertainment.com

Koffee Krazy

- What are you thinking about right now?
- Coffee?.... ice cream?.... pastries?... espresso?.... sandwiches?
- We have all this & more!
- Great for staff meetings
- We proudly serve Allann Bros. Coffee & Umpqua Ice Cream
- Easy access parking & outdoor seating

KOFFEE KRAZY

9113 S.W. Barbur Blvd.
Portland, OR
(503)244-3202

Offer Conditions: Valid anytime.

00605340

Francesca's Coffee House

- We proudly serve Koloo's coffee
- Homemade soup from 11:30 a.m.-2 p.m.
- Espresso, mocha's & lattes
- Fresh baked pastries & goodies
- Awesome gift shop
- Phone orders welcome

Francesca's Coffee House

1220 N. Pacific Hwy.
(located in Al's Garden Ctr.)
Woodburn, OR
(503)981-0665

Offer Conditions: Valid anytime.

00633108

Incahoots

- Organic coffee & espresso drinks
- Over 100 teas
- Coffee & tea accessories
- Flowers, plants, gifts, books & music
- Mon.-Sat. 9:30 a.m.-5:30 p.m.
- Closed Sunday

Plants ❀ Flowers ❀ Gifts
incahoots

905 N.E. Baker St.
McMinnville, OR
(503)472-4923

Offer Conditions: Valid anytime. Specials excluded.

00653362

Seasons Coffee, Tea & Remedies

Enjoy one complimentary MENU ITEM when a second MENU ITEM of equal or greater value is purchased.

Offer Conditions on reverse side.

Valid now thru November 1, 2010

113 N. Main, Ridgefield, WA
(360)887-7260

D124

---

entertainment.com

Leann's Lattes

Enjoy one BEVERAGE ORDER at 50% off the regular price - maximum discount $5.00.

Offer Conditions on reverse side.

Valid now thru November 1, 2010

2375 NW Hwy 99W, McMinnville, OR
(503)435-1264

D125

---

entertainment.com

Coffee on the Corner

Enjoy any FOOD/BEVERAGE ORDER at 50% off the regular price.

Offer Conditions on reverse side.

Valid now thru November 1, 2010

Up To $5.00 Value

3021 NE 72nd Dr., Ste. 11, Vancouver, WA
(360)891-4835

D126

Seasons Coffee, Tea & Remedies

- Serving Portland Roasting Coffees, Mighty Leaf Tea & variety of goodies to sooth your soul!
- Dryers Ice Cream & fruit smoothies
- Friendly atmosphere
- Live entertainment most weekends - see www.oldlibertytheater.com
- Have cart, will cater!

COFFEE, TEA & REMEDIES

113 N. Main
Ridgefield, WA
(360)887-7260

Offer Conditions: Valid anytime.

00633045

Leann's Lattes

- Latte, Espresso, Mocha, Cappuccino
- Americano, Italian Soda, Cremosa, Granita
- Iced or Hot Espresso Shakes
- Open daily

2375 NW Hwy 99W
(in Wal-Mart parking lot)
McMinnville, OR
(503)435-1264

Offer Conditions: Valid anytime.

00352294

Coffee on the Corner

- Espresso - coffee - tea - blended cold drinks - bagels - pastries - sandwiches - soups - salads - specialties
- Box lunches, too!

3021 NE 72nd Dr., Ste. 11
(4th Plain & Andresen)
Vancouver, WA
(360)891-4835

Offer Conditions: Valid anytime.

00498322

Space Monkey Coffee

Enjoy one complimentary
MENU ITEM when a second
MENU ITEM of equal or greater
value is purchased.
Offer Conditions on reverse side.

PRINT MORE ONLINE

Valid now thru November 1, 2010

Up To $5.00 Value

SPACE MONKEY COFFEE

5511 S.E. 72nd Ave., Portland, OR
(503)772-3028

D127

Delightful Coffee

Enjoy one BEVERAGE ORDER
at 50% off the regular price.
Offer Conditions on reverse side.

Valid now thru November 1, 2010

Up To $5.00 Value

6115 S.W. Murray Blvd., Beaverton, OR
(503)520-1804

D128

Karma Cafe Espresso & Bubble Tea

Enjoy one complimentary
MENU ITEM when a second
MENU ITEM of equal or greater
value is purchased.
Offer Conditions on reverse side.

Valid now thru November 1, 2010

Up To $5.00 Value

KARMA CAFE
ESPRESSO & BUBBLE TEA

www.karmacafe.net

8220 S.E. Harrison St., #115, Portland, OR
(503)772-1500

D129

More Offers Online!

FAST FOOD & CARRYOUT

entertainment.com

Space Monkey Coffee
- Live music on weekends
- Local art on display
- Fair trade organic coffee
- French press coffees
- Across from Mt. Scott Pool & Community Center
- Family & community oriented

SPACE MONKEY COFFEE

5511 S.E. 72nd Ave.
(By Mt. Scott Pool)
Portland, OR
(503)772-3028

Offer Conditions: Valid anytime.

00619042

Delightful Coffee
- Frappe, mochas, lattes & espresso
- Many flavors to choose from
- Pastries, cookies & bagels
- Smoothies, assorted juices & teas
- Open daily

6115 S.W. Murray Blvd.
Beaverton, OR
(503)520-1804

Offer Conditions: Valid anytime.

00496063

Karma Cafe Espresso & Bubble Tea
- Open Mon. - Sat. 8 a.m. - 11 p.m. & Sun. 9 a.m. - 8 p.m.
- Free Wi-Fi access
- We serve Stumptown Coffee

KARMA CAFE
ESPRESSO & BUBBLE TEA

8220 S.E. Harrison St., #115
(Universal Center - 82nd & Harrison)
Portland, OR
(503)772-1500

Offer Conditions: Valid anytime.

00608693

Cinnabon

Enjoy ONE FOUR PACK CLASSIC EXPRESS when a second FOUR PACK CLASSIC EXPRESS of equal or greater value is purchased.
Offer Conditions on reverse side.

Valid now thru November 1, 2010

www.cinnabon.com

See Reverse Side for Locations

D130

Wetzel's Pretzels

Enjoy one complimentary MENU ITEM when a second MENU ITEM of equal or greater value is purchased.
Offer Conditions on reverse side.

PRINT MORE ONLINE

Valid now thru November 1, 2010

FREE MENU ITEM

www.wetzels.com

2201 Lloyd Ctr., Portland, OR
(503) 281-6630

D131

Upper Crust Bread Company

Enjoy UP TO 2 DOZEN COOKIES at 50% off the regular price or 50% off the regular price of any MUFFINS OR CINNAMON ROLLS - maximum discount $5.00.
Offer Conditions on reverse side.

Valid now thru November 1, 2010

41 B. Ave., Lake Oswego, OR
(503) 697-9747

D132

More Offers Online!

FAST FOOD & CARRYOUT

entertainment.com

Cinnabon

- World famous cinnamon rolls
- Try our classic Cinnabon or a Minibon, Caramel Pecanbon or Cinnabon Stix
- Each Cinnabon is baked fresh before your eyes & served hot out of the oven
- Express packs are packed & ready to take home to your family & friends

2497 S.E. Burnside Rd.
(Inside Fred Meyer)
Gresham, OR
(503)492-3487

23105 S.W. Tualatin Valley Hwy.
(Inside Fred Meyer)
Hillsboro, OR
(503)649-0880

401 Salem Center Dr.
(Salem Center Mall)
Salem, OR
(503)585-6100

8700 N.E. Vancouver Mall Dr.,
Ste. 137
(Westfield Shpg. Towne)
Vancouver, WA
(360)253-9743

Offer Conditions: Valid anytime.

00631837

Wetzel's Pretzels

- Always served fresh
- Over 100 million rolled!
- Try our garlic, cheese or cinnamon varieties
- Dip your pretzel in pizza sauce, cheddar cheese or even caramel

2201 Lloyd Ctr.
Portland, OR
(503)281-6630

Offer Conditions: Valid anytime.

00682708

Upper Crust Bread Company

- A cut above the rest
- Dedicated to providing the best bread, cookies & other pastries
- Located in Lake Oswego on State St., next to Jamba Juice

41 B. Ave.
Lake Oswego, OR
(503)697-9747

Offer Conditions: Valid anytime.

00384537

Low Carb Nation Gourmet Market & Creamery

Enjoy one complimentary MENU ITEM when a second MENU ITEM of equal or greater value is purchased.

Offer Conditions on reverse side.

Up$ **$5**^{00} To Value

www.lowcarbnation.com

17937 S.W. McEwan Rd., #100, Tigard, OR
(503)639-6262

Valid now thru November 1, 2010

D133

Honeybaked

Enjoy one complimentary SANDWICH when a second SANDWICH of equal or greater value is purchased.

Offer Conditions on reverse side.

FREE SANDWICH

THE HONEYBAKED HAM COMPANY

See Reverse Side for Locations

Valid now thru November 1, 2010

D134

All Sports Pizzeria

Enjoy any one PIZZA at 50% off the regular price.

Offer Conditions on reverse side.

50%OFF

ALL SPORTS PIZZERIA

121 E. 4th St., La Center, WA
(360)263-6426

Valid now thru November 1, 2010

D135

Low Carb Nation Gourmet Market & Creamery

- The Northwest's largest selection of low-carb & sugar free food
- Taste why people drive for miles for our ice cream!!
- Try our famous ice cream, milkshakes or homemade ice cream sandwiches
- Only 1 Weight Watcher point per cup
- Browse our other low carb, low fat, low calorie & sugar free products
- Open 10 a.m.-7 p.m. daily

LOW CARB *Nation*
Gourmet Market & Creamery

17937 S.W. McEwan Rd., #100
(I-5 exit 290 Lake Oswego)
Tigard, OR
(503)639-6262

Offer Conditions: Valid anytime.

00579813

Honeybaked

- Open for lunch and dinner, 7 days a week
- Sandwiches, soups and salads made fresh daily
- Ham and Turkey sandwiches, dinners, roasts and ribs
- Ready to serve Ham
- National shipping call: 1-800-367-2426

THE HONEYBAKED HAM
Est. 1957
COMPANY

11657 SW Beaverton
Hillsdale Hwy
(Beaverton Towne Square)
Beaverton, OR
(503)646-4446

5331 SW Macadam,
Suite 276
(Water Tower Building)
Portland, OR
(503)243-1181

480 Center St NE
(City Center Mall)
Salem, OR
(503)585-5300

Offer Conditions: Valid anytime.

00741160

All Sports Pizzeria

- Pizza by the slice or by the whole
- Choose from our delicious selection of toppings
- Game room available for private parties
- Great place to bring your school team, family or just yourself

ALL SPORTS PIZZERIA

121 E. 4th St.
La Center, WA
(360)263-6426

Offer Conditions: Valid anytime.

00731177

ENTERTAINMENT & SPORTS INDEX

ENTERTAINMENT & SPORTS INDEX

To search by area, see the **Neighborhood Index** located at the back of your book.

Entertainment & Sports Index

Looking for a certain merchant?
Go to **www.entertainment.com** to search for hundreds
of online printable coupons not found in your book.

OR

Visit **www.entertainment.com/choice** to tell us about
a place you'd like to see a coupon for.

To search by area, see the **Neighborhood Index** located at the back of your book

= **Print more coupons online at www.entertainment.com**, up to once a month
with these Repeat Savings® merchants. See the Rules of Use for more details.

KID'S CLUB FUN & FITNESS

3 levels of The ULTIMATE adventure...

JUNGLELAND BALLOCITY

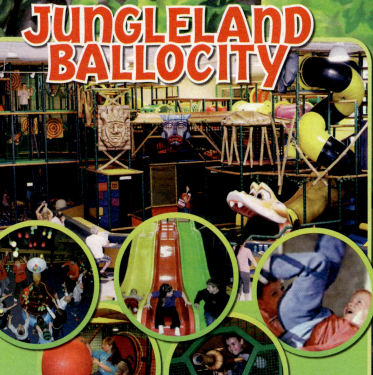

Call us! (360) 546-KIDS (5437)

www.kidsclubfunandfitness.com

13914 NW 3RD CT. • VANCOUVER, WA 98685

KID'S CLUB FUN & FITNESS

Birthday Parties!

So Many Great Themes!

- Princess Ballerina
- Bounce House
- Jungle Safari
- Super Hero
- Pirate
- Gladiator
- Pool Party
- Weird Science
- Funtastic Gymnastics

We take care of EVERYTHING, you just bring the kid

ALL Kids Club Parties include:
- private party room
- all setup & cleanup
- all paper goods
- party hosts

Deluxe and Ultimate upgrades available!!!

Call us! (360) 546-KIDS (5437)
www.kidsclubfunandfitness.com

13914 NW 3RD CT. • VANCOUVER, WA 98685

jazzercise®

Burn up to 500 calories in one
60-minute total body workout
that's pure fun.

jazzercise.com • (800)FIT-IS-IT

ENTERTAINMENT & SPORTS

**Think Jazzercise faded out with acid wash? Think again.
Blast fat and rock your core with this fusion of jazz dance, resistance
training, Pilates, yoga, and kickboxing.
Start redefining your body today.**

jazzercise.com • (800)FIT-IS-IT

Discounted Movie Tickets!

Two Easy Ways:

1 *REDEEM THE COUPONS FROM YOUR BOOK RIGHT AT THE THEATRE'S BOX OFFICE.*

Present your coupon at the time of purchase and get an instant discount.

2 *GET DISCOUNTED MOVIE TICKETS MAILED DIRECTLY TO YOUR HOME.*

Go to **www.entertainment.com/movies** to purchase discounted movie tickets online. With discounts as much as 35% off general admission it's easier than ever to get value delivered to you, and it makes a great gift too!

www.entertainment.com/movies

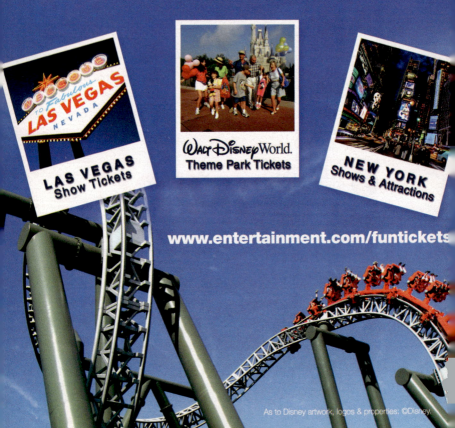

Save Up to 50% on Theme Parks, Shows & Attractions Nationwide.

LAS VEGAS
Show Tickets

Walt Disney World.
Theme Park Tickets

NEW YORK
Shows & Attractions

www.entertainment.com/funtickets

MOVIE TICKETS
REDEEM AT THEATRE

Purchase up to two(2) *VIP Super Saver Admission Tickets
or only $7.00 each. Upgrade to an "UNRESTRICTED"
Premiere Super Saver Admission Ticket
for only $1.50 extra per ticket.

Limit 2 Admission Tickets Per Coupon.

Subject to Rules of Use. Coupons VOID if purchased,
sold or bartered for cash.

See reverse side offer details.

E3

Valid now thru November 1, 2010

Offer validity is governed by the Rules of Use and excludes defined holidays.
Offers are not valid with other discount offers, unless specified.

MOVIE TICKETS
REDEEM AT THEATRE

Purchase up to two(2) *VIP Super Saver Admission Tickets
for only $7.00 each. Upgrade to an "UNRESTRICTED"
Premiere Super Saver Admission Ticket
for only $1.50 extra per ticket.

Limit 2 Admission Tickets Per Coupon.

Subject to Rules of Use. Coupons VOID if purchased,
sold or bartered for cash.

See reverse side offer details.

E4

Valid now thru November 1, 2010

Offer validity is governed by the Rules of Use and excludes defined holidays.
Offers are not valid with other discount offers, unless specified.

MOVIE TICKETS
REDEEM AT THEATRE

Purchase up to two(2) *VIP Super Saver Admission Tickets
or only $7.00 each. Upgrade to an "UNRESTRICTED"
Premiere Super Saver Admission Ticket
for only $1.50 extra per ticket.

Limit 2 Admission Tickets Per Coupon.

Subject to Rules of Use. Coupons VOID if purchased,
sold or bartered for cash.

See reverse side offer details.

E5

Valid now thru November 1, 2010

Offer validity is governed by the Rules of Use and excludes defined holidays.
Offers are not valid with other discount offers, unless specified.

MOVIE TICKETS
REDEEM AT THEATRE

Purchase up to two(2) *VIP Super Saver Admission Tickets
for only $7.00 each. Upgrade to an "UNRESTRICTED"
Premiere Super Saver Admission Ticket
for only $1.50 extra per ticket.

Limit 2 Admission Tickets Per Coupon.

Subject to Rules of Use. Coupons VOID if purchased,
sold or bartered for cash.

See reverse side offer details.

E6

Valid now thru November 1, 2010

Offer validity is governed by the Rules of Use and excludes defined holidays.
Offers are not valid with other discount offers, unless specified.

MOVIE TICKETS
REDEEM AT THEATRE

Purchase up to two(2) *VIP Super Saver Admission Tickets
r only $7.00 each. Upgrade to an "UNRESTRICTED"
Premiere Super Saver Admission Ticket
for only $1.50 extra per ticket.

Limit 2 Admission Tickets Per Coupon.

Subject to Rules of Use. Coupons VOID if purchased,
sold or bartered for cash.

See reverse side offer details.

E7

Valid now thru November 1, 2010

er validity is governed by the Rules of Use and excludes defined holidays.
ers are not valid with other discount offers, unless specified.

MOVIE TICKETS
REDEEM AT THEATRE

Purchase up to two(2) *VIP Super Saver Admission Tickets
for only $7.00 each. Upgrade to an "UNRESTRICTED"
Premiere Super Saver Admission Ticket
for only $1.50 extra per ticket.

Limit 2 Admission Tickets Per Coupon.

Subject to Rules of Use. Coupons VOID if purchased,
sold or bartered for cash.

See reverse side offer details.

E8

Valid now thru November 1, 2010

Offer validity is governed by the Rules of Use and excludes defined holidays.
Offers are not valid with other discount offers, unless specified.

Visit www.REGmovies.com for locations and showtime information.

VIP Super Saver ticket is not valid during the first 12 days of "Selected" new release films, special engagements or where prohibited by contractual obligations. **$1.50 UPGRADE FEE MAY BE PAID AT THE BOX OFFICE FOR ADMISSION TO THESE "SELECTED" NEW RELEASE FILMS. Not valid for special events or private screenings. Surcharge Fees apply to all IMAX, Large Format or 3-D Films and Manhattan, NY locations.** Regal Entertainment Group reserves the right to change any upgrade or surcharge fee without notice.

ET1009251996

00770115

Visit www.REGmovies.com for locations and showtime information.

VIP Super Saver ticket is not valid during the first 12 days of "Selected" new release films, special engagements or where prohibited by contractual obligations. **$1.50 UPGRADE FEE MAY BE PAID AT THE BOX OFFICE FOR ADMISSION TO THESE "SELECTED" NEW RELEASE FILMS. Not valid for special events or private screenings. Surcharge Fees apply to all IMAX, Large Format or 3-D Films and Manhattan, NY locations.** Regal Entertainment Group reserves the right to change any upgrade or surcharge fee without notice.

ET1009251996

00770115

Visit www.REGmovies.com for locations and showtime information.

VIP Super Saver ticket is not valid during the first 12 days of "Selected" new release films, special engagements or where prohibited by contractual obligations. **$1.50 UPGRADE FEE MAY BE PAID AT THE BOX OFFICE FOR ADMISSION TO THESE "SELECTED" NEW RELEASE FILMS. Not valid for special events or private screenings. Surcharge Fees apply to all IMAX, Large Format or 3-D Films and Manhattan, NY locations.** Regal Entertainment Group reserves the right to change any upgrade or surcharge fee without notice.

ET1009251996

00770115

Visit www.REGmovies.com for locations and showtime information.

VIP Super Saver ticket is not valid during the first 12 days of "Selected" new release films, special engagements or where prohibited by contractual obligations. **$1.50 UPGRADE FEE MAY BE PAID AT THE BOX OFFICE FOR ADMISSION TO THESE "SELECTED" NEW RELEASE FILMS. Not valid for special events or private screenings. Surcharge Fees apply to all IMAX, Large Format or 3-D Films and Manhattan, NY locations.** Regal Entertainment Group reserves the right to change any upgrade or surcharge fee without notice.

ET1009251996

00770115

Visit www.REGmovies.com for locations and showtime information.

VIP Super Saver ticket is not valid during the first 12 days of "Selected" new release films, special engagements or where prohibited by contractual obligations. **$1.50 UPGRADE FEE MAY BE PAID AT THE BOX OFFICE FOR ADMISSION TO THESE "SELECTED" NEW RELEASE FILMS. Not valid for special events or private screenings. Surcharge Fees apply to all IMAX, Large Format or 3-D Films and Manhattan, NY locations.** Regal Entertainment Group reserves the right to change any upgrade or surcharge fee without notice.

ET1009251996

00770115

Visit www.REGmovies.com for locations and showtime information.

VIP Super Saver ticket is not valid during the first 12 days of "Selected" new release films, special engagements or where prohibited by contractual obligations. **$1.50 UPGRADE FEE MAY BE PAID AT THE BOX OFFICE FOR ADMISSION TO THESE "SELECTED" NEW RELEASE FILMS. Not valid for special events or private screenings. Surcharge Fees apply to all IMAX, Large Format or 3-D Films and Manhattan, NY locations.** Regal Entertainment Group reserves the right to change any upgrade or surcharge fee without notice.

ET1009251996

00770115

Coupons void if purchased, sold or bartered. Discounts exclude tax, tip and/or alcohol, where applicable.

MOVIE TICKETS
REDEEM AT THEATRE

Purchase up to two(2) *VIP Super Saver Admission Tickets for only $7.00 each. Upgrade to an "UNRESTRICTED" Premiere Super Saver Admission Ticket for only $1.50 extra per ticket.

Limit 2 Admission Tickets Per Coupon.

Subject to Rules of Use. Coupons VOID if purchased, sold or bartered for cash.

See reverse side offer details.

E9

Valid now thru November 1, 2010

MOVIE TICKETS
REDEEM AT THEATRE

Purchase up to two(2) *VIP Super Saver Admission Tickets for only $7.00 each. Upgrade to an "UNRESTRICTED" Premiere Super Saver Admission Ticket for only $1.50 extra per ticket.

Limit 2 Admission Tickets Per Coupon.

Subject to Rules of Use. Coupons VOID if purchased, sold or bartered for cash.

See reverse side offer details.

E10

Valid now thru November 1, 2010

MOVIE TICKETS
REDEEM AT THEATRE

Purchase up to two(2) *VIP Super Saver Admission Tickets for only $7.00 each. Upgrade to an "UNRESTRICTED" Premiere Super Saver Admission Ticket for only $1.50 extra per ticket.

Limit 2 Admission Tickets Per Coupon.

Subject to Rules of Use. Coupons VOID if purchased, sold or bartered for cash.

See reverse side offer details.

E11

Valid now thru November 1, 2010

MOVIE TICKETS
REDEEM AT THEATRE

Purchase up to two(2) *VIP Super Saver Admission Tickets for only $7.00 each. Upgrade to an "UNRESTRICTED" Premiere Super Saver Admission Ticket for only $1.50 extra per ticket.

Limit 2 Admission Tickets Per Coupon.

Subject to Rules of Use. Coupons VOID if purchased, sold or bartered for cash.

See reverse side offer details.

E12

Valid now thru November 1, 2010

MOVIE TICKETS
REDEEM AT THEATRE

Purchase up to two(2) *VIP Super Saver Admission Tickets for only $7.00 each. Upgrade to an "UNRESTRICTED" Premiere Super Saver Admission Ticket for only $1.50 extra per ticket.

Limit 2 Admission Tickets Per Coupon.

Subject to Rules of Use. Coupons VOID if purchased, sold or bartered for cash.

See reverse side offer details.

E13

Valid now thru November 1, 2010

MOVIE TICKETS
REDEEM AT THEATRE

Purchase up to two(2) *VIP Super Saver Admission Tickets for only $7.00 each. Upgrade to an "UNRESTRICTED" Premiere Super Saver Admission Ticket for only $1.50 extra per ticket.

Limit 2 Admission Tickets Per Coupon.

Subject to Rules of Use. Coupons VOID if purchased, sold or bartered for cash.

See reverse side offer details.

E14

Valid now thru November 1, 2010

Visit www.REGmovies.com for locations and showtime information.

VIP Super Saver ticket is not valid during the first 12 days of "Selected" new release films, special engagements or where prohibited by contractual obligations. **$1.50 UPGRADE FEE MAY BE PAID AT THE BOX OFFICE FOR ADMISSION TO THESE "SELECTED" NEW RELEASE FILMS. Not valid for special events or private screenings. Surcharge Fees apply to all IMAX, Large Format or 3-D Films and Manhattan, NY locations.** Regal Entertainment Group reserves the right to change any upgrade or surcharge fee without notice.

ET1009251996

00770115

Visit www.REGmovies.com for locations and showtime information.

VIP Super Saver ticket is not valid during the first 12 days of "Selected" new release films, special engagements or where prohibited by contractual obligations. **$1.50 UPGRADE FEE MAY BE PAID AT THE BOX OFFICE FOR ADMISSION TO THESE "SELECTED" NEW RELEASE FILMS. Not valid for special events or private screenings. Surcharge Fees apply to all IMAX, Large Format or 3-D Films and Manhattan, NY locations.** Regal Entertainment Group reserves the right to change any upgrade or surcharge fee without notice.

ET1009251996

00770115

Visit www.REGmovies.com for locations and showtime information.

VIP Super Saver ticket is not valid during the first 12 days of "Selected" new release films, special engagements or where prohibited by contractual obligations. **$1.50 UPGRADE FEE MAY BE PAID AT THE BOX OFFICE FOR ADMISSION TO THESE "SELECTED" NEW RELEASE FILMS. Not valid for special events or private screenings. Surcharge Fees apply to all IMAX, Large Format or 3-D Films and Manhattan, NY locations.** Regal Entertainment Group reserves the right to change any upgrade or surcharge fee without notice.

ET1009251996

00770115

Visit www.REGmovies.com for locations and showtime information.

VIP Super Saver ticket is not valid during the first 12 days of "Selected" new release films, special engagements or where prohibited by contractual obligations. **$1.50 UPGRADE FEE MAY BE PAID AT THE BOX OFFICE FOR ADMISSION TO THESE "SELECTED" NEW RELEASE FILMS. Not valid for special events or private screenings. Surcharge Fees apply to all IMAX, Large Format or 3-D Films and Manhattan, NY locations.** Regal Entertainment Group reserves the right to change any upgrade or surcharge fee without notice.

ET1009251996

00770115

Visit www.REGmovies.com for locations and showtime information.

VIP Super Saver ticket is not valid during the first 12 days of "Selected" new release films, special engagements or where prohibited by contractual obligations. **$1.50 UPGRADE FEE MAY BE PAID AT THE BOX OFFICE FOR ADMISSION TO THESE "SELECTED" NEW RELEASE FILMS. Not valid for special events or private screenings. Surcharge Fees apply to all IMAX, Large Format or 3-D Films and Manhattan, NY locations.** Regal Entertainment Group reserves the right to change any upgrade or surcharge fee without notice.

ET1009251996

00770115

Visit www.REGmovies.com for locations and showtime information.

VIP Super Saver ticket is not valid during the first 12 days "Selected" new release films, special engagements or where prohibited by contractual obligations. **$1.50 UPGRADE FEE MAY BE PAID AT THE BOX OFFICE FOR ADMISSION TO THESE "SELECTED" NEW RELEASE FILMS. Not valid for special events or private screenings. Surcharge Fees apply to all IMAX, Large Format or 3-D Films and Manhattan, NY locations.** Regal Entertainment Group reserves the right to change any upgrade or surcharge fee without notice.

ET1009251996

00770115

MOVIE TICKETS
REDEEM AT THEATRE

REGAL
ENTERTAINMENT
G R O U P™
REGAL CINEMAS   UNITED ARTISTS Theatres™   EDWARDS THEATRES

urchase up to two(2) *VIP Super Saver Admission Tickets
or only $7.00 each. Upgrade to an "UNRESTRICTED"
Premiere Super Saver Admission Ticket
for only $1.50 extra per ticket.

Limit 2 Admission Tickets Per Coupon.

Subject to Rules of Use. Coupons VOID if purchased,
sold or bartered for cash.

See reverse side offer details.

E15

Valid now thru November 1, 2010

ffer validity is governed by the Rules of Use and excludes defined holidays.
fers are not valid with other discount offers, unless specified.

MOVIE TICKETS
REDEEM AT THEATRE

REGAL
ENTERTAINMENT
G R O U P™
REGAL CINEMAS   UNITED ARTISTS Theatres™   EDWARDS THEATRES

Purchase up to two(2) *VIP Super Saver Admission Tickets
for only $7.00 each. Upgrade to an "UNRESTRICTED"
Premiere Super Saver Admission Ticket
for only $1.50 extra per ticket.

Limit 2 Admission Tickets Per Coupon.

Subject to Rules of Use. Coupons VOID if purchased,
sold or bartered for cash.

See reverse side offer details.

E16

Valid now thru November 1, 2010

Offer validity is governed by the Rules of Use and excludes defined holidays.
Offers are not valid with other discount offers, unless specified.

MOVIE TICKETS
REDEEM AT THEATRE

REGAL
ENTERTAINMENT
G R O U P™
REGAL CINEMAS   UNITED ARTISTS Theatres™   EDWARDS THEATRES

urchase up to two(2) *VIP Super Saver Admission Tickets
r only $7.00 each. Upgrade to an "UNRESTRICTED"
Premiere Super Saver Admission Ticket
for only $1.50 extra per ticket.

Limit 2 Admission Tickets Per Coupon.

Subject to Rules of Use. Coupons VOID if purchased,
sold or bartered for cash.

See reverse side offer details.

E17

Valid now thru November 1, 2010

er validity is governed by the Rules of Use and excludes defined holidays.
fers are not valid with other discount offers, unless specified.

MOVIE TICKETS
REDEEM AT THEATRE

REGAL
ENTERTAINMENT
G R O U P™
REGAL CINEMAS   UNITED ARTISTS Theatres™   EDWARDS THEATRES

Purchase up to two(2) *VIP Super Saver Admission Tickets
for only $7.00 each. Upgrade to an "UNRESTRICTED"
Premiere Super Saver Admission Ticket
for only $1.50 extra per ticket.

Limit 2 Admission Tickets Per Coupon.

Subject to Rules of Use. Coupons VOID if purchased,
sold or bartered for cash.

See reverse side offer details.

E18

Valid now thru November 1, 2010

Offer validity is governed by the Rules of Use and excludes defined holidays.
Offers are not valid with other discount offers, unless specified.

MOVIE TICKETS
REDEEM AT THEATRE

REGAL
ENTERTAINMENT
G R O U P™
REGAL CINEMAS   UNITED ARTISTS Theatres™   EDWARDS THEATRES

rchase up to two(2) *VIP Super Saver Admission Tickets
only $7.00 each. Upgrade to an "UNRESTRICTED"
Premiere Super Saver Admission Ticket
for only $1.50 extra per ticket.

Limit 2 Admission Tickets Per Coupon.

Subject to Rules of Use. Coupons VOID if purchased,
sold or bartered for cash.

See reverse side offer details.

E19

Valid now thru November 1, 2010

er validity is governed by the Rules of Use and excludes defined holidays.
ers are not valid with other discount offers, unless specified.

MOVIE TICKETS
REDEEM AT THEATRE

REGAL
ENTERTAINMENT
G R O U P™
REGAL CINEMAS   UNITED ARTISTS Theatres™   EDWARDS THEATRES

Purchase up to two(2) *VIP Super Saver Admission Tickets
for only $7.00 each. Upgrade to an "UNRESTRICTED"
Premiere Super Saver Admission Ticket
for only $1.50 extra per ticket.

Limit 2 Admission Tickets Per Coupon.

Subject to Rules of Use. Coupons VOID if purchased,
sold or bartered for cash.

See reverse side offer details.

E20

Valid now thru November 1, 2010

Offer validity is governed by the Rules of Use and excludes defined holidays.
Offers are not valid with other discount offers, unless specified.

Visit www.REGmovies.com for locations and showtime information.

VIP Super Saver ticket is not valid during the first 12 days of "Selected" new release films, special engagements or where prohibited by contractual obligations. **$1.50 UPGRADE FEE MAY BE PAID AT THE BOX OFFICE FOR ADMISSION TO THESE "SELECTED" NEW RELEASE FILMS. Not valid for special events or private screenings. Surcharge Fees apply to all IMAX, Large Format or 3-D Films and Manhattan, NY locations.** Regal Entertainment Group reserves the right to change any upgrade or surcharge fee without notice.

ET1009251996

00770115

Visit www.REGmovies.com for locations and showtime information.

VIP Super Saver ticket is not valid during the first 12 days of "Selected" new release films, special engagements or where prohibited by contractual obligations. **$1.50 UPGRADE FEE MAY BE PAID AT THE BOX OFFICE FOR ADMISSION TO THESE "SELECTED" NEW RELEASE FILMS. Not valid for special events or private screenings. Surcharge Fees apply to all IMAX, Large Format or 3-D Films and Manhattan, NY locations.** Regal Entertainment Group reserves the right to change any upgrade or surcharge fee without notice.

ET1009251996

00770115

Visit www.REGmovies.com for locations and showtime information.

VIP Super Saver ticket is not valid during the first 12 days of "Selected" new release films, special engagements or where prohibited by contractual obligations. **$1.50 UPGRADE FEE MAY BE PAID AT THE BOX OFFICE FOR ADMISSION TO THESE "SELECTED" NEW RELEASE FILMS. Not valid for special events or private screenings. Surcharge Fees apply to all IMAX, Large Format or 3-D Films and Manhattan, NY locations.** Regal Entertainment Group reserves the right to change any upgrade or surcharge fee without notice.

ET1009251996

00770115

Visit www.REGmovies.com for locations and showtime information.

VIP Super Saver ticket is not valid during the first 12 days of "Selected" new release films, special engagements or where prohibited by contractual obligations. **$1.50 UPGRADE FEE MAY BE PAID AT THE BOX OFFICE FOR ADMISSION TO THESE "SELECTED" NEW RELEASE FILMS. Not valid for special events or private screenings. Surcharge Fees apply to all IMAX, Large Format or 3-D Films and Manhattan, NY locations.** Regal Entertainment Group reserves the right to change any upgrade or surcharge fee without notice.

ET1009251996

00770115

Visit www.REGmovies.com for locations and showtime information.

VIP Super Saver ticket is not valid during the first 12 days of "Selected" new release films, special engagements or where prohibited by contractual obligations. **$1.50 UPGRADE FEE MAY BE PAID AT THE BOX OFFICE FOR ADMISSION TO THESE "SELECTED" NEW RELEASE FILMS. Not valid for special events or private screenings. Surcharge Fees apply to all IMAX, Large Format or 3-D Films and Manhattan, NY locations.** Regal Entertainment Group reserves the right to change any upgrade or surcharge fee without notice.

ET1009251996

00770115

Visit www.REGmovies.com for locations and showtime information.

VIP Super Saver ticket is not valid during the first 12 days "Selected" new release films, special engagements or where prohibite by contractual obligations. **$1.50 UPGRADE FEE MAY BE PAID AT T BOX OFFICE FOR ADMISSION TO THESE "SELECTED" NEW RELEA FILMS. Not valid for special events or private screenings. Surcharg Fees apply to all IMAX, Large Format or 3-D Films and Manhatta NY locations.** Regal Entertainment Group reserves the right to chan any upgrade or surcharge fee without notice.

ET1009251996

00770115

Bullwinkle's/ Family Fun Center

Enjoy one complimentary ATTRACTION when a second ATTRACTION of equal or greater value is purchased.

Offer Conditions on reverse side.

Valid now thru November 1, 2010

FREE ATTRACTION

www.fun-center.com

29111 S.W. Town Center Loop W., Wilsonville, OR
(503)685-5000

E21

Bullwinkle's/ Family Fun Center

Enjoy one complimentary ATTRACTION when a second ATTRACTION of equal or greater value is purchased.

Offer Conditions on reverse side.

Valid now thru November 1, 2010

FREE ATTRACTION

www.fun-center.com

29111 S.W. Town Center Loop W., Wilsonville, OR
(503)685-5000

E22

Bullwinkle's/ Family Fun Center

Enjoy one complimentary DAY PASS when a second DAY PASS of equal or greater value is purchased.

Offer Conditions on reverse side.

Valid now thru November 1, 2010

FREE DAY PASS

www.fun-center.com

29111 S.W. Town Center Loop W., Wilsonville, OR
(503)685-5000

E23

Bullwinkle's/ Family Fun Center

- Open year round
- A fun experience for the entire family
- Miniature golf, bumper boats, go-karts, batting cages, 28' rock wall, sling shot, lazer tag, Kidoplis-soft play, aracde games, great prizes and so much more!
- Stop by Bullwinkle's restaurant for great pizza and burgers
- Perfect for group parties, corporate events or any time!

29111 S.W. Town Center Loop W.
Wilsonville, OR
(503)685-5000

00764754

Offer Conditions: Valid anytime.

Offer validity is governed by the Rules of Use and excludes defined holidays. Offers are not valid with other discount offers, unless specified. Coupons void if purchased, sold or bartered. Discounts exclude tax, tip and/or alcohol, where applicable.

Bullwinkle's/ Family Fun Center

- Open year round
- A fun experience for the entire family
- Miniature golf, bumper boats, go-karts, batting cages, 28' rock wall, sling shot, lazer tag, Kidoplis-soft play, aracde games, great prizes and so much more!
- Stop by Bullwinkle's restaurant for great pizza and burgers
- Perfect for group parties, corporate events or any time!

29111 S.W. Town Center Loop W.
Wilsonville, OR
(503)685-5000

00764754

Offer Conditions: Valid anytime.

Offer validity is governed by the Rules of Use and excludes defined holidays. Offers are not valid with other discount offers, unless specified. Coupons void if purchased, sold or bartered. Discounts exclude tax, tip and/or alcohol, where applicable.

Bullwinkle's/ Family Fun Center

- Open year round
- A fun experience for the entire family
- Miniature golf, bumper boats, go-karts, batting cages, 28' rock wall, sling shot, lazer tag, Kidoplis-soft play, aracde games, great prizes and so much more!
- Stop by Bullwinkle's restaurant for great pizza and burgers
- Perfect for group parties, corporate events or any time!

29111 S.W. Town Center Loop W.
Wilsonville, OR
(503)685-5000

00764756

Offer Conditions: Valid anytime.

Offer validity is governed by the Rules of Use and excludes defined holidays. Offers are not valid with other discount offers, unless specified. Coupons void if purchased, sold or bartered. Discounts exclude tax, tip and/or alcohol, where applicable.

Cinetopia

Enjoy up to 4 Living Room
Theater TICKETS at $9.50 each.

Offer Conditions on reverse side.

Movie Tickets

CINETOPIA

Valid now thru November 1, 2010

11700 SE 7th Street, Vancouver, WA
(360)213-2800

E24

Cinetopia

Enjoy up to 4 Grand Auditorium
Tickets at $7.50 each.

Offer Conditions on reverse side.

Movie Tickets

CINETOPIA

Valid now thru November 1, 2010

11700 SE 7th Street, Vancouver, WA
(360)213-2800

E25

Northern Lights Theatre Pub

Enjoy one complimentary
ADMISSION when a second
ADMISSION of equal or greater
value is purchased.

Offer Conditions on reverse side.

FREE ADMISSION

www.northernlightstheatrepub.com

3893 Commercial St. SE, Salem, OR
(503)585-4232

E26

Valid now thru November 1, 2010

More Offers Online!

ENTERTAINMENT & SPORTS

entertainment.com

Cinetopia

- Extra wide leather seating
- Digital super high definition movies
- Premium concessions, hot food and gourmet popcorn bar
- Come experience the Northwest's finest

11700 SE 7th Street
Vancouver, WA
(360)213-2800

Offer Conditions: Valid anytime. Not valid with Starred Attractions; 21 and over please.

00752755

Cinetopia

- Extra wide leather seating
- Digital super high definition movies
- Premium concessions, hot food and gourmet popcorn bar
- Come experience the Northwest's finest

CINETOPIA

11700 SE 7th Street
Vancouver, WA
(360)213-2800

Offer Conditions: Valid anytime. Not valid with Starred Attractions.

00752756

Northern Lights Theatre Pub

- All ages matinees
- Birthday party packages
- Pizza, burritos & wraps
- Full line of desserts
- Micro brews
- Fine wines

3893 Commercial St. SE
Salem, OR
(503)585-4232

Offer Conditions: Valid anytime.

00657484

entertainment.com

Familycinemas.com
Enjoy up to FOUR
ADMISSIONS at $4.00 each.
See reverse for Offer Details.

THEATRE BONUS

familycinemas.com

www.familycinemas.com

See Reverse Side for Locations

Valid now thru November 1, 2010

E27

---

entertainment.com

Familycinemas.com
Enjoy up to FOUR
ADMISSIONS at $4.00 each.
See reverse for Offer Details.

THEATRE BONUS

familycinemas.com

www.familycinemas.com

See Reverse Side for Locations

Valid now thru November 1, 2010

E28

entertainment.com

Familycinemas.com
Enjoy up to FOUR
ADMISSIONS at $4.00 each.
See reverse for Offer Details.

THEATRE BONUS

familycinemas.com

www.familycinemas.com

See Reverse Side for Locations

Valid now thru November 1, 2010

E29

Familycinemas.com

- Family environment, family prices
- See our Oregonian listing for restrictions
- Tigard-Joy Theatre (503)653-9999-2
- Oak Grove - 8, (503)653-9999-1

Entertainment® Order Back
Please order all tickets you will need together.
Enclose one coupon for every four tickets ordered.
Write one check for the Familycinemas.com entire order

TO: Familycinemas.com FMB119
      10117 S.E. Sunnyside Road, Suite F
      Clackamas, OR 97015
Please send _____ tickets at $4.00 each:

ORDERS WILL NOT BE FILLED WITHOUT SELF ADDRESSED STAMPED ENVELOPE

Name: _____
Address: _____
Day Phone: _____
City: _____
State: _____ ZIP: _____

E-mail Address (optional): _____

- Order before October 1, 2009. Tickets will be mailed within 21 days of receipt of order.
- Prices subject to change without notice.
- Tickets on availability basis.

Offer Details: Valid anytime. Starred attractions & special engagements excluded; Not redeemable at the theatre box office; Mail order only before Oct. 1, 2009; On availability basis.

00711746

Offer validity is governed by the Rules of Use and excludes defined holidays. Offers are not valid with other discount offers, unless specified. Coupons void if purchased, sold or bartered. Discounts exclude tax, tip and/or alcohol, where applicable.

Familycinemas.com

- Family environment, family prices
- See our Oregonian listing for restrictions
- Tigard-Joy Theatre (503)653-9999-2
- Oak Grove - 8, (503)653-9999-1

Entertainment® Order Back
Please order all tickets you will need together.
Enclose one coupon for every four tickets ordered.
Write one check for the Familycinemas.com entire order

TO: Familycinemas.com FMB119
      10117 S.E. Sunnyside Road, Suite F
      Clackamas, OR 97015
Please send _____ tickets at $4.00 each:

ORDERS WILL NOT BE FILLED WITHOUT SELF ADDRESSED STAMPED ENVELOPE

Name: _____
Address: _____
Day Phone: _____
City: _____
State: _____ ZIP: _____

E-mail Address (optional): _____

- Order before October 1, 2009. Tickets will be mailed within 21 days of receipt of order.
- Prices subject to change without notice.
- Tickets on availability basis.

Offer Details: Valid anytime. Starred attractions & special engagements excluded; Not redeemable at the theatre box office; Mail order only before Oct. 1, 2009; On availability basis.

00711746

Offer validity is governed by the Rules of Use and excludes defined holidays. Offers are not valid with other discount offers, unless specified. Coupons void if purchased, sold or bartered. Discounts exclude tax, tip and/or alcohol, where applicable.

Familycinemas.com

- Family environment, family prices
- See our Oregonian listing for restrictions
- Tigard-Joy Theatre (503)653-9999-2
- Oak Grove - 8, (503)653-9999-1

Entertainment® Order Back
Please order all tickets you will need together.
Enclose one coupon for every four tickets ordered.
Write one check for the Familycinemas.com entire order

TO: Familycinemas.com FMB119
      10117 S.E. Sunnyside Road, Suite F
      Clackamas, OR 97015
Please send _____ tickets at $4.00 each:

ORDERS WILL NOT BE FILLED WITHOUT SELF ADDRESSED STAMPED ENVELOPE

Name: _____
Address: _____
Day Phone: _____
City: _____
State: _____ ZIP: _____

E-mail Address (optional): _____

- Order before October 1, 2009. Tickets will be mailed within 21 days of receipt of order.
- Prices subject to change without notice.
- Tickets on availability basis.

Offer Details: Valid anytime. Starred attractions & special engagements excluded; Not redeemable at the theatre box office; Mail order only before Oct. 1, 2009; On availability basis.

00711746

Offer validity is governed by the Rules of Use and excludes defined holidays. Offers are not valid with other discount offers, unless specified. Coupons void if purchased, sold or bartered. Discounts exclude tax, tip and/or alcohol, where applicable.

Players

Enjoy one complimentary HOUR OF PLAY when a second HOUR OF PLAY of equal or greater value is purchased.

Offer Conditions on reverse side.

Up To $8.00 Value

www.eatdrinkbowlplay.com

17880 SW McEwan, Lake Oswego, OR
(503)726-4263

E30

Valid now thru November 1, 2010

Me Too! Cafe

Enjoy one complimentary ADMISSION when a second ADMISSION of equal or greater value is purchased.

Offer Conditions on reverse side.

FREE ADMISSION

Café for Grown-ups – Play-time for Kids!

16755 Baseline Rd. #102, Beaverton, OR
(503)439-6586

E31

Valid now thru November 1, 2010

Action Acres

Enjoy one complimentary Full Day Rental Package when a second Full Day Rental Package of equal or greater value is purchased.

Offer Conditions on reverse side.

$35.00 Value

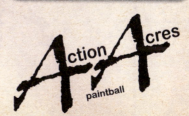

paintball

10381 S Mulino Rd, Canby, OR
(503)266-5733

E32

Valid now thru November 1, 2010

Players

- We are experts at entertaining all ages
- Players offers 12 state of the art bowling lanes & comfortable lounge seating
- Test your skills & challenge your friends on the hottest video games in our arcade
- Kick back and catch the game in our sports bar
- Hang out with your friends & shoot some pool
- Parties are a blast at players & our party packages won't break the bank

17880 SW McEwan
(1/4 mile E. off I-5 at the Lower Boones Ferry/Durham exit)
Lake Oswego, OR
(503)726-4263

Offer Conditions: Valid anytime.

00779088

Me Too! Cafe

- Cafe for grown-ups...playtime for kids
- A friendly, comfortable environment where you can relax while your kids play
- Your kids will love our fun, educational, attended childcare area

16755 Baseline Rd. #102
(Down the street from Beaverton Costco)
Beaverton, OR
(503)439-6586

Offer Conditions: Valid anytime.

00747178

Action Acres

- Includes admission, equipment and 500 paintballs
- Five acres of cars, crates, bunkers and 40x40 ft Fort FTP
- Action, adventure and tons of family fun!

10381 S Mulino Rd
Canby, OR
(503)266-5733

Offer Conditions: Valid anytime.

00744492

Thrill-Ville USA

Enjoy one complimentary UNLIMITED RIDE PASS when a second UNLIMITED RIDE PASS of equal or greater value is purchased or for those who prefer - one ALL-YOU-CAN-SLIDE PASS when a second ALL-YOU-CAN-SLIDE PASS of equal or greater value is purchased.

Offer Conditions on reverse side.

ALL-YOU-CAN RIDE/SLIDE PASS

Thrill - Ville USA

Valid now thru November 1, 2010

8372 Enchanted Way, Turner, OR
(503)363-4095

E33

Portland Children's Museum

Enjoy one complimentary ADMISSION when a second ADMISSION of equal or greater value is purchased.

Offer Conditions on reverse side.

FREE ADMISSION

where imagination lives
Portland Children's Museum
www.PortlandChildrensMuseum.org

Valid now thru November 1, 2010

4015 S.W. Canyon Rd., Portland, OR
(503)223-6500

E34

Hallie Ford Museum of Art

Enjoy one complimentary ADMISSION when a second ADMISSION of equal or greater value is purchased.

Offer Conditions on reverse side.

FREE ADMISSION

www.willamette.edu/museum_of_art/index

Valid now thru November 1, 2010

900 State St., Salem, OR
(503)370-6855

E35

Thrill-Ville USA

- Come out & ride "The Ripper", Oregon's most thrilling, awesome & hair-raising roller coaster
- Cool off on our exhilarating giant waterslides, then enjoy our vast array of classic rides, kiddie rides & thrill rides
- Call for park hours

Thrill - Ville USA

8372 Enchanted Way
Turner, OR
(503)363-4095

Offer Conditions: Valid anytime. Weather permitting.

00151900

Portland Children's Museum

- Hands-on exhibits for children ages 6 mos. thru 10 years & their families
- Make a splash in WATER WORKS, join the construction crew in BUILDING BRIDGETOWN, shop for groceries/serve a meal in the KID CITY MARKET & CAFE
- Museum Hours: Mon.-Sat., 9 a.m.-5 p.m., Sun. 11 a.m.-5 p.m.
- Closed Monday, except on some Portland Public School holidays (Sept.-Feb.)

where imagination lives

Portland Children's Museum
4015 S.W. Canyon Rd.
(opposite the Oregon Zoo)
Portland, OR
(503)223-6500

Offer Conditions: Valid anytime except Portland Public School holidays.

00469904

Hallie Ford Museum of Art

- Museum open Tues - Sat 10am - 5pm
- Sun 1pm - 5pm
- Exhibits, collections & archives

900 State St.
Salem, OR
(503)370-6855

Offer Conditions: Valid anytime.

00718255

Ripley's Believe It or Not

Enjoy one complimentary ADMISSION when a second ADMISSION of equal or greater value is purchased.

Offer Conditions on reverse side.

Up To $**10**⁰⁰ Value

250 S.W. Bay Blvd., Newport, OR
(541)265-2206

Valid now thru November 1, 2010

E36

Clark County Historical Museum

Enjoy up to 4 ADMISSIONS at 50% off the regular price.

Offer Conditions on reverse side.

50%OFF

CLARK COUNTY
HISTORICAL MUSEUM

www.cchmuseum.org

1511 Main St, Vancouver, WA
(360)993-5679

Valid now thru November 1, 2010

E37

Pearson Air Museum

Enjoy one complimentary ADMISSION when a second ADMISSION of equal or greater value is purchased.

Offer Conditions on reverse side.

FREE ADMISSION

Vancouver National
HISTORIC RESERVE
Pearson Air Museum

1115 E. 5th St., Vancouver, WA
(360)694-7026

Valid now thru November 1, 2010

E38

Ripley's Believe It or Not

- Step into a world of discoveries by the world famous explorer, Robert L. Ripley
- Seeing is believing

RipLey's
Believe It or Not!®

250 S.W. Bay Blvd.
Newport, OR
(541) 265-2206

Offer Conditions: Valid anytime. Not valid with any other discount offer.

00659362

Clark County Historical Museum

- Open Tues-Sat 11am-4pm
- The Museum features permanent and changing exhibits and a research library specializing in Clark County and Pacific Northwest history.
- In 2009 the Museum celebrates the centennial of its 1909 Carnegie Library Building
- Visit our website at www.cchmuseum.org for special 100th anniversary events throughout the year.

CLARK COUNTY
HISTORICAL MUSEUM

1511 Main St
Vancouver, WA
(360) 993-5679

Offer Conditions: Valid anytime.

00752749

Pearson Air Museum

- The oldest operating Airfield in the U.S.
- New facility with 2 aircraft hangars, theatre & educational rooms
- Children's hands-on Activity Center
- Open Wed.-Sat., 10 a.m. 5 p.m.

Vancouver National
HISTORIC RESERVE
Pearson Air Museum

1115 E. 5th St.
(200 yds. East of Fort Vancouver Stockade)
Vancouver, WA
(360) 694-7026

Offer Conditions: Valid anytime.

00469933

Rice Northwest Museum Of Rocks & Minerals

Enjoy one complimentary ADMISSION when a second ADMISSION of equal or greater value is purchased.

Offer Conditions on reverse side.

FREE ADMISSION

www.ricenwmuseum.org

26385 Groveland Dr., Hillsboro, OR
(503)647-2418

Valid now thru November 1, 2010

E39

Maryhill Museum

Enjoy one complimentary ADMISSION when a second ADMISSION of equal or greater value is purchased.

Offer Conditions on reverse side.

FREE ADMISSION

MARYHILL MUSEUM OF ART
ON · THE · COLUMBIA · RIVER

www.maryhillmuseum.org

35 Maryhill Museum Dr., Goldendale, WA
(509)773-3733

Valid now thru November 1, 2010

E40

Oregon Sports Hall of Fame & Museum

Enjoy up to 4 ADMISSIONS at 50% off the regular price.

Offer Conditions on reverse side.

Up To 50% OFF

Oregon Sports Hall of Fame & Museum

www.oregonsportshall.org

321 S.W. Salmon, Portland, OR
(503)227-7466

PRINT MORE ONLINE

Valid now thru November 1, 2010

E41

More Offers Online!

ENTERTAINMENT & SPORTS

entertainment.com

Rice Northwest Museum Of Rocks & Minerals

- Nationally recognized as the finest rock & minerals museum in the Pacific Northwest
- A fun filled discovery for all ages
- Minerals, meleorites, petrified wood, gem stones & more
- See website for more information

26385 Groveland Dr.
Hillsboro, OR
(503)647-2418

Offer Conditions: Valid anytime. Not valid with any other discounts or promotions.

00731178

Maryhill Museum

- Historic castle overlooking the Columbia River
- Highlights include Rodin sculpture, Native American artifacts, chess sets, European & American classical Realism paintings & Sam Hill history
- Season runs March 15th - Nov. 15th
- Open daily 9:00 a.m. - 5:00 p.m. including holidays
- Group rates available - or call for information

35 Maryhill Museum Dr.
Goldendale, WA
(509)773-3733

Offer Conditions: Valid anytime.

00007322

Oregon Sports Hall of Fame & Museum

- Fun for all ages & the entire family
- Highly interactive & emotional exhibits
- World class sports museum located in the heart of Portland
- Please call or visit www.oregonsportshall.org for hours & special event information

Oregon Sports Hall of Fame & Museum

321 S.W. Salmon
Portland, OR
(503)227-7466

Offer Conditions: Valid anytime.

00232778

Columbia Gorge Discovery Center & Museum

Enjoy one complimentary ADMISSION when a second ADMISSION of equal or greater value is purchased.

Offer Conditions on reverse side.

Valid now thru November 1, 2010

Up$ **13**.00 To Value

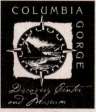

www.gorgediscovery.org

5000 Discovery Dr., The Dalles, OR
(541) 296-8600

E42

Columbia Gorge Interpretive Center

Enjoy one complimentary ADMISSION when a second ADMISSION of equal or greater value is purchased.

Offer Conditions on reverse side.

PRINT MORE ONLINE

Valid now thru November 1, 2010

FREE ADMISSION

COLUMBIA GORGE INTERPRETIVE CENTER

info@columbiagorge.org

990 S.W. Rock Creek Dr. Stevenson, WA
(509) 427-8211 or (800) 991-2338

E43

Western Antique Aeroplane & Automobile Museum

Enjoy one complimentary ADMISSION when a second ADMISSION of equal or greater value is purchased.

Offer Conditions on reverse side.

NEW

Valid now thru November 1, 2010

FREE ADMISSION

www.waaamuseum.org

1600 Air Museum Rd., Hood River, OR
(541) 308-1600

E44

Columbia Gorge Discovery Center & Museum

- Discover...
- The contents of 30 tons of Lewis & Clark's cargo
- 10,000 years of Native Amercian history & pioneer life
- Explore the geologic splendor of the Columbia River Gorge
- Interactive exhibits, films & live presentations
- Cafe with terrace, picnic area, outdoor trails, store & free parking

00307150

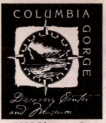

5000 Discovery Dr.
(exit 82 off of I-84)
The Dalles, OR
(541)296-8600

Offer Conditions: Valid anytime. Not valid with any other discounts or promotions.

Columbia Gorge Interpretive Center

- American Indian Culture
- Oregon Trail Saga
- Timber & Fishing Industries
- World's Largest Rosary Collection
- The Museum with a heart in the heart of the Gorge

00209793

COLUMBIA GORGE INTERPRETIVE CENTER

990 S.W. Rock Creek Dr. Stevenson, WA (509)427-8211 or (800)991-2338

Offer Conditions: Valid anytime.

Western Antique Aeroplane & Automobile Museum

- Nestled in the Hood River Valley along the Columbia River you will find the opportunity to step back in time and see life as it was in the era of early flight and transportation
- One of the nations largest collections of flying Antique Aeroplanes and Antique Automobiles

00761228

1600 Air Museum Rd.
(at the Hood River Airport)
Hood River, OR
(541)308-1600

Offer Conditions: Valid anytime.

The Science Factory Children's Museum

Enjoy one complimentary ADMISSION when a second ADMISSION of equal or greater value is purchased.

Offer Conditions on reverse side.

Valid now thru November 1, 2010

FREE ADMISSION

Science FACTORY
Eugene, Oregon
www.sciencefactory.org

2300 Leo Harris Pkwy., Eugene, OR
(541)682-7888

E45

U. of O. Museum of Natural & Cultural History

Enjoy one complimentary ADMISSION when a second ADMISSION of equal or greater value is purchased.

Offer Conditions on reverse side.

Valid now thru November 1, 2010

FREE ADMISSION

O MUSEUM OF NATURAL AND CULTURAL HISTORY
University of Oregon

natural-history.uoregon.edu/

1680 E. 15th Ave., Eugene, OR
(541)346-3024

E46

Historic Deepwood Estate

Enjoy one complimentary HOUSE TOUR ADMISSION when a second HOUSE TOUR ADMISSION of equal or greater value is purchased.

Offer Conditions on reverse side.

Valid now thru November 1, 2010

ONE HOUSE TOUR ADMISSION

Historic Deepwood Estate

www.historicdeepwoodestate.org

1116 Mission St. S.E., Salem, OR
(503)363-1825

E47

The Science Factory Children's Museum

- Where imagination gets in gear!
- Over 50 interactive hands-on exhibits & a state-of-the-art planetarium
- A wonderful opportunity for children to explore, create & discover
- Ongoing camps, classes & other educational programs available
- See our website for more information & special programs: www.sciencefactory.org

THE Science FACTORY
Eugene, Oregon
2300 Leo Harris Pkwy.
Eugene, OR
(541)682-7888

Offer Conditions: Valid anytime. Special events excluded.

00602950

U. of O. Museum of Natural & Cultural History

- Experience a place where past is present
- Find yourself face-to-face with traditional items & learn the stories behind them
- Explore over 15,000 years of Northwest cultural history, with sights, sounds & language
- Open: Wednesday -Sunday 11 a.m.-5 p.m.
- Closed Monday & Tuesday

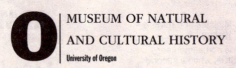

O MUSEUM OF NATURAL AND CULTURAL HISTORY
University of Oregon

1680 E. 15th Ave.
Eugene, OR
(541)346-3024

Offer Conditions: Valid anytime.

00726000

Historic Deepwood Estate

- Stroll 5.5 acres of 1930's English-styled gardens & nature trails
- Tour one of Oregon's finest examples of Queen Anne architecture
- Enjoy 1894 oak woodwork, stained glass & carriage house
- National Register of Historic Places
- A City of Salem Park & Community Museum

Historic Deepwood Estate

1116 Mission St. S.E.
Salem, OR
(503)363-1825

Offer Conditions: Valid anytime. Special events excluded.

00087882

The Museum at Warm Springs

Enjoy one complimentary ADMISSION when a second ADMISSION of equal or greater value is purchased.

Offer Conditions on reverse side.

PRINT MORE ONLINE

Valid now thru November 1, 2010

FREE ADMISSION

2189 Hwy. 26, Warm Springs, OR
(541)553-3331

E48

Wildlife Safari

Enjoy one complimentary ADMISSION when a second ADMISSION of equal or greater value is purchased.

Offer Conditions on reverse side.

Valid now thru November 1, 2010

FREE ADMISSION

1790 Safari Rd., Winston, OR
(541)679-6761

E49

Steve Smith Outdoors

Enjoy one complimentary RIVER FISHING TRIP ECO/TOUR when a second RIVER FISHING TRIP ECO/TOUR of equal or greater value is purchased.

Offer Conditions on reverse side.

Valid now thru November 1, 2010

UP TO $125 VALUE

Steve Smith

OUTDOORS

www.stevesmithoutdoors.com

Troutdale, OR
(503) 661-3474

E50

More Offers Online!

ENTERTAINMENT & SPORTS

entertainment.com

The Museum at Warm Springs

- Museum opened March, 1993
- Over 2500 tribal artifacts
- Large-scale scenes of ancient tribal life
- Changing exhibitions
- Museum shop
- Award-winning architecture
- Open daily, 10 a.m.-5 p.m.
- Closed Thanksgiving, Christmas & New Year's Day

The Museum At Warm Springs

2189 Hwy. 26
Warm Springs, OR
(541)553-3331

Offer Conditions: Valid anytime.

00144715

Wildlife Safari

- Drive through our 600 acre wild animal park where hundreds of exotic animals roam free
- Be sure to visit the village, more animal exhibits, gift shop, restaurant and children's zoo
- Check www.wildlifesafari.org for updated activities and events

WILDLIFE SAFARI

1790 Safari Rd.
Winston, OR
(541)679-6761

Offer Conditions: Valid anytime. Not valid with any other discount offer.

00142022

Steve Smith Outdoors

- Enjoy day or overnight fishing trips/tours with professional guide Steve Smith
- Fishing & white water guide service since 1979
- Find out more at www.stevesmithoutdoors.com

Steve Smith

OUTDOORS

Troutdale, OR
(503) 661-3474

Offer Conditions: Valid anytime.

00721730

Willamette Shore Trolley

- Scheduled trains run May through end of October
- Step back in time & ride historic trolley cars between Portland's Lake Oswego
- Great for special events
- Call for regular schedule

311 N. State St.
Lak Oswego, OR
(503)697-7436

Offer Conditions: Valid anytime. Excludes special excursions & charters.

00731176

Portland Classical Chinese Garden

- Garden of Awakening Orchids
- An urban oasis created to nurture & inspire residents of a busy city
- Elegant pavilions, ponds, walkways & arched bridges
- Open 10:00 a.m. - 5:00 p.m. Nov. 1 - March 31, 9:00 a.m. - 6:00 p.m. April 1 - Oct. 31

PORTLAND CLASSICAL
CHINESE GARDEN
garden of awakening orchids

239 N.W. Everett
(located at N.W. 3rd & Everett)
Portland, OR
(503)228-8131

Offer Conditions: Valid anytime.

00458039

Pump It Up

- The inflatable party zone!
- Perfect for parties, team building or just plain fun!
- For ages 2 to adult
- Giant, fun-filled inflatable play structures
- Don't forget to bring your socks
- See website for schedule & more information

PUMP IT UP
"THE INFLATABLE PARTY ZONE"
25749 S.W. Canyon Creek Rd., #700
Wilsonville, OR
(503)582-1331

Offer Conditions: Valid anytime. This location only.

00716522

JJ Jump

Enjoy one complimentary ADMISSION when a second ADMISSION of equal or greater value is purchased.

Offer Conditions on reverse side.

FREE ADMISSION

where the party's always jump'n!

See Reverse Side for Locations

Valid now thru November 1, 2010

E54

All About Fun

Enjoy 25% off the regular price of any INFLATABLE RENTAL or CASINO EQUIPMENT RENTAL PACKAGE.

Offer Conditions on reverse side.

UP TO $150 VALUE

ALL ABOUT FUN ENTERTAINMENT & EVENTS

www.allaboutfun.info

See Reverse Side for Locations

Valid now thru November 1, 2010

E55

Sykart Indoor Racing Center

Enjoy one complimentary 10 MINUTE SESSION when a second 10 MINUTE SESSION of equal or greater value is purchased.

Offer Conditions on reverse side.

Up To $15.00 Value

Sykart indoor racing center

8205 S.W. Hunziker St., Tigard, OR
(503)684-5060

Valid now thru November 1, 2010

E56

JJ Jump
- Where the party's always jumping!
- 4000 sq ft of inflatable fun in Clackamas, 6000 sq ft of fun in Vancouver!
- JJ Jump is fun for all ages- perfect for parties, team and corporate events
- Climb, zip, joust, bungee and slide at JJ Extreme
- See www.jjjump.com for more details

where the party's always jump'n!

9057 SE Jannsen Rd
(Clackamas Business Center)
Clackamas, OR
(503) 723-3600

7500 NE 16th Ave, Suite 2-C
(Northgate Complex)
Vancouver, OR
(360) 213-2524

Offer Conditions: Valid anytime.

00742303

All About Fun
- We come to you!
- Bounce houses & amazing inflatables
- Interactive fun
- Casino parties & so much more delivered right to your door
- Perfect for birthdays, graduation, church or corporate junctions!
- See www.allaboutfun.info for more!

(503) 516-3878

www.allaboutfun.info

Offer Conditions: Valid anytime. Excludes disc jockey services & all live entertainment including casino dealer.

00712941

Sykart Indoor Racing Center
- The only indoor go-kart track in Oregon
- Ideal for family fun or competitive racing
- Perfect for team building, corporate meetings or parties
- Karts reach speeds up to 35 mph through a 1/4 mile track
- Children 8-14 must complete kids driving school before racing (held every Sun. Call for details)

8205 S.W. Hunziker St.
Tigard, OR
(503) 684-5060

Offer Conditions: Valid anytime. Not valid with any other discounts or promotions.

00608452

Chuck E. Cheese's

Buy 40 GAME TOKENS and get 40 GAME TOKENS FREE, for a maximum total of 80 tokens.
Offer Conditions on reverse side.

40 GAME TOKENS

See Reverse Side for Locations

Valid now thru November 1, 2010

E57

Wunderland

Enjoy one complimentary GAME ROOM ADMISSION when a second GAME ROOM ADMISSION of equal or greater value is purchased.
Offer Conditions on reverse side.

FREE GAME ROOM ADMISSION

WUNDERLAND

See Reverse Side for Locations

Valid now thru November 1, 2010

E58

Wunderland

Enjoy one complimentary GAME ROOM ADMISSION when a second GAME ROOM ADMISSION of equal or greater value is purchased.
Offer Conditions on reverse side.

FREE GAME ROOM ADMISSION

WUNDERLAND

See Reverse Side for Locations

Valid now thru November 1, 2010

E59

Chuck E. Cheese's
- Family fun pizza restaurant
- Pizza, sandwiches, salad bar
- A variety of kiddie rides & skill games
- Sky crawl & ball pits
- Ask about our birthday party packages

CHUCK E. CHEESE'S.

4145 S.W. 110th Ave.
Beaverton, OR
(503)643-2002

9120 S.E. Powell
Portland, OR
(503)774-7000

Offer Conditions: Valid anytime. One coupon per customer per visit.

00034761

Wunderland
- Amusement center & video adventures
- Great fun for parties & birthdays
- Regular admission charge
- Check location for hours

WUNDERLAND

Beaverton Center 4070
S.W. Cedar Hills Blvd.
Beaverton, OR
(503)626-1665

Avalon Theatres 3451
S.E. Belmont
Portland, OR
(503)238-1617

Market Center 1657
Hawthorne N.E.
Salem, OR
(503)399-9410

Milwaukee Cinemas
11011 S.E. Main St.
Milwaukee, OR
(503)653-2222

Gateway 103rd & N.E.
Halsey St.
Portland, OR
(503)255-7333

Offer Conditions: Valid anytime. Not valid with any other discount offer.

00033783

Wunderland
- Amusement center & video adventures
- Great fun for parties & birthdays
- Regular admission charge
- Check location for hours

WUNDERLAND

Beaverton Center 4070
S.W. Cedar Hills Blvd.
Beaverton, OR
(503)626-1665

Avalon Theatres 3451
S.E. Belmont
Portland, OR
(503)238-1617

Market Center 1657
Hawthorne N.E.
Salem, OR
(503)399-9410

Milwaukee Cinemas
11011 S.E. Main St.
Milwaukee, OR
(503)653-2222

Gateway 103rd & N.E.
Halsey St.
Portland, OR
(503)255-7333

Offer Conditions: Valid anytime. Not valid with any other discount offer.

00033783

Malibu Raceway
Enjoy up to 100 ARCADE TOKENS at 50% off the regular price.
Offer Conditions on reverse side.

www.maliburaceway.com

9405 S.W. Cascade Ave., Beaverton, OR
(503)641-8122

Valid now thru November 1, 2010

E60

Malibu Raceway
Enjoy one 5 LAP PACKAGE at 50% off the regular price.
Offer Conditions on reverse side.

www.maliburaceway.com

9405 S.W. Cascade Ave., Beaverton, OR
(503)641-8122

Valid now thru November 1, 2010

E61

Malibu Raceway
Enjoy up to 5 BATTING CAGE TOKENS at 50% off the regular price.
Offer Conditions on reverse side.

www.maliburaceway.com

9405 S.W. Cascade Ave., Beaverton, OR
(503)641-8122

Valid now thru November 1, 2010

E62

Malibu Raceway
- Racing, games & more!
- Virage drivers must present a valid drivers license or have successfully completed Malibu's Car Control Clinic
- Sprint drivers must be at least 4' 6" tall
- All new drivers must purchase a lifetime Malibu racing license

9405 S.W. Cascade Ave.
Beaverton, OR
(503) 641-8122

Offer Conditions: Valid anytime. Arcade tokens must be purchased at the front desk.

00584895

Offer validity is governed by the Rules of Use and excludes defined holidays. Offers are not valid with other discount offers, unless specified. Coupons void if purchased, sold or bartered. Discounts exclude tax, tip and/or alcohol, where applicable.

Malibu Raceway
- Racing, games & more!
- Virage drivers must present a valid drivers license or have successfully completed Malibu's Car Control Clinic
- Sprint drivers must be at least 4' 6" tall
- All new drivers must purchase a lifetime Malibu racing license

9405 S.W. Cascade Ave.
Beaverton, OR
(503) 641-8122

Offer Conditions: Valid anytime.

00584894

Offer validity is governed by the Rules of Use and excludes defined holidays. Offers are not valid with other discount offers, unless specified. Coupons void if purchased, sold or bartered. Discounts exclude tax, tip and/or alcohol, where applicable.

Malibu Raceway
- Racing, games & more!
- Virage drivers must present a valid drivers license or have successfully completed Malibu's Car Control Clinic
- Sprint drivers must be at least 4' 6" tall
- All new drivers must purchase a lifetime Malibu racing license

9405 S.W. Cascade Ave.
Beaverton, OR
(503) 641-8122

Offer Conditions: Valid anytime.

00584878

Offer validity is governed by the Rules of Use and excludes defined holidays. Offers are not valid with other discount offers, unless specified. Coupons void if purchased, sold or bartered. Discounts exclude tax, tip and/or alcohol, where applicable.

entertainment.com

Enjoy one complimentary ADMISSION when a second ADMISSION of equal or greater value is purchased.

Offer Conditions on reverse side.

Valid now thru November 1, 2010

FREE ADMISSION

PORTLAND PARKS & RECREATION

www.PortlandParks.org

www.portlandparks.org

See Reverse Side for Locations

E63

entertainment.com

Mountain Air Miniature Golf

Enjoy up to 4 ROUNDS of MINIATURE GOLF at 50% off the regular price.

Offer Conditions on reverse side.

PRINT MORE ONLINE

Valid now thru November 1, 2010

50% OFF

Mountain Air Miniature Golf

www.mountainairoregon.com

60183 E. Sleepy Hollow Dr., Sandy, OR
(503)622-4759

E64

entertainment.com

Safari Sam's

Enjoy one complimentary ROUND OF MINIATURE GOLF when a second ROUND OF MINIATURE GOLF of equal or greater value is purchased.

Offer Conditions on reverse side.

Valid now thru November 1, 2010

FREE ROUND OF MINIATURE GOLF

16260 S.W. Langer Dr., Sherwood, OR
(503)925-8000

E65

- Celebrate birthdays with our pool party packages
- Water work-out classes
- Adult lap swims, family swims, & open play swims
- Call (503)823-5130 for pool information

PORTLAND PARKS
& RECREATION
www.PortlandParks.org

Portland
Buckman Pool
320 S.E. 16th
(503)823-3668

Columbia Pool
7701 N. Chautauqua Blvd.
(503)823-3669

Creston Pool
S.E. 44th & Powell
(503)823-3672

Dishman Pool
77 N.E. Knott
(503)823-3673

Grant Pool
2300 N.E. 33rd
(503)823-3674

Montavilla Pool
8219 N.E. Glisan
(503)823-3675

Mt. Scott Pool
5530 S.E. 72nd
(503)823-3676

Peninsula Pool
6400 N. Albina
(503)823-3677

Pier Pool
N. Seneca & St. Johns
(503)823-3678

Sellwood Pool
S.E. 7th & Miller
(503)823-3679

South West C.C. Pool
6820 S.W. 45th Ave.
(503)823-2840

Wilson Pool
1151 S.W. Vermont
(503)823-3680

Offer Conditions: Valid for any "open play swim" or "family swim". Valid for up to four free admissions.

00495978

Mountain Air Miniature Golf

- An Oregon trail themed 18 hole miniature golf course
- Open March-October with seasonal events
- Located in the beautiful Mt. Hood Forest
- Great for families & friends
- Horseshoe pits, gift shop, snack bar
- See website for more information & directions

Mountain Air Miniature Golf
60183 E. Sleepy Hollow Dr.
(Hwy. 26 at mile marker 36)
Sandy, OR
(503)622-4759

Offer Conditions: Valid anytime.

00635943

Safari Sam's

- Featuring over 40 of the hottest new redemption & arcade games.
- 18-hole "jungle themed" mini golf course. 3,000 sq. ft.
- Jungle gym play structure.
- Birthday party packages available.

16260 S.W. Langer Dr.
(Sherwood Plaza)
Sherwood, OR
(503)925-8000

Offer Conditions: Valid anytime.

00490221

Steakburger Golf-O-Rama

Enjoy one complimentary ROUND OF MINIATURE GOLF when a second ROUND OF MINIATURE GOLF of equal or greater value is purchased.

Offer Conditions on reverse side.

$8.00 Value

steakburger

Golf-O-Rama

Valid now thru November 1, 2010

7120 N.E. Hwy. 99, Vancouver, WA
(360)694-3421

E66

Eagle Landing Golf Course

Enjoy one complimentary ROUND OF MINIATURE GOLF when a second ROUND OF MINIATURE GOLF of equal or greater value is purchased.

Offer Conditions on reverse side.

FREE ROUND OF MINIATURE GOLF

PRINT MORE ONLINE

Valid now thru November 1, 2010

10220 S.E. Causey Ave., Happy Valley, OR
(503)698-7888

E67

Eagle Landing Golf Course

Enjoy one complimentary GREEN FEE when a second GREEN FEE of equal or greater value is purchased.

Offer Conditions on reverse side.

FREE GREEN FEE

PRINT MORE ONLINE

Valid now thru November 1, 2010

10220 S.E. Causey Ave., Happy Valley, OR
(503)698-7888

E68

Steakburger Golf-O-Rama

- 18 or 36 Hole miniature golf course adjacent to Steakburger
- Enjoy great family fun with great eats too!
- Vancouver's original miniature golf course located in Hazel Dell
- Proud to be a part of Vancouver's family community for over 45 years
- Great fun for the whole family
- Family owned & operated since 1962

steakburger

Golf-O-Rama

7120 N.E. Hwy. 99
Vancouver, WA
(360)694-3421

Offer Conditions: Valid anytime. Excludes other promotions. One coupon/card per customer per visit; Please present coupon/card at time of purchase.

00653468

Eagle Landing Golf Course

- Experience our brand new scenic 27 hole, Par 3 course & 36 hole miniature golf course
- Great fun for the entire family!
- There's no other golf facility in Oregon like Eagle Landing!

10220 S.E. Causey Ave.
(Sunnyside Rd. exit; east to Stevens Rd. north)
Happy Valley, OR
(503)698-7888

Offer Conditions: Valid anytime.

00583863

Eagle Landing Golf Course

- Experience our brand new scenic 27 hole, Par 3 course & 36 hole miniature golf course
- Great fun for the entire family!
- There's no other golf facility in Oregon like Eagle Landing!

10220 S.E. Causey Ave.
(Sunnyside Rd. exit; east to Stevens Rd. north)
Happy Valley, OR
(503)698-7888

Offer Conditions: Valid anytime.

00583840

Ultrazone Laser Tag

Enjoy one complimentary LASER TAG GAME when a second LASER TAG GAME of equal or greater value is purchased.

Offer Conditions on reverse side.

Valid now thru November 1, 2010

FREE LASER TAG GAME

"Portland's Best Laser Tag"

www.ultrazoneportland.com

16074 S.E. McLoughlin Blvd., Milwaukie, OR
(503)652-1122

E69

Laserport

Enjoy one complimentary LASER TAG PLAY SESSION when a second LASER TAG PLAY SESSION of equal or greater value is purchased.

Offer Conditions on reverse side.

Valid now thru November 1, 2010

ONE LASER TAG PLAY SESSION

Birthday Parties, Corporate Events and Just Plain Fun

6540 S.W. Fallbrook Pl., Beaverton, OR
(503)526-9501

E70

Sherwood Ice Arena

Enjoy one complimentary ADMISSION when a second ADMISSION of equal or greater value is purchased.

Offer Conditions on reverse side.

Valid now thru November 1, 2010

FREE ADMISSION

www.sherwoodicearena.com

20407 S.W. Borchers Dr., Sherwood, OR
(503)625-5757

E71

ENTERTAINMENT & SPORTS

More Offers Online!

entertainment.com

Ultrazone Laser Tag

- Huge 5000 square foot arena built on 2 levels
- Incredible special effects
- Fantastic Birthday Parties!
- Corporate bookings
- Team building & coaching
- Youth group events for church, school & scouts

"Portland's Best Laser Tag"

16074 S.E. McLoughlin Blvd.
(Holly Farm Ctr. - Near Oak Grove 8 Cinema)
Milwaukie, OR
(503)652-1122

Offer Conditions: Valid anytime.

00073033

Laserport

- 4,100 sq. ft. fully fogged arena
- Strobes, laser beams & flourescent lighting
- Over 40 of the hottest video games available
- Special parties & team building packages available for your needs

Birthday Parties, Corporate Events and Just Plain Fun

6540 S.W. Fallbrook Pl.
Beaverton, OR
(503)526-9501

Offer Conditions: Valid anytime. Not valid with any other discounts or promotions.

00236459

Sherwood Ice Arena

- Portland's newest skating rink
- Valid during any Public Session
- We offer a Learn to Skate program
- Youth & Adult Hockey for all ages & skill levels
- Snack Bar that features Longbottom Coffee & Espresso
- Northwest skate authority full service pro shop

20407 S.W. Borchers Dr.
Sherwood, OR
(503)625-5757

Offer Conditions: Valid anytime. Skate rental extra.

00396684

Mountain View Ice Arena

Enjoy one complimentary
ADMISSION when a second
ADMISSION of equal or greater
value is purchased.

Offer Conditions on reverse side.

FREE ADMISSION

www.mtviewice.com

14313 S.E. Mill Plain Blvd., Vancouver, WA
(360)896-8700

Valid now thru November 1, 2010

E72

Mountain View Ice Arena

Enjoy one complimentary
ADMISSION when a second
ADMISSION of equal or greater
value is purchased.

Offer Conditions on reverse side.

FREE ADMISSION

www.mtviewice.com

14313 S.E. Mill Plain Blvd., Vancouver, WA
(360)896-8700

Valid now thru November 1, 2010

E73

Skateworld

Enjoy up to TWO ADMISSIONS
when up to TWO ADMISSIONS
of equal or greater value is
purchased.

Offer Conditions on reverse side.

UP TO TWO ADMISSIONS

See Reverse Side for Locations

Valid now thru November 1, 2010

E74

Mountain View Ice Arena

- Valid during public skating session times
- Admission $6.50; 5 & under $3.25
- Skate Rental $2.25
- www.mtviewice.com

14313 S.E. Mill Plain Blvd.
Vancouver, WA
(360)896-8700

00275829

Offer Conditions: Valid during public skating session times.

Offer validity is governed by the Rules of Use and excludes defined holidays. Offers are not valid with other discount offers, unless specified. Coupons void if purchased, sold or bartered. Discounts exclude tax, tip and/or alcohol, where applicable.

Mountain View Ice Arena

- Valid during public skating session times
- Admission $6.50; 5 & under $3.25
- Skate Rental $2.25
- www.mtviewice.com

14313 S.E. Mill Plain Blvd.
Vancouver, WA
(360)896-8700

00275829

Offer Conditions: Valid during public skating session times.

Offer validity is governed by the Rules of Use and excludes defined holidays. Offers are not valid with other discount offers, unless specified. Coupons void if purchased, sold or bartered. Discounts exclude tax, tip and/or alcohol, where applicable.

Skateworld

- Classes & lockers available
- Private parties & fundraisers
- Pro shop, snack shop
- Call for schedule information

1220 N.E. Kelley
Gresham, OR
(503)667-1647

4395 S.W. Witch Hazel Rd.
Hillsboro, OR
(503)640-1333

3188 Gateway Loop
Springfield, OR
(541)746-8424

2219 Talley Way
Kelso, WA
(360)577-7999

00035613

Offer Conditions: Valid any regular public session.

Offer validity is governed by the Rules of Use and excludes defined holidays. Offers are not valid with other discount offers, unless specified. Coupons void if purchased, sold or bartered. Discounts exclude tax, tip and/or alcohol, where applicable.

Oaks Amusement Park

- Great birthday packages
- Private & class lessons
- Pre-school only mornings
- Largest floor on the West Coast
- Live Wurlitzer Organ music
- Call for session times

7805 S.E. Oaks Pkwy.
Portland, OR
(503)233-5777

Offer Conditions: Valid during any regular public session. Conventional skat
rental included.

00015400

Silver Creek Lanes

- High Tech Sound & Lighting; Wall to Wall Music Videos
- Fun for casual bowlers; Exceptional for league bowlers
- A competitive shot, newest synthetic lanes & equipment
- Advanced Pro Shop; IPBSIA ball drilling certified
- Visit www.Silvercreeklanes,org for directions and more information

SILVER CREEK LANES
500 W. C St.
Silverton, OR
(503)873-5316

Offer Conditions: Valid anytime. Not valid with other discounts or promotion

00780404

Big Al's

- Visit the next generation of entertainment
- 60,000 sq. ft. of awe-inspiring fun
- 30 tradtional bowling lanes
- 12 lounge-style bowling lanes
- Up-scale sports bar and grill with 8'x36' Jumbo-tron
- Full menu with a variety of amazing appetizers, impressive entrees and delectable desserts
- See www.ilovebigals.com for more information

16615 S.E. 18th St.
Vancouver, WA
(360)944-6118

Offer Conditions: Valid Monday through Thrusday. Valid Monday-Thursday
only; based on lane availability. Use Code #4001.

00765987

AMF Bowling Centers

Enjoy one complimentary
GAME OF BOWLING when a
second GAME OF BOWLING
of equal or greater value is
purchased.
Offer Conditions on reverse side.

Valid now thru November 1, 2010

FREE GAME OF BOWLING

Need fun? Add bowling.
amf.com

For the AMF Bowling Center nearest you, visit
us on the web at www.amf.com E78

AMF Bowling Centers

Enjoy $2.00 off one XTREME
GAME OR SESSION.
Offer Conditions on reverse side.

Valid now thru November 1, 2010

$2.00 VALUE

Need fun? Add bowling.
amf.com

For the AMF Bowling Center nearest you, visit
us on the web at www.amf.com E79

AMF Bowling Centers

Enjoy $2.00 off GIO'S TEAM
PIZZA.
Offer Conditions on reverse side.

Valid now thru November 1, 2010

$2.00 VALUE

Need fun? Add bowling.
amf.com

For the AMF Bowling Center nearest you, visit
us on the web at www.amf.com E80

AMF Bowling Centers
- Fun for all ages
- Bumper bowling for kids
- Adult & youth bowling leagues
- Birthday parties
- Xtreme bowling
- Automatic scoring
- Great food choices featuring our very own Gio's Pizza
- All new Grip & Sip menu from our full service bar including signature drinks

00691864

For the AMF Bowling Center nearest you, visit us on the web at www.amf.co

Offer Conditions: Valid anytime. Offer good for up to 6 people. Shoe rental not included. One coupon/card per customer per visit. Not valid during Xtreme league or tournament bowling, birthday parties or group events. Offer valid at participating AMF Bowling Center locations. No valid at 300 Brand locations.

AMF Bowling Centers
- Fun for all ages
- Bumper bowling for kids
- Adult & youth bowling leagues
- Birthday parties
- Xtreme bowling
- Automatic scoring
- Great food choices featuring our very own Gio's Pizza
- All new Grip & Sip menu from our full service bar including signature drinks

00712719

For the AMF Bowling Center nearest you, visit us on the web at www.amf.co

Offer Conditions: Valid during Xtreme Bowling. Offer good for up to 6 people. Shoe rental not included. One coupon/card per customer per visit. Offer valid at participating AMF Bowling Center locations. Not valid at 300 Brand locations.

AMF Bowling Centers
- Fun for all ages
- Bumper bowling for kids
- Adult & youth bowling leagues
- Birthday parties
- Xtreme bowling
- Automatic scoring
- Great food choices featuring our very own Gio's Pizza
- All new Grip & Sip menu from our full service bar including signature drinks

00712894

For the AMF Bowling Center nearest you, visit us on the web at www.amf.co

Offer Conditions: Valid anytime. Not valid at 300 Brand Center locations. Off is valid where Gio's Pizza is served.

Sunset Lanes

Enjoy one complimentary GAME OF BOWLING when a second game of equal or greater value is purchased - valid for up to 5 people.

Offer Conditions on reverse side.

Valid now thru November 1, 2010

FREE GAME OF BOWLING

www.sunsetlanes.com

12770 SW Walker Rd, Beaverton, OR
(503) 646-1116

E81

Rainbow Lanes

Enjoy up to 4 GAMES (open bowling) at 50% off the regular price.

Offer Conditions on reverse side.

Valid now thru November 1, 2010

50% OFF

2748 19th Pl, Forest Grove, OR
(503) 357-6321

E82

Allen's Crosley Lanes

Enjoy up to 4 GAMES (open bowling) at 50% off the regular price.

Offer Conditions on reverse side.

Valid now thru November 1, 2010

50% OFF

Family Fun Bowling Center

2400 E. Evergreen, Vancouver, WA
(360) 693-4789

E83

Sunset Lanes
- 36 lanes with 12 lanes of Boutique bowling lounge seating
- Cosmic bowling with laser lights, back lights and your favorite music videos on 54" flat screens and 12 jumbo-tron screens at the end of your lanes
- Arcade with your favorite video games and redemption prize center
- Full food and bar menu with your favorite drinks and a fantastic entrees and appetizers

12770 SW Walker Rd
Beaverton, OR
(503)646-1116

00752007

Offer Conditions: Valid anytime. Not valid Friday or Saturday after 6pm.

Rainbow Lanes
- Newly remodeled 16 lane bowling center
- Newly re-surfaced lanes, couch seating, automatic scoring
- Pro shop, Silver certified coach
- Lottery, snack bar
- Friendly, helpful staff

2748 19th Pl
(Behind Safeway)
Forest Grove, OR
(503)357-6321

00747446

Offer Conditions: Valid anytime.

Allen's Crosley Lanes

Family Fun Bowling Center
Allen's Crosley Lanes
2400 E. Evergreen
Vancouver, WA
(360)693-4789

00731180

Offer Conditions: Valid anytime. Not valid during leagues and tournaments; Not valid with Cosmic Bowl.

Columbia Lanes

Enjoy up to 4 GAMES (open bowling) at 50% off the regular price.

Offer Conditions on reverse side.

Valid now thru November 1, 2010

213 E. Second St., The Dalles, OR
(541)296-8003

E84

Bailey's Classic Lanes

Enjoy up to 4 GAMES (open bowling) at 50% off the regular price.

Offer Conditions on reverse side.

Bailey's Classic Lanes

Valid now thru November 1, 2010

11605 Se Mcgillivray Blvd, Vancouver, OR
(360)882-6921

E85

Mt. Hood Lanes

Enjoy up to 4 GAMES (open bowling) at 50% off the regular price.

Offer Conditions on reverse side.

Valid now thru November 1, 2010

2311 E Powell Blvd, Gresham, OR
(503)492-9820

E86

More Offers Online!

ENTERTAINMENT & SPORTS

entertainment.com

Columbia Lanes

- Complete youth program
- Complete pro shop
- 16 Lanes & bumpers
- Cosmic bowling every Friday & Saturday night
- Custom graphics
- Oregon lottery & video games
- Beer & wine

Columbia Lanes

213 E. Second St.
The Dalles, OR
(541) 296-8003

Offer Conditions: Valid anytime.

00459408

Bailey's Classic Lanes

- We do it for the love of bowling
- Pro shop, leagues and open bowling
- Available for private and corporate parties

Bailey's Classic Lanes

11605 Se Mcgillivray Blvd
Vancouver, OR
(360) 882-6921

Offer Conditions: Valid anytime.

00752640

Mt. Hood Lanes

- 24 lanes of fun family entertainment
- Totally smoke free
- Full service lounge and restaurant
- Lessons available

2311 E Powell Blvd
Gresham, OR
(503) 492-9820

Offer Conditions: Valid anytime. Not valid with Cosmic Bowl; shoe rental not included.

00751360

Milwaukie Bowl

Enjoy up to 4 GAMES (open bowling) at 50% off the regular price.

Offer Conditions on reverse side.

50%OFF

Milwaukie Bowl

Valid now thru November 1, 2010

3056 S.E. Harrison St., Milwaukie, OR
(503)654-7719

E87

Tiger Bowl

Enjoy up to 4 GAMES (open bowling) at 50% off the regular price.

Offer Conditions on reverse side.

50%OFF

Tiger Bowl

Valid now thru November 1, 2010

211 N. Parkway, Battle Ground, WA
(360)687-2101

E88

Woodburn Lanes

Enjoy up to 4 GAMES (open bowling) at 50% off the regular price.

Offer Conditions on reverse side.

50%OFF

WOODBURN LANES

Valid now thru November 1, 2010

435 N. Pacific Hwy., Woodburn, OR
(503)981-1500

E89

Milwaukie Bowl

Milwaukie Bowl
- Your fun is our business!
- Offering tournament, leagues, lessons, pro shop & just plain fun!

3056 S.E. Harrison St.
Milwaukie, OR
(503) 654-7719

Offer Conditions: Valid anytime. Not valid during leagues and tournaments.

00731684

Tiger Bowl

Tiger Bowl
- Open bowl
- Leagues
- Lessons
- Rock & Bowl - Fri. & Sat. nights
- Call for open lane times

211 N. Parkway
(2 Blocks N. of Main St.)
Battle Ground, WA
(360) 687-2101

Offer Conditions: Valid anytime. Not valid during leagues and tournaments; Excludes Rock & Bowl.

00729929

WOODBURN LANES

Woodburn Lanes
- Woodburn's ONLY 12 lane bowling alley
- Rental & pro shop
- Beer, wine, snacks, lottery & arcade
- ATM on site
- Glo-Bowl Fri. & Sat. nights

435 N. Pacific Hwy.
Woodburn, OR
(503) 981-1500

Offer Conditions: Valid anytime. Not vaild with Glo-Bowl; Not valid during leagues and tournaments.

00731682

Triangle Bowl

Enjoy up to 4 GAMES (open bowling) at 50% off the regular price.

Offer Conditions on reverse side.

Valid now thru November 1, 2010

700 Triangle Center, Longview, WA
(360)425-4060

E90

The Hilander

Enjoy up to 4 GAMES (open bowling) at 50% off the regular price.

Offer Conditions on reverse side.

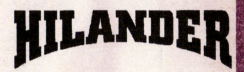

Valid now thru November 1, 2010

www.thehilander.com

200 Kelso Dr., Kelso, WA
(360)423-1500

E91

The Hilander

Enjoy one LASER TAG SESSION without charge, upon payment for the same of equal or greater value.

Offer Conditions on reverse side.

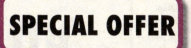

Valid now thru November 1, 2010

www.thehilander.com

200 Kelso Dr., Kelso, WA
(360)423-1500

E92

Triangle Bowl
- 32 Lanes of pure fun!
- League & open bowling
- Pro shop
- Lounge & snack bar

700 Triangle Center
Longview, WA
(360)425-4060

Offer Conditions: Valid anytime.

00753800

The Hilander
- Bowling, laser tag & so much more!
- 23 sensational bowling lanes
- Fun center with carousel, games, human habitrail & more
- Full restaurant & lounge, snack bar & gift shop

200 Kelso Dr.
Kelso, WA
(360)423-1500

Offer Conditions: Valid anytime.

00753780

The Hilander
- Bowling, laser tag & so much more!
- 23 sensational bowling lanes
- Fun center with carousel, games, human habitrail & more
- Full restaurant & lounge, snack bar & gift shop

HILANDER

200 Kelso Dr.
Kelso, WA
(360)423-1500

Offer Conditions: Valid anytime.

00753770

Warpaint

Enjoy 3 FREE HOURS OF
PAINTBALL for up to 5 people.
Offer Conditions on reverse side.

3 FREE HOURS OF PAINTBALL

www.warpaintpb.com

Valid now thru November 1, 2010

3046 Portland Rd. NE, Salem, OR
(503)585-9477   E93

Pioneer Paintball Park

Enjoy one complimentary Field
Day Pass when a second Field
Day Pass of equal or greater
value is purchased.
Offer Conditions on reverse side.

One FIELD DAY PASS

Valid now thru November 1, 2010

19712 S.E. Canyon Valley Rd., Sandy, OR
(503)668-0250   E94

Oregon Ballet Theatre

Enjoy Up to 4 ADMISSIONS in
AREAS 3 or 4 at 50% off the
regular price.
Offer Conditions on reverse side.

50% OFF

OREGONBALLETTHEATRE
CHRISTOPHER STOWELL / ARTISTIC DIRECTOR

Valid now thru November 1, 2010

818 S.E. 6th Ave., Portland, OR
(503)222-5538   E95

Warpaint

- Indoor and Outdoor fields
- 20,000 square feet of play area
- Play the Congo, Tombstone, Camelot & more
- Available 24 hours, 7 days a week for private events
- Players under 18 years require parental consent form

3046 Portland Rd. NE
Salem, OR
(503)585-9477

Offer Conditions: Valid anytime. Not valid for special events; call for availability; paintballs extra; Valid for indoor and outdoor fields; paintballs must be purchased at $5.00 per 100 rounds; not valid with any other discounts or promotions; not valid on BYOP days.

00769027

Offer validity is governed by the Rules of Use and excludes defined holidays. Offers are not valid with other discount offers, unless specified. Coupons void if purchased, sold or bartered. Discounts exclude tax, tip and/or alcohol, where applicable.

Pioneer Paintball Park

- 2 Paint Ball fields - one speed, one wooded
- Paint ball markers, paintballs and CO2 available for rental
- Please call for field reservation and availability
- Great for beginners and families - ideal for groups of 6 or more

19712 S.E. Canyon Valley Rd.
Sandy, OR
(503)668-0250

Offer Conditions: Valid anytime.

00755540

Offer validity is governed by the Rules of Use and excludes defined holidays. Offers are not valid with other discount offers, unless specified. Coupons void if purchased, sold or bartered. Discounts exclude tax, tip and/or alcohol, where applicable.

Oregon Ballet Theatre

- George Balanchine's The Nutcracker at Portland Keller Auditorium
- For performance and ticket information call 503-222-5538
- Limited performaces and seating locations - no upgrades available

Entertainment® Order Back
PLEASE ENCLOSE A SEPARATE CHECK FOR THIS ATTRACTION. PLEASE PRINT.

TO: OREGON BALLET
     818 SE 6th Ave.
     Portland, OR 97214

Please send ☐ 2 or ☐ 4 tickets at 50% off the regular price for:

December 17 at 7:30pm	December 21 at 2:00pm	December 21 at 7:30pm
December 22 at 2:00pm	December 22 at 7:30pm	December 23 at 2:00pm
December 23 at 7:30pm	December 24 at 12:00pm	

Enclosed is my check payable to OREGON BALLET THEATRE for $ _____ , or charge my :
☐ VISA   ☐ Master Card   ☐ American Express   ☐ DISCOVER

Credit Card Number: _____ Expiration Date: _____

Signature: _____

Name: _____

Address: _____

Phone: _____

City: _____

State: _____ ZIP: _____

Email: _____

Offer Conditions: Valid for Listed Performance Dates Only. Valid for any Monday -Thursday performance of George Balanchine's The Nutcracker 2009; Subject to availability; Redeem ONLY in person or mail order at Oregon Ballet Theatre ticket office, no phone orders or reservations accepted; $3 handling charge per ticket; limit total of 4 tickets; Tickets go on sale July 2009.

00779499

Offer validity is governed by the Rules of Use and excludes defined holidays. Offers are not valid with other discount offers, unless specified. Coupons void if purchased, sold or bartered. Discounts exclude tax, tip and/or alcohol, where applicable.

Oregon Children's Theatre

Enjoy one complimentary CHILDREN'S ADMISSION when an adult or senior admission is purchased.

Offer Conditions on reverse side.

Valid now thru November 1, 2010

FREE CHILDREN'S ADMISSION

Oregon Children's Theatre

explore the stage

www.octc.org

600 S.W. 10th Ave., Ste. 313, Portland, OR
(503)228-9571

E96

Portland Center Stage

Enjoy one complimentary TICKET when a second TICKET of equal or greater value is purchased.

Offer Conditions on reverse side.

Valid now thru November 1, 2010

Up To $63.00 Value

PORTLANDCENTERSTAGE

www.pcs.org

128 NW 11th Ave., Portland, OR
(503)445-3700

E97

Tears Of Joy Theatre

Enjoy one complimentary ADMISSION when a second ADMISSION of equal or greater value is purchased.

Offer Conditions on reverse side.

Valid now thru November 1, 2010

FREE ADMISSION

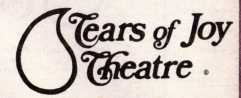

Tears of Joy Theatre ®

www.tojt.org

Portland Center For Performing Arts 1111 S.W. Broadway,
Portland, OR
(503)248-0557

E98

Oregon Children's Theatre

- Oregon Children's Theatre invites you to explore the stage!
- 2009-2010 Season includes:
- Charlie and the Chocolate Factory: Oct 31 – Nov 22, 2009.
- Giggle, Giggle, Quack: Jan 30-Feb 21, 2010
- The True Story of the Three Little Pigs: Feb 27-Mar 21, 2010
- Small Steps: The Sequel to Holes: April 24 - May 16, 2010
- Sideways Stories from Wayside School, May 15 - Jun 6, 2010

Oregon Children's Theatre

explore the stage

600 S.W. 10th Ave., Ste. 313
(Box Office)
Portland, OR
(503)228-9571

Offer Conditions: Valid anytime. Valid for listed 2009-2010 performances; offer exlcudes price level one in the Newmark Theatre; valid for advance ticket sales only at the OCT box office; not valid with any other offer; subject to availability.

00770671

Portland Center Stage

- Portland Center Stage inspires our community by bringing unexpected stories to life
- 599 Seat main stage, 200 seat studio
- Box Office Hours: 10 a.m. - 5:30 p.m. Mon. - Fri.; 12 p.m. - 5:30 p.m. Sat. & Sun.
- Visit our website

PORTLANDCENTERSTAGE

128 NW 11th Ave.
Portland, OR
(503)445-3700

Offer Conditions: Valid anytime. Subject to availability; Not valid with any other discounts or promotions.

00742030

Tears Of Joy Theatre

- Our mission is to produce, develop & present puppet theatre that celebrates the diversity of world cultures
- We entertain & enrich the lives of over 225,000 children each year
- Please visit our website
- Tears Of Joy Theatre is where imagination begins

Portland Center For Performing Arts 1111 S.W. Broadway
Portland, OR
(503)248-0557

Offer Conditions: Valid anytime.

00729162

Columbia Dance
Royal Durst Theatre
- "Come dance with us"
- One of Clark County's premier art groups
- A non-profit pre-professional dance company with dancers from around the country
- Please visit our website for events & schedule

Columbia Dance

3101 Main St.
Vancouver, WA
(360)737-1922

Offer Conditions: Valid any performance. On availability basis.

00672512

Oregon Chorale
- 50 talented and dedicated Musicians perform symphonic concerts December, March & June
- For concert info go to www.oregonchorale.org or call (503)939-8441
- Director: Bernd R. Kuehn

OREGON CHORALE
(503)939-8441 Portland, OR

Offer Conditions: Valid anytime.

00501067

Pacific University Performing Arts Series
- Pacific University Performing Arts Series
- Enjoy a variety of musical concerts
- For information regarding performances & dates, call the Taylor-Meade Performing Arts Center at McCready Hall in Forest Grove at (503)352-2918
- Please add $4.00 handling charge for all mail orders

Pacific University Performing Arts Series

2043 College Way
Forest Grove, OR
(503)352-2918

Offer Conditions: Valid for any Pacific University Arts Series event in the September 2009 - May 2010 season. On availability basis.

00010786

Inclimb

Enjoy one complimentary
ADMISSION when a second
ADMISSION of equal or greater
value is purchased.

Offer Conditions on reverse side.

Valid now thru November 1, 2010

FREE ADMISSION

www.inclimb.com

**555 N.W. Arizona Ave., Ste. 50, Bend, OR
(541)388-6764**

E102

Inclimb

Enjoy one complimentary
ADMISSION when a second
ADMISSION of equal or greater
value is purchased.

Offer Conditions on reverse side.

Valid now thru November 1, 2010

FREE ADMISSION

www.inclimb.com

**555 N.W. Arizona Ave., Ste. 50, Bend, OR
(541)388-6764**

E103

Portland Symphonic Choir

Enjoy one complimentary
ADMISSION when a second
ADMISSION of equal or greater
value is purchased.

Offer Conditions on reverse side.

Valid now thru November 1, 2010

Up To $20.00 Value

Founded in 1946
www.pschoir.org

Concerts at St Mary's Cathedral (503)223-1217

E104

Inclimb
- No age minimum or maximum
- Kids must have liability waiver
- Indoor rock climbing gym
- Membership club & drop-in's welcome
- Instruction for all levels
- Corporate team building
- www.inclimb.com

**555 N.W. Arizona Ave., Ste. 50
Bend, OR
(541)388-6764**

Offer Conditions: Valid anytime. Not valid with any other discounts or promotions; On availability basis.

00600665

Inclimb
- No age minimum or maximum
- Kids must have liability waiver
- Indoor rock climbing gym
- Membership club & drop-in's welcome
- Instruction for all levels
- Corporate team building
- www.inclimb.com

**555 N.W. Arizona Ave., Ste. 50
Bend, OR
(541)388-6764**

Offer Conditions: Valid anytime. Not valid with any other discounts or promotions; On availability basis.

00600665

Portland Symphonic Choir
- Celebrating over 60 years of choral excellence
- Programs subject to change
- Call (503) 223-1217 for ticket/concert information or visit www.pschoir.org

Founded in 1946
Concerts at St Mary's Cathedral (503)223-1217

Offer Conditions: Valid anytime. On availability basis.

00012307

Marylhurst Symphony

Enjoy up to 4 ADMISSIONS at 50% off the regular price.

Offer Conditions on reverse side.

Valid now thru November 1, 2010

17600 Hwy. 43, Marylhurst, OR
(503)699-6263

E105

Columbia Symphony Orchestra

Enjoy one complimentary ADMISSION when a second ADMISSION of equal or greater value is purchased.

Offer Conditions on reverse side.

www.columbiasymphony.org

(503)234-4077

Valid now thru November 1, 2010

E106

Pacific Crest Wind Symphony

Enjoy up to 4 ADMISSIONS at 50% off the regular price.

Offer Conditions on reverse side.

www.pcws.org

Valid now thru November 1, 2010

For schedule & ticket information, call:
(503)285-7621

E107

Marylhurst Symphony

- Marylhurst Symphony is made up of community & university players
- It has been a tradition since 1968
- To schedule an audition call (503)699-6263

17600 Hwy. 43
(Marylhurst University)
Marylhurst, OR
(503)699-6263

Offer Conditions: Valid any performance. Tickets may be purchased day of concert at box office; Excludes season tickets & reserved tables; Valid for any Marylhurst Symphony concert.

00517260

Columbia Symphony Orchestra

- Performances at First United Methodist Church - 1838 S.W. Jefferson, Portland, OR
- Concerts begin promptly at 7:30 p.m., pre-concert lectures at 6:45 p.m.
- Concert dates subject to change, please call for updated information
- Check our website for performances
- www.columbiasymphony.org

Entertainment® Order Back

TO: **Columbia Symphony Orchestra**
      P.O. Box 6559
      Portland, OR 97228

Please send (2) tickets for the price of one. Please send ☐ two $30.00 adult tickets or ☐ two $25.00 senior tickets.
☐ Friday, October 16, 2009   ☐ Sunday, October 18, 2009   ☐ Friday, November 20, 2009
☐ Sunday, November 22, 2009   ☐ Friday, February 19, 2010   ☐ Friday, March 19, 2010
☐ Sunday, March 21, 2010   ☐ Friday, April 30, 2010

Enclosed is my check payable to COLUMBIA SYMPHONY ORCHESTRA for $_____, or charge my :
☐ VISA   ☐ Master Card   ☐ Discover   ☐ American Express

Credit Card Number: _____ Expiration Date: _____

Signature: _____

Name: _____

Address: _____

Phone: _____

City:_____State: _____ZIP:_____

Email: _____

ORDER WILL NOT BE FILLED WITHOUT SELF-ADDRESSED, STAMPED ENVELOPE

Offer Conditions: Valid for performances listed. Mail order preferred.

00005940

Pacific Crest Wind Symphony

- Organized in 1988, this highly acclaimed 40-member organization plays the finest contemporary & classical symphonic band literature
- Come & discover the best kept secret in the Northwest
- www.pcws.org
- For schedule & ticket information, call: (503) 285-7621
- Tickets available by phone or at the door

For schedule & ticket information, call: **(503)285-7621**

Offer Conditions: Valid any performance. Group rates available.

00010785

Metropolitan Youth Symphony

Enjoy up to 4 ADMISSIONS at 50% off the regular price.

Offer Conditions on reverse side.

www.playmys.org

4800 S.W. MacAdam Ave., Portland, OR
(503)239-4566

E108

Valid now thru November 1, 2010

Portland Rose Festival, Rose Cup Races

Enjoy one complimentary ADMISSION when a second ADMISSION of equal or greater value is purchased--Up to 4 free admissions.

Offer Conditions on reverse side.

UP TO FOUR FREE ADMISSIONS

www.rosefestival.org

1940 N. Victory Blvd., Portland, OR
(503)227-2681

E109

Valid now thru November 1, 2010

Smucker's Stars on Ice

Enjoy 40% OFF the regular price of UP TO 4 RESERVED TICKETS.

Offer Conditions on reverse side.

Tracking Code: EPS

40% OFF

www.starsonice.com

Visit www.starsonice.com for show dates, performance times, & locations

E110

Valid now thru November 1, 2010

Metropolitan Youth Symphony

- MYS office hours are Tues. - Fri. 9 a.m. - 3 p.m.
- See www.playmys.org for performance dates & information

Metropolitan Youth Symphony

**4800 S.W. MacAdam Ave.
Portland, OR
(503)239-4566**

Offer Conditions: Valid anytime. Tickets redeemable at box office up to 2 days prior to performance; Season tickets & Dress Circle tickets excluded; Valid for any Metropolitan Youth Symphony performance.

00517258

Portland Rose Festival, Rose Cup Races

- Annual Rose Festival Rose Cup Races at Portland International Raceway
- Over 300 amateur race entries
- June 2010 - see www.rosefestival.org for more information
- Discounted tickets availabe by mail order only

Entertainment® Order Back

To: Portland Rose Festival
     5603 S.W. Hood Ave.
     Portland, OR 97239

Ticket Type: Regular Price:
☐ Three-day $16.00
☐ Sunday only admission $8.00
☐ Saturday only admission $5.50
☐ Friday only admission $4.00

Please send ☐ two or ☐ four tickets at 50% off the regular price.

Enclosed is my check payable to Portland Rose Festival Assn. for $ _____ , or charge my:

☐ VISA   ☐ Master Card   ☐ American Express

Credit Card Number: _____   Exp. Date: _____

Signature: _____

Name: _____

Address: _____

Phone: _____

City: _____

State: _____   ZIP: _____

• Mail order before May 25, 2010. Prices are subject to change.

Offer Conditions: Valid anytime. Valid June 2010; mail order by May 25, 2010; prices subject to change; limit four admissions per coupon; mail order only; on availability basis.

00776145

Smucker's Stars on Ice

- In 2010, this all-new show will feature the brightest stars from the Vancouver Olympic Games!
- Experience the excitement of seeing the world's best skaters with a fresh new look - as they perform live just for you, for one night only!

Visit www.starsonice.com for show dates, performance times, & locations

Offer Conditions: Valid for performances March 1, 2010 thru July 30, 2010 only. Valid for tickets $55 or under. Redeem at Box Office or to redeem on-line, use redemption code EPS during checkout; No refunds or exchanges; Date & time subject to change; Tickets subject to availability; Not valid on ticket presales or previously purchased tickets; Cannot be combined with any other offer.

00777495

PGE Park - Portland Timbers

Enjoy up to 4 RESERVED
TICKETS VALID THE MONTHS
OF APRIL, MAY OR JUNE at
50% off the regular price.
Offer Conditions on reverse side.

Valid now thru November 1, 2010

1844 S.W. Morrison St. PGE Park, Portland, OR
(503)553-5555

E111

PGE Park - Portland Beavers

Enjoy up to 4 RESERVED
TICKETS at 50% off the regular
price.
Offer Conditions on reverse side.

Valid now thru November 1, 2010

1844 S.W. Morrison St., PGE Park, Portland, OR
(503)553-5555

E112

PGE Park - Portland Beavers

Enjoy up to 4 RESERVED
TICKETS FOR GAMES PLAYED
SUNDAY THROUGH
WEDNESDAY at 50% off the
regular price.
Offer Conditions on reverse side.

Valid now thru November 1, 2010

1844 SW Morrison St, Portland, OR
(503)553-5555

E113

PGE Park - Portland Timbers

- Visit www.portlandtimbers.com for game times and schedule

**1844 S.W. Morrison St. PGE Park
Portland, OR
(503)553-5555**

00779999

Offer Conditions: Valid April, May and June Regular Season Only. Excludes playoffs, general admission, exhibition games and US Open Cup; some blackout dates may apply; not valid with any other discount or promotion; redeem at PGE Park Box Office ONLY; upgrades available; Valid for regular season games only.

Offer validity is governed by the Rules of Use and excludes defined holidays. Offers are not valid with other discount offers, unless specified. Coupons void if purchased, sold or bartered. Discounts exclude tax, tip and/or alcohol, where applicable.

PGE Park - Portland Beavers

- Visit www.PortlandBeavers.com for games, times and schedule

**1844 S.W. Morrison St., PGE Park
Portland, OR
(503)553-5555**

00780008

Offer Conditions: Valid for regular season games only. Excludes club seats, general admission, playoff and exhibition games; some blackout dates may apply; Redeem at PGE Park Box Office ONLY; not valid with any other discount or promotion.

Offer validity is governed by the Rules of Use and excludes defined holidays. Offers are not valid with other discount offers, unless specified. Coupons void if purchased, sold or bartered. Discounts exclude tax, tip and/or alcohol, where applicable.

PGE Park - Portland Beavers

- Visit www.PortlandBeavers.com for games, times and schedule

**1844 SW Morrison St
(PGE Park)
Portland, OR
(503)553-5555**

00780009

Offer Conditions: Valid for regular season games played Sunday through Wednessday only. Excludes club seats, general admission, playoff and exhibition games; some blackout dates may apply; Redeem at PGE Park Box Office ONLY; not valid with any other discount or promotion.

Offer validity is governed by the Rules of Use and excludes defined holidays. Offers are not valid with other discount offers, unless specified. Coupons void if purchased, sold or bartered. Discounts exclude tax, tip and/or alcohol, where applicable.

Body Vox

Enjoy one complimentary
TICKET when a second TICKET
of equal or greater value is
purchased.

Offer Conditions on reverse side.

Up To $46.00 Value

Body Vox

Valid now thru November 1, 2010

www.bodyvox.com

1300 NW Northrup, Portland, OR
(503) 229-0627

E114

Concordia University

Enjoy up to 4 ADMISSIONS of
Women's basketball, soccer, or
volleyball at 50% off the regular
price.

Offer Conditions on reverse side.

Up To $10.00 Value

CONCORDIA **CU** UNIVERSITY
ATHLETIC DEPARTMENT

Valid now thru November 1, 2010

2811 NE Holman, Portland, OR
(503) 280-8582

E115

Concordia University

Enjoy up to 4 ADMISSIONS of
Men's basketball or soccer at
50% off the regular price.

Offer Conditions on reverse side.

Up To $10.00 Value

CONCORDIA **CU** UNIVERSITY
ATHLETIC DEPARTMENT

Valid now thru November 1, 2010

2811 NE Holman, Portland, OR
(503) 280-8582

E116

Body Vox

- Breathtakingly physical; highly original; passionately lyrical; frequently whimsical
- Body Vox combines dance, storytelling, cinema and comedy for truly memorable entertainment
- "Side splittingly funny and magnificently danced." Dance Magazine
- "A hymn to impulsive uninhibited creative expression." The Los Angeles Times
- 10th Anniversary season, join the celebration

Body Vox

1300 NW Northrup
Portland, OR
(503) 229-0627

Offer Conditions: Valid anytime. Based on availability. Friday and Saturday evenings excluded.; Not valid with any other discounts or promotions.

00744477

Concordia University

- Concordia University preparing leaders for the transformation of society
- Proud member of the Cascade Collegiate Conference
- One of the most exciting games in town

CONCORDIA **CU** UNIVERSITY

ATHLETIC DEPARTMENT

2811 NE Holman
Portland, OR
(503) 280-8582

Offer Conditions: Valid on any regular season game.

00316802

Concordia University

- Concordia University preparing leaders for the transformation of society
- Proud member of the Cascade Collegiate Conference
- One of the most exciting games in town

CONCORDIA **CU** UNIVERSITY

ATHLETIC DEPARTMENT

2811 NE Holman
Portland, OR
(503) 280-8582

Offer Conditions: Valid on any regular season game.

00316797

George Fox University Bruin Basketball

Enjoy up to 4 ADMISSIONS at 50% off the regular price.

Offer Conditions on reverse side.

www.georgefox.edu

See Reverse Side for Locations

Valid now thru November 1, 2010

E117

Cascade College Thunderbirds

Enjoy one complimentary ADMISSION when a second ADMISSION of equal or greater value is purchased.

Offer Conditions on reverse side.

FREE ADMISSION

CASCADE COLLEGE THUNDERBIRDS

91st. & Glisan, Portland, OR
(503)257-1212

Valid now thru November 1, 2010

E118

P.S.U. Basketball, Volleyball, Wrestling

Enjoy one complimentary GENERAL ADMISSION when a second GENERAL ADMISSION of equal or greater value is purchased.

Offer Conditions on reverse side.

FREE GENERAL ADMISSION

Portland State University
WOMEN'S
BASKETBALL or VOLLEYBALL or MEN'S WRESTLING

P.S.U. Gymnasium (S.W. 10th & Hall) Portland, OR (503) 725-3307

Valid now thru November 1, 2010

E119

More Offers Online!

ENTERTAINMENT & SPORTS

entertainment.com

George Fox University Bruin Basketball

- Exciting college men's & women's basketball
- Tickets on availability basis
- $5 adults, $3 students, $1 seniors & children
- No reservations accepted

GEORGE FOX UNIVERSITY BRUIN BASKETBALL

Wheeler Sports Center E. Fulton St. Newberg, OR

Please call sports information director for a schedule at: (503)554-2926

Offer Conditions: Valid any regular season home game. Redeem at ticket office; On availability basis.

00154501

Cascade College Thunderbirds

- Games are held on campus at 9101 E. Burnside St.
- For schedules on-line at www.cascade.edu or call our sports hotline at (503)257-1212

91st. & Glisan Portland, OR (503)257-1212

Offer Conditions: Valid anytime. Valid for men or women¿s basketball, volleyball, or soccer games.

00480206

P.S.U. Basketball, Volleyball, Wrestling

- For information & schedule call (503) 725-3307
- Volleyball, basketball & wrestling held at P.S.U. gym - S.W. 10th & Hall

Portland State University
WOMEN'S BASKETBALL or VOLLEYBALL or MEN'S WRESTLING

P.S.U. Gymnasium (S.W. 10th & Hall) Portland, OR (503) 725-3307

Offer Conditions: Valid any regular season home game. Playoffs & special events excluded; On availability basis; Redeem for Stott Center Games only at ticket office same day.

00029323

Lewis & Clark College - Football & Basketball

Enjoy one complimentary ADULT ADMISSION when a second ADULT ADMISSION of equal or greater value is purchased.

Offer Conditions on reverse side.

Valid now thru November 1, 2010

FREE ADULT ADMISSION

Lewis & Clark College

FOOTBALL & BASKETBALL

www.lclark.edu

615 S.W. Palatine Hill Rd., Portland, OR
(503) 768-7060

E120

Lakewood Theatre Company

Enjoy one complimentary ADULT ADMISSION when a second ADULT ADMISSION of equal or greater value is purchased.

Offer Conditions on reverse side.

Valid now thru November 1, 2010

FREE ADULT ADMISSION

 LAKEWOOD THEATRE COMPANY

www.lakewood-center.org

368 S. State St., Lake Oswego, OR
(503) 635-3901

E121

Meriwether National Golf Club

Enjoy one complimentary GREEN FEE when 3 GREEN FEES of equal or greater value are purchased.

Offer Conditions on reverse side.

Valid now thru November 1, 2010

Up To $36.00 Value

MERIWETHER NATIONAL GOLF CLUB

www.meriwethergolfclub.com

5200 S.W. Rood Bridge Rd., Hillsboro, OR
(503) 648-4143

E122

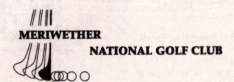

entertainment.com

Camas Meadows Golf Club

Enjoy one complimentary GREEN FEE when 3 GREEN FEES of equal or greater value are purchased.

Offer Conditions on reverse side.

Valid now thru November 1, 2010

FREE GREEN FEE

www.camasmeadows.com

4105 NW Camas Meadows Drive, Camas, OR
(360)833-2000

E123

entertainment.com

Camas Meadows Golf Club

Enjoy one complimentary BUCKET OF BALLS when a second BUCKET OF BALLS of equal or greater value is purchased.

Offer Conditions on reverse side.

Valid now thru November 1, 2010

FREE BUCKET OF BALLS

www.camasmeadows.com

4105 NW Camas Meadows Drive, Camas, OR
(360)833-2000

E124

---

entertainment.com

Claremont Golf Club

Enjoy one complimentary GREEN FEE when 3 GREEN FEES of equal or greater value are purchased.

Offer Conditions on reverse side.

Valid now thru November 1, 2010

FREE GREEN FEE

www.claremontgolfclub.com

15800 NW Country Club Dr., Portland, OR
(503)690-4589

E125

More Offers Online!

ENTERTAINMENT & SPORTS

entertainment.com

Camas Meadows Golf Club

- 6518 yard, par 72, Championship golf course
- Camas Meadows offers an exciting combination of challenging course design and incredible scenery
- 4 sets of tees for golfers of all levels
- Pro shop, restaurant, leagues and lessons available on site in our beautiful clubhouse
- See www.camasmeadows.com for more informaiton and directions

4105 NW Camas Meadows Drive
Camas, OR
(360)833-2000

Offer Conditions: Valid all hours Monday-Thursday and Friday - Sunday after 2pm. Golf cart excluded.

00776372

Camas Meadows Golf Club

- Camas Meadows Golf Club offers over an acre of seasonal grass tees as well as a 300 Yard, heated, lit, and covered driving range open year round
- Pro shop, restaurant, leagues and lessons available on site in our beautiful clubhouse
- See www.camsmeadows.com for more information and directions

4105 NW Camas Meadows Drive
Camas, OR
(360)833-2000

Offer Conditions: Valid anytime. Must redeem in the main clubhouse proshop

00776371

Claremont Golf Club

- 9 hole, par 36 course amongst beautiful lakes, residential and park -like setting
- Lessons available

15800 NW Country Club Dr.
Portland, OR
(503)690-4589

Offer Conditions: Valid anytime. Not valid during leagues and tournaments.

00764740

Hood River Golf & Country Club

Enjoy one complimentary GREEN FEE when a second GREEN FEE of equal or greater value is purchased.

Offer Conditions on reverse side.

FREE GREEN FEE

Valid now thru November 1, 2010

1850 Country Club Rd., Hood River, OR
(541)386-3009

E126

Charbonneau Golf Club

Enjoy one complimentary GREEN FEE when 3 GREEN FEES of equal or greater value are purchased.

Offer Conditions on reverse side.

FREE GREEN FEE

CHARBONNEAU GOLF CLUB

Valid now thru November 1, 2010

32020 SW Charbonneau Dr., Wilsonville, OR
(503)694-1246

E127

Sunset Grove Golf Club

Enjoy one complimentary GREEN FEE when a second GREEN FEE of equal or greater value is purchased.

Offer Conditions on reverse side.

FREE GREEN FEE

Valid now thru November 1, 2010

41615 N.W. Osterman Rd., Forest Grove, OR
(503)357-6044

E128

Hood River Golf & Country Club

- Open to the public
- Full service restaurant & lounge
- Full service Pro-shop
- Less than an hour from Portland

1850 Country Club Rd.
Hood River, OR
(541)386-3009

Offer Conditions: Valid anytime. On availability basis.

00194514

Charbonneau Golf Club

- Discover the best kept "public" golf secret in the state of Oregon
- You'll find an enchanting mix of lakes, sculptured fairways & fastidiously manicured greens
- 27 holes (three nines!) of challenging par three & four holes to mix & match
- Grass driving range, practice bunker for Sand Wedges & 3 practice greens are also available

CHARBONNEAU GOLF CLUB

32020 SW Charbonneau Dr.
Wilsonville, OR
(503)694-1246

Offer Conditions: Valid Monday - Friday after 12 p.m. Not valid during league and tournaments; Advance tee times required.

00495333

Sunset Grove Golf Club

- Regulation 9 hole course
- Beer & wine available
- Pro shop & club rentals
- Snacks & golf carts available
- We do not charge additional tournament fees!
- No fee for walk-alongs!

41615 N.W. Osterman Rd.
Forest Grove, OR
(503)357-6044

Offer Conditions: Valid anytime. For holidays-see Rules of Use; Not valid during leagues and tournaments.

00634550

Colwood National Golf Course

Enjoy one complimentary GREEN FEE when 3 GREEN FEES of equal or greater value are purchased.

Offer Conditions on reverse side.

Valid now thru November 1, 2010

FREE GREEN FEE

COLWOOD NATIONAL GOLF CLUB

www.colwoodgolfclub.com

7313 N.E. Columbia Blvd., Portland, OR
(503)254-5515

E129

Mint Valley Golf Course

Enjoy one complimentary GREEN FEE when 3 GREEN FEES of equal or greater value are purchased.

Offer Conditions on reverse side.

Valid now thru November 1, 2010

FREE GREEN FEE

MINT VALLEY
—GOLF COURSE—

mint-valley.com

4002 Pennsylvania St, Longview, WA
(360)442-5442

E130

Cedars on Salmon Creek

Enjoy one complimentary GREEN FEE when 3 GREEN FEES of equal or greater value are purchased.

Offer Conditions on reverse side.

Valid now thru November 1, 2010

FREE GREEN FEE

Cedars on Salmon Creek

15001 NE 181st St, Brush Prairie, WA
(360)687-4233

E131

Colwood National Golf Course

- Colwood's beautiful park-like setting makes it a welcoming oasis in the heart of the city
- Offering 18 hole, regulation length course, driving range & putting green
- Open year round, advance reservation recommended
- Carts available
- Full service pro shop & instruction

COLWOOD NATIONAL GOLF CLUB

7313 N.E. Columbia Blvd.
Portland, OR
(503)254-5515

Offer Conditions: Valid anytime. Not valid for leagues or tournaments; Valid all weekday hours, weekends after 12 p.m.

00620291

Mint Valley Golf Course

- One of the finest public golf courses in the state of Washington
- Well-bunkered greens, water hazards, and tall trees will test every skill level.
- 18-hole championship golf course; 6-hole, par 3, Pitch 'n' Putt course
- Covered driving range with grass tees, pro shop and restaurant

MINT VALLEY
—GOLF COURSE—

4002 Pennsylvania St
Longview, WA
(360)442-5442

Offer Conditions: Valid anytime.

00751346

Cedars on Salmon Creek

- A public golf course in a resort setting
- 18 hole, par 72 championship course
- Beautiful clubhouse with pro- shop, dining and lounge
- Driving range and lessons available

Cedars on Salmon Creek

15001 NE 181st St
Brush Prairie, WA
(360)687-4233

Offer Conditions: Valid anytime. Golf cart excluded. Not valid during leagues and tournaments; valid all weekday hours, weekends after 12 p.m..

00741965

Colonial Valley Golf Course

Enjoy one complimentary
GREEN FEE when a second
GREEN FEE of equal or greater
value is purchased.
Offer Conditions on reverse side.

FREE GREEN FEE

Colonial Valley Golf Course

PRINT MORE ONLINE

Valid now thru November 1, 2010

75 Nelson Way, Grants Pass, OR
(541)479-5568

E132

Colonial Valley Golf Course

Enjoy one complimentary
GREEN FEE when a second
GREEN FEE of equal or greater
value is purchased.
Offer Conditions on reverse side.

FREE GREEN FEE

Colonial Valley Golf Course

PRINT MORE ONLINE

Valid now thru November 1, 2010

75 Nelson Way, Grants Pass, OR
(541)479-5568

E133

The Children's Course

Enjoy one complimentary
GREEN FEE when a second
GREEN FEE of equal or greater
value is purchased.
Offer Conditions on reverse side.

FREE GREEN FEE

the **Children's Course**
Teaching life's values through golf.

NEW

Valid now thru November 1, 2010

www.thechildrenscourse.org

19825 River Rd., Gladstone, OR
(503)722-1530

E134

Colonial Valley Golf Course

- Oregon's best kept secret
- Open to the public year round (wheather permitting)
- 9 hole, executive course with driving range
- Party and banquet facilities available

Colonial Valley Golf Course

75 Nelson Way
Grants Pass, OR
(541)479-5568

Offer Conditions: Valid anytime.

00197735

Colonial Valley Golf Course

- Oregon's best kept secret
- Open to the public year round (wheather permitting)
- 9 hole, executive course with driving range
- Party and banquet facilities available

Colonial Valley Golf Course

75 Nelson Way
Grants Pass, OR
(541)479-5568

Offer Conditions: Valid anytime.

00197735

Offer validity is governed by the Rules of Use and excludes defined holidays. Offers are not valid with other discount offers, unless specified. Coupons void if purchased, sold or bartered. Discounts exclude tax, tip and/or alcohol, where applicable.

The Children's Course

- Home of The First Tee
- Family friendly 9 hole, par 3 golf course
- Dedicated to teaching life's values through golf
- Our teaching and learning facility offers programs, lessons and camps for all levels

19825 River Rd.
Gladstone, OR
(503)722-1530

Offer Conditions: Valid anytime.

00756017

FUNdaMental Golf & Learning Center

- Covered tees, grass tees & target greens
- Full service golf shop with equipment for the beginner to the expert
- Lessons available with PGA Golf Professionals
- Visit our website

21661 S. Beavercreek Rd.
Oregon City, OR
(503)632-3986

Offer Conditions: Valid anytime.

00719353

Vanco Golf Range

- Practice range conveniently located in Vancouver
- Putting & chopping greens
- Lessons available
- Pro shop

703 N. Devine Rd.
Vancouver, WA
(360)693-8811

Offer Conditions: Valid anytime.

00678081

Swingers Club

- Have some fun at the Swingers Club!
- Driving range with targets including a revolving car
- Call for hours of operation
- A great place to warm up your game!

SWINGERS CLUB

14189 Union Mills Rd.
Mulino, OR
(503)829-4653

Offer Conditions: Valid anytime.

00614121

Mt. Hood SkiBowl

Enjoy one ADULT NIGHT LIFT TICKET without charge when a second ADULT NIGHT LIFT TICKET is purchased.

Offer Conditions on reverse side.

FREE ADULT NIGHT LIFT TICKET

Valid now thru November 1, 2010

87000 Hwy 26 E, Government Camp, OR
(503) 222-BOWL

E138

---

entertainment
entertainment.com

Mt. Hood Adventure Park at SkiBowl

Enjoy one ADULT ALPINE SLIDE ONE RIDE TICKET without charge, upon payment for the same of equal or greater value.

Offer Conditions on reverse side.

FREE ADULT ALPINE SLIDE ONE RIDE TICKET

Valid now thru November 1, 2010

87000 E. Hwy. 26, Government Camp, OR
(503) 222-BOWL

E139

Mt. Hood SkiBowl Snow Tubing & Adventure Park

Enjoy one ALL DAY/ALL NIGHT TUBING TICKET - OPEN TO CLOSE without charge, upon payment for the same of equal or greater value.

Offer Conditions on reverse side.

ALL DAY / ALL NIGHT TUBING TICKET - OPEN TO CLOSE

Valid now thru November 1, 2010

87000 Hwy 26 E, Government Camp, OR
(503) 222-BOWL

E140

More Offers Online!

ENTERTAINMENT & SPORTS

entertainment.com

Mt. Hood SkiBowl

- Portland's closest ski area!
- Check out the Upper Bowl! 4 Minute ride to PURE vertical
- 300 Acres of outback skiing - 3 mile lit skyline trail
- Night skiing at 3:30 p.m., ski until 10 p.m., Fri. & Sat. til 11 p.m.
- Snow tubing & adventure park with Zipline & Kiddy Snowmobiles
- Discounts available for groups
- Call (503) 222-2695 or go to www.skibowl.com for resort details

00742928

87000 Hwy 26 E
Government Camp, OR
(503)222-BOWL

Offer Conditions: Valid Sunday though Thursday evening. All school holiday periods excluded. One coupon per customer per visit. Discounts available for groups, parties, meetings and more! Call 503-222-2695 or go to www.skibowl.com for resort details..

Mt. Hood Adventure Park at SkiBowl

- Over 20 attractions, where you are in control!
- Take the Sky Chair, then choose the track of your choice - for a ride on the Northwest's only 1/2 mile dual Alpine slide
- Indy Karts, Kiddy-Jeeps, Mini & Disc Golf, Freefall Bungee, Rapid Riser, Quad Sling Shot, Zipline, Summer Tube Hill, Batting Cages, Kids Super Play Zone, Lift-Assisted Mountain Bike Park & more!

00740943

87000 E. Hwy. 26
Government Camp, OR
(503)222-BOWL

Offer Conditions: Valid anytime. Valid anytime June, July and September; Va" Monday through Friday in the month of August.

Mt. Hood SkiBowl Snow Tubing & Adventure Park

- Snow Tube Hill and Express Tow
- Extreme Tube hill
- Toddler hill
- Horsedrawn sleigh rides
- 500' long high adrenaline Zipline
- Kids snowmobile track; Adult snowmobile rentals
- 2-Story, 2400 sq ft indoor play zone
- Call for current weather conditions and operating schedule at (503) 222-BOWL

00740381

87000 Hwy 26 E
Government Camp, OR
(503)222-BOWL

Offer Conditions: Valid anytime. Valid Saturday and Sunday; Not valid holida" or school holiday periods; Tickets include Epress Tow.

Mt Hood Meadows Ski Resort

Enjoy one complimentary MIDWEEK LEARN TO SKI OR SNOWBOARD PACKAGE when a second MIDWEEK LEARN TO SKI OR SNOWBOARD PACKAGE of equal or greater value is purchased.

Offer Conditions on reverse side.

Valid now thru November 1, 2010

FREE LEARN TO SKI OR SNOWBOARD PACKAGE

MT. HOOD MEADOWS SKI RESORT

www.skihood.com

14040 Hwy 35, Mt. Hood, OR
(503) 227-SNOW

E141

Mt Hood Meadows Ski Resort

Enjoy one complimentary MIDWEEK SHIFT (Monday-Friday) LIFT TICKET AND EQUIPMENT (ski or snowboard) RENTAL when a second MIDWEEK SHIFT (Monday-Friday) LIFT TICKET AND EQUIPMENT (ski or snowboard) RENTAL of equal or greater value is purchased.

Offer Conditions on reverse side.

Valid now thru November 1, 2010

FREE MIDWEEK SHIFT LIFT TICKET / RENTAL

MT. HOOD MEADOWS SKI RESORT

www.skihood.com

14040 Hwy 35, Mt. Hood, OR
(503) 227-SNOW

E142

Mt Hood Meadows Ski Resort

Enjoy one complimentary NIGHT LIFT TICKET and EQUIPMENT (ski or snowboard) RENTAL PACKAGE when a second NIGHT LIFT TICKET AND EQUIPMENT (ski or snowboard) RENTAL PACKAGE of equal or greater value is purchased (excludes Saturday nights).

Offer Conditions on reverse side.

Valid now thru November 1, 2010

FREE NIGHT LIFT TICKET & EQUIPMENT RENTAL

MT. HOOD MEADOWS SKI RESORT

www.skihood.com

14040 Hwy 35, Mt. Hood, OR
(503) 227-SNOW

E143

Mt Hood Meadows Ski Resort

- Oregon's Premier Ski Experience!
- 35 miles S. of Hood River on Hwy 35
- 67 miles E. of Portland
- Always check for lift operation schedule and conditions
- Ski Area: 503-337-2222 ; Snow Phone: 503-227-SNOW (7669)
- www.skihood.com

00780173

14040 Hwy 35
Mt. Hood, OR
(503)227-SNOW

Offer Conditions: Valid 2009/2010 Season -some restrictions apply. Ages 13 & older. Valid Monday- Friday; Includes Beginner Lift Ticket, 2 Hour Lesson & Ski or Snowboard equipment rental; Excludes December 28, 2009 - January 1, 2010, January 18, 2010, February 15, 2010; Valid Winter 2009/Spring 2010 season only; Offer must be used same day; Must be purchased at regular price at ski area. Cannot be combined with any other discounts or special offers.

Mt Hood Meadows Ski Resort

- Oregon's Premier Ski Experience!
- 35 miles south of Hood River on Hwy 35
- 67 miles east of Portland
- Always check for lift operation schedule and conditions
- Ski Area: 503-337-2222 ; Snow Phone: 503-227-SNOW (7669)
- www.skihood.com

00780171

14040 Hwy 35
Mt. Hood, OR
(503)227-SNOW

Offer Conditions: Valid 2009/2010 Season -some restrictions apply. Excludes December 28, 2009 - January 1, 2010, January 18, 2010, February 15, 2010; Valid Winter 2009/Spring 2010 season only; Offer must be used same day; Must be purchased at regular price at ski area. Can not be combined with any other discounts or special offers.

Mt Hood Meadows Ski Resort

- Oregon's Premier Ski Experience!
- 35 miles south of Hood River on Hwy 35
- 67 miles east of Portland
- Always check for lift operation schedule and conditions
- Ski Area: 503-337-2222 ; Snow Phone: 503-227-SNOW (7669)
- www.skihood.com

00780172

14040 Hwy 35
Mt. Hood, OR
(503)227-SNOW

Offer Conditions: Valid 2009/2010 Season -some restrictions apply. Not available Saturday nights; Excludes December 31, 2009, January 17, 2010, February 14, 2010; Valid Winter 2009/Spring 2010 season only; Offer must be used same day; Must be purchased at regular price at ski area. Can not be combined with any other discounts or special offers.

Club Sport

Enjoy ONE FREE DAY PASS.
Offer Conditions on reverse side.

Valid now thru November 1, 2010

SPECIAL OFFER

18120 SW Lower Boones Ferry Rd., Tigard, OR
(503)968-4500

E144

Eastmoreland Racquet Club

Enjoy one complimentary MEMBERSHIP ENROLLMENT FEE and FIRST MONTH DUES FREE.
Offer Conditions on reverse side.

$953.50 VALUE

Eastmoreland Racquet Club

Valid now thru November 1, 2010

3015 S.E. Berkley Place, Portland, OR
(503)653-0820

E145

Clackamas River Racquet Club

Enjoy one complimentary MEMBERSHIP ENROLLMENT FEE and FIRST MONTH DUES FREE.
Offer Conditions on reverse side.

$596.00 VALUE

Clackamas River Racquet Club

Valid now thru November 1, 2010

790 82nd Dr., Gladstone, OR
(503)657-1806

E146

Club Sport
- Your complete family fitness center
- Basketball, volleyball, soccer & hockey with sports leagues & tournaments
- Indoor & outdoor aquatics center
- Racquetball & squash courts, rock climbing & group exercise
- Personal training & nutrition counseling
- Corporate team building, parties & socials

00388313

18120 SW Lower Boones Ferry Rd.
Tigard, OR
(503)968-4500

Offer Conditions: Valid anytime. Must be 21 yrs. or older; Local residents & 1st time guests only; By appointment only.

Eastmoreland Racquet Club
- 6 Indoor courts, 6 outdoor courts, including 2 clay courts
- USPTA Tennis pros
- Lessons available
- Fitness facilities with aerobics, cardio & free weights
- Seasonal outdoor pool
- Massage & daycare available
- Dual memberships available with Clackamas River Racquet Club
- Call for more information on our wide selection of summer camps & year-round programs

00405292

Eastmoreland Racquet Club

**Eastmoreland Racquet Club
3015 S.E. Berkley Place
Portland, OR
(503)653-0820**

Offer Conditions: Valid anytime. Not valid with other specials or promotions.

Clackamas River Raquet Club
- Tennis, racquetball & fitness
- 4 Indoor tennis courts & 3 new, state-of-the-art racquetball courts
- USPTA Tennis Pros
- Lessons available
- Cardio, Nautilus, free weights, aerobics
- Massage & daycare available
- Dual membership available with Eastmoreland Racquet Club
- Call for membership information

00405304

Clackamas River Racquet Club

**Clackamas River Raquet Club
790 82nd Dr.
Gladstone, OR
(503)657-1806**

Offer Conditions: Valid anytime. Not valid with other specials or promotions.

entertainment.com

Inflatable Kingdom

Enjoy one complimentary HOURLY PLAY SESSION when a second HOURLY PLAY SESSION of equal or greater value is purchased.

Offer Conditions on reverse side.

Valid now thru November 1, 2010

Up To $8.00 Value

"Party on the Red Carpet!"

www.inflatablekingdom.com

6830 SW Bonita Rd., Tigard, OR
(503)718-0994

E147

entertainment.com

Shooter's Pool Hall at the Island Casino

Enjoy one complimentary HOURLY PLAY SESSION when a second HOURLY PLAY SESSION of equal or greater value is purchased.

Offer Conditions on reverse side.

Valid now thru November 1, 2010

FREE HOURLY PLAY SESSION

Shooter's Pool Hall
AT THE ISLAND CASINO

See Reverse Side for Locations

E148

entertainment.com

Hot Shots Billiards

Enjoy one complimentary HOUR OF POOL when a second HOUR OF POOL of equal or greater value is purchased.

Offer Conditions on reverse side.

PRINT MORE ONLINE

Valid now thru November 1, 2010

FREE HOUR OF POOL

www.hotshotspool.com

4900 S.W. Western Ave., Beaverton, OR
(503)644-8869

E149

Inflatable Kingdom

- Party on the red carpet!
- Jump on in to our premium selection of inflatable games and entertainment
- Perfect for your next party, corporate event or a day out to play!
- See our website for all our fun options and packages

**6830 SW Bonita Rd.
Tigard, OR
(503) 718-0994**

Offer Conditions: Valid anytime.

00751358

Shooter's Pool Hall at the Island Casino

- Located in the Island Casinos

**8524 W. Gage Blvd
Kennelwick, WA
(509) 374-3289**

**1125 Commerce Ave
Longview, WA
(360) 501-4328**

Offer Conditions: Valid anytime.

00757471

Hot Shots Billiards

- The place where people from all ages come to have fun!
- 20 Pocket billiard tables & games room
- Over The Rail Cafe with complete menu
- Pro Shop with the very best selection of pool & billiard equipment

**4900 S.W. Western Ave.
Beaverton, OR
(503) 644-8869**

Offer Conditions: Valid anytime. Up to 4 people; Offer valid only upon payment of 1st hour of pool.

00367213

FREE HOURLY PLAY SESSION

Break Time Billiards & Cafe

Break Time Billiards & Cafe

Enjoy One Hourly Play Session when a second Hourly Play Session of equal or greater value is purchased.

Offer Conditions on reverse side.

Valid now thru November 1, 2010

14411 S.W. Pacific Hwy., Tigard, OR
(503)443-6166

E150

UP TO $345.00 VALUE

Academy of Modern Martial Arts

Enjoy any INTRODUCTORY SESSION at 50% off the regular price.

Offer Conditions on reverse side.

ACADEMY OF MODERN MARTIAL ARTS

KARATE   KICKBOXING   GRAPPLING   MMA   TAI CHI

www.martialarts-fitness.com

333 S. State St., Ste. A&B, Lake Oswego, OR
(503)697-7482

Valid now thru November 1, 2010

E151

$36.00 Value

Yoga Bhoga

Enjoy 6 LESSONS at 50% off the regular price.

Offer Conditions on reverse side.

YOGA BHOGA

www.yogabhoga.com

1401 S.E. Morrison, Portland, OR
(503)422-6230

Valid now thru November 1, 2010

E152

More Offers Online!

ENTERTAINMENT & SPORTS

entertainment.com

Break Time Billiards & Cafe

- 20 Pool tables
- One 12 ft. snooker table
- One 10 ft. billiard table
- Pool cue rentals
- Cafe
- Clean, family environment
- Great for all ages!
- Video games
- Open 7 days a week

Break Time Billiards & Cafe

14411 S.W. Pacific Hwy.
Tigard, OR
(503)443-6166

Offer Conditions: Valid anytime. Special events excluded.

00605348

Academy of Modern Martial Arts

- Be Safe - Be Strong - Be Fit
- Experience real confidence from real training for real life
- Enjoy increased flexibility, greater strength & improved focus
- Classes in Self Defense, Aerobic Kickboxing, Grappling, MMA & Tai Chi, training can be tailored to you
- Classes & private instruction for men, women, teens & children
- Call to begin your training now

ACADEMY OF MODERN MARTIAL ARTS

| KARATE | KICKBOXING | GRAPPLING | MMA | TAI CHI |

333 S. State St., Ste. A&B
(Inside the Lake Place Shpg. Ctr.)
Lake Oswego, OR
(503)697-7482

Offer Conditions: Valid anytime.

00654774

Yoga Bhoga

- Daily drop-in classes for all levels
- Gentle beginning and back care yoga
- Intermediate classes
- Advanced power yoga and Ashtanga classes

YOGA BHOGA

1401 S.E. Morrison
Portland, OR
(503)422-6230

Offer Conditions: Admissions valid anytime.

00781702

Evergreen Dance Academy

Enjoy ONE MONTH OF LESSONS at 50% off the regular price.

Offer Conditions on reverse side.

Up To $**60**$ ^{00} Value

Evergreen Dance Academy

At Bally Sports Club
www.evergreendanceacademy.com

16096 SE 15th St., Vancouver, WA
(360)891-1698

Valid now thru November 1, 2010

E153

Fire Mountain Yoga

Enjoy any 5 LESSONS at 50% off the regular price.

Offer Conditions on reverse side.

50%OFF

Fire Mountain YOGA

www.firemountainyoga.com

707 S.E. Parkcrest Ave., Ste. C-330, Vancouver, WA
(360)882-4979

Valid now thru November 1, 2010

E154

Lake Oswego Academy of Dance

Enjoy one complimentary MONTH OF ANY DANCE CLASS when a second MONTH OF ANY DANCE CLASS of equal or greater value is purchased.

Offer Conditions on reverse side.

ONE MONTH OF ANY DANCE CLASS

LAKE OSWEGO ACADEMY OF DANCE

16250 S.W. Bryant Rd., Lake Oswego, OR
(503)697-3673

Valid now thru November 1, 2010

E155

Evergreen Dance Academy

- Offering a variety of classes & times, see our web site for details
- Youth & adult ballet & hip hop
- Creative dance for 4 -5 years

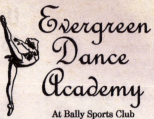

Evergreen Dance Academy

At Bally Sports Club
16096 SE 15th St.
(At Bally Sports Club)
Vancouver, WA
(360)891-1698

Offer Conditions: Valid anytime.

00729930

Fire Mountain Yoga

- Hot yoga studio
- Posture stretches that strengthen muscles, ligament & joints while at the same time stimulate organs, glands & nerves, moving blood to 100% of the body
- See www.firemountainyoga.com for more information, directions & class times

707 S.E. Parkcrest Ave., Ste. C-330
Vancouver, WA
(360)882-4979

Offer Conditions: Valid anytime.

00709157

Lake Oswego Academy of Dance

- Rated in the top 3 dance studios in the Portland area
- Dance lessons for all ages, featuring ballet, jazz, tap, hip hop, combination classes & more
- Summer dance classes & camps available for all ages
- #1 Place to have a dance birthday party

LAKE OSWEGO ACADEMY OF DANCE

16250 S.W. Bryant Rd.
Lake Oswego, OR
(503)697-3673

Offer Conditions: Valid anytime. New students only. Must present coupon at the time of registration.

00161869

Oregon Gymnastics Academy

Enjoy one complimentary MONTH OF CLASS when a second MONTH OF CLASS of equal or greater value is purchased.

Offer Conditions on reverse side.

ONE MONTH OF CLASS

www.ogagym.org

16305 N.W. Bethany Ct., Ste. 109, Beaverton, OR
(503)531-3409

Valid now thru November 1, 2010

E156

Bikram's Yoga College of India - Hall Street

Enjoy any 5 LESSONS at 50% off the regular price.

Offer Conditions on reverse side.

50%OFF

www.bikramyogahallstreet.com

3665 S.W. Hall Blvd., Beaverton, OR
(503)526-8828

Valid now thru November 1, 2010

E157

Aerobic Kickboxing

Enjoy ONE MONTH LESSONS at 50% off the regular price.

Offer Conditions on reverse side.

Up To $25.00 Value

Aerobic Kickboxing

PRINT MORE ONLINE

397 N. State St., Lake Oswego, OR
(503)697-7482

Valid now thru November 1, 2010

E158

Oregon Gymnastics Academy

- Since 1978
- Classes from birth to adult
- Boys & girls gymnastics
- Rythmic gymnastics, tumbling & trampoline programs
- Birthday parties & parent's night out

OREGON GYMNASTICS ACADEMY

16305 N.W. Bethany Ct., Ste. 109
Beaverton, OR
(503)531-3409

Offer Conditions: Valid anytime. New students only; Annual insurance fee extra.

00496112

Bikram's Yoga College of India - Hall Street

- Experience Bikram's Yoga
- Routine of 26 postures & 2 breathing exercises through a 90 minutes class
- Heated room encourages increased circulation & flexibility
- Open your mind, challenge your body
- Awaken your spirit, change your life

3665 S.W. Hall Blvd.
Beaverton, OR
(503)526-8828

Offer Conditions: Valid anytime.

00708664

Aerobic Kickboxing

- Burn an incredible 800 calories per hour!
- Total body workout makes it easy to stay on track with your fitness goals
- Aerobic Kickboxing simply & safely blends the fundamental self defense moves of kickboxing into a fantastic body shaping system

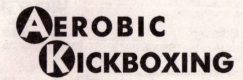

397 N. State St.
Lake Oswego, OR
(503)697-7482

Offer Conditions: Valid anytime.

00655067

The Gym - Nest
- "Gynmnastics"©
- The world's greatest sport
- The Gym-Nest, Ltd. has been in Hillsboro for over 20 years
- Classes for all ages from 2 thru adult, both boys & girls
- Come train with our qualified instructors in an atmosphere designed for fun, safety & learning

THE GYM-NEST
GYMNASTICS

1414 SE 18th #100
Hillsboro, OR
(503)640-6378

Offer Conditions: Valid anytime. New students only; Annual insurance fee extra.

00368907

Norm Stoll School of Dance
- Learn ballroom, country/western, disco, swing, foxtrot & waltz
- Also featuring mambo, cha cha & other Latin dances
- Wedding, cruise & reunion dances
- Class & private lessons
- No contracts
- Call (503) 284-8336 for information

NORM STOLL SCHOOL OF DANCE

3830 N.E. Hancock
(Hollywood District; just off 39th & Sandy)
Portland, OR
(503)284-8336

Offer Conditions: Valid anytime. Pre-registration required; On availability basis.

00015379

Willamette Sailing Club
- The only small boat sailing club within the greater Portland area
- Minutes from downtown
- Club memberships, moorage & racing
- Sailing classes from beginner to advanced
- Classes are offered April thru September
- Credit cards accepted

Willamette Sailing School

6336 S.W. Beaver Ave. Portland, OR 97239 (503) 730-SAIL (7245)
(just off Macadam near Willamette Park) www.willamettesailingclub.com &
wss_sailors@yahoo.com

Offer Conditions: Valid anytime. On availability basis; Pre-registration required; New Customers only.

00077136

Vancouver Yoga Center

Enjoy ONE MONTH UNLIMITED YOGA PACKAGE at 50% OFF the regular price.

Offer Conditions on reverse side.

www.vancouveryogacenter.com

202 E. McLoughlin Blvd., Vancouver, WA
(360)521-1609

Valid now thru November 1, 2010

E162

Professional Martial Arts Association

Enjoy 50% of the regular price of 1 MONTH LESSONS .

Offer Conditions on reverse side.

50% OFF

www.professionalmartialarts.com

See Reverse Side for Locations

Valid now thru November 1, 2010

E163

Gamefly.com

Enjoy A FREE 15-Day Trial To GameFly.com.

Offer Conditions on reverse side.

15 DAY FREE TRIAL

Valid now thru November 1, 2010

Visit www.gamefly.com/ent092 to redeem your free 15 day trial.

E164

Vancouver Yoga Center

- Dedicated to honoring & preserving the ancient wisdom of the East
- Committed to teaching & practicing principles to reclaim good health & inner harmony
- Yoga & healing arts
- Special workshops & personalized programs
- See our website for more details & class schedule

202 E. McLoughlin Blvd.
Vancouver, WA
(360)521-1609

Offer Conditions: Valid anytime.

00621277

Professional Martial Arts Association

- Offering Professional Martial Arts lessons for over 30 years
- Self-Defense
- Sports tournament
- Weapons training
- Conditioning
- Weight training & cardio fitness
- Nutritional education
- Perfect for men, women & children
- See website for more info.

CALIFORNIA
Redding
3025 Bechelli Lane, #1
(Total Self-Defense)
(530)221-7425

OREGON
Beaverton
9985 S.W. 125th Ave.
(Professional Martial Arts of Beaverton)
(503)629-6313

Hillsboro
2575 N.E. Kathryn St., #12
(American Freestyle Martial Arts)
(503)681-4990

Oregon City
18131 S. Fischer Mill Rd.
(Northwest Martial Arts)
(503)813-7900

Portland
17115 S.E. Foster Rd.
(Karate World of Oregon)
(503)813-7900

5607 S.E. Woodstock
(Zakira Martial Arts)
(503)772-4581

9212 S.E. Ramona St.
(Professional Martial Arts of Portland)
(503)771-3000

Salem
483 53rd Place N.E.
(Professional Martial Arts of Salem)
(503)581-5768

Message Phone for all locations: (971)226-9614

Offer Conditions: Valid anytime.

00658843

Gamefly.com

- Video Game Rentals Delivered to Your Door
- Free Shipping
- No Late Fees
- New Releases and Classic Games
- Cancel Anytime

Visit www.gamefly.com/ent092 to redeem your free 15 day trial.

Offer Conditions: Offer ends 9/1/2010. Limit one account per person/household. Must be 18 years or older with a valid credit card. Valid in 50 U.S. States and D.C. only and cannot be combined with any other offer. New GameFly members only (not valid for existing or former members). Subject to additional terms and conditions at www.gamefly.com/terms.

00774849

North Clackamas Aquatic Park

Enjoy one complimentary ADMISSION when a second ADMISSION of equal or greater value is purchased.

Offer Conditions on reverse side.

Valid now thru November 1, 2010

FREE ADMISSION

North Clackamas Aquatic Park

www.pdxsurf.com

7300 S.E. Harmony Rd., Milwaukie, OR
(503)557-SURF

E165

West Coast Game Park Safari

Enjoy one complimentary ADULT ADMISSION when a second ADULT ADMISSION of equal or greater value is purchased.

Offer Conditions on reverse side.

Valid now thru November 1, 2010

FREE ADULT ADMISSION

WEST COAST
GAME PARK
The Original Walk-Thru Safari

www.gameparksafari.com

46914 Hwy. 101 S., Bandon, OR
(541)347-3106

E166

Wild Cat Adventures Whale Watching

Enjoy one complimentary WHALE WATCHING TOUR when a second WHALE WATCHING TOUR of equal or greater value is purchased.

Offer Conditions on reverse side.

Valid now thru November 1, 2010

FREE WHALE WATCHING TOUR

WildCat Adventures

Whale Watching

Ride The Big Red Cat

www.wildcat-adventures.com

1234 Wharf Street, Victoria, BC
(250)384-9998

E167

North Clackamas Aquatic Park

- All indoor, one-of-a-kind, park offers 400,000 gallons of fun!
- Wave pool provides real surf action
- 6 lane competition/lap pool
- 3 waterslides, dive pool and whirlpool
- Meeting rooms, patio/picnic area and restaurant
- Call or see our website for more information

North Clackamas Aquatic Park

NORTH CLACKAMAS PARKS & RECREATION DISTRICT

7300 S.E. Harmony Rd.
(Behind Toys 'R Us)
Milwaukie, OR
(503)557-SURF

Offer Conditions: Valid anytime. Valid on any BIG SURF Swim Session. Group rentals and birthday packages excluded.

00768611

West Coast Game Park Safari

- America's largest wild animal petting park
- Over 450 animals, 75 different species from around the world
- Meet & pet special cub, pups or kits
- Walk among 100's of free roaming wildlife, offering unsurpassed wildlife adventure that will amaze & entertain visitors of all ages
- Open daily Mar.-Nov.
- Call for winter hours
- For more details log onto www.gameparksafari.com

WEST COAST GAME PARK
The Original Walk-Thru **Safari**

46914 Hwy. 101 S.
Bandon, OR
(541)347-3106

Offer Conditions: Valid anytime.

00144697

Wild Cat Adventures Whale Watching

- Features 2 full sized washrooms
- Comfortable seating for 54 passengers
- Wind jackets provided
- Onboard naturalist
- Onboard P.A. system
- Hydrophone to listen to whales

WildCat Adventures
Whale Watching
Ride The Big Red Cat

1234 Wharf Street
Victoria, BC
(250)384-9998

Offer Conditions: Valid anytime. On availability basis; Reservations recommended.

00479474

TRAVEL & HOTELS

More Offers at
www.entertainment.com/travel

American Airlines®
AA.com

✂

SAVE $10 off any fare* worldwide for up to six (6) passengers!

Go to www.entertainment.com/AA10 to receive your Discount Code.

Then go see the world!

Valid now thru December 31, 2010
F1   Subject to Rules of Use. Not valid with other discount offers, unless specified. Coupon VOID if purchased, sold or bartered for cash.

*Visit **AA.com/women** for the latest information about special discounts, promotions and the most up-to-date travel finds in major cities around the globe.*

Choose from exciting destinations such as:

- Caribbean
- Mexico
- Hawaii
- Europe
- Las Vegas
- Canada
- Ski destinations
- Costa Rica
- Belize
- Florida
- And many more!

American Airlines Vacations℠
AAVacations.com

You must be a registered member at www.entertainment.com to take advantage of these great offers from American Airlines.

NOW FLYING TO YOUR FAVORITE BEACHES

Fly to Florida, Mexico, or the Caribbean on USA3000 Airlines and

SAVE $5⁰⁰

off your next ticket when you book online with the promo code EB1.

To receive your fare savings, log on to

USA3000.COM

F3

Hotel Savings
Programs

Choose the one that's right for you!

Guaranteed Best Rate Program

Mail-in Rebate

Receive a special **Entertainment® Member Rebate of up to $250** with the Guaranteed Best Rate Program, affiliated with **hotels.com**.

See pp. G2–G29 or book online at www.entertainment.com/travel.

or

Direct to Hotel Program

Call Direct and Save

Call the hotel directly to **save up to 50% Off** full-priced rates or **10% Off** Best Available Rate at thousands of hotels from coast to coast.

See pp. G30–G51 to call the hotel's listed number.

or

Hotel Chain Savings Program

Favorite Hotel Chains

Save 10% or more on your next stay at your favorite hotel chain. It's easy!

See pp. G52–G53 for special 800 numbers or book online at www.entertainment.com/hotelchains.

Book.
Save.
Repeat.

Get the Guaranteed Best Rate* at more than 53,000 hotels worldwide.

- Call or visit us online at
  www.entertainment.com/travel
  to get the lowest hotel rates—guaranteed.

- This amazing offer includes low rates at
  our hotel partners starting on page G5.

- Plus thousands more hotels online.

Book your Guaranteed Best Rate today.

**Call 1-800-50-HOTEL or visit
www.entertainment.com/travel**

hotels.con

Call 1-800-50-HOTEL
or visit **www.entertainment.com/travel**

*See **Rebate Rules** on page G4 and the Guaranteed Best Rate Program Rules of Use on page C

Get up to $250 in mail-in rebates.

That's on top of your already low hotel rates! Here's how it works:

1. Book a Guaranteed Best Rate*, either on the phone or online.

2. Complete your stay at your reserved hotel.

3. Send in your rebate form within 60 days and make sure to include your booking number.

Up to $125 for phone bookings:

2 Nights .... $15 Rebate
3 or 4 Nights .... $25 Rebate
5, 6 or 7 Nights .... $40 Rebate
8 or 9 Nights .... $70 Rebate
10+ Nights .... $125 Rebate

Up to $250 for online bookings:

2 Nights .... $30 Rebate
3 or 4 Nights .... $50 Rebate
5, 6 or 7 Nights .... $80 Rebate
8 or 9 Nights ...... $140 Rebate
10+ Nights .... $250 Rebate

Guaranteed Best Rate Certificate*

Name _____

Hotel _____

Date of Stay _____ / __ / _____ to _____ / __ / _____
                 mm/dd/yyyy   mm/dd/yyyy

Booking Number_____

Fill out this rebate form and mail to: REBATE
                               2201 E. LAMAR BLVD.
                               ARLINGTON, TX 76006

*See reverse side for Rebate Rules of Use.

hôtels.com

Guaranteed Best Rate Certificate*

Name _____

Hotel _____

Date of Stay _____ / __ / _____ to _____ / __ / _____
                 mm/dd/yyyy   mm/dd/yyyy

Booking Number_____

Fill out this rebate form and mail to: REBATE
                               2201 E. LAMAR BLVD.
                               ARLINGTON, TX 76006

*See reverse side for Rebate Rules of Use.

hôtels.com

...e **Rebate Rules** on page G4 and the Guaranteed Best Rate Program Rules of Use on page G28.

Guaranteed savings.
All year long.

Now that you're an Entertainment® Member you can take advantage of the Guaranteed Best Rate Program* again and again. Start saving today by booking any of the hotels in the following directory from pages G5 through G27. Or visit us online for thousands more hotel choices.

Book your Guaranteed Best Rate today.

Call 1-800-50-HOTEL or visit www.entertainment.com/travel

Rebate Rules of Use

1. You must book and confirm a Guaranteed Best Rate hotel to be eligible for rebate offer. No call-in or fax rebates will be accepted.

2. Rebate is valid only for reservations booked through the Guaranteed Best Rate Program and **paid in full** at time of booking.

3. After checkout, please cut out and mail completed rebate certificate to: Rebate, 2201 E. Lamar Blvd., Arlington, TX 76006.

4. Not valid with any other offer, including, but not limited to, frequent flyer miles.

5. Form must be mailed in to collect rebates. Rebates will be credited back to your credit card.

6. One rebate per booking number.

7. Envelope must be postmarked within 60 days after your checkout date.

8. "Booking" means a completed stay of consecutive nights at the same property, booked on one calendar day.

9. Our interpretation of the rules of this offer is final.

Rebate Rules of Use

1. You must book and confirm a Guaranteed Best Rate hotel to be eligible for rebate offer. No call-in or fax rebates will be accepted.

2. Rebate is valid only for reservations booked through the Guaranteed Best Rate Program and **paid in full** at time of booking.

3. After checkout, please cut out and mail completed rebate certificate to: Rebate, 2201 E. Lamar Blvd., Arlington, TX 76006.

4. Not valid with any other offer, including, but not limited to, frequent flyer miles.

5. Form must be mailed in to collect rebates. Rebates will be credited back to your credit card.

6. One rebate per booking number.

7. Envelope must be postmarked within 60 days after your checkout date.

8. "Booking" means a completed stay of consecutive nights at the same property, booked on one calendar day.

9. Our interpretation of the rules of this offer is final.

United States of America

Alabama

Birmingham

MEDICAL CENTER INN – UAB
800 11th St S

HILTON BIRMINGHAM PERIMETER PARK
8 Perimeter Park S

EMBASSY SUITES HOTEL BIRMINGHAM
2300 Woodcrest Pl

Alaska

Anchorage

MILLENNIUM ALASKAN HOTEL ANCHORAGE
4800 Spenard Rd

HILTON GARDEN INN ANCHORAGE
100 Tudor Rd

Fairbanks

WESTMARK FAIRBANKS, A HOLLAND AMERICA LINE COMPANY
813 Noble St

FAIRBANKS QUALITY INN & SUITES
1521 S Cushman St

Arizona

Flagstaff

RODEWAY INN & SUITES FLAGSTAFF
2285 E Butler Ave

RADISSON WOODLANDS HOTEL
1175 W Route 66

LITTLE AMERICA FLAGSTAFF
2515 E Butler Ave

Grand Canyon Village
(South Rim)

THE GRAND HOTEL
Hwy 64

BEST WESTERN GRAND CANYON SQUIRE INN
100 Hwy 64

Phoenix

CROSSLANDS PHOENIX WEST
4861 W McDowell Rd

SHERATON CRESCENT HOTEL
2620 W Dunlap Ave

RESIDENCE INN BY MARRIOTT PHOENIX ARPT.
801 N 44th St

POINTE HILTON SQUAW PEAK RESORT
7677 N 16th St

FOUR POINTS SHERATON HOTEL PHOENIX
10220 N Metro Pkwy E

EMBASSY SUITES PHOENIX – ARPT. AT 44TH STREET
1515 N 44th St

ECONO LODGE PHOENIX ARPT.
3037 E Van Buren St

DOUBLETREE GUEST SUITES PHOENIX – GATEWAY CENTER
320 N 44th St

COMFORT INN – PHOENIX
5050 N Black Canyon Hwy

Scottsdale

MARRIOTT SUITES SCOTTSDALE OLD TOWN
7325 E 3rd Ave

3 PALMS RESORT OASIS
7707 E McDowell Rd

Sedona

RIDGE ON SEDONA GOLF RESORT
55 Sun Ridge Cir

RADISSON POCO DIABLO RESORT
1752 S Hwy 179

HILTON SEDONA RESORT & SPA
90 Ridge Trail Dr

Tucson

EMBASSY SUITES PALOMA VILLAGE
3110 East Skyline Dr

DAYS INN SUITES TUCSON AZ
1440 S Craycroft Rd

HOTEL ARIZONA
181 W Broadway Blvd

HILTON EL CONQUISTADOR GOLF & TENNIS RESORT
10000 N Oracle Rd

Arkansas

Hot Springs

CLARION RESORT ON THE LAKE
4813 Central Ave

Little Rock

STUDIOPLUS LITTLE ROCK – WEST
10800 Kanis Rd

RESIDENCE INN BY MARRIOTT LITTLE ROCK WEST
1401 S Shackleford Rd

THE PEABODY LITTLE ROCK
3 Statehouse Plz

California

Anaheim

RAMADA LIMITED SUITES CONVENTION CENTER
2141 S Harbor Blvd

EDEN ROC INN & SUITES
1830 S West St

HOTEL MENAGE ANAHEIM BOUTIQUE HOTEL
1221 S Harbor Blvd

HILTON ANAHEIM
777 W Convention Way

DISNEY'S PARADISE PIER HOTEL – ON DISNEYLAND RESORT PROPERTY
1717 S Disneyland Dr

DISNEYLAND HOTEL – ON DISNEYLAND RESORT PROPERTY
1150 W Magic Way

DESERT PALMS HOTEL & SUITES
631 W Katella Ave

BEST WESTERN STOVALL'S INN
1110 W Katella Ave

Bakersfield

SLEEP INN & SUITES BAKERSFIELD
6257 Knudsen Dr

HILTON GARDEN INN BAKERSFIELD
3625 Marriott Dr

ECONO LODGE BAKERSFIELD
350 Oak St

Call 1-800-50-HOTEL
or visit **www.entertainment.com/travel**

Big Bear Lake

THE TIMBERLINE LODGE
39921 Big Bear Blvd

CASTLE WOOD COTTAGES
547 Main St

Carmel

CARMEL INN & SUITES
5th & Junipero

QUAIL LODGE RESORT
8205 Valley Greens Dr

Fremont

HOMESTEAD FREMONT – FREMONT BLVD SOUTH
46080 Fremont Blvd

EXTENDED STAY DELUXE FREMONT – NEWARK
5375 Farwell Pl

EXTENDED STAY AMERICA FREMONT – WARM SPRINGS
46312 Mission Blvd

Fresno

LA QUINTA INN & SUITES FRESNO RIVERPARK
330 E Fir Ave

EXTENDED STAY AMERICA FRESNO – NORTH
7135 N Fresno St

CROSSLAND FRESNO – WEST
3460 W Shaw Ave

Hollywood

QUALITY INN HOLLYWOOD
1520 N La Brea Ave

HOLLYWOOD ROOSEVELT
7000 Hollywood Blvd

BEST WESTERN HOLLYWOOD HILLS HOTEL
6141 Franklin Ave

Long Beach

QUEEN MARY HOTEL
1126 Queens Hwy

HYATT REGENCY LONG BEACH
200 S Pine Ave

Los Angeles

SU CASA AT VENICE BEACH
431 Ocean Front Walk

O HOTEL
819 S Flower St

ECONO LODGE HOLLYWOOD
777 N Vine St

CUSTOM HOTEL
8639 Lincoln Blvd

CINEMA SUITES BED & BREAKFAST
925 S Fairfax Ave

HOTEL PALOMAR LOS ANGELES – WESTWOOD – A KIMPTON HOTEL
10740 Wilshire Blvd

THE WESTIN BONAVENTURE HOTEL AND SUITES
404 S Figueroa St

THE HISTORIC MAYFAIR HOTEL LOS ANGELES
1256 W 7th St

SHERATON GATEWAY HOTEL LOS ANGELES ARPT.
6101 W Century Blvd

RAMADA INN WILSHIRE
3900 Wilshire Blvd

FOUR POINTS BY SHERATON LAX ARPT.
9750 Airport Blvd

COURTYARD BY MARRIOTT LAX
6161 W Century Blvd

BEST WESTERN DRAGON GATE INN
818 N Hill St

Modesto

SPRINGHILL SUITES BY MARRIOTT MODESTO
1901 W Orangeburg Ave

RODEWAY INN MODESTO
936 McHenry Ave

Monterey

MARRIOTT MONTEREY
350 Calle Principal

HOWARD JOHNSON EXPRESS – MONTEREY
1240 Munras Ave

HOTEL PACIFIC
300 Pacific St

DAYS INN MONTEREY – FISHERMANS WHARF/AQUARIUM
1288 Munras Ave

Napa

MARRIOTT NAPA VALLEY HOTEL & SPA
3425 Solano Ave

HILTON GARDEN INN NAPA
3585 Solano Ave

Oakland

HOMEWOOD SUITES BY HILTON OAKLAND – WATERFRONT
1103 Embarcadero

MARRIOTT OAKLAND CITY CENTER
1001 Broadway

THE INN AT JACK LONDON SQUARE
233 Broadway

Ontario

TRAVELODGE ONTARIO
1150 N Grove Ave

KNIGHTS INN ONTARIO
1120 E Holt Blvd

Palm Springs

EXTENDED STAY AMERICA PALM SPRINGS – ARPT.
1400 E Tahquitz Canyon Way

HOLIDAY INN PALM SPRINGS
1800 E Palm Canyon Dr

Sacramento

TOWNEPLACE SUITES MARRIOTT CAL EXPO
1784 Tribute Rd

HOMESTEAD SACRAMENTO – SOUTH NATOMAS
2810-2830 Gateway Oaks Dr

Choose from 53,000 more hotels by phone.

FOUR POINTS SACRAMENTO INTL ARPT.
4900 Duckhorn Dr

EXTENDED STAY AMERICA SACRAMENTO – ARDEN WAY
2100 Harvard St

COURTYARD BY MARRIOTT SACRAMENTO CAL EXPO
1781 Tribute Rd

CLARION HOTEL MANSION INN DOWNTOWN
700 16th St

HILTON SACRAMENTO ARDEN WEST
2200 Harvard St

San Diego

HOMEWOOD SUITES BY HILTON SAN DIEGO/DEL MAR
11025 Vista Sorrento Pkwy

HOMESTEAD SAN DIEGO – MISSION VALLEY
7444 Mission Valley Rd

HARD ROCK HOTEL SAN DIEGO
207 5th Ave

BEST WESTERN BAYSIDE INN
555 W Ash St

San Francisco

GAYLORD SUITES
620 Jones St

AMERICAS BEST VALUE INN & SUITES – SOMA
10 Hallam St

THE WESTIN ST. FRANCIS
335 Powell St

THE POWELL HOTEL
28 Cyril Magnin St

SIR FRANCIS DRAKE HOTEL – A KIMPTON HOTEL
450 Powell St

THE STANFORD COURT, A RENAISSANCE HOTEL
905 California St

THE WHITCOMB, A HISTORIC HOTEL OF AMERICA
1231 Market St

JW MARRIOTT SAN FRANCISCO
500 Post St

Santa Barbara

THE SANDMAN INN
3714 State St

HOLIDAY INN EXPRESS SANTA BARBARA
17 W Haley St

CASA DEL MAR INN B&B
18 Bath St

Santa Monica

HOLIDAY INN SANTA MONICA BEACH AT THE PIER
120 Colorado Ave

OCEAN VIEW HOTEL
1447 Ocean Ave

South Lake Tahoe

HOLIDAY INN EXPRESS HWY 50 JCT
3961 Lake Tahoe Blvd

LAKE TAHOE – DAYS INN SKI RESORT/ GOLF AREA
3530 Lake Tahoe Blvd

Call 1-800-504-6835
or visit **www.entertainment.com/travel**

SHERATON SAN DIEGO HOTEL AND MARINA
1380 Harbor Island Dr

CROWNE PLAZA HANALEI SAN DIEGO – MISSION VALLEY
2270 Hotel Cir N

RAMADA LIMITED SAN DIEGO ARPT.
1403 Rosecrans St

OLD TOWN WESTERN INN & SUITES
3889 Arista St

HYATT REGENCY MISSION BAY SPA & MARINA
1441 Quivira Rd

HILTON SAN DIEGO RESORT & SPA
1775 E Mission Bay Dr

COMFORT INN ARPT. AT OLD TOWN
1955 San Diego Ave

COMFORT INN & SUITES HOTEL CIRCLE – SEAWORLD
2201 Hotel Cir S

BEST WESTERN GOLDEN TRIANGLE INN
5550 Clairemont Mesa Blvd

KING GEORGE HOTEL – UNION SQUARE
334 Mason at Geary

HOTEL NIKKO SAN FRANCISCO
222 Mason St

HOTEL METROPOLIS – A PERSONALITY HOTEL
25 Mason St

San Jose

HOMESTEAD SAN JOSE – DOWNTOWN
1560 N 1st St

EXTENDED STAY DELUXE SAN JOSE – SOUTH – EDENVALE
6189 San Ignacio Ave

HOLIDAY INN SILICON VALLEY
399 Silicon Valley Blvd

EXTENDED STAY AMERICA SAN JOSE – SANTA CLARA
2131 Gold St

AMERICAS BEST VALUE INN SAN JOSE CONVENTION CENTER
1415 Monterey Hwy

Colorado

Aspen

HOTEL JEROME, A ROCKRESORT
330 E Main St

ASPEN MEADOWS RESORT
845 Meadows Rd

Boulder

NEW WEST INNS
970 28th St

HOMEWOOD SUITES BOULDER CO
4950 Baseline Rd

Breckenridge

THE VILLAGE HOTEL
535 S Park Ave

RESORTQUEST AT BLUE SKY
42 Snowflake Dr

BEAVER RUN RESORT & CONFERENCE CENTER
620 Village Rd

United States

Get up to $250 in mail-in rebates.
See page G4 for details.

hotels.com

Colorado Springs

HAMPTON INN & SUITES COLORADO SPRINGS/AIR FORCE ACADEMY
1307 Republic Dr

CROSSLAND COLORADO SPRINGS – ARPT.
3490 Afternoon Cir

COMFORT INN COLORADO SPRINGS
2115 Aerotech Dr

Crested Butte

LODGE AT MOUNTAINEER SQUARE
620 Gothic Rd

Denver

HOLIDAY INN EXPRESS & SUITES DENVER ARPT.
7010 Tower Rd

CROSSLAND DENVER – CHERRY CREEK
4850 Leetsdale Dr

CROSSLAND DENVER – THORNTON
8750 Grant St

RENAISSANCE DENVER HOTEL
3801 Quebec St

RED LION HOTEL DENVER CENTRAL
4040 Quebec St

RAMADA INN DOWNTOWN
1150 E Colfax Ave

HYATT REGENCY DENVER AT COLORADO CONVENTION CENTER
650 15th St

Grand Junction

WILLOW POND BED & BREAKFAST
662 26 Rd

TWO RIVERS INN
141 N 1st St

COURTYARD BY MARRIOTT GRAND JUNCTION
765 Horizon Ct

Steamboat Springs

THE STEAMBOAT GRAND RESORT HOTEL & CONDOMINIUMS
2300 Mount Werner Cir

FAIRFIELD INN & SUITES BY MARRIOTT
3200 S Lincoln St

Telluride

RIVER CLUB CONDOS
550 Depot Ave

TELLURIDE MOUNTAINSIDE INN
333 S Davis St

MOUNTAIN LODGE AT TELLURIDE
457 Mountain Village Blvd

Vail

VAIL PLAZA HOTEL & CLUB
16 Vail Rd

THE ARRABELLE AT VAIL SQUARE, A ROCKRESORT
675 Lionshead Pl

DESTINATION RESORTS VAIL
612 Lionshead Pl

MONTANEROS CONDOMINIUMS
641 W Lionshead Cir

Winter Park

WINTER PARK PREMIER TOWNHOMES
Various Addresses

SNOWBLAZE RESORT & ATHLETIC CLUB
79114 US Hwy 40 (Main St)

Connecticut

Hartford

HOMEWOOD SUITES HARTFORD DOWNTOWN
338 Asylum St

THE GOODWIN HOTEL
1 Haynes St

HILTON HARTFORD
315 Trumbull St

District of Columbia

Washington

WASHINGTON PLAZA HOTEL
10 Thomas Cir NW

WASHINGTON MARRIOTT
1221 22nd St NW

THE WESTIN GRAND WASHINGTON DC
2350 M St NW

THE WATERGATE HOTEL
2650 Virginia Ave NW

THE HENLEY PARK HOTEL
926 Massachusetts Ave NW

THE FAIRMONT WASHINGTON DC
2401 M St NW

RENAISSANCE MAYFLOWER HOTEL
1127 Connecticut Ave NW

OMNI SHOREHAM HOTEL
2500 Calvert St NW

RENAISSANCE M STREET
1143 New Hampshire Ave NW

HYATT REGENCY WASHINGTON DC
400 New Jersey Ave NW

HILTON WASHINGTON
1919 Connecticut Ave NW

HOLIDAY INN WASHINGTON – CAPITOL
550 C St SW

COURTYARD BY MARRIOTT WASHINGTON DC NORTHWEST
1900 Connecticut Ave NW

Florida

Boca Raton

HOMESTEAD BOCA RATON – COMMERCE
501 NW 77th St

RENAISSANCE BOCA RATON HOTEL
2000 NW 19th St

EMBASSY SUITES BOCA RATON
661 NW 53rd St

DOUBLETREE GUEST SUITES BOCA RATON
701 NW 53rd St

Clearwater

HOMESTEAD ST. PETERSBURG – CLEARWATER
2311 Ulmerton Rd

Fort Lauderdale

Enjoy the sights of Fort Lauderdale

- Warm weather and pristine beaches
- A variety of water sports
- Museums, galleries and restaurants

Call 1-800-50-HOTEL (46835)

or book online at **www.entertainment.com/travel**

Choose from 53,000 more hotels online.

EXTENDED STAY AMERICA ST. PETERSBURG – CLEARWATER
3089 Executive Dr

HOLIDAY INN EXPRESS HOTEL & SUITES CLEARWATER
2580 Gulf To Bay Blvd

Cocoa Beach

FOUR POINTS COCOA BEACH
4001 N Atlantic Ave

HILTON COCOA BEACH OCEANFRONT
1550 N Atlantic Ave

HOLIDAY INN EX STES COCOA BCH
5575 N Atlantic Ave

Daytona Beach

SHORELINE ALL SUITES INN
2435 S Atlantic Ave

HAMPTON INN DAYTONA SHORES – OCEANFRONT
3135 S Atlantic Ave

EXTENDED STAY DELUXE DAYTONA BEACH – INTERNATIONAL SPEEDWAY
255 Bill France Blvd

RAMADA INN FORT LAUDERDALE – ARPT./CRUISEPORT
2275 W State Rd 84 Marina Mile

PELICAN GRAND BEACH RESORT
2000 N Ocean Blvd

MARRIOTT'S BEACHPLACE TOWERS
21 S Fort Lauderdale Beach Blvd

Fort Myers

FAIRFIELD INN BY MARRIOTT FORT MYERS
7090 Cypress Ter

COURTYARD FORT MYERS AT I-75/ GULF COAST TOWN CENTER
10050 Gulf Center Dr

COUNTRY INN & SUITES BY CARLSON FORT MYERS ARPT.
9401 Marketplace Rd

COMFORT INN FORT MYERS
4171 Boatways Rd

Fort Myers Beach

PINK SHELL BEACH RESORT & SPA
275 Estero Blvd

JACKSONVILLE PLAZA HOTEL & SUITES
14585 Duval Rd

Kissimmee

MIKE DITKA RESORTS – RUNAWAY BEACH CLUB
3000 Bonfire Beach Dr

THE PALMS HOTEL & VILLAS
3100 Parkway Blvd

SUMMER BAY RESORT
17805 US Hwy 192

ROYAL CELEBRATION INN ON LAKE CECILE
4944 W Irlo Bronson Memorial Hwy

RADISSON RESORT ORLANDO – CELEBRATION
2900 Parkway Blvd

ROYALE PARC SUITES – A QUALITY SUITES HOTEL
5876 W Irlo Bronson Memorial Hwy

GALLERIA PALMS ORLANDO
3000 Maingate Ln

AMERICAS BEST VALUE INN
7514 W Irlo Bronson Memorial Hwy

CELEBRITY RESORTS DAYTONA BEACH
3711 S Atlantic Ave

CASTAWAYS BEACH RESORT
2043 S Atlantic Ave

Destin

EMERALD GRANDE
10 Harbor Blvd

DESTIN INN & SUITES
713 Hwy 98 E

Fort Lauderdale

HOLIDAY INN EXP CONVENTION CTR – FORT LAUDERDALE
1500 SE 17th Causeway

RODEWAY INN & SUITES ARPT.
2440 W State Rd 84

IL LUGANO SUITE HOTEL
3333 NE 32nd Ave

EXTENDED STAY AMERICA FORT LAUDERDALE – PLANTATION
7755 SW 6th St

RAMADA PLAZA FORT LAUDERDALE
5100 N State Rd 7

HOLIDAY INN FORT MYERS BEACH
6890 Estero Blvd

OUTRIGGER BEACH RESORT
6200 Estero Blvd

DIAMONDHEAD BEACH RESORT
2000 Estero Blvd

LOVERS KEY BEACH CLUB BY JE HOTELS & RESORTS INC
8701 Estero Blvd

Jacksonville

RESIDENCE INN BY MARRIOTT JACKSONVILLE BUTLER BOULEVARD
10551 Deerwood Park Blvd

RED ROOF INN JACKSONVILLE – ORANGE PARK
6099 Youngerman Cir

HILTON GARDEN INN JACKSONVILLE ARPT.
13503 Ranch Rd

COURTYARD BY MARRIOTT BUTLER BOULEVARD
4670 Lenoir Ave S

Lake Buena Vista

WALT DISNEY WORLD SWAN
1200 Epcot Resort Blvd

HILTON ORLANDO RESORT LAKE BUENA VISTA
1751 Hotel Plaza Blvd

BUENA VISTA PALACE HOTEL & SPA
1900 N Buena Vista Dr

Miami

MOTEL BLU
7700 Biscayne Blvd

EXTENDED STAY AMERICA MIAMI – ARPT. – DORAL
7750 NW 25th St

HILTON MIAMI ARPT.
5101 Blue Lagoon Dr

FAIRFIELD INN BY MARRIOTT MIAMI ARPT. WEST/DORAL AREA
3959 NW 79th Ave

HOLIDAY INN MIAMI – INTERNATIONAL ARPT. (NORTH)
1111 S Royal Poinciana Blvd

Miami Beach

VILLA HARDING BY BOUTIQUE RENTALS
8118 Harding Ave

METROPOLE SUITES – SOUTH BEACH
635 Collins Ave

THE RITZ-CARLTON, SOUTH BEACH
1 Lincoln Rd

THE DEAUVILLE BEACH RESORT
6701 Collins Ave

MARCO POLO RAMADA PLAZA BEACH RESORT
19201 Collins Ave

HOWARD JOHNSON PLAZA DEZERLAND BEACH & SPA
8701 Collins Ave

FOUR POINTS BY SHERATON MIAMI BEACH
4343 Collins Ave

COURTYARD BY MARRIOTT MIAMI BEACH OCEANFRONT
3925 Collins Ave

Naples

PARK SHORE RESORT
600 Neapolitan Way

HAWTHORN SUITES NAPLES
3557 Pine Ridge Rd

BEST WESTERN NAPLES PLAZA HOTEL
6400 Dudley Dr

Orlando

RED ROOF INN ORLANDO CONV CTR
9922 Hawaiian Ct

HOMESTEAD STUDIO SUITES ORLANDO – JOHN YOUNG PARKWAY
4101 Equity Row

CROSSLAND ORLANDO – UNIVERSITY OF CENTRAL FLORIDA
12350 E Colonial Dr

CRESTWOOD SUITES – DISNEY ORLANDO
8010 Presidents Dr

COMFORT SUITES UCF/ RESEARCH PARK
12101 Challenger Pkwy

WYNDHAM ORLANDO RESORT
8001 International Dr

WESTGATE LAKES UNIVERSAL STUDIOS AREA
10000 Turkey Lake Rd

UNIVERSAL'S LOWES ROYAL PACIFIC RESORT
6300 Hollywood Way

SHERATON ORLANDO DOWNTOWN HOTEL
60 S Ivanhoe Blvd

RESIDENCE INN BY MARRIOTT ORLANDO SEAWORLD
11000 Westwood Blvd

RAMADA INN INTERNATIONAL DR
6500 International Dr

ORLANDO CONTINENTAL PLAZA HOTEL
6825 Visitor's Cir at Intl. Dr

INTERNATIONAL PLAZA RESORT & SPA
10100 International Dr

ENCLAVE SUITES AT ORLANDO BY SKY HOTELS & RESORTS
6165 Carrier Dr

COMFORT INN INTERNATIONAL
8134 International Dr

BAYMONT INN & SUITES ORLANDO – UNIVERSAL STUDIOS
5625 Major Blvd

HYATT PLACE ORLANDO/UNIVERSAL
5895 Caravan Ct

St. Petersburg

HOLIDAY INN EXPRESS ST. PETERSBURG NORTH (I-275)
2171 54th Ave N

RAMADA INN ST. PETERSBURG
5005 34th St N

Tampa

RODEWAY INN TAMPA
210 E Fowler Ave

HOMESTEAD TAMPA – NORTH ARPT.
5401 E Beaumont Center Blvd

EXTENDED STAY DELUXE TAMPA – ARPT.
4811 Memorial Hwy

EMBASSY SUITES TAMPA BRANDON
10220 Palm River Rd

TAHITIAN INN, CAFÉ & SPA
601 S Dale Mabry Hwy

SAILPORT WATERFRONT SUITES
2506 N Rocky Point Dr

BAY HARBOR HOTEL
7700 W Courtney Campbell Cswy

HOWARD JOHNSON – TAMPA ARPT.
2055 N Dale Mabry Hwy

HILTON TAMPA ARPT. WESTSHORE
2225 N Lois Ave

HAMPTON INN & SUITES TAMPA – YBOR CITY DOWNTOWN
1301 E 7th Ave

HOLIDAY INN EXPRESS HOTEL & SUITES TAMPA – ANDERSON ROAD
9402 Corporate Lake Dr

DAYS INN NORTH OF BUSCH GARDENS
701 E Fletcher Ave

West Palm Beach

RESIDENCE INN BY MARRIOTT WEST PALM BEACH
2461 Metrocentre Blvd

HAWTHORN SUITES WEST PALM
301 Lamberton Dr

HOLIDAY INN PALM BEACH – ARPT. CONFERENCE CENTER
1301 Belvedere Rd

COURTYARD BY MARRIOTT WEST PALM BEACH
600 Northpoint Pkwy

BEST WESTERN PALM BEACH LAKES
1800 Palm Beach Lakes Blvd

Georgia

Atlanta

THE ELLIS ON PEACHTREE
176 Peachtree St NW

HOMESTEAD STUDIO SUITES ATLANTA NORTH DRUID HILLS
1339 Executive Park Dr NE

HAMPTON INN ATLANTA – GEORGIA TECH – DOWNTOWN
244 North Ave NW

THE WESTIN HOTEL ATLANTA ARPT.
4736 Best Rd

HOLIDAY INN EXPRESS EMORY UNIV
2183 N Decatur Rd

MICROTEL INN & SUITES BUCKHEAD
1840 Corporate Blvd NE

HYATT REGENCY ATLANTA DOWNTOWN
265 Peachtree St NE

HILTON ATLANTA ARPT.
1031 Virginia Ave

EMBASSY SUITES ATLANTA – BUCKHEAD
3285 Peachtree Rd NE

SPRINGHILL SUITES SAVANNAH I-95
4 Gateway Blvd E

HOLIDAY INN EXPRESS HISTORIC DISTRICT
199 E Bay St

HILTON GARDEN INN SAVANNAH MIDTOWN
5711 Abercorn St

HILTON GARDEN INN SAVANNAH HISTORIC
321 W Bay St

EXTENDED STAY AMERICA SAVANNAH – MIDTOWN
5511 Abercorn St

DOUBLETREE HISTORIC SAVANNAH
411 W Bay St

CONFEDERATE HOUSE
808 Drayton St

THE WESTIN SAVANNAH HARBOR RESORT & SPA
1 Resort Dr

THE PROMENADE – A HISTORIC SAVANNAH HOTEL
412 W Bay St

KAUAI SANDS HOTEL
420 Papaloa Rd

ASTON ALOHA BEACH HOTEL FORMERLY RESORTQUEST
3-5920 Kuhio Hwy

WYNDHAM BALI HAI VILLAS
4970 Pepelani Loop

Koloa

ASTON AT POIPU KAI FORMERLY RESORTQUEST
1775 Poipu Rd

OUTRIGGER KIAHUNA PLANTATION
2253 Poipu Rd

GRAND HYATT KAUAI RESORT & SPA
1571 Poipu Rd

CASTLE KIAHUNA PLANTATION & BEACH BUNGALOWS
2253B Poipu Rd

Lahaina

THE KAPALUA VILLAS MAUI
500 Office Rd

Call 1-800-504-6835
or visit www.entertainment.com/travel

Macon

RAMADA MACON
4755 Chambers Rd

QUALITY INN & SUITES MACON
115 Riverside Pkwy

EXTENDED STAY DELUXE MACON – NORTH
3980 Riverside Dr

Marietta

HOMESTEAD ATLANTA MARIETTA – POWERS FERRY ROAD
2239 Powers Ferry Rd SE

EXTENDED STAY AMERICA ATLANTA – MARIETTA – WINDY HILL
1967 Leland Dr SE

HYATT REGENCY SUITES ATLANTA NORTHWEST
2999 Windy Hill Rd SE

Savannah

THE OLDE SAVANNAH INN
217 E Gaston St

BEST WESTERN SAVANNAH GATEWAY
1 Gateway Blvd E

Hawaii

Big Island

KING KAMEHAMEHA'S KONA BEACH HOTEL
5660 Palani Rd

CASTLE KONA BALI KAI, A CONDOMINIUM RESORT
76-6246 Alii Dr

NANILOA VOLCANOES RESORT
93 Banyan Dr

HILO SEASIDE HOTEL
126 Banyan Way

Kauai

KAUAI MARRIOTT RESORT AND BEACH CLUB
3610 Rice St Kalapaki Bch

ASTON KAUAI BEACH AT MAKAIWA FORMERLY RESORTQUEST
650 Aleka Loop

WESTIN KAANAPALI OCEAN RESORT VILLAS
6 Kai Ala Dr

SHERATON MAUI RESORT
2605 Kaanapali Pkwy

ROYAL LAHAINA RESORT
2780 Kekaa Dr

ASTON MAUI KAANAPALI VILLAS FORMERLY RESORTQUEST
45 Kai Ala Dr

ASTON MAHANA AT KAANAPALI FORMERLY RESORTQUEST
110 Kaanapali Shores Pl

THE RITZ-CARLTON, KAPALUA
1 Ritz Carlton Dr

HYATT REGENCY MAUI RESORT & SPA
200 Nohea Kai Dr

Maui

MAUI VISTA RESORT
2191 S Kihei Rd

MAUI KAMAOLE – MAUI CONDO & HOME
2777 S Kihei Rd

United States

Get up to $250 in mail-in rebates.
See page G4 for details.

hôtels.com

ASTON MAUI LU RESORT
575 S Kihei Rd

Oahu

WAIKIKI SAND VILLA HOTEL
2375 Ala Wai Blvd

WAIKIKI GATEWAY HOTEL
2070 Kalakaua Ave

WAIKIKI BEACH MARRIOTT RESORT & SPA
2552 Kalakaua Ave

SHERATON PRINCESS KAIULANI
120 Kaiulani Ave

SHERATON WAIKIKI
2255 Kalakaua Ave

ASTON WAIKIKI BEACH HOTEL FORMERLY RESORTQUEST
2570 Kalakaua Ave

CASTLE QUEEN KAPIOLANI HOTEL
150 Kapahulu Ave

ILIKAI HOTEL
1777 Ala Moana Blvd

OHANA WAIKIKI BEACHCOMBER HOTEL
2300 Kalakaua Ave

HAWAII PRINCE HOTEL WAIKIKI
100 Holomoana St

AQUA WAIKIKI WAVE
2299 Kuhio Ave

AQUA PALMS & SPA
1850 Ala Moana Blvd

AQUA WAIKIKI MARINA
1700 Ala Moana Blvd

HOLIDAY INN WAIKIKI
1830 Ala Moana Blvd

Idaho

Boise

SAFARI INN DOWNTOWN
1070 W Grove St

RESIDENCE INN BY MARRIOTT BOISE WEST
7303 W Denton St

OWYHEE PLAZA HOTEL
1109 Main St

Ketchum

CLARION INN OF SUN VALLEY
600 N Main St

Meridian

SANDMAN INN & SUITES
1575 S Meridian Rd

Post Falls

RED LION TEMPLINS HOTEL
414 E 1st Ave

Illinois

Bloomington

HAWTHORN SUITES BLOOMINGTON
1 Lyon Ct

EXTENDED STAY AMERICA BLOOMINGTON – NORMAL
1805 S Veterans Pkwy

Chicago

THE SILVERSMITH HOTEL
10 S Wabash Ave

SPRINGHILL SUITES CHICAGO O'HARE BY MARRIOTT
8101 W Higgins Rd

UNIVERSITY QUARTERS BED & BREAKFAST
6137 S Kimbark Ave, 1st Floor

RESIDENCE INN BY MARRIOTT DOWNTOWN CHICAGO RIVER NORTH
410 N Dearborn St

PRATT SHORE
1137 W Pratt

WYNDHAM CHICAGO
633 N Saint Clair St

SWISSOTEL – CHICAGO
323 E Wacker Dr

SHERATON CHICAGO HOTEL AND TOWERS
301 E North Water St

TRAVELODGE HOTEL DOWNTOWN
65 E Harrison St

SENECA HOTEL & SUITES
200 E Chestnut St

RAFFAELLO HOTEL
201 E Delaware Pl

MARRIOTT CHICAGO MIDWAY ARPT.
6520 S Cicero Ave

HYATT REGENCY CHICAGO
151 E Wacker Dr

EMBASSY SUITES CHICAGO DOWNTOWN – LAKEFRONT
511 N Columbus Dr

AFFINIA CHICAGO
166 E Superior St

HOLIDAY INN EXPRESS CHICAGO – MAGNIFICENT MILE
640 N Wabash Ave

Peoria

EXTENDED STAY AMERICA PEORIA – NORTH
4306 N Brandywine Dr

Rosemont

SHERATON GATEWAY SUITES CHICAGO O'HARE
6501 Mannheim Rd

HYATT REGENCY O'HARE
9300 Bryn Mawr Ave

Schaumburg

HOMESTEAD CHICAGO – SCHAUMBURG – CONVENTION CENTER
51 E State Pkwy

HOLIDAY INN EXPRESS CHICAGO – SCHAUMBURG
1550 N Roselle Rd

Schiller Park

O'HARE INN & SUITES
4101 Mannheim Rd

Indiana

Huntingburg

QUALITY INN HUNTINGBURG
406 E 22nd St

Kansas City

Enjoy the sights of Kansas City

- World-famous barbecue
- Museums, zoos and art galleries
- The bustling River Market

Call 1-800-50-HOTEL (46835)
or book online at **www.entertainment.com/travel**

Indianapolis

EXTENDED STAY AMERICA INDIANAPOLIS – NORTHWEST – COLLEGE PARK
9030 Wesleyan Rd

EXTENDED STAY AMERICA INDIANAPOLIS – NORTH
9750 Lake Shore Dr E

HAMPTON INN INDIANAPOLIS – DWTN CIRCLE CENTRE
105 S Meridian St

FAIRFIELD INN & SUITES BY MARRIOTT INDIANAPOLIS ARPT.
5220 W Southern Ave

DAYS INN INDIANAPOLIS
3910 Payne Branch Rd

COMFORT SUITES INDIANAPOLIS
7035 Western Select Dr

CLARION HOTEL & CONFERENCE CENTER
2930 Waterfront Pkwy

BEST WESTERN CROSSROADS
7610 Old Trails Rd

OMNI SEVERIN HOTEL
40 Jackson Pl

HYATT PLACE INDIANAPOLIS/KEYSTONE
9104 Keystone Crossing

HILTON INDIANAPOLIS DOWNTOWN
120 W Market St

FAIRFIELD INN & SUITES BY MARRIOTT INDIANAPOLIS ARPT.
5220 W Southern Ave

EMBASSY SUITES INDIANAPOLIS DOWNTOWN
110 W Washington St

DAYS INN INDIANAPOLIS
8275 Craig St

COURTYARD BY MARRIOTT INDIANAPOLIS AT THE CAPITOL
320 N Senate Ave

COMFORT INN & SUITES NORTH AT THE PYRAMIDS
9090 Wesleyan Rd

Iowa

Cedar Rapids

QUALITY INN CEDAR RAPIDS
4747 1st Ave SE

COUNTRY INN CEDAR RAPIDS ARPT
9100 Atlantic Dr SW

COMFORT INN SOUTH
390 33rd Ave SW

HAWTHORN SUITES LTD – CEDAR RAPIDS
4444 Czech Ln NE

Davenport

CLARION HOTEL CONFERENCE CENTER
5202 N Brady St

Des Moines

MARRIOTT DES MOINES
700 Grand Ave

QUALITY INN & SUITES EVENT
929 3rd St

RAMADA NORTHWEST
5000 Merle Hay Rd

Sioux City

COMFORT INN SIOUX CITY
4202 S Lakeport St

Kansas

Kansas City

CHATEAU AVALON
701 Village West Pkwy

HOLIDAY INN EXPRESS VILLAGE WEST
1931 Prairie Crossing Parallel

Overland Park

HOMEWOOD SUITES KANSAS CITY/OVERLAND PARK
10556 Marty St

SETTLE INN OVERLAND PARK
4401 W 107th St

EMBASSY SUITES KANSAS CITY – OVERLAND PARK
10601 Metcalf Ave

COURTYARD BY MARRIOTT OVERLAND PARK CONVENTION CENTER
11001 Woodson St

Topeka

ECONO LODGE TOPEKA
2950 SW Topeka Blvd

QUALITY INN – TOPEKA
1240 SW Wanamaker Rd

HOLIDAY INN WEST – TOPEKA
605 SW Fairlawn Rd

Wichita

STUDIOPLUS WICHITA – EAST
9450 E Corporate Hills Dr

COURTYARD BY MARRIOTT WICHITA EAST
2975 N Webb Rd

THE BROADVIEW HOTEL
400 W Douglas Ave

HOLIDAY INN EXPRESS HOTEL & SUITES WICHITA ARPT.
1236 S Dugan Rd

Kentucky

Bowling Green

RAMADA INN
4767 Scottsville Rd

Call 1-800-50-HOTEL
or visit www.entertainment.com/travel

DAYS INN BOWLING GREEN KY
4617 Scottsville Rd

Lexington

SLEEP INN LEXINGTON
1920 Plaudit Pl

MICROTEL INN LEXINGTON
2240 Buena Vista Rd

DOUBLETREE GUEST SUITES LEXINGTON
2601 Richmond Rd

EXTENDED STAY AMERICA LEXINGTON – TATES CREEK
3575 Tates Creek Rd

RAMADA LTD LEXINGTON KY
2261 Elkhorn Rd

RAMADA CONFERENCE CENTER
2143 N Broadway

HYATT REGENCY LEXINGTON
401 W High St

FOUR POINTS BY SHERATON LEXINGTON
1938 Stanton Way

United States

Get up to $250 in mail-in rebates. See page G4 for details.

hotels.com

COURTYARD BY MARRIOTT LEXINGTON NORTH
775 Newtown Ct

Louisville

TRAVELODGE LOUISVILLE ARPT.
3315 Bardstown Rd

SPRINGHILL SUITES BY MARRIOTT LOUISVILLE – HURSTBOURNE
10101 Forest Green Blvd

HAWTHORN SUITES
751 Cypress Station Dr

EXTENDED STAY AMERICA LOUISVILLE – HURSTBOURNE
9801 Bunsen Way

EXTENDED STAY AMERICA LOUISVILLE – ST. MATTHEWS
1401 Browns Ln

COUNTRY INN & SUITES LOUISVILLE ARPT.
2850 Crittenden Dr

THE BROWN HOTEL
335 W Broadway

HOLIDAY INN LOUISVILLE – I-65 SOUTH – ARPT.
2715 Fern Valley Rd

RAMADA DOWNTOWN NORTH
1041 Zorn Ave

MARRIOTT LOUISVILLE DOWNTOWN
280 W Jefferson St

GALT HOUSE HOTEL
141 N 4th St

DAYS INN CENTRAL/UNIVERSITY/ EXPO CENTER
1620 Arthur St

CLARION HOTEL & CONFERENCE CENTER
9700 Bluegrass Pkwy

Louisiana

Baton Rouge

CROSSLAND BATON ROUGE – SHERWOOD FOREST
11140 Boardwalk Dr

EXTENDED STAY AMERICA BATON ROUGE – CITIPLACE
6250 Corporate Blvd

COMFORT SUITES BATON ROUGE
1755 Oneal Ln

SHERATON BATON ROUGE CONVENTION CENTER HOTEL
102 France St

Bossier City

CROSSLAND SHREVEPORT – BOSSIER CITY
3070 E Texas St

RESIDENCE INN SHV – BOSSIER CITY BY MARRIOTT
1001 Gould Dr

DIAMONDJACKS CASINO & RESORT
711 DiamondJacks Blvd

BOSSIER INN & SUITES
750 Isle of Capri Blvd

Houma

FAIRFIELD INN BY MARRIOTT HOUMA
1530 Martin Luther King Blvd

QUALITY HOTEL HOUMA
210 S Hollywood Rd

Kenner

EXTENDED STAY AMERICA NEW ORLEANS – KENNER
2300 Veterans Blvd

HILTON GARDEN INN NEW ORLEANS ARPT.
4535 Williams Blvd

New Orleans

BEST WESTERN SAINT CHARLES INN
3636 St. Charles Ave

AMERICAS BEST VALUE INN
2820 Tulane Ave

W NEW ORLEANS
333 Poydras St

THE INN ON BOURBON RAMADA PLAZA HOTEL
541 Bourbon St

LOEWS NEW ORLEANS HOTEL
300 Poydras St

LE PAVILLON HOTEL
833 Poydras St

INTERNATIONAL HOUSE
221 Camp St

HOTEL PROVINCIAL
1024 Rue Chartres

HAMPTON INN NEW ORLEANS – DOWNTOWN
226 Carondelet St

EMBASSY SUITES HOTEL NEW ORLEANS
315 Julia St

HOLIDAY INN NEW ORLEANS – FRENCH QUARTER
124 Royal St

COUNTRY INN & SUITES NEW ORLEANS FRENCH QUARTER
315 Magazine St

Shreveport

SAM'S TOWN HOTEL & CASINO
315 Clyde Fant Pkwy

BEST WESTERN CHATEAU SUITE HOTEL
201 Lake St

Maine

Portland

HOWARD JOHNSON PLAZA – PORTLAND
155 Riverside St

CLARION HOTEL PORTLAND
1230 Congress St

Maryland

Annapolis

THE WESTIN ANNAPOLIS
100 Westgate Cir

EXTENDED STAY AMERICA ANNAPOLIS – NAVAL ACADEMY
1 Womack Dr

Choose from 53,000 more hotels by phone.

HISTORIC INNS OF ANNAPOLIS
58 State Cir

DOUBLETREE ANNAPOLIS
210 Holiday Ct

Baltimore

THE WESTIN BALTIMORE WASHINGTON ARPT. – BWI
1110 Old Elkridge Landing Rd

SPRINGHILL SUITES MARRIOTT BALTIMORE DOWNTOWN/ INNER HARBOR
16 S Calvert St

PHOENIX RISIN' BED & BREAKFAST
1429 Bolton St

HOMEWOOD SUITES BY HILTON BALTIMORE INNER HARBOR
625 S President St

HILTON GARDEN INN AT BALTIMORE INNER HARBOR
625 S President St

TREMONT PLAZA HOTEL
222 Saint Paul Pl

THE TREMONT PARK HOTEL
8 E Pleasant St

Linthicum Heights

HAMPTON INN BALTIMORE – WASHINGTON INTERNATIONAL ARPT.
829 Elkridge Landing Rd

EMBASSY SUITES HOTEL BALTIMORE AT BWI ARPT.
1300 Concourse Dr

COUNTRY INN & SUITES BY CARLSON – BWI ARPT.
1717 W Nursery Rd

COMFORT SUITES BWI ARPT.
815 Elkridge Landing Rd

HILTON BALTIMORE BWI ARPT.
1739 W Nursery Rd

Massachusetts

Boston

HOLIDAY INN BOSTON AT BEACON HILL
5 Blossom St

RENAISSANCE BOSTON WATERFRONT HOTEL
606 Congress St

MILLENNIUM BOSTONIAN HOTEL BOSTON
Faneuil Hall Marketplace

HYATT REGENCY BOSTON
1 Avenue de Lafayette

EMBASSY SUITES BOSTON LOGAN ARPT.
207 Porter St

DOUBLETREE GUEST SUITES BOSTON
400 Soldiers Field Rd

Hyannis

HYANNIS HARBOR HOTEL
213 Ocean St

HERITAGE HOUSE HOTEL
259 Main St

Michigan

Ann Arbor

THE KENSINGTON COURT
610 Hilton Blvd

COMFORT INN & SUITES ANN ARBOR
2376 Carpenter Rd

Call 1-800-504-6835
or visit www.entertainment.com/travel

SLEEP INN & SUITES BWI ARPT.
6055 Belle Grove Rd

HYATT REGENCY BALTIMORE
300 Light St

DAYS INN INNER HARBOR
100 Hopkins Pl

COURTYARD BY MARRIOTT BALTIMORE DOWNTOWN
1000 Aliceanna St

BROOKSHIRE INN & SUITES
120 E Lombard St

HOLIDAY INN EXPRESS BALTIMORE AT THE STADIUMS
1701 Russell St

Bethesda

DOUBLETREE HOTEL BETHESDA
8120 Wisconsin Ave

MARRIOTT BETHESDA
5151 Pooks Hill Rd

HYATT REGENCY BETHESDA
1 Bethesda Metro Ctr

CASA DO ZEQUITA – BED & BREAKFAST
1534 Commonwealth Ave

THE LIBERTY HOTEL
215 Charles St

BERKELEY RESIDENCE
40 Berkeley St

BEACON HILL HOTEL & BISTRO
25 Charles St

THE WESTIN BOSTON WATERFRONT
425 Summer St

THE LENOX HOTEL BOSTON
710 Boylston St

THE COLONNADE HOTEL – SUMMIT HOTEL
120 Huntington Ave

SHERATON BOSTON HOTEL
39 Dalton St

RADISSON BOSTON HOTEL
200 Stuart St

NINE ZERO – A KIMPTON HOTEL
90 Tremont St

BEST WESTERN EXECUTIVE PLAZA
2900 Jackson Ave

Detroit

MOTORCITY CASINO HOTEL
2901 Grand River Ave

OMNI DETROIT HOTEL RIVER PLACE
1000 River Place Dr

MILNER HOTEL
1526 Centre St

HOLIDAY INN EXPRESS HOTEL & SUITES – DETROIT DOWNTOWN
1020 Washington Blvd

STAY INN & SUITES DOWNTOWN DETROIT
3250 E Jefferson Ave

Minnesota

Duluth

FAIRFIELD INN BY MARRIOTT DULUTH
901 Joshua Ave

DULUTH SPIRIT MOUNTAIN RED ROOF INN
9315 Westgate Blvd

United States

Get up to $250 in mail-in rebates.
See page G4 for details.

hotels.con

Minneapolis

HISTORIC KING INN
2400 Stevens Ave S

CHAMBERS
901 Hennepin Ave

THE MARQUETTE BY HILTON
710 Marquette Ave

RADISSON UNIVERSITY HOTEL
615 Washington Ave SE

MILLENNIUM HOTEL MINNEAPOLIS
1313 Nicollet Ave

GRAND HOTEL MINNEAPOLIS
615 2nd Ave S

COMFORT SUITES MINNEAPOLIS
425 S 7th St

DOUBLETREE MINNEAPOLIS PARK PLACE HOTEL
1500 Park Place Blvd

THE DEPOT MINNEAPOLIS, A MARRIOTT RENAISSANCE HOTEL
225 3rd Ave S

Rochester

QUALITY INN & SUITES ROCHESTER
1620 1st Ave SE

GUESTHOUSE INN ROCHESTER
435 16th Ave NW

EXTENDED STAY AMERICA ROCHESTER – SOUTH
55 Woodlake Dr SE

COURTYARD BY MARRIOTT ROCHESTER MAYO CLINIC AREA/ SAINT MARYS
161 13th Ave SW

COUNTRY INN & SUITES BY CARLSON ROCHESTER SOUTH
77 Woodlake Dr SE

Mississippi

Biloxi

TREASURE BAY CASINO & HOTEL
1980 Beach Blvd

ISLE OF CAPRI CASINO RESORT BILOXI
151 Beach Blvd

IP CASINO RESORT SPA
850 Bayview Ave

Tunica

SAM'S TOWN TUNICA
1477 Casino Strip Resorts Blvd

AMERICA'S BEST VALUE INN – TUNICA RESORTS
4250 Casino Center Dr

Missouri

Branson

SUPER 8 BRANSON CENTRAL
3470 Keeter St

HOLIDAY INN EXPRESS BRANSON – GREEN MOUNTAIN DRIVE
2801 Green Mountain Dr

QUALITY INN BRANSON
2834 W SR 76

ECONO LODGE BRANSON
230 S Wildwood Dr

HILTON BRANSON CONVENTION CENTER
200 E Main St

HILLBILLY INN
1166 W Hwy 76

FOXBOROUGH INN
235 Expressway Lane Taney

RADISSON HOTEL BRANSON
120 S Wildwood Dr

Kansas City

HYATT REGENCY CROWN CENTER
2345 McGee St

HOLIDAY INN EXPRESS ARPT.
11130 NW Ambassador Dr

EXTENDED STAY AMERICA KANSAS CITY – ARPT.
11712 NW Plaza Cir

CROSSLAND KANSAS CITY – NORTHEAST – WORLDS OF FUN
4301 N Corrington Ave

INTERCONTINENTAL AT THE PLAZA
401 Ward Pkwy

Springfield

SLEEP INN MEDICAL DISTRICT
233 E Camino Alto

COMFORT INN & SUITES
2815 N Glenstone Ave

BAYMONT INN & SUITES SPRINGFIELD ARPT.
2445 N Airport Plaza Ave

St. Louis

THE WESTIN ST. LOUIS
811 Spruce St

QUALITY INN ST. LOUIS ARPT. HOTEL
10232 Natural Bridge Rd

MILLENNIUM HOTEL ST. LOUIS
200 S 4th St

HOLIDAY INN SELECT DOWNTOWN CONVENTION CENTER
811 N 9th St

CROWNE PLAZA RIVERFRONT AT THE ARCH
200 N 4th St

COURTYARD BY MARRIOTT ST. LOUIS DOWNTOWN
2340 Market St

Montana

Billings

HOLIDAY INN THE GRAND MONTANA BILLINGS
5500 Midland Rd

Great Falls

EXTENDED STAY AMERICA GREAT FALLS – MISSOURI RIVER
800 River Dr S

Nebraska

Lincoln

ECONO LODGE LINCOLN
1140 W Cornhusker Hwy

COUNTRY INN & SUITES BY CARLSON LINCOLN NORTH
5353 N 27th St

HOLIDAY INN EXPRESS LINCOLN
1133 Belmont Ave

Omaha

STUDIOPLUS OMAHA – WEST
9006 Burt St

MOTEL 6 WEST CENTRAL
3511 S 84th St

COUNTRY INN SUITES OMAHA
11818 Miami St

Nevada
Henderson

WINGATE BY WYNDHAM – HENDERSON
3041 Saint Rose Pkwy

THE RITZ-CARLTON LAKE LAS VEGAS
1610 Lake Las Vegas Pkwy

Las Vegas

HAMPTON INN LAS VEGAS/ SUMMERLIN
7100 Cascade Valley Ct

HOLIDAY INN EXPRESS LAS VEGAS WEST
8669 W Sahara Ave

RIVIERA HOTEL & CASINO
2901 Las Vegas Blvd S

RIO ALL-SUITE HOTEL & CASINO
3700 W Flamingo Rd

PARIS LAS VEGAS
3655 Las Vegas Blvd S

PALACE STATION HOTEL & CASINO
2411 W Sahara Ave

NEW YORK NEW YORK HOTEL & CASINO
3790 Las Vegas Blvd S

MONTE CARLO RESORT & CASINO
3770 Las Vegas Blvd S

MIRAGE RESORT & CASINO
3400 Las Vegas Blvd S

MGM GRAND HOTEL & CASINO
3799 Las Vegas Blvd S

BEST WESTERN MARDI GRAS HOTEL & CASINO
3500 Paradise Rd

MANDALAY BAY RESORT & CASINO
3950 Las Vegas Blvd S

LUXOR HOTEL & CASINO
3900 Las Vegas Blvd S

ARIZONA CHARLIE'S DECATUR – CASINO HOTEL & SUITES
740 S Decatur Blvd

Laughlin

TROPICANA EXPRESS
2121 S Casino Dr

HARRAH'S HOTEL & CASINO
2900 S Casino Dr

Reno

GRAND SIERRA RESORT & CASINO
2500 E 2nd St

QUALITY INN SOUTH RENO
1885 S Virginia St

SILVER LEGACY RESORT CASINO
407 N Virginia St

SANDS REGENCY HOTEL & CASINO
345 N Arlington Ave

New Hampshire
Manchester

COMFORT INN ARPT.
298 Queen City Ave

Call 1-800-50-HOTEL
or visit www.entertainment.com/travel

WYNN LAS VEGAS
3131 Las Vegas Blvd S

TROPICANA HOTEL & CASINO – LAS VEGAS
3801 Las Vegas Blvd S

TI – TREASURE ISLAND HOTEL & CASINO
3300 Las Vegas Blvd S

THE PALMS CASINO RESORT
4321 W Flamingo Rd

SUPER 8 MOTEL – LAS VEGAS/NELLIS
4435 Las Vegas Blvd N

STRATOSPHERE TOWER – CASINO & RESORT HOTEL
2000 Las Vegas Blvd S

ST. TROPEZ ALL SUITE HOTEL
455 E Harmon Ave

SAM'S TOWN HOTEL & GAMBLING HALL
5111 Boulder Hwy

SAHARA LAS VEGAS HOTEL & CASINO
2535 Las Vegas Blvd S

AIRPORT INN LAS VEGAS
5125 Swenson St

HOWARD JOHNSON INN – LAS VEGAS STRIP
1401 Las Vegas Blvd S

HARRAH'S HOTEL & CASINO LAS VEGAS
3475 Las Vegas Blvd S

FOUR QUEENS HOTEL & CASINO
202 Fremont St

FLAMINGO LAS VEGAS
3555 Las Vegas Blvd S

FITZGERALDS CASINO LAS VEGAS
301 Fremont St

EXCALIBUR HOTEL CASINO
3850 Las Vegas Blvd S

EMERALD SUITES S LAS VEGAS BLVD
9145 Las Vegas Blvd S

CIRCUS CIRCUS HOTEL & CASINO
2880 Las Vegas Blvd S

BELLAGIO
3600 Las Vegas Blvd S

SPRINGHILL SUITES BY MARRIOTT MANCHESTER
975 Perimeter Rd

New Jersey
Atlantic City

SURFSIDE RESORT HOTEL
18 S Mount Vernon Ave

THE TRUMP TAJ MAHAL CASINO FEATURING CHAIRMAN TOWER
1000 Boardwalk at Virginia Ave

TRUMP PLAZA HOTEL & CASINO
Mississippi Ave at the Boardwalk

TROPICANA CASINO & RESORT
Brighton Ave & Boardwalk

SHERATON ATLANTIC CITY
2 Miss America Way

RESORTS CASINO HOTEL ATLANTIC CITY
1133 Boardwalk

QUALITY INN CASINO CITY
500 N Albany Ave

hŏtels.cor

FLAGSHIP – FANTASEA RESORTS
60 N Maine Ave

BORGATA HOTEL CASINO & SPA
1 Borgata Way

ATLANTIC CITY HILTON CASINO RESORT
Boston at the Boardwalk

Newark

WYNDHAM GARDEN HOTEL
NEWARK ARPT.
550 Route 1 S

FAIRFIELD INN & SUITES BY MARRIOTT
NEWARK LIBERTY INT ARPT.
618 Routes 1 & 9 S

COMFORT SUITES NEWARK
1348 McCarter Hwy

New Mexico
Albuquerque

HOLIDAY INN EXPRESS – BALLOON
FIESTA PARK
5401 Alameda Blvd NE

HILTON ALBUQUERQUE
1901 University Blvd NE

RODEWAY INN ALBUQUERQUE
13141 Central Ave NE

HOTEL ALBUQUERQUE AT OLD TOWN
800 Rio Grande Blvd NW

Santa Fe

HOTEL SANTA FE
1501 Paseo de Peralta

HOTEL PLAZA REAL
125 Washington Ave

New York
Albany

EXTENDED STAY AMERICA
ALBANY – CAPITAL
1395 Washington Ave

74 STATE, AN ASCEND COLLECTION
74 State St

HILTON GARDEN INN ALBANY ARPT.
800 Albany Shaker Rd

HAMPTON INN & SUITES
ALBANY – DOWNTOWN
25 Chapel St

CLARION HOTEL OF ALBANY
3 Watervliet Ave Ext

HOLIDAY INN EXPRESS
ALBANY DOWNTOWN
300 Broadway

Buffalo

HYATT REGENCY BUFFALO
2 Fountain Plz

COMFORT SUITES BUFFALO
901 Dick Rd

BEST WESTERN THE INN
AT BUFFALO ARPT.
4630 Genesee St

ADAM'S MARK BUFFALO
120 Church St

Jamaica

CLARION HOTEL JAMAICA
138-05 Jamaica Ave

RAMADA PLAZA HOTEL – JFK ARPT.
Van Wyck Expy

HILTON GARDEN INN
QUEENS/JFK ARPT.
14818 134th St

DOUBLETREE HOTEL JFK ARPT.
135-30 140th St

New York City

THE SHOREHAM HOTEL
33 W 55th St

THE PIERRE, A TAJ HOTEL
2 E 61st St

THE PENINSULA NEW YORK
700 5th Ave

THE MUSE NEW YORK –
A KIMPTON HOTEL
130 W 46th St

THE CARLYLE, A ROSEWOOD HOTEL
35 E 76th St

THE ALEX
205 E 45th St

MILFORD PLAZA
700 8th Ave

NEW YORK HELMSLEY
212 E 42nd St

SALISBURY HOTEL
123 W 57th St

ROOSEVELT HOTEL NEW YORK
45 E 45th St

RADISSON MARTINIQUE
ON BROADWAY
49 W 32nd St

HOTEL 373 FIFTH AVENUE
373 5th Ave

HOTEL MELA
120 W 44th St

HOLIDAY INN MANHATTAN
DOWNTOWN
138 Lafayette St

PARK CENTRAL NEW YORK HOTEL
870 7th Ave

NEW YORK MARRIOTT DOWNTOWN
85 West St

MURRAY HILL EAST SUITES
149 E 39th St

BROADWAY PLAZA HOTEL
1155 Broadway

Niagara Falls

ECONO LODGE AT THE FALLS NORTH
5919 Niagara Falls Blvd

TRAVELODGE NIAGARA FALLS
9401 Niagara Falls Blvd

QUALITY HOTEL & SUITES
AT THE FALLS
240 Rainbow Blvd

INN ON THE RIVER
7001 Buffalo Ave

HOWARD JOHNSON CLOSEST TO THE
FALLS & CASINO
454 Main St

HOLIDAY INN NIAGARA FALLS
SCENIC DOWNTOWN
114 Buffalo Ave

New York

Enjoy the sights of New York

- Galleries and museums
- Broadway theatre district
- The Big Apple's incredible architecture

Call 1-800-50-HOTEL (46835)
or book online at **www.entertainment.com/travel**

Choose from 53,000 more hotels by phone.

**FALLSIDE HOTEL &
CONFERENCE CENTER**
401 Buffalo Ave

CROWNE PLAZA NIAGARA FALLS
300 3rd St

Rochester

HAMPTON INN ROCHESTER – NORTH
500 Center Place Dr

**EXTENDED STAY AMERICA
ROCHESTER – HENRIETTA**
700 Commons Way

RADISSON HOTEL ROCHESTER ARPT.
175 Jefferson Rd

HYATT REGENCY ROCHESTER
125 Main St E

CLARION RIVERSIDE HOTEL
120 Main St E

Syracuse

THE GENESEE GRANDE HOTEL
1060 E Genesee St

PARKVIEW HOTEL
713 E Genesee St

Durham

**STUDIO PLUS DURHAM –
RESEARCH TRIANGLE PARK**
2504 Hwy 54

**RED ROOF INN DURHAM RESEARCH
TRIANGLE PARK**
4405 APEX Hwy 55 E

**HOMESTEAD DURHAM – RESEARCH
TRIANGLE PARK**
4515 NC Hwy 55

HOLIDAY INN EXPRESS HOTEL & SUITES
4912 S Miami Blvd

Raleigh

STUDIOPLUS NORTH RALEIGH
921 Wake Towne Dr

MICROTEL INN & SUITES RALEIGH
1209 Plainview Dr

**HOMESTEAD RALEIGH –
NORTH RALEIGH**
3531 Wake Forest Rd

**EXTENDED STAY AMERICA
RALEIGH – NORTH RALEIGH**
911 Wake Towne Dr

MILLENNIUM HOTEL CINCINNATI
150 W 5th St

**HILTON CINCINNATI
NETHERLAND PLAZA**
35 W 5th St

Cleveland

**EXTENDED STAY AMERICA
CLEVELAND – BEACHWOOD**
3820 Orange Pl

**WYNDHAM CLEVELAND AT
PLAYHOUSE SQUARE**
1260 Euclid Ave

THE GLIDDEN HOUSE
1901 Ford Dr

RENAISSANCE CLEVELAND HOTEL
24 Public Sq

Columbus

**TOWNEPLACE SUITES BY
MARRIOTT GAHANNA**
695 Taylor Rd

**SPRINGHILL SUITES BY MARRIOTT
COLUMBUS ARPT. GAHANNA**
665 Taylor Rd

Call 1-800-504-6835
or visit www.entertainment.com/travel

North Carolina

Charlotte

**STUDIO PLUS CHARLOTTE –
UNIVERSITY PLACE**
123 McCullough Dr

**HOLIDAY INN CHARLOTTE –
BILLY GRAHAM PARKWAY**
321 W Woodlawn Rd

**HOMESTEAD STUDIO SUITES
CHARLOTTE ARPT.**
710 Yorkmont Rd

GREENLEAFE INN
5820 Monroe Rd

COMFORT SUITES UNIVERSITY AREA
7735 University City Blvd

AMERICAS BEST VALUE INN – ARPT.
3200 Queen City Dr

MARRIOTT CHARLOTTE CITY CENTER
100 W Trade St

COUNTRY INN & SUITES – CHARLOTTE
2541 Little Rock Rd

COMFORT SUITES ARPT.
3424 Mulberry Church Rd

COMFORT SUITES PAVILION RALEIGH
1309 Corporation Pkwy

North Dakota

Fargo

COMFORT INN EAST FARGO
1407 35th St S

HOLIDAY INN FARGO
3803 13th Ave S

Ohio

Cincinnati

**EXTENDED STAY AMERICA
CINCINNATI – BLUE ASH – NORTH**
11145 Kenwood Rd

**EXTENDED STAY AMERICA
CINCINNATI – BLUE ASH – SOUTH**
4260 Hunt Rd

HOLIDAY INN EASTGATE
4501 Eastgate Blvd

THE GARFIELD SUITES HOTEL
2 Garfield Pl

**QUALITY INN & SUITES
COLUMBUS NORTH**
1001 Schrock Rd

**FAIRFIELD INN BY MARRIOTT
COLUMBUS OSU**
3031 Olentangy River Rd

**EXTENDED STAY AMERICA
COLUMBUS – WORTHINGTON**
7465 High Cross Blvd

**COUNTRY INN & SUITES
COLUMBUS WEST**
1155 Evans Way Ct

THE BLACKWELL
2110 Tuttle Park Pl

HYATT ON CAPITOL SQUARE
75 E State St

Oklahoma

Oklahoma City

**EXTENDED STAY DELUXE
OKLAHOMA CITY – NORTHWEST**
4811 NW Expy

HOLIDAY INN EXP OKLAHOMA CITY
7601 C A Henderson Blvd

Tulsa

STUDIO PLUS TULSA – CENTRAL
7901 E 31st Ct

RAMADA TULSA ARPT. EAST
1010 N Garnett Rd

HAMPTON INN & SUITES WOODLAND HILLS
7141 S 85th E Ave

EXTENDED STAY AMERICA TULSA – CENTRAL
3414 S 79th St E

PRESIDENTIAL SUITES
8338 E 61st St

Oregon
Lincoln City

SILETZ BAY LODGE
1012 SW 51st St

THE ASHLEY INN & SUITES
3430 NE Hwy 101

Portland

EXTENDED STAY AMERICA PORTLAND – GRESHAM
17777 NE Sacramento St

COMFORT SUITES PORTLAND SOUTHWEST
11340 SW 60th Ave

RIVERPLACE, A LARKSPUR COLLECTION HOTEL
1510 SW Harbor Way

MARRIOTT PORTLAND DOWNTOWN WATERFRONT
1401 SW Naito Pkwy

MARK SPENCER HOTEL
409 SW 11th Ave

Pennsylvania
Harrisburg

COMFORT INN RIVERFRONT
525 S Front St

Philadelphia

RAMADA PHILADELPHIA
11580 Roosevelt Blvd

RODEWAY INN PHILADELPHIA
1208 Walnut St

SHERATON PHILADELPHIA CITY CENTER HOTEL
2 Franklin Plaza 17th & Race Sts

RADISSON PLAZA WARWICK HOTEL
1701 Locust St

PARK HYATT PHILADELPHIA
1415 Chancellor St

MARRIOTT PHILADELPHIA ARPT.
1 Arrivals Rd

LATHAM HOTEL – PHILADELPHIA
135 S 17th St

HILTON GARDEN INN PHILADELPHIA CITY CENTER
1100 Arch St

COURTYARD BY MARRIOTT PHILADELPHIA DOWNTOWN
21 N Juniper St

CLUB QUARTERS IN PHILADELPHIA
1628 Chestnut St

Pittsburgh

QUALITY INN UNIVERSITY CENTER
3401 Blvd of the Allies

HOLIDAY INN EXPRESS PITTSBURGH NORTH
10 Landings Dr

RESIDENCE INN BY MARRIOTT PITTSBURGH ARPT.
1500 Park Lane Dr

HYATT REGENCY PITTSBURGH INTERNATIONAL ARPT.
1111 Airport Blvd

Rhode Island
Newport

HYATT REGENCY NEWPORT
1 Goat Island

MARRIOTT NEWPORT
25 America's Cup Ave

South Carolina
Charleston

HAWTHORN SUITES CHARLESTON
2455 Savannah Hwy

EXTENDED STAY AMERICA NORTH CHARLESTON – ARPT.
5059 N Arco Ln

THE FRANCIS MARION HOTEL
387 King St

Hilton Head Island

HOLIDAY INN HILTON HEAD ISLAND (OCEANFRONT)
1 S Forest Beach Dr

PLAYERS CLUB HOTEL
35 DeAllyon Ave

MARRIOTT HILTON HEAD GOLF RESORT
1 Hotel Cir

COMFORT INN SOUTH FOREST BEACH
2 Tanglewood Dr

HILTON HEAD ISLAND BEACH & TENNIS RESORT
40 Folly Field Rd

Myrtle Beach

WESTGATE MYRTLE BEACH
415 S Ocean Blvd

HOLIDAY INN W HARD ROCK PKWY
101 Hard Rock Pkwy

COMFORT SUITES MYRTLE BEACH
710 Frontage Rd E

South Dakota
Rapid City

DAKOTA PINES INN
1313 N Lacrosse St

ALEX JOHNSON
523 6th St

Sioux Falls

TRAVELODGE HOTEL SIOUX FALLS
3300 W Russell St

Tennessee

Chattanooga

THE CHATTANOOGAN
1201 S Broad St

FAIRFIELD INN BY MARRIOTT CHATTANOOGA
2350 Shallowford Village Dr

EXTENDED STAY AMERICA CHATTANOOGA – ARPT.
6240 Airpark Dr

Memphis

HOMEWOOD SUITES MEMPHIS EAST
5811 Poplar Ave

HOMESTEAD MEMPHIS – POPLAR AVENUE
6500 Poplar Ave

HAMPTON INN & SUITES MEMPHIS/ SHADY GROVE
962 S Shady Grove Rd

EXTENDED STAY AMERICA MEMPHIS – MT MORIAH
6520 Mount Moriah Rd Ext

MEMPHIS HOTEL
6101 Shelby Oaks Dr

Nashville

EXTENDED STAY AMERICA NASHVILLE – VANDERBILT
3311 W End Ave

CROSSLAND NASHVILLE – ARPT. – BRILEY PKWY
1210 Murfreesboro Pike

DAYS INN NASHVILLE – OPRYLAND AREA
2460 Music Valley Dr

RADISSON HOTEL OPRYLAND
2401 Music Valley Dr

MILLENNIUM MAXWELL HOUSE NASHVILLE
2025 Metrocenter Blvd

HILTON NASHVILLE DOWNTOWN
121 4th Ave S

GAYLORD OPRYLAND RESORT & SPA
2800 Opryland Dr

Texas

Amarillo

HOLIDAY INN EXP STES AMARILLO
2806 Wolflin Ave

Arlington

HILTON ARLINGTON/SIX FLAGS
2401 E Lamar Blvd

COURTYARD BY MARRIOTT ARLINGTON BALLPARK
1500 Nolan Ryan Expy

HOLIDAY INN ARLINGTON – NORTHEAST
1311 Wet N Wild Way

Austin

PARK LANE GUEST HOUSE
221 Park Ln

HOMESTEAD AUSTIN – DOWNTOWN – TOWN LAKE
507 S 1st St

EXTENDED STAY DELUXE AUSTIN – METRO
6300 E Hwy 290

HILTON AUSTIN
500 E 4th St

Corpus Christi

RED ROOF INN & SUITES CORPUS CHRISTI
3030 Buffalo St

RAILWAY INN & SUITES CORPUS CHRISTI
4343 Ocean Dr

Dallas

THE RITZ-CARLTON, DALLAS
2121 McKinney Ave

W DALLAS – VICTORY
2440 Victory Park Ln

THE WESTIN HOTEL GALLERIA
13340 Dallas Pkwy

RADISSON HOTEL DALLAS EAST
11350 Lyndon B Johnson Fwy

MCM ELEGANTÉ HOTEL & SUITES
2330 W Northwest Hwy

HYATT REGENCY DALLAS
300 Reunion Blvd

HOLIDAY INN DALLAS MARKET CENTER
4500 Harry Hines Blvd

BAYMONT INN & SUITES LOVE FIELD
2370 W Northwest Hwy

El Paso

WINGATE BY WYNDHAM EL PASO
6351 Gateway Blvd W

STUDIOPLUS EL PASO – WEST
990 Sunland Park Dr

MARRIOTT EL PASO
1600 Airway Blvd

Fort Worth

COUNTRY INN STES FORT WORTH
2200 Mercado Dr

RENAISSANCE FORT WORTH WORTHINGTON HOTEL
200 Main St

Call 1-800-50-HOTEL
or visit **www.entertainment.com/travel**

RADISSON HOTEL FORT WORTH – FOSSIL CREEK
2540 Meacham Blvd

HILTON DOWNTOWN FORT WORTH
815 Main St

Galveston

COMFORT INN & STES GALVESTON
6302 Seawall Blvd

HOLIDAY INN SUNSPREE RESORT GALVESTON BEACH
1702 Seawall Blvd

Houston

LA QUINTA INN & SUITES HOUSTON GALLERIA
1625 W Loop S

INTERCONTINENTAL HOUSTON
2222 W Loop S

HOMESTEAD HOUSTON – WILLOWBROOK
13223 Champions Centre Dr

HOMEWOOD SUITES BY HILTON HOUSTON NEAR THE GALLERIA
2950 Sage Rd

ee **Rebate Rules** on page G4 and the Guaranteed Best Rate Program Rules of Use on page G28.

hotels.com

COURTYARD MARRIOTT HOUSTON I-10
12401 Katy Fwy

SHERATON SUITES HOUSTON GALLERIA
2400 W Loop S

WINGATE BY WYNDHAM HOUSTON – WILLOWBROOK
9050 Mills Rd

BAYMONT INN HOUSTON HOBBY ARPT.
9902 Gulf Fwy

CROSSLAND HOUSTON – NORTHWEST
5959 Guhn Rd

EXTENDED STAY AMERICA HOUSTON – NASA
1410 Nasa Rd

Irving

WYNDHAM DFW ARPT. NORTH
4441 W Hwy 114

HOMESTEAD STUDIO SUITES DALLAS – LAS COLINAS CARNABY STREET
5315 Carnaby St

HOLIDAY INN EXPRESS IRVING NORTH – LAS COLINAS
333 W John W Carpenter Fwy

CROSSLAND DALLAS – IRVING
3440 W Walnut Hill Ln

San Antonio

HOLIDAY INN RIVER WALK
217 N Saint Marys St

REST INN
5530 E I-10

LA QUINTA INN SAN ANTONIO CONVENTION CENTER
303 Blum St

HILTON SAN ANTONIO HILL COUNTRY HOTEL & SPA
9800 Westover Hills Blvd

AMERICAS BEST VALUE INN – AT&T CENTER
3645 N Pan Am Expy

OMNI HOTEL – SAN ANTONIO
9821 Colonnade Blvd

QUALITY INN NEAR SEAWORLD
323 SW Loop 410

South Padre Island

DAYS INN SOUTH PADRE ISLAND
3913 Padre Blvd

SOUTH PADRE BEACH RESORT
100 Padre Blvd

Utah
Salt Lake City

HOMESTEAD SALT LAKE CITY – SUGAR HOUSE
1220 E 2100 S

HAMPTON INN DOWNTOWN
425 S 300 W

HOLIDAY INN EXPRESS SALT LAKE CITY
4465 Century Dr

SHILO INN DOWNTOWN SALT LAKE CITY
206 S West Temple

HOTEL MONACO SALT LAKE CITY – A KIMPTON HOTEL
15 W 200 S

EMBASSY SUITES HOTEL
110 W 600 S

SKY HARBOR SUITES
1876 W North Temple

Virginia
Alexandria

CROWNE PLAZA OLD TOWN
901 N Fairfax St

MORRISON HOUSE BOUTIQUE HOTEL – A KIMPTON HOTEL
116 S Alfred St

Arlington

HYATT ARLINGTON
1325 Wilson Blvd

RESIDENCE INN BY MARRIOTT PENTAGON CITY
550 Army Navy Dr

SHERATON NATIONAL HOTEL
900 S Orme St

Norfolk

HAMPTON INN & SUITES NORFOLK ARPT.
1511 Usaa Dr

AMERICAS BEST VALUE INN
235 N Military Hwy

DOUBLETREE HOTEL NORFOLK ARPT.
880 N Military Hwy

BEST WESTERN HOLIDAY SANDS INN
1330 E Ocean View Ave

Richmond

THE BERKELEY HOTEL RICHMOND
1200 E Cary St

HOMESTEAD RICHMOND – MIDLOTHIAN
241 Arboretum Pl

EXTENDED STAY DELUXE RICHMOND – I-64 – WEST BROAD STREET
6807 Paragon Pl

DOUBLETREE HOTEL RICHMOND DOWNTOWN
301 W Franklin St

HOLIDAY INN EXPRESS RICHMOND DOWNTOWN
201 E Cary St

Virginia Beach

SPRINGHILL SUITES VIRGINIA BEACH OCEANFRONT
901 Atlantic Ave

MARJAC SUITES
2201 Atlantic Ave

EXTENDED STAY AMERICA VIRGINIA BEACH – INDEPENDENCE BLVD
4548 Bonney Rd

HILTON VIRGINIA BEACH OCEANFRONT
3001 Atlantic Ave

DOUBLETREE HOTEL VIRGINIA BEACH
1900 Pavilion Dr

CROWNE PLAZA VIRGINIA BEACH – NORFOLK
4453 Bonney Rd

Canada
Enjoy the sights of Canada
- Big-city action and nightlife
- World-class museums
- National parks and scenic drives

Call 1-800-50-HOTEL (46835)
or book online at **www.entertainment.com/travel**

Williamsburg

QUALITY INN COLONY
309 Page St

WILLIAMSBURG DAYS INN CENTRAL
1900 Richmond Rd

RAMADA INN 1776
725 Bypass Rd

HOLIDAY INN EXPRESS HOTEL & SUITES WILLIAMSBURG
1452 Richmond Rd

Washington

Bellevue

HOMESTEAD SEATTLE – BELLEVUE
3700 132nd Ave SE

HYATT REGENCY BELLEVUE
900 Bellevue Way NE

THE WESTIN BELLEVUE
600 Bellevue Way NE

Seattle

EXTENDED STAY AMERICA SEATTLE – NORTHGATE
13330 Stone Ave N

RODEWAY INN & SUITES
9201 NE Vancouver Mall Dr

EXTENDED STAY AMERICA PORTLAND – VANCOUVER
300 NE 115th Ave

Wisconsin

Green Bay

COMFORT SUITES GREEN BAY
1951 Bond St

GREEN BAY – DAYS INN LAMBEAU FIELD
1978 Holmgren Way

BEST WESTERN MIDWAY HOTEL
780 Armed Forces Dr

Madison

EXTENDED STAY AMERICA MADISON – WEST
617 Junction Rd

HOLIDAY INN HOTEL STES MADISON
1109 Fourier Dr

MICROTEL MADISON
2139 E Springs Dr

West Virginia

Charleston

HOLIDAY INN CHARLESTON
600 Kanawha Blvd E

Wyoming

Cheyenne

HOLIDAY INN CHEYENNE – I-80
204 W Fox Farm Rd

KNIGHTS INN CHEYENNE
1719 Central Ave

Jackson Hole

PARKWAY INN
125 N Jackson St

RUSTIC INN AT JACKSON HOLE
475 N Cache

Canada

Alberta

Banff

THE FAIRMONT BANFF SPRINGS
405 Spray Ave

Call 1-800-504-6835
or visit www.entertainment.com/travel

SHERATON SEATTLE HOTEL
1400 6th Ave

RENAISSANCE SEATTLE HOTEL
515 Madison St

EXECUTIVE HOTEL PACIFIC
400 Spring St

BEST WESTERN EXECUTIVE INN SEATTLE CENTER
200 Taylor Ave N

LA QUINTA INN SEATTLE SEA-TAC
2824 S 188th St

Tacoma

CROSSLAND TACOMA – HOSMER
8801 S Hosmer St

EXTENDED STAY AMERICA TACOMA – SOUTH
2120 S 48th St

COURTYARD BY MARRIOTT TACOMA DOWNTOWN
1515 Commerce St

Vancouver

COMFORT INN & SUITES DOWNTOWN
401 E 13th St

Milwaukee

WYNDHAM MILWAUKEE ARPT. HOTEL & CONVENTION CENTER
4747 S Howell Ave

DOUBLETREE MILWAUKEE CITY CENTER
611 W Wisconsin Ave

RADISSON HOTEL MILWAUKEE NORTH SHORE
7065 N Port Washington Rd

RAMADA MILWAUKEE ARPT.
6331 S 13th St

HYATT REGENCY MILWAUKEE
333 W Kilbourn Ave

BEST WESTERN INN TOWNE HOTEL
710 N Old World 3rd St

Wisconsin Dells

ECONO LODGE WISCONSIN DELLS
350 W Munroe Ave

COMFORT INN WISCONSIN DELLS
703 N Frontage Rd

INNS OF BANFF
600 Banff Ave

BANFF CARIBOU LODGE & SPA
521 Banff Ave

CHARLTON'S CEDAR COURT
513 Banff Ave

Calgary

SANDMAN HOTEL & SUITES – CALGARY ARPT.
25 Hopewell Way NE

MARRIOTT CALGARY
110 9th Ave SE

HYATT REGENCY CALGARY
700 Centre St SE

HOWARD JOHNSON EXPRESS INN – CALGARY
5307 MacLeod Trail SW

EXECUTIVE ROYAL INN N CALGARY
2828 23 St NE

DAYS INN – CALGARY SOUTH
3828 MacLeod Trail S

HOLIDAY INN CALGARY – MACLEOD TRAIL SOUTH
4206 MacLeod Trail SE

Canada

hotels.com

Canmore

HOTEL OF THE ROCKIES
1 Silvertip Trail

QUALITY RESORT CHATEAU CANMORE
1720 Bow Valley Trail

RADISSON HOTEL CONFERENCE CENTER CANMORE
511 Bow Valley Trail

Edmonton

TRAVELODGE EDMONTON WEST
18320 Stony Plain Rd NW

THE SUTTON PLACE HOTEL EDMONTON
10235 101 St

SANDMAN HOTEL WEST EDMONTON
17635 Stony Plain Rd NW

HOLIDAY INN CONVENTION CENTER – EDMONTON
4520 76 Ave NW

CROWNE PLAZA EDMONTON – CHATEAU LACOMBE
10111 Bellamy Hill NW

Jasper

THE FAIRMONT JASPER PARK LODGE
Old Lodge Rd

MOUNT ROBSON INN
902 Connaught Dr

Lake Louise

DEER LODGE
109 Lake Louise Dr

THE FAIRMONT CHATEAU LAKE LOUISE
111 Lake Louise Dr

British Columbia

Kamloops

RAMADA INN KAMLOOPS
555 Columbia St W

HOLIDAY INN EXPRESS KAMLOOPS
1550 Versatile Dr

Kelowna

LAKE OKANAGAN RESORT
2751 Westside Rd

RECREATION INN & SUITES
1891 Parkinson Way

DELTA GRAND OKANAGAN LAKEFRONT RESORT & CONFERENCE CENTER
1310 Water St

HOLIDAY INN EXPRESS KELOWNA, BC
2429 Hwy 97 N

Richmond

TRAVELODGE VANCOUVER ARPT.
3071 St. Edwards Dr

SANDMAN VANCOUVER ARPT.
3233 St. Edwards Dr

RADISSON HOTEL VANCOUVER ARPT.
8181 Cambie Rd

Vancouver

THE FAIRMONT WATERFRONT
900 Canada Pl

THE SUTTON PLACE HOTEL – VANCOUVER
845 Burrard St

THE GREENBRIER HOTEL
1393 Robson St

RAMADA HOTEL & SUITES METROTOWN
3484 Kingsway

SHERATON VANCOUVER WALL CENTRE
1088 Burrard St

BOSMANS HOTEL
1060 Howe St

BEST WESTERN DOWNTOWN VANCOUVER
718 Drake St

HOLIDAY INN VANCOUVER CENTRE
711 Broadway W

Victoria

DELTA VICTORIA OCEAN POINTE RESORT & SPA
45 Songhees Rd

HARBOUR TOWERS HOTEL & SUITES
345 Quebec St

BEST WESTERN CARLTON PLAZA HOTEL
642 Johnson St

QUEEN VICTORIA HOTEL & SUITES
655 Douglas St

Whistler

WHISTLER VILLAGE INN & SUITE
4429 Sundial Pl

FOUR SEASONS RESORT WHISTLER
4591 Blackcomb Way

ADARA HOTEL
4122 Village Green

Manitoba

Winnipeg

PLACE LOUIS RIEL SUITE HOTEL
190 Smith St

THE FAIRMONT WINNIPEG
2 Lombard Pl

HOLIDAY INN WINNIPEG SOUTH
1330 Pembina Hwy

HILTON SUITES WINNIPEG ARPT.
1800 Wellington Ave

Nova Scotia

Halifax

PRINCE GEORGE HOTEL
1725 Market St

FOUR POINTS BY SHERATON HALIFAX
1496 Hollis St

BEST WESTERN CHOCOLATE LAKE HOTEL
20 St. Margaret's Bay Rd

LORD NELSON HOTEL & SUITES
1515 S Park St

Ontario

Barrie

DAYS INN BARRIE
60 Bryne Dr

Mississauga

NOVOTEL TORONTO MISSISSAUGA CENTRE
3670 Hurontario St

BEST WESTERN TORONTO ARPT. HOTEL
5825 Dixie Rd

Niagara Falls

RADISSON HOTEL & SUITES FALLSVIEW
6733 Fallsview Blvd

SHERATON FALLSVIEW HOTEL & CONFERENCE CENTER
6755 Fallsview Blvd

GREAT WOLF LODGE, RIPLEY'S WATER PARK RESORT
3950 Victoria Ave

MICHAEL'S INN BY THE FALLS
5599 River Rd

AMERICANA WATERPARK RESORT & SPA
8444 Lundy's Ln

THE FALLS PLAZA HOTEL NIAGARA FALLS
6045 Stanley Ave

MARRIOTT NIAGARA FALLS FALLSVIEW HOTEL & SPA
6740 Fallsview Blvd

HOLIDAY INN HOTEL & SUITES DOWNTOWN OTTAWA
111 Cooper St

Toronto

METROPOLITAN HOTEL
108 Chestnut St

THE SUITES AT 1 KING WEST
1 King St W

NOVOTEL TORONTO CENTRE
45 The Esplanade

BOND PLACE HOTEL
65 Dundas St E

HOLIDAY INN EXPRESS TORONTO – DOWNTOWN
111 Lombard St

HOLIDAY INN SELECT TORONTO ARPT.
970 Dixon Rd

COMFORT SUITES CITY CENTRE
200 Dundas St E

THE FAIRMONT ROYAL YORK
100 Front St W

STRATHCONA HOTEL
60 York St

LE MERIDIEN VERSAILLES – MONTREAL
1808 Sherbrooke St W

BEST WESTERN VILLE MARIE MONTREAL
3407 Rue Peel

HOLIDAY INN SELECT MONTRÉAL CENTRE-VILLE
99 Viger Ave & St. Urban St

GRAND PLAZA MONTREAL CENTRE-VILLE
505 Sherbrooke St E

RESIDENCE MARRIOTT MONTREAL ARPT.
6500 Place Robert-Joncas

W MONTREAL
901 Square Victoria

FAIRMONT THE QUEEN ELIZABETH
900 Rene-Levesque Blvd W

HOTEL LE ROBERVAL
505 Boul Rene-Levesque E

INTERCONTINENTAL MONTREAL
360 Rue Saint-Antoine W

LE NOUVEL HOTEL
1740 Boul Rene-Levesque W

OAKES HOTEL OVERLOOKING THE FALLS
6546 Fallsview Blvd

TRAVELODGE AT THE FALLS
4943 Clifton Hill

SHERATON ON THE FALLS
5875 Falls Ave

EMBASSY SUITES NIAGARA FALLS FALLSVIEW
6700 Fallsview Blvd

Ottawa

LES SUITES HOTEL OTTAWA
130 Besserer St

ARC THE HOTEL
140 Slater St

LORD ELGIN HOTEL
100 Elgin St

TRAVELODGE OTTAWA HOTEL & CONFERENCE CENTRE
1376 Carling Ave

DELTA OTTAWA HOTEL & SUITES
361 Queen St

Windsor

CAESARS WINDSOR
377 Riverside Dr E

HOLIDAY INN DOWNTOWN WINDSOR
430 Ouellette Ave

Quebec

Montreal

HOTEL LE CANTLIE SUITES
1110 Rue Sherbrooke W

HOTEL DE LA MONTAGNE
1430 Rue de la Montagne

DELTA MONTREAL
475 Ave du President-Kennedy

THE OMNI MONT – ROYAL HOTEL
1050 Sherbrooke St W

FOUR POINTS BY SHERATON MONTREAL CENTRE-VILLE
475 Sherbrooke St W

NOVOTEL MONTREAL CENTRE
1180 Rue de la Montagne

Quebec

HOTEL CLARENDON
57 Rue Ste-Anne

HOTEL PUR
395 Rue de la Couronne

LOEWS LE CONCORDE
1225 Cours du General de Montcalm

Saskatchewan

Saskatoon

SANDMAN HOTEL SASKATOON
310 Circle Dr W

RAMADA HOTEL GOLF DOME
806 Idylwyld Dr N

International

Aruba

Palm Beach

ARUBA MARRIOTT RESORT & STELLARIS CASINO
L G Smith Blvd 101

HYATT REGENCY ARUBA RESORT & CASINO
Juan E Irausquin Blvd 85

Australia

Melbourne

RADISSON ON FLAGSTAFF GARDENS MELBOURNE
380 William St

TRAVELODGE SOUTHBANK MELBOURNE
Corner of Southgate Ave/Riverside Quay

Sydney

DIAMANT BOUTIQUE HOTEL SYDNEY
14 Kings Cross Rd

SYDNEY HARBOUR MARRIOTT
30 Pitt St

Austria

Vienna

AMBASSADOR HOTEL
Kaerntner Strasse 22

TOURHOTEL MARIAHILF
Mariahilfer Strasse 156

Bahamas

Cable Beach

WYNDHAM NASSAU RESORT
West Bay St Cable Beach

SHERATON NASSAU BEACH RESORT
1 West Bay St – Cable St

Belgium

Brussels

LE MERIDIEN BRUSSELS
Carrefour de l'Europe 3

ROYAL WINDSOR HOTEL GRAND PLACE
Rue Duquesnoy 5-7

RADISSON SAS ROYAL HOTEL
47 Rue du Fosse aux Loups

SHERATON BRUSSELS HOTEL & TOWERS
Place Rogier 3

China

Beijing

COURTYARD BY MARRIOTT HOTEL BEIJING
3c Chongwenmen Wai St

PRIME HOTEL BEIJING
2 Wangfujing Ave Dongcheng District

Czech Republic

Prague

K&K HOTEL FENIX
Ve Smeckach 30

RAMADA PRAGUE CITY CENTRE
Vaclavske Namesti 41

HILTON PRAGUE OLD TOWN
V Celnici 7

Dominican Republic

Santo Domingo

HILTON SANTO DOMINGO
George Washington Ave 500

France

Bordeaux

QUALITY HOTEL ST. CATHERINE
27 Rue du Parlement Sainte Catherine

Paris

BEST WESTERN MERCEDES
128 Avenue de Wagram

ASTOR SAINT-HONORÉ
11 Rue d'Astorg

HOTEL DU LOUVRE
Place Andre Malraux

HILTON ARC DE TRIOMPHE PARIS
51-57 Rue de Courcelles

HOLIDAY INN PARIS – BASTILLE
11-13 Rue de Lyon

NOVOTEL PARIS TOUR EIFFEL
61 Quai de Grenelle

Germany

Berlin

BERLIN MARK HOTEL
Meinekestr 18-19

SWISSOTEL BERLIN
Augsburger Strasse 44

Frankfurt

INTERCITYHOTEL FRANKFURT
Poststr 8

FLEMING'S HOTEL FRANKFURT – MESSE
Mainzer Landstr 87-89

Greece

Athens

AIROTEL PARTHENON
6 Makri St

NOVOTEL ATHENES
4-6 Michail Voda Et Makedonias

Ireland

Dublin

MORRISON
Quay Ormond

THE FITZWILLIAM HOTEL
St. Stephens Green

PARAMOUNT HOTEL
Parliament St. Essex Gate

Italy

Florence

MONTEBELLO SPLENDID HOTEL
Via Garibaldi 14

HOTEL ADLER CAVALIERI
Via Della Scala 40

Rome

**GRAND HOTEL OLYMPIC –
AURUM HOTEL**
Via Properzio 2/a

BETTOJA HOTEL MEDITERRANEO
Via Cavour 15

STARHOTELS MICHELANGELO
Via Della Stazione Di San Pietro 14

Venice

HOTEL AI MORI D'ORIENTE
Fondamenta Della Sensa

BEST WESTERN ALBERGO SAN MARCO
Sestiere San Marco 877

Japan

Tokyo

HOTEL SUNROUTE PLAZA SHINJUKU
2-3-1 Yoyogi

SHINAGAWA PRINCE HOTEL
4-10-30 Takanawa Minato-ku

Puerto Vallarta

**FIESTA AMERICANA –
PUERTO VALLARTA**
Carretera Aeropuerto Km 2 5

**VILLA DEL PALMAR BEACH
RESORT & SPA**
Blvd Francisco Medina Ascencio
Km 2 5

Portugal

Lisbon

TIARA PARK ATLANTIC LISBOA
Rue Castilho 149

PESTANA PALACE
Rua Jau 54

Singapore

Singapore

**ROYAL PLAZA ON SCOTTS –
A SUMMIT HOTEL**
25 Scotts Rd

HILTON SINGAPORE
581 Orchard Rd

MORNINGTON HOTEL STOCKHOLM CITY
Nybrogatan 53

ALEXANDRA HOTEL
Magnus Ladulasgatan 42

Switzerland

Geneva

GRAND HOTEL KEMPINSKI GENEVA
19 Quai du Mont Blanc

Zurich

WELLENBERG SWISS Q HOTEL
Niederdorf Strasse 10

HOTEL BASILEA
Zaehringerstrasse 25

United Kingdom

Edinburgh

THE KNIGHT RESIDENCE
12 Lauriston St

London

THE STRAND PALACE
372 The Strand

Call 1-800-504-6835
or visit www.entertainment.com/travel

Mexico

Acapulco

LAS BRISAS ACAPULCO
Carretera Escenica, Clemente Mejia
#5255

FIESTA AMERICANA VILLAS ACAPULCO
Av Costera Miguel Aleman 97

Cabo San Lucas

HOTEL FINISTERRA
Domocilio Conocido

Cancun

**FIESTA AMERICANA
GRAND CORAL BEACH**
Blvd Kukulcan Km 9 5

GRAN MELIA CANCUN
Blvd Kukulkan Km 16 5

RIU CANCUN ALL INCLUSIVE
Blvd Kukulcán Km 8 5

Spain

Barcelona

ROYAL RAMBLAS
Ramblas 117-119

HOTEL BARCELONA UNIVERSAL
Del Paral.lel, Del 76-78

HOTEL BARCELONA PRINCESS
Avinguda Diagonal 1

Madrid

BEST WESTERN ATLANTICO
Gran Via 38

HOTEL GRAN VERSALLES
Covarrubias 4

HOTEL MARIA ELENA PALACE
Aduana 19

Sweden

Stockholm

SHERATON STOCKHOLM HOTEL
Tegelbacken 6, Box 195

THE GRAND AT TRAFALGAR SQUARE
8 Northumberland Ave

**THE SHAFTESBURY PREMIER
LONDON HYDE PARK**
78-82 Westbourne Terrace

**EXPRESS BY HOLIDAY INN
LONDON WIMBLEDON SOUTH**
200 High St

HILTON LONDON METROPOLE
225 Edgware Rd

Virgin Islands

Charlotte Amalie

WYNDHAM SUGAR BAY RESORT & SPA
6500 Estate Smith Bay

THE RITZ-CARLTON, ST. THOMAS
6900 Great Bay

St. Thomas

**BEST WESTERN EMERALD
BEACH RESORT**
8070 Lindbergh Bay

Get up to $250 in mail-in rebates. See page G4 for details.

hôtels.com

Guaranteed Best Rate Program Rules of Use*

Best Rate Guarantee

- Prepaid hotel reservations are guaranteed to be the lowest rate you can find. If there is a lower rate publicly available online for the same dates and the same hotel and room category, you must contact us prior to the property's cancellation deadline at 1-800-50-HOTEL (1-800-504-6835). Deadlines vary by property and travel dates. Please refer to your booking confirmation for the applicable deadline. Bookings that cannot be cancelled are not subject to this guarantee. If your booking qualifies for this guarantee, we will either, at our discretion, refund the difference or cancel the reservation without penalty.

Bookings

- Properties and locations are subject to change. Rooms are subject to availability. Bed type and smoking preferences cannot be guaranteed.

- You may be required to prepay with a major credit card.

- All prices are quoted and billed in U.S. dollars unless otherwise specified and are subject to change.

Changes & Cancellations

- To change or cancel your reservation, call 1-800-50-HOTEL (1-800-504-6835). You may still be subject to change and cancellation fees imposed by the properties.

- Some peak seasonal dates may not be discounted.

- Guaranteed Best Rate Program hotels are not subject to any additional discounts, except the rebate. See page G4.

Book. Save. Repeat.

Book the Guaranteed Best Rate.*

Call or visit us online to get the absolute lowest hotel rates at our hotel partners starting on page G5, plus thousands more online.

Get up to $250 in rebates.

Just fill out and send in the rebate forms found on page G3. The more you stay, the more you earn. Visit page G4 for complete details.

Call 1-800-50-HOTEL

or visit **www.entertainment.com/travel**

*Call the hotel directly to **save up to 50% Off full-priced rates** or **10% Off Best Available Rate** at thousands of hotels from coast to coast.*

How to Book Your Stay:

✔ Call the Hotel
at the number indicated in the following directory sample, or go to www.entertainment.com/enthotels for full program listings. Be sure to identify yourself as an **"Entertainment® Member."**

Discount: As a member, participating hotels will offer you a discount of Up To 50% off the full-priced (rack) room rate or 10% off Best Available Rate (available to the general public), whichever provides the greater value — *subject to Entertainment® Direct to Hotel Program room availability. Discounts vary by hotel.

The **"$"** indicates the hotel's full-priced (rack) room rate before the discount.
$ = $30–$60**   **$$** = $61–$100**   **$$$** = $101–$150**   **$$$$** = $151+**
**U.S. Funds (Canadian Hotels in Canadian Funds)*
(Rates subject to change. Hotel room rates may fluctuate throughout the year due to seasonal factors.)

Program Room Availability: Reservations with the Entertainment® rate are accepted until the hotel projects to be 80% or more occupied on your selected dates. If "R14" or "R30" appears in the listing, reservations will only be accepted when made within 14 or 30 days of arrival.

✔ Confirm Your Reservation
and discounted room rate by asking for a confirmation number. Be sure to ask for the hotel's policy on deposits, cancellations and late arrival guarantees. Entertainment Publications, LLC does not control the hotel's management policy. **Advance reservations are necessary** to use the Entertainment Direct to Hotel Program.

✔ Check In
and present your Entertainment® Membership Card.

Information You Need to Know

- Remaining flexible with your travel dates may offer the greatest opportunity for the Entertainment® rate. Discounts may not be available for every night of your stay, especially if traveling during peak seasons, holiday weeks, New Year's Eve, conventions or special events such as Mardi Gras, 2010 Olympic games and other major sporting events.

- If the Entertainment rate is not available, check alternate dates, call back closer to your travel date, or contact other hotels listed for that area. Be sure to activate your Entertainment® Membership Card and view a complete listing of participating hotels on **www.entertainment.com/enthotels**.

- Entertainment® Direct to Hotel Program rates do not apply to walk-ins, group/convention rates, packages, travel agency bookings, special amenities, taxes/fees, meal plans or any rates found on the Internet, and cannot be combined with any other discount rate programs.

- Hotels offering discounts on "any room" may exclude special room types such as suites and premium rooms.

- Only one room can be discounted per Entertainment® Membership Card and the card is non-transferable.

- Hotels participate in the program on an individual basis. You must call the number indicated for the hotel in the following directory listing and state that you are an **"Entertainment® Member"** to be eligible for the Entertainment rate, if available.

- The Guaranteed Best Rate rebate is not applicable to Entertainment Direct to Hotel Program bookings.

- **Advance reservations are required** and you must present your Entertainment Membership Card.

entertainment
Direct to Hotel

Call the hotel directly to **save up to 50% Off full-priced rates** or **10% Off Best Available Rate** at thousands of hotels from coast to coast.

United States of America

Alabama

Go to entertainment.com/enthotels for this state's hotel listings.

Alaska

Anchorage

DAYS INN DOWNTOWN, $$$$
321 E. 5th Ave., Anchorage. Valid September thru May. (907)276-7226

SHERATON ANCHORAGE HOTEL & SPA, $$$$
401 E. 6th Ave., Anchorage. Valid for 10% off the best available rate. Special events excluded. (907)276-8700

Arizona

Phoenix

EMBASSY SUITES PHOENIX - SCOTTSDALE, $$$$
4415 E. Paradise Village Pkwy., Paradise Valley. Valid for one suite. Jan.-March & special events excluded. (602)765-5800

FOUR POINTS BY SHERATON PHOENIX NORTH, $$$$
10220 N. Metro Pkwy. E., Phoenix. Valid for 10% off the best available rate. (602)997-5900

HYATT PLACE PHOENIX/NORTH, $$$$
10838 N 25th Ave, Phoenix. Valid for one room. R30. (602)997-8800, (888)492-8847

RADISSON HOTEL PHOENIX CITY CENTER, $$$$
3600 N. 2nd Ave., Phoenix. Special events excluded. 1/31- 2/3 excl. (602)604-4900

WYNDHAM PHOENIX, $$$$
50 E. Adams, Phoenix. Valid for any room or suite. (602)333-5000, (800)359-7253

Scottsdale

HAMPTON INN, $$
10101 N. Scottsdale Rd., Scottsdale. Valid for one standard room. Jan 15 - April 1 excl. (480)443-3233, (877)776-6464

MARRIOTT'S CAMELBACK INN RESORT & GOLF CLUB, $$$$
5402 E. Lincoln Dr., Scottsdale. Valid May thru December. R30. (480)948-1700, (800)24C-AMEL

SCOTTSDALE LINKS RESORT, $$$$
16858 N. Perimeter Dr., Scottsdale. Valid for one suite. (480)563-0500

SHERATON'S DESERT OASIS, $$$$
17700 North Hayden Road, Scottsdale. R30. (480)515-5888, (866)207-8599

THE INN AT PIMA, $$
7330 N. Pima Rd., Scottsdale. Valid for one standard room or suite. Jan 15 - April 1 excl. (480)948-3800, (800)344-0262

THE WESTIN KIERLAND VILLAS, $$$$
15620 North Clubgate Dr., Scottsdale. R30. (480)624-1700, (866)837-4273

Sedona

L'AUBERGE DE SEDONA, $$$$
301 L'Auberge Ln., Sedona. Valid for on lodge room. Valid Monday thru Friday. Holidays & special events excl. (928)282-1661, (800)217-9389

PREMIERE VACATION CLUB AT BELL ROCK, $$$$
6246 State Route 179, Sedona. Valid for any room or suite. Valid Sunday thru Thursday. (928)282-4161, (800)521-3131

VILLAS OF SEDONA, $$$$
55 Nothview, Sedona. Valid for any room or suite. Holidays excl. R30. (928)204-3400, (800)874-8770

Tempe

HYATT PLACE TEMPE/PHOENIX AIRPORT, $$$
1413 Rio Salado Pkwy., Tempe. Valid for one room. Valid Friday, Saturday & Sunday. Special events excluded. R30. (480)804-9544, (888)492-8847

TEMPE MISSION PALMS, $$$$
60 E. 5th St., Tempe. (480)894-1400, (800)547-8705

Tucson

DOUBLETREE HOTEL REID PARK, $$$$
445 S. Alvernon Way, Tucson. (520)881-4200

HYATT PLACE TUCSON AIRPORT, $$$$
6885 S Tucson Blvd, Tucson. Valid for one room. Special events excluded. R30. (520)295-0405, (888)492-8847

OMNI TUCSON NATIONAL GOLF RESORT & SPA, $$$$
2727 W. Club Dr., Tucson. Valid for one deluxe room. Valid April thru December. R30. (520)297-2271, (800)THE-OMNI

THE LODGE AT VENTANA CANYON, $$$$
6200 N. Clubhouse Lane, Tucson. Valid for one suite. (520)577-1400, (800)828-5701

Arkansas

Little Rock

RESIDENCE INN BY MARRIOTT, $$$
1401 S. Shackleford, Little Rock. Valid for any one bedroom. Valid Friday & Saturday. (501)312-0200

WYNDHAM RIVERFRONT LITTLE ROCK, $$$
2 Riverfront Pl., North Little Rock. Valid for one standard room. (501)371-9000, (866)657-4458

California

Anaheim

ANAHEIM JOLLY ROGER HOTEL, $$$
640 W. Katella Ave, Anaheim. July, holidays & special events excl. (714)782-7500, (800)446-1555

BEST WESTERN ANAHEIM INN, $$$
1630 S. Harbor Blvd., Anaheim. (714)774-1050, (800)854-8175

BEST WESTERN RAFFLES INN, $$$$
2040 S. Harbor Blvd., Anaheim. (714)750-6100, (888)859-0189

CLARION HOTEL MAINGATE, $$$$
616 Convention Way, Anaheim. Special events & conventions excl. R30. (714)750-3131, (800)231-6215

COURTYARD ANAHEIM, $$$$
2045 S. Harbor Blvd., Anaheim. July, holidays & special events excl. (714)740-2645, (800)479-6680

HOLIDAY INN HOTEL & SUITES ANAHEIM, $$$$
1240 S. Walnut St., Anaheim. (714)535-0300, (888)859-0390

✦ **HOWARD JOHNSON PLAZA HOTEL - DISNEYLAND $$$**
1380 S. Harbor Blvd., Anaheim. (714)776-6120, (800)422-4228

PORTOFINO INN & SUITES, $$$$
1831 S. Harbor Blvd, Anaheim. July, holidays & special events excl. (714)782-7600, (888)368-7971

RAMADA MAINGATE AT THE PARK, $$$$
1650 S. Harbor Blvd., Anaheim. Valid for one standard room. Holidays excl. (714)772-0440, (800)854-6097

Bakersfield

CLARION HOTEL BAKERSFIELD, $$$
3540 Rosedale Hwy., Bakersfield. (661)326-1111, (888)326-1121

FOUR POINTS BY SHERATON BAKERSFIELD, $$$$
5101 California Ave., Bakersfield. Valid for 10% off the best available rate. Special events excluded. (661)325-9700

Big Bear Lake

SLEEPY FOREST COTTAGES, $$$$
426 Eureka Dr., Big Bear Lake. Valid for one cottage. Valid April-November & Sunday thru Thursday December-March. Min stay 2 nts on Friday & Saturday. Holidays excl. (909)866-7444, (800)544-7454

SNOW LAKE LODGE, $$$$
41579 Big Bear Blvd., Big Bear. Valid for one condo. Holidays excl. (714)779-7900, (800)854-2324

Discount subject to Program room availability. See **Program Guidelines** on pages G30–G31.

Remember to identify yourself as an Entertainment® Member.

Be Sure To Activate Your Card For Full Program Listings
Go To: www.entertainment.com/enthotels
Check out our ✦Featured Properties

Buena Park

KNOTTS BERRY FARM RESORT HOTEL, $$$$
7675 Crescent Ave., Buena Park. (714)995-1111, (866)752-2444

PORTOLA INN & SUITES, $$$
7921 Orangethorpe Ave., Buena Park. Special events excluded. (714)739-5885

Carmel/Monterey

CAROUSEL MOTEL, $$$$
110 Riverside Ave., Santa Cruz. Valid Sunday thru Friday September thru June. (831)425-7090

HYATT REGENCY MONTEREY RESORT & SPA, $$$$
1 Old Golf Course Rd., Monterey. Valid Sunday thru Thursday. Holidays & special events excl. (831)372-1234

PACIFIC GROVE PLAZA, $$$$
620 Lighthouse Ave., Pacific Grove. Valid for any room or suite. Valid Sunday thru June. Holidays excluded. R30. (831)373-0562

Costa Mesa

HILTON COSTA MESA, $$$$
3050 Bristol St., Costa Mesa. Suites & executive level excl. R30. (714)540-7000

HOLIDAY INN COSTA MESA/ORANGE COUNTY AIRPORT, $$$$
3131 S. Bristol Street, Costa Mesa. Valid Thursday thru Sunday. (714)557-3000, (800)221-7220

Desert Hot Springs

DESERT HOT SPRINGS SPA HOTEL, $$$
10805 Palm Dr., Desert Hot Springs. (760)329-6000, (800)808-7727

MIRACLE SPRINGS RESORT & SPA, $$$$
10625 Palm Dr., Desert Hot Springs. (760)251-6000, (800)400-4414

Fresno

AMERICA'S BEST VALUE INN, $$
4141 N. Blackstone Ave., Fresno. (559)222-4445, (800)762-9071

PICCADILLY INN SHAW, $$$$
2305 W. Shaw, Fresno. Suites excluded. (559)226-3850, (800)HOT-ELUS

Los Angeles

HILTON CHECKERS LOS ANGELES, $$$$
535 S. Grand Ave, Los Angeles. Valid Thursday thru Monday. Special events excluded. Tuesday & Wednesday excl. (213)624-0000, (800)423-8549

HOLIDAY INN EXPRESS WEST LOS ANGELES, $$$$
11250 Santa Monica Blvd., Los Angeles. (310)478-1400, (888)859-0441

MIYAKO HOTEL LOS ANGELES, $$$$
328 E. First St., Los Angeles. (213)617-2000, (800)228-6596

OMNI LOS ANGELES HOTEL AT CALIFORNIA PLAZA, $$$$
251 S. Olive St., Los Angeles. Valid for one deluxe room. Special events & New Years Eve excluded. (213)617-3300, (800) THE-OMNI

SHERATON CERRITOS, $$$$
12725 Center Court Dr., Cerritos. Special events excluded. (562)809-1500

SPORTSMEN'S LODGE HOTEL, $$$$
12825 Ventura Blvd., North Hollywood. Suites, special events & holidays excl. (818)769-4700, (800)821-8511

Los Angeles Int'l Airport

FOUR POINTS BY SHERATON LOS ANGELES WESTSIDE, $$$$
5990 Green Valley Cir., Culver City. Valid Friday, Saturday & Sunday. Valid for 10% off the best available rate. R30. (310)641-7740

FOUR POINTS SHERATON LOS ANGELES INT'L APRT, $$$$
9750 Airport Blvd., Los Angeles. Valid for any room or suite. (310)645-4600, (800)529-4683

RESIDENCE INN MANHATTAN BEACH/LAX, $$$$
1700 N. Sepulveda Blvd., Manhattan Beach. Valid for one suite. July-Aug 22 excluded. (310)421-3100

✦TRAVELODGE HOTEL AT LAX $$
5547 W. Century Blvd., Los Angeles. (310)649-4000, (800)421-3939

Napa

NAPA VALLEY MARRIOTT HOTEL & SPA, $$$$
3425 Solano Ave., Napa. Special events excluded. (707)253-8600

Napa Valley

THE CHABLIS INN, $$$
3360 Solano Ave., Napa. Valid for one standard room. Valid Sunday thru Thursday November - June. (707)257-1944, (800)443-3490

Oakland

FOUR POINTS BY SHERATON EMERYVILLE, $$$$
1603 Powell St., Emeryville. Valid for 10% off the best available rate. (510)547-8414

SHERATON GATEWAY SFO, $$$$
600 Airport Blvd., Burlingame. Valid for 10% off the best available rate. Special events excluded. (650)340-8500

Ontario

HYATT PLACE - ONTARIO MILLS, $$$$
4760 E. Mills Circle, Ontario. Valid for one room. Valid Friday, Saturday & Sunday. Special events excluded. R30. (909)980-2200, (888)492-8847

ONTARIO AIRPORT MARRIOTT, $$$$
2200 E. Holt Blvd., Ontario. Valid Friday, Saturday & Sunday. Special events excluded. (909)975-5000

Palm Springs

DESERT ISLE RESORT, $$$$
2555 E. Palm Canyon Dr., Palm Springs. Valid for any room or suite. Holidays excl. R30. (760)327-8469, (800)874-8770

PALM SPRINGS TENNIS CLUB RESORT, $$$$
701 W. Baristo Rd., Palm Springs. Valid for one condo. Holidays excluded. (714)779-7900, (800)854-2324

Pleasanton

FOUR POINTS BY SHERATON - PLEASANTON, $$$$
5115 Hopyard, Pleasanton. Valid for 10% off the best available rate. (925)460-8800

HYATT SUMMERFIELD SUITES-PLEASANTON, $$$$
4545 Chabot Dr., Pleasanton. Valid for one suite. (925)730-0070, (866)974-9288

Sacramento

GOVERNORS INN, $$$
210 Richards Blvd., Sacramento. Valid Friday, Saturday & Sunday. (916)448-7224

RED LION HOTEL SACRAMENTO, $$$$
1401 Arden Way, Sacramento. Suites excluded. (916)922-8041

San Clemente

HOLIDAY INN EXPRESS SAN CLEMENTE, $$$
35 Via Pico Plaza, San Clemente. (949)498-8800, (888)859-0190

SAN CLEMENTE INN, $$$
2600 Avenida del Presidente, San Clemente. Valid for any room or suite. Valid Sunday thru Thursday. Holidays excluded. R30. (949)492-6103, (800)874-8770

San Diego

✦AMERICA'S BEST VALUE INN-MISSION BAY/SEAWORLD $$$
4545 Mission Bay Dr., San Diego. Holidays & special events excl. (858)483-4222

✦BEST WESTERN ISLAND PALMS HOTEL & MARINA $$$$$
2051 Shelter Island Dr., San Diego. Valid for marina view room or suite. (619)222-0561, (800)345-9995

✦DAYS HOTEL - HOTEL CIRCLE/SEA WORLD $$$
543 Hotel Circle S., San Diego. (619)297-8800, (800)227-4743

HOLIDAY INN EXPRESS OLD TOWN SAN DIEGO, $$$$
3900 Old Town Ave., San Diego. Special events excluded. (619)299-7400

✦HOLIDAY INN SAN DIEGO BAYSIDE $$$$
4875 N. Harbor Dr., San Diego. Valid for one deluxe room. R30. (619)224-3621, (800)662-8899

Be Sure To Activate Your Card For Full Program Listings
Go To: www.entertainment.com/enthotels
Check out our ✦Featured Properties

THE WESTIN WESTMINSTER, $$$$
10600 Westminster Blvd., Westminster. Valid for 10% off the best available rate. (303)410-5000

Connecticut

Danbury

DANBURY MARON HOTEL & SUITES, $$$
42 Lake Ave. Ext, (off I-84 at Exit 4), Danbury. Valid Sunday thru Thursday. (203)791-2200

SHERATON, $$$$
18 Old Ridgebury Rd., Danbury. Valid for any room or suite. (203)794-0600

Hartford

CROWNE PLAZA HARTFORD DOWNTOWN, $$$$
50 Morgan St., Hartford. Valid for one standard room. (860)549-2400

SHERATON HARTFORD, $$$$
100 E. River Dr., East Hartford. Valid for 10% off the best available rate. Holidays excl. (860)528-9703

Stamford

SHERATON SAMFORD, $$$$
2701 Summer St., Stamford. Valid for 10% off the best available rate. (203)359-1300

Stratford

HOMEWOOD SUITES BY HILTON, $$$$
6905 Main St., Stratford. Valid for one suite. (203)377-3322

Delaware

Go to entertainment.com/enthotels for this state's hotel listings.

District Of Columbia

Washington D.C.

✦BEACON HOTEL & CORPORATE QUARTERS, $$$$
1615 Rhode Island Ave. NW, Washington. Valid for any room or suite. Valid Friday, Saturday, Sunday & holidays. (202)296-2100, (800)821-4367

DOUBLETREE GUEST SUITES WASHINGTON DC, $$$$
801 New Hampshire Ave., NW, Washington. Valid for one suite. (202)785-2000

GEORGE WASHINGTON UNIVERSITY INN, $$$$
824 New Hampshire Ave, NW, Washington. Valid for any room or suite. (202)337-6620, (800)426-4455

GEORGETOWN SUITES, $$$$
1111 30th St. NW., Washington. Valid for one suite. April, May & October excluded. (202)298-7800, (800)348-7203

HOTEL LOMBARDY, $$$$
2019 Pennsylvania Ave., NW, Washington. (202)828-2600, (800)424-5486

OMNI SHOREHAM HOTEL, $$$$
2500 Calvert St. N.W., Washington. Valid for one deluxe room. (202)234-0700, (800)THE-OMNI

✦ST. GREGORY LUXURY HOTEL & SUITES, $$$$
2033 M Street NW, Washington. Valid for any room or suite. Valid Friday, Saturday, Sunday & holidays. (202)530-3600, (800)829-5034

THE FAIRFAX AT EMBASSY ROW, $$$$
2100 Massachusetts Ave. N.W., Washington. Valid for 10% off the best available rate. R30. (202)293-2100, (800)325-3589

Florida

Boca Raton

HOLIDAY INN EXPRESS BOCA RATON WEST, $$$$
8144 W. Glades Rd., Boca Raton. Dec 20-Jan 1 & Feb 1-April 15 excl. R30. (561)482-7070

LA BOCA CASA, $$$
365 N. Ocean Blvd., Boca Raton. Valid for any room or suite. Holidays excluded. R30. (561)392-0885, (800)874-8770

Deerfield Beach

BERKSHIRE BEACH CLUB, $$$
500 North A1A, Deerfield Beach. Valid for one condo. Holidays excl. R30. (949)859-2181, (800)874-8770

HOWARD JOHNSON PLAZA RESORT, $$$$
2096 N.E. 2nd St., Deerfield Beach. Valid for one standard room. Jan 31 - Feb 26 excl. R30. (954)428-2850, (800)426-0084

Florida Keys

OCEAN POINTE SUITES AT KEY LARGO, $$$$
500 Burton Dr., Tavernier. Valid for one suite. Special events & holidays excl. R30. (305)853-3000

THE WESTIN KEY WEST RESORT & MARINA, $$$$
245 Front St., Key West. Valid for 10% off the best available rate. Special events excluded. R30. (305)294-4000

Ft. Lauderdale

FT. LAUDERDALE BEACH RESORT, $$$$
909 Breakers Ave., Ft. Lauderdale. Valid for any room or suite. Holidays excl. R30. (954)566-8800, (800)874-8770

OCEAN MANOR BEACH RESORT, $$$$
4040 Galt Ocean Dr., Ft. Lauderdale. (954)566-7500, (800)955-0444

THE WESTIN BEACH RESORT, FORT LAUDERDALE, $$$$
321 N. Ft. Lauderdale Beach Blvd., Ft. Lauderdale. Valid for any room or suite. (954)467-1111, (888)627-7108

Hollywood

COMFORT INN - AIRPORT/CRUISE PORT, $$$$
2520 Stirling Rd., Hollywood. Jan. 15 - April 30 excluded. (954)922-1600, (800)333-1492

THE WESTIN DIPLOMAT RESORT & SPA, $$$$
3555 S. Ocean Dr., Hollywood. Valid for 10% off the best available rate. (954)602-6000, (888)627-9057

Jacksonville

FOUR POINTS SHERATON JACKSONVILLE BAYMEADOWS, $$$
8520 Baymeadows Rd., Jacksonville. Valid for 10% off the best available rate. Special events excluded. R30. (904)562-4920

OMNI JACKSONVILLE HOTEL, $$$$
245 Water St., Jacksonville. Valid for one deluxe room. Special events excl. (904)355-6664, (800)THE-OMNI

Kissimmee

BEST WESTERN LAKESIDE, $$$
7769 West Irlo Bronson Memorial Highway, Kissimmee. Holidays & special events excl. (407)396-2222, (800)848-0801

FUN SPOTS HOTEL AT FOUNTAIN PARK, $$
5150 W. Irlo Bronson Hwy., Kissimmee. (407)396-1111, (800)327-9179

HOWARD JOHNSON MAINGATE RESORT WEST, $$
8660 W. Irlo Bronson Memorial Hwy., Kissimmee. Valid Sunday thru Thursday. Special events & holidays excl. (407)396-4500, (800)638-7829

KNIGHTS INN MAINGATE, $
7475 W. Irlo Bronson Memorial Hwy, Kissimmee. Holidays & special events excl. (407)396-4200, (800)944-0062

MAGIC TREE, $$$$
2795 N. Old Lake Wilson Rd., Kissimmee. Valid for one condo. (714)779-7900, (800)854-2324

MASTERS INN KISSIMMEE, $$
5367 W. Irlo Bronson Hwy., Kissimmee. Valid for one standard room. (407)396-4020, (800)633-3434

✦QUALITY SUITES® ROYALE PARC SUITES $$$$
5876 W. Irlo Bronson Hwy (US192), Kissimmee. Valid for one 1 or 2 bedroom suites. (407)396-8040, (800)848-4148

SERALAGO HOTEL & SUITES MAIN GATE EAST, $$
5678 Irlo Bronson Memorial Hwy., Kissimmee. (407)396-4488, (800)366-5437

✦VENTURA RESORT RENTALS $$$$
5946 Curry Ford Rd., Orlando. Valid for one home or condo. (407)273-8770, (800)311-9736

Discount subject to Program room availability. See **Program Guidelines** on pages G30–G31.   G35

Call the hotels at the number listed for Entertainment® Membership rate availability.

Lake Buena Vista

◆ **WALT DISNEY WORLD SWAN & DOLPHIN $$$$**
1500 Epcot Resorts Blvd., Lake Buena Vista. Dec 25-Jan 1 excl. (407)934-4000, (800)227-1500

Miami

HOLIDAY INN EXPRESS, $$$$
5125 NW 36th St., Miami Springs. Feb excl. Special events excluded. (305)887-2153

HYATT PLACE MIAMI AIRPORT WEST/ DORAL, $$$
3655 NW 82nd St, Miami. Valid for one room. Holidays & special events excl. R30. (305)718-8292, (888)492-8847

HYATT SUMMERFIELD SUITES MIAMI AIRPORT, $$$$
5710 Blue Lagoon Dr., Miami. Valid for one suite. Special events excluded. R30. (305)269-1922, (866)974-9288

Miami Beach

DORCHESTER HOTEL AND SUITES, $$$$
1850 Collins Ave., Miami Beach. Suites excluded. (305)503-1442, (800)829-3003

SOUTH SEAS HOTEL, $$$
1751 Collins Ave., Miami Beach. Holidays & special events excl. R30. (305)538-1411, (800)345-2678

Orlando

COMFORT INN - LAKE BUENA VISTA, $$
8442 Palm Parkway, Orlando. Valid for one double room. (407)996-7300

◆ **COURTYARD BY MARRIOTT @ VISTA CENTRE, $$$$**
8501 Palm Parkway, Orlando. (407)239-6900, (866)790-2197

CYPRESS POINTE RESORT, $$$$
8651 Treasure Cay Ln., Orlando. Valid for any room or suite. Holidays excl. R30. (407)238-2300, (800)874-8770

DOUBLETREE CASTLE ORLANDO, $$$$
8629 International Dr., Orlando. (407)345-1511, (800)952-2785

HAWTHORN SUITES HOTEL, $$$
6435 Westwood Blvd., Orlando. Valid for one-bedroom suite. (407)351-6600, (800)331-5530

HYATT PLACE ORLANDO CONVENTION CENTER, $$$$
8741 International Dr, Orlando. Valid for one room. Holidays & special events excl. R30. (407)370-4720, (888)492-8847

MASTERS INN INTERNATIONAL DRIVE, $$$
8222 Jamaican Ct., Orlando. (407)345-1172, (800)633-3434

MONUMENTAL MOVIELAND, $$$
6233 International Dr., Orlando. Holiday periods excl. (407)351-3900, (800)327-2114

RENAISSANCE ORLANDO RESORT AT SEAWORLD, $$$$
6677 Sea Harbor Dr., Orlando. Valid for any room or suite. (407)351-5555

SHERATON SAFARI HOTEL & SUITES, $$$$
11205 S. Apopka Vineland Rd., Orlando. Valid for 10% off the best available rate. (407)239-0444, (800)423-3297

STAYBRIDGE SUITES - ORLANDO/ LAKE BUENA VISTA, $$$$
8751 Suiteside Dr., Lake Buena Vista. Valid for one suite. (407)238-0777, (800)866-4549

Sarasota

COMFORT INN, $$
5778 Clark Rd., Sarasota. R30. (941)921-7750

DAYS INN SARASOTA I-75, $$$$
5774 Clark Rd., Sarasota. Valid for one standard room. Holiday weeks & special events excl. (941)921-7812

St. Pete Beach

◆ **TRADEWINDS ISLAND GRAND BEACH RESORT $$$$**
5500 Gulf Blvd., St. Pete Beach. Standard Rooms & Holiday periods excl. R30. (727)363-2212, (877)300-5520

◆ **TRADEWINDS SANDPIPER HOTEL & SUITES $$$$**
6000 Gulf Blvd., St. Pete Beach. Standard Rooms & Holiday periods excl. R30. (727)363-2212, (877)300-5520

Tampa

EMBASSY SUITES TAMPA - AIRPORT/ WESTSHORE, $$$$
555 North Westshore Blvd., Tampa. Valid for one suite. Special events excluded. (813)875-1555

HYATT PLACE TAMPA/BUSCH GARDENS, $$$$
11408 N 30th St, Tampa. Valid for one room. Special events excl. R30. (813)979-1922, (888)492-8847

MASTERS INN TAMPA FAIRGROUNDS, $$
6626 Dr. Martin Luther King Blvd., Tampa. (813)623-6667, (800)633-3434

THE WESTIN TAMPA BAY AIRPORT, $$$$
7627 Courtney Campbell Cswy., Tampa. Valid Friday, Saturday & Sunday. Valid for 10% off the best available rate. Special events excluded. (813)281-0000, (888)627-8647

Atlanta

HAMPTON INN PERIMETER, $$$
769 Hammond Dr., Atlanta. (404)303-0014

HYATT PLACE ATLANTA/PERIMETER CENTER, $$$$
1005 Crestline Pkwy., Atlanta. Valid for one room. R30. (770)730-9300, (888)492-8847

OMNI HOTEL AT CNN CENTER, $$$$
100 CNN Center, Atlanta. Valid for one deluxe room. (404)659-0000, (800) THE-OMNI

REGENCY SUITES - MIDTOWN ATLANTA, $$$$
975 W. Peachtree St., Atlanta. Valid for one suite. (404)876-5003, (800)642-3629

SHERATON SUITES GALLERIA ATLANTA, $$$$
2844 Cobb Pkwy., Atlanta. Valid for 10% off the best available rate. (770)955-3900, (800)325-3535

Hartsfield Int'l Airport

HYATT PLACE ATLANTA AIRPORT SOUTH, $$$$
1899 Sullivan Rd, College Park. Valid for one room. Special events excl. R30. (770)994-2997, (888)492-8847

WESTIN HOTEL ATLANTA AIRPORT, $$$$
4736 Best Rd., Atlanta. Holidays & special events excl. (404)762-7676

Savannah

FOUR POINTS BY SHERATON HISTORIC SAVANNAH, $$$$
520 W. Bryan St., Savannah. Valid for 10% off the best available rate. Special events, Memorial & Labor Day weekends excl. (912)790-1000

INN AT ELLIS SQUARE A DAYS HOTEL, $$$
201 W Bay St., Savannah. Valid for any room or suite. (912)236-4440

Big Island

◆ **ASTON KONA BY THE SEA $$$$**
75-6106 Alii Drive, Kailua-Kona. (808)327-2300, (866)774-2924

◆ **ASTON SHORES AT WAIKOLOA $$$$**
69-1035 Keana Place, Waikoloa. (808)886-5001, (866)774-2924

◆ **ASTON WAIKOLOA COLONY VILLAS $$$$**
69-555 Waikoloa Beach Dr., Waikoloa. (808)886-8899, (866)774-2924

CASTLE HALII KAI AT WAIKOLOA, $$$$
69-1029 Nawahine Pl., Waikoloa. Min stay 2 nts. (808)545-3510, (800)367-5004

KONA SEASIDE HOTEL, $$$
76-5646 Palani Rd., Kailua-Kona. Standard rooms excl. (808)329-2455, (800)560-5558

Be Sure To Activate Your Card For Full Program Listings
Go To: www.entertainment.com/enthotels
Check out our ✦Featured Properties

OUTRIGGER KANALOA AT KONA, $$$$
78-261 Manukai St., Kailua-Kona. Valid for one suite. R30. (303)369-7777, (800)462-6262

Kauai

✦**ASTON ALOHA BEACH HOTEL $$$$**
3-5920 Kuhio Hwy., Kapaa. (808)823-6000, (866)774-2924

✦**ASTON AT POIPU KAI $$$$**
1775 Poipu Rd., Koloa. (808)742-7424, (866)774-2924

✦**ASTON ISLANDER ON THE BEACH $$$$**
440 Aleka Place, Kapaa. (808)822-7417, (866)774-2924

✦**ASTON KAUAI BEACH AT MAKAIWA $$$$**
650 Aleka Loop, Kapaa. (808)822-3455, (866)774-2924

✦**ASTON WAIMEA PLANTATION COTTAGES $$$$**
9400 Kaumualii Hwy., #367, Waimea. (808)338-1625, (866)774-2924

CASTLE KIAHUNA PLANTATION & BEACH BUNGALOWS, $$$$
2253B Poipu Rd., (East Entrance), Koloa. Valid for one bedroom garden view & garden view deluxe. (808)545-3510, (800)367-5004

Maui

✦**ASTON AT PAPAKEA RESORT $$$$**
3543 Lower Honoapiilani Rd., Kaanapali. (808)669-4848, (866)774-2924

✦**ASTON AT THE MAUI BANYAN $$$$**
2575 South Kihei Rd., Kihei. (808)875-0004, (866)774-2924

✦**ASTON KAANAPALI SHORES $$$$**
3445 Lower Honoapiilani Rd., Kaanapali. (808)667-2211, (866)774-2924

✦**ASTON MAHANA AT KAANAPALI $$$$**
110 Kaanapali Shores Place, Kaanapali. Min stay 3 nts. (808)661-8751, (866)774-2924

✦**ASTON MAUI HILL $$$$**
2881 South Kihei Rd., Kihei. (808)879-6321, (866)774-2924

✦**ASTON MAUI KAANAPALI VILLAS $$$$**
45 Kai Ala Dr., Kaanapali. (808)667-7791, (866)774-2924

✦**ASTON MAUI LU $$$**
575 South Kihei Rd., Kihei. (808)879-5881, (866)774-2924

✦**ASTON PAKI MAUI $$$$**
3615 Lower Honoapiilani Rd., Kaanapali. Min stay 3 nts. (808)669-8235, (866)774-2924

CASTLE KAMAOLE SANDS, $$$$
2695 S. Kihei Rd., Kihei. Min 2 nts stay. (808)545-3510, (800)367-5004

✦**MAUI SUNSET $$$**
1032 S. Kihei Rd., Kihei. Valid for one condo. R30. (425)454-9923, (800)233-3310

Molokai

CASTLE KALUAKOI VILLAS, $$$$
1121 Kaluakoi Rd., Maunaloa. Special events excl. (808)545-3510, (800)367-5004

MARC MOLOKAI SHORES, $$$$
Kamehameha Hwy., Star Rte., Kaunakakai. Valid for one suite. (808)922-9700, (800)535-0085

Oahu

✦**ASTON AT THE EXECUTIVE CENTRE HOTEL $$$$**
1088 Bishop Street, Honolulu. (808)539-3000, (866)774-2924

✦**ASTON AT THE WAIKIKI BANYAN $$$$**
201 Ohua Ave., Honolulu. (808)922-0555, (866)774-2924

✦**ASTON PACIFIC MONARCH $$$$**
2427 Kuhio Ave., Honolulu. (808)923-9805, (866)774-2924

✦**ASTON WAIKIKI BEACH HOTEL $$$$**
2570 Kalakaua Ave., Honolulu. (808)922-2511, (866)774-2924

✦**ASTON WAIKIKI BEACH TOWER $$$$**
2470 Kalakaua Ave., Honolulu. (808)926-6400, (866)774-2924

✦**ASTON WAIKIKI CIRCLE HOTEL $$$$**
2464 Kalakaua Ave., Honolulu. (808)923-1571, (866)774-2924

✦**ASTON WAIKIKI JOY HOTEL $$$**
320 Lewers Street, Honolulu. (808)923-2300, (866)774-2924

✦**ASTON WAIKIKI SUNSET $$$$**
229 Paoakalani Ave., Honolulu. (808)922-0511, (866)774-2924

CASTLE MAILE SKY COURT, $$$$
2058 Kuhio Ave., Honolulu. (808)545-3510, (800)367-5004

CASTLE WAIKIKI SHORE, $$$$
2161 Kalia Rd., Honolulu. Min stay 2 nts. (808)545-3510, (800)367-5004

OHANA WAIKIKI BEACHCOMBER, $$$$
2300 Kalakaua Ave., Honolulu. R30. (303)369-7777, (800)462-6262

THE LOTUS AT DIAMOND HEAD, $$$$
2885 Kalakaua Ave., Honolulu. (808)545-3510, (800)367-5004

Idaho

Boise

BEST WESTERN VISTA INN AT THE AIRPORT, $$
2645 Airport Way, Boise. Valid September thru May. R30. (208)336-8100, (800)727-5006

DOUBLETREE CLUB HOTEL, $$$
475 W ParkCenter Blvd., Boise. Valid for one standard room. (208)345-2002

HYATT PLACE BOISE/TOWNE SQUARE MALL, $$$
925 N Milwaukee St, Boise. Valid for one room. R30. (208)375-1200, (888)492-8847

RESIDENCE INN BY MARRIOTT - BOISE CENTRAL, $$$
1401 Lusk Ave., Boise. Valid for one studio suite. R30. (208)344-1200

Idaho Falls

GUESTHOUSE INN & SUITES, $$
850 Lindsay Blvd., Idaho Falls. (208)523-6260, (800)852-7829

RED LION HOTEL ON THE FALLS, $$$
475 River Parkway, Idaho Falls. Valid September thru May. R30. (208)523-8000, (800)325-4000

Sandpoint

QUALITY INN, $$$
807 N. 5th Ave., Sandpoint. Max stay 3 nts. Valid October thru May. Holiday Periods excl. (208)263-2111, (866)519-7683

SUPER 8 SANDPOINT, $$
476841 Hwy. 95 N., Sandpoint. (208)263-2210

Illinois

Chicago

ALLEGRO CHICAGO, A KIMPTON HOTEL, $$$
171 W. Randolph, Chicago. (312)236-0123, (800)643-1500

HILTON CHICAGO, $$$$
720 S. Michigan Ave., Chicago. (312)922-4400

OMNI CHICAGO HOTEL, $$$$
676 N. Michigan Ave., Chicago. Valid for one suite. (312)944-6664, (800)THE-OMNI

SHERATON CHICAGO HOTEL & TOWERS, $$$$
301 E. North Water St., Chicago. Valid for 10% off the best available rate. (312)464-1000

THE PALMER HOUSE HILTON, $$$$
17 E. Monroe St., Chicago. (312)726-7500

THE WESTIN MICHIGAN AVENUE CHICAGO, $$$$
909 North Michigan Ave., Chicago. Valid for 10% off best available rate. (312)943-7200

Discount subject to Program room availability. See **Program Guidelines** on pages G30–G31.

G37

Call the hotels at the number listed for Entertainment® Membership rate availability.

Call the hotel directly to **save up to** **50% Off** **full-priced rates** *or* **10% Off Best Available Rate** *at thousands of hotels from coast to coast.*

Des Plaines

ALOFT CHICAGO O'HARE, $$$$
9700 Balmoral Ave., Rosemont. (847)671-4444

BEST WESTERN DES PLAINES, $$$
1231 Lee, Des Plaines. (847)297-2100

WYNDHAM O'HARE, $$$$
6810 Mannheim Rd., Rosemont. (847)297-1234, (877)999-3223

Indiana

Indianapolis

ADAM'S MARK INDIANAPOLIS, $$$$
2544 Executive Dr., Indianapolis. (317)248-2481

COMFORT INN & SUITES, $$$$
9090 Wesleyan Rd., Indianapolis. Valid Sunday thru Thursday. Indy 500 & special events excl. R30. (317)875-7676

HAMPTON INN NORTHEAST, $$
6817 E. 82nd St., Indianapolis. R30. (317)576-0220

HYATT PLACE INDIANAPOLIS AIRPORT, $$$$
5500 Bradbury Ave, Indianapolis. Valid for one room. Valid Friday, Saturday & Sunday. R30. (317)227-0950, (888)492-8847

MARRIOTT INDIANAPOLIS EAST, $$$$
7202 E. 21st St., Indianapolis. Advance purchase rates excl. (317)352-1231

WESTIN INDIANAPOLIS, $$$$
50 S. Capitol Ave., Indianapolis. Valid for 10% off the best available rate. Special events excluded. (317)262-8100

Iowa

Des Moines

COUNTRY INN & SUITES DES MOINES - WEST, $$$
1350 NW 118th St., Clive. Special events excluded. R30. (515)223-9254

HOLIDAY INN AIRPORT, $$$
6111 Fleur Dr., Des Moines. (515)287-2400, (800)248-4013

SETTLE INN & SUITES - ALTOONA, $$
2101 Adventureland Dr., Altoona. R30. (515)967-7888, (888)222-8224

SHERATON WEST DES MOINES, $$$$
1800 50th St., West Des Moines. Valid for 10% off the best available rate. Special events excluded. (515)223-1800

Kansas

Overland Park

COMFORT INN & SUITES, $$$
7200 W 107th Ave., Overland Park. Special events excluded. (913)648-7858

HYATT PLACE OVERLAND PARK/ CONVENTION CTR., $$$$
5001 W 110th St, Overland Park. Valid for one room. Valid Friday, Saturday & Sunday. R30. (913)491-9002, (888)492-8847

SETTLE INN - OVERLAND PARK, $$
4401 W 107th St., Overland Park. R30. (913)381-5700

Wichita

HILTON WICHITA AIRPORT, $$$$
2098 Airport Rd., Wichita. Valid for one standard room. (316)945-5272, (800)247-4458

THE INN AT TALLGRASS, $$$
2280 N. Tara, Wichita. Valid for one suite. (316)684-3466

Kentucky

Lexington

COURTYARD BY MARRIOTT LEXINGTON NORTH, $$$
775 Newtown Court, Lexington. Valid May thru August & November thru March. (859)253-4646

FOUR POINTS SHERATON, $$$$
1938 Stanton Way, Lexington. Valid for any room or suite. (859)259-1311

HILTON SUITES OF LEXINGTON GREEN, $$$$
245 Lexington Green Circle, Lexington. April, Sept 8-21, Oct & Nov 5-17 excl. R30. (859)271-4000

Louisville

BEST WESTERN AIRPORT EAST, $$
1921 Bishop Ln., Louisville. Valid for one standard room. Kentucky Derby & Special events excl. (502)456-4411

HOLIDAY INN HURSTBOURNE, $$$
1325 Hurstbourne Pkwy., Louisville. Valid Friday, Saturday & Sunday. Special events excl. R30. (502)426-2600

HYATT PLACE LOUISVILLE/EAST, $$$$
701 S Hurstbourne Pkwy, Louisville. Valid for one room. R30. (502)426-0119, (888)492-8847

Louisiana

New Orleans

HOLIDAY INN - FRENCH QUARTER, $$$$
124 Royal St., New Orleans. R30. (504)529-7211, (800)747-3279

HOTEL MONTELEONE, $$$$
214 Rue Royal, New Orleans. (504)523-3341, (800)535-9595

HOTEL PROVINCIAL, $$$$
1024 Rue Chartres, New Orleans. R30. (504)581-4995, (800)535-7922

OMNI ROYAL ORLEANS, $$$$
612 St. Louis St., New Orleans. Valid for one deluxe room. Valid Sunday thru Thursday. Mardi Gras, Dec 31-Jan 3 & special events excl. (504)529-5333, (800) THE-OMNI

QUALITY INN & SUITES MAISON ST. CHARLES, $$$$
1319 St. Charles Ave., New Orleans. Holidays & special events excl. R30. (504)522-0187

ROYAL SONESTA HOTEL, $$$$
300 Bourbon St., New Orleans. Valid Sunday thru Thursday. R30. (504)586-0300

Maine

Go to entertainment.com/enthotels for this state's hotel listings.

Maryland

Baltimore

COMFORT INN BWI, $$$
6921 Baltimore Annapolis Blvd., Baltimore. Valid for one standard room. Special events excluded. R30. (410)789-9100

HAMPTON INN & SUITES BALTIMORE, $$$$
131 E. Redwood St., Baltimore. (410)539-7886

PEABODY COURT-A CLARION HOTEL, $$$$
612 Cathedral St., Baltimore. Special events excl. R30. (410)727-7101

SLEEP INN SUITES BWI, $$$
6055 Belle Grove Rd., Baltimore. Special events excluded. R30. (410)789-7223

Gaithersburg

COMFORT INN SHADY GROVE, $$$$
16216 Frederick Rd., Gaithersburg. (301)330-0023, (888)605-9100

HYATT SUMMERFIELD SUITES-GAITHERSBURG, $$$$
200 Skidmore Blvd., Gaithersburg. Valid for one suite. (301)527-6000, (866)974-9288

Rockville

CROWNE PLAZA ROCKVILLE, $$$$
3 Research Ct., Rockville. Valid for one suite. Special events excluded. R30. (301)840-0200

Towson

HOLIDAY INN TOWSON, $$$
1100 Cromwell Bridge Rd., Towson. (410)823-4410

◆ **SHERATON BALTIMORE NORTH $$$$**
903 Dulaney Valley Rd., Towson. Valid for 10% off the best available rate. Special events excluded. (410)321-7400

Discount subject to Program room availability. See **Program Guidelines** on pages G30–G31.

Remember to identify yourself as an Entertainment® Member.

Be Sure To Activate Your Card For Full Program Listings
Go To: www.entertainment.com/enthotels
Check out our ✦Featured Properties

Massachusetts

Boston

COLONNADE HOTEL, $$$$
120 Huntington Ave., Boston. (617)424-7000, (800)962-3030

COPLEY SQUARE HOTEL, $$$$
47 Huntington Ave., Boston. (617)536-9000, (800)225-7062

EMBASSY SUITES BOSTON - AT LOGAN AIRPORT, $$$$
207 Porter St., Boston. Valid for one suite. Special events excluded. (617)567-5000

OMNI PARKER HOUSE, $$$$
60 School St., Boston. Valid for one deluxe room. (617)227-8600, (800)THE-OMNI

SHERATON BOSTON, $$$$
39 Dalton St., Boston. Valid for 10% off the best available rate. (617)236-2000

Cape Cod Area

CAPE COD HOLIDAY ESTATES, $$$
97 Four Seasons Dr., Mashpee. Valid for any room or suite. Holidays excluded. R30. (508)477-3377, (800)874-8770

SEASHORE PARK INN, $$$$
24 Canal Rd., Orleans. R30. (508)255-2500, (800)772-6453

Michigan

Acme

GRAND TRAVERSE RESORT & SPA, $$$$
100 Grand Traverse Village Blvd., Acme. Condos excl. June, July & August weekends excl. R30. (231)938-2100, (800)748-0303

Detroit

OMNI DETROIT HOTEL RIVER PLACE, $$$$
1000 River Place Dr., Detroit. Valid for one deluxe room. (313)259-9500, (800) THE-OMNI

THE INN ON FERRY STREET, $$$$
84 E Ferry St., Detroit. R30. (313)871-6000

WESTIN BOOK CADILLAC DETROIT, $$$$
1114 Washington Blvd., Detroit. Valid for 10% off the best available rate. Special events excluded. (313)442-1600, (888)627-7150

Grand Rapids

BEST WESTERN HOSPITALITY HOTEL & SUITES, $$
5500 28th Street SE, Grand Rapids. Valid for any room or suite. (616)949-8400

HYATT PLACE GRAND RAPIDS/ WYOMING, $$$
2150 Metro Lane, Wyoming. Valid for one room. Max stay 5 days. R30. (616)724-1234

Mackinac Island

MISSION POINT RESORT, $$$$
1 Lakeshore Dr., Mackinac Island. Valid Sunday thru Thursday. (800)833-7711

Mackinaw City

BEST WESTERN DOCKSIDE, $$$
505 S. Huron St., Mackinaw City. Valid Sunday thru Thursday. July, August, holidays & special events excl. (231)436-5001, (800)774-1794

HOLIDAY INN EXPRESS, $$
364 Louvigny, Mackinaw City. Valid September thru May. Holidays & Special events excl. (231)436-7100, (866)394-8339

Sterling Heights

✦BEST WESTERN STERLING INN, $$$$
34911 Van Dyke Ave., Sterling Heights. Valid for one standard room. Valid Sunday thru Friday. Jacuzzi rooms, New Year's Eve, holiday weeks & school breaks excl. Valid for 10% off best available rate. (586)979-1400, (800)953-1400

Traverse City

BEST WESTERN FOUR SEASONS, $$$
305 Munson Ave., Traverse City. Valid Sunday thru Thursday September thru May. Holidays & special events excl. (231)946-8424, (888)499-3060

PARK PLACE HOTEL, $$$$
300 E. Front St., Traverse City. R30. (231)946-5000, (800)748-0133

Troy

HILTON DETROIT/TROY, $$$$
5500 Crooks Rd., Troy. Valid Friday, Saturday & Sunday. R30. (248)879-2100

SOMERSET INN, $$$$
2601 W. Big Beaver, Troy. (248)643-7800, (800)228-8769

Minnesota

Duluth

INN ON LAKE SUPERIOR, $$$
350 Canal Park Dr., Duluth. Valid for one standard room. Valid Sunday thru Thursday October thru June. (218)726-1111, (888)668-4352

SHERATON DULUTH HOTEL, $$$
301 E. Superior St., Duluth. Valid for 10% off the best available rate. (218)733-5660, (888)627-8122

Eagan

HILTON GARDEN INN - EAGAN, $$$
1975 Rahncliff Ct., Eagan. Valid September thru May. Stay 'n Fly pkgs excl. R30. (651)686-4605, (800)500-4232

STAYBRIDGE SUITES EAGAN, $$$$
4675 Rahncliff Rd., Eagan. Valid for one suite. Valid Thursday - Sunday September thru May. R30. (651)994-7810

Minneapolis

HOLIDAY INN EXPRESS & SUITES - GOLDEN VALLEY, $$$
6020 Wayzata Blvd., Golden Valley. Valid for any room or suite. Valid September thru May. R30. (763)545-8300, (800)688-5977

HOTEL IVY, $$$$
201 S. 11th St., Minneapolis. Valid for 10% off the best available rate. (612)746-4600

LE BOURGET AERO SUITES, $$$$
7770 Johnson Ave. S, Bloomington. R30. (952)893-9999, (800)449-0409

NORTHLAND INN, $$$$
7025 Northland Dr., Brooklyn Park. Valid for one two-room suite. Max stay 7 nts. R30. (763)536-8300, (800)441-6422

RADISSON UNIVERSITY HOTEL - MPLS, $$$$
615 Washington Ave. SE, Minneapolis. Suites excluded. R30. (612)379-8888

THE WESTIN MINNEAPOLIS, $$$$
88 S. 6th St., Minneapolis. Valid for 10% off the best available rate. Special events excluded. (612)333-4006

St. Paul

HAMPTON INN SHOREVIEW, $$$
1000 Gramsie Rd., Shoreview. Valid September thru May. R30. (651)482-0402, (877)233-3194

HILTON GARDEN INN - SHOREVIEW, $$$
1050 Gramsie Rd., Shoreview. Valid September thru May. R30. (651)415-1956, (877)746-7384

Mississsippi

Go to entertainment.com/enthotels for this state's hotel listings.

Missouri

Branson

BARRINGTON HOTEL & SUITES, $$
263 Shepherd of the Hills Expressway, Branson. Valid for one standard room. Valid March thru December. (417)334-8866, (800)760-8866

RADISSON HOTEL BRANSON, $$$
120 S. Wildwood Dr., Branson. (417)335-5767, (888)566-5290

✦SETTLE INN RESORT & CONFERENCE CENTER $$
3050 Green Mountain Dr., Branson. Valid for one standard room. (417)335-4700, (800)677-6906

Kansas City

COURTYARD KANSAS CITY, $$$$
4600 JC Nichols Pkwy., Kansas City. R30. (816)285-9755

Discount subject to Program room availability. See **Program Guidelines** on pages G30–G31.

Call the hotels at the number listed for Entertainment® Membership rate availability.

entertainment
Direct to Hotel

Call the hotel directly to **save up to** **50% Off** **full-priced rates** *or* **10% Off Best Available Rate** *at thousands of hotels from coast to coast.*

FOUR POINTS BY SHERATON KANSAS CITY AIRPORT, $$$$
11832 N.W. Plaza Cir., Kansas City. (816)464-2345

HYATT PLACE KANSAS CITY AIRPORT, $$$
7600 NW 97th Terrace, Kansas City. Valid for one room. Special events excluded. R30. (816)891-0871, (888)492-8847

SHERATON SUITES COUNTRY CLUB PLAZA, $$$$
770 W. 47th St., Kansas City. Valid for 10% off the best available rate. Holidays & special events excl. (816)931-4400, (800)325-3535

St. Louis

CLUBHOUSE INN & SUITES, $$$
1970 Craig Rd., St. Louis. R30. (314)205-8000

OMNI MAJESTIC HOTEL, $$$$
1019 Pine Street, St. Louis. Valid for one deluxe room. (314)436-2355, (800)THE-OMNI

ST. LOUIS MARRIOTT WEST, $$$$
660 Maryville Centre Dr., St. Louis. Valid for one standard room. Valid Friday, Saturday & Sunday. (314)878-2747

Montana

Go to entertainment.com/enthotels for this state's hotel listings.

Nebraska

Lincoln

BEST WESTERN CROWN INN, $$
6501 N 28th St., Lincoln. Valid September thru May. R30. (402)438-4700, (800)398-3619

SETTLE INN - LINCOLN, $$
7333 Husker Circle, Lincoln. Valid September thru May. R30. (402)435-8100, (800)824-6004

Omaha

CAROL HOTEL OMAHA, $$
4888 S. 118th St. at I-80, Omaha. Suites excluded. New Year's Eve excl. R30. (402)895-1000, (800)662-4280

CROWNE PLAZA, $$$$
655 N 108th Ave, Omaha. Valid for one standard room. (402)496-0850

RESIDENCE INN BY MARRIOTT - OMAHA, $$$
6990 Dodge St., Omaha. Valid for one studio suite. Valid Friday, Saturday & Sunday. R30. (402)553-8898

Nevada

Las Vegas

ELEMENT BY WESTIN LAS VEGAS/ SUMMERLIN, $$$$
10555 Discovery Dr., Las Vegas. Valid for 10% off the best available rate. Special events excluded. (702)589-2000

GOLDEN GATE HOTEL & CASINO, $
One Fremont St., Las Vegas. Valid Sunday thru Thursday. (702)385-1906, (800)426-1906

HYATT PLACE LAS VEGAS, $$$$
4520 Paradise Rd, Las Vegas. Valid for one room. R30. (702)369-3366, (888)492-8847

THE JOCKEY CLUB, $$$$
3700 Las Vegas Blvd. S., Las Vegas. Valid for one condo. Holidays excl. (714)779-7900, (800)854-2324

Reno

CELEBRITY RESORTS RENO, $$$
140 Court St., Reno. R30. (407)996-3070, (866)507-1427

DAYS INN, $$
701 E. 7th St., Reno. Valid Sunday thru Thursday. Special events & holiday wknds excl. (775)786-4070

HARRAH'S LAKE TAHOE, $$$$
Hwy. 50, South Lake Tahoe. Valid Sunday thru Thursday. Special events & holiday wknds excl. R30. (775)588-6611, (800)427-7247

KINGSBURY CROSSING, $$$$
133 Deer Run Ct., Stateline. Valid for one condo. Holidays excluded. (714)779-7900, (800)854-2324

New Hampshire

Go to entertainment.com/enthotels for this state's hotel listings.

New Jersey

Atlantic City

QUALITY HOTEL ATLANTIC CITY WEST, $$$$
8029 Black Horse Pike, West Atlantic City. Valid Sunday thru Thursday September thru May. R30. (609)641-3546, (800)999-9466

QUALITY INN CASINO CITY, $$$
500 N. Albany Ave., Atlantic City. Valid Sunday thru Thursday September thru May. R30. (609)344-9085

Morristown

HYATT SUMMERFIELD SUITES MORRISTOWN, $$$$
194 Park Ave, Morristown. Valid for one suite. Special events excluded. R30. (973)971-0008, (866)974-9288

WESTIN GOVERNOR MORRIS, $$$$
2 Whippany Rd., Morristown. Valid Friday, Saturday & Sunday. Valid for 10% off the best available rate. Holidays & special events excl. (973)539-7300

Parsippany

HOLIDAY INN HOTEL & SUITES PARSIPPANY, $$$
707 Rte. 46 E., Parsippany. Valid for one standard room. Valid Thursday thru Sunday. (973)263-2000

HOTEL SIERRA PARSIPPANY, $$$$
299 Smith Rd., Parsippany. Valid for one suite. (973)428-8875, (800)474-3772

Princeton

HOLIDAY INN PRINCETON, $$$$
100 Independence Way, Princeton. Valid Friday, Saturday, Sunday & holidays. (609)520-1200

HOMEWOOD SUITES PRINCETON, $$$$
3819 US 1 South, Princeton. R30. (609)720-0550

HYATT PLACE PRINCETON, $$$$
3565 US Highway 1, Princeton. Valid for one room. R30. (609)720-0200, (888)492-8847

Secaucus

HOLIDAY INN HARMON MEADOW, $$$$
300 Plaza Dr., Secaucus. (201)348-2000, (800)222-2676

HYATT PLACE - SECAUCUS, $$$$
575 Park Plaza Dr, Secaucus. Valid Friday, Saturday & Sunday. R30. (201)422-9480, (888)492-8847

West Atlantic City

CLARION HOTEL & CONVENTION CENTER, $$$
6821 Black Horse Pike, Atlantic City West. Valid for one standard room. Valid Sunday thru Thursday. (609)272-0200

HOLIDAY INN EXPRESS, $$$
6811 Black Horse Pike, Atlantic City West. Valid for one standard room. Valid Sunday thru Thursday. (609)484-1500

New Mexico

Albuquerque

COMFORT INN EAST, $$
13031 Central Ave. N.E., Albuquerque. Oct. 1-15 & New Mexico state fair dates excl. (505)294-1800, (800)748-EAST

DAYS INN, $$
2120 Menual Blvd. N.E., Albuquerque. Valid for standard or double room. Valid Sunday thru Thursday. Special events & holidays excl. (505)884-0250

HAWTHORN INN & SUITES, $$
1511 Gibson Blvd., SE, Albuquerque. Special events excluded. (505)242-1555

HYATT PLACE ALBUQUERQUE AIRPORT, $$$
1400 Sunport Blvd SE, Albuquerque. Valid for one room. Valid Friday, Saturday & Sunday. R30. (505)242-9300, (888)492-8847

HYATT PLACE ALBUQUERQUE UPTOWN, $$$$
6901 Arvada NE, Albuquerque. Valid for one room. R30. (505)872-9000, (888)492-8847

Discount subject to Program room availability. See **Program Guidelines** on pages G30–G31.

Be Sure To Activate Your Card For Full Program Listings
Go To: www.entertainment.com/enthotels
Check out our ✦Featured Properties

Santa Fe

AMERICAS BEST VALUE LAMPLIGHTER INN, $$
2405 Cerrillos Rd., Santa Fe. Valid September thru June. Holidays & Indian Market excl. (505)471-8000, (800)767-5267

FORT MARCY HOTEL SUITES, $$$$
320 Artist Rd., Santa Fe. Valid for one suite. Holidays & special events excl. R30. (505)988-2800, (888)570-2775

INN OF THE GOVERNORS, $$$$
101 W. Alameda, Santa Fe. Valid for deluxe room or mini suites. Some blackout dates may apply. R30. (505)982-4333, (800)234-4534

VILLAS DE SANTA FE, $$$$
400 Griffin St., Santa Fe. Valid for 1br condo. Min stay 2 nts. R30. (888)333-1962

New York

Albany

COMFORT INN & SUITES ALBANY, $$$
1606 Central Ave., Albany. R30. (518)869-5327, (800)233-9444

HILTON GARDEN INN ALBANY AIRPORT, $$$$
800 Albany Shaker Rd., Albany. (518)464-6666

HOLIDAY INN ALBANY ON WOLF ROAD, $$$$
205 Wolf Rd., Albany. Valid Friday, Saturday, Sunday & holidays September thru June. (518)458-7250

HOWARD JOHNSON HOTEL ALBANY CENTRAL, $$$
1614 Central Avenue, Albany. Special events excluded. Valid September thru June. (518)869-0281, (800)293-3794

La Guardia Airport

CROWNE PLAZA LAGUARDIA, $$$$
104-04 Ditmars Blvd., East Elmhurst. Suite excluded. R30. (718)457-6300

PAN AMERICAN HOTEL, $$$
79-00 Queens Blvd., Elmhurst. (718)446-7676, (800)937-7374

Lake Placid

COMFORT INN ON LAKE PLACID, $$$
2125 Saranac Ave., Lake Placid. Valid for one standard room. Suites excluded. Valid Sunday thru Thursday September 6 - June 30. Holidays excluded. (518)523-9555, (800)858-4656

LAKE PLACID CLUB LODGES, $$$$
30 Lake Placid Club Way, Lake Placid. Valid for any room or suite. Holidays excluded. R30. (518)523-3361, (800)874-8770

Long Island

HOWARD JOHNSON INN, $$$
450 Moreland Rd., Commack. Special events & holidays excl. (631)864-8820

SHERATON LONG ISLAND HOTEL, $$$$
110 Vanderbilt Motor Pkwy., Hauppauge. Valid for 10% off the best available rate. Special events excluded. (631)231-1100

New York City/Manhattan

FOUR POINTS SHERATON MANHATTAN SOHO VILLAGE, $$$$
66 Charlton St., New York. Valid for 10% off the best available rate. (212)229-9988

HILTON GARDEN INN CHELSEA, $$$$
119 W. 28th St., New York. Valid Sunday & Monday. R30. (212)564-2181, (866)430-9291

MILBURN HOTEL, $$$$
242 W. 76th. St., New York. Valid for one suite. R30. (212)362-1006, (800)833-9622

OMNI BERKSHIRE PLACE, $$$$
21 E. 52nd St. & Madison Ave., New York. Valid for one deluxe room. Valid Friday, Saturday, Sunday & holidays. R30. (212)753-5800, (800)THE-OMNI

TRAVEL INN HOTEL, $$$$
515 W. 42nd St., New York. (212)695-7171

Rochester

BEST WESTERN ROCHESTER MARKETPLACE, $$
940 Jefferson Rd., Rochester. Special events excluded. (585)427-2700

HOLIDAY INN EXPRESS - ROCHESTER, $$$
Brighton/Pittsford Area 2835 Monroe Ave., Rochester. (585)784-8400, (877)514-6835

ROCHESTER PLAZA HOTEL & CONFERENCE CENTER, $$$$
70 State Street, Rochester. Valid for any standard room. (585)546-3450

North Carolina

Charlotte

FOUR POINTS BY SHERATON CHARLOTTE, $$$$
315 E. Woodlawn Rd., Charlotte. Valid for 10% off the best available rate. Special events excluded. (704)522-0852

HYATT SUMMERFIELD SUITES-CHARLOTTE A/P, $$$$
4920 S. Tryon St., Charlotte. Valid for one suite. (704)525-2600, (866)974-9288

OMNI CHARLOTTE HOTEL, $$$$
132 E. Trade St., Charlotte. Valid for one deluxe room. Special events excluded. Valid Friday, Saturday & Sunday. (704)377-0400, (800)THE-OMNI

Durham

COMFORT INN UNIVERSITY, $$
3508 Mount Moriah Rd., Durham. (919)490-4949

SHERATON IMPERIAL HOTEL, $$$$
4700 Emperor Blvd., Durham. Valid Friday, Saturday & Sunday. Valid for 10% off the best available rate. Special events excluded. (919)941-5050

Raleigh

COMFORT SUITES RALEIGH, $$$$
4400 Capital Blvd., Raleigh. Valid for one suite. Special events excl. R30. (919)876-2211, (800)543-5497

HOLIDAY INN CRABTREE VALLEY, $$$
4100 Glenwood Ave., Raleigh. (919)782-8600

RESIDENCE INN BY MARRIOTT, $$$
1000 Navaho Dr., Raleigh. Valid for studio queen suites. Valid Friday, Saturday, Sunday & holidays. (919)878-6100

North Dakota

Go to entertainment.com/enthotels for this state's hotel listings.

Ohio

Cincinnati

GARFIELD SUITES HOTEL, $$$
2 Garfield Place, Cincinnati. Valid for one suite. R30. (513)421-3355, (800)367-2155

HOLIDAY INN I-275 NORTH, $$$
3855 Hauck Rd., Cincinnati. (513)563-8330

HYATT PLACE CINCINNATI/BLUE ASH, $$$$
11435 Reed Hartman Hwy, Cincinnati. Valid for one room. R30. (513)489-3666, (888)492-8847

Cleveland

CROWNE PLAZA CLEVELAND - CITY CENTRE, $$$
777 St. Clair Ave., Cleveland. Valid for one standard room. Special events excluded. (216)771-7600

WYNDHAM CLEVELAND AT PLAYHOUSE SQUARE, $$$$
1260 Euclid Ave., Cleveland. Valid for one standard room. (216)615-7500, (800) WYN-DHAM

Columbus

BEST WESTERN COLUMBUS NORTH, $$
888 E. Dublin-Granville Rd., Columbus. Suites excluded. (614)888-8230

HOLIDAY INN ON THE LANE, $$$
328 W. Lane Ave., Columbus. Valid October thru June. (614)294-4848

WESTIN COLUMBUS, $$$$
310 S. High St., Columbus. Valid for 10% off the best available rate. Special events excluded. (614)228-3800

Miamisburg

✦HOLIDAY INN DAYTON MALL, $$$
31 Prestige Plaza Dr., Miamisburg. Valid for up to 35% off the rack rate. Special events excluded. (937)434-8030

Discount subject to Program room availability. See **Program Guidelines** on pages G30–G31.   G41

Call the hotels at the number listed for Entertainment® Membership rate availability.

Call the hotel directly to **save up to 50% Off** **full-priced rates** *or* **10% Off Best Available Rate** *at thousands of hotels from coast to coast.*

Oklahoma

Oklahoma City

CLARION MERIDIAN HOTEL & CONVENTION CENTER, $$
737 S. Meridian, Oklahoma City. R30. (405)942-8511

FOUR POINTS BY SHERATON OKLAHOMA CITY AIRPORT, $$$
6300 E. Terminal Dr., Oklahoma City. Valid for 10% off the best available rate. Special events excluded. (405)681-3500, (800)325-3535

HYATT PLACE OKLAHOMA CITY AIRPORT, $$$$
1818 S. Meridian Ave, Oklahoma City. Valid for one room. R30. (405)682-3900, (888)492-8847

Tulsa

BEST WESTERN TRADE WINDS CENTRAL INN, $$
3141 E. Skelly Dr., Tulsa. Valid for one standard room. (918)749-5561, (800)685-4564

HYATT PLACE/TULSA SOUTHERN HILLS, $$$$
7037 S. Zurich Ave., Tulsa. Valid for one room. Valid Friday, Saturday & Sunday. Special Events excl. R30. (918)491-4010, (888)492-8847

Oregon

Clackamas

DAYS INN PORTLAND SOUTH, $$
9717 SE Sunnyside Rd., Clackamas. Valid for one standard room. (503)654-1699, (800)241-1699

✦**MONARCH HOTEL & CONFERENCE CENTER, $$$**
12566 SE 93rd Ave, Clackamas. Jacuzzi suites excluded. Valid weekends/holidays. R30. (503)652-1515, (800)492-8700

Eugene

PHOENIX INN SUITES EUGENE, $$$$
850 Franklin Blvd., Eugene. Valid for one suite. Special events excluded. R30. (541)344-0001, (800)344-0131

VALLEY RIVER INN, $$$$
1000 Valley River Way, Eugene. Special events excluded. (541)473-1000, (800)543-8266

Grants Pass

BEST WESTERN INN AT THE ROGUE, $$$$
8959 Rogue River Hwy., Grants Pass. Max stay 5 nts. Suites excluded. (541)582-2200

HOLIDAY INN EXPRESS GRANTS PASS, $$$$
105 NE Agness Ave., Grants Pass. Valid September thru May. Special events excluded. R30. (541)471-6144, (800)838-7666

Lincoln City

✦**CROWN PACIFIC INN EXPRESS $$$**
1070 SE 1st St., Lincoln City. Suites excluded. Valid October thru May & valid Sunday thru Thursday June thru September. Holidays excl. (541)994-7559, (800)359-7559

✦**INN AT SPANISH HEAD RESORT HOTEL $$$$**
4009 S.W. Hwy. 101, Lincoln City. Valid Sunday thru Thursday September thru June. Min stay 2 nts. (541)996-2161, (800)452-8127

Portland

HILTON PORTLAND & EXECUTIVE TOWER, $$$$
921 SW Sixth Ave., Portland. Valid weekends/holidays. New Year's Eve excl. (503)226-1611

RADISSON HOTEL PORTLAND AIRPORT, $$$
6233 NE 78th Ct., Portland. Valid for one standard room. Special events excluded. (503)251-2000, (800)994-7878

RED LION HOTEL PORTLAND - CONVENTION CENTER, $$$
1021 N.E. Grand Ave., Portland. Suites excluded. (503)235-2100, (800)343-1822

RESIDENCE INN LLOYD CENTER, $$$$
1710 NE Multnomah St., Portland. Valid for one studio suite. Valid Friday, Saturday & Sunday. R30. (503)288-1400

SHERATON PORTLAND AIRPORT HOTEL, $$$$
8235 NE Airport Way, Portland. R30. (503)281-2500, (800)808-9497

THRIFTLODGE, $$
949 E. Burnside St., Portland. (503)234-8411

Seaside

GEARHART BY THE SEA, $$$
1157 N. Marion at 10th, Gearhart. Valid for one condo. Valid October thru May. Holiday & school vacation periods excl. Min stay 2 nts. (503)738-8331, (800)547-0115

THE TIDES, $$$$
2316 Beach Dr., Seaside. Valid for one suite. Valid September 15-June 15. Special events, holiday weeks & school breaks excl. min stay 2 nts. (503)738-6317, (800)548-2846

Pennsylvania

Allentown

COMFORT SUITES, $$$
3712 Hamilton Blvd., Allentown. Valid for one suite. Valid weekends September thru May. Special events wknds excl. R30. (610)437-9100

FOUR POINTS BY SHERATON ALLENTOWN AIRPORT, $$$$
3400 Airport Rd., Allentown. Valid for 10% off the best available rate. Special events excluded. (610)266-1000

Harrisburg

FOUR POINTS BY SHERATON HARRISBURG, $$$$
800 E. Park Dr., Harrisburg. Valid for 10% off the best available rate. Special events excluded. (717)561-2800

HILTON HARRISBURG, $$$$
One N. Second St., Harrisburg. Valid Friday, Saturday, Sunday & holidays. Special events excluded. R30. (717)233-6000

Lancaster

BEST WESTERN EDEN RESORT & SUITES, $$$
222 Eden Rd., Lancaster. Suites excluded. Valid November-May. (717)569-6444, (866)890-2339

TRAVELODGE, $$
2101 Columbia Ave., Lancaster. July-Aug, Oct, holidays & special events excl. (717)397-4201

Philadelphia

FOUR POINTS BY SHERATON PHILADELPHIA AIRPORT, $$$$
4101 Island Ave., Philadelphia. Valid for 10% off the best available rate. Special events excluded. (215)492-0400, (800)368-7764

HOLIDAY INN EXPRESS MIDTOWN, $$$$
1305 Walnut St., Philadelphia. Valid Friday, Saturday, Sunday & holidays. New Year's Eve excl. Penn relays, Army-Navy & Greek wknds excl. (215)735-9300

OMNI HOTEL AT INDEPENDENCE PARK, $$$$
401 Chestnut St., Philadelphia. Valid for one deluxe room. Valid Friday, Saturday, Sunday & holidays. (215)925-0000, (800) THE-OMNI

Pittsburgh

INN AT GREENTREE, $$$
401 Holiday Dr., Pittsburgh. R30. (412)922-8100

OMNI WILLIAM PENN, $$$$
530 William Penn Place, Pittsburgh. Valid for one deluxe room. (412)281-7100, (800) THE-OMNI

QUALITY SUITES, $$$
700 Mansfield Ave., Pittsburgh. Valid for one studio suite. Valid Friday, Saturday, Sunday & holidays. R30. (412)279-6300

Pocono Mountains Area

CHATEAU RESORT & CONFERENCE CENTER, $$$$
300 Camelback Rd., Tannersville. Valid Sunday thru Thursday. Holidays excl. R30. (800)245-5900

TANGLEWOOD RESORT, $$$
Junction of Rte. 6 & 507, Hawley. Valid for any room or suite. Holidays excluded. R30. (570)226-6161, (800)874-8770

Discount subject to Program room availability. See **Program Guidelines** on pages G30–G31.

Remember to identify yourself as an Entertainment® Member.

Be Sure To Activate Your Card For Full Program Listings
Go To: www.entertainment.com/enthotels
Check out our ✦Featured Properties

Rhode Island

Newport

HOTEL VIKING NEWPORT, $$$$
One Bellevue Ave., Newport. Special events excluded. (401)847-3300, (800)556-7126

WELLINGTON RESORT, $$$
551 Thames St., Newport. Valid for any room or suite. Holidays excluded. R30. (401)849-1770, (800)874-8770

Providence

HOTEL DOLCE VILLA, $$$$
63 DePasquale Plaza, Providence. (401)383-7031

South Carolina

Charleston

BEST WESTERN SWEETGRASS INN, $$$$
1540 Savannah Hwy., Charleston. Valid November thru March & Sunday-Thursday April thru October. (843)571-6100

QUALITY SUITES NORTH CHARLESTON, $$$$
5225 N. Arco Lane, North Charleston. Valid for one suite. (843)747-7300

Hilton Head Island

COMFORT INN, $$$$
2 Tanglewood Dr., Hilton Head Island. Spring Break, Summer holiday wknds & special events excl. R30. (843)842-6662, (800)52B-EACH

PLAYERS CLUB RESORT, $$
35 DeAllyon Ave., Bldg. 200, Hilton Head. Valid for any room or suite. Valid Sunday thru Thursday. Holidays excluded. R30. (843)842-6640, (800)874-8770

THE BREAKERS, $$$
27C Coligny Plaza, Hilton Head Island. Valid for one condo. Min stay 3 nts. (800)845-6802

Myrtle Beach

OCEAN VILLAS BEACH & RAQUET CLUB, $$$$
7509 N. Ocean Blvd., Myrtle Beach. Valid for any room or suite. Holidays excl. R30. (843)449-0837, (800)874-8770

SHERATON'S BROADWAY PLANTATION, $$$$
3301 Robert M. Grissom Parkway, Myrtle Beach. R30. (843)916-8855, (866)207-8602

South Dakota

Go to entertainment.com/enthotels for this state's hotel listings.

Tennessee

Memphis

FRENCH QUARTER SUITES, $$$
2144 Madison Ave., Memphis. Valid for one suite. Valid Sunday thru Thursday. Special events & holidays excl. R30. (901)728-4000, (800)843-0353

HYATT PLACE MEMPHIS/PRIMACY PARKWAY, $$$$
1220 Primacy Pkwy, Memphis. Valid for one room. R30. (901)680-9700, (888)492-8847

THE WESTIN MEMPHIS BEALE STREET, $$$$
170 Lt. George W. Lee Ave., Memphis. Valid Thursday thru Sunday. Valid for 10% off the best available rate. Special events excluded. (901)334-5900

Nashville

BEST WESTERN MUSIC ROW, $$$
1407 Division St., Nashville. (615)242-1631

HOLIDAY INN SELECT OPRYLAND AIRPORT, $$$
2200 Elm Hill Pike, Nashville. (615)883-9770

HYATT PLACE NASHVILLE AIRPORT, $$$$
721 Royal Parkway, Nashville. Valid for one room. Valid Sunday & Monday. R30. (615)493-5200, (888)492-8847

RESIDENCE INN, $$$
2300 Elm Hill Pike, Nashville. Valid for one suite. (615)889-8600

SHERATON NASHVILLE DOWNTOWN, $$$$
623 Union St., Nashville. Valid for 10% off the best available rate. Special events excluded. (615)259-2000

Texas

Austin

HYATT SUMMERFIELD SUITES AUSTIN/ARBORETUM, $$$$
10001 N. Capital of Texas Hwy., Austin. Valid for one suite. Valid Friday, Saturday & Sunday. Special events excluded. R30. (512)342-8080, (866)974-9288

NORTH AUSTIN PLAZA HOTEL & SUITES, $$
6911 Interstate Hwy 35 N, Austin. (512)459-4251, (800)306-4629

OMNI AUSTIN HOTEL DOWNTOWN, $$$$
700 San Jacinto, Austin. Valid for one deluxe room. (512)476-3700, (800)THE-OMNI

Corpus Christi

HOLIDAY INN NORTH PADRE, $$$
15202 Windward Dr., Corpus Christi. Valid for one standard room. Valid September thru May. R30. (361)949-8041, (888)949-8041

OMNI CORPUS CHRISTI HOTEL MARINA TOWER, $$$$
707 N. Shoreline Blvd., Corpus Christi. Valid for one deluxe room. (361)887-1600, (800)THE-OMNI

Dallas

DOUBLETREE HOTEL DALLAS-CAMPBELL CENTRE, $$$$
8250 N. Central Expy, Dallas. Special events excluded. (214)691-8700

EMBASSY SUITES, $$$$
3880 W. Northwest Hwy., Dallas. Valid for one suite. (214)357-4500

HILTON GARDEN INN DALLAS/ MARKET CENTER, $$$$
2325 N. Stemmons Fwy., Dallas. (214)634-8200

HYATT PLACE DALLAS NORTH, $$$$
5229 Spring Valley Rd, Dallas. Valid for one room. R30. (972)716-2001, (888)492-8847

HYATT SUMMERFIELD SUITES DALLAS/UPTOWN, $$$$
2914 Harry Hines Blvd., Dallas. Valid Friday, Saturday & Sunday. Special events excluded. (214)965-9990

OMNI DALLAS HOTEL AT PARK WEST, $$$$
1590 LBJ Fwy., Dallas. Valid for one deluxe room. (972)869-4300, (800)THE-OMNI

SHERATON DALLAS, $$$$
400 N. Olive St., Dallas. Valid for 10% off the best available rate. (214)922-8000

Dallas/Ft. Worth Airport

ALOFT LAS COLINAS, $$$$
122 E. John Carpenter Fwy., Irving. (972)717-6100

HYATT PLACE LAS COLINAS, $$$$
5455 Green Park Dr, Irving. Valid for one room. R30. (972)550-7400, (888)492-8847

OMNI MANDALAY HOTEL AT LAS COLINAS, $$$$
221 E. Las Colinas Blvd., Irving. Valid for one deluxe room. (972)556-0800, (800)THE-OMNI

Ft. Worth

DFW MARRIOTT AT CHAMPIONS CIRCLE, $$$
3300 Championship Pkwy, Ft. Worth. Special events, New Year's Eve & Race Days excluded. (817)961-0800, (866)348-3984

HYATT PLACE FT. WORTH/CITYVIEW, $$$$
5900 Cityview Blvd, Ft. Worth. Valid for one room. R30. (817)361-9797, (888)492-8847

Discount subject to Program room availability. See **Program Guidelines** on pages G30–G31.   G43

Call the hotels at the number listed for Entertainment® Membership rate availability.

Houston

COURTYARD HOUSTON, $$$$
2504 N. Loop West, Houston. (713)688-7711

CROWNE PLAZA HOUSTON DOWNTOWN, $$$$
1700 Smith, Houston. (713)739-8800

ELEMENT HOUSTON VINTAGE PARK, $$$$
14555 Vintage Preserve Pkwy., Houston. Valid for 10% off the best available rate. Special events excluded. (281)379-7300

HOUSTONIAN HOTEL, CLUB & SPA, $$$$
111 N. Post Oak Ln., Houston. (713)680-2626, (800)231-2759

HYATT SUMMERFIELD SUITES HOUSTON/GALLERIA, $$$$
3440 Sage Rd., Houston. Valid for one suite. Special events excluded. R30. (713)629-9711, (866)974-9288

OMNI HOUSTON HOTEL, $$$$
Four Riverway, Houston. Valid for one deluxe room. (713)871-8181, (800)THE-OMNI

SHERATON HOUSTON BROOKHOLLOW, $$$$
3000 North Loop West, Houston. Valid Friday, Saturday & Sunday. Valid for 10% off the best available rate. Special events excluded. (713)688-0100

Houston Intercontinental Airport

COUNTRY INN & SUITES INTERCONTINENTAL AIRPORT, $$$
15555B John F Kennedy Blvd., Houston. (281)987-2400

HILTON HOUSTON NORTH HOTEL, $$$$
12400 Greenspoint Dr., Houston. Valid for one standard room. (281)875-2222, (866)933-7829

San Antonio

HILTON SAN ANTONIO AIRPORT, $$$$
611 N.W. Loop 410, San Antonio. (210)340-6060

HOTEL VALENCIA RIVERWALK, $$$$
150 E. Houston St., San Antonio. (210)227-9700, (866)842-0100

HYATT PLACE SAN ANTONIO NORTHWEST, $$$$
4303 Hyatt Place Dr., San Antonio. Valid for one room. Special events excluded. R30. (210)561-0099, (888)492-8847

OMNI LA MANSION DEL RIO, $$$$
112 College St., San Antonio. Valid for one deluxe room. Valid Sunday thru Thursday. (210)518-1000, (800)THE-OMNI

Utah

Park City

BEST WESTERN LANDMARK INN, $$$
6560 N. Landmark Dr., Park City. Valid April thru December 15. Special events & holidays excl. (435)649-7300, (800)548-8824

LODGE AT THE MOUNTAIN VILLAGE, $$$$
1415 Lowell Ave., Park City. 4-bedroom condos excl. Min stay 2 nts. Valid April 1 thru December 1. R30. (435)649-0800, (800)824-5331

Salt Lake City

BEST WESTERN EXECUTIVE INN, $$
280 W. 7200 S., Salt Lake City. Valid for one regular room. R30. (801)566-4141, (800)253-0512

CRYSTAL INN DOWNTOWN, $$$$
230 W. 500 South, Salt Lake City. Valid for one standard room. Special events excluded. R30. (801)328-4466, (800)366-4466

HILTON SALT LAKE CITY CENTER, $$$$
255 S. West Temple, Salt Lake City. Valid for one standard room. Special events excluded. (801)328-2000, (877)776-4936

SHERATON SALT LAKE CITY HOTEL, $$$$
150 W. 500 S., Salt Lake City. Valid for 10% off the best available rate. (801)401-2000

THE KIMBALL, $$
150 N. Main St., Salt Lake City. Holidays excl. R30. (949)587-2299, (800)874-8770

Vermont

Go to entertainment.com/enthotels for this state's hotel listings.

Virginia

Alexandria

WASHINGTON SUITES ALEXANDRIA, $$$$
100 S. Reynolds St., Alexandria. Valid for any room or suite. Valid Friday, Saturday, Sunday & holidays. (703)370-9600, (877)736-2500

Arlington

SHERATON NATIONAL HOTEL, $$$$
900 Orme St., Arlington. Valid Sunday thru Thursday. Valid for 10% off the best available rate. Special events excluded. (703)521-1900, (866)716-8115

Norfolk

SHERATON NORFOLK WATERSIDE, $$$$
777 Waterside Dr., Norfolk. Valid Friday, Saturday & Sunday. Valid for 10% off the best available rate. Special events excluded. (757)622-6664, (888)627-8042

Richmond

HYATT PLACE RICHMOND/ ARBORETUM, $$$
201 Arboretum Place, Richmond. Valid for one room. R30. (804)560-1566, (888)492-8847

OMNI RICHMOND HOTEL, $$$$
100 S. 12th St., Richmond. Special events excluded. (804)344-7000, (800)THE-OMNI

Roanoke

HYATT PLACE ROANOKE AIRPORT, $$$$
5040 Valley View Blvd., Roanoke. Valid for one room. Special events & VA Tech's home football games & graduation. R30. (540)366-4700, (888)492-8847

QUALITY INN ROANOKE AIRPORT, $$
6626 Thirlane Rd., Roanoke. (540)366-8861

Virginia Beach

HOLIDAY INN SUN SPREE, $$$$
39th & Oceanfront, Virginia Beach. Memorial Day, July 4th, Labor Day wknds, & New Year's Eve excl. R30. (757)428-1711

◆ **VIRGINIA BEACH RESORT HOTEL & CONFERENCE CTR. $$$$**
2800 Shore Dr., Virginia Beach. Valid for one suite. Holidays & special events excl. June thru August wknds excl. R30. (757)481-9000, (800)468-2722

Washington/Dulles Int'l Airport

HOTEL SIERRA WASHINGTON DULLES, $$$$
45520 Dulles Plaza, Sterling. Valid for one suite. (703)435-9002, (800)474-3772

HYATT PLACE STERLING, $$$$
21481 Ridgetop Circle, Sterling. Valid for one room. R30. (703)444-3909, (888)492-8847

Washington

Bellevue

HOTEL SIERRA BELLEVUE, $$$$
3244 139th Ave. S.E., Bellevue. Valid for one suite. (425)747-2705, (800)474-3772

SHERATON BELLEVUE HOTEL, $$$$
100 112th Ave. N.E., Bellevue. Valid for 10% off the best available rate. (425)455-3330, (800)235-4458

Leavenworth

◆ **DER RITTERHOF MOTOR INN, $$$**
190 Hwy. 2, Leavenworth. Valid October thru June. Festivals excl. R30. (509)548-5845, (800)255-5845

Seattle

BEST WESTERN PIONEER SQUARE HOTEL, $$$$
77 Yesler Way, Seattle. Suites excluded. Valid November thru April. Sporting events & special events excl. R30. (206)340-1234, (800)800-5514

Discount subject to Program room availability. See **Program Guidelines** on pages G30–G31.

Remember to identify yourself as an Entertainment® Member.

Be Sure To Activate Your Card For Full Program Listings
Go To: www.entertainment.com/enthotels
Check out our ✦Featured Properties

HOMEWOOD SUITES - DOWNTOWN, $$$$
206 Western Ave. W., Seattle. Valid for one suite. Special events excluded. (206)281-9393

MAYFLOWER PARK HOTEL, $$$$
405 Olive Way, Seattle. Max stay 3 nts. R30. (206)623-8700, (800)426-5100

TRAVELODGE - SEATTLE CENTER, $$$
200 6th Ave. N., Seattle. Valid September thru May. (206)441-7878

Seattle/Tacoma Int'l Airport

BEST WESTERN AIRPORT EXECUTEL, $$$
20717 International Blvd., Seattle. Valid for one standard room. R14. (206)878-3300, (800)648-3311

HILTON SEATTLE AIRPORT & CONFERENCE CENTER, $$$$
17620 International Blvd., Seattle. R30. (206)244-4800

Spokane

BEST WESTERN PEPPERTREE AIRPORT INN, $$$
3711 S. Geiger Blvd., Spokane. Family & spa suites excluded. Valid September thru May. (509)624-4655, (800)799-3933

COMFORT INN NORTH, $$$
7111 N. Division, Spokane. Suites excluded. (509)467-7111

QUALITY INN - DOWNTOWN 4TH AVE, $$$
110 E. 4th Ave., Spokane. Valid for one standard room. (509)838-6101, (800)980-6101

RAMADA, $$$
8909 Airport Dr., Spokane. Suites excluded. Valid September thru May. R30. (509)838-5211

TRAVELODGE SPOKANE FALLS, $$$
W-33 Spokane Falls Blvd., Spokane. Special events excl. (509)623-9727, (888)824-0292

West Virginia

Go to entertainment.com/enthotels for this state's hotel listings.

Wisconsin

Green Bay

DAYS INN LAMBEAU FIELD, $$
1978 Holmgren Way, Green Bay. Valid for one double room. Valid Sunday thru Thursday. July, Aug & Packer events excl. (920)498-8088, (800)329-7466

HOTEL SIERRA GREEN BAY, $$$$
333 Main St., Green Bay. Valid for one suite. (920)432-4555

Lake Geneva

GRAND GENEVA RESORT & SPA, $$$$
7036 Grand Geneva Way, (Hwy. 50 & Hwy. 12), Lake Geneva. Valid for one deluxe room. Suites excl. Holidays excl. (262)248-8811, (800)558-3417

TIMBER RIDGE LODGE WATERPARK, $$$$
7020 Grand Geneva Way, (Hwy. 50 East of 12 on Grand Geneva Way), Lake Geneva. Valid for one suite. Valid Sunday - Thursday Labor Day thru Memorial Day. Holiday periods excluded. (262)249-3400, (866)636-4502

Madison

CLARION SUITES CENTRAL, $$$
2110 Rimrock Rd., Madison. Valid for one studio suite. Special events excluded. (608)284-1234

SHERATON MADISON HOTEL, $$$$
706 John Nolen Dr., Madison. Valid for 10% off the best available rate. Special events excluded. (608)251-2300

Milwaukee

BEST WESTERN INN TOWNE HOTEL, $$$
710 N. Old World Third St., Milwaukee. (414)224-8400, (877)ITH-OTEL

HOSPITALITY INN, $$$
4400 S. 27th St., Milwaukee. Valid for one suite. Specialty & whirlpool suites excl. (414)282-8800, (800)825-8466

HYATT PLACE MILWAUKEE AIRPORT, $$$$
200 W. Grange Ave, Milwaukee. Valid for one room. Valid Friday, Saturday & Sunday. R30. (414)744-3600, (888)492-8847

WYNDHAM MILWAUKEE AIRPORT HOTEL & CONV. CTR., $$$$
4747 South Howell Ave., Milwaukee. (414)481-8000, (800)558-3862

Wisconsin Dells

AMERICAN WORLD HOTEL & RV RESORT, $$$
400 County Rd. & Hwy. 12, Wisconsin Dells. Valid for one deluxe room. Suites excluded. July-August, Memorial & Labor Day wknds excluded. R30. (608)253-4451

ATLANTIS WATERPARK HOTEL & SUITES, $$$
1570 Wisconsin Dells Pkwy., Wisconsin Dells. Valid for double suite. Valid Sunday thru Friday September thru May. Holiday weeks & special events excl. (608)253-6606, (800)800-6179

WINTERGREEN RESORT & CONFERENCE CENTER, $$
60 Gasser Rd., Wisconsin Dells. Valid Sunday thru Thursday September thru May. Holidays excluded. R30. (608)254-2285, (800)648-4765

Wyoming

Go to entertainment.com/enthotels for this state's hotel listings.

Canada

Alberta

Banff

BANFF PARK LODGE RESORT & CONFERENCE CENTRE, $$$$
222 Lynx St., Banff. Valid for one superior room. Valid Sunday thru Friday October thru June. Dec 25-Jan 3 excl. (403)762-4433, (800)661-9266

BANFF ROCKY MOUNTAIN RESORT, $$$$
1029 Banff Ave., Banff. Valid Sunday thru Thursday October thru May 19. Holiday periods excl. (403)762-5531, (800)661-9563

Calgary

BLACKFOOT INN, $$$$
5940 Blackfoot Trail SE, Calgary. Max stay 7 nts. June 9-12 & July 2-13 excl. (403)252-2253, (800)661-1151

✦**CARRIAGE HOUSE INN $$$$**
9030 MacLeod Trail South, Calgary. Executive rooms excl. (403)253-1101, (800)661-9566

DELTA CALGARY AIRPORT, $$$$
2001 Airport Rd. N.E., Calgary. Valid for any room or suite. (403)291-2600

FOUR POINTS BY SHERATON CALGARY WEST, $$$$
8220 Bowridge Crescent N.W., Calgary. Valid Sunday thru Thursday. Valid for 10% off the best available rate. Special events excluded. (403)288-4441, (877)288-4441

SANDMAN HOTEL CALGARY CITY CENTRE, $$$
888 - 7th Ave., SW, Calgary. (403)237-8626, (800)726-3626

SHERATON SUITES CALGARY EAU CLAIRE, $$$$
255 Barclay Parade S.W., Calgary. Valid for any room or suite. Special events excluded. (403)266-7200, (888)784-8370

Edmonton

CROWNE PLAZA - CHATEAU LACOMBE, $$$$
10111 Bellamy Hill, Edmonton. Valid for any room or suite. (780)428-6611, (800)661-8801

DAYS INN DOWNTOWN EDMONTON, $$$
10041 - 106 St., Edmonton. (780)423-1925, (800)267-2191

DELTA EDMONTON SOUTH HOTEL & CONFERENCE CTR, $$$$
4404 Gateway Blvd., Edmonton. (780)434-6415, (800)661-1122

Discount subject to Program room availability. See **Program Guidelines** on pages G30–G31.   G45

Call the hotels at the number listed for Entertainment® Membership rate availability.

HOWARD JOHNSON HOTEL, $$$
15540 Stony Plain Rd., Edmonton.
(780)484-3333, (800)556-4156

SANDMAN HOTEL EDMONTON, $$$
17635 Stony Plain Rd., Edmonton.
(780)483-1385, (800)726-3626

THE FAIRMONT HOTEL MACDONALD, $$$$
10065-100 St., Edmonton. Specialty suites excl. Valid Friday & Saturday. (780)424-5181, (800)441-1414

British Columbia

Golden

BEST WESTERN MOUNTAINVIEW INN, $$$$
1024 - 11th St. N., Golden. (250)344-2333

THE PRESTIGE MOUNTAINSIDE RESORT, $$$$
1049 Trans Canada Hwy. N., Golden. Holidays & special events excluded. (250)344-7990, (877)737-8443

Harrison Hot Springs

HARRISON HOT SPRINGS RESORT & SPA, $$$$
100 Esplanade Ave., Harrison Hot Springs. Valid Sunday thru Thursday. (604)796-2244, (800)663-2266

Kelowna

HOLIDAY INN EXPRESS, $$$$
2429 Hwy. 97 North, Kelowna. Valid for one standard room. Valid October thru June. (250)763-0500, (800)465-0200

SANDMAN HOTEL & SUITES KELOWNA, $$$
2130 Harvey Ave., Kelowna. (250)860-6409, (800)726-3626

Richmond

✦ **BEST WESTERN RICHMOND INN CONFERENCE CENTRE $$$$**
7551 Westminster Hwy., Richmond. Valid for one standard room. (604)273-7878, (800)663-0299

FOUR POINTS VANCOUVER AIRPORT, $$$$
8368 Alexandra Rd., Richmond. Valid for 10% off the best available rate. Feb. 4-28, 2010 & special events excl. (604)214-0888, (888)281-8888

✦ **MARRIOTT VANCOUVER AIRPORT $$$$**
7571 Westminster Hwy., Richmond. February 2010 excl. (604)276-2112, (877)323-8888

RADISSON HOTEL VANCOUVER AIRPORT, $$$$
8181 Cambie Rd., Richmond. (604)276-8181

SANDMAN HOTEL VANCOUVER AIRPORT, $$$
3233 St. Edwards Dr., Richmond. (604)303-8888, (800)726-3626

Valemount

PREMIER MOUNTAIN LODGE & SUITES, $$$$
1495 6th Ave., Valemount. Valid September thru May. (256)566-4445, (888)830-7888

Vancouver

BEST WESTERN CHATEAU GRANVILLE, $$$$
1100 Granville St., Vancouver. Valid for one tower room. (604)669-7070, (800)663-0575

EMPIRE LANDMARK HOTEL & CONFERENCE CENTRE, $$$$
1400 Robson St., Vancouver. Not Valid February & March 2010. (604)687-0511, (800)830-6144

FOUR SEASONS HOTEL VANCOUVER, $$$$
791 W. Georgia St., Vancouver. Suites excluded. (604)689-9333

HOLIDAY INN VANCOUVER CENTRE, $$$$
711 W. Broadway, Vancouver. (604)879-0511

✦ **PAN PACIFIC HOTEL VANCOUVER $$$$**
#300-999 Canada Place, Vancouver. (604)662-8111, (800)663-1515

RENAISSANCE VANCOUVER HOTEL HARBOURSIDE, $$$$
1133 West Hastings St., Vancouver. (604)689-9211, (800)905-8582

✦ **SHERATON VANCOUVER WALL CENTRE HOTEL $$$$**
1088 Burrard St., Vancouver. (604)331-1000, (800)663-9255

✦ **WESTIN GRAND VANCOUVER $$$$**
433 Robson St., Vancouver. Feb 8- Mar 1, 2010 excl. (604)602-1999, (888)680-9393

Victoria

INN AT LAUREL POINT, $$$$
680 Montreal Street, Victoria. Valid for any room or suite. (250)386-8721, (800)663-7667

PAUL'S MOTOR INN, $$$
1900 Douglas St., Victoria. (250)382-9231

QUEEN VICTORIA HOTEL & SUITES, $$$$
655 Douglas St., Victoria. Valid for one suite. (250)386-1312, (800)663-7007

✦ **ROYAL SCOT HOTEL & SUITES $$$$**
425 Quebec St., Victoria. Valid for any room or suite. Holidays, holiday weeks & special events excl. (250)388-5463, (800)663-7515

✦ **THE JAMES BAY INN $$$**
270 Government St., Victoria. Valid for any room or suite. Special events excl. (250)384-7151, (800)836-2649

✦ **VICTORIA REGENT HOTEL $$$$**
1234 Wharf St., Victoria. Valid for any room or suite. R30. (250)386-2211, (800)663-7472

Whistler

BEST WESTERN LISTEL WHISTLER HOTEL, $$$$
4121 Village Green, Whistler. Valid May-November & Sunday thru Thursday December-April. R30. (604)932-1133, (800)663-5472

DELTA WHISTLER VILLAGE SUITES, $$$$
4308 Main St., Whistler. Valid for one suite. Valid May thru November & Sunday thru Thursday December thru April. (604)905-3987, (888)299-3987

THE WESTIN RESORT & SPA WHISTLER, $$$$
4090 Whistler Way, Whistler. Valid for 10% off the best available rate. (604)905-5000, (888)634-5577

Manitoba

Winnipeg

CARLTON INN, $$
220 Carlton St., Winnipeg. (204)942-0881, (877)717-2885

RAMADA MARLBOROUGH HOTEL, $$$
331 Smith St., Winnipeg. Special events & holidays excl. (204)942-6411, (800)667-7666

Nova Scotia

Halifax

CAMBRIDGE SUITES HOTEL, $$$$
1583 Brunswick St., Halifax. (902)420-0555, (800)565-1263

FOUR POINTS BY SHERATON HALIFAX, $$$$
1496 Hollis St., Halifax. Valid Friday, Saturday & Sunday. Valid for 10% off the best available rate. Special events excluded. (902)423-4444, (866)444-9494

HOLIDAY INN SELECT HALIFAX CENTRE, $$$$
1980 Robie St., Halifax. Suites & executive floor excluded. R30. (902)423-1161, (888)810-7288

WESTIN NOVA SCOTIAN, $$$$
1181 Hollis St., Halifax. Valid Friday, Saturday & Sunday. Valid for 10% off the best available rate. (902)496-8585, (877)993-7846

Ontario

Niagara Falls

BEST WESTERN CAIRN CROFT HOTEL, $$$$
6400 Lundy's Lane, Niagara Falls. Valid October thru June. R30. (905)356-1161, (800)263-2551

DOUBLETREE FALLSVIEW RESORT & SPA BY HILTON, $$$
6039 Fallsview Blvd., Niagara Falls. Valid Sunday thru Thursday October 15 thru May. (905)358-3817

Discount subject to Program room availability. See **Program Guidelines** on pages G30–G31.

Remember to identify yourself as an Entertainment® Member.

Be Sure To Activate Your Card For Full Program Listings
Go To: www.entertainment.com/enthotels
Check out our ✦Featured Properties

QUALITY HOTEL & CONFERENCE CENTRE, $$$
5807 Ferry St., Niagara Falls. (905)353-1010, (800)215-5691

Lester B. Pearson International Airport

DELTA TORONTO AIRPORT WEST, $$$$
5444 Dixie Rd., Toronto. (905)624-1144, (800)737-3211

SHERATON GATEWAY TORONTO, $$$$
P.O. Box 3000 Toronto International Airport, Toronto. Valid for 10% off the best available rate. (905)672-7000, (888)627-7092

THE WESTIN BRISTOL PLACE-TORONTO AIRPORT, $$$$
950 Dixon Rd., Toronto. Valid for one standard room. (416)675-9444

Ottawa

ALBERT AT BAY SUITE HOTEL, $$$$
435 Albert St., Ottawa. Valid for one suite. R30. (613)238-8858, (800)267-6644

BEST WESTERN VICTORIA PARK SUITES, $$$$
377 O'Connor St., Ottawa. Valid for one suite. R30. (613)567-7275, (800)465-7275

LES SUITES HÔTEL - OTTAWA, $$$$
130 Besserer St., Ottawa. Valid for one suite. (613)232-2000, (800)267-1989

Toronto

CROWNE PLAZA TORONTO DON VALLEY, $$$$
1250 Eglinton Ave. E., Toronto. Valid for one standard room. (416)449-4111, (877)474-6835

DELTA CHELSEA, $$$$
33 Gerrard St. W., Toronto. (416)595-1975, (800)243-5732

✦FOUR POINTS BY SHERATON TORONTO LAKESHORE $$$$
1926 Lake Shore Blvd. W., Toronto. Valid for 10% off the best available rate. Special events excluded. (416)766-4392, (800)463-9929

✦HOWARD JOHNSON HOTEL TORONTO/MARKHAM $$$
555 Cochrane Dr., Markham. Special events excl. (905)479-5000, (877)703-4656

NOVOTEL TORONTO NORTH YORK, $$$$
3 Park Home Ave., North York. (416)733-2929

WESTIN HARBOUR CASTLE, $$$$
1 Harbour Square, Toronto. Suites & executive club floor excluded. (416)869-1600

Quebec
Montreal

HOLIDAY INN MONTREAL - MIDTOWN, $$$$
420 Sherbrooke St. W., Montreal. June 7 - 10 & Dec 30 - 31 excl. (514)842-6111, (800)387-3042

HOLIDAY INN SELECT MONTRÉAL CENTRE-VILLE, $$$$
99 Viger W., Montreal. Suites & executive floor excluded. (514)878-9888, (888)878-9888

HÔTEL DU FORT, $$$$
1390 rue du Fort, Montreal. (514)938-8333, (800)565-6333

HYATT REGENCY MONTREAL, $$$$
1255, Jeanne-Mance P.O. Box 130, Montreal. (514)982-1234, (800)233-1234

Quebec City

BEST WESTERN CITY CENTRE/CENTRE-VILLE, $$$$
330 rue de la Couronne, Quebec City. (418)649-1919, (800)667-5345

DELTA QUEBEC, $$$$
690 Rene Levesque Blvd. E., Quebec City. (418)647-1717

HÔTEL UNIVERSEL, $$$$
2300 ch. Sainte-Foy, Quebec. Valid for any room or suite. (418)653-5250, (800)463-4495

Saskatchewan
Saskatoon

SANDMAN HOTEL SASKATOON, $$$
310 Circle Dr. W., Saskatoon. (306)477-4844, (800)726-3626

SASKATOON INN HOTEL & CONFERENCE CENTRE, $$$$
2002 Airport Dr., Saskatoon. (306)242-1440, (800)667-8789

SHERATON CAVALIER HOTEL, $$$$
612 Spadina Crescent East, Saskatoon. Valid for 10% off the best available rate. Special events excluded. (306)652-6770

Caribbean
Antigua/Barbuda
Mamora Bay

ST. JAMES'S CLUB, $$$$
P.O. Box 63, Mamora Bay. Christmas, New Year's, President's & Easter wks excl. Bonus: 25% off the all-inclusive rate. (954) 481-8787, (800)345-0356

St. Johns

GALLEY BAY RESORT, $$$$
Five Island Village, P.O. Box 305, St. John's. Valid for one room. Enjoy one room at 25% off the all-inclusive rack rate. Christmas, New Year's, President's & Easter wks excl. (954) 481-8787, (800) 345-0356

VERANDAH RESORT & SPA, $$$$
St. John's. Holiday weeks excluded. (954)481-8787, (800)345-0356

British Virgin Islands
Road Town, Tortola

LONG BAY BEACH RESORT & VILLAS, $$$$
P.O. Box 433, Road Town, Tortola. Christmas, New Year's, President's & Easter wks excl. (954) 481-8787, (800) 345-0356

Puerto Rico
Rio Mar

RIO MAR BEACH GOLF RESORT & SPA, A WYNDHAM, $$$$
6000 Rio Mar Blvd., Rio Grande. Dec 20-Jan 1 & President's week excl. (787)888-6000, (800)4 RIO-MAR

Saint Lucia
Castries

WINDJAMMER LANDING VILLA BEACH RESORT, $$$$
P.O. Box 1504, Castries. Christmas, New Year's, President's & Easter wks excl. Bonus: 25% off the all-inclusive rate. (954) 481-8787, (800) 345-0356

Saint Vincent & Grenadines
Palm Island

PALM ISLAND RESORT, $$$$
Palm Island. Valid for one room. Enjoy one room at 25% off the all-inclusive rack rate. Christmas, New Year's, President's & Easter wks excl. (954) 481-8787, (800) 345-0356

Virgin Islands
St. Thomas

POINT PLEASANT RESORT, $$$$
6600 Estate Smith Bay #4, St. Thomas. Valid for one suite. Dec 20-Jan 2 excl. (340)775-7200, (800) 524-2300

WYNDHAM SUGAR BAY RESORT & SPA, $$$$
6500 Estate Smith Bay, St. Thomas. Valid for one standard room. Holiday wks excl. (340)777-7100, (800)WYN-DHAM

Discount subject to Program room availability. See **Program Guidelines** on pages G30–G31.   G47

Call the hotels at the number listed for Entertainment® Membership rate availability.

entertainment.
Direct to Hotel

Call the hotel directly to **save up to** *50% Off* **full-priced rates** *or* **10% Off Best Available Rate** *at thousands of hotels from coast to coast.*

Entertainment International®

Africa

Morocco

Marrakech

LA MAISON DES OLIVIERS HOTEL, $$$$
Km 6 Route de l'ourika, Marrakech.
Valid for any room or suite. Valid April
thru December. 21-22437-5405, Fax:21-22437-5406.

Mozambique

Maputo

HOTEL TIVOLI, $$$
Avenida 25 De Setembro 1321, Maputo.
Special events excluded. 258-21-307600,
Fax:258-21-307609.

Namibia

Windhoek

VONDELHOF GUESTHOUSE, $$
2 Puccini Street, Windhoek. R30. 264 61
248320, Fax:264 61 240373.

Asia

People's Republic of China

Beijing

**COMMUNE BY THE GREAT WALL
KEMPINSKI BEIJING, $$$$**
Exit 16 at Shuiguan Badaling Hwy., Beijing.
Valid for one standard room. Special
events excl. August excl. R30. 8610-8118-1888, Fax:8610-8118-1866.

SINO-SWISS HOTEL BEIJING, $$$$
P.O. Box 6913 Xiao Tianzhu Nan Rd.,
Beijing. 86-10-6456-5588, Fax:86-10-6456-1588.

Chongqing

HARBOUR PLAZA CHONGQING, $$$$
Wu-Yi Rd. Yuzhong District, Chongqing.
86-23-6370-0888, Fax:86-23-6370-0778.

Haikou City, Hainan

CROWN SPA RESORT HAINAN, $$$$
No. 1 Qiongshan Ave., East Riverside,
Haikou City, Hainan. 86-898-6596-6888,
Fax:86-898-6596-0456.

Hohhot

HOLIDAY INN HOHHOT, $$$
33 Zhong Shan West Rd., Hohhot. R30.
86-471-6351888, Fax:86-471-6351666.

Shanghai

**BEST WESTERN SHANGHAI RUITE
HOTEL, $$$**
1888 Yishan Rd. Minhang District,
Shanghai. Special events excl. 86-21-511717, Fax:86-21-511568.

CENTRAL HOTEL SHANGHAI, $$$$
555 Jiujiang Road, Shanghai. Valid for any
room or suite. 86-21-5396-5000, Fax:86-21-5396-5188.

Zhengzhou

CROWNE PLAZA ZHENGZHOU, $$$
115A Jinshui Rd., Zhengzhou. Valid for any
room or suite. 86-371-6595-0055, Fax:86-371-6599-0770.

HOLIDAY INN ZHENGZHOU, $$$$
115 Jinshui Rd., Zhengzhou. 86-371-6595-0055, Fax:86-371-6599-0770.

Vietnam

Ho Chi Minh

**HOTEL EQUATORIAL HO CHI MINH
CITY, $$$**
242 Tran Binh Trong, District 5, Ho Chi
Minh. 84-8-839-7777, Fax:84-8-839-0011.

HOTEL MAJESTIC - SAIGON, $$$$
1 Dong Khoi Street, District 1, Ho Chi
Minh. 848-8295-517, Fax:848-8295-510.

Australia

Queensland

Surfers Paradise

AUSTRALIS SOVEREIGN HOTEL $$$$
138 Ferny Ave., Surfers Paradise. Excluding
special events & peak seasons. 61-7-5579-3888.

**SURFERS PARADISE MARRIOTT RESORT
& SPA $$$$**
158 Ferny Ave., Surfers Paradise. Excluding
24 Dec to 18 Jan, Indy Carnival and Magic
Millions. 61-7-5592-9800.

South Australia

Sydney

MEDINA GRAND SYDNEY $$$$
511 Kent St., Sydney. Min. stay 2 nts.
61-2-9274-0000.

VIBE HOTEL SYDNEY $$$$
111 Goulburn St., Sydney. Min. stay 2 nts.
61-2-8272-3300.

Central America

Belize

Dangriga

JAGUAR REEF LODGE, $$$$
P.O. Box 297, Dangriga. Valid for any room
or suite. Holiday & special events excl.
R30. 510-523-7276, Fax:510-520-7040.

Costa Rica

Samara

MIRADOR DE SAMARA, $$
Samara, Apt. #5, Samara. Valid for any
room or suite. Valid only May, June,
August, September, October & November.
506 2656 0044, Fax:506 2656 0046.

San Jose

ABRIL HOSTAL, $
Matute Gomez, 300 East #2540, San Jose.
506-253-8542, Fax:506-233-6397.

HOTEL 1492, $
Calle 31-33 Ave 1; 2985 Barrio Escalante,
San Jose. (506)225-3752, Fax:(506)280-6206.

Europe

Austria

Polling

GEINBERG SUITES, $$$
Aigelsberg 3, Polling. Valid for one studio
suite. 43-7723-6303, Fax:43-7723-6303-4.

Salzburg

SHERATON SALZBURG HOTEL, $$$$
Auerspergstrasse 4, Salzburg. 43-662-889990, Fax:43-662-881776.

Vienna

GRABEN HOTEL, $$$$
Dorotheergasse 3, Vienna. 43-1-5121-5310, Fax:43-1-5121-53120.

HOTEL REGINA, $$$$
Rooseveltplatz 15, Vienna. 43-1-404460,
Fax:43-1-408-8392.

HOTEL ROYAL, $$$$
Singerstrasse 3, Vienna. 43-1-515680,
Fax:43-1-513-9698.

Belgium

Brussels

CHELTON HOTEL BRUSSELS, $$$$
48 rue Veronese, Brussels. 32-2-735-20-32, Fax:32-2-735-07-66.

HOTEL BRISTOL STEPHANIE, $$$$
Avenue Louise 91-93, Brussels. 32-2-543-33-11, Fax:32-2-538-03-07.

Discount subject to Program room availability. See **Program Guidelines** on pages G30–G31.

Remember to identify yourself as an Entertainment® Member.

Be Sure To Activate Your Card For Full Program Listings
Go To: www.entertainment.com/enthotels
Check out our ✦Featured Properties

Ostend

BEST WESTERN HOTEL IMPERIAL, $$$$
Van Iseghemlaan 76, Ostend. 32-59-806767, Fax:32-59-807838.

Czech Republic

Prague

BEST WESTERN HOTEL KINSKY GARDEN, $$$$
Holeckova 7, Prague. 420-2-5731-1173, Fax:420-2-5731-1184.

HOTEL ARTESSE, $$$$
Arbesovo Nam 2/1028, Prague. Valid for any room or suite. 420-775-023423, Fax:420-226-015-413.

HOTEL ESPLANADE PRAGUE, $$$$
Washingtonova 1600/19, Prague. Minimum 3 nts stay. Special events excluded. 420-224-501-111, Fax:420-224-229-306.

HOTEL NERUDA, $$$$
Nerudova 44, Prague. 420-257-535-557, Fax:420-257-531-492.

France

Angers

HOTEL DE FRANCE, $$$$
8 Place de la Gare, Angers. 33-2-4188-4942, Fax:33-2-4187-1950.

Belleme

HOTEL DU GOLF BELLEME, $$
Les Sablons, Belleme. 33-2-3385-1313, Fax:33-2-3385-1314.

Bordeaux

QUALITY HOTEL ST. CATHERINE, $$$$
27 Rue du Parlement St. Catherine, Bordeaux. 33-5-5681-9512, Fax:33-5-5644-5051.

Paris

ABOTEL APOLLINAIRE MONTPARNASSE, $$$
39 Rue Delambre, Paris. Valid for one suite. 33-1-4727-1515, Fax:33-1-4727-0587.

ABOTEL BLACKSTON OPERA, $$$$
12 Rue de Parme, Paris. 33-1-4727-1515, Fax:33-1-4727-0587.

ABOTEL JARDINS D'EIFFEL, $$$$
8 Rue Amelie, Paris. Valid for one suite. 33-1-4727-1515, Fax:33-1-4727-0587.

ABOTEL LUTECE SAINT GERMAIN, $$$$
2, rue Berthollet, Paris. 33-1-4727-1515, Fax:33-1-4727-0587.

HOTEL ARAMIS SAINT-GERMAIN, $$$$
124 Rue de Rennes, Paris. 33-1-4548-0375, Fax:33-1-4544-9929.

HOTEL BERSOLYS SAINT-GERMAIN, $$$$
28 rue de Lille, Paris. 33-1-4727-1515, Fax:33-1-4727-0587.

HOTEL MONCEAU ELYSEES, $$$$
108, rue de Courcelles, Paris. 33-1-4727-1515, Fax:33-1-4727-0587.

HOTEL OPERA LAFAYETTE, $$$$
80, ru La Fayette, Paris. 33-1-4727-1515, Fax:33-1-4727-0587.

HOTEL WESTMINSTER, $$$$
13 Rue de la Paix, Paris. 33-1-4261-5746, Fax:33-1-4260-3066.

ROYAL HOTEL, $$$$
33 Ave. de Friedland, Paris. 33-1-4359-0814, Fax:33-1-4563-6992.

Germany

Bad Zwischenahn

CONCORDE HOTEL RESTAURANT AM BADEPARK, $$
Am Badepark 5, Bad Zwischenahn. 49-4403-6960, Fax:49-4403-696373.

RINGHOTEL AMSTERDAM, $$
Wiefelsteder Str. 18, Bad Zwischenahn. 49-4403-9340, Fax:49-4403-934234.

Berlin

PARK HOTEL BLUB BERLIN, $$$$
Buschkrugallee 60-62, Berlin. 49-30-6000-3600, Fax:49-30-6000-3777.

Fuerth-Nuremberg

AMBIENT HOTEL AM EUROPAKANAL, $$$$
Unterfarrnbacher Strasse 222, Fuerth-Nuremberg. Valid for any room or suite. 49-911-973720, Fax:49-911-9737215.

Karben-Frankfurt.M.

COMFORT INN FRANKFURT-KARBEN, $$$
St. Egreve Strasse 25-27, Karben-Frankfurt.M. 49-6039-8010, 888-406-4368, Fax:49-6039-938-408.

Munich-Eching

GOLDEN TULIP HOTEL OLYMP, $$$
Weilandstrasse 3, Eching, Munich-Eching. 49-89-327-100, Fax:49-89-327-10112.

Greece

Athens

CROWNE PLAZA ATHENS CITY CENTRE, $$$$
50 Michalacopoulou St., Athens. 30-210-727-8000, Fax:30-210-727-8600.

DIVANI PALACE ACROPOLIS HOTEL, $$$$
19-25 Parthenonos Street, Athens. 30-210-928-0100, Fax:30-210-921-4993.

THE ROYAL OLYMPIC HOTEL, $$$$
28-34 Diakou Str, Athens. 30-210-922-6411, Fax:30-210-923-3317.

Hungary

Budapest

HOTEL GLORIA, $$$
Blathy Otto U. 22, Budapest. Special events excluded. 36-1-210-4120, Fax:36-1-210-4129.

HOTEL MEDITERRAN, $$$
Budaorsi ut 20/a, Budapest. 36-1-372-7020, Fax:36-1-372-7021.

Iceland

Husavik

FOSSHOTEL HUSAVIK, $$$$
Ketilsbraut 22, Husavik. 354-464-1220.

FOSSHOTEL LAUGAR, $$$$
Husavik. Valid June thru August. 354-464-6300.

Reykjavik

FOSSHOTEL BARON, $$$$
Baronsstigur 2, Reykjavik. 354-562-3204.

FOSSHOTEL LIND, $$$$
Raudarastigur 18, Reykjavik. 354-562-3350.

Italy

Cannizzaro

SHERATON CATANIA HOTEL & CONFERENCE CENTRE, $$$$
Via Antonello da Messina 45, Cannizzaro. 39-095-271557, Fax:39-095-271380.

Florence

HOTEL BERCHIELLI, $$$$
Lungarno Acciaouli 14, Florence. 39-055-264061, Fax:39-055-218636.

HOTEL BRUNELLESCHI, $$$
Via de' Calzaioli Piazza Santa Elisabetta, Florence. 39-055-27370, Fax:39-055-219653.

HOTEL GOLF, $$$$
Viale Fratelli Rosselli 56, Florence. 39-055-281818, Fax:39-055-268432.

HOTEL VILLA CASAGRANDE, $$$$
Via Del Puglia, 61 50063 Figline Valdarno - Firenze, Florence. 39-055-952554, Fax:39-055-954-4322.

Milan

ATAHOTEL EXECUTIVE, $$$$
Via Don Luigi Sturzo 45, Milan. 39-02-62941, Fax:39-02-2901-0238.

FOUR POINTS SHERATON MILAN CENTER, $$$$
Via Cardano 1, Milan. 39-02-667461, Fax:39-02-667-46165.

Discount subject to Program room availability. See **Program Guidelines** on pages G30–G31.   G49

Call the hotels at the number listed for Entertainment® Membership rate availability.

Entertainment International®

Montecatini Terme

HOTEL ERCOLINI & SAVI, $$$$
Via San Martino 18, Montecatini Terme.
39-0572-70331, Fax:39-0572-71624.

HOTEL MANZONI, $$$$
Viale Manzoni, Montecatini Terme.
39-0572-70175, Fax:39-0572-911012.

Perugia

PARK HOTEL PERUGIA, $$$$
Via A. Volta Nr 1, Perugia. 39-075-599-0444, Fax:39-075-599-0455.

SANGALLO PALACE HOTEL, $$$$
Via Masi N9, Perugia. 39-075-5730202, Fax:39-075-5730068.

Rapallo

EXCELSIOR PALACE HOTEL, $$$$
Via San Michele di Pagana, 8, Rapallo.
39-0185-230666, Fax:39-0185-230214.

Rome

GRAND HOTEL PLAZA, $$$$
Via Del Corso 126, Rome. 39-06-69921111, Fax:39-06-69941575.

HOTEL ARTEMIDE, $$$$
Via Nazionale 22, Rome. 39-06-489911, Fax:39-06-48991700.

HOTEL SAVOY, $$$$
Via Ludovisi 15, Rome. 39-06-421551, Fax:39-06-42155555.

Todi

HOTEL EUROPALACE TODI, $$$
Loc Pian Di Porto, 144/1, Todi. Easter, special events & suites excl. 39-075-898-7474, Fax:39-075-898-7476.

Venice

ALBERGO SAN MARCO, $$$
Piazza San Marco 877, Venice. 39-041-5204277, Fax:39-041-5238447.

HOTEL BISANZIO, $$$$
Riva Schiavoni, Venice. 39-041-5203-100, Fax:39-041-5204-114.

Luxembourg

Clervaux

HOTEL INTERNATIONAL, $$$
10 Grand Rue, Clervaux. 352-929-391, Fax:352-920-492.

Luxembourg

GRAND HOTEL CRAVAT, $$$$
29 Boulevard Roosevelt, Luxembourg.
352-221-975, Fax:352-226-711.

Netherlands

Amsterdam

THE GRESHAM MEMPHIS HOTEL, $$$$
De Lairessestraat 87, Amsterdam. 31-20-673-3141, Fax:31-20-673-7312.

Oranjewoud

GOLDEN TULIP TJAARDA ORANJEWOUD, $$$
Koningin Julianaweg 98, Oranjewoud.
31-513-433533, Fax:31-513-433599.

Utrecht

PARK PLAZA UTRECHT, $$$
Westplein 50, Utrecht. 31-30-292-5200, Fax:31-30-292-5199.

Portugal

Lisbon

HOLIDAY INN LISBOA, $$$$
Avenida Antonio Jose de Almeida, 28-A, Lisbon. 351-21-0044000, Fax:351-21-793-6672.

HOTEL PRINCIPE LISBOA, $$
Ave Duque D'Avila, 201, Lisbon. Valid for one room. R30. 351-21-35-92050, Fax:351-21-35-92055.

Porto

RESIDENCIAL DOS ALIADOS, $$
Rua Elisio de Melo, 27, Porto. Valid for one standard room. R30. 351 222 004 853, Fax:351 222 002 710.

Spain

Barcelona

HOTEL AUGUSTA VALLES, $$$$
Autopista A-7, Barcelona. 34-938-456050, Fax:34-938-456061.

HOTEL RIVOLI RAMBLAS, $$$$
Rambla de los Estudios 128, Barcelona.
34-93-481-7676, Fax:34-93-317-5053.

Madrid

ARTURO SORIA SUITES, $$$
Juan Perez Zuniga 20, Madrid. Valid for any room or suite. 34-91-291-1500, Fax:34-91-367-0421.

SUITES PRADO HOTEL, $$$
Manuel Fernandez Y Gonzalez 10, Madrid.
34-914-202318, Fax:34-914-200559.

Seville

GRAN HOTEL LAR, $$$$
Plaza de Carmen Benitez, 3, Seville.
34-954-410361, Fax:34-954-410452.

Sweden

Goteborg

HOTEL ALLEN, $$$
Parkgatan 10, Goteborg. 46-31-101450, Fax:46-31-7119160.

Malmo

CONTINENTAL HOTEL, $$$$
Hospitalsgatan 2, Malmo. 46-40-121977, Fax:46-40-122766.

HOTELL BALTZAR, $$$
Baltzargatan 45, 211 36 Malmo. 46-40-6655700, Fax:46-40-665-5710.

Stockholm

HOTEL ESPLANADE, $$$$
Strandvagen 7A, Stockholm. 46-8-6630740, Fax:46-8-6625992.

SHERATON STOCKHOLM HOTEL & TOWER, $$$$
Tegelbacken 6, Stockholm. 46-8-4123400, Fax:46-8-412-3409.

Mexico

Distrito Federal

Mexico City

SHERATON MARIA ISABEL HOTEL & TOWERS, $$$$
Paseo de la Reforma 325, Mexico City.
Valid for 10% off the best available rate.
Special events excluded. 52-55-5242-5555, Fax:52-55-5242-5602.

W MEXICO CITY, $$$$
Campos Eliseos 252 Chapultepec, Polanco, Mexico City. Valid Friday, Saturday & Sunday. Valid for 10% off the best available rate. 52-55-91381800, Fax:52-55-91381899.

Guerrero

Acapulco

CALINDA BEACH ACAPULCO HOTEL, $$$
1260 Costera Miguel Aleman, Acapulco.
52-744-4840410, Fax:52-744-4844676.

EL TROPICANO, $$
Ave. Costera Miguel Aleman #510, Acapulco. Valid Jan 5 thru December 19. Holy week excl. 52-744-4841332, Fax:52-744-4841308.

Jalisco

Puerto Vallarta

HOLIDAY INN PUERTO VALLARTA, $$$$
Blvd. Francisco Medina km. 3.5, Puerto Vallarta. 52-322-226-1700, Fax:52-322-224-5683.

Discount subject to Program room availability. See **Program Guidelines** on pages G30–G31.

Remember to identify yourself as an Entertainment® Member.

Be Sure To Activate Your Card For Full Program Listings
Go To: www.entertainment.com/enthotels
Check out our ✦Featured Properties

SHERATON BUGANVILIAS RESORT & CONV. CENTER, $$$$
Blvd. Fco. Medina Ascencio #999, Puerto Vallarta. (818)842-6155, (800)433-5451, Fax:(818)843-2423.

THE WESTIN RESORT & SPA, PUERTO VALLARTA, $$$$
Paseo de la Marina Sur 205, Puerto Vallarta. Valid for 10% off the best available rate. 52 322 2260 1100, Fax:52 322 2261 144.

Quintana Roo

Cancun

BEACH PALACE, $$$$
Blvd. Kukulcan KM 11.5, Zona Hotelera, Cancun. Valid for one suite. (305)374-6882, (800)635-1836, Fax:(305)593-0464.

CANCUN PALACE, $$$$
Blvd. Kukulcan KM 14.5, Zona Hotelera, Cancun. (305)374-6882, (800)635-1836, Fax:(305)593-0464.

CARIBE INTERNACIONAL, $$
Yaxchilan Ave. #36, Cancun. Valid April 20 thru December 20. 52-998-8843747, Fax:52-998-8841993.

LE BLANC SPA RESORT, $$$$
Blvd. Kukulcan KM-10, Zona Hotelera, Cancun. (305)374-6882, (800)635-1836, Fax:(305)593-0464.

MOON PALACE GOLF & SPA RESORT, $$$$
Carretera Cancun-Chetumal KM 340, Cancun. (305)374-6882, (800)635-1836, Fax:(305)593-0464.

OMNI CANCUN HOTEL & VILLAS, $$$$
Blvd. Kukulkan, L-48, KM. 16.5, M. 53, Cancun. Valid for one deluxe room. Dec 26 - Jan 2 & Holidays excl. 52-998-881-0600, 800-446-8977, Fax:52-998-885-0059.

SUN PALACE, $$$$
Blvd. Kukulcan KM 20, Zona Hotelera, Cancun. Valid for one suite. (305)374-6882, (800)635-1836, Fax:(305)593-0464.

Playa del Carmen

AVENTURA SPA PALACE, $$$$
KM 72 Carretera Cancun-Tulum, Riviera Maya. (305)374-6882, (800)635-1836, Fax:(305)593-0464.

PLAYACAR PALACE, $$$$
Fracc. Playacar, Bahia del Espíritu Santo Esq Abraira de Arriva, Playa del Carmen. (305)374-6882, (800) 635-1836, Fax:(305)593-0464.

XPU-HA PALACE, $$$$
Km 265 Carretera Chetumal-Puerto Juarez, Riviera Maya. (305)374-6882, (800)635-1836, Fax:(305)593-0464.

Puerto Aventuras

OMNI PUERTO AVENTURAS BEACH RESORT, $$$$
KM. 269.5 Carretera Chetumal-Cancun, Puerto Aventuras. Valid for one deluxe room. Dec 26 - Jan 2 & Holidays excl. 52-984-875-1950, Fax:52-984-875-1958.

Sinaloa

Mazatlan

HOWARD JOHNSON HOTEL - DON PELAYO, $$
Avenida Del Mar #1111, Mazatlan. Valid for any room or suite. Easter week excl. 52-669-983-2221, Fax:52-669-984-0799.

TORRES MAZATLAN, $$$$
Av. Sabalo Cerritos Esq Lopez Portillo, Mazatlan. Valid for one condo. Min stay 2 nts. R30. (888)333-1962, Fax:(425)635-0768.

New Zealand

Auckland

COPTHORNE HOTEL AUCKLAND HARBOUR CITY $$$$
196-200 Quay St., Auckland. 64-9-309-4420.

HOTEL GRAND CHANCELLOR AUCKLAND $$$$
1 Hobson St., Auckland. 64-9-356-1000.

South America

Argentina

Buenos Aires

PARK TOWER BUENOS AIRES, $$$$
Avenida Leandro N. Alem 1193, Buenos Aires. Valid for 10% off the best available rate. 54-11-43189100, Fax:54-11-43189150.

SHERATON BUENOS AIRES HOTEL & CONVENTION CTR., $$$$
San Martin 1225, Buenos Aires. Valid for 10% off the best available rate. 54-11-43189000, Fax:54-11-43189353.

TRIBECA BUENOS AIRES APART, $$$
Bartolome Mitre 1265, Buenos Aires. 54-11-4372-5444, Fax:54-11-4372-5444.

Brazil

Buzios

HIBISCUS BEACH, $$$
Rua 1, #22 Quadra C, Caixa Postal: 112.255, Buzios. Valid for one standard room. Valid May 3rd to December 19th. 55-22-2623-6221, Fax:55-22-2623-6221.

Sao Paolo

SHERATON SAO PAULO WTC HOTEL $$$$
Nações Unidas Avenue, 12.559, Sao Paolo. Valid for 10% off best available rate. Special events excl. 55-11-3055-8000.

Colombia

Bogota

HOTEL HAMILTON, $$$$
Carrera 14, No. 81-20, Bogota. Valid for one suite. June 16-July 14 & Dec-Jan 14 excl. 57-1-621-5455, Fax:57-1-2188.

Cali

RADISSON ROYAL CALI HOTEL, $$$
Carrera 100B #11A-99, Cali. Valid Friday, Saturday, Sunday, holidays & Easter week. 57-2-3307777, Fax:57-2-3306477.

United Kingdom

England

Banbury

THE BANBURY HOUSE HOTEL, $$$
Oxford Rd., Banbury. 44-1295-259361, Fax:44-1295-270954.

Birmingham

PRIME LODGE, $$$$
Nechells Pakrway, Birmingham. 44-121-333-6088, Fax:44-121-359-4943.

Blackpool, Lancashire

GRAND METROPOLE HOTEL - BLACKPOOL, $$$$
Princess Parade, Promenade, Blackpool, Lancashire. Min stay 2 nts. R30. 44-845-8381002, Fax:44-845-8380721.

THE SAVOY HOTEL, $$$$
Queens Promenade, Blackpool, Lancashire. Min stay 2 nts. R30. 44-845-8386079, Fax:44-845-8386022.

Coventry

BRITANNIA HOTEL COVENTRY, $$$$
Fairfax Street, Coventry. Min stay 2 nts. R30. 44-2476-633733, Fax:44-2476-520172.

ROYAL COURT HOTEL, $$$$
Tamworth Road, Keresley, Coventry. Min stay 2 nts. R30. 44-2476-334171, Fax:44-2476-333478.

London

BERJAYA EDEN PARK HOTEL, $$$$
35-39 Inverness Terrace, London. 44-20-7221-2220, Fax:44-20-7221-2286.

PLAZA ON THE RIVER CLUB & RESIDENCE, $$$$
18 Albert Embankment, London. 44 20 7769 2525, Fax:44 20 7769 2400.

THE INTERNATIONAL HOTEL, $$$$
Marsh Wall, London. Min stay 2 nts. R30. 44-20-7712-0100, Fax:44-20-7712-0102.

Norwich

QUALITY HOTEL NORWICH, $$$$
2 Barnard Rd., Norwich. Valid for one room. 44 160 374 1161, Fax:44 160 374 1500.

Otterburn

PERCY ARMS HOTEL, $$$$
Main Road, Otterburn. 44-1830-520261, Fax:44-1830-520567.

Discount subject to Program room availability. See **Program Guidelines** on pages G30–G31.

G51

Call the hotels at the number listed for Entertainment® Membership rate availability.

Hotel Chain Savings

SAVE 10% or MORE...

...at your favorite hotel chain

Save 10% off the "Best Available Rate" at over 6,500 participating locations **worldwide** every time you travel. Whether you are looking for an upscale hotel, an all-inclusive resort or something more cost-effective, we have the right hotel for you...and at the right price. So start saving now.

(877) 670-7088
ID# 1000 000181

HOW TO SAVE

1. Call the hotel chain of your choice or book online at **www.entertainment.com/hotelchains***
2. Provide agent with special ID number
3. Make your reservation & receive your savings

CHOICE HOTELS INTERNATIONAL ™

Combining convenience with value—that's what makes Choice Hotels® the right place for you. Choice offers attractive rooms, valued amenities, friendly hospitality, and affordable rates at more than 5,800 hotels. With upscale, midscale, economy and extended stay brands, Choice hotels meet the needs of today's travelers.

(800) 533-2100
ID# 00803210

Save 10% or more off the Best Flexible Rate when you book in advance.* With almost 4,000 hotels in nearly 100 countries, InterContinental Hotels Group is pleased to offer Great Hotels Guest Love®. (*5% or more savings at Staybridge Suites and Candlewood Suites.)

(877) 580-2943
REQUEST THE BEST
AVAILABLE RATE

Red Roof is invested in delivering a memorable experience to our guests. Having recently completed a nationwide renovation to our 350 properties, our goal is to provide our customers a savings without sacrificing comfort. We invite you to experience our warm and welcoming spirit firsthand. The next time you make travel plans, think red and save 15% on your stay at Red Roof.

(888) 503-7695
ID# 534795

With more than 4,100 Best Western hotels in 80 countries—we are The World's Largest Hotel Chain®, so wherever you travel in the world, you will find a familiar, friendly and comfortable hotel awaiting your arrival.

(800) 441-1114
MVP# 00162370

Get away, your way!
Choose from over 6,000 hotels worldwide at...

SAVE NOW
on Great Hotels Guests Love®

InterContinental® Hotels & Resorts
Enjoy authentic, enriching experiences with superior, understated service at over 150 locations around the world.

Crowne Plaza® Hotels & Resorts
Upscale hotels in major cities, offering business travelers high levels of comfort, service and amenities.

Hotel Indigo®
Offers travelers an upscale boutique experience, where each hotel is locally reflective and refreshingly different.

Holiday Inn® Hotels & Resorts
Signs of change are everywhere from our iconic signage to our genuine service, our lobbies and our linens— you'll see and feel the difference the moment you arrive.

Holiday Inn® Express
A fresh, clean, uncomplicated hotel choice providing free Internet access, a free hot breakfast, and a comfortable room that will leave you refreshed and recharged.

Holiday Inn Club Vacations™
With spacious, beautifully appointed villas and a wide variety of resort amenities, it's easy to enjoy the ultimate vacation experience with your family and friends.

Staybridge Suites®
All-suite hotel offering comfortable, stylish accommodations with free breakfast buffet, free Wireless Anywhere, and evening receptions.

Candlewood Suites®
Extended-stay hotel with studio and one-bedroom suites, full kitchens, free high-speed Internet, and free guest laundry. *Consider us home.®*

Save 10% or more off the Best Flexible Rate when you book in advance.*

With over 4,000 hotels in nearly 100 countries, InterContinental Hotels Group is pleased to offer Great Hotels Guests Love®. (*5% or more savings at Staybridge Suites and Candlewood Suites.)

Call (877) 580-2943 or visit Entertainment.com to Book Today!
Coupon not required. 14-Day Advanced Purchase Rate is non-refundable and subject to availability.
See www.holidayinn.com/advpurchase for complete terms and conditions.

InterContinental Hotels Group

Valid now thru December 31, 2010

Subject to Rules of Use. Not valid with other discount offers, unless specified. Coupons VOID if purchased, sold or bartered for cash.   H2

Leaving lasting impressions℠

Make memories that will last a lifetime when you escape to Aston Hotels & Resorts. Located on 4 beautiful islands, Aston's 25 hotels and condominium resorts are moments away from the best beaches, restaurants, and activities in paradise. Getting away has never been a better value.

For reservations, call **866.774.2924** and ask for the Entertainment® Rate.

ASTON
Hotels & Resorts

Oahu

Maui

Kauai

Big Island

Friendly. Value. Choice Hotels®.

SAVE 10%
on your next hotel stay!

No matter where you travel in the United States or Canada—you are never far away from a Choice Hotels® property.

Many locations offer FREE Breakfast, Newspapers and Wireless Internet.

Valid only at participating locations. Discount rate applies to regular (rack) non-discounted room rates and is subject to program room availability. Advance reservations required. Blackout dates and other restrictions may apply. This discount cannot be used in conjunction with any other discount promotional room rate. The toll-free number listed is valid only for booking the promotional rate that accompanies the ID# listed. Not valid for group travel.

CHOICE HOTELS INTERNATIONAL ™

SAVE 10%
on your next hotel stay!

Two Ways to Save:

1. **Call 800-533-2100**, *mention code: 00803210*

2. **Book online at www.entertainment.com/choicehotels**

Valid now thru December 30, 2010

Subject to Rules of Use. Not valid with other discount offers, unless specified. Coupons VOID if purchased, sold or bartered for cash.

H4

ENDLESS VACATION RENTALS
BY WYNDHAM WORLDWIDE

Condos, Villas and Cottages Around the World!

Orlando

Mexico

Italy

Caribbean

25% Off the Ultimate Nickelodeon Vacation

Pack your bags knowing that this year's Orlando family vacation won't cost a fortune. Take advantage of a suite deal from the Nickelodeon Family Suites. For more information about the hotel, visit www.nickhotel.com.

For reservations, call 877-NICK-KID
(877-642-5543)
Ask for the Entertainment® Rate.

VALID NOW THRU DECEMBER 31, 2010. ASK FOR THE ENTERTAINMENT® RATE. SUBJECT TO RULES OF USE. COUPONS VOID IF PURCHASED, SOLD OR BARTERED FOR CASH. VALID ONE ROOM PER COUPON. BLACKOUT DATES APPLY. NOT VALID WITH OTHER DISCOUNT OFFERS OR SPECIAL RATES. ©VIACOM INTERNATIONAL INC. ALL RIGHTS RESERVED. NICKELODEON AND ALL RELATED TITLES, LOGOS AND CHARACTERS ARE TRADEMARKS OF VIACOM INTERNATIONAL INC. SPONGEBOB SQUAREPANTS CREATED BY STEPHEN HILLENBURG.

NICKELODEON
Family Suites
Orlando's Entertainment Destination

These deals are something to smile about

Save up to $200*USD **off your next vacation rental!†**
Book online www.EVRentals.com/evrbudgetoffer or
call 1-877-670-7088, prompt 3
Use promo code: EVRBudgetOffer

plus

Save up to 30% off your Budget car rental!
Visit budget.com or call 1-888-724-6212
Mention Budget Corporate Discount (BCD) # X443037 when making a reservation.

Valid now thru December 31, 2010

H8   Subject to Rules of Use. Not valid with other discount offers, unless specified. Coupons VOID if purchased, sold or bartered for cash.

SkyMall...Going beyond the ordinary.

Shop from thousands of innovative products from over 50 stores with just one delivery charge.

See the latest arrivals at skymall.com

Air + Hotel + Entertainment® = Savings

Entertainment® Members get exclusive savings on vacation packages. Offers available only at

www.Entertainment.com/Expedia

Save $100 on a 5-night vacation

- Book any vacation package with air + hotel
- Minimum package price of $2,000
- Book online and enter code entbook100

H16

Save $50 on a 3-night vacation

- Book any 3-night vacation including air + hotel
- Minimum package price of $1,300
- Book online and enter code entbook50

H17

Terms and Conditions
Special offers are available only at participating hotels. Discounts will be subtracted from the price of the hotel component of any air + hotel vacation package at the time of booking on www.Entertainment.com/Expedia. The discount is based upon the total price, excluding taxes and other fees. Offers are subject to availability and may be discontinued without notice. Additional restrictions and blackout dates may apply. Package prices vary by date and departure city. See www.Entertainment.com/Expedia for full terms and conditions.

Call 1-800-237-1078
or visit **www.Entertainment.com/Expedia**

Valid now thru December 31, 2010
Subject to Rules of Use. Not valid with other discount offers, unless specified. Coupons VOID if purchased, sold or bartered for cash.

ORBITZ®

Super savings when you book your flight and hotel together!

Orbitz Packages could include flights from:
Alaska Airlines | Continental | Frontier Airlines | United | And more!!

$200 OFF
7+ Nights Flight + Hotel
Mexico, Caribbean, or Hawaii*
Promo Code: 200ENTERTAIN

H18

*Book a qualifying Mexico, Caribbean, or Hawaii flight + hotel package between July 1, 2009, and December 31, 2010, for 7 or more nights for travel between July 1, 2009, and December 31, 2010, via Orbitz and instantly receive $200 off your booking through the use of the promotion code. To display qualifying packages, click "I have a promotion code." and enter the promotion code, then look for packages marked with the icon "COUPON." Limit one discount per hotel room and one promotion code per booking. Discounts are not redeemable for cash for any reason. Any attempt at fraud will be prosecuted to the fullest extent of the law. Void where prohibited, taxed or restricted. Orbitz reserves the right to change or limit the promotion in its sole discretion.

Valid now thru December 31, 2010
Subject to Rules of Use. Not valid with other discount offers, unless specified. Coupons VOID if purchased, sold or bartered for cash.

A Luxury You Can Afford.

SAVE up to $100
on your next Apple Vacation!

Save $100 on vacations of 6 nights or more and $50 on vacations of 5 nights or less. Vacation certificate is per booking and is good towards the purchase of any complete Apple Vacations' air and hotel package to Mexico and the Caribbean.

All bookings must be made via
www.applevacations.com/entertainment
or via 1-800-597-4982

Identify yourself as an Entertainment® Member and provide promo code **ENT10**.

APPLE VACATIONS.com

CANCUN | RIVIERA MAYA | BAHAMAS | BERMUDA | PUNTA CANA
LA ROMANA | CAP CANA | JAMAICA | PUERTO VALLARTA

H19

priceline.com®

I HAVE WAYS OF
MAKING YOU SAVE

Instant Bonus
Cash Coupon
for
Entertainment® Members

H20

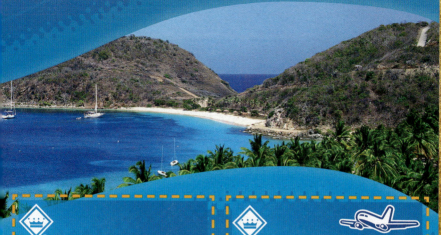

CUSTOMIZED VACATIONS MADE EASY.

Flights, hotels, car reservations, show tickets, attraction passes, and more—all in one place for one low price. Now offering online check-in!

SAVE UP TO $125

Entertainment® Members can save up to $125 when you book a Southwest Airlines Vacations flight + hotel package online at:

southwestvacations.com/entertainment

Offer not combinable with any other offers. Savings valid if booked 8/1/09-12/24/10 for travel 8/6/09-12/31/10. Five-day advance purchase required. Seats may be limited and may not be available on some flights that operate during peak travel times and holiday periods. Discounts are valid per reservation before taxes are applied. Restrictions apply. All Rapid Rewards rules and regulations apply. The Mark Travel Corporation is the tour operator for Southwest Airlines Vacations. CST 2009218-20 WNV044976

Valid now thru December 31, 2010

H21   Subject to Rules of Use. Not valid with other discount offers, unless specified. Coupons VOID if purchased, sold or bartered for cash.

Save up to $125 with United Vacations!

Book your package at www.unitedvacations.com/entertainment
Promotion code applies.

United Vacations provides complete vacation packages including air, hotel, rental car & attraction tickets to popular destinations such as the Caribbean, Hawaii, Las Vegas, Mexico, Canada, Europe and throughout the United States.

UNITED VACATIONS®

The savings amount is applied per reservation and is based on the original purchase price of the vacation, before the discount. The savings are available on vacations totaling $750 or more purchased 8/1/09-12/24/10 for travel 8/1/09-12/29/10, with the correct promotion code. Maximum savings amount is $125. Savings are not available for travel to Mexico and the Caribbean 11/20-11/27/09; 12/19/09-1/3/2010. Offer is not valid for North Pacific, South Pacific or Latin America destinations. Offer is non-combinable and not retroactive. All offers are based on availability and are subject to change without notice. Additional restrictions and blackout dates may apply. For full details, see the United Vacations Terms & Conditions.   CST# 2009218-20 uv045071.gew

Valid now thru December 29, 2010

Subject to Rules of Use. Not valid with other discount offers, unless specified. Coupons VOID if purchased, sold or bartered for cash.

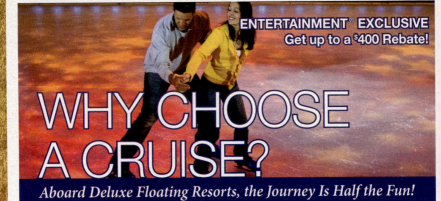

WHY CHOOSE A CRUISE?

Aboard Deluxe Floating Resorts, the Journey Is Half the Fun!

*Your travel dollar goes a lot farther with a cruise vacation. Choose a cruise and you'll **save hundreds compared to a hotel-based vacation** and avoid the hassles of airplane and train travel. For every kind of traveler, there's a cruise ship offering a tailored range of modern amenities and fun activities. So you're sure to find a sailing perfect for you, whether you're dreaming of a family trip, romantic escape, adventure with friends, relaxing retreat, or a luxury getaway.*

BEST VALUE IN TRAVEL

One Low Price Includes:
- All Meals & Basic Beverages Onboard
- Visit Multiple Ports – Unpack Once!
- Stateroom – Some with a Balcony
- Day/Night Activities for All Ages
- Vegas-Style Theater, Magic & Comedy
- Supervised Kids' Clubs
- Entry to Nightclubs, Piano Bars & More
- Art Galleries & Auctions
- Game Rooms, Lounges & Library
- Pools, Hot Tubs, Gym & More

THE MOST VARIETY!

Amazing Ship Amenities:
- Surfing Wave & Beach Pools
- Ice-Skating Rink
- Rock-Climbing Wall
- Mini-Golf & Golf Simulator
- Bowling, Billiards & More
- Grass Lawns & Gardens
- Spiral Waterslide & Kids' Pools
- 10-Story Atriums & Shops
- Casino w/Slots & Tables (fee)
- Spa w/Lavish Treatments (fee)

(*Amenities vary by ship)

UNMATCHED CONVENIENCE!

Within Reach, Easy & Fun for All:
- Cruise from Close to Home – **22 U.S. Departure Ports**
- Drive, Don't Fly to Your Home Port – **SAVE HUNDREDS!**
- Real Comfort & Fun upon Boarding – Unlike Air Travel
- Awake in a New Destination Most Days!
- Ships Can Avoid Storms – Your Vacation Is Saved!
- **Dining Options Galore** – Gourmet, Buffet, Café & More
- **Stateroom Options** – Suite, Balcony, Oceanview, Inter-Connecting & More
- **Perfect for Groups** – Family Reunions, Church Groups, Clubs & Conventions

ENTERTAINMENT® EXCLUSIVE
Get up to a $400 Rebate!

FEATURED FLEETS

110% Best Price Guarantee!

NORWEGIAN CRUISE LINE®
FREESTYLE CRUISING®

Go Freestyle Cruising℠ for more freedom to play as you please at sea. Choose when and where you'll dine, whether in casual or formal attire, and enjoy a variety of imaginative amenities aboard the youngest fleet.

- Up to 13 restaurants & hip nightclubs
- Only bowling lanes at sea
- Vegas-style casino & shows
- Theme parties, comedy classes & more
- Pools, spa, gym & more
- Kids' club & 2-story Nintendo Wii™ screen

FUN & FAMILY: *Perfect balance for all ages*

LUXURY: *The ultimate experience at sea*

CRYSTAL ⚜ CRUISES

SILVERSEA

PREMIUM: *Sophisticated, yet affordable*

SPECIALTY: *Intimate ships visiting smaller & unique ports*

Book Online — http://entertainment.cruises.com   Call our Expert Agents 24/7: 1-800-887-9042

Celebrity X® Cruises®

Indulge in red-carpet treatment for far less than you think. Inventive amenities and a mix of casual country club style with upscale flair have made Celebrity one of the most award-winning fleets.

- World-renowned cuisine by Michel Roux
- Butler service in all suites
- Champagne & martini bars
- iPod® rentals & music library
- Half-acre lawns for picnics, croquet & more

Call our Expert Agents 24/7:
1-800-887-9042
Book Online or Print More Rebate Forms:
http://entertainment.cruises.com

1. Madame Tussauds – Hollywood, CA
2. Madame Tussauds – Las Vegas, NV
3. Madame Tussauds – Washington, DC
4. Madame Tussauds – New York, NY
5. LEGOLAND® California – Carlsbad, CA
6. SEA LIFE™ Aquarium – Carlsbad, CA
7. LEGOLAND Discovery Center – Chicago,

www.Madame-Tussauds.com

Receive 25% OFF adult and child ticket price when you present this offer at admissions. Offer is not valid on groups of 15 and over. Cannot be combined with other offers. Not valid for advance ticket purchases. Expires 12/31/10.

Codes: MTNY & MTDC 5340/5341
MTLV & MTH 6605

Madame Tussauds

MADAME TUSSAUDS IS A PART OF THE MERLIN ENTERTAINMENTS GROUP.

(760) 918-LEGO
www.LEGOLAND.com

Original coupon must be surrendered at time of purchase at a LEGOLAND® California Resort ticket booth to receive $5 off one-day admission for up to six. Cannot be combined with other discounts or offers. Restrictions apply. Expires 12/31/10.

10078

LEGOLAND.
CALIFORNIA

©2009 The LEGO Group. LEGOLAND® California IS A PART OF THE MERLIN ENTERTAINMENTS GROUP.

(866) 929-8111
www.LEGOLANDdiscoveryCenter.com

Original Coupon must be exchanged at the ticket booth at the time of purchase to receive $5 off up to six admissions. Valid only on the day of purchase at LEGOLAND Discovery Center Chicago. Offer cannot be applied to pre-purchased or online ticket sales, or combined with any other discounts or offers. No photocopies or facsimiles will be accepted. Additional restrictions may apply. Not for resale. Expires 12/31/10. Code: 1094

LEGOLAND.
Discovery Center
CHICAGO
SCHAUMBURG

©2009 The LEGO Group. LEGOLAND DISCOVERY Center IS A PART OF THE MERLIN ENTERTAINMENTS GROUP.

(760) 918-LEGO
www.SEALIFEUS.com

Original coupon must be surrendered at time of purchase at a LEGOLAND® California Resort ticket booth to receive 25% off one-day admission for up to six. Cannot be combined with other discounts or offers. Restrictions apply. Expires 12/31/10.

10077

AQUARIUM
SEA LIFE
LEGOLAND CALIFORNIA RESORT

SEA LIFE IS A PART OF THE MERLIN ENTERTAINMENTS GROUP.

Save on Great Amusement Park Thrills!

Cedar Fair parks bring you the ultimate in family excitement, including a total of 122 amazing coasters! From the sun-drenched fun of Knott's Berry Farm in California to the the world record-breaking roller coasters of Cedar Point to the family-pleasing children's areas at Kings Island, you'll experience the best in amusement park thrills!

For the best deal on a whole season of amusement park fun, and free parking, we recommend the Platinum Pass, valid at all Cedar Fair amusement parks and outdoor waterparks across North America.

For more information, visit cedarfair.com, or call the phone numbers on the reverse side. Cedar Fair is traded on the NYSE under the ticker symbol "FUN."

Cedar Fair
Entertainment Company

FUN From Coast to Coast

Cedar Fair
Entertainment Company™

Cedar Point®
Sandusky, OH • cedarpoint.com
(419) 627-2350

Knott's® Berry Farm
Buena Park, CA • knotts.com
(714) 220-5200

Kings Island®
Cincinnati, OH • visitkingsisland.com
(800) 333-8080

Canada's Wonderland®
Toronto, ON
canadaswonderland.com
(905) 832-8131

Kings Dominion®
Richmond, VA • kingsdominion.com
(804) 876-5561

California's Great America
Santa Clara, CA • cagreatamerica.com
(408) 988-1776

Carowinds®
Charlotte, NC • carowinds.com
(800) 888-4386

**Dorney Park® &
Wildwater Kingdom**
Allentown, PA • dorneypark.com
(610) 395-3724

Valleyfair®
Shakopee, MN • valleyfair.com
(952) 445-6500

Worlds of Fun®
Kansas City, MO • worldsoffun.com
(816) 454-4545

Michigan's Adventure®
Muskegon, MI • miadventure.com
(231) 766-3377

Please check
www.entertainment.com
for updated discounts
through the year!

One coupon per visit per table. Present this coupon at time of purchase to receive discount off your total purchase. Not valid with any other offers or discounts. Not refundable or redeemable for cash. Excludes tax and gratuity. Excludes alcohol in states where prohibited by law. Valid at participating Planet Hollywood locations.

planethollywood.com

Subject to Rules of Use. Coupons VOID if purchased, sold or bartered for cash.

One coupon per visit per table. Present this coupon at time of purchase to receive discount off your total purchase. Not valid with any other offers or discounts. Not refundable or redeemable for cash. Excludes tax and gratuity. Excludes alcohol in states where prohibited by law. Valid at participating Planet Hollywood locations.

planethollywood.com

Subject to Rules of Use. Coupons VOID if purchased, sold or bartered for cash.

OWN A TIMESHARE?

Sell it for CASH!

Timeshares Only connects timeshare buyers, sellers and renters worldwide.
FREE Info Kit - Call Today!

1-800-880-1323

Subject to Rules of Use. Not valid with other discount offers, unless specified. Coupons VOID if purchased, sold or bartered for cash.

Serving 33 airports in over 50 cities and surrounding communities

supershuttle.com   **execucar.com**

Subject to Rules of Use. Not valid with other discount offers, unless specified. Coupons VOID if purchased, sold or bartered for cash.

Buca
di BEPPO
Italian Restaurant

$10 *off*

ANY PURCHASE OF $20 OR MORE

VISIT BUCADIBEPPO.COM FOR LOCATIONS AND RESERVATIONS.

TRY *BUCA TO GO!*
Our entire menu is now available for take out.

Valid now thru November 1, 2010

See reverse side for details

H35

Buca
di BEPPO
Italian Restaurant

$10 *off*

ANY PURCHASE OF $20 OR MORE

VISIT BUCADIBEPPO.COM FOR LOCATIONS AND RESERVATIONS.

TRY *BUCA TO GO!*
Our entire menu is now available for take out.

Valid now thru November 1, 2010

See reverse side for details

H36

Buca
di BEPPO
Italian Restaurant

$10 *off*

ANY PURCHASE OF $20 OR MORE

VISIT BUCADIBEPPO.COM FOR LOCATIONS AND RESERVATIONS.

TRY *BUCA TO GO!*
Our entire menu is now available for take out.

Valid now thru November 1, 2010

See reverse side for details

H37

_____

Signature

One coupon per visit per table. Present this coupon at time of purchase to receive discount off your total purchase. Not valid with any other offers or discounts. Not refundable or redeemable for cash. Excludes tax, gratuity and purchase of gift cards. Excludes alcohol in states where prohibited by law. Valid for dine in or Buca To Go. **ENTPub$OFF**

Subject to Rules of Use. Coupons VOID if purchased, sold or bartered for cash.

_____

Signature

One coupon per visit per table. Present this coupon at time of purchase to receive discount off your total purchase. Not valid with any other offers or discounts. Not refundable or redeemable for cash. Excludes tax, gratuity and purchase of gift cards. Excludes alcohol in states where prohibited by law. Valid for dine in or Buca To Go. **ENTPub$OFF**

Subject to Rules of Use. Coupons VOID if purchased, sold or bartered for cash.

_____

Signature

One coupon per visit per table. Present this coupon at time of purchase to receive discount off your total purchase. Not valid with any other offers or discounts. Not refundable or redeemable for cash. Excludes tax, gratuity and purchase of gift cards. Excludes alcohol in states where prohibited by law. Valid for dine in or Buca To Go. **ENTPub$OFF**

Subject to Rules of Use. Coupons VOID if purchased, sold or bartered for cash.

Smart renters.
Big savings.

Save every time at the airport and right in your neighborhood with Budget's reusable offers!

$20 Off
a Weekly Rental
PLUS a Free Upgrade

Get up to 20% off plus an extra $20 off AND a free one-car group upgrade. Mention **BCD # X443000** and **CPN # MUGZ366**.

For reservations, visit **budget.com/entertainment** or call 1-888-724-6212.

Budget

Valid now thru June 30, 2011
See reverse side for details   H38

Free Day
of *where2*

Get up to 20% off plus a free day of a *where2* GPS. Mention **BCD # X443000** and **CPN # MUGZ371**.

For reservations, visit **budget.com/entertainment** or call 1-888-724-6212.

Budget

Valid now thru June 30, 2011
See reverse side for details   H39

$25 Off
a Weekly Rental

Get up to 20% off plus an extra $25 off when you rent a premium or above car. Mention **BCD # X443000** and **CPN # MUGZ367**.

For reservations, visit **budget.com/entertainment** or call 1-888-724-6212.

Budget

Valid now thru June 30, 2011
See reverse side for details   H40

$35 Off
a 10+ Day Rental

Get up to 20% off plus an extra $35 off a minimum ten consecutive day rental. Mention **BCD # X443000** and **CPN # MUGZ368**.

For reservations, visit **budget.com/entertainment** or call 1-888-724-6212.

Budget

Valid now thru June 30, 2011
See reverse side for details   H41

Get even more out of your travel with our great services, including:

 **where2**®

Audible turn-by-turn directions, the latest news, the nearest pizza place, real-time traffic reports* and so much more when you rent a *where2* GPS unit.

Budget flicks·to·go

Rent a portable DVD player when you rent a car from Budget.**

*Real-time traffic feature available in select cities.
**Budget rents DVD player only.

These services are optional and may be subject to availability at select locations for an additional fee.

 **Budget**

Terms and Conditions: Offer applies to one day free of the daily charges of a *where2* unit when rented for a minimum three consecutive days. The savings of up to 20% applies only to the time and mileage charges of the rental. Taxes, concession recovery fees, vehicle license recovery fee, customer facility charges ($10/contract in CA) may apply and are extra. Optional products such as LDW ($29.99/day or less, except in Louisiana $49.99/day) and refueling are extra. One coupon per rental. Offer valid at participating Budget airport and neighborhood locations in the contiguous U.S. and Canada. **An advance reservation is required.** Offer may not be available during holiday and other blackout periods. May not be used in conjunction with any other coupon, promotion or offer except your Entertainment* member discount. Renter must show proof of membership at time of rental. Offer subject to vehicle availability at the time of reservation and may not be available on some rates at some times. For reservations made on budget.com, free day of *where2* rental will be applied at time of rental. Renter must meet Budget age, driver and credit requirements. Minimum age may vary by location. An additional daily surcharge may apply for renters under 25 years old. **Rental must begin by 6/30/11.**

Budget features Ford and Lincoln Mercury vehicles.
©2009 Budget Rent A Car System, Inc.
A global system of corporate and licensee-owned locations.   17538

Subject to Rules of Use. Not valid with other discount offers, unless specified. Coupons VOID if purchased, sold or bartered for cash.

Terms and Conditions: Coupon valid on a compact (group B) through a full-size four-door (group E) car with a one-time, one-car group upgrade. Maximum upgrade to premium (group G). Dollars off applies to the time and mileage charges only on a minimum five consecutive day rental period. Taxes, concession recovery fees, vehicle license recovery fee, customer facility charges ($10/contract in CA) may apply and are extra. Optional products such as LDW ($29.99/day or less, except in Louisiana $49.99/day) and refueling are extra. Coupon must be surrendered at time of rental; one coupon per rental. **A 24-hour advance reservation is required.** May not be used in conjunction with any other coupon, promotion or offer except your Entertainment* member discount. Renter must show proof of membership at time of rental. The savings of up to 20% applies to the time and mileage charges only. Coupon valid at participating Budget airport and neighborhood locations in the contiguous U.S., Canada and New Zealand. Offer subject to vehicle availability at time of reservation and may not be available on some rates at some times. The upgraded car is subject to vehicle availability at the time of rental and may not be available on some rates at some times. For reservations made on budget.com, dollars off and upgrade will be applied at time of rental. Renter must meet Budget age, driver and credit requirements. Minimum age may vary by location. An additional daily surcharge may apply for renters under 25 years old. Fuel charges are extra. **Rental must begin by 6/30/11.**

Budget features Ford and Lincoln Mercury vehicles.
©2009 Budget Rent A Car System, Inc.
A global system of corporate and licensee-owned locations.   17538

Subject to Rules of Use. Not valid with other discount offers, unless specified. Coupons VOID if purchased, sold or bartered for cash.

Terms and Conditions: Coupon valid on a compact (group B) and higher car, excluding groups S and X. Dollars off applies to the time and mileage charges only on a minimum ten consecutive day rental period. Taxes, concession recovery fees, vehicle license recovery fee, customer facility charges ($10/contract in CA) may apply and are extra. Optional products such as LDW ($29.99/day or less, except in Louisiana $49.99/day) and refueling are extra. One coupon per rental. **An advance reservation is required.** May not be used in conjunction with any other coupon, promotion or offer except your Entertainment* member discount. Renter must show proof of membership at time of rental. The savings of up to 20% applies to the time and mileage charges only. Coupon valid at participating Budget airport and neighborhood locations in the contiguous U.S., Canada and New Zealand. Offer subject to vehicle availability at time of reservation and may not be available on some rates at some times. For reservations made on budget.com, dollars off will be applied at time of rental. Renter must meet Budget age, driver and credit requirements. Minimum age may vary by location. An additional daily surcharge may apply for renters under 25 years old. **Rental must begin by 6/30/11.**

Budget features Ford and Lincoln Mercury vehicles.
©2009 Budget Rent A Car System, Inc.
A global system of corporate and licensee-owned locations.   17538

Subject to Rules of Use. Not valid with other discount offers, unless specified. Coupons VOID if purchased, sold or bartered for cash.

Terms and Conditions: Coupon valid on a premium (group G) and above car, excluding groups S and X. Dollars off applies to the time and mileage charges only on a minimum five consecutive day rental period. Taxes, concession recovery fees, vehicle license recovery fee, customer facility charges ($10/contract in CA) may apply and are extra. Optional products such as LDW ($29.99/day or less, except in Louisiana $49.99/day) and refueling are extra. One coupon per rental. **An advance reservation is required.** May not be used in conjunction with any other coupon, promotion or offer except your Entertainment* member discount. Renter must show proof of membership at time of rental. The savings of up to 20% applies to the time and mileage charges only. Coupon valid at participating Budget airport and neighborhood locations in the contiguous U.S., Canada and New Zealand. Offer subject to vehicle availability at time of reservation and may not be available on some rates at some times. For reservations made on budget.com, dollars off will be applied at time of rental. Renter must meet Budget age, driver and credit requirements. Minimum age may vary by location. An additional daily surcharge may apply for renters under 25 years old. **Rental must begin by 6/30/11.**

Budget features Ford and Lincoln Mercury vehicles.
©2009 Budget Rent A Car System, Inc.
A global system of corporate and licensee-owned locations.   17538

Subject to Rules of Use. Not valid with other discount offers, unless specified. Coupons VOID if purchased, sold or bartered for cash.

$40 Off
a Weekly Rental

Get up to 20% off plus an extra $40 off convertibles, premium SUVs and full-size SUVs. Mention **BCD # X443000** and **CPN # MUGZ369**.

For reservations, visit **budget.com/entertainment** or call 1-888-724-6212.

Valid now thru June 30, 2011
See reverse side for details   H42

$75 Off
a Long-Term Rental

Get up to 20% off plus an extra $75 off a minimum 30-day rental. Mention **BCD # X443000** and **CPN # MUGZ370**.

For reservations, visit **budget.com/entertainment** or call 1-888-724-6212.

Valid now thru June 30, 2011
See reverse side for details   H43

Up to 10% Off
International Rentals

Get up to 10% off rentals in Latin America, the Caribbean, Mexico, Europe, the Middle East, Africa, Asia, Australia and New Zealand. Mention **BCD # X443000**.

For reservations, visit **budget.com/entertainment** or call 1-888-724-6212.

Valid now thru June 30, 2011
See reverse side for details   H44

$20 Off
a Weekly Rental

Get up to 20% off plus an extra $20 off when you rent a compact or above car. Mention **BCD # X443000** and **CPN # MUGZ365**.

For reservations, visit **budget.com/entertainment** or call 1-888-724-6212.

Valid now thru June 30, 2011
See reverse side for details   H45

Free
Weekend Day

Get up to 20% off plus your third weekend day free. Mention **BCD # X443000** and **CPN # TUGZ129**.

For reservations, visit **budget.com/entertainment** or call 1-888-724-6212.

Valid now thru June 30, 2011
See reverse side for details   H46

Free
Single Upgrade

Get up to 20% off plus a free one-car group upgrade. Mention **BCD # X443000** and **CPN # UUGZ032**.

For reservations, visit **budget.com/entertainment** or call 1-888-724-6212.

Valid now thru June 30, 2011
See reverse side for details   H47

Terms and Conditions: Coupon valid for $75 off a monthly or mini-lease rental at participating Budget airport and neighborhood locations in the contiguous U.S., Canada and New Zealand. Offer applies to a minimum 30-day rental period of an intermediate (group C) or above car, excluding groups S and X. Offer applies to the time and mileage charges on the first month of a minimum 30 and maximum 330 consecutive day rental. Taxes, concession recovery fees, vehicle license recovery fee, customer facility charges ($10/contract in CA) may apply and are extra. Optional products such as LDW ($29.99/day or less, except in Louisiana $49.99/day) and refueling are extra. One coupon per rental period. **An advance reservation is required.** Offer is subject to vehicle availability at time of reservation and may not be available on some rates at some times. For reservations made on **budget.com**, dollars off will be applied at time of rental. May not be used in conjunction with any other coupon, promotion or offer except your Entertainment® member discount. Renter must show proof of membership at time of rental. The savings of up to 20% applies to the time and mileage charges only. Renter must meet Budget age, driver and credit requirements. Minimum age may vary by location. An additional daily surcharge may apply for renters under 25 years old. **Rental must begin by 6/30/11.**

Terms and Conditions: Coupon valid on a convertible (group K), premium SUV (group L) or full-size SUV (group Z). Dollars off applies to the time and mileage charges only on a minimum five consecutive day rental period. Taxes, concession recovery fees, vehicle license recovery fee, customer facility charges ($10/contract in CA) may apply and are extra. Optional products such as LDW ($29.99/day or less, except in Louisiana $49.99/day) and refueling are extra. One coupon per rental. **An advance reservation is required.** May not be used in conjunction with any other coupon, promotion or offer except your Entertainment® member discount. Renter must show proof of membership at time of rental. The savings of up to 20% applies to the time and mileage charges only. Coupon valid at participating Budget locations in the contiguous U.S. and Canada. Offer subject to vehicle availability at time of reservation and may not be available on some rates at some times. For reservations made on **budget.com**, dollars off will be applied at time of rental. Renter must meet Budget age, driver and credit requirements. Minimum age may vary by location. An additional daily surcharge may apply for renters under 25 years old. **Rental must begin by 6/30/11.**

Terms and Conditions: Coupon valid on a compact (group B) or above car, excluding groups S and X. Dollars off applies to the time and mileage charges only on a minimum five consecutive day rental period. Taxes, concession recovery fees, vehicle license recovery fee, customer facility charges ($10/contract in CA) may apply and are extra. Optional products such as LDW ($29.99/day or less, except in Louisiana $49.99/day) and refueling are extra. One coupon per rental. **An advance reservation is required.** May not be used in conjunction with any other coupon, promotion or offer except your Entertainment® member discount. Renter must show proof of membership at time of rental. The savings of up to 20% applies to the time and mileage charges only. Coupon valid at participating Budget airport and neighborhood locations in the contiguous U.S., Canada and New Zealand. Offer subject to vehicle availability at time of reservation and may not be available on some rates at some times. For reservations made on **budget.com**, dollars off will be applied at time of rental. Renter must meet Budget age, driver and credit requirements. Minimum age may vary by location. An additional daily surcharge may apply for renters under 25 years old. **Rental must begin by 6/30/11.**

Terms and Conditions: To take advantage of this offer, **Budget Corporate Discount (BCD) X443000** must be used at time of reservation. Offer is available for U.S. and Canadian residents only at participating locations in Latin America, the Caribbean, Mexico, Europe, the Middle East, Africa, Asia, Australia and New Zealand. Taxes, optional items and other surcharges may apply. Renter must meet Budget age, driver and credit requirements. Minimum age may vary by location. An additional daily surcharge may apply for renters under 25 years old. Offer cannot be used in conjunction with any other promotional offer or discount except your Entertainment® member discount. Renter must show proof of membership at time of rental. The savings of up to 10% applies to the time and mileage charges only. Offer is subject to availability and subject to change without notice. Europe, the Middle East, Africa and Asia blackout dates: 4/4/09–4/13/09, 12/18/09–1/3/10, 3/5/10–4/5/10, 12/17/10–1/2/11, 4/16/11–4/25/11. **Rental must begin by 6/30/11.**

Terms and Conditions: Coupon valid for a one-time, one-car group upgrade on a compact (group B) through a full-size four-door (group E) car. Maximum upgrade to premium (group G). The upgraded car is subject to vehicle availability at the time of rental and may not be available on some rates at some times. Coupon valid at participating Budget airport and neighborhood locations in the contiguous U.S., Canada and New Zealand. One coupon per rental. **A 24-hour advance reservation is required.** May not be used in conjunction with any other coupon, promotion or offer except your Entertainment® member discount. Renter must show proof of membership at time of rental. The savings of up to 20% applies to the time and mileage charges only. For reservations made on budget.com, upgrade will be applied at time of rental. Renter must meet Budget age, driver and credit requirements. Minimum age may vary by location. An additional daily surcharge may apply for renters under 25 years old. Fuel charges are extra. **Rental must begin by 6/30/11.**

Terms and Conditions: Offer of one weekend day free applies to the time and mileage charges only of the third consecutive day of a minimum three-day weekend rental on a compact (group B) through a full-size four-door (group E) car. Taxes, concession recovery fees, vehicle license recovery fee, customer facility charges ($10/contract in CA) may apply and are extra. Optional products such as LDW ($29.99/day or less, except in Louisiana $49.99/day) and refueling are extra. Weekend rental period begins noon Thursday, and car must be returned by Monday 11:59 p.m. or a higher rate will apply. A Saturday night keep is required. Coupon cannot be used for one-way rentals; one coupon per rental. Offer may not be used in conjunction with any other coupon, promotion or offer except your Entertainment® member discount. Renter must show proof of membership at time of rental. The savings of up to 20% applies to the time and mileage charges only. Coupon valid at participating Budget airport and neighborhood locations in the contiguous U.S. (excluding the New York Metro area) and Canada. **An advance reservation is required.** Offer may not be available during holiday and other blackout periods. Offer is subject to vehicle availability at the time of reservation and may not be available on some rates at some times. For reservations made on **budget.com**, free day will be applied at time of rental. Renter must meet Budget age, driver and credit requirements. Minimum age may vary by location. An additional daily surcharge may apply for renters under 25 years old. **Rental must begin by 6/30/11.**

REUSABLE SAVINGS
AT THE AIRPORT
AND IN YOUR NEIGHBORHOOD

 AVIS We try harder.

$25 OFF
A WEEKLY RENTAL

Enjoy up to 25% off plus an extra discount of $25 when you rent an intermediate car or above. Mention **AWD # B790000** and **CPN # MUGA225**.

For reservations, visit
avis.com/entertainment
or call 1-800-245-8572.

Valid now thru June 30, 2011
See reverse side for details   H48

 AVIS We try harder.

$30 OFF
A WEEKLY RENTAL

Enjoy up to 25% off plus an extra discount of $30 when you rent a premium car or above. Mention **AWD # B790000** and **CPN # MUGA226**.

For reservations, visit
avis.com/entertainment
or call 1-800-245-8572.

Valid now thru June 30, 2011
See reverse side for details   H49

 AVIS We try harder.

$40 OFF
A WEEKLY RENTAL

Enjoy up to 25% off plus an extra discount of $40 when you rent a convertible, a premium SUV or full-size SUV. Mention **AWD # B790000** and **CPN # MUGA227**.

For reservations, visit
avis.com/entertainment
or call 1-800-245-8572.

Valid now thru June 30, 2011
See reverse side for details   H50

 **AVIS** We try harder.

FREE DAY OF
where2 ®

Enjoy up to 25% off plus a free day of a *where2* GPS. Mention **AWD # B790000** and **CPN # MUGA230**.

For reservations, visit
avis.com/entertainment
or call 1-800-245-8572.

Valid now thru June 30, 2011
See reverse side for details   H51

Plus, enjoy the ride with our premium services:

Avoid traffic*, find a florist, make dinner reservations with hands free calling, and much more when you re a where2 GPS unit.

Bring along your favorite movies and stay entertaine on long drives with a portable DVD rental.**

*Real-time traffic feature available in select cities.
**Avis rents DVD player only.

These services are optional and may be subject to availability at select locations for an additional fee.

AVIS *We try harder.*

$75 OFF
A LONG-TERM RENTAL

Enjoy up to 25% off plus an extra discount of $75 when you rent for at least 30 days. Mention **AWD # B790000** and **CPN # MUGA229**.

For reservations, visit
avis.com/entertainment
or call 1-800-245-8572.

Valid now thru June 30, 2011
See reverse side for details   H52

 **AVIS** *We try harder.*

UP TO 30% OFF
INTERNATIONAL RENTALS

Enjoy up to 30% off rentals in Europe, the Middle East, Africa, Asia, Latin America, the Caribbean, Mexico, Australia and New Zealand. Mention **AWD # B790000**.

For reservations, visit
avis.com/entertainment
or call 1-800-245-8572.

Valid now thru June 30, 2011
See reverse side for details   H53

 AVIS *We try harder.*

$40 OFF
A 10-DAY RENTAL

Enjoy up to 25% off plus an extra discount of $40 when you rent for a minimum of ten consecutive days. Mention **AWD # B790000** and **CPN # MUGA228**.

For reservations, visit
avis.com/entertainment
or call 1-800-245-8572.

Valid now thru June 30, 2011
See reverse side for details   H54

 AVIS *We try harder.*

FREE WEEKEND DAY

Enjoy up to 25% off plus your third weekend day free. Mention **AWD # B790000** and **CPN # TUGA136**.

For reservations, visit
avis.com/entertainment
or call 1-800-245-8572.

Valid now thru June 30, 2011
See reverse side for details   H55

 AVIS *We try harder.*

THIRD RENTAL DAY FREE

Enjoy up to 25% off plus your third rental day free. Mention **AWD # B790000** and **CPN # TUGA137**.

For reservations, visit
avis.com/entertainment
or call 1-800-245-8572.

Valid now thru June 30, 2011
See reverse side for details   H56

 **AVIS** *We try harder.*

FREE SINGLE UPGRADE

Enjoy up to 25% off plus a free one-car group upgrade. Mention **AWD # B790000** and **CPN # UUGA001**.

For reservations, visit
avis.com/entertainment
or call 1-800-245-8572.

Valid now thru June 30, 2011
See reverse side for details   H57

Terms and Conditions: To take advantage of this offer, **Avis Worldwide Discount number (AWD) B790000** must be used at time of reservation. Offer is available for U.S. and Canadian residents only at participating locations in Europe, the Middle East, Africa, Asia, Latin America, the Caribbean, Mexico, Australia and New Zealand. Taxes, optional items and other surcharges may apply. Renter must meet Avis age, driver and credit requirements. Minimum age may vary by location. An additional daily surcharge may apply for renters under 25 years old. Offer cannot be used in conjunction with any other promotional offer, discount or AWD except your Entertainment® member discount. Renter must show proof of membership at time of rental. The savings of up to 30% applies to the time and mileage charges only. Offer is subject to availability and subject to change without notice. Europe, Middle East, Africa and Asia blackout dates: 12/18/09–1/4/10, 3/27/10–4/11/10. Australia blackout dates: 9/1/09–6/1/10, 12/18/09–1/4/10, 3/27/10–4/11/10. **Rental must begin by 6/30/11.**

Avis features GM vehicles.
©2009 Avis Rent A Car System, LLC   17537

Subject to Rules of Use. Not valid with other discount offers, unless specified. Coupons VOID if purchased, sold or bartered for cash.

Terms and Conditions: Coupon valid for $75 off a monthly or mini-lease rental at participating Avis airport and neighborhood locations in the contiguous U.S., Canada and New Zealand. Offer applies to a minimum 30-day rental period of an intermediate (group C) or above car, excluding groups S and X. Offer applies to the time and mileage charges on the first month of a minimum 30 and maximum 330 consecutive day rental. Taxes, concession recovery fees, vehicle license recovery fee, customer facility charges ($10/contract in CA) may apply and are extra. Optional products such as LDW ($29.99/day or less, except in Louisiana $49.99/day) and refueling are extra. One coupon per rental period. **An advance reservation is required.** Offer is subject to vehicle availability at time of reservation and may not be available on some rates at some times. For reservations made on **avis.com**, dollars off will be applied at time of rental. May not be used in conjunction with any other coupon, promotion or offer except your Entertainment® member discount. Renter must show proof of membership at time of rental. The savings of up to 25% applies to the time and mileage charges only. Renter must meet Avis age, driver and credit requirements. Minimum age may vary by location. An additional daily surcharge may apply for renters under 25 years old. **Rental must begin by 6/30/11.**

Avis features GM vehicles.
©2009 Avis Rent A Car System, LLC   17537

Subject to Rules of Use. Not valid with other discount offers, unless specified. Coupons VOID if purchased, sold or bartered for cash.

Terms and Conditions: Offer of one weekend day free applies to the time and mileage charges only of the third consecutive day of a minimum three-day weekend rental on an intermediate (group C) through a full-size four-door (group E) car. Taxes, concession recovery fees, vehicle license recovery fee, customer facility charges ($10/contract in CA) may apply and are extra. Optional products such as LDW ($29.99/day or less, except in Louisiana $49.99/day) and refueling are extra. Weekend rental period begins Thursday, and car must be returned by Monday 11:59 p.m. or a higher rate will apply. A Saturday night keep is required. Coupon cannot be used for one-way rentals; one coupon per rental. Offer may not be used in conjunction with any other coupon, promotion or offer except your Entertainment® member discount. Renter must show proof of membership at time of rental. The savings of up to 25% applies to the time and mileage charges only. Coupon valid at participating Avis airport and neighborhood locations in the contiguous U.S. and Canada (excluding the New York Metro area). **An advance reservation is required.** Offer may not be available during holiday and other blackout periods. Offer is subject to vehicle availability at the time of reservation and may not be available on some rates at some times. For reservations made on **avis.com**, free day will be applied at time of rental. Renter must meet Avis age, driver and credit requirements. Minimum age may vary by location. An additional daily surcharge may apply for renters under 25 years old. **Rental must begin by 6/30/11.**

Avis features GM vehicles.
©2009 Avis Rent A Car System, LLC   17537

Subject to Rules of Use. Not valid with other discount offers, unless specified. Coupons VOID if purchased, sold or bartered for cash.

Terms and Conditions: Coupon valid on an intermediate (group C) and above car, excluding groups S and X. Dollars off applies to the time and mileage charges only on a minimum ten consecutive day rental period. Taxes, concession recovery fees, vehicle license recovery fee, customer facility charges ($10/contract in CA) may apply and are extra. Optional products such as LDW ($29.99/day or less, except in Louisiana $49.99/day) and refueling are extra. One coupon per rental. **An advance reservation is required.** May not be used in conjunction with any other coupon, promotion or offer except your Entertainment® member discount. Renter must show proof of membership at time of rental. The savings of up to 25% applies to the time and mileage charges only. Coupon valid at participating Avis airport and neighborhood locations in the contiguous U.S., Canada, Australia and New Zealand. Offer subject to vehicle availability at time of reservation and may not be available on some rates at some times. For reservations made on **avis.com**, dollars off will be applied at time of rental. Renter must meet Avis age, driver and credit requirements. Minimum age may vary by location. An additional daily surcharge may apply for renters under 25 years old. **Rental must begin by 6/30/11.**

Avis features GM vehicles.
©2009 Avis Rent A Car System, LLC   17537

Subject to Rules of Use. Not valid with other discount offers, unless specified. Coupons VOID if purchased, sold or bartered for cash.

Terms and Conditions: Coupon valid for a one-time, one-car group upgrade on an intermediate (group C) through a full-size four-door (group E) car. Maximum upgrade to premium (group G). The upgraded car is subject to vehicle availability at the time of rental and may not be available on some rates at some times. Coupon valid at participating Avis airport and neighborhood locations in the contiguous U.S., Canada, Australia and New Zealand. One coupon per rental. **A 24-hour advance reservation is required.** May not be used in conjunction with any other coupon, promotion or offer except your Entertainment® member discount. Renter must show proof of membership at time of rental. The savings of up to 25% applies to the time and mileage charges only. For reservations made on **avis.com**, upgrade will be applied at time of rental. Renter must meet Avis age, driver and credit requirements. Minimum age may vary by location. An additional daily surcharge may apply for renters under 25 years old. Fuel charges are extra. **Rental must begin by 6/30/11.**

Avis features GM vehicles.
©2009 Avis Rent A Car System, LLC   17537

Subject to Rules of Use. Not valid with other discount offers, unless specified. Coupons VOID if purchased, sold or bartered for cash.

Terms and Conditions: Offer of one day free applies to the time and mileage charges only of the third consecutive day of a minimum three consecutive day rental on an intermediate (group C) through full-size four-door (group E) car. A Saturday night keep is required. The savings of up to 25% applies to the time and mileage charges only. Taxes, concession recovery fees, vehicle license recovery fee, customer facility charges ($10/contract in CA) may apply and are extra. Optional products such as LDW ($29.99/day or less, except in Louisiana $49.99/day) and refueling are extra. Coupon cannot be used for one-way rentals; one coupon per rental. Offer may not be used in conjunction with any other coupon, promotion or offer except your Entertainment® member discount. Renter must show proof of membership at time of rental. The savings of up to 25% applies to the time and mileage charges only. Offer valid at participating Avis airport and neighborhood locations in the contiguous U.S. (excluding the New York Metro area) and Canada. **An advance reservation is required.** Offer may not be available during holiday and other blackout periods. Offer subject to vehicle availability at the time of reservation and may not be available on some rates at some times. For reservations made on **avis.com**, free day will be applied at time of rental. Renter must meet Avis age, driver and credit requirements. Minimum age may vary by location. An additional daily surcharge may apply for renters under 25 years old. **Rental must begin by 6/30/11.**

Avis features GM vehicles.
©2009 Avis Rent A Car System, LLC   17537

Subject to Rules of Use. Not valid with other discount offers, unless specified. Coupons VOID if purchased, sold or bartered for cash.

The Road Calls,
And So Do The Savings.

Spend a few minutes clipping these coupons
and you'll spend less money on your next rental.

**Find more savings from Enterprise
at entertainment.com/enterprise.**

We'll pick you up.

10% OFF
Standard Daily Rates!

We'll pick you up.

enterprise.com/ent10 • 1 888 446-9952
Reference customer # ENT10DG

Must present original coupon at time of rental.
Valid now thru June 30, 2011
See reverse side for details   H58

10% OFF
Weekly Rates!

We'll pick you up.

enterprise.com/ent10 • 1 888 446-9952
Reference customer # ENT10WG

Must present original coupon at time of rental.
Valid now thru June 30, 2011
See reverse side for details   H59

Great Cars. Low Rates. Free Pick-up.

- Economy to luxury cars, minivans, trucks and more
- Everyday low rates, plus weekend and holiday specials
- Free pick-up and return to/from your home, office or repair shop
- 24-hour roadside assistance
- More than 6,500 locations, including all major airports
- Largest fuel-efficient rental fleet*

Find more savings from Enterprise at entertainment.com/enterprise.

We'll pick you up.

*Based on 334,000 cars in North America with an EPA highway fuel efficiency of 28 MPG or better. Pick-up and drop-off service is subject to geographic and other restrictions. ©2009 Enterprise Rent-A-Car Company

Free Weekend Day.

FYI: Offer valid for one 24-hour day's rate on advance reservations for a Full Size or smaller car. Valid at participating North American neighborhood locations only for rentals ending on or before June 30, 2011. A three-day minimum rental that includes one Saturday night is required. Up to two additional days may be added at standard daily rates. Not valid at airport locations. Rates are as posted at time of reservation at enterprise.com/ent10 or by calling 1 888 466-9952 and referencing customer number ENTFWDG. Credit applies to the standard weekend rental rate only. Offer does not apply to taxes, surcharges, excess mileage fees, vehicle licensing fees and optional products and services, including damage waiver at $30 or less per day and additional driver fees. In the USA, check your auto policy and/or credit card agreement for rental vehicle coverage. **Original coupon must be redeemed at the time of rental** and may not be used in conjunction with any other coupon, offer or discounted rate, including weekend special rates. Vehicles are subject to availability. Other restrictions, including holiday and blackout dates, may apply. Normal rental qualifications apply. Pick-up and drop-off services are subject to geographic and other restrictions. Void where prohibited. Cash value: 1/100¢.

15% Off Daily Or Weekly Household Truck Rentals.

FYI: Discount applies to daily and weekly rates for trucks at a participating Enterprise Commercial Trucks location in your area. Rates are as posted at time of reservation by calling 1 888 541-2950. Valid for rentals starting on or after July 1, 2009, and ending by June 30, 2011. A 30-day maximum rental applies. Offer applies to time and mileage rates only and does not apply to taxes or surcharges, excess mileage fees, recovery fees and optional products and services such as damage waiver and refueling fees. **Original coupon must be redeemed at the time of rental** and may not be used with any other coupon, offer or discounted rate. Standard rental qualifications apply. Vehicles subject to availability. Other restrictions may apply. Void where prohibited. Cash value: 1/100¢.

Car Buying Offer.

FYI: $200 gas card will be issued within 30 business days upon purchase (or financing) of vehicle. Offer valid only on Enterprise vehicles purchased through 6/30/11. Offer void when 7-Day Repurchase Agreement is activated. No cash advances. Cannot be combined with any other offers. Not valid on previous purchases. **Offer not available in CA, LA, OR, WV, KS, KY, OH, OK, TX and VA or other states where prohibited by law.** This coupon must be presented at time of sale to redeem the offer. **Enterprise Account Executive, please source to: EBO7799.**

The "e" logo, Enterprise, and "Haggle-free buying. Worry-free ownership." are trademarks of the Enterprise Rent-A-Car Company.

All other trademarks are the property of their respective owners.
©2009 Enterprise Rent-A-Car-Company.

MORE FOR YOUR MONEY
SAVE UP TO 25%
AND USE THE COUPONS BELOW TO SAVE EVEN MORE.

Book your rental at Alamo.com/offer/ent10 or call 1-800-237-0984.
Then all you have to do is remember to bring your coupons, and remember this
CONTRACT ID: 7014777. IT WILL SAVE YOU UP TO 25%.
Get more great coupons at entertainment.com/alamo.

SELF-SERVICE KIOSK

- Skip the rental counter
- Check in at the kiosk
- Choose your car
- Then go, go, go

FOUR MORE
WAYS TO SAVE.

Book your rental at Alamo.com/offer/ent10 or call 1-800-237-0984.
Then all you have to do is remember to bring your coupons, and remember this
CONTRACT ID: 7014777. IT WILL SAVE YOU UP TO 25%.
Get more great coupons at entertainment.com/alamo.

$25 OFF
ANY SPECIALTY RENTAL
(3-day minimum, Saturday
night required)

Contract ID: 7014777
Coupon Code: AD8876FJG

Valid now thru June 30, 2011
See reverse side for details   H65

$15 OFF
ANY RENTAL
(3-day minimum, Saturday
night required)

Contract ID: 7014777
Coupon Code: AD8854FJB

Valid now thru June 30, 2011
See reverse side for details   H66

$10 OFF
ANY RENTAL
(2-day minimum, Saturday
night required)

Contract ID: 7014777
Coupon Code: AD8881FJB

Valid now thru June 30, 2011
See reverse side for details   H67

FREE
WEEKEND DAY
(3-day minimum, Saturday
night required)

Contract ID: 7014777
Coupon Code: AF2262FJV

Valid now thru June 30, 2011
See reverse side for details   H68

THE DEALS
DON'T STOP HERE.

Get more great coupons at
entertainment.com/alamo.

"A good deal just got a good deal better."

Combine a discount of up to **25% off** with any of these coupons!
Use Contract ID: 5027958

Book online today at nationalcar.com/offer/ent10 or 1-888-575-6279.
For additional coupons, visit www.entertainment.com/national.

"Your membership awaits."

Register for your complimentary **Emerald Club** membership today at **nationalcar.com** and start enjoying all the benefits of membership today:

- Bypass the counter and choose your own car
- Enjoy special tiered benefits
- Receive speedy and automatic e-receipts
- Choose your rewards
- Access one-click reservations and expedited service
- Register additional drivers for no fee

National, the "flag" and Emerald Club are trademarks of Vanguard Trademark Holdings USA LLC. The choose your own car feature is available at select locations only and subject to The Emerald Club membership terms and conditions. The Emerald Club and its services require a signed Master Rental Agreement on file. ©2009 Vanguard Car Rental USA Inc. All rights reserved.

"Go like a Pro.
Save like one, too."

Combine a discount of up to **25% off** with any of these coupons!
Use Contract ID: 5027958

Book online today at nationalcar.com/offer/ent10 or 1-888-575-6279.
For additional coupons, visit www.entertainment.com/national.

$20 OFF
Weekend Rental
Use Coupon ID: ND1317FJY
Three-day minimum rental that
includes a Saturday night.

Valid now thru June 30, 2011
See reverse side for details   **H71**

$40 OFF
a 10-Day Rental
Use Coupon ID: ND1283FJA
Ten-day minimum rental.

Valid now thru June 30, 2011
See reverse side for details   **H72**

FREE DAY
w/5-Day Rental
that includes a Saturday night.
Use Coupon ID: NF6197FJD

Valid now thru June 30, 2011
See reverse side for details   **H73**

$20 OFF
Weekly Rental
Use Coupon ID: ND1294FJV
Five-day minimum rental that
includes a Saturday night.

Valid now thru June 30, 2011
See reverse side for details   **H74**

40 Dollars Off:

Rent a compact or larger size vehicle for a minimum of 10 days. Valid through June 30, 2011. One coupon per National rental and void once redeemed. Discount applies to base rate, which does not include taxes (including GST/VAT), other governmentally-authorized or imposed surcharges, license recoupment/air tax recovery and concession recoupment fees, airport and airport facility fees, fuel, additional driver fee, one-way rental charge, or optional items. Offer is subject to standard rental conditions. Blackout dates may apply. 24-Hour advance reservation required. Not valid with any other discount or promotional rate, except your Entertainment® discount. Subject to availability and valid only at participating U.S. and Canadian locations. Some countries may convert coupon value into local currency. Coupon VOID if bought, bartered or sold for cash. Void where prohibited.

Must present original coupon at time of rental.

20 Dollars Off Weekend:

Rent a compact or larger size vehicle through June 30, 2011. Three (3) day minimum, five (5) day maximum with Saturday night keep required. One coupon per National rental and void once redeemed. Discount applies to base rate, which does not include taxes (including GST/VAT), other governmentally-authorized or imposed surcharges, license recoupment/air tax recovery and concession recoupment fees, airport and airport facility fees, fuel, additional driver fee, one-way rental charge, or optional items. Offer is subject to standard rental conditions. Blackout dates may apply. 24-hour advance reservation required. Not valid with any other discount or promotional rate, except your Entertainment® discount. Subject to availability and valid only at participating U.S. and Canadian locations. Some countries may convert coupon value into local currency. Coupon VOID if bought, bartered or sold for cash. Void where prohibited.

Must present original coupon at time of rental.

20 Dollars Off:

Rent a compact or larger size vehicle for a minimum of five (5) days. Valid through June 30, 2011. One coupon per National rental and void once redeemed. Discount applies to base rate, which does not include taxes (including GST/VAT), other governmentally-authorized or imposed surcharges, license recoupment/air tax recovery and concession recoupment fees, airport and airport facility fees, fuel, additional driver fee, one-way rental charge, or optional items. Offer is subject to standard rental conditions. Blackout dates may apply. 24-hour advance reservation required. Not valid with any other discount or promotional rate, except your Entertainment® discount. Subject to availability and valid only at participating U.S. and Canadian locations. Some countries may convert coupon value into local currency. Coupon VOID if bought, bartered or sold for cash. Void where prohibited.

Must present original coupon at time of rental.

Free Day:

Valid for compact or larger vehicle through June 30, 2011, with a five (5) day minimum rental. One coupon per National rental and void once redeemed. Free day is prorated against base rate for entire rental period, which does not include taxes, other governmentally-authorized or imposed surcharges, license recoupment/air tax recovery and concession recoupment fees, airport and airport facility fees, fuel, additional driver fee, one-way rental charge, or optional items. Offer is subject to standard rental conditions. Blackout dates may apply. 24-hour advance reservation required. Not valid with any other discount or promotional rate, except your Entertainment® discount. Subject to availability and valid only at participating U.S. and Canadian locations. Some countries may convert coupon value into local currency. Offer not valid in Manhattan, N.Y. Coupon VOID if bought, bartered or sold for cash. Void where prohibited.

Must present original coupon at time of rental.

Say "Entertainment®" and save 2 ways with Hertz.

Automatic Discounts.
Partner Offers.

Visit www.hertz.com/entertainment for special value offers.

$20 Off

WEEKLY RENTALS OF ANY CAR CLASS

Go to hertz.com for low web rates.
Enter your rental location, rental dates and arrival information.
Check: I have a discount (CDP, PC, Coupon or other code)
Enter CDP# **ENTERTAINMENT (or 205521)** and PC# 116196

For phone reservations:
Call 1-888-999-7125
or call your travel agent.

Valid now thru June 30, 2011
See reverse side for details   H75

Save Up to $15

WEEKEND RENTALS OF ANY CAR CLASS
$5 a Day, Up to $15 off

Go to hertz.com for low web rates.
Enter your rental location, rental dates and arrival information.
Check: I have a discount (CDP, PC, Coupon or other code)
Enter CDP# **ENTERTAINMENT (or 205521)** and PC# 116200

For phone reservations:
Call 1-888-999-7125
or call your travel agent.

Valid now thru June 30, 2011
See reverse side for details   H76

Save Up to $20

WEEKEND RENTALS OF PREMIUM AND HIGHER CAR CLASSES
$5 a Day, Up to $20 off

Go to hertz.com for low web rates.
Enter your rental location, rental dates and arrival information.
Check: I have a discount (CDP, PC, Coupon or other code)
Enter CDP# **ENTERTAINMENT (or 205521)** and PC# 116185

For phone reservations:
Call 1-888-999-7125
or call your travel agent.

Valid now thru June 30, 2011
See reverse side for details   H77

$30 Off Weekly

HERTZ FUN COLLECTION
HERTZ GREEN COLLECTION
HERTZ PRESTIGE COLLECTION

Go to hertz.com for low web rates.
Enter your rental location, rental dates and arrival information.
Check: I have a discount (CDP, PC, Coupon or other code)
Enter CDP# **ENTERTAINMENT (or 205521)** and PC# 116163

For phone reservations:
Call 1-888-999-7125
or call your travel agent.

Valid now thru June 30, 2011
See reverse side for details   H78

Join Hertz #1 Club®.

Enjoy faster rentals.
Earn Hertz #1 Awards®.
Earn and redeem points for free rental day and weekend certificates.
Visit www.hertz.com/entertainment for more special offers.

Mention offer PC# 116200 and CDP# ENTERTAINMENT

When calling your travel agent, mention CDP# 205521.

Advance reservations required as blackout periods may apply. Subject to availability, this offer is redeemable at participating Hertz locations in the U.S., Canada and Puerto Rico. This offer has no cash value, may not be used with Pre-pay Rates, Tour Rates or Insurance Replacement Rates and cannot be combined with any other certificate, voucher, offer or promotion. Hertz age, driver, credit and weekend rate qualifications for the renting location apply. Taxes, tax reimbursement, age differential charges, fees and optional service charges, such as refueling, are not included. Discounts apply to time and mileage charges only. Discounts in local currency on redemption. Offer valid for vehicle pickup through 6-30-11.

Subject to Rules of Use. Not valid with other discount offers, unless specified. Coupons VOID if purchased, sold or bartered for cash.

Mention offer PC# 116196 and CDP# ENTERTAINMENT

When calling your travel agent, mention CDP# 205521.

Advance reservations required as blackout periods may apply. Subject to availability, this offer is redeemable at participating Hertz locations in the U.S., Canada and Puerto Rico. This offer has no cash value, may not be used with Pre-pay Rates, Tour Rates or Insurance Replacement Rates and cannot be combined with any other certificate, voucher, offer or promotion. Hertz age, driver, credit and weekly rate qualifications for the renting location apply. Taxes, tax reimbursement, age differential charges, fees and optional service charges, such as refueling, are not included. Discounts apply to time and mileage charges only. Discounts in local currency on redemption. Offer valid for vehicle pickup through 6-30-11.

Subject to Rules of Use. Not valid with other discount offers, unless specified. Coupons VOID if purchased, sold or bartered for cash.

Mention offer PC# 116163 and CDP# ENTERTAINMENT

When calling your travel agent, mention CDP# 205521.

Advance reservations required.Blackout periods may apply. Subject to availability, offer is redeemable at select Hertz locations in the U.S. and Canada (excluding Fun Collection in Canada). Not all vehicles, vehicle equipment and services are available at all locations. Offer has no cash value, may not be used with Pre-pay Rates, Tour Rates or Insurance Replacement Rates and cannot be combined with any other certificate, voucher, offer or promotion. Hertz age, driver, credit and weekly rate qualifications for the renting location apply. Taxes, tax reimbursement, age differential charges, fees and optional service charges, such as refueling, are not included. Discounts apply to time and mileage charges only. Discounts in local currency on redemption. Offer valid for vehicle pickup through 6-30-11.

Subject to Rules of Use. Not valid with other discount offers, unless specified. Coupons VOID if purchased, sold or bartered for cash.

Mention offer PC# 116185 and CDP# ENTERTAINMENT

When calling your travel agent, mention CDP# 205521.

Advance reservations required as blackout periods may apply. Subject to availability, this offer is redeemable at participating Hertz locations in the U.S., Canada and Puerto Rico. This offer has no cash value, may not be used with Pre-pay Rates, Tour Rates or Insurance Replacement Rates and cannot be combined with any other certificate, voucher, offer or promotion. Hertz age, driver, credit and weekend rate qualifications for the renting location apply. Taxes, tax reimbursement, age differential charges, fees and optional service charges, such as refueling, are not included. Discounts apply to time and mileage charges only. Discounts in local currency on redemption. Offer valid for vehicle pickup through 6-30-11.

Subject to Rules of Use. Not valid with other discount offers, unless specified. Coupons VOID if purchased, sold or bartered for cash.

$10 Off

WEEKEND RENTALS AT
HERTZ LOCAL EDITION
We'll even come and get you!*

Go to hertz.com for low web rates.
Enter your rental location, rental dates and arrival information.
Check: I have a discount (CDP, PC, Coupon or other code)
Enter CDP# **ENTERTAINMENT (or 205521)** and PC# 130126

For phone reservations:
Call 1-888-999-7125
or call your travel agent.

Valid now thru June 30, 2011
See reverse side for details   H79

$15 Off

WEEKLY RENTALS AT
HERTZ LOCAL EDITION
We'll even come and get you!*

Go to hertz.com for low web rates.
Enter your rental location, rental dates and arrival information.
Check: I have a discount (CDP, PC, Coupon or other code)
Enter CDP# **ENTERTAINMENT (or 205521)** and PC# 130130

For phone reservations:
Call 1-888-999-7125
or call your travel agent.

Valid now thru June 30, 2011
See reverse side for details   H80

$25 Off

WEEKLY RENTALS OF
PREMIUM AND HIGHER CLASSES

Go to hertz.com for low web rates.
Enter your rental location, rental dates and arrival information.
Check: I have a discount (CDP, PC, Coupon or other code)
Enter CDP# **ENTERTAINMENT (or 205521)** and PC# 130152

For phone reservations:
Call 1-888-999-7125
or call your travel agent.

Valid now thru June 30, 2011
See reverse side for details   H81

$50 Off

MONTHLY RENTALS OF
ANY CAR CLASS

Go to hertz.com for low web rates.
Enter your rental location, rental dates and arrival information.
Check: I have a discount (CDP, PC, Coupon or other code)
Enter CDP# **ENTERTAINMENT (or 205521)** and PC# 130141

For phone reservations:
Call 1-888-999-7125
or call your travel agent.

Valid now thru June 30, 2011
See reverse side for details   H82

Save Up to $15

WEEKEND RENTALS OF
ANY CAR CLASS VEHICLE
$5 a Day, Up to $15 off

Go to hertz.com for low web rates.
Enter your rental location, rental dates and arrival information.
Check: I have a discount (CDP, PC, Coupon or other code)
Enter CDP# **ENTERTAINMENT (or 205521)** and PC# 116200

For phone reservations:
Call 1-888-999-7125
or call your travel agent.

Valid now thru June 30, 2011
See reverse side for details   H83

$20 Off

WEEKLY RENTALS OF
ANY CAR CLASS

Go to hertz.com for low web rates.
Enter your rental location, rental dates and arrival information.
Check: I have a discount (CDP, PC, Coupon or other code)
Enter CDP# **ENTERTAINMENT (or 205521)** and PC# 116196

For phone reservations:
Call 1-888-999-7125
or call your travel agent.

Valid now thru June 30, 2011
See reverse side for details   H84

Mention offer PC# 130130 and CDP# ENTERTAINMENT

*Hertz Local Edition pick up and return available in local areas only.

When calling your travel agent, mention CDP# 205521.

Advance reservations required as blackout periods may apply. Subject to availability, this offer is redeemable at participating Hertz locations in the U.S., Canada and Puerto Rico. This offer has no cash value, may not be used with Pre-pay Rates, Tour Rates or Insurance Replacement Rates and cannot be combined with any other certificate, voucher, offer or promotion. Hertz age, driver, credit and weekly rate qualifications for the renting location apply. Taxes, tax reimbursement, age differential charges, fees and optional service charges, such as refueling, are not included. Discounts apply to time and mileage charges only. Discounts in local currency on redemption. Offer valid for vehicle pickup through 6-30-11.

Subject to Rules of Use. Not valid with other discount offers, unless specified. Coupons VOID if purchased, sold or bartered for cash.

Mention offer PC# 130126 and CDP# ENTERTAINMENT

Offer applies to minimum 2-day weekend rentals of any car class.
*Hertz Local Edition pick up and return available in local areas only.

When calling your travel agent, mention CDP# 205521.

Advance reservations required. Blackout periods may apply. Subject to availability, offer is redeemable at Hertz Local Edition locations in the U.S. and Canada. Offer has no cash value, may not be used with Pre-pay Rates, Tour Rates or Insurance Replacement Rates and cannot be combined with any other certificate, voucher, offer or promotion. Hertz age, driver, credit and weekend rate qualifications for the renting location apply. Taxes, tax reimbursement, age differential charges, fees and optional service charges, such as refueling, are not included. Discounts apply to time and mileage charges only. Discounts in local currency on redemption. Offer valid for vehicle pickup through 6-30-11.

Subject to Rules of Use. Not valid with other discount offers, unless specified. Coupons VOID if purchased, sold or bartered for cash.

Mention offer PC# 130141 and CDP# ENTERTAINMENT

When calling your travel agent, mention CDP# 205521.

Advance reservations required as blackout periods may apply. Subject to availability, this offer is redeemable at participating Hertz locations in the U.S., Canada and Puerto Rico. This offer has no cash value, may not be used with Pre-pay Rates, Tour Rates or Insurance Replacement Rates and cannot be combined with any other certificate, voucher, offer or promotion. Hertz age, driver, credit and monthly rate qualifications for the renting location apply. Taxes, tax reimbursement, age differential charges, fees and optional service charges, such as refueling, are not included. Discounts apply to time and mileage charges only. Discounts in local currency on redemption. Offer valid for vehicle pickup through 6-30-11.

Subject to Rules of Use. Not valid with other discount offers, unless specified. Coupons VOID if purchased, sold or bartered for cash.

Mention offer PC# 130152 and CDP# ENTERTAINMENT

When calling your travel agent, mention CDP# 205521.

Advance reservations required as blackout periods may apply. Subject to availability, this offer is redeemable at participating Hertz locations in the U.S., Canada and Puerto Rico. This offer has no cash value, may not be used with Pre-pay Rates, Tour Rates or Insurance Replacement Rates and cannot be combined with any other certificate, voucher, offer or promotion. Hertz age, driver, credit and weekly rate qualifications for the renting location apply. Taxes, tax reimbursement, age differential charges, fees and optional service charges, such as refueling, are not included. Discounts apply to time and mileage charges only. Discounts in local currency on redemption. Offer valid for vehicle pickup through 6-30-11.

Subject to Rules of Use. Not valid with other discount offers, unless specified. Coupons VOID if purchased, sold or bartered for cash.

Mention offer PC# 116196 and CDP# ENTERTAINMENT

When calling your travel agent, mention CDP# 205521.

Advance reservations required as blackout periods may apply. Subject to availability, this offer is redeemable at participating Hertz locations in the U.S., Canada and Puerto Rico. This offer has no cash value, may not be used with Pre-pay Rates, Tour Rates or Insurance Replacement Rates and cannot be combined with any other certificate, voucher, offer or promotion. Hertz age, driver, credit and weekly rate qualifications for the renting location apply. Taxes, tax reimbursement, age differential charges, fees and optional service charges, such as refueling, are not included. Discounts apply to time and mileage charges only. Discounts in local currency on redemption. Offer valid for vehicle pickup through 6-30-11.

Subject to Rules of Use. Not valid with other discount offers, unless specified. Coupons VOID if purchased, sold or bartered for cash.

Mention offer PC# 116200 and CDP# ENTERTAINMENT

When calling your travel agent, mention CDP# 205521.

Advance reservations required as blackout periods may apply. Subject to availability, this offer is redeemable at participating Hertz locations in the U.S., Canada and Puerto Rico. This offer has no cash value, may not be used with Pre-pay Rates, Tour Rates or Insurance Replacement Rates and cannot be combined with any other certificate, voucher, offer or promotion. Hertz age, driver, credit and weekend rate qualifications for the renting location apply. Taxes, tax reimbursement, age differential charges, fees and optional service charges, such as refueling, are not included. Discounts apply to time and mileage charges only. Discounts in local currency on redemption. Offer valid for vehicle pickup through 6-30-11.

Subject to Rules of Use. Not valid with other discount offers, unless specified. Coupons VOID if purchased, sold or bartered for cash.

RETAIL & SERVICES

christopher & banks

AÉROPOSTALE

BEAUTY.COM
THE WORLD OF BEAUTY ONLINE™

ProFlowers®

PetCareRx
America's Most Affordable Pet Pharmacy

BIRTHDAY EXPRESS
THE ORIGINAL CHILDREN'S PARTY SOURCE

HICKORY FARMS
EST. 1951

COMPUSA.com

Lillian Vernon since 1951

FTD

Oriental Trading
celebrating over **75** years of fun

R
RadioShack.

NEW YORK & COMPANY

AÉROPOSTALE

get **$10off**

your next purchase
of $50 or more

AÉROPOSTALE
aeropostaie.com

AÉROPOSTALE

get

$10off

your next purchase
of $50 or more

95555811

Discount applies to purchases after all discounts have been applied but before applicable taxes. May not be combined with other discount offers. Not valid for purchases of gift cards or previous purchases. Not valid for online
purchases. Purchases over 50 items are considered bulk purchases and are not eligible for this discount. No cash
value. Aéropostale employees not eligible. Duplication or reproduction of this coupon in any manner voids the coupon and Aéropostale has no obligation to accept it. Please present this coupon to receive discount. Limit one coupon
per customer. Redeemable at Aéropostale stores in the U.S., Puerto Rico and Canada only. Valid now to 12/31/2010.

AÉROPOSTALE   aeropostale.com

Subject to Rules of Use. Not valid with other discount offers, unless specified. Coupons VOID if purchased, sold or bartered for cash.

JUNIORS • PLUS • ACCESSORIES • LINGERIE • SHOES • KIDS
check out www.rainbowshops.com for a store nearest you!

Rainbow

www.rainbowshops.com

One coupon per transaction, not to be combined with any other offer. Coupon may only be used once and must be presented at time of purchase. Coupon discount excludes employee discounts, layaways and the purchase of gift cards. **Cashier:** After ringing all items, select one line item to receive the 2010 ENT. COUPON discount then press modify key (5) and choose code 25-2010 ENT. COUPON. The 20% line item discount will automatically be taken off of that line item. Press Total and complete the sale normally. Only one line item per transaction may receive the 2010 ENT. COUPON discount.

Subject to Rules of Use. Not valid with other discount offers, unless specified. Coupons VOID if purchased, sold or bartered for cash.

Rainbow

www.rainbowshops.com

One coupon per transaction, not to be combined with any other offer. Coupon may only be used once and must be presented at time of purchase. Coupon discount excludes employee discounts, layaways and the purchase of gift cards. **Cashier:** After ringing all items, select one line item to receive the 2010 ENT. COUPON discount then press modify key (5) and choose code 25-2010 ENT. COUPON. The 20% line item discount will automatically be taken off of that line item. Press Total and complete the sale normally. Only one line item per transaction may receive the 2010 ENT. COUPON discount.

Subject to Rules of Use. Not valid with other discount offers, unless specified. Coupons VOID if purchased, sold or bartered for cash.

wet *seal.*
FIT IN. STAND OUT.™

FREE
STANDARD SHIPPING
on orders over $15 online only

wet *seal.*
wetseal.com/ent2010

Valid now thru December 31, 2010   See reverse side for details   I5

25%OFF
any one item in stores only

wet *seal.*

Valid now thru December 31, 2010   See reverse side for details   I6

FIT IN. STAND OUT.™

GO TO:
wetseal.com/ent2010

ONLINE ONLY

wet seal®

```
2  89346  61200  3
```

IN STORES ONLY

NAME

PHONE

EMAIL

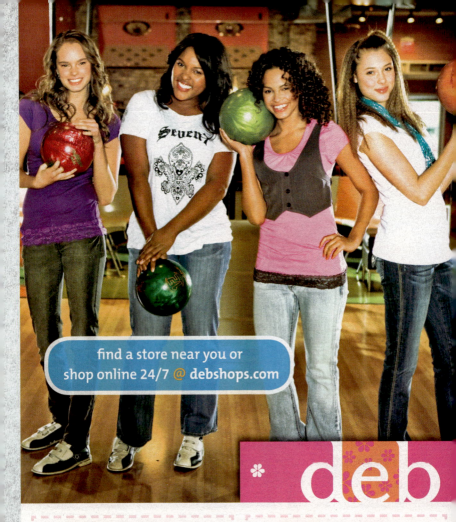

www.579.com

www.579.com

free

standard shipping of **$15 or more**

online only
www.ardenb.com/ent10

ARDEN B.

Valid now thru December 31, 2010   See reverse side for details   I11

$**10**off

your purchase of **$50 or more**

in stores only

ARDEN B.

Valid now thru December 31, 2010   See reverse side for details   I12

ARDEN B.

go to **ardenb.com/ent10**

online only

ARDEN B.

NAME

PHONE

EMAIL

```
2 89346 61300 0
```

in stores only

By giving us your email address and phone number, you are agreeing to receive promotional emails and text messages from Arden B. You can opt out anytime by clicking the "opt-out" link in any email or text message.

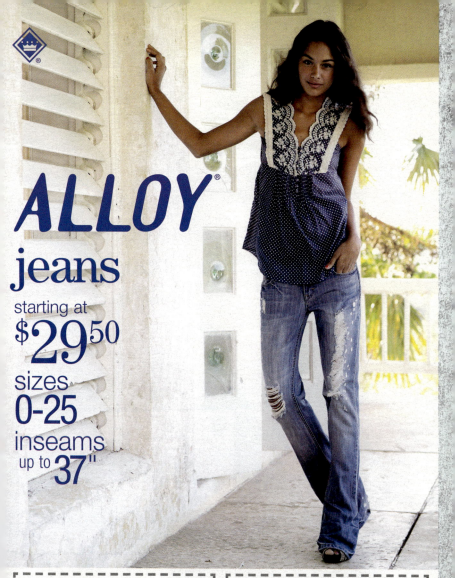

ALLOY®

jeans

starting at

$29⁵⁰

sizes

0-25

inseams

up to **37"**

Great style is
your obsession.
Great price
is ours.

CHADWICKS™

TURN HEADS SAVE MONEY

$25 OFF

YOUR PURCHASE OF $75 OR MORE

Doubles to $50 when you spend $150 or more

NEW YORK & COMPANY

Valid at any New York & Company store and online at nyandcompany.com

Valid now through December 31, 2010
See reverse side for details   I16

$25 OFF

YOUR PURCHASE OF $75 OR MORE

Doubles to $50 when you spend $150 or more

NEW YORK & COMPANY

Valid at any New York & Company store and online at nyandcompany.com

Valid now through December 31, 2010
See reverse side for details   I17

$25 OFF

YOUR PURCHASE OF $75 OR MORE

Doubles to $50 when you spend $150 or more

NEW YORK & COMPANY

Valid at any New York & Company store and online at nyandcompany.com

Valid now through December 31, 2010
See reverse side for details   I18

$25 OFF

YOUR PURCHASE OF $75 OR MORE

Doubles to $50 when you spend $150 or more

NEW YORK & COMPANY

Valid at any New York & Company store and online at nyandcompany.com

Valid now through December 31, 2010
See reverse side for details   I19

$25 OFF YOUR PURCHASE OF $75 OR MORE
Doubles to $50 when you spend $150 or more

Only one certificate, coupon or discount per customer (pre-tax). Not valid on previous purchases, redlines, New York & Company Collection, Store Closing Sale, City Deals, gift wrapping & boxes, shipping fees, gift card purchases. Not redeemable for cash, or accepted as payment for any credit card account. Coupon may be used only once. Discount applied at time of purchase will be taken off each item returned. The discount may not be reapplied to items being exchanged except for size or color. Valid in USA only. Void if copied. Cash value of 1/100 cent. Expires 12/31/10.

Redeeming this coupon is easy. To receive $25 off $75, use promotion code 1854 in stores and online. To receive $50 off $150, use promotion code 1855 in stores and online. Online: Enter the code on the checkout page. Your discount will appear on the following page.

NEW YORK & COMPANY

Subject to Rules of Use. Not valid with other discount offers, unless specified. Coupons VOID if purchased, sold or bartered for cash.

$25 OFF YOUR PURCHASE OF $75 OR MORE
Doubles to $50 when you spend $150 or more

Only one certificate, coupon or discount per customer (pre-tax). Not valid on previous purchases, redlines, New York & Company Collection, Store Closing Sale, City Deals, gift wrapping & boxes, shipping fees, gift card purchases. Not redeemable for cash, or accepted as payment for any credit card account. Coupon may be used only once. Discount applied at time of purchase will be taken off each item returned. The discount may not be reapplied to items being exchanged except for size or color. Valid in USA only. Void if copied. Cash value of 1/100 cent. Expires 12/31/10.

Redeeming this coupon is easy. To receive $25 off $75, use promotion code 1856 in stores and online. To receive $50 off $150, use promotion code 1857 in stores and online. Online: Enter the code on the checkout page. Your discount will appear on the following page.

NEW YORK & COMPANY

Subject to Rules of Use. Not valid with other discount offers, unless specified. Coupons VOID if purchased, sold or bartered for cash.

$25 OFF YOUR PURCHASE OF $75 OR MORE
Doubles to $50 when you spend $150 or more

Only one certificate, coupon or discount per customer (pre-tax). Not valid on previous purchases, redlines, New York & Company Collection, Store Closing Sale, City Deals, gift wrapping & boxes, shipping fees, gift card purchases. Not redeemable for cash, or accepted as payment for any credit card account. Coupon may be used only once. Discount applied at time of purchase will be taken off each item returned. The discount may not be reapplied to items being exchanged except for size or color. Valid in USA only. Void if copied. Cash value of 1/100 cent. Expires 12/31/10.

Redeeming this coupon is easy. To receive $25 off $75, use promotion code 1858 in stores and online. To receive $50 off $150, use promotion code 1859 in stores and online. Online: Enter the code on the checkout page. Your discount will appear on the following page.

NEW YORK & COMPANY

Subject to Rules of Use. Not valid with other discount offers, unless specified. Coupons VOID if purchased, sold or bartered for cash.

$25 OFF YOUR PURCHASE OF $75 OR MORE
Doubles to $50 when you spend $150 or more

Only one certificate, coupon or discount per customer (pre-tax). Not valid on previous purchases, redlines, New York & Company Collection, Store Closing Sale, City Deals, gift wrapping & boxes, shipping fees, gift card purchases. Not redeemable for cash, or accepted as payment for any credit card account. Coupon may be used only once. Discount applied at time of purchase will be taken off each item returned. The discount may not be reapplied to items being exchanged except for size or color. Valid in USA only. Void if copied. Cash value of 1/100 cent. Expires 12/31/10.

Redeeming this coupon is easy. To receive $25 off $75, use promotion code 1860 in stores and online. To receive $50 off $150, use promotion code 1861 in stores and online. Online: Enter the code on the checkout page. Your discount will appear on the following page.

NEW YORK & COMPANY

Subject to Rules of Use. Not valid with other discount offers, unless specified. Coupons VOID if purchased, sold or bartered for cash.

FASHION BUG

LOOK GREAT. SPEND LESS.

Come see our new collection and save!

It's all about looking great and spending less with **new lower prices** on everything in the store.

Plus, use the coupons below to save even more in stores and online.

FASHION BUG

LOOK GREAT. SPEND LESS.

Chic on a Shoestring

Come see our fashionable collection… all at new lower prices.

Who says frugal can't be fabulous!

09-0530A1 WK 22 © Charming Shoppes, Inc. 2009

sensuality
REFINED

A complete collection of intimates
with your curves in mind.

CACIQUE
(KA'-SEEK)
Only at LANE BRYANT

christopher & banks

www.christopherandbanks.com/ent

$15 off

your regular and sale price purchase of $60 or more

* Exclusive Designs

* Exceptional Value

* Wardrobe Solutions

misses 4–16   petite 4P–16P
(select stores)

christopher & banks™

www.christopherandbanks.com/ent

the  commitment

Style Everyday. Value Everyday. That's smart.

Lorna Nagler
President & CEO

cj banks™
size 14 & more...

www.cjbanks.com/ent

$15 off
*your regular and sale price
purchase of $60 or more*

* Exclusive Designs

* Exceptional Value

* Wardrobe Solutions

women's sizes 14–24

www.cjbanks.com/ent

the **cj**
commitment

Style Everyday. Value Everyday. That's smart.

Lorna Nagler
President & CEO

CATHERINES®

Classic and current fashions for today's plus size woman

Visit catherines.com for the store nearest you.

CATHERINES®

Classic and current fashions for today's plus size woman

Visit catherines.com for the store nearest you.

THE TERRITORY AHEAD

Exceptional Clothing for Men & Women

Call 800-882-4323 for a FREE catalog

www.territoryahead.com

Garnet Hill

original designs in clothing and home decor

women's & kids' apparel • designer footwear • exclusive bedding • home decor

we've got it!®
comfort, fit & value for sizes 12w to 44w

woman within

check us out!

get more **spend**less
more sizes
more styles
more value

visit womanwithin.com/ent
for a free catalog call 800-248-2000

TRAVELSMITH®

CLOTHING, GEAR, AND ADVICE TO GO

SAVE UP TO $30
OFF YOUR FIRST ORDER

TO ORDER CALL
800-950-1600

OR VISIT US AT
TRAVELSMITH.COM

Growing Up with
garnet hill
- colorful clothing
- home furnishings • fun accessories

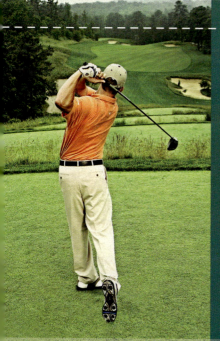

SHOES.COM

shoes.com is your go-to, one-stop shop for the best selection of men's shoes, women's shoes and kids' shoes. Featuring hundreds of your favorite brands and thousands of must-have styles and colors, we've got your shoe needs covered, no matter what the occasion.

FREE Shipping
FREE Returns

Finish Line.

finishline.com

finishline.com

Save 16% Online!

SHOP NFLSHOP.COM

www.NFLShop.com/ent16

store.nascar.com/ent16

www.NBAStore.com/ent16

shop.NHL.com/ent16

Buy Online.
Pick Up In-Store.

Sears

Click on savings.

Visit **Entertainment.com/Target** to find unbelievable savings on Target.com finds.

The latest and greatest items for less.

Valid now thru December 31, 2010

I44

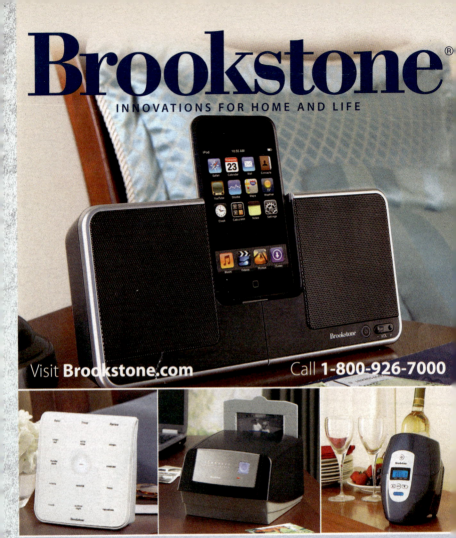

Brookstone®

INNOVATIONS FOR HOME AND LIFE

Visit **Brookstone.com**   Call **1-800-926-7000**

Domesticator®
Where Style & Value Come Home

$10 OFF
any $60 purchase*

$15 OFF
any $90 purchase*

$20 OFF
any $120 purchase*

domestications.com/D10ENT
1-800-859-9445
(mention code: D10ENT)

*Minimum purchase required. Discount applied to merchandise total exclusive of tax, delivery and service charges. This one-time use offer is applicable towards new orders only. Does not apply to the purchase of Clearance merchandise or Gift Cards and may not be combined with other promotions (except the Domestications® Buyers' Club discount).

148

Valid now thru December 31, 2010
Subject to Rules of Use. Not valid with other discount offers, unless specified. Coupons VOID if purchased, sold or bartered for cash.

$5 off*

ACE
The helpful place.

your next $25 purchase or more of regular priced merchandise

Valid now through December 31, 2010

$5.00 COUPON

8003 3523

*At participating Ace Hardware stores. Coupon not valid on sale and clearance priced merchandise or in combination with any other coupon offer. Valid for one transaction only. May not be used toward rental items, in-store services, online purchases, for the purchase of the Ace Gift Card, city stickers or for previously purchased merchandise. Not redeemable for cash. Coupon may not be sold or transferred. Void if photocopied or duplicated. **Cashier:** Scan "$5 off" barcode in the body of the transaction or key in the number beneath the barcode.

79 .109601_0309

Subject to Rules of Use. Not valid with other discount offers, unless specified. Coupons VOID if purchased, sold or bartered for cash.

FRONTGATE®

OUTFITTING AMERICA'S FINEST HOMES

Visit us at frontgate.com or call 1-800-626-6488 for a free catalog.

BED BATH & BEYOND®

WORLD MARKET®

Unique, authentic and always affordable.

Bring home a brand new look for a whole lot less.

WORLDMARKET.COM

WORLD MARKET®

Unique, authentic and always affordable.

How would you describe our gourmet marketplace? Deliciously authentic, pleasantly surprising and just the best selection of foreign fare you can find without hopping a plane.

Savor the flavors of Italy without the pricey airfare.

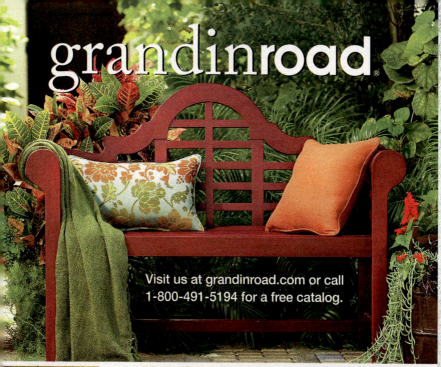

grandinroad®

Visit us at grandinroad.com or call
1-800-491-5194 for a free catalog.

155

BALLARD DESIGNS.

Unique, classically inspired furnishings
and accents for the home.
- **Home & Office Organization**
- **Lighting • Rugs • Wall Decor & more...**

3 ways to **save** on 1000s of **window fashions!**

$150 OFF $1000

$100 OFF $750

$50 OFF $400

Offer Details: Save up to $150 on any smith+noble or Christopher Lowell Collection window treatment purchase. Save $150 off a $1000+ purchase; save $100 off a $750+ purchase; save $50 off a $400+ purchase. Minimum eligible purchase is $400; minimum discount is $50; maximum discount is $150. Mention offer code SAVE-9TCB when ordering, or enter during online checkout. May only be used once per household and cannot be combined with any other offer. Expires 11:59 P.M. PST, 12/31/2010.

 now featuring the **Christopher Lowell** COLLECTION **exclusively at** smith+noble®

smith+noble®

america's leading resource for window treatments®

call today! 866.878.7806

Valid now thru December 31, 2010

Subject to Rules of Use. Not valid with other discount offers, unless specified. Coupons VOID if purchased, sold or bartered for cash.

IMPROVEMENTS®

...for your home, for your life

Outdoor
Privacy Screen

Wolfgang Puck

FUSIONBEAUTY
TOMORROW'S TECHNOLOGY FOR BEAUTY TODAY

SEPHORA
colorful palette

dyson

Shop HSN for amazing products, top brands and unique finds in beauty, jewelry, fashion, cookware, home, crafts, fitness, sports and more. Enjoy Easy Returns, a 30-day money-back guarantee and 24/7 customer service.

To order, visit hsn.com/entertainment or call 1.800.436.8080.

there's no place like... HSN

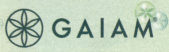

GAIAM

Live green.
Live fit.
Live well.

Natural & Organic Fiber Bedding

Yoga & Pilates Media & Tools

Eco-Friendly Clothing

Fair Trade & Ecological Home Décor

Health & Wellbeing Solutions

Live happy.

gaiam.com   800-869-3603

Take along a where2® GPS!

Great trucks, less bucks.®

where2 is optional and is available at select locations for an additional fee.
Cargo Vans available for local rentals at select locations.

Exclusive Offer for Entertainment® Customers
DIRECTV's Best Deal!

 FREE DVR or HD Receiver Upgrade**
With CHOICE XTRA™ package or above.

FREE Standard Professional Installation
In up to 4 rooms

 OVER 30 Premium Movie Channels
With PREMIER™ package

 265+ All-Digital Channels Includes Locals††
With PREMIER™ package

Packages start at only $29⁹⁹ mo
for FAMILY PKG.

Offers end 12/31/10, on approved credit, credit card required. New customers only (lease required, must maintain programming, DVR and HD Access). Hardware available separately. Lease fee $5.00/mo. for second and each additional receiver. $19.95 Handling & Delivery fee may apply.

Call now for the Best Deal available!
1-800-750-5797
DIRECTSTARTV – An Authorized DIRECTV Dealer

DIRECTV SATELLITE TELEVISION

I65

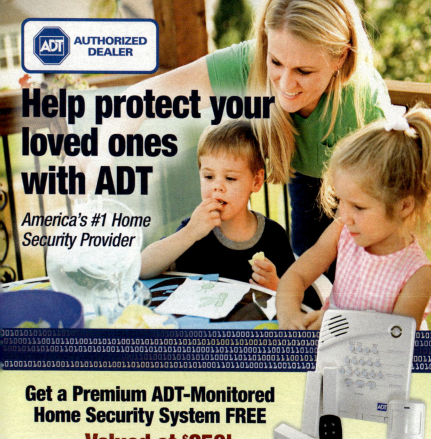

AUTHORIZED DEALER

Help protect your loved ones with ADT

America's #1 Home Security Provider

Get a Premium ADT-Monitored Home Security System FREE
– Valued at $850!

With $99 Customer Installation Charge and purchase of alarm monitoring services.

Local Installation • Best National Offers
Call Today! 1-866-211-1120

SECURITY CHOICE
ADT Authorized Company

PLUS, order your ADT-monitored Home Security System today and get a $100 VISA Gift Card!

Exclusive offer from Security Choice with purchase and installation of an ADT-monitored Home Security System. After mail-in redemption.

Call Today! 1-866-211-1120

Valid now thru December 31, 2010

Subject to Rules of Use. Not valid with other discount offers, unless specified. Coupons VOID if purchased, sold or bartered for cash.

168

Have Movies Delivered Right To Your Mailbox

BLOCKBUSTER® BY MAIL

BLOCKBUSTER® By Mail gives you the convenience of online DVD rentals with no due dates or late fees. See reverse for more information.

Use the coupons below to save on game and movie rentals at a participating BLOCKBUSTER store.

Get Movies Delivered with BLOCKBUSTER® By Mail

SELECT MOVIES ▸ RECEIVE BY MAIL ▸ MAIL BACK OR EXCHANGE IN-STORE *for discounted rentals* ▸ NEXT DVD ON THE WAY

- **Rent DVDs online from over 90,000 titles**
- **No due dates or late fees**
- **Free shipping**

Start your FREE trial at www.blockbuster.com/bbmepb10

Sometimes you're **Wolverine**. Sometimes you're **Harry Potter on Blu-ray**. Sometimes you're **Bridget Jones**.

And every so often, you're **shredding a few choice Guitar Hero licks before a crowd of 60,000**.

Be what you want, when you want.
The best selection of movies and games available.

LOCATE A STORE NEAR YOU

www.hollywoodvideo.com

+CEBFRNM10

Free Movie or Game Rental With New Membership.
Good on any one movie or game with new membership sign-up. Limit one coupon per membership account. May not be combined with any other offer. Valid at all Hollywood Video stores, with the exception of Game Crazy stores. Membership terms and conditions apply. Customers responsible for applicable taxes and additional rental period charges. See store for details. Cash value 1/100 of a cent. This coupon must be relinquished at the time of redemption and may not be printed, reproduced, sold or transferred. Coupon expires 12/31/10. ©2009 Hollywood Entertainment Corporation.

+CEBR1G110

Rent 2 Movies or Games, Get 1 Free
One coupon per account. Free rental must be lesser value item in transaction. May not be combined with any other offer. Valid at all Hollywood Video stores, with the exception of Game Crazy stores. Membership terms and conditions apply. Customers responsible for applicable taxes and additional rental period charges. See store for details. Cash value 1/100 of a cent. This coupon must be relinquished at the time of redemption and may not be printed, reproduced, sold or transferred. Coupon expires 12/31/10. ©2009 Hollywood Entertainment Corporation.

Sometimes you're **Wolverine**. Sometimes you're **Harry Potter on Blu-ray**. Sometimes you're **Bridget Jones**.

And every so often, you're **shredding a few choice Guitar Hero licks before a crowd of 60,000**.

Be what you want, when you want.
The best selection of movies and games available.

LOCATE A STORE
NEAR YOU
www.moviegallery.com

+CEBFRNM10

Free Movie or Game Rental With New Membership.
Free membership required. Not valid with any other offers, specials, or discounts. Limit one coupon per membership account. May not be combined with any other offer. Valid at all Movie Gallery stores. Membership terms and conditions apply. Customer responsible for applicable taxes and extended viewing/replay fees. See store for details. Cash value 1/100¢. This coupon must be relinquished at the time of redemption and may not be printed, reproduced, sold or transferred. Coupon expires 12/31/10.
©2009 Movie Gallery US, LLC

+CEBR1G110

Rent 2 Movies or Games, Get 1 Free
Good on all movies and games. Free rental must be of equal or lesser value. Limit one coupon per membership account per visit. May not be combined with any other offer. Valid at all Movie Gallery stores. Membership terms and conditions apply. Customer responsible for applicable taxes and extended viewing/replay fees. See store for details. Cash value 1/100¢. This coupon must be relinquished at the time of redemption and may not be printed, reproduced, sold or transferred. Coupon expires 12/31/10.
©2009 Movie Gallery US, LLC

NETFLIX

FREE MOVIE RENTALS

- DVD Rentals Delivered
- No Late Fees
- Over 100,000 DVD Titles
- Free Shipping Both Ways

2 weeks FREE

Rent
what you want

Just point and click to add
movies & TV episodes
to your list from
over 100,000 titles.

Receive
what you wanted

We rush DVDs from our list
with fast, free delivery
in about 1 business day.

Watch
when you want

Keep each movie
as long as you want.

Exchange
as often as you want

Simply return 1 movie in
its prepaid envelope
to get another –
as often as you like.

PLUS

Streaming
to your TV

As a bonus to your DVDs by mail,
instantly watch some movies on your TV
over the Internet – anytime!

FREE 2-WEEK TRIAL

DVDs by mail plus instantly watch movies (some new releases)
& TV episodes (including current season) on your PC, Mac or TV.

Go to:
http://www.netflix.com/ent2010

Valid now thru December 31, 2010

Subject to Rules of Use. Not valid with other discount offers, unless specified. Coupons VOID if purchased, sold or bartered for cash.

177

TigerDirect.com®

The Best Computer Deals...
Anywhere!

TigerDirect.com offers a huge selection of computer products and electronics at the lowest prices. Log on to our website for detailed product specs, photo galleries, manuals, user ratings and more!

the all-new
COMPUSA.com®
PCs, TVs and More!

The Best Deals on:

Laptops & Netbooks,
Desktop PCs,
LCD Monitors,
Hi-Definition TVs
& Home Theater,
MP3 Players,
Digital Cameras,
Cell Phones,
GPS Systems...

And Do-It-Yourself:

Components, Networking,
Memory Upgrades

179

BORDERS®

the books you love... and more

Whether you're visiting a Borders store or Borders.com, you'll always find millions of great titles to choose from. From fitness to finance, cooking to classics, there's something for everyone!

plus, shop **Borders.com** and get
free shipping
on purchases of $25 or more

BORDERS

MILLIONS OF TITLES.
MILLIONS OF REASONS TO
RELAX AND ENJOY.

Borders is your home for millions of great titles. So curl up with a good book, relax to your favorite tune, or enjoy a new movie— at your local Borders store and Borders.com, you'll find everything you love!

New Technology,
Hot brands,
Expert Advice.

Stop by Your
Neighborhood
RadioShack Today.

RadioShack.

RadioShack®

Over 5,000 retail locations nationwide. For a store near you, call 1-800-THE-SHACK® or visit us at www.RadioShack.com.

$10 OFF A PURCHASE OF $40 OR MORE.

Must present this coupon to receive offer. Offer valid through 12/31/10 at participating stores. Limit one coupon per person per visit. iPod®, gaming hardware/software, mobile phones, gift cards, services, special orders, and online and phone orders excluded. May not be combined with certain other discounts. No cash value. No photocopies. Void where prohibited. Call 1-800-THE-SHACK® or go to www.RadioShack.com to find the store nearest you.

RSS Instructions: If the ticket total is $40.00 or more, use a Line Item Price Change to reduce the price of a product by $10.00. Select reason code "7. Promo/Coupon" and scan the barcode for the comment or type in the number under the barcode.

ENTA2010

RadioShack®

$15 OFF A PURCHASE OF $60 OR MORE.

Must present this coupon to receive offer. Offer valid through 12/31/10 at participating stores. Limit one coupon per person per visit. iPod®, gaming hardware/software, mobile phones, gift cards, services, special orders, and online and phone orders excluded. May not be combined with certain other discounts. No cash value. No photocopies. Void where prohibited. Call 1-800-THE-SHACK® or go to www.RadioShack.com to find the store nearest you.

RSS Instructions: If the ticket total is $60.00 or more, use a Line Item Price Change to reduce the price of a product by $15.00. Select reason code "7. Promo/Coupon" and scan the barcode for the comment or type in the number under the barcode.

ENTB2010

RadioShack®

Join today and receive **30 FREE PRINTS** along with free online photo storage and photo sharing.

Already a member? **ENJOY 10% OFF** your order of personalized photo books, gifts, stationery and more.

PICTURE NEW WAYS TO SHARE EVERY MOMENT.
30 FREE 4X6 PRINTS FOR NEW CUSTOMERS

Visit shutterfly.com/ent2010
Valid now through December 31, 2010

20% off
custom photo gifts

Share your memories and save 20% on personalized photo books, mugs, calendars, jewelry, and over 100 photo products!

To save 20%, enter coupon code **ENTERTAIN10** at checkout.

New customers get **50 FREE** prints at:
www.snapfish.com/entertain10

50 free
digital camera prints

fromyouflowers·com™
flowers | plants | gifts | and more!

SAVE $15 on a dozen long stem roses!

SAVE $10 on all other flowers and gifts!

say it with flowers!

fromyouflowers·com/ent | **1.800.758.9353** mention code ENT

thinking of you • i miss you • i love you • happy anniversary • just because

---

the teleflora difference.

their bouquet   our bouquet

Arrangements never arrive in a box.
Arrangements always hand-arranged and hand-delivered.
Vases always included, many are keepsakes.
ALL arrangements available for same-day delivery.
Flowers, gift baskets, plants and more.
Bouquets starting at $29.99.

teleflora ®

Coupons can be used all year!
Starting at $29.99.
Vase always included.

800.281.9541
www.ent.flowerclub.com

Order online SAVE $15

teleflora ®

promo code: save15
www.ent.flowerclub.com

Valid now thru December 31, 2010
Subject to Rules of Use. Not valid with other discount offers, unless specified. Coupons VOID if purchased, sold or bartered for cash.

I98

Order by phone SAVE $10

teleflora ®

promo code: save10
800.281.9541

Valid now thru December 31, 2010
Subject to Rules of Use. Not valid with other discount offers, unless specified. Coupons VOID if purchased, sold or bartered for cash.

I99

SAVE $15
ON ANY BOUQUET
www.florist.com/ent2010

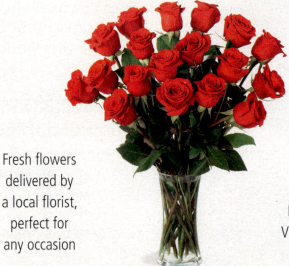

Fresh flowers
delivered by
a local florist,
perfect for
any occasion

Birthday
Anniversary
Sympathy
Mother's Day
Valentine's Day
Christmas

FLORIST.COM

Valid now through December 31, 2010

SAVE $15
WHEN YOU ORDER ONLINE
www.florist.com/ent2010

Valid now through December 31, 2010   I100

SAVE $10
ON ALL ORDERS WHEN
YOU CALL 1-800-425-0622
mention promo code 18020

Valid now through December 31, 2010   I101

We Specialize in Same-Day Nationwide Delivery

Save up to 50%
at bloomstoday.com/ent10

bloomstoday™

Family Owned & Operated · National & Local Delivery Guaranteed

Visit **bloomstoday.com/ent10** or call **1-800-890-3670 (code ENT10)**

birthday · anniversary · sympathy · get well · congratulations · friendship

Fresh flowers and gifts?
Yep, we got 'em!

SAVOR THE BEST HICKORY FARMS EVER AND SAVE $10.

100% Satisfaction Guaranteed
On Time Delivery
Perfect Arrival Presentation
Free Personalized Gift Card

Wedding Berries™

Fancy Combo

Hand-Dipped Strawberries on sale for $24.99

Fancy Berries™

Cheesecake Trio & Fancy Berries™

Birthday Berries™

Swizzled 'N Sweet Berries

Harry & David

Send a sweet, juicy surprise for birthdays, anniversaries, holidays and celebrations throughout the year.

Our famous Royal Riviera® Pear Gift.

NEW to the Family: Save 10% at Cushmans.com/go/ent2010
Cushman's Fruit Company is a DBA of Harry and David

To find the Store nearest you:
Call 877-233-1000
or visit HarryandDavid.com

Valid only in a Harry & David retail store. Offer not valid with any other offers, discounts or promotions and cannot be applied to previous purchases, In-store Catalog orders, Catalog, Phone, or Internet purchases or for the purchase of gift cards. Not valid (a) on wine sales in Ohio or (b) where prohibited by law. All applicable taxes apply. Limit one coupon per customer and one purchase per coupon. Cash value: 1/20 of a cent.
Harry & David is a DBA of Harry and David.

0 00000 16700 0

Coupon code: 167000

Subject to Rules of Use. Not valid with other discount offers, unless specified. Coupon VOID if copied, purchased, sold, or bartered. Valid now through December 31, 2010.

CHERRY MOON FARMS®

A Brand of ProFlowers®

Spa Baskets

Hand-Dipped Berries

Fruit Baskets
& Organic
Fruit

Quality
Gifts
From
$24⁹⁹

100% Satisfaction Guarantee

Special Offer!
We'll include **3 Free Gifts**
when you order the Classic Fruit Basket

wine.com™

Ranked #1 online wine store by *Internet Retailer* magazine.

Visit www.wine.com/ent2010 now for your exclusive promo codes.
See site for details and restrictions.

$5 off $75 or more

$10 off $100 or more

10% off any 6- or 12-month wine club

15% off any gift basket or wine gift set

Wolferman's

10% off
any online purchase

wolfermans.com/go/ent2010

Because everything
begins with breakfast.ˢᴹ

I124

Offer valid only for a Wolferman's® product purchase made via the redemption method listed above. Offer applies to merchandise total only (excluding delivery & processing and taxes). Cannot be applied to previous purchases or to the purchase of gift cards. Delivery & processing charges are based on regular price of merchandise. No cash value. Limit one coupon per customer and one purchase per coupon. Offer valid through December 31, 2010.

©2009, Harry and David. Wolferman's is a registered trademark and service mark, and a division and DBA of Harry and David.

 ⦿ blue nile

10% OFF FINE JEWELRY AND FREE SHIPPING

VISIT WWW.ENTERTAINMENT.COM/BLUENILE

Blue Nile is the largest online retailer of certified diamonds and fine jewelry. Receive 10% off your purchase of select fine jewelry.*

*Offer is not valid for any loose diamonds, pre-set engagement rings, gift certificates, polishing cloth, or watch purchases. See www.entertainment.com/bluenile for complete offer terms.

Valid now thru December 31, 2010

I125

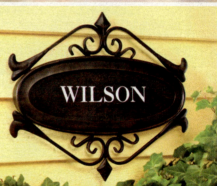

Personalized Gifts

for Life's Celebrations

Oriental Trading

celebrating over **75** years of fun

From novelties to crafts, parties to classrooms... discover thousands of ways to have fun every day!

Play! Choose from over 40,000 fun items online!

Party! Find their favorites in themed party packs!

10% off
any order $59 or more!
Checkout Code: OTCENT

or go to
entertainment.com/orientaltrading
for exclusive offers!

LOWEST PRICE **110%** GUARANTEE

visit **orientaltrading.com**
call **800-228-2269**

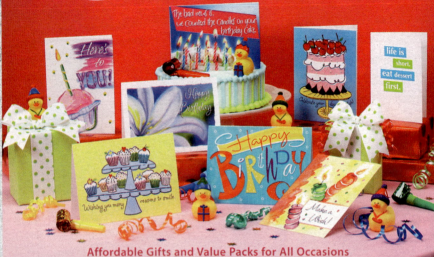

celebrate life's special moments™

Current

Affordable Gifts and Value Packs for All Occasions

Seasonal Gifts	Home Décor	Gift Wrap & Accessories

Visit us at currentcatalog.com or call 1-800-848-2848 for a free catalog.

Simply the Best Pet Insurance!

PETSMART

save $10

on a Bath, Brush & More grooming package

Grooming

- Package includes shampoo, blow-dry, brush, nail trim and ear cleaning
- PetSmart® safety-certified PetStylists trained in breed-specific and customized services
- Convenient hours seven days a week and evenings

Valid now thru December 31, 2010

See reverse side for details

I135

PETSMART

save $10

on any 6- or 8-week training course

Training

- PetSmart® Accredited Training Instructors skilled in canine behavior and problem solving
- Positive reinforcement for fun and effective learning
- Our SmartPet Promise℠: If you're not 100% satisfied, you can take the class again for free

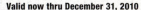

Valid now thru December 31, 2010

See reverse side for details

I136

PETSMART

save $10

on a PetSmart PetsHotel® overnight stay or one session of Doggie Day Camp℠

PetSmart PetsHotel®
with Doggie Day Camp℠

- PetSmart® safety-certified caregivers on-site 24/7
- Doggie Day Camp provides your pooch with hours of supervised play and exercise when you can't be there
- Veterinarians always on call

Valid now thru December 31, 2010

See reverse side for details

I137

Please visit grooming.petsmart.com or call 1-877-4-PetSmart for current locations and more information. Simply call any of our locations to book your appointment and bring in this certificate to receive offer.

Valid through 12/31/10 at PetSmart in U.S. with coupon on any Bath, Brush & More only. Limit one coupon per transaction. Void if copied. No credit or cash back. Non-transferable. Not valid with any other discount or offer. Based on availability. Must show proof of current PetSmart required vaccinations. For the safety of all animals and associates, and at the discretion of PetSmart, some pets may not be permitted. We reserve the right to refuse or limit this service. Terms and conditions of this offer are subject to change at the sole discretion of PetSmart.

4 15141 80561 0

Subject to Rules of Use. Not valid with other discount offers, unless specified. Coupons VOID if purchased, sold or bartered for cash.

Please visit training.petsmart.com or call 1-877-4-PetSmart for current locations and more information. Simply call any of our locations to book your appointment and bring in this certificate to receive offer.

Valid through 12/31/10 at PetSmart in U.S. with coupon for $10 off any 6- or 8-week training course. Limit one coupon per transaction. Void if copied. No credit or cash back. Non-transferable. Not valid with any other discount or offer. Based on availability. Must show proof of current PetSmart required vaccinations. For the safety of all animals and associates, and at the discretion of PetSmart, some pets may not be permitted. We reserve the right to refuse or limit this service. Terms and conditions of this offer are subject to change at the sole discretion of PetSmart.

4 15141 80761 4

Subject to Rules of Use. Not valid with other discount offers, unless specified. Coupons VOID if purchased, sold or bartered for cash.

Please visit petshotel.com or call 1-877-4-PetSmart for current locations and more information. Simply call any of our locations to book your reservation and bring in this certificate to receive offer.

Valid through 12/31/10 at PetSmart PetsHotel in U.S. with coupon for $10 off one day or night in a dog atrium or kitty cottage or $10 off one session of Doggie Day Camp. Coupon value may be applied toward a suite. Limit one coupon per transaction. Void if copied. No credit or cash back. Non-transferable. Not valid with any other discount or offer. Based on availability. Must show proof of current PetSmart required vaccinations. For the safety of all animals and associates, and at the discretion of PetSmart, some pets may not be permitted. Dogs must pass a health and behavior assessment and be at least four months old to participate in Doggie Day Camp. We reserve the right to refuse or limit this service. Terms and conditions of this offer are subject to change at the sole discretion of PetSmart.

4 15141 80661 7

Subject to Rules of Use. Not valid with other discount offers, unless specified. Coupons VOID if purchased, sold or bartered for cash.

VisionDirect.com ®

The lowest prices around on contact lenses!

Get an additional **10% off &**
free shipping on your order!

Use coupon code **ENT10BK** at checkout.

Free standard shipping on orders of $99 or more. 10% off discount expires December 31, 2010. Discount will be deducted from your subtotal. Discount does not apply to shipping charges or applicable sales tax, and cannot be combined with some offers. Offers cannot be transferred or redeemed for cash and are void where prohibited by law. Restrictions may apply. See site for details.

I140

Saving on prescriptions is easy.

1. Detach and fill out the card below. **2.** Show the card to the pharmacist each time you submit your prescription. **3.** You save. Once your prescription is filled you pay the discounted price. It's that easy.

card can be used repeatedly

PharmacyID pharmacyid.com

Use this card to save money on prescriptions

ID: _____
print your Entertainment® card number (found in the front of your book)

NAME: _____
print your full name

DISCOUNTS ONLY — NOT INSURANCE
Full payment of discounted price required at time of sale.
Pharmacy Help Desk **1-800-875-9032**

RX BIN: 014559
RX GRP: PD01

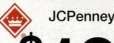

JCPenney₀ Optical

ALL BRANDS ON SALE!

10% OFF
All Contact Lenses

Must present ad to receive contac lens offer.

Valid prescription required. See optician for details.
Contact lenses not available in AR. Offer ends December 31, 2010.

drugstore·com™
the **uncommon** drugstore

- Shop our site for over 40,000 items – including everyday essentials and hard-to-find favorites!
- Free shipping*
- 5% back in drugstore dollars™

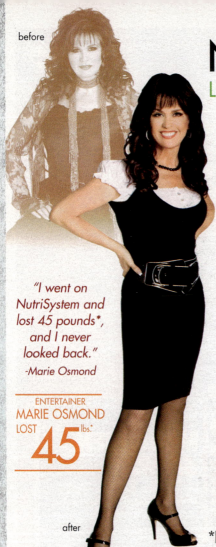

before

Nutrisystem®

Lose weight. Save money.™

NutriSystem is **hundreds of dollars less** than other weight loss programs

Choose from up to 170 menu items—including gourmet, restaurant-quality, fresh-frozen meals!

Lose weight with healthy recipes created with good carbs and high fiber to help you *feel fuller longer.*

- NO counting calories, carbs, or points
- FREE online membership including weight loss tips and tools, menu planning, and live chat sessions with registered dietitians
- Plus! Round-the-clock access to weight loss coaches absolutely FREE

"I went on NutriSystem and lost 45 pounds*, and I never looked back."
-Marie Osmond

ENTERTAINER
MARIE OSMOND
LOST **45** lbs.*

after

MONEY BACK GUARANTEE!

Try our food! If you don't like it, call within 7 days of receipt of your first order and return the three weeks of food for a **FULL REFUND** of the purchase price, less shipping. Call or see website for details.

*Results not typical.
On NutriSystem you add in fresh grocery items.

JCPenney® Portraits

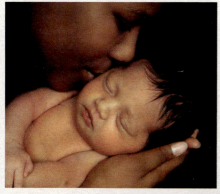

Make an appointment online
Visit **jcpportraits.com** or call your local studio

FREE 8x10
and **50% off** your
total portrait purchase

JCPenney® Portraits

Valid now thru December 31, 2010
See reverse side for details

I148

FREE 8x10
and **50% off** your
total portrait purchase

JCPenney® Portraits

Valid now thru December 31, 2010
See reverse side for details

I149

JCPenney® Portraits

fun portrait products

Designs may vary.

FREE 8x10

and **50% off** your total portrait purchase

Offer expires 12/31/10. Sitting fee $9.99 per person, FREE for Portrait Club members. Present at time of sitting. Valid for 50% off entire portrait purchase, including enhanced portraits and fees. Not valid on reorders, studio events, merchandise, media, with other offers or online orders. **PC1811421**

JCPenney® Portraits

Subject to Rules of Use. Not valid with other discount offers, unless specified. Coupons VOID if purchased, sold or bartered for cash.

FREE 8x10

and **50% off** your total portrait purchase

Offer expires 12/31/10. Sitting fee $9.99 per person, FREE for Portrait Club members. Present at time of sitting. Valid for 50% off entire portrait purchase, including enhanced portraits and fees. Not valid on reorders, studio events, merchandise, media, with other offers or online orders. **PC1811421**

JCPenney® Portraits

Subject to Rules of Use. Not valid with other discount offers, unless specified. Coupons VOID if purchased, sold or bartered for cash.

Sweet smiles sweet deals

10x20

 PORTRAIT STUDIO

Schedule your appointment online at Targetportraits.com
or call 1-888-887-8994 for the location nearest you

Stack up the savings

multi-image
frame sold separately

be squared

designs may vary

single-image
frame sold separately

©2009 Target Stores. The Bullseye Design and Target are registered trademarks of Target Brands, Inc. All rights reserved. 100023-01

◎ PORTRAIT STUDIO

TARGET PORTRAIT STUDIO COUPON   EXPIRES 12/31/10

50%off
Portrait Purchase

Present at sitting. No sitting fees. Valid for 50% off entire portrait purchase, including enhanced portraits. Not valid with other coupon offers, on reorders, studio events, merchandise, media or online orders. Limit one offer per coupon. Void if copied, transferred, purchased, sold or prohibited by law. No cash value. **Cashier: Change price of each item to reduce 50% off. Select ad substitute as your reason.**   PC24317

◎ PORTRAIT STUDIO

Subject to Rules of Use. Not valid with other discount offers, unless specified. Coupons VOID if purchased, sold or bartered for cash.

TARGET PORTRAIT STUDIO COUPON   EXPIRES 12/31/10

50%off
Portrait Purchase

Present at sitting. No sitting fees. Valid for 50% off entire portrait purchase, including enhanced portraits. Not valid with other coupon offers, on reorders, studio events, merchandise, media or online orders. Limit one offer per coupon. Void if copied, transferred, purchased, sold or prohibited by law. No cash value. **Cashier: Change price of each item to reduce 50% off. Select ad substitute as your reason.**   PC24317

◎ PORTRAIT STUDIO

Subject to Rules of Use. Not valid with other discount offers, unless specified. Coupons VOID if purchased, sold or bartered for cash.

Capture the *Smiles.* Save 30%.

 picture people | Unique personalities.
Unique portraits.

Your *one-stop* framing solution.

A beautiful Trilogy series,
one beautiful frame

Only $99

Save
BIG on our top Web deals!

20% OFF ANY PURCHASE OF $50 OR MORE.*

www.ebags.com/entertainment2010

I156

DIAMONDS INTERNATIONAL

www.ShopDI.com

FINE JEWELRY | DIAMONDS | WATCHES Save $50 Off $300 (Code EB850) or 15% Off Sitewide (Code EB815). Go to www.shopdi.com/?ent=1 and enter code at checkout.

I157

RitzCamera

TAKE 5% OFF YOUR ONLINE ORDER, PLUS FREE SHIPPING & TAX ON QUALIFYING ORDERS OVER $100. (Online only and exclusions apply.) Visit www.entertainment.com/ritz

I158

GET 18% OFF YOUR ENTIRE ORDER TODAY! (Online only and exclusions apply.) www.FogDog.com/ent18

I159

GET 17% OFF YOUR ENTIRE ORDER TODAY! (Online only and exclusions apply.) www.ProGolf.com/ent17

I160

RETAIL & SERVICES INDEX

RETAIL & SERVICES INDEX

To search by area, see the **Neighborhood Index** located at the back of your book.

= **Print more coupons online at www.entertainment.com**, up to once a month, with these Repeat Savings® merchants. See the Rules of Use for more details.

no-risk fundraisers

Set up your fundraiser the right way with a company you can trust— and no upfront cost!

Coupon Products

Easy to sell; people enjoy the savings!

A uniquely yummy way to raise money and delight everyone!

Otis Spunkmeyer
Cookie Dough

Up to 50% profit! Premium giftwrap, chocolates, gourmet foods and specialty gifts.

Legendary Giftwrap

Exceed your fundraising goal with our quick, easy, profitable fundraisers. Contact us for more information.

www.entertainment.com/info2010
1-866-862-0069

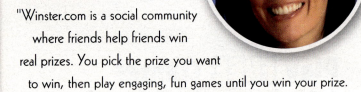

"Winster.com is a social community where friends help friends win real prizes. You pick the prize you want to win, then play engaging, fun games until you win your prize.

"Our games foster a sense of community because players *cooperate* with each other, rather than *compete* with each other. At Winster.com, you play *with* your friends, not *against* them."

Winnie Winster, Founder and Host

www.winster.com/ent

PLAY NOW

To register and play, you must:

- Be at least 18 years of age.

- Have an email account through which you can send and receive personal and private email messages.

- Have uninterrupted and unrestricted access to the Internet.

- Be able to run current versions of Javascript and Macromedia Flash programs in Microsoft's Internet Explorer or a compatible browser, and have cookies and pop-ups enabled.

Additional terms and conditions can be found at www.winster.com/terms.html

Subject to Rules of Use. Coupons VOID if purchased, sold or bartered for cash.

Hard-to-find Sizes!

* Women´s 5–13, 4A to 4E
* Men´s 6 ½–17, 2A to 6E

Over 100,000 pairs in Stock!

Since 1957 Peltz Shoes has offered the best values in footwear for the whole family!

Your life. Your story.

For locations near you visit FLASHPORTRAITS.COM

Personal. Exceptional.

F L A S H!
digital·portraits

Your life. Your story.

For locations near you visit FLASHPORTRAITS.COM

HOW TO DO WITH INSTEAD OF WITHOUT

WHEN YOU BUY DIRECT FROM THE SOURCE, YOUR BUDGET GOES A LOT FURTHER.

Now is the time to learn how to do more with your money. For 38 years, DirectBuy Club members have been avoiding the traditional retail mark-ups that stores force you to pay. Any store can pretend to have a sale. Unless you know what something really costs, you'd never really know if you are getting a good deal or not. That's the DirectBuy Club difference.

Join the over 400,000 families in North America that have said NO to unknown retail mark-ups. With over 160 locations, chances are there's a DirectBuy Club near you.

DirectBuy Club members choose from over 700 of their favorite brands for their homes at direct insider prices. No hidden retail mark-ups. Ever. That's a smarter, fairer way to shop.

Call or go online now to receive your **FREE personal invitation** to attend an upcoming Open House Tour. We'll even send you our **FREE Insider's Guide to Buying Direct,** full of the insider information retailers don't want you to know.

HOME IMPROVEMENT I HOME FURNISHINGS I FLOORING I ENTERTAINMENT & OUTDOOR I ACCESSORIES

Valid now thru December 31, 2010
See reverse side for details

DIRECT INSIDER PRICES
DirectBuy®
The Home Improvement & Furnishings Club

Call Now For Your **FREE** Visitor's Pass & **FREE** Insider's Guide to Buying Direct!

mydbclub.com | **1.800.313.1106**

J4

RETAIL

WITH THE DIRECTBUY CLUB
YOU HAVE THE DIRECT
ROUTE TO MAKING A
HOUSE YOUR HOME

160+ DIRECTBUY CLUB LOCATIONS ACROSS NORTH AMERICA

"I have been a member of Direct-Buy for 7 years. What can I say... my home looks like a magazine cover thanks to DirectBuy. The money that I saved allowed me to buy drop dead beautiful furniture that I could not have afforded otherwise."

Maggie Kane
DirectBuy Club Member
since 2003

HOME IMPROVEMENT | HOME FURNISHINGS | FLOORING | ENTERTAINMENT & OUTDOOR | ACCESSORIES

DIRECT INSIDER PRICES

DirectBuy®

The Home Improvement & Furnishings Club

Call Now For Your **FREE** Visitor's Pass & **FREE** Insider's Guide to Buying Direct!

mydbclub.com | **1.800.313.1106**

BLACK & DECKER
Factory Store

GREAT PRODUCTS, YEAR-ROUND SAVINGS!

BLACK & DECKER
Factory Store

- GREAT SELECTION OF PRODUCTS -
- SAVINGS ALL YEAR -
- SHIPPING IS AVAILABLE -

*Discounts do not apply. Not valid with gift card sales.

BLACK & DECKER
Factory Store

- GREAT SELECTION OF PRODUCTS -
- SAVINGS ALL YEAR -
- SHIPPING IS AVAILABLE -

*Clearance items are any items with price ending in 5, 6, 7, or 8.
No other discounts apply. Not valid with gift card sales.

A Lot More Than Oil Changes

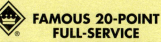

SERVICES

Trust Your Cars To Us!

At Oil Can Henry's, you'll relax in the comfort of your own car, enjoy a free newspaper and watch on the CastrolCam video monitor as our trained technicians complete your service.

GRESHAM 750 NW Eastman Pkwy.
HAZEL DELL 6302 NE Highway 99
HILLSBORO 2505 SE TV Highway
HILLSBORO 6685 SE TV Highway
MILWAUKIE 14800 SE Webster Rd.
ORCHARDS 5800 NE Gher Rd.
PORTLAND 10030 SW Capitol Hwy.
PORTLAND 440 NE Weidler St.

PORTLAND 2016 NW 26th Ave.
TANASBOURNE 2055 NW Town Center
TIGARD 12398 SW Scholls Ferry Rd.
TUALATIN 19417 SW Boones Ferry Rd.
VANCOUVER 19007 SE 1st St.
WEST LINN 2175 8th Court
WEST LINN 19323 Willamette Dr.

Driving directions and hours at www.oilcanhenrys.com

RADIATOR FLUSH
SAVE $10

Valid at participating Portland and Vancouver locations.

Subject to Rules of Use. Coupons VOID if purchased, sold or bartered for cash.

AUTOMATIC TRANSMISSION FLUSH
SAVE $10

Valid at participating Portland and Vancouver locations.

Subject to Rules of Use. Coupons VOID if purchased, sold or bartered for cash.

FAMOUS 20-POINT FULL-SERVICE OIL CHANGE
SAVE $7

Valid at participating Portland and Vancouver locations.

Subject to Rules of Use. Coupons VOID if purchased, sold or bartered for cash.

FAMOUS 20-POINT FULL-SERVICE OIL CHANGE
SAVE $7

Valid at participating Portland and Vancouver locations.

Subject to Rules of Use. Coupons VOID if purchased, sold or bartered for cash.

ECO CAR WASH
Express

Biodegradable Soaps

Brushless Soft Cloth

3 Minutes or Less

GO GREEN
ECO EDDY
WASH ECO
™

Hello, I'm ECO Eddy and I work diligently to make ECO Car Wash the #1 environmental car wash. Through our auto manufacturer approved 3-minute brushless wash, ECO Car Wash minimizes our carbon footprint by investing in innovative technology. Go Green, Wash ECO!

SERVICES

ECO CAR WASH

Express

Express MONEY SAVER

$3⁸⁰ per wash
*Limited Time

5 for $19⁰⁰

ecocarwash.com

MONEY SAVER

3-Minute Brushless Wash

Washing Cars 7 Days a Week
Summer (March 11 - October 17)
7am - 8pm
Winter (October 18 - March 10)
7am - 6:30pm

Recycled Water

Bio-Degradable **Wash Solutions**

Renewable Energy

ECO CAR WASH *Express*	ECO CAR WASH *Express*	ECO CAR WASH *Express*
5020 SE 82nd Ave. Portland, OR 97266-4802 Ph: 503.771.1864 16942 SE Powell Blvd. Portland, OR 97236-1769 Ph: 503.666.6782 12118 N Jantzen Dr. Portland, OR 97217-8160 Ph: 503.247.3322 18128 NE Glisan Portland, OR 97230-7252 Ph: 503.666.9596	5020 SE 82nd Ave. Portland, OR 97266-4802 Ph: 503.771.1864 16942 SE Powell Blvd. Portland, OR 97236-1769 Ph: 503.666.6782 12118 N Jantzen Dr. Portland, OR 97217-8160 Ph: 503.247.3322 18128 NE Glisan Portland, OR 97230-7252 Ph: 503.666.9596	5020 SE 82nd Ave. Portland, OR 97266-4802 Ph: 503.771.1864 16942 SE Powell Blvd. Portland, OR 97236-1769 Ph: 503.666.6782 12118 N Jantzen Dr. Portland, OR 97217-8160 Ph: 503.247.3322 18128 NE Glisan Portland, OR 97230-7252 Ph: 503.666.9596
Subject to Rules of Use. Coupons VOID if purchased, sold or bartered for cash.	Subject to Rules of Use. Coupons VOID if purchased, sold or bartered for cash.	Subject to Rules of Use. Coupons VOID if purchased, sold or bartered for cash.

- The brushless & environmentally friendly wash
- Simoniz Tire Shine
- Clearshield/Clearcoat Protection
- Triple Polish Shine
- Underbody Wash
- Ride-Thru Exterior Wash

www.washmanusa.com
Office phone (503) 255-9111

40% OFF

the regular price of "THE WORKS" EXTERIOR CAR WASH

Subject to Rules of Use. Coupons VOID if purchased, sold or bartered for cash. See reverse side for details.

Enjoy 40% OFF the regular price of "THE WORKS" EXTERIOR CAR WASH.
PLU #355

Valid May 2010

Enjoy 40% OFF the regular price of "THE WORKS" EXTERIOR CAR WASH.
PLU #355

Valid November 2009

Enjoy 40% OFF the regular price of "THE WORKS" EXTERIOR CAR WASH.
PLU #355

Valid June 2010

Enjoy 40% OFF the regular price of "THE WORKS" EXTERIOR CAR WASH.
PLU #355

Valid December 2009

Enjoy 40% OFF the regular price of "THE WORKS" EXTERIOR CAR WASH.
PLU #355

Valid July 2010

Enjoy 40% OFF the regular price of "THE WORKS" EXTERIOR CAR WASH.
PLU #355

Valid January 2010

Enjoy 40% OFF the regular price of "THE WORKS" EXTERIOR CAR WASH.
PLU #355

Valid August 2010

Enjoy 40% OFF the regular price of "THE WORKS" EXTERIOR CAR WASH.
PLU #355

Valid February 2010

Enjoy 40% OFF the regular price of "THE WORKS" EXTERIOR CAR WASH.
PLU #355

Valid September 2010

Enjoy 40% OFF the regular price of "THE WORKS" EXTERIOR CAR WASH.
PLU #355

Valid March 2010

Enjoy 40% OFF the regular price of "THE WORKS" EXTERIOR CAR WASH.
PLU #355

Valid October 2010

Enjoy 40% OFF the regular price of "THE WORKS" EXTERIOR CAR WASH.
PLU #355 J9

Valid April 2010

SERVICES

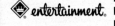

carwash WASHMAN

OREGON

Sandy
37055 Hwy. 26
(Sandy Marketplace Center)

Gresham
1655 NE Burnside
(off Division)

24161 SE 242nd & Stark

Milwaukie
14373 SE McLoughlin
(Oak Grove)

Portland
1616 SE MLK & Clay

1530 NE MLK Jr. Blvd. & Weidler

2920 SE 10th & Powell
(Ross Island)

315 NE 82nd Ave. & Glisan

11461 NE Holman & Airport Way

11838 SE Division
(by 122 NE)

Salem
260 Lancaster Dr. NE
(Next to Oil Can Henry's)

WASHINGTON

Longview
1039 15th Ave.

www.washmanusa.com

Air Pride, Inc.
72DEGREES®
HEATING & AIR CONDITIONING

(503) 655-0556

TECHNICIAN SEAL OF
SAFETY
YOUR SYMBOL OF TRUST
TM

✓ DRUG TESTED
✓ BACKGROUND CHECKED
✓ PROFESSIONALLY TRAINED

Got Questions??? We've got answers at:
www.72DegreesAirPride.com

CCB# 154359

SERVICES

 GE Security

Next Generation Home Security!
FREE Month & FREE Smoke Detector

Completely Wireless
Totally wireless sensors and our unique cellular link provide unmatched protection.

24x7 Monitoring
No hidden fees. No extra charges. Simple and affordable.

Remote & Online Access
Remotely control your system from anywhere with your iPhone, BlackBerry or personal computer.

 Mention "Entertainment32" when you call to get your FREE smoke detector and FREE month of monitoring!

FREE MONTH & FREE SMOKE DETECTOR!* *($100 Value)*

Sign up for FrontPoint and receive your first month of service absolutely free! Only FrontPoint can provide you with next generation security that is virtually impossible for a burglar to defeat—and offer you next generation features so you'll be more connected while you're away than ever before. Call today for a free consultation!

CALL 866-480-4024 | **VISIT** http://1980.fpoffer.com

*Orders received by FrontPoint on or before the 24th of each month will not be charged for monthly service in the current month; the first monthly charge will occur on or about the 1st of the following month. Orders received after the 24th of each month will not be charged for monthly service in the current month or the following month; the first monthly charge will occur on or about the 1st of the second following month. For example, an order received on January 1-24 will be charged for monthly service on February 1st & an order received on January 25-31 will be charged for monthly service on March 1. Offer valid through 12/31/10. Standard monitoring agreement required. FrontPoint is a fully licensed alarm company and operates in the United States and Canada. For full licensing information, please visit us online at www.frontpointsecurity.com/licensing or contact us at (703) 776-9100. Any trademarks used herein are property of their respective owners. FrontPoint Security Solutions, LLC, 1568 Spring Hill Road, Suite 100, McLean, VA 22102.

Valid now thru December 31, 2010

J11

Everything You See Here Is  FREE

25 Small Magnets Reg. $12.99
10 Large Magnets Reg. $12.99
NOW FREE

10 Holiday Cards Starting at $12.99
10 Invitations Starting at $7.99
NOW FREE

BONUS: FREE Photo Uploads

1 T-Shirt
Reg. $9.49
NOW FREE

1 Wall Calendar
Reg. $15.99
NOW FREE

1 Small Rubber Stamp
Reg. $12.99
NOW FREE

Plus, Get
25%–80% OFF
Site-Wide!
ORDER NOW

Order NOW at:
www.vistaprint.com/entbook

beard's
FRAMING

Your Neighborhood Framers
for More Than 35 Years!

www.beards.com

22% OFF

Enjoy **22% OFF** the
regular price of **"THE WORKS"**
FULL SERVICE CAR WASH.
(interior & exterior)

www.washmanusa.com

Valid anytime.

22% OFF
Enjoy **22% OFF** the
regular price of **"THE WORKS"**
FULL SERVICE CAR WASH.
(interior & exterior)
www.washmanusa.com
PLU #356
Valid May 2010

22% OFF
Enjoy **22% OFF** the
regular price of **"THE WORKS"**
FULL SERVICE CAR WASH.
(interior & exterior)
www.washmanusa.com
PLU #356
Valid November 2009

22% OFF
Enjoy **22% OFF** the
regular price of **"THE WORKS"**
FULL SERVICE CAR WASH.
(interior & exterior)
www.washmanusa.com
PLU #356
Valid June 2010

22% OFF
Enjoy **22% OFF** the
regular price of **"THE WORKS"**
FULL SERVICE CAR WASH.
(interior & exterior)
www.washmanusa.com
PLU #356
Valid December 2009

22% OFF
Enjoy **22% OFF** the
regular price of **"THE WORKS"**
FULL SERVICE CAR WASH.
(interior & exterior)
www.washmanusa.com
PLU #356
Valid July 2010

22% OFF
Enjoy **22% OFF** the
regular price of **"THE WORKS"**
FULL SERVICE CAR WASH.
(interior & exterior)
www.washmanusa.com
PLU #356
Valid January 2010

22% OFF
Enjoy **22% OFF** the
regular price of **"THE WORKS"**
FULL SERVICE CAR WASH.
(interior & exterior)
www.washmanusa.com
PLU #356
Valid August 2010

22% OFF
Enjoy **22% OFF** the
regular price of **"THE WORKS"**
FULL SERVICE CAR WASH.
(interior & exterior)
www.washmanusa.com
PLU #356
Valid February 2010

22% OFF
Enjoy **22% OFF** the
regular price of **"THE WORKS"**
FULL SERVICE CAR WASH.
(interior & exterior)
www.washmanusa.com
PLU #356
Valid September 2010

22% OFF
Enjoy **22% OFF** the
regular price of **"THE WORKS"**
FULL SERVICE CAR WASH.
(interior & exterior)
www.washmanusa.com
PLU #356
Valid March 2010

22% OFF
Enjoy **22% OFF** the
regular price of **"THE WORKS"**
FULL SERVICE CAR WASH.
(interior & exterior)
www.washmanusa.com
PLU #356
Valid October 2010

22% OFF
Enjoy **22% OFF** the
regular price of **"THE WORKS"**
FULL SERVICE CAR WASH.
(interior & exterior)
www.washmanusa.com
PLU #356 J14
Valid April 2010

SERVICES

Complete Car Care
The Way You Want It.

BASIC **PREFERRED** **SUPREME**

We give you options and help you choose what's right for you, your car and your budget.

- Batteries • Belts • Brakes
- Cooling System Service • CV Joints
- Exhaust • Oil Change • Shocks & Struts
- Tires • Transmission Fluid Service
- Wheel Alignment • Wheel Balance

meineke®
car care center

At Meineke, You're Always The Driver™

SERVICES

J15

FREE UNDERCAR INSPECTION & ESTIMATE
Nationwide Lifetime Guarantees
Open Mon.–Sat., 7:30 a.m. to 6:00 p.m.

SPECIAL FINANCING TERMS AVAILABLE
Ask About The Benefits!

For additional money-saving offers, visit us at www.meineke.com.

BEAVERTON
13203 SW Canyon Rd.
(503) 644-3522

NEWBERG
705 North Springbrook Rd.
(503) 537-9592

PORTLAND
1807 SE Powell Blvd.
(503) 232-6121

TIGARD
13707 SW Pacific Hwy., Ste. 100
(503) 624-9298

HILLSBORO
2901 SE 73rd Ave.
(503) 848-3231

OREGON CITY
19368 S. Molalla Ave.
(503) 656-2333

PORTLAND
206 North Lombard Street
(503) 283-9170

VANCOUVER
2300 E. 4th Plain Blvd.
(360) 693-9038

LAKE OSWEGO
17705 SW Boones Ferry Rd.
(503) 635-6656

PORTLAND
145 Southeast 82nd
(503) 254-6539

SALEM
558 Market Street NE
(503) 585-9820

VANCOUVER
15510 East Mill Plain Blvd.
(360) 260-8585

MCMINNVILLE
2175 NE 27th Street
(503) 472-9702

PORTLAND
10717 SE 82nd Ave.
(503) 652-9061

SHERWOOD
13985 SW Tualatin-Sherwood Rd.
(503) 625-4831

Washman
AUTO SPA
EXPRESS
DETAILS

Your Car Will LOVE You For It!

www.washmanusa.com

Washman
AUTO SPA
EXPRESS
DETAILS

Enjoy one AUTO DETAIL at 14% off the regular price.

www.washmanusa.com
Winter Coupon valid now through March 2010.

14% OFF

Valid now thru 3/31/10
See reverse side for details

Washman
AUTO SPA
EXPRESS
DETAILS

Enjoy one AUTO DETAIL at 14% off the regular price.

www.washmanusa.com
Spring Coupon valid April 2010 through June 2010.

14% OFF

Valid now thru 4/1/10–6/30/10
See reverse side for details

Washman
AUTO SPA
EXPRESS
DETAILS

Enjoy one AUTO DETAIL at 14% off the regular price.

www.washmanusa.com
Summer Coupon valid July 2010 through September 2010.

14% OFF

Valid now thru 4/1/10–9/30/10
See reverse side for details

Washman
AUTO SPA
EXPRESS
DETAILS

Enjoy one AUTO DETAIL at 14% off the regular price.

www.washmanusa.com
Fall Coupon valid October 2010 through December 2010.

14% OFF

Valid now thru 10/1/10–12/31/10 2010
See reverse side for details   J16

SERVICES

(503) 255-911

washmanusa.com

1655 NE Burnside
(off Division)
Gresham, OR

37055 Hwy. 26
(Sandy Marketplace Center)
Sandy, OR

11838 SE Division St.
(off 122nd)
Portland, OR

14373 SE McLoughlin
Milwaukie, OR

1430 NE MLK Jr. Blvd.
Portland, OR

314 NE 82nd
Portland, OR

www.washmanusa.com

Music Millennium

Enjoy 15% off the regular price of any PURCHASE (sale items excluded) - maximum discount $25.00.

Offer Conditions on reverse side.

Up To $25.00 Value

Valid now thru November 1, 2010

3158 E. Burnside St., Portland, OR
(503)231-8943

J17

Game Crazy

Enjoy 20% off the regular price of ANY USED GAME purchase - maximum discount $25.00.

Offer Conditions on reverse side.

Up To $25.00 Value

Valid now thru November 1, 2010

See Reverse Side for Locations

J18

FYE

$3 off any CD OR DVD regularly priced $12.99 and up.

Offer Conditions on reverse side.

$3.00 Value

for your entertainment
music • movies • games • more

Valid now thru November 1, 2010

Valid at All Participating Locations

J19

Music Millennium

- Voted best independent recorded music store in the country, 1992, 1997, and 2000 by Album Network Magazine
- New CD's, vinyl, cassettes and DVD's
- Buy and sell used CD's, vinyl, cassettes and DVD's
- Knowledgeable staff
- A place where the music and people still matter
- Portland's recorded music store since 1969

3158 E. Burnside St.
Portland, OR
(503)231-8943

00768396

Offer Conditions: Valid anytime. Excludes Red Tag items; Not valid with any other discount offer.

Offer validity is governed by the Rules of Use and excludes defined holidays. Offers are not valid with other discount offers, unless specified. Coupons void if purchased, sold or bartered. Discounts exclude tax, tip and/or alcohol, where applicable.

Game Crazy

- The ultimate neighborhood gaming store
- World's largest selection of new, used & classic games & consoles
- Play ANY game before you buy
- Get more for your trade - GUARANTEED
- Always 12 FREE rentals at Hollywood Video ($72.00 value) with a new or used console purchase

Valid at All Participating Locations

Log on to www.gamecrazy.com for store locations, tournaments, news, chat and more

Game Crazy is located at select Hollywood Video stores

00400430

Offer Conditions: Valid anytime.

Offer validity is governed by the Rules of Use and excludes defined holidays. Offers are not valid with other discount offers, unless specified. Coupons void if purchased, sold or bartered. Discounts exclude tax, tip and/or alcohol, where applicable.

FYE

for your entertainment
music • movies • games • more
Valid at All Participating Locations

00593867

Offer Conditions: Valid anytime. Limit 1 per transaction; Not to include electronics, game hardware, CD singles, gift cards/coins, sale items or special orders; Attention TWE Associate: Redemption instructions: Press discount key. Enter $3. Scan item. Select TWE coupon and enter promotion code 803800000000.

Offer validity is governed by the Rules of Use and excludes defined holidays. Offers are not valid with other discount offers, unless specified. Coupons void if purchased, sold or bartered. Discounts exclude tax, tip and/or alcohol, where applicable.

Dick's Sporting Goods
$20 off any purchase of $100 or more.
Offer Conditions on reverse side.

$20.00 Value

EVERY SEASON STARTS AT

DICK'S SPORTING GOODS

Valid now thru November 1, 2010   J20

Dick's Sporting Goods
$15 off any purchase of $75 or more.
Offer Conditions on reverse side.

$15.00 Value

EVERY SEASON STARTS AT

DICK'S SPORTING GOODS

Valid now thru November 1, 2010   J21

---

entertainment
entertainment.com

Dick's Sporting Goods
$10 off any purchase of $50 or more.
Offer Conditions on reverse side.

$10.00 Value

EVERY SEASON STARTS AT

DICK'S SPORTING GOODS

Valid now thru November 1, 2010   J22

Dick's Sporting Goods

9 11111 11233 2

00769315

Offer Conditions: Valid anytime. Limit one coupon per customer. Minimum purchase of $100 before sales tax. Total amount of coupon must be redeemed at one time. Cannot be combined with any other offers, coupons, team discounts or Guaranteed In-Stock markdown, or used for licenses or previously purchased merchandise. Coupon valid on in-store purchases only. Not redeemable for cash, gift cards or store credit. No reproductions or rain checks accepted. Excludes firearms, ammunition, Under Armour, The North Face, DC, Nike Pro, LIVESTRONG, AF1, Hyperdunk and Jordan, adidas Originals, Ugg, Merrell, Burton, Callaway Golf, Odyssey, Titleist, Cobra and select new-release TaylorMade merchandise and championship merchandise. Some additional exclusions may apply. See store for details. ASSOCIATE: Scan barcode and take a group discount markdown. Valid through 12/31/10.

Offer validity is governed by the Rules of Use and excludes defined holidays. Offers are not valid with other discount offers, unless specified. Coupons void if purchased, sold or bartered. Discounts exclude tax, tip and/or alcohol, where applicable.

Dick's Sporting Goods

9 11111 11295 0

00769313

Offer Conditions: Valid anytime. Limit one coupon per customer. Minimum purchase of $75 before sales tax. Total amount of coupon must be redeemed at one time. Cannot be combined with any other offers, coupons, team discounts or Guaranteed In-Stock markdown, or used for licenses or previously purchased merchandise. Coupon valid on in-store purchases only. Not redeemable for cash, gift cards or store credit. No reproductions or rain checks accepted. Excludes firearms, ammunition, Under Armour, The North Face, DC, Nike Pro, LIVESTRONG, AF1, Hyperdunk and Jordan, adidas Originals, Ugg, Merrell, Burton, Callaway Golf, Odyssey, Titleist, Cobra and select new-release TaylorMade merchandise and championship merchandise. Some additional exclusions may apply. See store for details. ASSOCIATE: Scan barcode and take a group discount markdown. Valid through 12/31/2010.

Offer validity is governed by the Rules of Use and excludes defined holidays. Offers are not valid with other discount offers, unless specified. Coupons void if purchased, sold or bartered. Discounts exclude tax, tip and/or alcohol, where applicable.

Dick's Sporting Goods

9 11111 11334 6

00769290

Offer Conditions: Valid anytime. Limit one coupon per customer. Minimum purchase of $50 before sales tax. Total amount of coupon must be redeemed at one time. Cannot be combined with any other offers, coupons, team discounts or Guaranteed In-Stock markdown, or used for licenses or previously purchased merchandise. Coupon valid on in-store purchases only. Not redeemable for cash, gift cards or store credit. No reproductions or rain checks accepted. Excludes firearms, ammunition, Under Armour, The North Face, DC, Nike Pro, LIVESTRONG, AF1, Hyperdunk and Jordan, adidas Originals, Ugg, Merrell, Burton, Callaway Golf, Odyssey, Titleist, Cobra and select newrelease TaylorMade merchandise and championship merchandise. Some additional exclusions may apply. See store for details. ASSOCIATE: Scan barcode and take a group discount markdown. Valid through 12/31/2010.

Offer validity is governed by the Rules of Use and excludes defined holidays. Offers are not valid with other discount offers, unless specified. Coupons void if purchased, sold or bartered. Discounts exclude tax, tip and/or alcohol, where applicable.

Game Trader

Enjoy 20% off any USED GAME at the regular price - maximum discount $25.00.

Offer Conditions on reverse side.

Up To $25.00 Value

Valid now thru November 1, 2010

3205 S.W. Cedar Hills Blvd., Ste. 57, Beaverton, OR
(503)641-5511   J23

---

entertainment.com

Learning Palace

Enjoy 20% off the regular price of any PURCHASE (sale items excluded).

Offer Conditions on reverse side.

Up To $25.00 Value

Educational Materials, Learning Toys & Games
www.learningpalace.com

See Reverse Side for Locations

Valid now thru November 1, 2010   J24

---

entertainment.com

Kazoodles

Enjoy 20% off the regular price of any PURCHASE (sale items excluded) - maximum discount $25.00.

Offer Conditions on reverse side.

Up To $25.00 Value

kid-powered toys

Valid now thru November 1, 2010

575 W. 8th St., Vancouver, WA
(360)699-9200   J25

Game Trader
- Sony Playstation, PS2, Sega Dreamcast, Nintendo 64
- Game Boy, Game Gear, Neo, Geo, Atari, Sega Genesis
- Super NES, Nintendo, Game Boy Advance, X-Box & more

3205 S.W. Cedar Hills Blvd., Ste. 57
(Cedar Hills Crossing)
Beaverton, OR
(503)641-5511

Offer Conditions: Valid anytime.

00431625

Learning Palace
- Teacher's resource books
- Toys that teach
- Classroom charts
- Flashcards, floor puzzles and art supplies
- Thomas and Friends trains and accessories
- Playmobil
- See our website www.learningpalace.com for more information

Learning Palace
Educational Materials, Learning Toys & Games

OREGON
Beaverton
3861 S.W. 117th
(503)644-9301
Clackamas
11750 S.E. 82nd Ave.
(Clackamas Corner)
(503)794-5696
Eugene
65 Division
(Santa Clara Sq.)
(541)689-9793

Gresham
818 N.W. Eastman Pkwy.
(Gresham Town Fair)
(503)661-0865
Portland
9971 NE Cascades Parkway
(Near IKEA/Airport Way)
(503)251-1833
Salem
3832 Center St., N.E.
(Evergreen Plaza)
(503)587-8992

WASHINGTON
Vancouver
7809 N.E. Vancouver Plaza Dr.
(Vancouver Plaza)
(360)896-1574

Offer Conditions: Valid anytime. In store purchases only; not valid with any other offer; excludes purchase orders, special orders and online orders.

00765325

Kazoodles
- Where learning comes wrapped in fun
- Quality developmental toys, games & books
- Ravensburger, Coralle Thomas, Manhatten, Bryer
- A bundle of fun - come on in & explore

575 W. 8th St.
Vancouver, WA
(360)699-9200

Offer Conditions: Valid anytime.

00721244

Play it Again Sports

- We buy, sell, trade & consign used & new sporting goods

9244 Beaverton
Hillsdale Hwy.
Beaverton, OR
(503)292-4552

1422 N.W. 9th
Corvallis, OR
(541)754-7529

2598 Willamette St.
Eugene, OR
(541)342-4041

10355 N.E. Halsey St.
Portland, OR
(503)254-4993

1991 Lancaster Dr., N.E.
(next to Chuck E. Cheese)
Salem, OR
(503)378-7283

8101 N.E. Parkway Dr.
Vancouver, WA
(360)260-9440

Offer Conditions: Valid anytime.

00389587

NW Ambush

- All your paintball needs, PLUS- skateboards, snowboards, mountainboards & more
- Certified airsmiths
- Parts & repairs also available
- Let us help connect you to your neighborhood paintball team

NW Ambush
Paintball
Skateboards

711 E. Main St.
Battle Ground, WA
(360)666-0029

Offer Conditions: Valid anytime.

00729193

Side Saddle Tack Shop

- Specializes in English & Western saddlery
- Also, a wide selection of barn & farm equipment
- Wide variety of books & videos
- Open Mon.-Fri., 8 a.m.-6 p.m., Sat., 8 a.m.-5:30 p.m., & closed Sunday

Sidesaddle
T·A·C·K·S·H·O·P

10414 N.E. Halsey
Portland, OR
(503)256-1964

Offer Conditions: Valid anytime.

00519296

Mill End Store

- In business since 1918. Mill End Store carries fabrics of all kinds - bridal/costume, fashion/gourmet, cotton, home decor, flat folds, plus notions & yarns. If it is fashion forward, casual, formal, retro or vintage Mill End Store has it all! Come shop & enjoy. Open daily, Visa & Mastercard accepted

Mill End Store
No bigger display of fabrics in America.

4955 S.W. Western Ave. Beaverton, OR (503)646-3000	9701 S.E. McLoughlin Blvd. Milwaukie, OR (503)786-1234

Offer Conditions: Valid anytime. Regular priced in-store merchandise only; Good for fabric and notions only.

00742490

Nan's Glad Rags

- Resale clothing for EVERY woman (petite to plus)
- Shop our clean, spacious & organized store
- Fun, new, current jewelry
- Name brand & designer fashions
- Cash/Trade for women's quality seasonal clothing & accessories - call for details
- It's Nan-tastic!!
- www.nansgladrags.com

21325 S.W. Tualatin Valley Hwy.
Aloha, OR
(503)642-9207

Offer Conditions: Valid anytime.

00589610

The Tao of Tea

- Begin your journey...
- International teaware collection includes: Yixing Purple Clayware, Indian teaware, Kasoras, Gung-Fu tea sets & much more
- Leaf room carries 120 varieties of teas, including rare & limited production teas
- Appreciate the "art" of tea
- The leaf, the art, the way...

The Tao of Tea

The leaf,
the art,
the way...

2112 N.W. Hoyt Portland, OR (503)223-3563	239 N.W. Everett St. Portland, OR (503)224-8455	3430 S.E. Belmont St. Portland, OR (503)736-0119

Offer Conditions: Valid anytime.

00460084

Magazine Outlet

CHOOSE FROM OVER
50 TITLES, ALL YOUR
FAVORITES INCLUDING
SPORTS ILLUSTRATED AND
MORE, UP TO $100 OFF THE
NEWSSTAND PRICE.

Offer Conditions on reverse side.

GET 6 MONTHS OF ISSUES, JUST $2!

magazineoutlet

Valid now thru November 1, 2010

Visit www.magazineoutlet.com/ENT6M2B

J32

Magazine Outlet

CHOOSE FROM OVER
50 TITLES, ALL YOUR
FAVORITES INCLUDING
MARIE CLAIRE AND MORE,
UP TO $100 OFF THE
NEWSSTAND PRICE.

Offer Conditions on reverse side.

GET 6 MONTHS OF ISSUES, JUST $2

magazineoutlet

Valid now thru November 1, 2010

Visit www.magazineoutlet.com/ENT6M2B

J33

Magazine Outlet

CHOOSE FROM OVER
50 TITLES, ALL YOUR
FAVORITES INCLUDING
ENTERTAINMENT WEEKLY
AND MORE, UP TO $100 OFF
THE NEWSSTAND PRICE.

Offer Conditions on reverse side.

GET 6 MONTHS OF ISSUES, JUST $2

magazineoutlet

Valid now thru November 1, 2010

Visit www.magazineoutlet.com/ENT6M2B

J34

Rodda Paint

Enjoy 20% off the regular price of any PURCHASE (sale items excluded) - maximum discount $100.00.

Offer Conditions on reverse side.

it's the finish that counts

www.roddapaint.com

See Reverse Side for Locations

Valid now thru November 1, 2010

J35

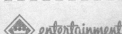

Rodda Paint

Enjoy one complimentary 1 GALLON of HORIZON PAINT when 2 GALLONS of HORIZON PAINT of equal or greater value are purchased.

Offer Conditions on reverse side.

FREE 1 GALLON OF HORIZON PAINT

it's the finish that counts

www.roddapaint.com

See Reverse Side for Locations

Valid now thru November 1, 2010

J36

Rodda Paint

Enjoy 20% off the regular price of any WINDOW COVERING PURCHASE.

Offer Conditions on reverse side.

20% OFF

it's the finish that counts

www.roddapaint.com

See Reverse Side for Locations

J37

Valid now thru November 1, 2010

Rodda Paint
- Local Northwest manufacturer
- Quality paints & stains
- Wallpaper & window coverings
- 44 locations throughout WA, OR, ID & AK
- Since 1932
- 1-800-452-2315

00714238

Valid at Rodda Paint Company Stores   See www.RoddaPaint.com for locations

Offer Conditions: Valid anytime. Store SKU: ENT COUPON; Coupon valid only at Rodda Paint Company stores; Not valid with any other offers or sale items; Coupon not valid for Ultimate Exterior, Spray Equipment Purchase or Rental; Valid on retail accounts only.

Offer validity is governed by the Rules of Use and excludes defined holidays. Offers are not valid with other discount offers, unless specified. Coupons void if purchased, sold or bartered. Discounts exclude tax, tip and/or alcohol, where applicable.

Rodda Paint
- Local Northwest manufacturer
- Quality paints & stains
- Wallpaper window coverings
- 44 locations throughout WA, OR, ID & AK
- Since 1932
- 1-800-452-2315

00714247

Valid at Rodda Paint Company Stores   See www.RoddaPaint.com for locations

Offer Conditions: Valid anytime. Limit ONE GALLON per customer. Store SKU: ENT COUPON; Coupon valid only at Rodda Paint Company stores; Valid only on Horizon products; Not valid with any other discounts, sale items or promotion; Valid on retail accounts only.

Offer validity is governed by the Rules of Use and excludes defined holidays. Offers are not valid with other discount offers, unless specified. Coupons void if purchased, sold or bartered. Discounts exclude tax, tip and/or alcohol, where applicable.

Rodda Paint
- Local Northwest manufacturer
- Quality paints & stains
- Wallpaper & window coverings
- 44 locations throughout WA, OR, ID & AK
- Since 1932
- 1-800-452-2315

00714258

Valid at Rodda Paint Company Stores   See www.RoddaPaint.com for locations

Offer Conditions: Valid anytime. Store SKU: ENT COUPON; Coupon valid only at Rodda Paint Company stores; Not valid with any other offers, sale items, installation or promotions; Valid only on WINDOW COVERINGS; Valid on retail accounts only.

Offer validity is governed by the Rules of Use and excludes defined holidays. Offers are not valid with other discount offers, unless specified. Coupons void if purchased, sold or bartered. Discounts exclude tax, tip and/or alcohol, where applicable.

Sherwin-Williams®

$3.00 off regular priced Purdy 2 1/2" XL Glide Angle Sash Brush; item# 813-6863.
Offer Conditions on reverse side.

Valid now thru November 1, 2010

Valid at All Participating Locations

J38

Sherwin-Williams®

15% off regular priced items.
Offer Conditions on reverse side.

15% OFF

Valid now thru November 1, 2010

Valid at All Participating Locations

J39

Sherwin-Williams®

$10 off a purchase of $50 or more on non-sale merchandise.
Offer Conditions on reverse side.

$10 OFF

Valid now thru November 1, 2010

Valid at All Participating Locations

J40

Sherwin-Williams®

- Become a Preferred Customer to receive:
- Exclusive discounts
- How-to advice
- Color & decorating tips
- Register at sherwin-williams.com or at your neighborhood Sherwin-Williams® paint store. Ask Sherwin-Williams™

Valid at All Participating Locations

00773337

Offer Conditions: Retail sales only. Limit one per household. While supplies last. May not be combined with any other offer. Valid only for Purdy 2 1/2" XL Glide Angle Sash Brush item# 813-6863. Valid at all Sherwin-Williams and Sherwin-Williams operated retail paint stores. Not valid at Sherwin-Williams Automotive Finishes locations or Product Finishes facilities. Must present & surrender coupon at time of redemption. Coupon has no cash value. Void if copied, transferred, purchased or sold. Offer expires 11/01/10. ©2009 The Sherwin-Williams Company.

Offer validity is governed by the Rules of Use and excludes defined holidays. Offers are not valid with other discount offers, unless specified. Coupons void if purchased, sold or bartered. Discounts exclude tax, tip and/or alcohol, where applicable.

Sherwin-Williams®

- Become a Preferred Customer to receive:
- Exclusive discounts
- How-to advice
- Color & decorating tips
- Register at sherwin-williams.com or at your neighborhood Sherwin-Williams® paint store. Ask Sherwin-Williams™

Valid at All Participating Locations

00773333

Offer Conditions: Retail sales only. May not be combined with any other offer or used toward sale merchandise. Limit one per household. Excludes ceiling paint, primers, Minwax® Wood Finish Quarts, Design Basics™ paint, floor covering, window treatments, wall covering, special orders, ladders, spray equipment & accessories and gift cards. Valid at Sherwin-Williams operated retail paint stores. Not valid at Sherwin-Williams Automotive Finishes locations or Product Finishes facilities. Not valid on previous purchases. Void if copied, transferred, purchased or sold. Offer expires 11/1/10. (c)2009 The Sherwin-Williams Company.

Offer validity is governed by the Rules of Use and excludes defined holidays. Offers are not valid with other discount offers, unless specified. Coupons void if purchased, sold or bartered. Discounts exclude tax, tip and/or alcohol, where applicable.

Sherwin-Williams®

- Become a Preferred Customer to receive:
- Exclusive discounts
- How-to advice
- Color & decorating tips
- Register at sherwin-williams.com or at your neighborhood Sherwin-Williams® paint store. Ask Sherwin-Williams™

Valid at All Participating Locations

00773322

Offer Conditions: Retail sales only. May not be combined with any other offer or used toward sale merchandise. All savings pre-tax. Limit one per household. Excludes Multi-Purpose primer, Design Basics™ paint and gift cards. Valid at Sherwin-Williams operated retail paint stores. Not valid at Sherwin-Williams Automotive Finishes locations or Product Finishes facilities. Not valid on previous purchases. Void if copied, transferred, purchased or sold. Offer expires 11/1/10. (c)2009 The Sherwin-Williams Company.

Offer validity is governed by the Rules of Use and excludes defined holidays. Offers are not valid with other discount offers, unless specified. Coupons void if purchased, sold or bartered. Discounts exclude tax, tip and/or alcohol, where applicable.

Sherwin-Williams®
$10 off a purchase of $50 or more on non-sale merchandise.
Offer Conditions on reverse side.

Valid now thru November 1, 2010

$10 OFF

SHERWIN WILLIAMS®

Valid at All Participating Locations

J41

Tranquility Ponds
Enjoy 20% off the regular price of any PURCHASE (sale items excluded) - maximum discount $100.00.
Offer Conditions on reverse side.

PRINT MORE ONLINE

Valid now thru November 1, 2010

Up$ **100** $\frac{00}{}$ Value To

Tranquility **PONDS**

See Reverse Side for Locations

J42

Dad's Candy Shoppe
Enjoy 20% off the regular price of any PURCHASE (sale items excluded) - maximum discount $25.00.
Offer Conditions on reverse side.

PRINT MORE ONLINE

Valid now thru November 1, 2010

Up$ **25** $\frac{00}{}$ Value To

Dad's Candy Shoppe

514 E. 9th, Newberg, OR
(503) 537-0753

J43

Sherwin-Williams®
- Become a Preferred Customer to receive:
- Exclusive discounts
- How-to advice
- Color & decorating tips
- Register at sherwin-williams.com or at your neighborhood Sherwin-Williams® paint store. Ask Sherwin-Williams™

Valid at All Participating Locations

5 35777 16491 9

00773322

Tranquility Ponds
- Your do-it-yourself waterfall & pond supply store
- Indoor/outdoor fountains, table-top fountains & ponds
- Fish, plants & garden ornaments
- Liners, filters, pumps & water treatments
- Friendly, helpful staff

Tranquility PONDS

227 E. Fairview
Meridian, ID
(208)888-6191

2050 E. Serene #610-2
Las Vegas, NV
(702)270-3791

11435 S.W. Canyon Rd.
Beaverton, OR
(503)641-0432

10309-A S.E. 82nd
Portland, OR
(503)788-2642

1001 S. IH 35
Round Rock, TX
(512)310-5800

10211 N.E. 4th Plain
Vancouver, WA
(360)260-0887

Offer Conditions: Valid anytime.

00576522

Dad's Candy Shoppe
- Old-fashioned & difficult to find candy
- Over 17 kinds of handmade chocolates
- From Abbazaba to Zoygs
- Over 20 flavors of suckers
- Locally owned & operated

Dad's Candy Shoppe

514 E. 9th
Newberg, OR
(503)537-0753

Offer Conditions: Valid anytime.

00635972

Harbor Freight Tools

Enjoy 10% off your entire
PURCHASE.

Offer Conditions on reverse side.

www.harborfreightusa.com

Valid now thru November 1, 2010

Valid at all Harbor Freight Tools Retail Stores
Only

J44

Harbor Freight Tools

Enjoy 10% off your entire
PURCHASE.

Offer Conditions on reverse side.

www.harborfreightusa.com

Valid now thru November 1, 2010

Valid at all Harbor Freight Tools Retail Stores
Only

J45

Harbor Freight Tools

Enjoy 15% off your entire
PURCHASE.

Offer Conditions on reverse side.

www.harborfreightusa.com

Valid now thru November 1, 2010

Valid at all Harbor Freight Tools Retail Stores
Only

J46

Harbor Freight Tools

20174819

Valid at all Harbor Freight Tools Retail Stores Only

Offer Conditions: Valid anytime. One coupon per customer visit; Copies of this coupon will not be accepted.

00714994

Offer validity is governed by the Rules of Use and excludes defined holidays. Offers are not valid with other discount offers, unless specified. Coupons void if purchased, sold or bartered. Discounts exclude tax, tip and/or alcohol, where applicable.

- -

Harbor Freight Tools

20174819

Valid at all Harbor Freight Tools Retail Stores Only

Offer Conditions: Valid anytime. One coupon per customer visit; Copies of this coupon will not be accepted.

00714994

Offer validity is governed by the Rules of Use and excludes defined holidays. Offers are not valid with other discount offers, unless specified. Coupons void if purchased, sold or bartered. Discounts exclude tax, tip and/or alcohol, where applicable.

- -

Harbor Freight Tools

19804160

Valid at all Harbor Freight Tools Retail Stores Only

Offer Conditions: Valid anytime. One coupon per customer per visit; Copies of this coupon will not be accepted.

00714993

Offer validity is governed by the Rules of Use and excludes defined holidays. Offers are not valid with other discount offers, unless specified. Coupons void if purchased, sold or bartered. Discounts exclude tax, tip and/or alcohol, where applicable.

Floor Factors

Enjoy 20% off the regular price of any PURCHASE (sale items excluded).

Offer Conditions on reverse side.

www.floorfactors.com

Valid now thru November 1, 2010

1320 N.W. 17th Ave., Portland, OR
(503)222-9393

J47

Frame Central

Enjoy 30% off purchases at Frame Central.

Offer Conditions on reverse side.

Valid now thru November 1, 2010

See Reverse Side for Locations

J48

Salut! Wine Co.

Enjoy 20% off the regular price of any PURCHASE (sale items excluded) - maximum discount $25.00.

Offer Conditions on reverse side.

Valid now thru November 1, 2010

16020 S.E. Mill Plain Blvd., #105, Vancouver, WA
(360)891-5505

J49

More Offers Online!

RETAIL

entertainment.com

Floor Factors

- A Portland business since 1980
- Residential & commercial
- Vinyl, marmoleum, laminate, ceramic tile
- Carpet, pre-finished hardwood, window coverings
- Open Mon.-Fri. 8 a.m.-5 p.m., Sat. 10 a.m.-2 p.m.

FLOOR FACTORS

1320 N.W. 17th Ave.
Portland, OR
(503)222-9393

Offer Conditions: Valid anytime.

00520381

Frame Central

- 1-Day Custom Framing
- DIY Custom Framing
- Framed art
- Wall Frames
- Photo Frames
- Mirrors
- Pre-cut Mats to Go
- www.framecentral.com
- Shop our online art store at www.framecentralart.com

(frame CENTRAL)

OREGON
Beaverton
16157 N.W. Cornell Rd.
(503)439-8961
Gresham
200 N.W. Burnside
(503)491-5883
Portland
11384 S.E. 82nd Ave.
(503)353-0388

1238 N.W. Davis
(503)546-9087
3265 N.W. Yeon St.
(503)219-9222
6639 S.W. Macadam
(503)245-1000
Tigard
12260 S.W. Main St.
(503)968-2668

WASHINGTON
Seattle
305 N.E. 45th St.
(206)632-0073
901 E. Pike
(206)720-2054
Tacoma
2901 S. 38th St.
(253)474-4647

Offer Conditions: Valid anytime. Save an additional 5% off our EVERYDAY 25% less prices. Offers cannot be combined. Excludes C&C, work in progress and special framing packages.

00771398

Salut! Wine Co.

- Offering a wide selection of wine & wine accessories
- Discover wines from around the world
- Wine tasting every Friday
- Full catering services
- Private events & dinners
- Visit us online for complete information

Salut! WINE Co.

16020 S.E. Mill Plain Blvd., #105
Vancouver, WA
(360)891-5505

Offer Conditions: Valid anytime.

00589415

LaRog Jewelers

- Ask for your FREE GIFT with repair
- Your keepsakes are safe with us
- Our expert goldsmiths perform jewelry repairs on the premises

13033 SE 84th St
(Sunnybrook Center across from the Clackamas Costco)
Clackamas, OR
(503)774-8991

9225 SW Hall Blvd
(Corner of Hall and Greenburg)
Tigard, OR
(503)684-4824

Offer Conditions: Valid anytime. Custom designs excluded; Ask for your FREE GIFT with repair.

00740944

Portland Luggage

- Portland Luggage is the Northwest's largest & most complete luggage store
- Representing the finest in selection & value since 1916
- We offer the finest luggage, business & computer cases, a variety of leather bags, travel accessories & gifts for that savvy traveler in your life
- For business or travel, the best adventures begin at Portland Luggage

11645 S.W. Beaverton Hillsdale Hwy.
Beaverton, OR
(503)641-3456

440 S.W. 4th Ave.
Portland, OR
(503)226-3255

Offer Conditions: Valid anytime. Not valid on certain Tumi, Hartmann, & Andiamo products or repairs; Other exclusions may apply.

00513525

The Ultimate Tan and Spa

- A salon for men and women
- 8 convenient locations
- See our website www.theultimatetanandspa.com for more information

THE ULTIMATE
Tan and Spa

Cornelius
1886 SW Baseline Rd.
(503)992-0211

Hillsboro
2935 SE 73rd Ave.
(503)356-9800

McMinnville
911 NE Hwy 99 E
(503)435-2600

Newberg
705 N. Springbrook Rd., #106
(503)537-9800

Sherwood
20649 SW Roy Rogers Rd # 308
(503)625-4452

St. Helens
2296 Gable Rd.
(across from Wal-Mart)
(503)397-9722

Tigard
14250-1 SW Barrows Rd.
(503)579-6726

Wilsonville
8261 SW Wilsonville Rd., Ste. C
(503)685-7344

Offer Conditions: Valid anytime.

00780838

entertainment.com

www.chevrontexaco.com
See Reverse Side For Locations

Enjoy $1.00 OFF 8 Gallons or more of Plus or Supreme Unleaded Gasoline.

One coupon per month for 12 months

Quality gasoline & auto service

Convenient car washes

Food marts

Pay at the pump

Certified service technicians

When running on empty, nothing beats a quick visit at Chevron... stop in today!

Enjoy $1.00 OFF 8 Gallons or more of Plus or Supreme Unleaded Gasoline.

Valid May 2010

Chevron

Enjoy $1.00 OFF 8 Gallons or more of Plus or Supreme Unleaded Gasoline.

Valid June 2010

Chevron

Enjoy $1.00 OFF 8 Gallons or more of Plus or Supreme Unleaded Gasoline.

Valid July 2010

Chevron

Enjoy $1.00 OFF 8 Gallons or more of Plus or Supreme Unleaded Gasoline.

Valid Aug. 2010

Chevron

Enjoy $1.00 OFF 8 Gallons or more of Plus or Supreme Unleaded Gasoline.

Valid Sept. 2010

Chevron

Enjoy $1.00 OFF 8 Gallons or more of Plus or Supreme Unleaded Gasoline.

Valid Oct. 2010

Chevron

Enjoy $1.00 OFF 8 Gallons or more of Plus or Supreme Unleaded Gasoline.

Valid Nov. 2009

Chevron

Enjoy $1.00 OFF 8 Gallons or more of Plus or Supreme Unleaded Gasoline.

Valid Dec. 2009

Chevron

Enjoy $1.00 OFF 8 Gallons or more of Plus or Supreme Unleaded Gasoline.

Valid Jan. 2010

Chevron

Enjoy $1.00 OFF 8 Gallons or more of Plus or Supreme Unleaded Gasoline.

Valid Feb. 2010

Chevron

Enjoy $1.00 OFF 8 Gallons or more of Plus or Supreme Unleaded Gasoline.

Valid March 2010

Chevron

Enjoy $1.00 OFF 8 Gallons or more of Plus or Supreme Unleaded Gasoline.

Valid April 2010

Chevron

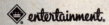

Not valid with any other discounts or promotions; Valid on Chevron credit card or cash sales only

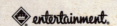

Not valid with any other discounts or promotions; Valid on Chevron credit card or cash sales only

entertainment.

Not valid with any other discounts or promotions; Valid on Chevron credit card or cash sales only

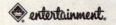

Not valid with any other discounts or promotions; Valid on Chevron credit card or cash sales only

entertainment.

Not valid with any other discounts or promotions; Valid on Chevron credit card or cash sales only

entertainment.

Not valid with any other discounts or promotions; Valid on Chevron credit card or cash sales only

entertainment.

Not valid with any other discounts or promotions; Valid on Chevron credit card or cash sales only

entertainment.

Not valid with any other discounts or promotions; Valid on Chevron credit card or cash sales only

entertainment.

Not valid with any other discounts or promotions; Valid on Chevron credit card or cash sales only

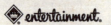

Not valid with any other discounts or promotions; Valid on Chevron credit card or cash sales only

entertainment.

Not valid with any other discounts or promotions; Valid on Chevron credit card or cash sales only

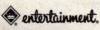

Not valid with any other discounts or promotions; Valid on Chevron credit card or cash sales only

OREGON
Beaverton
14470 S.W. Allen Blvd.
(503)646-9164

Gladstone
19200 S.E. McLougnlin Blvd.
(503)655-3116

Lake Oswego
15670 S.W. Upper Boones Ferry Rd.
(503)639-3003

17830 Lower Boones Ferry Rd.
(503)636-4345

Milwaukie
15710 S.E. McLoughlin
(503)659-1210

Newberg
3745 Portland Rd.
(503)554-0818

North Plains
10025 N.W. Glencoe Rd.
(503)647-0481

Portland
18081 N.E. Sandy Blvd.
(503)491-1999

Tualatin
9770 S.W. Sherwood Tualatin Rd.
(503)691-6300

West Linn
2115 8th Ct.
(503)557-1337

WASHINGTON
Vancouver
4804 St. Johns Rd.
(360)695-6609

610 N.E. 99th St.
(360)574-1372

entertainment®
entertainment.com

Proud of Being Locally Owned & Operated

www.thriftwaystores.com
See Reverse Side For Locations

Enjoy $5.00 off any purchase of $50.00 or more.

(one coupon per three months for 12 months)

Enjoy $5.00 off any purchase of $50.00 or more.

valid Nov. 2009 thru Jan. 2010
Thriftway

Enjoy $5.00 off any purchase of $50.00 or more.

valid Feb. 2010 thru April 2010
Thriftway

Enjoy $5.00 off any purchase of $50.00 or more.

valid May 2010 thru July 2010
Thriftway

Enjoy $5.00 off any purchase of $50.00 or more.

valid Aug. 2010 thru Oct. 2010
Thriftway

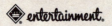

PLU# 5051

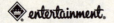

PLU# 5051

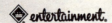

PLU# 5051

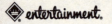

PLU# 5051

OREGON

Aloha
17675 S.W.
Farmington Rd.
(503)649-8597

Banks
660 S. Main St.
(503)324-2171

Bend
725 N.E.
Greenwood
(541)382-4421

Canby
225 N.E. 2nd
(503)266-2016

Estacada
280 S. Broadway
(503)630-3226

Hillsboro
661 S.E.
Baseline
(503)648-5122

John Day
631 W. Main St.
(541)575-1899

Lake Oswego
1377 S.W. McVey
Ave.
(503)636-2213

Madras
561 S.W. Fourth
(541)475-3637

Molalla
107 Robbins St.
(503)829-2322

Newberg
112 E. 1st
(503)538-8286

Newport
107 N. Coast
Hwy.
(541)265-6641

Philomath
1740 Main St.
(541)929-5897

Portland
12675 N.W.
Cornell Rd.
(503)646-9635

7410 S.W. Oleson
Rd.
(503)244-9061

Prineville
315 N.W. Third
St.
(541)447-6291

Redmond
224 S. Sixth St.
(541)548-2326

Sweet Home
621 Main St.
(541)367-6191

Terrebonne
8131 11th St.
(541)548-2603

Tigard
12220 S.W.
Scholls Ferry Rd.
(503)590-7048

Toledo
336 N.E. Hwy. 20
(541)336-5137

Welches
68280 E. Hwy.
26
(503)622-3244

West Linn
19133
Willamette Dr.
(503)635-6281

Willamina
112 W. Main St.
(503)876-2132

Wilsonville
8255 S.W.
Wilsonville Rd.
(503)682-9053

WASHINGTON
White Salmon
77 N.E. Wauna
(509)493-9494

Where Your Best Meals Begin™

See Reverse Side For Locations

Enjoy $5.00 OFF any PURCHASE of $50 or more.

(one coupon per two months for 12 months)

Enjoy $5.00 OFF any PURCHASE of $50 or more.

valid Nov. 2009 thru Dec. 2009
Haggen Food & Pharmacy

Enjoy $5.00 OFF any PURCHASE of $50 or more.

valid Jan. 2010 thru Feb. 2010
Haggen Food & Pharmacy

Enjoy $5.00 OFF any PURCHASE of $50 or more.

valid March 2010 thru April 2010
Haggen Food & Pharmacy

Enjoy $5.00 OFF any PURCHASE of $50 or more.

valid May 2010 thru June 2010
Haggen Food & Pharmacy

Enjoy $5.00 OFF any PURCHASE of $50 or more.

valid July 2010 thru Aug. 2010
Haggen Food & Pharmacy

Enjoy $5.00 OFF any PURCHASE of $50 or more.

valid Sept. 2010 thru Oct. 2010
Haggen Food & Pharmacy

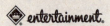

*Excludes alcoholic beverages, tobacco, U.S. Postage Stamps,
bus/commuter passes, money orders, container deposits,
lottery tickets, gift cards & pharmacy prescriptions*

0 00000 06424 8

---

*Excludes alcoholic beverages, tobacco, U.S. Postage Stamps,
bus/commuter passes, money orders, container deposits,
lottery tickets, gift cards & pharmacy prescriptions*

0 00000 06425 5

---

*Excludes alcoholic beverages, tobacco, U.S. Postage Stamps,
bus/commuter passes, money orders, container deposits,
lottery tickets, gift cards & pharmacy prescriptions*

0 00000 06426 2

---

*Excludes alcoholic beverages, tobacco, U.S. Postage Stamps,
bus/commuter passes, money orders, container deposits,
lottery tickets, gift cards & pharmacy prescriptions*

0 00000 06427 9

---

*Excludes alcoholic beverages, tobacco, U.S. Postage Stamps,
bus/commuter passes, money orders, container deposits,
lottery tickets, gift cards & pharmacy prescriptions*

0 00000 06428 6

---

*Excludes alcoholic beverages, tobacco, U.S. Postage Stamps,
bus/commuter passes, money orders, container deposits,
lottery tickets, gift cards & pharmacy prescriptions*

0 00000 06429 3

OREGON
Beaverton
18000 N.W. Evergreen Pkwy.
(Tanasbourne)
(503)690-5900

9055 S.W. Murray Blvd.
(Murray Hill)
(503)521-5800

Oregon City
19701 Hwy. 213
(503)451-7900

Tualatin
8515 S.W. Tualatin Sherwood Rd.
(503)612-8400

WASHINGTON
Arlington
20115 74th Ave. N.E.
(360)403-3800

Bellingham
1401 12th St.
(Fairhaven)
(360)733-4370

210 36th St.
(Sehome Village)
(360)676-1996

2814 Meridian
(Meridian Street)
(360)671-3300

2900 Woburn
(Barkley Village)
(360)676-5300

Burlington
757 Haggen Dr.
(360)814-1500

Ferndale
1815 Main St.
(360)380-9000

Lake Stevens
8915 Market Place N.E.
(425)377-7100

Marysville
3711 88th St. N.E.
(360)530-7700

Mount Vernon
2601 E. Division
(360)848-6999

Stanwood
26603 72nd Ave. N.W.
(360)629-4400

entertainment.com

Enjoy $5.00 OFF any PURCHASE of $50 or more.

valid Nov. 2009 thru Jan. 2010

Market of Choice

MARKET
OF
CHOICE

Enjoy $5.00 OFF any PURCHASE of $50 or more.

valid Feb. 2010 thru April 2010

Market of Choice

See Reverse Side For Locations

Enjoy $5.00 OFF any PURCHASE of $50 or more.

(one coupon per three months for 12 months)

Food for the way you live

Enjoy $5.00 OFF any PURCHASE of $50 or more.

valid May 2010 thru July 2010

Market of Choice

Enjoy $5.00 OFF any PURCHASE of $50 or more.

valid Aug. 2010 thru Oct. 2010

Market of Choice

J56

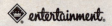

PLU #832; Excludes alcoholic beverages, tobacco, US postage stamps, container deposits, lottery tickets, gift certificate sales; Not valid with any other offer; Limit one offer per coupon; one coupon per customer; Final total of grocery purchase is determined after all your manufacturer's coupons and electronic checkout coupons have been deducted from your grand total at the cash register

---

PLU #832; Excludes alcoholic beverages, tobacco, US postage stamps, container deposits, lottery tickets, gift certificate sales; Not valid with any other offer; Limit one offer per coupon; one coupon per customer; Final total of grocery purchase is determined after all your manufacturer's coupons and electronic checkout coupons have been deducted from your grand total at the cash register

---

PLU #832; Excludes alcoholic beverages, tobacco, US postage stamps, container deposits, lottery tickets, gift certificate sales; Not valid with any other offer; Limit one offer per coupon; one coupon per customer; Final total of grocery purchase is determined after all your manufacturer's coupons and electronic checkout coupons have been deducted from your grand total at the cash register

---

PLU #832; Excludes alcoholic beverages, tobacco, US postage stamps, container deposits, lottery tickets, gift certificate sales; Not valid with any other offer; Limit one offer per coupon; one coupon per customer; Final total of grocery purchase is determined after all your manufacturer's coupons and electronic checkout coupons have been deducted from your grand total at the cash register

Ashland
1475 Siskiyou Blvd.
(541)488-2773

Eugene
1060 Green Acres Rd.
(541)344-1901

1960 Franklin Blvd.
(541)687-1188

2580 Willakenzie
(541)345-3349

67 West 29th Ave
(541)338-8455

Portland
8502 Terwilliger Blvd.
(503)892-7331

West Linn
5639 Hood St.
(503)594-2901

**9845 S.W. Barbur Blvd.
Portland, OR
(503)244-0670**

Enjoy $5.00 OFF any
PURCHASE of $50 or
more.

(one coupon per three months for 12 months)

Enjoy $5.00 OFF any PURCHASE of $50 or more.

valid Nov. 2009 thru Jan. 2010
Barbur World Foods, Inc.

Enjoy $5.00 OFF any PURCHASE of $50 or more.

valid Feb. 2010 thru April 2010
Barbur World Foods, Inc.

Enjoy $5.00 OFF any PURCHASE of $50 or more.

valid May 2010 thru July 2010
Barbur World Foods, Inc.

Enjoy $5.00 OFF any PURCHASE of $50 or more.

valid Aug. 2010 thru Oct. 2010
Barbur World Foods, Inc.

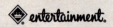

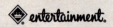

**9845 S.W. Barbur Blvd.
Portland, OR
(503) 244-0670**

Speedy Bright Dry Cleaners

Enjoy any DRY CLEANING ORDER at 50% off the regular price - maximum discount $10.00.

Offer Conditions on reverse side.

SPEEDY BRIGHT DRY CLEANERS

Valid now thru November 1, 2010

578 W Powell Blvd, Gresham, OR
(503)669-8447

J58

More Offers Online!

Superior Cleaners

Enjoy 20% OFF the regular price of any DRY CLEANING ORDER.

Offer Conditions on reverse side.

20%OFF

Super Cleaners

Valid now thru November 1, 2010

8409 S.E. Division St., Portland, OR
(503)771-7545

J59

SERVICES

Hazel Dell Car Wash

Enjoy any EXTERIOR "RIDE THRU" CAR WASH at 50% off the regular price.

Offer Conditions on reverse side.

Up To $8.00 Value

Hazel Dell Car Wash

www.finishlineautodetailing.com

8200 N.E. Hwy. 99, Vancouver, WA
(360)574-1636

J60

entertainment.com

Speedy Bright Dry Cleaners

- Pick-up & delivery available
- Alterations & tailoring
- Specialize in gown alterations & preservation

SPEEDY BRIGHT DRY CLEANERS

578 W Powell Blvd
Gresham, OR
(503)669-8447

Offer Conditions: Valid anytime. Leathers, suedes, furs, laundry & storage excluded.

00754122

Superior Cleaners

- Quality dry cleaning
- Leather, suede, drapery & wedding attire
- Must present coupon with incoming order
- Valid only at participating dry cleaners

Super Cleaners

Superior Cleaners
8409 S.E. Division St.
Portland, OR
(503)771-7545

Offer Conditions: Valid anytime. Laundered shirts, leather goods or any special promotions excluded. One per month for 12 months.

00325330

Hazel Dell Car Wash

- Choose from wash only, exterior plus, exterior deluxe or super deluxe
- All with soft cloth wash & towel dry
- Additional services available including full service & auto detail - see website for details

Hazel Dell Car Wash

8200 N.E. Hwy. 99
Vancouver, WA
(360)574-1636

Offer Conditions: Valid anytime.

00722828

Park Shuttle & Fly

Enjoy 20% off the regular price of PARKING - maximum discount $25.00.

Offer Conditions on reverse side.

Up $**25**⁰⁰ Value
To

PRINT MORE ONLINE

Valid now thru November 1, 2010

6455 N.E. 82nd Ave., Portland, OR
(503)255-6374

J61

Midas

Enjoy 20% off the regular price of any AUTOMOTIVE SERVICES - maximum discount $25.00.

Offer Conditions on reverse side.

Up $**25**⁰⁰ Value
To

PRINT MORE ONLINE

Valid now thru November 1, 2010

See Reverse Side for Locations

J62

Valvoline Express Care

Enjoy 20% off the regular price of any AUTOMOTIVE SERVICES - maximum discount $25.00.

Offer Conditions on reverse side.

Up $**25**⁰⁰ Value
To

PRINT MORE ONLINE

Valid now thru November 1, 2010

9330 N. Whitaker Rd., Portland, OR
(503)283-4009

J63

Park Shuttle & Fly

- 24 - Hour fast shuttle service
- Fenced, lighted & secure parking
- Baggage assistance
- Frequent & VIP customer program
- Hassle free airport parking

6455 N.E. 82nd Ave.
Portland, OR
(503)255-6374

00522083

Offer Conditions: Valid anytime.

Midas

- Brakes, mufflers, catalytic converters, struts, shocks, alignments, tires, batteries
- We can custom-tailor a maintenance package to meet your specific vehicle needs
- Let us help you keep a good thing going!

(MIDAS

OREGON
Beaverton
4325 S.W. Cedar Hills Blvd.
(503)643-5561
Gresham
135 N.W. Burnside
(503)667-5722
Hillsboro
146 S.E. Oak
(503)648-3304
Milwaukie
13840 S.E. McLoughlin
(503)659-2688

Portland
11520 S.E. 82nd Ave.
(Clackamas)
(503)659-9950
2326 N.E. Broadway
(503)288-6033
3635 S.E. 82nd Ave.
(Eastport)
(503)777-1753
Tigard
13055 S.W. Pacific Hwy
(503)684-1318

WASHINGTON
Longview
940 - 15th Ave.
(360)577-8174
Vancouver
5707 N.E. Gher Rd.
(Orchards)
(360)254-3153
6200 N.E. Hwy. 99
(Hazel Dell)
(360)696-0011
Valid at All Participating
Locations

Offer Conditions: Valid anytime.

00492884

Valvoline Express Care

- Full service - major or minor repair
- Instant oil change
- Brakes, tune-up, exhaust
- Quality parts & products
- Superior warranty by Valvoline

9330 N. Whitaker Rd.
Portland, OR
(503)283-4009

00710910

Offer Conditions: Valid anytime.

Limousine at Your Call

Enjoy 2 complimentary HOURS
OF LIMOUSINE SERVICE when
2 HOURS OF LIMOUSINE
SERVICE are purchased.
Offer Conditions on reverse side.

TWO HOURS LIMOUSINE SERVICE

Limousine AT-YOUR-CALL

www.limousineatyourcall.com

Valid now thru November 1, 2010

limousine@aol.com
www.limousineatyourcall.com (503)244-2689 J67

All Star Limousine

Enjoy 50% OFF the regular
price of 4 OR MORE HOURS
OF LUXURY LIMOUSINE
SERVICE.
Offer Conditions on reverse side.

50%OFF

ALL-STAR
LIMOUSINE SERVICE

www.allstarlimo.biz

503-222-1704 www.AllStarLimo.biz

Valid now thru November 1, 2010

J68

Avis

Enjoy up to 25% off plus an
extra discount of $30 when you
rent an intermediate through full-size
car. Mention AWD # B790000 and
CPN # MUFA001. For reservations,
visit avis.com/entertainment or call
1-800-245-8572. Valid now thru
November 1, 2010.
Offer Conditions on reverse side.

$30 OFF A WEEKLY RENTAL PLUS UP TO 25% OFF

We try harder.

avis.com

Valid at All Participating Locations

J69

Valid now thru November 1, 2010

Limousine at Your Call

- We are number 1 in Portland, Oregon
- Due to our popularity - minimum 7 day advance reservations required
- Professional chauffeurs for all events & occasions
- Surcharge for split times
- Rent 5 hours & we donate 5% to charity

limousine@aol.com www.limousineatyourcall.com (503) 244-2689

Offer Conditions: Valid anytime. 20% chauffeur gratuity not included; Does not include fuel surcharge.

00011460

All Star Limousine

- Portland-Vancouver's #1 Limousine Service
- Professional Chauffeurs
- Limousines for up to 14 passengers
- Founding and certified member of the Limousine Owners and Operators Of Oregon
- A member of EntertainmentLimos.com Network

ALL-STAR LIMOUSINE SERVICE

503-222-1704 www.AllStarLimo.biz

Offer Conditions: Valid anytime. Deposit required; excludes 20% chauffeur gratuity and fuel surcharges; advance reservations required.

00779537

Avis

AVIS

We try harder®

avis.com

This is what we do better:

* Free local pick-up service
* Direct billing to your Insurance company
* Open 7 days
* All vehicle types
* where2 GPS navigation

Offer Conditions: Coupon valid on an intermediate (group C) through full-size, four-door (group E) car. Dollars off applies to the time and mileage charges only on a minimum five consecutive day rental period. Taxes, concession recovery fees, vehicle license recovery fee, customer facility charges ($10/contract in CA) may apply and are extra. Optional products such as LDW ($29.99/day or less, except in Louisiana $49.99/day) and refueling are extra. One coupon per rental. An advance reservation is required. May not be used in conjunction with any other coupon, promotion or offer except your Entertainment member discount. Renter must show proof of membership at time of rental. The savings of up to 25% applies to the time and mileage charges only. Coupon valid at participating Avis locations in the contiguous U.S., and Canada. Offer subject to vehicle availability at time of reservation and may not be available on some rates at some times. For reservations made on avis.com, dollars off will be applied at time of rental. Renter must meet Avis age, driver and credit requirements. Minimum age may vary by location. An additional daily surcharge may apply for renters under 25 years old. Rental must begin by 11/1/10.

00774007

Budget Car Rental

Get up to 20% off plus an extra $25 off when you rent a compact or above car. Mention BCD # X443000 and CPN # MUGZ265. For reservations, visit budget.com/entertainment or call 1-888-724-6212. Valid now thru November 1, 2010.

Offer Conditions on reverse side.

$25 OFF A WEEKLY RENTAL PLUS UP TO 20% OFF

Valid now thru November 1, 2010

Valid at All Participating Locations

J70

Maid Brigade

Enjoy $18 OFF YOUR FIRST 4 REGULAR CLEANINGS.

Offer Conditions on reverse side.

Up To **$72.00** Value

Maid Brigade®

YOUR HOME. CLEANER.

green-clean
CERTIFIED

www.maidbrigade.com

Valid now thru November 1, 2010

See Reverse Side for Locations

J71

Extract Away Carpet Service, Inc.

Enjoy 20% off any CLEANING SERVICE - maximum discount $25.00.

Offer Conditions on reverse side.

Up To **$25.00** Value

≡EXTRACT ⊿AWAY

CARPET SERVICE INC.

PRINT MORE ONLINE

www.extractaway.com

(503) 640-6311

Valid now thru November 1, 2010

J72

Ability ChemDry

Enjoy 20% off any CLEANING SERVICES - maximum discount $25.00.

Offer Conditions on reverse side.

www.abilityclean.com

See Reverse Side for Locations

Valid now thru November 1, 2010

J73

Kumon Math & Reading Centers

Enjoy FREE REGISTRATION when you visit any of our listed Portland area centers.

Offer Conditions on reverse side.

www.kumon.com

See Reverse Side for Locations

Valid now thru November 1, 2010

J74

Family Home Pest Control

Enjoy 50% off the regular price of any INITIAL PEST CONTROL PURCHASE.

Offer Conditions on reverse side.

Family Home Pest Control

Serving families for 34 years

Valid now thru November 1, 2010

10151 S.W. Barbur Blvd. Ste. 201-D, Portland, OR
(503)452-9965

J75

Ability ChemDry

- Circle of Excellence Member
- Serving Greater Portland/Vancouver area
- Carpet, upholstery, tile & grout cleaning
- CRI approved "GOLD" truckmount technology & solutions
- Dries in less than 2 hours
- Serving Portland - Vancouver since 1982

(503)284-6858   (360)597-0129

Offer Conditions: Valid anytime.

00671382

Kumon Math & Reading Centers

- Imagine...accomplishing more each day than the day before
- Kumon Math and Reading unlocks your child's potential using a proven method that nurtures achievement
- Victories are frequent and rewarding
- For over 50 years, Kumon Instructors worldwide have helped millions of children achieve their most ambitious goals, and set even bigger ones

KUM☺N

OREGON
Beaverton
10170 SW Nimbus Ave. #H1
(503)639-7219

16755 SW Baseline Rd, Suite 105
(503)336-3709

Hillsboro
2350 NE Griffin Oaks St., Ste. 700
(503)473-3821

Lake Oswego
16063 SW Boones Ferry Rd
(503)635-2647

368 S. State St
(503)684-6168

Portland
6343-A SW Capitol Hwy
(503)336-1874

Sherwood
22566 SW Washington St
Suite 101
(503)639-7219

West Linn
1914 Willamette Falls Dr., Suite 210
(503)655-9717

WASHINGTON
Vancouver
9901 NE 7th Ave.
(360)576-0777

Offer Conditions: Valid anytime. Valid at these locations only.

00768631

Family Home Pest Control

- Carpenter ant and termite expert
- Free phone estimates (be sure to mention your coupon)
- Commercial and residential

Family Home Pest Control

Serving families for 34 years

10151 S.W. Barbur Blvd. Ste. 201-D
Portland, OR
(503)452-9965

Offer Conditions: Valid anytime. Contract may be required..

00764734

Membership Information

www.entertainment.com
Your comprehensive source for information about your Entertainment® membership and related products.

MEMBER SERVICES

(You must activate your online benefits using your Membership Card number and log in to access these services.)

TO ACTIVATE YOUR ONLINE BENEFITS
Go to www.entertainment.com/activate or call toll-free 866-208-1491
Have your Membership Card number ready.

FOR QUESTIONS REGARDING YOUR ENTERTAINMENT® MEMBERSHIP AND ITS MANY BENEFITS
Go to www.entertainment.com/questions

TO PURCHASE ADDITIONAL ENTERTAINMENT® MEMBERSHIP BOOKS AT MEMBER-ONLY PRICES (FOR GIFTS OR TRAVEL)
Go to www.entertainment.com/books

FOR OUR HOTEL PROGRAMS
Go to www.entertainment.com/travel

FOR THE LATEST MEMBER UPDATES AND OFFER INFORMATION
Go to www.entertainment.com/hotline

TO RECOMMEND A MERCHANT TO BE IN OUR PROGRAM
Go to www.entertainment.com/choice

FUNDRAISER/BUSINESS SERVICES

IF YOU ARE INTERESTED IN SELLING OUR PRODUCTS AS A FUNDRAISER
Go to www.fundraising.entertainment.com/2010

IF YOU ARE INTERESTED IN ADVERTISING IN THIS PROGRAM OR ON OUR WEB SITE
Go to www.entertainment.com/advertise

IF YOU ARE A BUSINESS INTERESTED IN CREATING A CUSTOM COUPON BOOK OR ONLINE SAVINGS PROGRAM...
Go to www.entertainment.com/pmd.

If our Web site does not address your question, or if you need to speak to one of our customer care representatives, please call

1-888-231-SAVE (7283)

Published by: Entertainment Publications, LLC • International Headquarters
1414 E. Maple Road • Troy, MI 48083

Rules of Use

Coupons are valid now through November 1, 2010,
unless otherwise stated on the discount offer.

1. **Entertainment® Membership Card...**Remove your membership card from the front of this book and activate for additional benefits online at www.entertainment.com/activate. Use your card to receive discounts for offers found in the Dining Out section that have ▒ in the upper right-hand corner of the offer page and with car rentals and select hotels.

2. **Additional Conditions...**Read the offer carefully for stated conditions, restrictions and exclusions. All offers are valid anytime except on defined holidays or unless the offer states otherwise. Certain offers are restricted to one offer per party, per visit. These additional conditions supersede other Rules of Use.

3. **How to Redeem Discount...**Present your coupon/membership card to a participating merchant at the time you request your bill to receive your discount. The merchant will retain your coupon or remove the card number from the back of your membership card to indicate you have used the discount offer. The least expensive item(s), up to the maximum value stated, will be deducted from your bill, or you will receive a percentage off the designated item(s), up to the maximum value stated, depending on the offer. For restaurants offering one complimentary "menu item" when a second is purchased, a "menu item" is a main course or entrée item. You may only use an offer once, and you may not combine the offer with any other discount or awards program/offer.

4. **Valid Dates and Times/Holidays...**Read the offer carefully for valid dates and times. Major holidays, including those defined below, and regional holidays observed by participating merchants, are excluded, even if the offer states "valid anytime":

New Year's Eve/Day	Valentine's Day	St. Patrick's Day	Easter
Mother's Day	Father's Day	Thanksgiving	Christmas Eve/Day

    Please check with the merchant regarding other holidays.

5. **Dining Discount Details...**Only one coupon/membership card may be used for every two people, **up to** a maximum of three coupons/membership cards per party, and separate checks are not allowed. Some restaurants include a "when dining alone" option in their offers. These offers are valid only when dining alone. Dining offers cannot be applied to children's menu items, discount-priced daily specials, senior citizen rates, Early Bird specials, carryout/takeout (except for fast food and some carryout-only merchants), and buffets, unless otherwise noted. Discounts on alcohol are prohibited. The discount will be applied only to the food portion of the bill.

6. **Tipping...**Tipping for satisfactory service should be 15–20% of the total bill before the discount amount is subtracted.

7. **Discounts...**Discounts exclude tax, tip and/or alcohol, where applicable.

8. **Hotel Discounts...**Please see the "Hotel Rules of Use" located in the Travel & Hotels section.

9. **Movie Theatre Discounts...**Some movie theatres are obligated by studio contracts to exclude discounts on certain movies. Please see individual offers for theatre exclusions, restrictions and conditions.

10. **Repeat Savings®...**You must activate your card at www.entertainment.com/activate to receive this benefit. Just look for ▬ PRINT MORE ONLINE on coupons in your Entertainment® edition for participating merchants or reference any index. Each coupon can only be redeemed once and will be retained by the merchant to indicate you have used the discount offer. Then, go to www.entertainment.com to print additional coupons for the merchant. Most offers may be printed one time per month, although availability may vary and participating merchants are subject to change. Offer value may vary and additional conditions and restrictions may apply. Simply click, print and redeem at these merchants. Coupons may not be reproduced, altered, traded or sold. Offers expire 14 days after printing.

11. **Printable Offers...**After activating your membership card online and logging on to www.entertainment.com, print coupons for new or additional offers, merchants not found in your membership book, and for Repeat Savings® merchants. Offers expire 14 days after printing.

12. **Free Offers...**In most cases, to qualify for a free offer or complimentary item, you must purchase goods or services from the merchant making the offer. Such offers may not be used in conjunction with any other discount or awards program/offer.

13. **Merchant Information...**All merchant information is valid as of May 1, 2009. Go to www.entertainment.com for important updates.

NEIGHBORHOOD INDEX

NEIGHBORHOOD INDEX

= **Print more coupons online at www.entertainment.com,** up to once a month,
with these Repeat Savings® merchants. See the Rules of Use for more details.

Neighborhood Index

= **Print more coupons online at www.entertainment.com**, up to once a month,
with these Repeat Savings® merchants. See the Rules of Use for more details.

Neighborhood Index

██████████ = Print more coupons online at www.entertainment.com, up to once a month, with these Repeat Savings® merchants. See the Rules of Use for more details.

NEIGHBORHOOD INDEX

Neighborhood Index

NEIGHBORHOOD INDEX

= **Print more coupons online at www.entertainment.com,** up to once a month, with these Repeat Savings® merchants. See the Rules of Use for more details.

Neighborhood Index

■ = **Print more coupons online at www.entertainment.com,** up to once a month, with these Repeat Savings® merchants. See the Rules of Use for more details.

NEIGHBORHOOD INDEX

Neighborhood Index

Here's a sampling of offers
you can only access at

www.entertainment.com...

NEIGHBORHOOD INDEX

= **Print more coupons online at www.entertainment.com,** up to once a month,
with these Repeat Savings® merchants. See the Rules of Use for more details.

ALPHABETICAL INDEX

To search by area, see the **Neighborhood Index** located at the back of your book.

         = **Print more coupons online at www.entertainment.com**, up to once a month, with these Repeat Savings® merchants. See the Rules of Use for more details.

Alphabetical Index

ALPHABETICAL INDEX

To search by area, see the **Neighborhood Index** located at the back of your book.

= **Print more coupons online at www.entertainment.com**, up to once a month, with these Repeat Savings® merchants. See the Rules of Use for more details.

Alphabetical Index

To search by area, see the **Neighborhood Index** located at the back of your book

ALPHABETICAL INDEX

Alphabetical Index

To search by area, see the **Neighborhood Index** located at the back of your book

ALPHABETICAL INDEX

Alphabetical Index

ALPHABETICAL INDEX

Looking for a certain merchant?

Go to www.entertainment.com to search for hundreds
of online printable coupons not found in your book.

OR

Visit www.entertainment.com/choice to tell us about
a place you'd like to see a coupon for.

To search by area, see the **Neighborhood Index** located at the back of your book.

= **Print more coupons online at www.entertainment.com,** up to once a month,
with these Repeat Savings® merchants. See the Rules of Use for more details.

Order Extra Editions & Out-of-Town Editions

Prices listed below reflect regular retail price and are shown in U.S. dollars. When calling **1-866-592-5991** toll-free to order extra editions, you will receive $5 off the prices listed below. If you choose to order online at **www.entertainment.com**, you will receive $5 off the price listed below plus **FREE SHIPPING** (a $5 value). You must have activated your membership at www.entertainment.com/activate and be signed in to take advantage of this free shipping offer. Please refer to the 3-digit code and edition name below when ordering.

Regular Retail Price listed below.

ALABAMA
106	Birmingham	$35

ARIZONA
047	Phoenix	$35
068	Tucson	$35

ARKANSAS
082	Little Rock	$35

CALIFORNIA
104	Bakersfield	$35
055	East Bay Area	$35
086	Fresno/Central Valley	$35
097	Inland Empire/Riverside/ Palm Springs	$35
110	Lake Tahoe/Reno	$35
016	Los Angeles/Long Beach	$35
102	Modesto/Stockton	$35
084	Monterey Peninsula	$35
014	Orange County	$40
042	Sacramento/Gold Country	$45
017	San Diego	$45
012	San Fernando/Santa Clarita	$35
073	San Francisco/San Mateo	$35
096	San Gabriel Valley	$35
010	San Jose/Santa Clara	$35
126	Sonoma/Marin	$35
088	Ventura/Santa Barbara	$35

COLORADO
141	Colorado Springs & Southern Colorado	$35
038	Denver Metro & Northern Colorado	$35

CONNECTICUT
080	Fairfield County	$35
046	Hartford	$35
144	New Haven	$35

DELAWARE
157	Delaware	$35

FLORIDA
137	Brevard County	$35
035	Ft. Lauderdale/ West Palm Beach	$35
075	Ft. Myers/Naples	$35
037	Gainesville	$35
036	Jacksonville	$35
154	Miami/Florida Keys	$35
153	Orlando	$35
118	Sarasota	$35
139	St. Petersburg/Pinellas/ West Pasco	$35
045	Tampa	$35

GEORGIA
028	Atlanta	$35
201	Augusta	$35

HAWAII
146	Hawaii	$35

IDAHO
085	Boise	$35

ILLINOIS
008	Chicago North/Northwest	$35
015	Chicago South/West	$35

INDIANA
078	Ft. Wayne/NE Indiana	$35
039	Indianapolis/ Central Indiana	$35
058	Northwest Indiana	$35
159	South Bend/Michiana	$35
056	Southern IN/Louisville	$35

IOWA
053	Des Moines	$35
302	Quad Cities	$35

KANSAS
105	Kansas City	$35
057	Wichita	$35

KENTUCKY
122	Lexington	$35
056	Louisville/Southern IN	$35

LOUISIANA
202	Baton Rouge	$35
321	Lafayette	$35
121	New Orleans	$35

MARYLAND
024	Baltimore	$35
022	Maryland/ Washington, D.C.	$35

MASSACHUSETTS
030	Boston	$35
124	Springfield/Western MA	$35
108	Worcester County/ Central MA	$35

MICHIGAN
001	Detroit Area	$35
150	Grand Rapids	$35
303	Saginaw	$35

MINNESOTA
091	Twin Cities	$35
123	Twin Ports	$35

MISSISSIPPI
304	Jackson	$35

MISSOURI
105	Kansas City	$35
134	Springfield/Branson	$35
013	St. Louis	$35

NEBRASKA
138	Omaha/Lincoln	$35

NEVADA
149	Las Vegas	$35
110	Reno/Lake Tahoe	$35

NEW HAMPSHIRE
128	Southern New Hampshire	$35

NEW JERSEY
048	Central/Middlesex	$35
094	Central/Monmouth	$35
076	NJ South	$35
052	North/Bergen	$35
026	North/Essex	$35
093	North/Morris	$35

NEW MEXICO
083	Albuquerque/Santa Fe	$40

NEW YORK
060	Albany	$35
109	Binghamton	$35
011	Buffalo	$35
111	Cortland/Ithaca	$35
033	Long Island/ Nassau/Suffolk	$35
087	Mid-Hudson Valley	$35
034	New York City	$35
044	Rochester	$35
074	Syracuse	$35
040	Westchester	$35

NORTH CAROLINA
043	Charlotte	$35
222	Fayetteville	$35
113	Greensboro	$35
112	Raleigh/Durham	$35

OHIO
006	Akron	$35
069	Canton	$35
002	Cincinnati Area	$35
004	Cleveland	$35
003	Columbus/Central OH	$35
005	Dayton/Springfield	$35
018	Toledo/NW Ohio/ SE Michigan	$35
131	Youngstown	$35

OKLAHOMA
160	Oklahoma City	$35
151	Tulsa	$35

OREGON
051	Oregon	$35
029	Portland/Vancouver	$35

PENNSYLVANIA
162	Harrisburg	$35
072	Lancaster/York	$35
062	Lehigh Valley	$35
156	NE Pennsylvania/Poconos	$35
031	Philadelphia North	$35
079	Philadelphia West	$35
007	Pittsburgh	$35
081	Reading/Pottsville	$35

RHODE ISLAND
155	Providence	$35

SOUTH CAROLINA
261	Charleston	$35
021	Columbia	$35
129	Greenville/Spartanburg	$35

TENNESSEE
116	Memphis	$
064	Nashville	$
205	Tri-Cities	$

TEXAS
142	Austin	$
140	Corpus Christi	$
145	Dallas	$
125	El Paso	$
147	Ft. Worth	$
019	Houston Area	$
152	San Antonio	$

UTAH
092	Utah	$

VERMONT
095	Vermont	$

VIRGINIA
063	Norfolk/VA Beach	$
070	North Virginia/ Washington, D.C.	$
158	Richmond	$

WASHINGTON
143	N. Puget Sound	$
050	S. Puget Sound	$
023	Seattle/Eastside	$
090	Spokane/N. Idaho	$

WEST VIRGINIA
115	Charleston Area	$
117	Huntington	$

WISCONSIN
077	Appleton/Green Bay	$
049	Madison	$
032	Milwaukee	$

INTERNATIONAL VALUES®

CANADA
065	Calgary	
066	Edmonton	
025	Greater Vancouver/ Fraser Valley	
130	Halifax	
059	Hamilton/Burlington/ Oakville	
089	Montréal et environs	
101	Okanagan Valley	
067	Ottawa/Outaouais	
135	Saskatchewan	
054	Toronto Area	
107	Victoria/ Mid Vancouver Island	
161	Winnipeg	

PUERTO RICO
100	San Juan	

Some editions will not be available until 11/1/09. Offer subject to availability. Credit card transactions are processed in U.S. funds and are subject to applicable exchange rates. May not be combined with any other offer. Offer expires 9/1/10.